OREGON
DISCOVERY GUIDE

A remarkably useful travel companion
for motorists, RVers and other explorers

By Don W. Martin and Betty Woo Martin

Pine Cone Press • Columbia, California

OTHER BOOKS BY DON AND BETTY MARTIN

NORTHERN CALIFORNIA DISCOVERY GUIDE ● Pine Cone Press (1993)
THE BEST OF NEVADA ● Pine Cone Press (1992)
THE BEST OF THE WINE COUNTRY ● Pine Cone Press (1991)
INSIDE SAN FRANCISCO ● Pine Cone Press (1991)
COMING TO ARIZONA ● Pine Cone Press (1991)
THE BEST OF ARIZONA ● Pine Cone Press (1990; revised 1993)
THE BEST OF THE GOLD COUNTRY ● Pine Cone Press (first printing, 1987; second printing, 1990; revised 1992)
SAN FRANCISCO'S ULTIMATE DINING GUIDE ● Pine Cone Press (1988)
THE BEST OF SAN FRANCISCO ● Chronicle Books (1986; revised 1990)

Library of Congress Cataloging-in-Publication Data
Martin, Don and Betty—
Oregon Discovery Guide
Includes index.
1. Oregon—description and travel
2. Oregon—history

ISBN 0-942053-10-9
Library of Congress catalog card number 92-91154

Cartography ● **Vicky Biernacki** and **Dave Bonnot**, Columbine Type and Design, Sonora, Calif.

THE COVER ● *The Cape Perpetua lookout near Yachats provides one of the Oregon Coast's most imposing vistas.* **—Arnold K. Martin**

Crater Lake, with its volcanic cinder cone of Wizard Island, is one of Oregon's many scenic gems. — **Betty Woo Martin**

Take time to see the sky
Find shapes in the clouds
Hear the murmur of the wind
And touch the cool water.
Walk softly
We are the intruders
Tolerated briefly
In an infinite universe.

—Jean Henderer,
National Park Service (retired)

This book is dedicated to those who came from another place, to become a part of the human fabric of Oregon, including my mother Irma Ann Martin and my late father, George E. Martin.

CONTENTS

INTRODUCTION

THIS BOOK WAS WRITTEN FOR YOU, whether you're among Oregon's several million annual visitors, or among its 2.8 million residents looking for new backyard discoveries.

If you're a resident, you've probably compiled a long list of places you intend to visit "when you get around to it." This book is designed to get you going.

If you're a visitor—or if you're contemplating a visit—the book will help sort out this captivating and complex state.

Further, this is a Discovery Guide, which separates the fun and the fascinating from the ordinary and the obvious. It was written for travelers with a sense of adventure, not for tourists who merely collect locations.

If you decided to create a microcosm of the great American West, you'd want to start with a piece of the Pacific Coast, and then move inland to include a lofty mountain range. You can't have a Western sampler without a chunk of desert, so you'd better add a generous section of the Great Basin.

For boundaries, you can use the ocean to the west, plus a couple of great rivers, one to the north and the other to the east. You might draw an artificial boundary across the bottom, to separate this sampler from that more crowded state to the south.

And there you'd have Oregon.

Perhaps no other state in the Union is so consistently appealing and so versatile. It's all here—the world's most beautiful seacoast, the mighty Columbia River, Hells Canyon of the Snake, the famous whitewater of the Rogue River, the indescribable gem of Crater Lake, the Cascade Range with its volcanoes born of the Ring of Fire, and the great High Desert that slopes away to the east. For touches of civilization and history, it offers the gold rush town of Jacksonville, the cultural bastion of Ashland, some remarkably good local wines and the cosmopolitan dignity of Portland.

Oregon is a manageable package, a handy rectangle about 345 miles wide and 275 miles deep. You can experience many of its highlights on a fly-drive vacation, or bring your RV and spend a leisurely several months discovering its wonders.

I've been exploring this place since I was a toddler, and I still make new discoveries with each visit. Although we live in California, I'm an Oregonian by birth, first seeing the light of day in Grants Pass a certain number of years ago. I grew up there, and I've return often to learn what's new in my native state. When Betty and I decided to do this discovery guide, we spent months prowling from coast to mountain to desert, from city to town to hamlet.

We've done it all, examined it all and explored it all. We've sorted through the wonders of this amazing state, and saved the very best of Oregon just for you.

Don W. Martin
Lithia Park
Ashland, Oregon

THE WAY THINGS WORK

When most folks go on vacation, they either drive from home in their family sedan or RV, or they fly to a city and rent a car. We have thus written this book for the way you travel, directing you to the state's most appealing areas. *The Oregon Discovery Guide* takes you mile by mile, with attendant maps, from one corner of the state to the other.

Along the way, we suggest interesting stops and detours to little discoveries that other guidebooks may have missed. In towns with visitor appeal, we review its lures, activities and places to sleep or camp, and we recommend some good restaurants.

ATTRACTIONS

As the book follows Oregon's highways and scenic byways, it takes attractions as they come, describing them briefly and listing hours and prices (if any). In communities that offer several lures, we suggest driving routes and list points of interest as you encounter them. We also indicate which are particularly appealing and which could best be bypassed if time is limited.

☺ *SPECIAL PLACES:* Our little smiling faces mark Oregon's special places—the best visitor lures in each area. These range from exceptionally well-done attractions and awesome vista points to wonderful woodland walks and undiscovered jewels. Several restaurants and lodgings earn grins in addition to their regular ratings because of their particular charm, exceptional facilities or food, great views or other distinctive features.

DINING

Our intent is to provide a selective dining sampler, not a complete list. Further, we generally focus on restaurants in or near visitor attractions. We won't send you to a neighborhood shopping center in search of a smashed beans and rice place. Of course, we do recommend tucked-away diners that have become legend for their food and atmosphere.

Our choices are based more on overviews of food, service and decor, not on the proper doneness of a specific pork chop. Further, we try to offer the typical Oregon dining experience. Recommendations dance from river-view Portland restaurants serving perfectly poached salmon to rustic rural roadhouses specializing in lumberjack flapjacks topped with wild blackberries.

Of course, one has to be careful when recommending restaurants. People's tastes differ, and your well-done fish may be someone else's art gum eraser. The chef might have a bad night, or your waitress might be recovering from one. Thus, your dining experience may be quite different from ours. Restaurants are graded with one to four wedges, for food quality, service and ambiance.

Δ **Adequate**—A clean café with basic but edible grub.

ΔΔ **Good**—A well-run establishment that offers fine food and service.

ΔΔΔ **Very good**—Substantially above average; excellent fare, served with a smile in a fine dining atmosphere.

ΔΔΔΔ **Excellent**—We've found heaven, and it has great halibut and a good wine list!

Price ranges are based on the tab for an average dinner, including soup or salad (but not wine or dessert). Obviously, cafés serving only breakfast and/or lunch are priced accordingly.

$—Average dinner for one is $9 or less
$$—$10 to $14
$$$—$15 to $24
$$$$—$25 and beyond
Ø—Smoke-free dining. Most restaurants have non-smoking sections; the symbol indicates a place that's non-smoking, or one that has a smoke-free dining room.

LODGING

Our sleeping selections are somewhat arbitrary, since the book can't list them all. Nor does it attempt to; the idea is to recommend facilities near points of interest as you drive through California. The guidebook suggests clean, well-run accommodations in all price ranges, near visitor attractions and recreational areas. In choosing pillow places, we often rely on the judgment of the American Automobile Association because we respect its high standards. We also include some budget lodgings that may fall short of Triple A ideals, but still offer a clean room for a fair price. Of course, one can't anticipate changes in management or the maid's day off, but hopefully your surprises will be good ones.

Historic inns tucked beneath evergreen groves or into coastal coves are part of the Oregon vacation experience, and we've made a point of seeking these out. The book also features bed & breakfast inns, which are cropping up like spring tulips. For a free B&B directory, write to: **Oregon Bed & Breakfast Directory,** 230 Red Spur Dr., Grants Pass, OR 97527.

We use little Monopoly © style symbols to rate the selected lodgings:
△ **Adequate**—Clean and basic; don't expect anything fancy.
△△ **Good**—A well-run place with comfortable beds and most essentials.
△△△ **Very good**—Substantially above average, often with facilities such as a pool, spa or restaurant.
△△△△ **Excellent**—An exceptional lodging with beautifully-appointed rooms and extensive amenities.
Ø—Non-Smoking rooms are available, or the entire facility is smoke-free (common with bed & breakfast inns). Incidentally, most B&Bs do not allow pets. Inquire when you make reservations so your poor pooch doesn't have to spend the night sulking in the back seat of your car.

Room prices were provided by the listed establishments. They are, of course, subject to change. Generally, the upper range indicates high season rates. Price codes below reflect the range for a standard room.
$—a double room for $35 or less
$$—$36 to $49
$$$—$50 to $74
$$$$—$75 to $99
$$$$$—$100 and beyond
It's always wise to make advance reservations, particularly during weekends and local celebrations (listed at the end of each community write-up). If you don't like the place and you're staying more than a day, you can always shop around after the first night and—hopefully—change lodgings.

CAMPING

Oregon offers a wonderful assortment of state park campgrounds, making it a *nirvana* for RVers and happy tenters. In fact, it has the most state parks in the entire nation. Oregon's national forests abound with campgrounds as well, particularly in the Cascade Range that stretches north to south, the Wallowas of northeastern Oregon and the Coast Range. Since the state attracts legions of happy campers, most communities have a goodly number of RV parks. For details, see "Getting camped" in Chapter one.

TIMES AND PRICES

Don't rely too much on times listed in this book because many establishments seem to change their hours more often than a dead-beat changes his address. Prices change, too, inevitably upward, so use those shown only as guidelines. Also, restaurants often suffer a high attrition rate, so don't be crushed if one that we have recommended has become a laundromat by the time you get there.

A FEW WORDS OF THANKS

In a sense, guidebooks are written by committee. The authors only provide the research, the adjectives and the editing, while hundreds of other sources furnish facts and background information. My photographer-brother **Arnie Martin** of Portland shot the cover photo and he and his wife **Carol** provided tips to aid in our exploration of the state. (That's Carol gracing our cover.) My sister **Virginia Martin Kennedy** of Medford offered her hospitality and clues to researching southwestern Oregon.

Others deserving mention are **Susan Bladholm**, public relations for the Oregon State Tourism Division; **Kent J. Taylor,** chief of interpretation for Crater Lake National Park; **Daniel B. Karnes,** area ranger for Oregon Dunes National Recreation Area, Dawn M. Edwards of the Portland District, Army Corps of Engineers; and **Jim Bocci**, public relations manager for Portland/Oregon Visitor Information. Dozens of folks at chambers of commerce, Oregon Welcome Centers, and visitor centers of the U.S. Forest Service, Bureau of Land Management, Army Corps of Engineers and state forest and fishery offices contributed to this work as well.

CLOSING INTRODUCTORY THOUGHTS:
Keeping up with the changes

Nobody's perfect, but we try. This guidebook contains thousands of facts and a few are probably wrong. If you catch an error, let us know.

Information contained herein was current at the time of publication, but of course things change. Drop us a note if you discover that an historic museum has become an auto repair shop or the other way around; or if a restaurant, motel or attraction has opened or closed. Further, we'd like to know if you discover a great undiscovered attraction, restaurant or hide-away resort. And we certainly want to learn if you have a bad experience at one of the places we've recommended.

All who provide useful information will earn a free copy of a Pine Cone Press publication. (See listing in the back of this book.)

Address your comments to:
> **Pine Cone Press**
> P.O. Box 1494
> Columbia, CA 95310

A BIT ABOUT THE AUTHORS

This is the ninth guidebook by the husband and wife team of Don and Betty Martin. Don, who provides most of the adjectives, has been a journalist since he was 17. He was a Marine correspondent in the Orient, then he worked on the editorial side of several West Coast newspapers. Later, he served as associate editor of the California State Automobile Association's travel magazine. A member of the Society of American Travel Writers, he now devotes his time to writing, photography, travel and—for some odd reason—collecting squirrel and chipmunk artifacts.

Betty, who does much of the research, photography and editing, offers the curious credentials of a doctorate in pharmacy and a California real estate broker's license. She's also a free-lance travel writer and photographer who has sold material to assorted newspapers and magazines.

A third and most essential member of the writing team is *Ickybod*, a green 1979 Volkswagen camper, the Martins' home on the road. Without *Ick*, they might have been tempted to solicit free lodging and meals, and this guidebook wouldn't be quite so honest.

TRAVEL TIPS

Whether you travel by car, RV or commercial transit, these tips will help make any trip anywhere more enjoyable and economical.

Reservations ● Whenever possible, make advance room reservations. Otherwise, you'll pay the "rack rate," the highest rate that a hotel or motel charges. Also, with a reservation, you won't be shut out if there's a convention or major local celebration.

Car rentals ● The same is true of rental cars; you'll often get a better rate by reserving your wheels ahead. **Important note:** Car rental firms may try to sell you "insurance" (actually collision damage waiver) to cover the vehicle. However, you may already have this protection through your own auto insurance company. Check before you go and take your policy or insurance card as proof of coverage.

Trip insurance ● If you're flying, trip insurance may be a good investment, covering lost luggage, accidents and missed flights (essential if you have a no-refund super saver). Most travel agencies can arrange this coverage.

Medical needs ● Always take spare prescription glasses and contacts. Take the prescriptions for your lenses and any drugs you may be taking. Don't forget sun protection, such as a wide-brimmed hat and sun block.

Cameras and film ● If you haven't used your camera recently, test it by shooting a roll of film before you go. Test and replace weak camera and flash batteries. If you're flying, hand-carry your camera and film through the security check.

Final checklist

There's more to trip departure than putting out the cat. Check off these essentials before you go:

___ Stop newspaper and other deliveries; put a hold on your mail.

___ Lock off or unplug your automatic garage door lifter.

___ Arrange for indoor plant watering, landscaping and pet care.

___ Make sure your phone answering machine is turned on; most of these devices allow you to pick up messages remotely.

___ Don't invite burglars by telling the world via answering machine or voice mail that you're gone. Put several lights on timers and make sure newspapers and mail don't accumulate outside.

___ If you're going on a long trip, arrange for future mortgage and other bill payments to avoid late charges.

___ Take perishable food from the refrigerator and lower the fridge and water heater temperatures to save energy.

___ Double-check the clothes you've packed (extra shoes, matching belts); make sure your shaving and cosmetic kits are complete.

___ Take more than one type of credit card, so you won't be caught short if one is lost or stolen.

___ Get travelers checks and/or take your bank card.

___ Have your car serviced, including a check of all belts, tires and fluid levels. For long desert stretches, take extra water and oil.

___ Turn out the lights, turn off the heat and put out the cat.

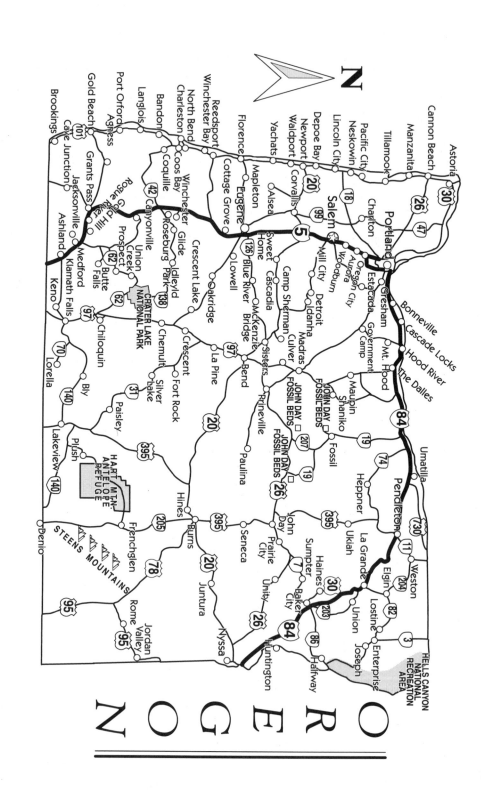

OREGON

Chapter One

OREGON

Getting to know you

THEY CALLED IT the Oregon Country and it was mostly a dream, a hope and a dare. It was a tantalizing goal at the end of a 2,000-mile dusty trail, a tree-shrouded landfall at the completion of a stomach-lurching voyage around Cape Horn.

Long before the Forty-niners scrambled to California and the silver barons dug their riches from Nevada's rocks, America's adventurers, dreamers and schemers headed for Oregon. They didn't know what that odd name meant (and historians still aren't sure), but they knew it was there. Captain Robert Gray had sailed up the Columbia River in 1792. Meriwether Lewis and William Clark, dispatched by President Jefferson to explore lands beyond his Louisiana Purchase, paddled down the Columbia and wintered near present-day Astoria in 1805-06.

What these early-day explorers found was a land in near-perfect balance, a lush paradise of thick timber, silken streams busy with trout and beaver, great prairies begging to be farmed and a magnificent coastline of sand, sea otters and rainforests.

The word spread and America's first major westward migration began in the mid-1800s. It continues to this day, sometimes to the consternation of Oregonians, who fear the loss of their uncrowded lands. With only one-tenth the population of California, Oregon is feeling the press of its neighbor to the south. *Don't Californicate Oregon,* reads an occasional bumper sticker.

However, like a beautiful woman, Oregon must accept the reality that it draws attention to itself, even without trying. Millions come to visit each year, from California, from across the Nation and beyond the sea. They want to view those coastal wilds, to become lost with their thoughts in the lush forests, to explore remarkably clean and pretty towns and cities, and to wander the wondrous tree plain of Eastern Oregon's high desert.

Officially, Oregon *does* try to draw attention to itself, and it succeeds very well. The Oregon Tourism Division conducts one of the most sophisticated and successful travel promotion programs in America, financed in part by a state lottery. Its statewide and regional travel guides will tempt you to start packing this instant. To request material, simply call **(800) 547-7842** nationwide, weekdays from 9 to 5 (Pacific Time). Or you can write: Oregon Tourism Division, 775 Summer St., NE, Salem, OR 97310. Folks at visitor information centers, well-marked and clustered at points of entry, will happily load you up with pounds of maps and brochures. Further, more than 130 chambers of commerce and visitor bureaus operate centers throughout the state.

With this convenient outpouring of information, Oregon is one of the easiest states in America to explore. Mild weather, while on the soggy side in some areas, encourages year-around visitation. It lends itself to discovery by car or RV, since its highways are well maintained. They're lined with state, county and regional parks that invite picnicking, camping, fishing, tubing, swimming, boating and general exploration.

Although it boasts some handsome cities and the world's largest outdoor drama festival, Oregon's greatest draw is its great outdoors. Selected slices of this land and water *au natural* are preserved in one of the nation's most extensive state park systems. The fabulous Oregon Coast—completely open to the public—is virtually lined with state parks.

GETTING THERE & ABOUT

By highway, Oregon's hard to miss. From any point east, just drive west until you hit Interstate 5 or U.S. 101 in California, and turn right. Interstate 84, tracing much of the route of the Oregon Trail, enters the state west of Boise, Idaho. It then swings northwest to follow the mighty Columbia through its famous gorge, which has been designated a National Scenic Area.

Interstate 5, skittering northwesterly through southwestern Oregon, then knifing northward to Portland and beyond, is the major north-south artery. Eight of ten Oregonians live near this non-stop freeway, most of them in the Willamette Valley between Eugene and Portland. U.S. 101 follows a parallel and much more scenic route up the Oregon Coast, a place so legendary that we spell it with a capital "C". To the east, U.S. 97 wanders northward in the rainshadow of the Cascade Range, taking visitors to our favorite part of the state—the ponderosa forests and volcanic wilds of central Oregon.

A series of west-east highways breech the high Cascades, linking the rainy coast and populated I-5 corridor with the interior. Even if you aren't tempted by Central Oregon's marvelous land of lava, ponderosa pines, captivating chipmunks and high desert, you should travel one or more of these west-to-east routes. You'll want to experience the beauty of the Cascades and their high mountain passes. Many follow rivers and creeks that are lined with campgrounds, woodsy resorts, picnic sites, fishing spots and chilly old swimming holes.

Beyond the middle, solitary highways whisk travelers across and about the Great Basin Desert of Oregon's east. They pass shanty ghost towns, dinosaur digs, craggy canyons, wildlife refuges and isolated mountain ranges that seem to float on the desert. If you *really* want to be alone, follow U.S. 395 north from Lakeview, through the solitary desert and into the remote mountain wilds of Chief Joseph Country in the northeastern corner.

Flying

Portland International Airport is served by several major carriers, and it's **Delta's** western hub; call (800) 221-1212. Other majors (with their 800 numbers) are **Alaska Airlines**, 426-0333; **American Airlines**, 433-7300; **America West**, 247-5692; **Braniff**, 272-6433; **Continental Airlines**, 525-0280; **Northwest Airlines**, 447-4747; **TWA**, 892-4141; **United Airlines**, 241-6522; and **USAir**, 428-4322. Other towns with scheduled airline service are **Salem, Eugene, Bend/Redmond, Pendleton, Coos Bay, Klamath Falls** and **Medford** (popular because of the Oregon Shakespeare Festival in next-door Ashland).

Horizon Air, (800) 547-9308, offers an extensive network of feeder lines from its Portland hub. **United Express**, (800) 241-6522, also serves several of Oregon's smaller communities.

Training

Amtrak's **Coast Starlight** runs between San Francisco and Seattle with stops in Klamath Falls, Chemult, Eugene Albany, Salem and Portland, offering one of the most scenic train rides in America. It's becoming so popular that you'd best book months in advance if you want a sleeper car. The **Pioneer** and **Empire Builder** serve Portland from the east, each traveling on opposite sides of the Columbia River Gorge. The Pioneer, on the Oregon side, calls on Ontario, Baker City, La Grande, Pendleton, Hermiston, the Dalles and Hood River. Call (800) USA-RAIL for Amtrak reservations.

Busing

Greyhound/Trailways operates a relatively frequent schedule with reasonably modern (and always smoke-free) buses along the busy I-5 corridor. However, bus service thins out considerably elsewhere in the state. Greyhound's 800 number is 531-5332. Assorted independent lines serve the rest of the state on a more or less irregular basis. Some have taken over abandoned Greyhound routes. For the latest on these, contact the Oregon Tourism Division (listed above).

If you'd like to get lost in the Sixties and still be assured of getting where you're going, the **Green Tortoise** runs a funky but clean and generally regular bus service. It operates between Ashland and Portland, with links from San Francisco; call (800) 227-4766.

Touring

Several firms offer guided bus and train tours that include pieces of Oregon; check with a travel agent for specifics. Two companies conducting outings within the state are **Tauk Tours,** 11 Wilton Rd., Westport, CT 06880, (203) 226-6911; and **Maupintour,** 1515 Saint Andrews Dr., Lawrence, KS 66046; (800) 255-6162.

Elderhostel, which specializes in learning vacations for seniors and often uses college dorms and classrooms, offers a series of classes at Southern Oregon College in Ashland and in Lakeview and Corvallis. The Ashland classes focus on the city's famed Shakespeare Festival and assorted other subjects. If you're 60 or older and you love to learn while traveling, contact Elderhostel at 75 Federal St., Boston, MA 02110-1941; (617) 426-8056.

When to come

Tourism is an important part of the state's economy, and most visitors come in summer. It doesn't get swamped with camera- clutchers like its neighbor to the south. However, most popular tourist areas are busy between Memorial Day and Labor Day, so make lodging and camping reservations. Best of all, you'll like the fall, when the crowds are gone and the kids have retreated to school. The state enjoys its finest weather then—balmy, wind- free days and crisp, cool nights. Late August through early October offer the best odds for sunshine in Portland and along the often-foggy Oregon Coast. Bear in mind, however, that some attractions and museums are closed or have reduced hours during the off-season.

What to wear

Come dressed in layers to best deal with the state's temperate but temperamental climate. Southwestern Oregon can get downright hot in summer, topping 100 degrees, while chilly sea breezes keep the coast cool in July. Expect occasional summer thundershowers in the Cascades and the Willamette and Rogue River valleys. Eastern Oregon offers warm, dry summers and crisp, cold winters. Snow is rarely a problem in the state, since it stays mostly to the higher elevations. The main highways are rarely closed by winter storms.

What to bring

If you plan to explore southeastern Oregon's desert, facilities are few and scattered, so take the usual precautions. Carry plenty of water and a survival kit in case of a mishap or breakdown. The kit should include first aid essentials, non- perishable foods, a can-opener, a powerful flashlight, small shovel, matches, aluminum foil (for signaling) and a space blanket so you can snooze in the shade of your car. Take extra engine oil, coolant, an emergency radiator sealant, spare belts, radiator hoses and tools to install these things.

Oregon's lodging and dining prices are relatively modest when compared with many other popular tourist states, and it has no sales tax. However, liquor prices are rather high because they're set by the state and sold in state stores. If you like a cocktail in your room before you adjourn to dinner, or a nip of brandy with the sunset, you may want to bring a supply of hard liquor.

GETTING CAMPED

We've toured throughout America and Canada and have never found a better selection of nicely located and well-maintained state-run camping areas. If you travel in a small, showerless RV as we do, you won't have to resort to commercial RV parks to avoid becoming gamey. Many state campgrounds have showers and a goodly number have electric, water and even sewer hookups, a rarity in other states' park systems. Some county parks maintain equally elaborate facilities.

Despite Oregon's relatively small population, its state park system is among the most-used in the nation. More than 200 parks are included in the network and 50 of them offer camping. Of these, 13 accept advance reservations between Memorial Day weekend and Labor Day weekend. Most are on the coast (see "Camping" in the Chapter 5 introduction). Campsites must be reserved by mail, and forms can be picked up at most chambers of commerce and other tourist information centers, state parks, motor vehicle and state police offices.

A call to the state's **Campsite Information Center** at (800) 452-5687 (within the state except in the Portland area, in summer from 8 to 4:30) will provide up-to-the-minute information on campsite availability. In Portland and outside the state, call (503) 238-7488. However, you can't make reservations by phone; that must be done with the form.

For campsite reservation forms and a detailed color brochure describing all 50 state campgrounds and other park facilities, contact: **State Parks & Recreation Department**, 525 Trade St. SE, Salem, OR 97310; (503) 378-8605. Brochures also are available through the Oregon Tourism Division and at most visitor information centers.

The **U.S. Forest Service** has dozens of campgrounds in Oregon and a few take reservations, up to 120 days in advance. For information, call (800) 283-CAMP. As in most states, forest service campgrounds generally do not have hookups, and many have chemical toilets. However the price is right—from $8 down to nothing—and many rival state park campgrounds in the beauty of their settings.

Obviously, the busy season for all campgrounds in Oregon is summer and the busiest areas are the coast and the Columbia River Gorge. Without a reservation, you'll be hard-pressed to find a state or national forest campground vacancy in these areas on summer weekends. However, commercial RV parks in these areas often have space. Surprisingly, the Cascade lakes area around Bend in central Oregon generally has space available on summer weekends, despite its great popularity. Most here are U.S. Forest Service campgrounds, since much of the area is in Deschutes National Forest.

HANDICAPPED TRAVELERS

People with mobility problems can get a special permit to use handicapped parking spaces by applying at any **Department of Motor Vehicles** office. Proof of impairment must be provided. These permits aren't limited to the driver; they can be used if any occupant of the car is physically impaired. Incidentally, there is a stiff fine if able-bodied persons park in handicapped spaces.

Golden Access Passes, available free to handicapped persons at national park and U.S. Forest service offices, provide half-price camping at national forest campgrounds and free admission to all national parks and monuments.

Among agencies that handicapped travelers will find useful are: **Travel Information Center,** 12th Street and Tabor Rd., Philadelphia, PA 19141, (215) 329-5715; **Society for the Advancement of Travel for the Handicapped,** 26 Court St., Brooklyn, NY 11242; (718) 858-5483; **American Foundation for the Blind,** 15 W. 16th St., New York, NY 10011; (800) 323-5463; and **Mobility International USA,** P.O. Box 3551, Eugene, OR 97403. Two federal government pamphlets, *Access Travel* and *Access to the National Parks,* are available by writing: **U.S. Government Printing Office,** Washington, DC 20402.

An extremely helpful publication is *Access to the World—A Travel Guide for the Handicapped* by Louise Weiss. Available at many bookstores, it's published by Holt, Rinehart & Winston of New York.

SENIOR TRAVELERS

Anyone 62 or older can obtain a free **Golden Age Pass** that provides half-price camping in U.S. Forest Service campgrounds and free admission to all national parks and monuments (similar to the Golden Access Pass for the handicapped).

Nearly every attraction and museum in Oregon and the rest of the country now provides senior discounts. They're also available on most public transit systems, and many restaurants and hotels offer reduced rates as well.

A fine organization that serves the interests of seniors is the **American Association of Retired Persons,** 1919 K Street Northwest, Washington, DC 22049; (202) 872-4700. For a nominal annual fee, AARP members receive information on travel and tour discounts and other stuff of interest to retired folk.

Elderhostel is a useful travel-oriented organization for 60- plus seniors; contact the organization at 75 Federal St., Boston, MA 02110-1941; (617) 426-8056. (See "Touring" above.)

WHERE TO DO WHAT WHEN

We've mentioned that Oregon is a year-around vacation land with relatively mild climate. Although I-5 through the Siskiyou Range to the south can be closed briefly by snow, it's re-opened after storms. Even roads to such lofty reaches as Crater Lake National Park are plowed after winter snows.

Snowfall is rare in the population corridor running from Ashland/Medford north to Portland, and along the Oregon Coast, Thus, one needn't worry about travel restrictions. Spring, with its dazzling rhododendron and azalea blooms, and autumn with its crisp, clear weather and touches of fall color should be great times to visit Oregon.

Should be?

One of the frustrations of off-season travel in Oregon is that many museums and other attractions hibernate. They shut down from mid-September or early October through the following spring. We began researching this book on a sunny day in May only to find that we had to return later and fill in a lot of blanks. Ranger programs and the boat rides at Crater Lake National Park were discontinued until summer, and several of Oregon's more interesting museums were still in hibernation.

Thus, for the Oregon vacationer who wants to do it all and see it all, this dictates a summer visit. The good news is that, unlike California, Hawaii and many other major vacation spots, facilities here aren't jammed between Memorial Day and Labor Day. Busy, but not jammed. Popular places do fill up on summer weekends, as Oregonians rush to enjoy their own days in the sun.

If you're limited to an off-season vacation, we'd suggest the Willamette Valley in the spring, when the azaleas and rhododendrons are stunning; peak blooming season is May. The Oregon Coast is most beautiful in the early fall, when sunshine frequently bathes those seastacks and tree-shrouded shorelines. You're also starting to get into the crab and clam season then. From winter through spring, you can watch the great procession

Anytime is a good time to explore coastal lures such as Samuel H. Boardman State Park. However, expect to get wet in winter. **— Betty Woo Martin**

of gray whales off the coast. If you need an Oregon fix in winter, gather up your skis and head for Mount Bachelor near Bend, one of the West's better ski resorts. Or do a metropolitan thing; museum, cultural and culinary lures thrive the year around in Portland, Eugene and Salem.

Ashland's noted Shakespeare festival runs from late February through October, although plays are held only in the two indoor theaters in spring and fall. The fabled Elizabethan outdoor theater functions from mid-June to early October. The festival's Portland theater runs through the winter.

Rain today, probably followed by tomorrow

You've likely heard the jokes about Oregon's rain. Natives are called Mossbacks, and they have webbed feet. Kids are let out of school when the sun shines because some have never seen it before.

Actually, the weather is as varied as Oregon's terrain, and most of the state enjoys sunny summers along with the rest of the country. You can take your pick of weather simply by moving from west to east across this rectangular state.

The Oregon Coast is indeed a rainy area, with pockets of verdant, dripping rainforests. Brookings, down near the Oregon border, gets nearly 90 inches a year and Astoria in the opposite corner is soaked with about 70. As we mentioned above, fall is the driest time of the year here.

Surprisingly, the I-5 corridor gets relatively little total rainfall, but *lots* of clouds. The Coast Range scrapes much of the moisture from the clouds, giving Portland an annual rainfall of about 37 inches, not much more than San Francisco and less than New York City. However clouds from those Pacific storms do make it over the rise, and Portland gets a lot of drizzle. Figure on 200 days of cloudiness and about 150 days of light rain a year in the Willamette Valley; less as you go south along the I-5 corridor.

Much of the corridor from Grants Pass to Portland experiences a ritual familiar to northern Californians—night and morning low cloudiness. It's generally safe to plan a picnic in summer, but expect overcast skies until noon many days, followed by sunny afternoons. Ashland and Medford, tucked a bit farther from the coast, have more sunshine. In fact, Ashland gets only 19 inches of rainfall a year. Medford and Ashland can get hot in summer, with the mercury often topping 100 degrees.

There's an advantage to the I-5 corridor cloudiness. It creates a temperature inversion, providing remarkably temperate climate throughout the year. Day-to-night extremes rarely vary more than 15 degrees, with low humidity.

Continuing eastward, you can luxuriate in the crisp, dry air of the rainshadow created by the Cascades and Siskiyou Range to the south. The eastern foothills offer the state's finest summer climate, with warm, sunny days and cool nights. Those lazy days of summer are disturbed only occasionally by brief showers rolling down from the mountains. Much of the foothill area is more than a 3,000 feet high, so hot days are rare.

Bend/Sunriver, central Oregon's major vacation mecca, receives just over ten inches of rainfall a year, and it declines as you continue eastward across the desert into Idaho. The trade-off as you travel farther east is cold winters, sometimes with icy winds. Although much of eastern Oregon is part of the Great Basin Desert, the high elevation and lack of insulating cloud cover often drives winter temperatures below zero.

Bring your booties and enjoy the sunshine.

ON BEING AN OREGONIAN

Oregon is more than a pleasing bundle of seastacks, surf, luxuriant forests and crisp high deserts. It's a condition, an attitude and an intriguing collection of contradictions. Cherishing their abundant natural resources, Oregonians are responsible for some of America's first and most rigid environmental codes.

America's beverage container law was born here, and Oregon was the first state to set aside a portion of highway funds for biking and walking lanes. Many communities require that a percentage of construction costs be used for parks, paths and art in public places. Thanks to the leadership of governors Mark Hatfield and Tom McCall, all of the state's ocean beaches— up to the vegetation line—are dedicated to "free and uninterrupted use" by the public.

During the 1960s, Oregon's liberal streak and moderate marijuana laws appealed to America's Flower Children. Zionistic religious cults have found sanctuary in its rural reaches. Many children of the sixties have remained to form rich pockets of arts, crafts and counter-culture, particularly in the university town of Eugene. A visit to the city's Saturday street market will convey you back to the sixties, complete with peace symbols, incense and tie-dyed tee-shirts.

Yet, the state fosters a conservative streak that at times borders on extremism. Oregon's leading industry, forestry, is on a collision course with its powerful environmental lobby. In recent years, the spotted owl has become the bird that lumberjacks love to hate. What many owlish rednecks are reluctant to admit, however, is that automation has put more of them out of work than logging restrictions.

Conservatism dominates Oregon's tax structure. It's one of the few states without a sales tax, and citizens recently passed a property tax limitation. Car registration fees are so cheap that hundreds of Californians cross the border to buy their autos, and they often register them to pretend Oregon addresses. (There's a stiff California penalty for getting caught.)

Oregon is not a state noted for a generous welfare system. Yet, it *is* acclaimed for its excellent public facilities, for its network of parks, trails and transit systems. Portland was one of America's first cities to establish a transit free zone in its urban core.

The state is still haven for good ole boys who lug their rifles and six-packs of Bud into the forests each fall to "git" their deer or elk. They rarely refer to the fact that they're killing nature's creatures. "I'm goin' out to git my elk this fall," they'll say, suggesting that the wildlife belongs to them, dead or alive. Thus, the state is at once liberal and provincial.

However, the good old boys and the nature-nurturing liberals agree on one thing: they want to protect the quality of life offered by Oregon's lush forests, crystalline streams and smog-free—if often overcast—skies. Whether they're pedaling along one of the many urban bike paths or stalking Bambi's dad with their 30.06, Oregonians love life out of doors.

THINGS OREGON

The state's attitude, climate and natural abundance have created several distinctive foods and crafts. As a visitor, you'll want to sample these, and bring home something more interesting than a souvenir ashtray.

Most towns of any size have "Oregon stores" which feature arts, folk crafts, wines, food specialties and other items unique to the state. It is no surprise that natural food stores thrive as well. The state's Mother Earth multi-grain baked goods are among the best we've tried anywhere. Here's a brief sampler of things Oregon:

Salmon • As you're likely aware, salmon are born in freshwater streams, then they journey to the ocean and live in saltwater for most of their adult life. Each fall, they return to their precise spot of birth to lay eggs, fertilize them, then perish. Oregon offers some of America's finest salmon rivers, and upstream hatcheries are working to keep them stocked. Fresh-caught salmon—be it Chinook, coho or sockeye—is a classic Oregon delicacy, in restaurants and fish markets. Many markets also feature smoked salmon. Of course, Oregon Coast places have an abundance of fresh seafood.

Berries • The Willamette Valley's cool climate is ideally suited to raspberries, blueberries, strawberries, gooseberries and a little-known black delicacy called the Marionberry. Visit one of the many roadside berry farms in the spring to stock up on freshly-picked fruit and related delicacies; U-pick farms are abundant as well. Berry jams, jellies and wines often are featured in the above-mentioned Oregon stores. Sauvie Island near Portland is a good place for the berries, along with rural communities on either side of I-5 to the south. Also, blackberries grow in wild abundance throughout the state, often finding their way into specialty foods. Fresh ones can find their way into your tummy if you tour the state's back roads during July and August.

Dungeness crab • Oregon's chilly coastal waters are ideal havens for this large, succulent critter, which is the crab of choice in every fish market and *fishhaus* from Astoria to San Diego.

Tillamook Cheese • World-famous, this rich cheddar comes from the lush pasturelands of the northwest Oregon Coast. True Tillamook is produced only by the Tillamook County Creamery Association, a dairy cooperative. A visit to the cheese factory in the town of that name is a required Oregon stop—unless you're on a low cholesterol diet. (See Chapter 6.)

Hazelnuts • Call them filberts, if you prefer. They thrive in orchards just south of Portland and many find their way to roadside fruit and vegetable stands. In fact, 97 percent of the national supply comes from the Willamette Valley. At the Pacific Hazelnut Factory, 14673 Ottaway Avenue at Highway 99E in Aurora, you can sample Oregon's favorite nuts and candies made from them. (Details in Chapter 3 under "Salem to Portland, the historic route.")

Earthy breads • Bakeries, whole earth and otherwise, are abundant in this state of gastronomical goodies. Check local bake shops for such specialties as hazelnut, cranberry and apple nut bread and delicious muffins large enough for a one-course breakfast. Albers Mill produces a line of Oregon brand breads that are available in supermarkets throughout the state.

Myrtlewood • You can't eat it, but you can take it home as a unique Oregon souvenir. Myrtlewood items appear in practically every gift and curio shop in the state, in shapes ranging from earrings and brooches to refrigerator magnets, bowls and vases. This distinctive fine grain, tawny colored wood grows only in the forests of southwestern Oregon, northwestern California and in parts of the Mideast. A member of the laurel family, it's locally called Oregon myrtle (although the Latin name is *Umbellularia californica*). Isaiah talks about it in the Bible: *Instead of the briar shall come up the Myrtle tree; and it shall be to the Lord for a name, for an everlasting sign that shall not be cut off.* For the best variety of myrtle souvenirs—presumably everlasting—check out the Oregon Myrtlewood Store in downtown Grants Pass (see Chapter 2).

The Trailblazers • Talk about things Oregon! The NBA's Portland Trailblazers is Oregon's only major sports franchise and the entire state has adopted the team with a frenzy of affection. "Blazer Believer" and "Blazer Mania" bumper stickers and signs are scattered from Brookings to Bend, from Lake Oswego to Lakeview. When the Blazers played the Chicago Bulls for the national title recently, most useful functions in the state came to a halt during game time. Every bar with a TV set became a castle of chaos. No, you can't take a Blazer home as a souvenir, but Blazer blazers aren't hard to come by.

Incidentally, there's an ironic twist to Oregon's Blazer Mania. The state is home to Nike footwear, and the Portland sales room has been fashioned into Nike Town, a mini sports museum. Guess who's the featured attraction? Michael Jordan, of those hated Bulls. (See Chapter 4 under "Attractions, downtown & nearby.")

The word on wine

In recent years, Oregon wines have earned the attention of serious sippers throughout the world. Indeed, some of the state's Pinot Noirs have outscored those of France and California. Chardonnay, Riesling, Cabernet Sauvignon and Gewürztraminer thrive here as well. This should come as no jolt to any serious enologist, since much of Oregon's "wine country" parallels France's vineyards in both climate and latitude.

All of the state's wineries are in the west, and most are cradled between the Coast Range and the Cascades. Most of these are in the Willamette Valley, with a handful around Roseburg and a few more in the Rogue River Valley of southwestern Oregon. The industry is rather new, dating back only a few decades.

If you're familiar with California's vast vinelands and tucked-together tasting rooms, you'll be either delighted or disappointed by an Oregon wine country tour. This state's wineries are quite small and widely scattered. In some areas, you'll have to log a lot of miles to visit several in a day.

Most are family owned and have rather limited production. A couple of Gallo's big vats probably turns out more wine in a year than the entire Oregon industry. Don't expect the castle-like tasting rooms and pleasantly musty cellars that are typical of California's Napa and Sonoma.

On the plus side, you'll enjoy an intimate and informative winetasting experience. You'll likely be talking to the winemaker or a member of the family. Wineries are rarely crowded; there's plenty of time and space to sip and chat. Further, the wines are excellent. In both price and quality, many are on a par with California premium varietals. Incidentally, Oregon produces some excellent light berry wines as well.

Spring through fall is the best time to go a-sipping, since some of the tasting rooms are closed in winter, or they limit their hours to weekends.

Oregon's wine industry takes itself very seriously, imposing some of the most rigid labeling laws in the world. Varietal wines must contain 90 percent of the named variety (except cabernet which typically is a blend) and vintage-labeled wine must contain 95 percent of grapes from the stated year. A wine can't be identified with a specific appellation unless all the grapes came from that area.

You'll find no "burgundies" or "champagnes" in Oregon, since laws prohibit the use of these names. (You may know that Burgundy, Champagne and Chablis are specific growing regions in France. The French are mightily miffed that many California and other American wineries have borrowed these names for generic use.)

An information-packed brochure, **Discover Oregon Wineries**, has descriptions and maps of 63 wineries open to the public. For a free copy, contact: Oregon Winegrowers Association, 1200 NW Front Ave., Suite 400, Portland, OR 97209; (503) 228-8403. Once in the wine country, you can pick up the **Oregon Wine Newspaper**, with feature articles, winery ads and lists of wineries and wine-related events. To get a copy by mail, call (503) 232-7607.

ON TO OREGON

Oregon's first tourist probably was Spain's globe-trotting navigator Juan Cabrillo, who sailed offshore in 1543. England's Sir Francis Drake followed in 1579 as he searched for the fabled Northwest Passage. There is no record as to whether either of them landed, although both were presumptuous enough to claim the area for their respective kings. Had they put ashore, they would have been met by one of the most highly-developed Native American societies on the continent.

With an abundance of food and a mild climate, the coastal tribes of western Canada and the American northwest created elaborate plank longhouses, spiritual totems and sophisticated tools, arts and crafts. East of the Cascades, the Great Basin Indians lived a more simple life, forced into a nomadic existence by the dry climate and elusive game. Southwestern Oregon's Native Americans were forest dwellers, adept hunters and so fierce that the French called them *Rogue.*

Oregon's original residents suffered the classic decline of all native peoples, decimated by the firepower and diseases of land-grabbing intruders. The noble, heartbreaking resistance led by northeastern Oregon's Chief Joseph is one of the most moving chapters in the saga of the American West.

History is vague on the meaning of the world "Oregon." It first appeared on a document in 1765, referring to a mythical river of the West and later applied to the Columbia drainage basin. One suggestion is that Spanish sailors exclaimed *"Orejon!"* (big ears) when they saw abalone shell inserts in the natives' lobes. That notion seems rather far-fetched, however. More logical—if less romantic—is that it's derived from "origin," a reference to its virgin forest lands.

Britain's Captain James Cook touched the Oregon Coast in 1778. His men began a sea otter trade with the locals, shipping pelts back to England and to China. This led eventually to the formation of the legendary Hudson's Bay Company that dominated Northwest trapping, settlement and politics for decades. America got its foot in the door when Captain Robert Gray discovered the mouth of a great river in 1785; he named it for his ship, *Columbia Rediviva.* Naturally, he claimed the entire drainage for the United States.

In 1803, Napoleon Bonaparte sold France's claim to the Mississippi River basin, called the Louisiana Territory, to the United States for $27,267,622 (including interest). When the boundaries finally were set, that came to about three cents per acre. President Jefferson launched Lewis and Clark's Corps of Discovery to see what one got for three cents an acre in those days. Specifically, he wanted them to explore the Missouri River portion of the Mississippi drainage, and press on to the Pacific, hoping to find a good land and water route across the continent "for the purposes of commerce.

What followed was one of the most remarkable expeditions in history. Gathering a crew of "good hunters, stout, healthy, unmarried young men," the 29-year-old Lewis and 33-year-old Clark made the first round-trip overland crossing of America, with few mishaps. Only one man was lost on the entire trip, probably to appendicitis.

The Bird Woman was no guide

En route, they picked up French trapper Toussaint Charbonneau as an interpreter, and his Native American wife, Sacajawea. Never a guide as some history books suggested, she served as a liaison between the group and other native peoples they met along the route. Seeing one of their own kind with these white strangers the Native Americans assumed the group traveled in peace. In fact, in her only attempt at guiding the explorers, she led them over the wrong pass and got them bogged down in a beaver marsh. It was the first and last time the "Bird Woman" attempted to direct the Corps of Discovery. Eventually finding the upstream Columbia, following it to the Pacific and wintering in Astoria, Lewis and Clark were the first Americans to get a detailed look at Oregon Country. They built a crude log fort, spent a winter poking about the Columbia basin, then headed home.

Acting on information they'd gathered, John Jacob Astor sent men and money in 1810 to establish the Pacific Fur Company, although he never set foot in Oregon himself. His company's overland trek paved the way for the legendary Oregon Trail. A short distance from Lewis and Clark's wintering ground, his crew built Fort Astor. It was to become Astoria, the first American settlement west of the Mississippi.

This precipitated an extended war of words—and occasional musket shots—between America and Great Britain over control of the Northwest. British gunboats on the Columbia chased Astor's colony out of Astoria during the War of 1812. Six years later, the British and Americans agreed on joint occupancy of this rich trapping country. In reality, the fur companies—mostly British-controlled—functioned as the local government. The powerful Hudson's Bay Company bought out its rival Canadian North West in 1821. For the next two decades, it ruled a fur trapping empire that reached from Alaska to California and east to the Rockies.

Beavers were the victim of choice for the fur traders, valuable for hats in Europe and eastern America, and for warm clothing in China. Oregon is in fact called the Beaver State, although that reference is no longer fashionable. (When we feel the need for a synonym, we call it the Emerald State because of its lush green forests. Next-door Washington has already claimed the "Evergreen State" title.)

A British-Canadian aids the gringos

Ironically, Oregon's most prominent early citizen was the Quebec-born chief factor of the Hudson's Bay Company, Dr. John McLoughlin. In the 1820s, he established Fort Vancouver on the north side of the Columbia (now in Washington state) as his operational headquarters. However, as Yankees began pouring into the land, following Astor's route, he realized that American domination of the area was inevitable. He defied company orders by aiding the Gringo settlers and missionaries who arrived at Fort Vancouver, providing shelter and extending credit for seed and farm tools. Guessing—incorrectly—that the Columbia River would be the dividing line between British and American holdings, he encouraged settlement to the south along the Willamette River. In fact, he bought land there himself. Forced out of the company in 1845 for his pro-American sympathies, he settled on his land, operated a flour mill and later became an American citizen.

Meanwhile the trickle of Yankee missionaries and settlers turned into a flood. Between 1840 and 1869, 250,000 to 300,000 pioneers followed the uncertainties of the Oregon Trail. One in ten perished en route, mostly from disease, thirst and hunger. Native Americans were responsible only for a few hundred pioneer deaths, while tens of thousands of them died at the hands of the whites.

In a bold move to outnumber Canadian and English settlers, America began giving away what it did not yet own. The Organic Act of 1843 granted 640 acres to each adult white American male. As land began running short, it was cut to 320 acres and then 160 by the 1850 Donation Land Act. After most of the Willamette Valley had been given away, settlers moved east of the Cascades to create great wheat farms that thrive to this day.

Women and all non-whites were excluded from this early land ownership. Thus, in one of history's meanest ironies, Native Americans could not own what they had occupied for centuries.

Pressure between American and English interests increased. "Fifty-four forty or fight" snarled the Yankees, wanting the border through the middle of present-day British Columbia. They settled on the forty-ninth parallel in 1846, and the Oregon Territory was created two years later. It initially included Washington and much of Idaho.

The California Gold Rush was both a boom and a bust to Oregon. It provided a ready market for its produce, wheat and lumber and at the same time drained a good percentage of the male population. Southern Oregon enjoyed its own brief gold rush in 1852. Miners headed for California with a load of Willamette vegetables found gold in a creek, giving birth to Jacksonville, named for the sitting President. Like most gold rush towns, it thrived and then died, leaving it its wake a lot of fine old brick buildings that now are the focal point of a national historic monument.

Although Oregon was granted statehood in 1859, it grew slowly in the following decades. Young Portland thrived as a seaport, but isolation kept the rest of the state in economic doldrums. Then the transcontinental tracks of the Northern Pacific Railroad arrived in 1883. With an overland outlet for its lumber, produce and wheat, the state began building a path of prosperity that continued well into this century. Lumbering and agriculture carried Oregon through the Depression in better shape than most states, and World War II brought shipbuilding industries to Portland. During the construction boom of the 1950s, Oregon became the nation's leading lumber producer.

Automation and that headline-grabbing owl have placed a chronic damper on the industry, causing serious economic slumps in the timber towns. Future clashes between environmentalists and lumber interests are inevitable; the tough trade-off between conservation and job loss likely will continue.

As a native Oregonian and now a keenly interested observer, I'm pleased to see that my old state is finding a better way. High tech industry is beginning to replace those jobs lost to Hooty Owl, and eastern Oregon's amber waves of grain are becoming even more of a breadbasket for growing world hunger. Tourism, the number three industry and gaining, brings in vital dollars, as well.

And that definitely gets our vote. After all, isn't that why we're all sitting here—us researching and writing this book, and you reading it?

Welcome to the Emerald State.

JUST THE FACTS

Size ● 96,961 square miles; tenth largest state. Measures 347 miles by 278 miles.

Population ● 2,847,000 (1990 census); largest city is Portland with 440,000 residents and 1,470,000 in the metropolitan area; next are Eugene with 112,700 and Salem with 107,800

Elevations ● Highest point is Mount Hood at 11,237 feet; lowest point is sea level.

Admitted to the Union ● February 14, 1859; became a territory in August, 1848.

Time zone ● Pacific.

Area code ● (503) statewide. So why do we keep repeating the silly thing? To label digits as phone numbers, and to separate local numbers from toll-free ones.

Traffic laws ● Same speed laws as most other states—55 on highways unless otherwise posted and 65 on rural freeways. Oregon State Police *do* use radar, but they aren't fanatics. Laws require trailers and slow-moving RVs to stay in the right lane of multi-lane highways, except to pass, and to use turn-outs on two-lane highways. Seat belts must be used by occupants of all private vehicles.

Taxes • Oregon is one of the few states with no sales tax.

Alcoholic beverages • Hard liquor is available only in state-operated stores, with high prices and rather arbitrary hours (never on Sunday). Wine and beer are available at various retail outlets. Booze is sold in bars from 7 a.m. to 2:30 a.m.; legal sipping age is 21. Interstate import limit is one quart (although there are no border checks.)

Go fish • Fishing license is required for anyone 14 and older. Nonresident fee is $35.75 a year, $21.75 for ten days and $5.25 a day, plus $5.50 for ten salmon tags and $5.50 each for halibut and sturgeon tags. For a copy of *Oregon Sportfishing Regulations,* contact the Oregon Department of Fish and Wildlife, 2501 SW First St. (P.O. Box 59), Portland, OR 97207; (503) 229-5400.

Official things • **State motto**—"The Union"; **state song**—"Oregon, My Oregon" (which I haven't heard anyone sing since I was a third-grader at Jones Creek School); **nickname**—the Beaver State; **state flower**—Oregon grape; **state tree**—Douglas fir; **state bird**—western meadowlark; **state animal**—beaver; **state fish**—Chinook salmon; **State rock**—thunderegg (Excuse me?); **state gem**—sunstone; **state bug**—swallowtail butterfly.

To learn more

Oregon Tourism Division, (800) 547-7842 nationwide; weekdays 9 to 5 Pacific Time. Or write: 775 NE Summer St., Salem, OR 97310. Ask for the state's excellent full-color travel guide, highway maps, regional guides and lists of chambers of commerce and area travel promotion agencies of places you plan to visit.

Oregon State Parks, call (800) 452-5687 (within the state except in the Portland area) in summer from 8 to 4:30 to learn about campsite availability. In Portland and outside the state, call (503) 238-7488, or write: Oregon State Parks, 525 Trade St. SE, Salem, OR 97310. (See **Getting camped** above for more details.)

National Forest campground reservations: call (800) 283-CAMP weekdays 9 to 6 and weekends 9 to 2 to learn which Forest Service campsites in Oregon can be reserved. Reservation fee is $6 plus the price of the site.

U.S. Forest Service, P.O. Box 3623 (319 Pine St. SW), Portland, OR 97208, (503) 221-2877, has an assortment of free and fee maps and brochures on its national forest areas in the state.

Bureau of Land Management, P.O. Box 2965, Portland, OR 97232, (503) 231-6273, offers maps and brochures of recreational areas within its domain.

Oregon Motor Hotel Association, 12724 Stark St., Portland OR 97233, (503) 255-5135, can furnish a list of the state's motels.

Pacific Northwest Ski Association, P.O. Box 34481, Kirkland, WA 98083, (206) 822-1770, can tell you where to skid the slopes.

Oregon Bed & Breakfast Association, 230 Red Spur Dr., Grants Pass, OR 97527, will send you a free copy of a directory to the state's B&Bs.

PHOTO TIPS: PRETTY AS A PICTURE?

As we travel, we've watched scores of people take hundreds of photos and shoot thousands of feet of videotape. We can tell by their set-ups that most of the shots will be poor and they'll be disappointed when they get back home. By following a few simple steps, you can greatly improve your images. These pointers won't make you a pro, but they'll bring better results the next time you point and shoot.

Still cameras

Most of these suggestions work with the simplest fixed focus cameras, even the disposables, in addition to more complex ones.

1. Get the light right. In photography, light is everything. Avoid shooting objects that are hit by direct sunlight; it washes them out. Try to catch light coming from an angle to accentuate shadows, giving depth and detail to your subject. Photo light is best from sunup to mid-morning and from mid-afternoon to sunset.

2. Frame your photos. Before you shoot, compose the image in the viewfinder. Eliminate distracting objects such as signs or utility poles by changing your position. Or, line up your shot so the offending sign is behind a bush. When shooting people, make sure a utility pole or tree isn't sprouting from your subject's head.

3. Create depth, not clutter. If you're shooting scenery, give dimension to the photo with something in the background (craggy mountains), the middleground (someone in the meadow) and the foreground (a tree limb to frame the photo). On the other hand, if you're focusing on a specific object such as wildlife or an intriguing rock formation, keep the photo simple; don't clutter it.

3. Take pictures, not portraits. Endless shots of Auntie Maude standing in front of the scenery and squinting into your lens are pretty boring. Everyone already knows what she looks like, so let professionals at home shoot the family portraits.

4. Put life in your lens. On the other hand, people *do* add life to scenic photos. Instead of posing them in front of the scenery, let them interact with it. The kids can scramble over the redwood log to show how big that sucker really is. Ask your mate to stroll from the historic building or perch carefully on the canyon rim. Maybe Aunt Maude can extend a tentative finger toward the prickly cactus. Also, have people wear bright clothes to add splashes of color to the photo.

Video cameras

1. Follow the above principles for lighting, framing and posing. You may want to create your own titles by shooting identifying signs.

2. Plan ahead. Think of what you're going to shoot before you pull the trigger. Be a good director and plot each sequence.

3. Hold her steady. You're shooting *moving* pictures, which means that the subjects should be moving, not the video camera. Keep it steady and let people walk in and out of the picture. Limit your panning; give viewers a chance to focus on the scenery.

4. Don't doom your zoom. A zoom lens is a tool, not a toy. Keep your zooming to a minimum, or you'll make your audience seasick.

Chapter Two

Southwestern Oregon

Woodlands, white water and "Will power"

. *FIFTY YEARS AGO*, the people of Oregon's southwestern corner felt so isolated from the rest of the state that they started a secessionist movement. Half joking but with serious undertones, they set about to create the State of Jefferson from Josephine and Jackson Counties. A couple of northern California counties, equally isolated from their state, were invited to join in.

Unfortunately, they picked a bad time to announce their plan to the world—the weekend of December 6 and 7, 1941.

Had they followed through with their scheme, they would have created a smaller version of the very state they wanted to shed. Indeed, these two counties comprise a sampler quilt of Oregon: a major river (the Rogue), tree-thatched mountains (the Siskiyous), a cultural center (Ashland), an historic mining town (Jacksonville), a major commercial center (Medford) and a river recreation gateway (Grants Pass). The area also contains some of the state's most striking coastline, which we will visit in Chapter 5.

If your time is limited and you want to sample an Oregon *rijsttafel* without covering the entire state, this is your corner. From here, a brief side-trip will take you Oregon's only national park, Crater Lake, just over the line in Klamath County.

Although the state's early history is focused around Astoria and Oregon City to the north, southwestern development soon followed, with the discovery of gold in 1852. Creeks around Jacksonville and other tributaries of the Rogue River were panned and dredged for several decades. Jacksonville ruled for half a century as the largest city in southern Oregon.

When the gold ran out, settlers found that the climate and soil in the broad valley of Bear Creek, a tributary to the Rogue, were ideal for agricul-

TRIP PLANNER

WHEN TO GO ● With benign climates, Jackson and Josephine counties are do-able the year around. Some museums and attractions close in the off-season, so Memorial Day through Labor Day is the best period to catch all the action. Ashland's Shakespeare Festival runs March through October.

WHAT TO SEE ● Ashland's Tudor-style downtown and beautiful Lithia Park, the old brickfront stores and historic mansions of Jacksonville, Harry and David's Country Store in Medford, Butte Creek Mill in Eagle Point, the scenic upper stretches of the Rogue River, Crater Lake at dawn, the House of Mystery in Gold Hill, downtown Grants Pass and its unusual Caveman Bridge, Hellgate Canyon of the lower Rogue.

WHAT TO DO ● Catch a play in Ashland and a concert at Jacksonville's Britt Festivals; tour the Oregon Belle Mine near Jacksonville; climb to the top of Medford's Lower Table Rock; hike portions of the upper and lower Rogue River trails; take a Crater Lake boat cruise and hike about Wizard Island; jet boat the Rogue or run it in a whitewater raft; tour the Oregon Caves.

Useful contacts

Ashland Visitors & Convention Bureau, P.O. Box 1360 (110 E. Main St.), Ashland, OR 97520; (503) 482-3486.

Britt Festivals, P.O. Box 1124, Medford, OR 97501; (800) 882-7488.

Crater Lake National Park, P.O. Box 7, Crater Lake, OR 97604; (503) 594-2211. For concessionaire services: **Crater Lake Lodge**, P.O. Box 128, Crater Lake, OR 97604; (503) 594-2511.

Grants Pass Visitors & Convention Bureau, 1439 NE Sixth St. (P.O. Box 1787), Grants Pass, OR 97526; (800) 547-5927 or (503) 476-5510.

Jacksonville Chamber of Commerce, P.O. Box 33 (185 N. Oregon St.), Jacksonville, OR 97530; (503) 899-8118.

Medford Visitors & Convention Bureau, 304 S. Central Ave., Medford, OR 97501; (800) 448-4856 or (503) 779-4847.

Oregon Caves National Monument, 19000 Caves Hwy., Cave Junction, OR 97523; (503) 592-2100. For concessionaire services: **Oregon Caves Company,** P.O. Box 128, Cave Junction, OR 97523; (503) 592-3400.

Oregon Shakespeare Festival, P.O. Box 158, Ashland, OR 97520; (503) 482-4331.

Rogue River Chamber of Commerce, P.O. Box 457, Rogue River, OR 97537; (503) 582-0242

Southern Oregon Reservation Center, P.O. Box 477, Ashland, OR 97520; (800) 547-8052 or (503) 488-1011; for lodging and Shakespeare Festival ticket packages.

Southwestern Oregon radio stations

KCMX-FM, 101.9, Ashland-Medford—classic pops & rock
KTMT-FM, 103.1, Medford—rock
KOVE-FM, 103.5, Medford—talk radio
KROG-FM, 105.1, Grants Pass—rock
KAGO-FM, 99.5, Medford—rock
KRWQ-FM, 100.3, Medford—country
KCNA-FM, 97.7 & 102.7, Cave Junction—pops oldies & news
KSOR-FM, 93.7 & 90.1, Ashland—National Public Radio
KOPE-FM, 103.5, Medford—news & talk
KCMX-AM, 940, Ashland-Medford—news & talk
KYJC-AM, 610, Medford—country.
KTMT-AM, 880, Medford—rock

ture and particularly for pear trees. To this day, orchards around Medford produce a good share of the nation's pears. And of course, the surrounding Siskiyou mountains offered timber. Medford and Grants Pass became—and still are—important lumbering areas.

Recent cutbacks in logging have dented the economies of the two communities. The surrounding Siskiyous shelter much of the old growth Douglas fir forest that is haven to the spotted owl. If you happen to saunter into one of the good old boy saloons along G Street in Grants Pass, you might want to discuss something other than what some locals call "that gawddamned bird." The weather or the Portland Trailblazers are safer subjects.

It's tough to make a buck here these days, the boys will tell you. The tourist business, however, is thriving. This area is, in fact, one of the most-visited regions of the state.

CALIFORNIA BORDER TO ASHLAND

Approaching Oregon from California on Interstate 5, you'll climb the thinly forested south slope of the Siskiyou Range. These mountains run cross-grain to the north-south Cascades, forming a lumpy border between the two states.

If you like hard liquor, you might want to engage in a southern Oregon ritual by stopping at **Hilt,** the last California town on the highway. The hard stuff is state-controlled and rather high-priced in Oregon, so many Oregonians come here to stock up. A former lumbering town, Hilt now consists of a service station, café and a small general store with a *large* booze department.

You'll enter Oregon about a mile beyond, just short of the Siskiyou Summit. For a sky-view side trip, take Exit 6 from I-5 up to **Mount Ashland,** southwestern Oregon's only ski resort. During a good snowfall year, the small facility's 22 beginner to advanced runs are open from Thanksgiving through Easter. Skiers enjoy awesome alpine views since all the runs are above a 7,000-foot base. Call (503) 482-2897 for ski details and (503) 482-2754 for recorded snow reports. Cross-country skiing and snowmobiling are available in the surrounding national forest.

In summer, the area offers hiking trails through thick Douglas fir and views of both the California and Oregon slopes of the Siskiyous. The road is winding but paved, navigable by most ordinary vehicles. After six miles, you'll pass **Mount Ashland Inn,** a wonderfully cozy retreat built of incense cedar logs, set in a forest thicket. For details, see "Where to sleep" in the Ashland section below.

Beyond the inn, continue winding upward to the ski resort, where the pavement ends. About a mile farther, on a well-maintained gravel road, is **Mount Ashland Campground**. This national forest facility has sites for tents and small RVs, with pit potties and water but no hookups. The area offers awesome views of California's **Mount Shasta,** swimming in a baby blue haze. From the camp, you can hike about half a mile up to the **Siskiyou Crest** for higher two-way views of the area, but it's a tough grind through manzanitas and over rocky outcroppings.

From the Mount Ashland turnoff, I-5 drops steeply toward the broad, forest-cradled **Bear Creek Valley**. Tourist publications tend to stretch the famous Rogue River Valley to include Medford and Ashland. However, it's wimpy little Bear Creek that drains this southeastern end of the basin. The legendary Rogue doesn't enter the picture until you reach the town of Gold Hill, well on your way to Grants Pass.

Reach for a lower gear as you sweep quickly down from the heights. Incidentally, that near-convex volcanic cone to the northeast is **Mount McLoughlin,** named for the "father" of Oregon. As your descent levels off, take Siskiyou Avenue (Business 99) to the home of the Oregon Shakespeare Festival, a remarkable haven of culture in this land of lumberjacks.

Ashland

Population: 16,775   **Elevation: 1,861 feet**

Your route takes you through the tidy, landscaped suburbs of this attractive community, and past the velvety lawns, immense shade trees and stately brick of **Southern Oregon State College.** You'll note as you drive along Siskiyou Avenue that Ashland is one of the more attractive small towns in the West. It's an orderly mix of suburbs and businesses, set against the wooded upslope of this broad valley. You'll find little of the ugly commercial sprawl on the edges that is typical of many of America's towns.

Approaching the business district, the route splits into two one-way streets—northbound Lithia Way and southbound Main Street. Just short of the small Lithia Creek bridge, veer to the left, following signs toward the **Shakespeare center**. You'll cross Main Street and pass a small plaza with a **visitor information** kiosk, which is staffed summer. The rest of the year, you can load up on brochures at the **Ashland visitor's bureau,** a couple of blocks south, next to the Black Swan Theatre at 110 E. Main St.; (503) 482-3486.

From the plaza, continue up Winburn Way alongside Lithia Park and find a parking space—which may be a challenge on summer afternoons. From here, everything of pressing interest is within a short walk, including the three theaters of the **Oregon Shakespeare Festival**, which perch on the park's edge.

☺ We nominate **Lithia Park** as the prettiest small-town west of the Rockies. Planned and planted by John McLaren, the master of San Francisco's Golden Gate Park, it's a lush greenbelt shaded by mature trees, following the course of sparkling Lithia Creek for more than a mile. It was financed by New York advertising mogul Jesse Winburn. He came to town in the 1920s, hoping to build a spa around Lithia Creek's effervescent—if rather sulfurous—waters.

These natural mineral waters can be sampled at a public fountain near the information kiosk. Lithia water is—along with anchovies, aged camembert and dry martinis—an acquired taste. (I was born 30 miles away and have visited Ashland hundreds of times, but I haven't yet acquired it.) Think of it as Perrier with a rotten egg finish.

Downtown Ashland, which nudges up against Lithia Park, is neon-free and spotlessly clean—with an attractive collection of shops, cafés, book stores and stylish boutiques. Of particular appeal are the **Chateaulin Wine and Gourmet Food Shop** at Main and Oak and the **Oregon Store** on Winburn just below the park, both offering samples of Oregon wines and specialty foods. Also check out **Paddington Station** at 125 E. Main Street, with a good selection of giftwares and café stalls, and **Blooms-bury Books and Coffee House** at 290 E. Main, the best of several local bookstores. Nearby is the **Rogue Brewery and Publichouse** at 31 S.

Water Street (488-5061), the area's only micro brewery. You can sip hearty malts and ales brewed on the premises, accompanied by appropriate beer-pub fare, and it's all smoke-free.

☺ Step into the polished wood lobby of the **Mark Antony Hotel** on Main Street, the town's only high rise and a registered historical landmark. It was opened in 1925 as the Lithia Springs Hotel by Mr. Winburn. Towering nine stories, it was the tallest structure between Portland and San Francisco. It faded during the Depression and was reopened as the Mark Antony, with an Elizabethan theme to match the festival. The lobby bar is a popular theatrical hangout, often offering live entertainment. You can dine at the Lithia Springs Restaurant and rent one of the refurbished oldstyle rooms (see listings below).

Some of Ashland's restaurants have sidewalk terraces over Lithia Creek; many are within a five-minute sprint of curtain call. The creekside walking path also serves as the site of an ongoing Elizabethan theme arts and crafts fair during the summer.

All *this* world is a stage

Even without the Shakespeare Festival, there is much to do and see in Ashland. Indeed, you could "do" the town and come away happy, having never set foot in one of the theaters. However, the Bard is the cause of it all and the reason for it all. More specifically, a diminutive, puckish teacher from Oregon State Normal School (now Southern Oregon State College) was the cause of it all. Angus L. Bowmer (as in *bow* and arrow) started the festival in 1935. He convinced town fathers to help finance a pair Shakespeare plays as part of the town's Fourth of July celebration.

From this has grown one of the largest and most remarkable outdoor theater festivals in the world. Remarkable, because Ashland is 300 miles from the nearest metropolitan core and because Oregon of the 1930s was hardly a bastion of culture. To repeat an oft-told tale, city officials agreed to underwrite Bowmer's plays only if boxing matches also were held to guarantee their investment. Of course, as in any fantasy come true, *Twelfth Night* and *The Merchant of Venice* outdrew the pugilists and made enough to cover their deficit. Shakespeare couldn't have scripted it better.

Directing the plays and sometimes playing the Puck he resembled, Angus continued building his festival until his retirement in 1971. He remained as advisor until he died eight years later.

Through the efforts of Bowmer and his successors, Ashland has become the most theatrically focused community in the world. In England's Stratford, the focus is on Shakespeare, the man. Here, it is on the play. Actually, it's on a variety of plays, ranging from the Bard to contemporary classics to *avant garde* experimental theater. About 350,000 people attend each year, choosing from dozen different plays, presented in three theaters during a nine- month season. More people buy more tickets to see more performances of more different plays than in any other place in the country. The ghost of Angus, unlike that of Hamlet's father, has to be smiling.

Critics rave about the shows, done in repertory by professional performers. The company consists of 500 paid staff, including 75 actors, supported by nearly a thousand volunteers. Most performers do at least three plays, often simultaneously. Othello in the afternoon may be a walk-on in a Noel

A new steeply-tiered pavilion improves accoustics and sightlines at the Oregon Shakespeare Festival's classic Elizabethan Theatre.

– Christopher Briscoe photo, courtesy Oregon Shakespeare Festival

Coward comedy at night. Some performers have multiple roles in the same play and make lightening changes that would impress a raceway pit crew.

"If you go into the quick-change room off cue, you might enter as a page and emerge as Queen Elizabeth," one of the performers quipped during a backstage tour.

For young dramatists, this is one of the most highly sought-after companies in the country. Alumni include George Peppard, William Hurt and Stacy Keach. The company has won a Tony Award for regional theater and a Presidential commendation for volunteerism. Other accolades include an ACLU award for refusing a National Endowment for the Arts grant because it had strings attached.

The festival could have used the money, but it certainly isn't poor. You'll note that everything about this facility is perfectly maintained, from the theaters to the landscaping on the bricked courtyard. Members donated $7.5 million to build a dramatic new Elizabethan Theatre seating pavilion to improve acoustics and sight lines. It opened in the summer of 1992.

Doing Shakespeare

☺ For drama buffs, a visit to Ashland can be total cultural immersion. You can see several plays within a week, attend drama-oriented lectures at Southern Oregon State College (including some Elderhostel courses), sit in on theatrical discussion groups and take backstage tours. Also, watch dancers and musicians perform before the plays, try on period costumes and play with props in the Festival Exhibit Center, nibble on Olde English savories, and buy "Will Power" T-shirts and Elizabethan souvenirs at the Tudor Guild Gift Shop. You can buy copies of every Bard play or cheat—as we do—by purchasing 12-page abridged versions to brush up your Shakespeare just before curtain.

The plays are offered in the state-of-the-art 600-seat Angus Bowmer Theatre and the intimate 140-seat Black Swan from late February to early November. The 1,200-seat outdoor Elizabethan Theatre—the oldest in America—functions from mid-June to early October. Take a wrap for the Elizabethan. It can get chilly, although the steeply-raked seating pavilion now provides better shelter.

Tickets should be reserved well in advance, particularly with the popularity of the new Elizabethan seating pavilion. One call does it all: **482-4331.** Or write: **Oregon Shakespeare Festival,** P.O. Box 158, Ashland, OR 97520. You'll receive a thick brochure that lists all the plays, performance times and related festival events such as lectures and Elizabethan feasts. It also lists area lodgings, restaurants, tours and other attractions. With brochure in hand and plans in mind, call the above number with your credit card ready to charge the tickets you want. (Children under five are not admitted to the theaters.)

Ticket prices at this writing were $24 and $18 in the Elizabethan and Bowmer, $24 in the Black Swan, and $36 for special Elizabethan boxes. During spring and fall, when only the Bowmer and Black Swan are operating, their seats are $2 less. Patrons seeing four or more plays from Sunday through Thursday in the spring and fall get a further discount.

The festival runs at about 95 percent capacity, so early planning is essential. If you don't have a ticket, you can join the daily ritual on the Shakespeare plaza near the box office. Hand-letter a sign indicating your needs and stand around looking hopeful. Other patrons often have spare tickets. Scalping is strictly frowned upon; expect to pay the going rate.

Another ritual that must be observed: *There is no late seating* in Ashland. When the door shuts, latecomers are shut out until intermission.

Backstage tours, well worth the $7.50 ($5 for kids 5-11), can be arranged on shorter notice. Conducted by performers and other festival personnel, they cover all three theaters and start daily at 10 a.m. The ticket price includes admission to the **Festival Exhibit Center**. It's a small museum of Shakespeare Festival lore, where you can view props from past performances, play with Brillo pad chain mail and styrofoam goblets, and try on costumes from past plays.

OTHER DRAMA GROUPS

The festival has inspired a cottage industry of drama in and about Ashland. Among them:

Actors' Theatre of Ashland does classic and contemporary drama; it was cited for excellence by National Public Radio and Drama-Logue Magazine; 295 E. Main St., Ashland, OR 97520; (503) 482-9659.

Ashland Community Theatre does an assortment of comedies and dramas in an arena theater; tickets at Paddington Station; (503) 482-0361.

Cygnet Theatre Group does dramas and comedies directed toward children; (503) 488-2945.

Lyric Theatre presents three Broadway-style musicals a year; (503) 488-1926.

Minshall Theatre, operated by the Actors' Theatre of Ashland, presents old fashioned melodramas and an annual Christmas play; it's at 101 Talent Avenue, midway between Ashland and Medford; (P.O. Box 353), Talent, OR 97540; (503) 482-9659.

Oregon Cabaret Theatre is a lively dinner theater troupe doing contemporary musicals; P.O. Box 1149, Ashland, OR 97520; (503) 488-2902.

Studio X offers intimate dramas and *avant garde* theater in a 70-seat "black box;" 208 Oak St., Ashland, OR 97520; (503) 488-2011.

Theatre at Southern is Southern Oregon State College's troupe, presenting a season of dramas and musicals; (503) 552-6348.

ACTIVITIES & OTHER ATTRACTIONS

Aerial flights • Adventures Aloft features hot-air balloon flights; (503) 582-2200. **Ashland Air** offers scenic flights over the valley from Ashland Municipal Airport, 403 Dead Indian Rd., (503) 488-1626.

Bicycling • Open Roads Bicycle Touring conducts extended bicycle trips in southwestern Oregon, with meals and lodging included; 264 Grant St., Ashland, OR 97520; (800) 831-5016. **Ashland Mountain Supply,** 31 N. Main St. just off the Plaza, has bike rentals; (503) 488-2749. The valley's **Bicentennial Bike Path** travels through town to the shores of Bear Creek, then heads for Medford.

Lumber mill tours • Croman Corporation offers tours of its milling operation every Wednesday; arrange in advance at the office at 146 Mistletoe Road, Ashland, or call (503) 482-1221.

Museums • Schneider Museum of Art on the campus of Southern Oregon State College, 1250 Siskiyou Blvd., is open Tuesday-Friday 11 to 5 and Saturday 1 to 5, closed Sunday, (503) 552-6245. **Swedenburg Cultural Resource Center** in the old Chappell-Swedenburg House offers displays on local archaeology; it's at Mountain Avenue and Siskiyou Boulevard, open weekdays 9 to 5.

River running and fishing • Noah's World of Water conducts whitewater trips and salmon and steelhead float trips on nearby rivers, P.O. Box 11, Ashland, OR 97520, (800) 858-2811 or (503) 488-2811. **Eagle Sun Rafting** offers whitewater trips and "snooze cruises" on the Rogue and Klamath rivers, P.O. Box 611, Ashland, OR 97520; (503) 482-5139. **River Trips Unlimited** has fishing, whitewater and scenic floats on the Rogue, 4140 Dry Creek Rd., Medford, OR 97504, (503) 779-3798. **Rogue/Klamath River Adventure** has whitewater outings on those streams with camping or lodging, P.O. Box 4295, Medford, OR 97501, (503) 779-3708. **Swisher Fly Fishing Service** features guided fishing trips on local rivers, 106 Suncrest, Talent, OR 97540, (503) 535-5177.

Various activities • The Adventure Center books an assortment of bike tours, ski packages, river trips, horseback rides and tours. Their booth is on the plaza at 40 N. Main St., Ashland, OR 97520; (800) 444-2819 or (503) 488-2819.

Wineries • Two wineries with tasting rooms are located on the edge of Ashland. **Weisinger's Vineyard** is four miles south at 3150 Siskiyou Blvd., (503) 488-5989; open daily 11 to 6 from June through September, and Wednesday-Sunday 11 to 5 the rest of the year. **Ashland Vineyards** is just east of I-5 near the airport at 2775 E. Main St., (503) 488-0088; open Tuesday-Sunday 11 to 5 from March through December.

WHERE TO DINE

Shakespeare Festival crowds support a startling number of restaurants. Many are geared to pre-theater dining, serving early and closing the kitchen early. Other than Chata in adjacent Talent, the listed diners are within a reasonable after-dinner hike to the theaters.

Alex's Plaza Restaurant • ΔΔ $$

35 N. Main St.; (503) 482-8818. American-continental; full bar service. Daily 11:30 to 9. MC/VISA. Early American setting, with a patio over the creek; busy menu ranges from Java ribs to Cantonese game hen. Attractive, cozy bar with a couch before a fireplace.

Ashland Bakery & Café • Δ $

38 E. Main St.; (503) 482-2117. American; wine and beer. Tuesday-Sunday 7 a.m. to 8 p.m., Monday 7 to 4. No credit cards. Cheerful café issuing assorted espressos, cappuccinos, pastries and tasty curiosities like spinach feta. A good quick-bite place between shows.

Beasy's Backroom • ΔΔ $$

139 E. Main St.; (503) 482-2141. American; full bar service. Monday-Saturday 5:30 to 9, Sunday 5 to 8:30. MC/VISA. Upstairs Western style restaurant with fare to match, such as Texas chicken, assorted steaks and fresh fish in lemon butter.

☺ Chata • ΔΔΔ $$$

1212 S. Pacific Highway, Talent; (503) 535-2575. Middle European; full bar service. Nightly from 5. MC/VISA. Pronounced *Hata*, it's something of a local legend, cozily tucked into an old home. It features dishes of Poland and assorted Baltic-Black Sea countries, such as hunters' stew with beef, smoked pork and sausage, and Rumanian cornmeal cakes with cheese and mushrooms.

☺ Chateaulin Cuisine Français • ΔΔΔ $$$

50 E. Main St.; (503) 482-2264. French; full bar service. Nightly 5 to 9:30, lighter fare until midnight. Major credit cards. One of Ashland's more expensive restaurants and possibly worth it; French country look with wainscoting, brick, café curtains and intimate booths. Both classic and *nouvelle* French cuisine emerge from an innovative constantly-changing menu.

ChinaKorea Restaurant • ΔΔ $$

139 E. Main St.; (503) 488-0235. Asian; full bar service. Tuesday-Saturday 5:30 to 9. MC/VISA. Upstairs restaurant beside Beasy's with a versatile Asian menu, ranging from Chinese orange sesame chicken to Mongolian barbecue and Korean dishes.

Greenleaf Restaurant • ΔΔ $

49 N. Main St.; (503) 482-2808. American; wine and beer. Daily from 10:30 a.m. MC/VISA. Bright, cheery rural American style, with brick accents and cozy booths. Whole earth menu features vegetarian dishes, frittatas, tofu, pasta and salads. Creekside seating.

Lithia Springs Restaurant • ΔΔΔ $$$

Main and First streets in the Mark Antony Hotel; (503) 482-1721. American-Mediterranean; full bar service. Daily 8 a.m. to 8 p.m. Major credit cards. Victorian style dining room done in white and green, with an imposing crystal chandelier. Innovative Greek-Italian-American *nouveau* menu, ranging from chicken piccata to *spanakopita* and smoked salmon in phyllo.

Macaroni's Ristorante ● △△ $$
58 E. Main St.; (503) 488-3359. Italian; wine and beer. Sunday-Thursday 5 to 9, Friday-Saturday 5 to 10. MC/VISA. Cute trattoria just below the theaters, with an outdoor patio. Calzones, pizzas, antipasto and other hearty Italian fare.

Munchie's ● △△ $
59 N. Main St.; (503) 488-2967. Mexican-American; wine and beer. Daily 9 to 9. MC/VISA. Popular "Mexican rathskeller," brick-trimmed and cozy, with assorted smashed beans and rice dishes, vegetarian specialties, home-baked pastries and breads, and salads. One of Ashland's better dining buys.

Thai Pepper ● △△△ $$
84 N. Main St.; (503) 482-8058. Thai; wine and beer. Nightly from 5. MC/VISA. The town's best Asian restaurant, with a bright interior. Creative Thai nouveau fare ranges from subtle to sizzling; try the Evil Jungle (spicy coconut beef curry) or sweet and sour shrimp with apple, cucumber and pineapple.

Underground Deli ● △ $ ∅
125 E. Main St. (in Paddington Station); (503) 488-2595. American; wine and beer. Tuesday-Sunday 7 a.m. to 8 p.m. A good spot for a breakfast muffin, lunch sandwich or light dinner; outside seating.

WHERE TO SLEEP
Ashland may have more bed & breakfast inns per capita than any other city on the planet. There were more than 40 at last count, and many occupy fine old Victorians. Most have summer and winter rates, generally indicated by the high and low ranges in the listing.

Ashland's Main Street Inn ● ⌂⌂ $$$
142 N. Main St., Ashland, OR 97520; (503) 488-0969. Couples and singles $50 to $85. Three rooms with private baths; continental breakfast. No credit cards. Refurbished 1883 Victorian three blocks from theaters. Rooms have period furnishings, refrigerators, TV and balconies.

☺ Chanticleer Inn ● ⌂⌂⌂⌂ $$$$$ ∅
120 Gresham St., Ashland, OR 97520; (503) 482-1919. Couples and singles $85 to $190. Six units with private baths; full breakfast. Elegantly done B&B in a 1920s Craftsman home with French country décor; a short walk to the theaters. Individually controlled heat, air conditioning and phones in rooms; elaborate formal gardens; river rock fireplace in living room.

Country Willows Inn ● ⌂⌂ $$$$ ∅
1313 Clay St., Ashland, OR 97520; (503) 488-1590. Couples $60 to $150, singles $5 less. Seven rooms with private baths; full breakfast. MC/VISA. Attractive ranch-style home with large yard and brook, about three miles from downtown. Modern and early American furnishings in air-conditioned rooms; pool, hot tub.

☺ Cowslip's Belle ● ⌂⌂⌂ $$$$ ∅
159 N. Main St., Ashland, OR 97520; (503) 488-2901. Couples $65 to $95, singles $5 less. Four rooms with private baths; full breakfast. MC/VISA.

Beautifully done B&B in a 1913 Craftsman bungalow, voted one of the 50 best in the country by an innkeepers magazine survey. Two rooms in main house and two in carriage house, furnished with antiques and Oriental rugs. Amenities include a garden and patio, porches and a library.

Edinburgh Lodge Bed & Breakfast • ⌂⌂⌂ $$$$ ∅
586 E. Main St., Ashland, OR 97520; (503) 643-4434. Couples and singles $65 to $95. Six rooms with private baths; full breakfast. MC/VISA. Attractively refurbished 1908 boarding house with early American décor, four blocks from theaters. Scottish style breakfasts with scones, berry crepes and baked herb eggs have been featured in *Sunset Magazine*.

Hersey House • ⌂⌂⌂ $$$$ ∅
452 N. Main St., Ashland, OR 97520; (503) 482-4563. Couples $94 to $104, bungalow from $120. Four units and bungalow, all with private baths; full breakfast. No credit cards. Attractive turn-of-the-century home fronted by a prim English garden, within a short walk of the theaters. Color-coordinated rooms with old English and American furnishings.

☺ McCall House • ⌂⌂⌂ $$$$ ∅
153 Oak St., Ashland, OR 97520; (503) 482-9296. Couples $85 to $150, singles $80 to $145. Seven rooms, some with private and some with shared baths; full breakfast. MC/VISA, DISC. Stylish Italianate Victorian mansion, nicely redone and listed on the National Register of Historic Places. Rooms in main house and carriage house furnished with heirloom antiques.

The Morical House • ⌂⌂⌂ $$$$ ∅
668 N. Main St., Ashland, OR 97520; (503) 482-2254. Couples $75 to $115, singles $65 to $105. Five units with private baths; full breakfast. MC/VISA. Restored 1880s farmhouse furnished with Eastlake antiques, leaded and stained glass windows and ornate woodwork. Huge yard with a 1.5-acre lawn, putting green and flower beds; valley and mountain views. A mile from the theaters.

☺ Mt. Ashland Inn • ⌂⌂⌂ $$$$ ∅
P.O. Box 944 (550 Mt. Ashland Rd.), Ashland, OR 97520; (503) 482-8707. Couples $80 to $130, singles $75 to $125. Five units with private baths; full breakfast. MC/VISA. Secluded hideaway high on the slopes of Mount Ashland, about 16 miles from town; crafted of cedar logs, with huge fieldstone fireplace, antiques and handcrafted furniture. Hearty country breakfasts featured in *Sunset Magazine*.

Romeo Inn • ⌂⌂⌂ $$$$$ ∅
295 Idaho St., Ashland, OR 97520; (503) 488-0884. Couples and singles $115 to $175. Six rooms with private baths; full breakfast. Opulent Cape Cod mansion tucked among ancient pines. Half acre of gardens with pool and spa; mountain and valley views. Large rooms with modern and antique furniture; king-sized beds; two suites with fireplaces.

Shrew's House • ⌂⌂⌂ $$$ ∅
570 Siskiyou Blvd., Ashland, OR 97520; (503) 482-9214. Couples $55 to $105, singles $45 to $95. Three rooms with private baths; full breakfast. MC/VISA. Guest rooms with private entrances in 1898 Victorian; modern amenities such as swimming pool, wet bars, refrigerators and spa tubs in the rooms. Eclectic antique furnishings; a few blocks from theaters.

Motels, hotels & assorted inns

Most of Ashland's motels are grouped along Siskiyou Boulevard at the south end of town, several blocks from the theaters. Some offer shuttles downtown. In addition to the establishments listed below, you'll find more than a dozen motels in Medford, ten miles to the northwest on I-5. For a list, contact the **Medford Visitors & Convention Bureau,** 304 S. Central Ave., Medford, OR 97501; (800) 448-4856 or (503) 779-4847.

All's Well & As You Like It ● △△△ $$$ ∅
637 and 649 E. Main St., Ashland, OR 97520; (503) 488-0874 and 488-5064. Couples and singles $90 in high season, $50 in low season. MC/VISA. Two refurbished turn of the century cottages, one with three bedrooms, one with four, all with private baths. Each house has kitchen facilities with microwave, hot tub, bikes and barbecues.

Ashland Hills Inn ● △△△ $$$ ∅
2525 Ashland St. (I-5 exit 14), Ashland, OR 97520; (800) 547-4747 or (503) 482-8310. Couples and singles $79 to $109, suites $125 to $225. Major credit cards. Ashland's most complete resort hotel with tennis, pool, spa, putting green, jogging track, horseshoe pits and free bicycles. Three miles from downtown; free shuttle to theaters and airport. **Dining room** and casual patio dining; open 7 a.m. to 9 p.m.; dinners $7.50 to $20; full bar service.

Best Western Bard's Inn ● △△ $$$ ∅
132 N. Main St., Ashland, OR 97520; (800) 528-1234 or (503) 482-0049. Couples and singles $48 to $85. Major credit cards. Attractive, well-maintained motel two blocks from Shakespeare festival; TV movies, room refrigerators and phones, pool and spa. **Restaurant** serves 7 a.m. to 2 p.m. and 5 to 10; dinners $8.50 to $15; full bar service.

☺ Buckhorn Springs ● △△ $$$ ∅
2200 Buckhorn Springs Rd., Ashland, OR 97520; (503) 488-2200. Couples and singles $50 to $150; includes full breakfast. MC/VISA, DISC. Century-old mineral springs resort in the mountains 12 miles above Ashland, restored to its original rustic charm. Lodge rooms and cabins with period furnishings—1900s through 1950s. The **restaurant** serves "wholesome, inventive meals" to guests, using organically grown ingredients. The resort, built in 1891, is listed on the National Register of Historic Places.

Columbia Hotel ● △ $$ ∅
262 1/2 E. Main St., Ashland, OR 97520; (503) 482-3726. Couples and singles $36 to $47. MC/VISA. Simply-furnished, clean rooms with vintage dècor, some with TV. Older refurbished downtown hotel, one block from theaters. One of Ashland's better lodging buys. All rooms non-smoking.

Curl-Up Motel ● △ $$ ∅
50 Lowe Rd., Ashland, OR 97520; (800) 482-4711 or (503) 482-4700. Couples $43 to $48, singles $37 to $43. Major credit cards. Very clean small motel five minutes from theaters; large rooms with TV and phones; free coffee; heated pool.

Mark Antony Hotel ● △△ $$$
212 E. Main St., Ashland, OR 97520; (800) 9-ANTONY or (503) 482-1721. Couples $62 to $94, suite $104; rates include continental breakfast. Ma-

jor credit cards. Historic hotel (described above) a short walk to the theaters. Rooms range from small and basic to rather stylish, with period furnishings. Elizabethan-Shakespearean dècor in the spacious lobby. **Restaurant** (listed above) and cocktail lounge.

Palm Motel ● △ $$ ∅
1065 Siskiyou Blvd., Ashland, OR 97520; (503) 482-9253. Couples and singles $36 to $44, kitchenettes $49 to $125, plus weekly rates. MC/VISA. Older motel with well-maintained rooms and housekeeping cottages across from Southern Oregon State College, about a mile from downtown. Lawns with picnic tables and barbecues.

Quality Inn Flagship ● △△ $$$ ∅
2520 Ashland Ave., Ashland, OR 97520; (800) 334-2330 or (503) 488-2330. Couples $50 to $80, singles $45 to $80, kitchenettes from $94. Major credit cards. Nicely furnished units with refrigerators, TV movies, VCRs, phones, fireplaces; heated pool, spa, laundry. Free continental breakfast.

Stratford Inn ● △△ $$$ ∅
555 Siskiyou Blvd., Ashland, OR 97520; (800) 547-4741 or (503) 488-2151. Couples $45 to $90, singles $40 to $85, kitchenettes and suites $59 to $139. Major credit cards. Attractive inn five blocks from theaters; TV/radios, room phones and refrigerators; indoor pool and spa; free morning coffee. All rooms non-smoking.

Timbers Motel ● △△ $$$ ∅
1450 Ashland St., Ashland, OR 97520; (503) 482-4242. Couples $50 to $60, singles $45 to $48, kitchenettes $62 to $72, suites $65 to $75. Major credit cards. A 28-unit motel with TV, room phones, some room refrigerators; pool.

Where to camp

Emigrant Lake Recreation Area ● *Highway 66, five miles east of Ashland, just beyond Glenyan KOA (listed below); (503) 776-7001. RV and tent sites, no hookups, $10. No reservations or credit cards.* Tree-shaded and well-spaced sites with flush potties, laundry, kids' playground and grassy lakeside picnic area. Water slide nearby; fishing, boating and swimming on the lake. Day use $2 per car.

Glenyan KOA ● *5310 Highway 66, Ashland, OR 97520; (503) 482-4138. Full hookups $19, water and electric $17.75, tent sites $15. Reservations accepted; MC/VISA.* Well maintained older park in wooded area with shaded, well-spaced units. Showers, pool, laundry, play area, convenience store.

Green Springs-Howard Prairie Loop

This 40-mile loop trip takes you east into the Siskiyous, up the scenically twisting Green Springs Route on Highway 66, then past a pair of mountain reservoirs. The route spirals steeply upward, but it's all paved and negotiable by just about anything with wheels.

To begin, pick up U.S. 66 near the airport (at the south Ashland I-5 exit) and head southeast, passing **Emigrant Lake** with its camping and recreation area (listed above). You'll quickly shed the brushy, oak lowlands and climb into the conifers, enjoying great views of the wild Siskiyous, surrounding you like a green storm- tossed sea. At **Green Springs Summit**, elevation 4,551 feet, you'll note an assortment of trailheads into the wilds, including the **Pacific Crest Scenic Trail** that travels from Canada to Mexico. (Take an extra pair of shoes.)

Just beyond the summit, you encounter the woodsy **Green Springs Inn,** with a down-home style restaurant that serves steaks, chops and seafood, from $12 to $20. It's also noted for hearty breakfasts and you can grab a sandwich or burrito for lunch. Grub is served from 9 to 9 daily in summer, with shorter hours in the off-season; it takes MC/VISA and AMEX. Nicely rustic lodge rooms go for $50 a night. There's also a luxury unit with a spa tub and fireplace for $95—a good place to cuddle with someone interesting.

Opposite the inn, turn left and drive three miles to **Hyatt Lake Recreation Area.** It's an ordinary-looking lake in a shallow basin but the surrounding forested mountains create a nice setting. There are several national forest campgrounds in the area with tree-shaded spots but no hookups, or you can find more complete facilities at **Hyatt Lake Resort.** Its offerings include a restaurant, rustic cabins for $45 a night, campsites with full hookups for $10 or no hookups for $8, plus coin laundry and showers. Motorboat and canoe rentals also are available. The lake is stocked with rainbow trout and bass; it's popular with local fisherpersons. For reservations and specifics, contact: Hyatt Lake Resort, P.O. Box 3120, Ashland, OR 97520; (503) 482-3331.

From Hyatt Lake, press on to **Howard Prairie Lake Recreation Area,** at yet another tree-rimmed reservoir, also offering swimming, boating and fishing. The **Howard Prairie Resort** has a lakeside campground with undeveloped sites for $10, water and electric for $11 and full hookups for $12. It doesn't accept reservations but will guarantee you a "dry site" until something with hookups becomes available. It's a *big* campground. One also can rent "prairie schooner" mobile cabins for $50 a night. It has boat rentals, plus a small café and gasoline. If you forget your tackle, you can rent a rod and buy the proper license here.

Return to Ashland via Dead Indian Road (an awful name that the county ought to change). It's less twisting than the Greensprings route, and the views aren't quite so dramatic. But you'll catch some nice glimpses of the Bear Creek Valley and Ashland as you descend.

ASHLAND TO JACKSONVILLE

From Ashland, head north on I-5 for about ten miles and jump off at Medford's Barnett Road interchange (exit 27). Then go left over the freeway to the log cabin **visitor center** operated by the Medford Visitors and Convention Bureau; it's open daily 9 to 5; (503) 779-4847. Brace yourself as you walk through the door, because the bureau's motto is "We hug visitors." Certainly better than being mugged. We'll get to this huggy community later, because we're bound for Jacksonville, one of only six cities in the country with a national historic landmark status.

☺ From the visitors bureau, follow the freeway frontage road (old Highway 99) for about a mile to **Harry and David's Original Country Store.** Original, indeed. Brothers Harry and David Holmes began running their family's Bear Creek Orchard in 1914, then branched out to mail-order gift packs to survive the Depression. With its culinary gift catalog and "Fruit of the Month Club," Bear Creek has become one of the world's largest purveyors of specialty foods.

The large country store is a wonderland for nibblers. Within this snack food Oz, we counted—and sampled—30 different items, ranging from butter toffee peanuts, roasted green peas and onion-garlic almonds to yogurt banana chips, cinnamon pretzels and (urp) sour gummy squigglies. These culinary curiosities are available in bulk or by the bag; take a pound of jalapeno peanuts home to Mom. The store also offers fresh produce, an awesome assortment of canned and otherwise prepared Oregon specialty foods, a deli specializing in smoked goods and bakery items, a restaurant and gift shop.

Tours of the huge packing facility are conducted weekdays; call (503) 776-2277 for reservations.

Nearby is **Jackson and Perkins,** the world's largest shipper of roses. Started in 1872, it's now part of the Bear Creek corporation. Don't believe that "rose by any other name" business until you've toured the 43,000-square-foot rose test garden. It's open to the public May through October.

Continue south on the frontage road to the next stoplight and turn right onto South Stage Road. You'll pass a bucolic panorama of orchards, pasturelands, an occasional fruit stand and prosperous looking country homes. The area offers a stunning display of white pear blossoms in the spring, usually in April. About five miles from Medford, you swing onto the main street of a town that yesterday didn't forget.

Jacksonville

Population: 1,989   **Elevation: 1,640 feet**

According to legend, a couple of prospectors headed from the Willamette Valley to a California mining camp in 1851 with a load of food and supplies, decided to camp beside a creek in this area. Rigging their mules the next morning, they found a nugget in one of the beast's hoof prints.

That sounds like a campfire story. But it is true that the pair hurried to California with their load, then returned and staked their claims. The word spread, of course, and within weeks, 2,000 gold-seekers were digging and panning feverishly in places called Ruth Gulch and Daisy Creek. The town of Tablerock Mountain was laid out, named for flat topped buttes several miles northeast. It later was changed to Jacksonville, in honor of Old Hickory.

Pursuing a course typical of most mining camps, it emerged as a shanty town of canvas, followed by more substantial wooden structures. These burned back to the dirt three times between 1873 and 1884. Taking a cue from California mining towns, residents switched to fireproof brick, with iron doors and shutters. Jacksonville thrived as the largest town in southern Oregon for decades, and was the seat of Jackson County for 70 years.

One of its most prominent residents was Swiss-born Peter Britt, a photographer, artist and horticulturist who arrived in 1852. He was the first to photograph Crater Lake and his pictures of that jewel led to its selection for national park status. This gentleman farmer-photographer built an impressive mansion surrounded by elaborate gardens, where he lived until his death in 1905. His mansion was burned but his gardens survive. In 1962, they became the setting for an annual music festival named in his honor.

After Jacksonville's gold played out, the town remained an important trading and agricultural center. Then in the 1880s, the new Oregon & California railroad bypassed it favor of the future community of Medford. As a final blow, Medford took away the county seat in 1927 and J'ville went to sleep. However, in hibernation there is preservation. Jacksonville's old iron

ASHLAND MEDFORD CRATER LAKE

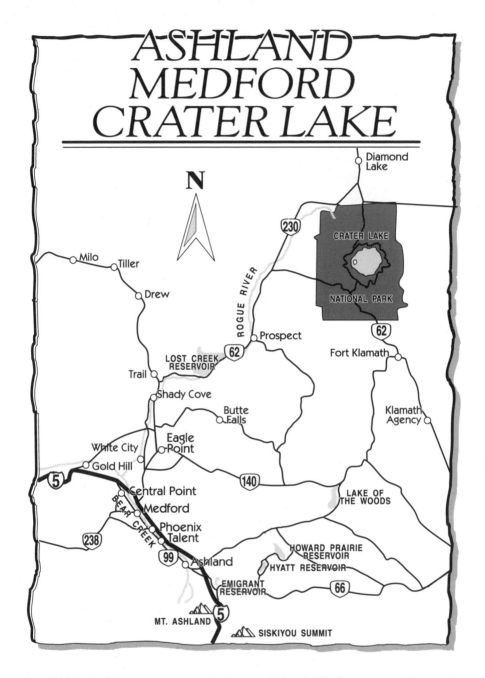

and brick buildings were spared the wrecking ball of progress. The entire town was declared a National Historic Landmark in 1967. More than 100 of its buildings are listed on the National Register of Historic Places.

A walk down California Street is a stroll into yesterday—sort of. Boutiques and shops such as Farrago Chocolates, the Mangy Moose Emporium and Calico Junction aren't authentic, although the structures that house them certainly are. Protected by its historic status, the town is refreshingly free of neon and gaudy signs. It does indulge in harmless tourist gimmicks such as carriage rides and a tour on a trackless cable car that somehow found its way here from San Francisco.

Three blocks of California Street are busy with boutiques, antique stores and restaurants. Brief strolls down side streets will deliver you to an assortment of old homes, including many restored Victorians. In the limelight of tourism, Jacksonville's neighborhoods have a prosperous old timey look. Walking tour maps will guide your feet past dozens of these old buildings.

A **visitors information center** is housed in the Rogue Valley Railway Depot at Oregon and C streets. It's open daily 10 to 4 from May through August and Saturday-Monday 10 to 4 the rest of the year; 899-8118.

THE MUSIC FESTIVAL

☺ Taking a cue from Ashland's success, locals established the Peter Britt Music Festival in the Britt Gardens in 1962. Now called the Britt Festivals, this summer-long showcase is held in an attractive outdoor pavilion, where patrons can listen to the stars under the stars. For ticket and schedule information, contact: **Britt Festivals**, P.O. Box 1124, Medford, OR 97501; (800) 882-7488 or (503) 6077. Tickets can be ordered by phone with credit cards, or FAX (503) 776-3712.

Initially a classical music festival, it has broadened its base to include jazz, *avant garde,* bluegrass, country, popular, theater and dance. Among those who have brightened the Britt Pavilion are Manhattan Transfer, Mason Williams, Pete Fountain, the Nitty Gritty Dirt Band, Mel Torme, the Everly Brothers and Joan Baez. Offerings range from Broadway musicals to Mozart marathons and San Francisco Japanese taiko drummers. Activities are scheduled from mid-June through early September.

Picnicking before the concerts on the outdoor pavilion's grassy slope adds a special dimension. For those who prefer to sit upright, reserved seats are available. In addition to personal picnicking, special catered picnic and champagne brunch concerts are scheduled.

Ticket prices range from $10 on the grass to $25 in the seats. Top name artists sell out early, so respond accordingly. Ticket outlets are at the pavilion box office, Farrago Chocolates at 157 California Street, the Adventure Center at 40 N. Main Street in Ashland, and at the Britt Festival office, behind Sears in the Medford Center shopping mall at Biddle Road and Stevens Street.

Like their Ashland cousins, the Britt people produce a detailed brochure. Obviously, a week of Bard and Britt can make for a fine Southwestern Oregon cultural trip.

OTHER ATTRACTIONS & ACTIVITIES

☺ **Jacksonville Museum of Southern Oregon History** ● *206 N. Fifth St. (at C Street); (503) 773-6536. Daily 10 to 5; admission $2.* Housed in the imposing three-story red brick former county courthouse, this is southwestern Oregon's finest museum. You'll find a mock-up of Britt's photo studio, frontier photos by Britt and others, exhibits on mining, the early Chinese, the Oregon & California Railroad that spelled J'ville's doom and a good collection of pioneer artifacts.

Peter Britt Gardens ● *First and Pine streets.* Britt's elaborate gardens are near the festival pavilion. You'll see the mortar and stone foundation walls of his Gothic mansion, plus extensive plantings by Britt, and others who have since tended the garden. From a huge redwood which Britt planted 130 years ago, you can follow a half-mile trail up to Jackson Creek and the remnants of Britt's diversion ditches and an abandoned railroad bed.

Beekman House ● *352 E. California St. (at Laurelwood); (503) 773-6536. Half-hour conducted tours $2, from Memorial Day to Labor Day weekend, daily from noon to 5.* Cornelius C. Beekman founded Oregon's second bank (still standing at Third and California streets), and he built this clapboard home for his family in 1873. Descendants owned it until 1959, so much of what you see is original. Costumed docents pose as folks of the period, talking as if yesterday were only yesterday. The smell of baking bread in the oven enhances the reality as the hired girl pauses from her chores to escort you about and introduce you to Julia Beekman.

Beekman Bank ● *California and Third Streets; (503) 773-6536. Self-guiding tours. Open Memorial Day through Labor Day weekend, noon to 5.* The bank, established in 1863, still contains most of its original furnishings, including gold scales and Wells Fargo memorabilia.

☺ **Jeremiah Nunan House** ● *635 Oregon St.; (503) 899- 1890. Guided tours Wednesday-Sunday 10:30 to 5 from mid-May through mid-September. Victorian Christmas ornament displays and Christmas shop open Friday-Sunday during November and December.* Jacksonville's most striking Victorian has enjoyed continuous occupancy since its construction in 1892. Present owners conduct half-hour tours through its lavish Victorian interior, a-brim with museum-quality antiques. Known as a "catalog house," it was ordered through a "wish book" by wealthy merchant Jeremiah Nunan, shipped in 14 boxcars from Tennessee and assembled at a cost of $7,800.

Gold mine tour ● *Oregon Belle Mine, P.O. Box 1774, Jacksonville, OR 95370; (503) 779-2239 or 899-9127. Adults $9, kids 12 and under, $5. Tickets at Farrago Chocolates, 157 California St.* This mine, about 20 minutes from town, has been worked for more than a century. You'll stroll into the cool, dark tunnels and learn of both early-day and modern mining techniques. You then get a quick lesson in gold refining as your guide demonstrates uses for the scatter of equipment outside. At the tour's end, visitors can become miners, with guaranteed results. You can buy a small sack of pulverized gold ore, pan it in a trough and take home your booty in a bottle.

Carriage tour ● *Jackson Carriage Service, Third and California streets; (503) 476-1426.* Hop aboard a vintage surrey and clip-clop around town; various prices for various lengths.

Trolley tours ● *Daily 10 to 4; adults $3.50, kids under 12, $1.50.* Fifty-minute narrated tours of Jacksonville are conducted aboard a derailed San Francisco cable car, departing hourly from Third and California street.

Historic walking tour maps ● They're available from the history museum, U.S. National Bank at California and Third streets and from the visitor center in the railway depot at Oregon and C streets.

WHERE TO DINE

Bella Union Restaurant & Lounge ● ∆∆ $$$
170 W. California St.; (503) 899-1770. American-continental; full bar service. Monday-Friday 11:30 to 10, Saturday 11 to 10, Sunday 10 to 10. MC/VISA. Attractive oldstyle diner with bentwood chairs and brick walls decorated with works of local artists. Outdoor patio is a popular lunch stop.

The historic mining town of Jacksonville still retains much of its yesterday look.
-- **Betty Woo Martin**

Resourceful dinner menu ranges from seafood fettuccini and rack of lamb to stuffed hazelnut chicken.

☺ Jacksonville Inn Dinner House ● ∆∆∆ $$$

175 E. California St.; (503) 899-1900. American-Italian; full bar service. Lunch Monday-Saturday 11 to 2, dinner Monday-Saturday 5 to 10 and Sunday 5 to 9, Sunday brunch 10 to 2. Major credit cards. Attractive Victorian dining room done in raw brick, warm woods and hanging plants; housed in a brick 1863 mercantile and bank building. Multi-course dinners offer prime rib, fresh seafood and Italian fare; outstanding wine list. Rated by Northwest magazines as one of Oregon's best restaurants.

McCully House Inn ● ∆∆∆ $$$ ∅

240 E. California St.; (503) 899-1942. American-continental; wine and beer. Lunch Wednesday-Saturday 11:30 to 2:30, dinner Wednesday-Sunday 5:30 to 8:30, Sunday brunch 9:30 to 2. MC/VISA, AMEX. Handsome Victorian dining room in a restored 1861 bed & breakfast inn. Menu ranges from shrimp jambalaya to pecan chicken.

Munchie's of Jacksonville ● ∆ $

150 S. Oregon St.; (503) 899-1029. Mexican-American; wine and beer. Daily 9 to 9. MC/VISA. A cousin to Ashland's Munchie's, with a similar inexpensive menu featuring Mexican fare, bakery goodies, vegetarian dishes, soups and salad. A good spot for a cheap fill up.

WHERE TO SLEEP

Jacksonville Inn • ⌂⌂ $$$ ∅

175 E. California St., Jacksonville, OR 97530; (503) 899-1900. Couples $80 to $175, singles from $60; includes full breakfast. Major credit cards. An 1861 brick mercantile converted into an inn with pleasing Victorian décor. Nine guest rooms nicely furnished with antiques; some a bit snug. TV, room phones. One-bedroom cottage with fireplace and spa. All rooms non-smoking. Restaurant listed above.

The Stage Lodge • ⌂⌂ $$

P.O. Box 1360 (830 N. Fifth St.), Jacksonville, OR 97530; (800) 253-8254 or (503) 899-3953. Couples $63 to $69. Major credit cards. Victorian style motel half a mile from the historic district. Large, neat rooms with TV and phones, modern with early American touches; some rooms with fireplaces.

Bed & breakfast inns

For a complete listing of Jacksonville-area B&Bs, contact the Jacksonville Bed & Breakfast Inn Association, P.O. Box 787, Jacksonville, OR 97530.

Arden Forest Inn • ⌂⌂ $$$ ∅

261 W. Hersey St., Ashland, OR 97520; (503) 488-1496. Couples $60 to $78, singles $55 to $62. Four units with private baths; full breakfast. MC/VISA, AMEX. Turn-of-the-century farmhouse with light, contemporary furnishings, accented by paintings of artist-owner. Library; surrounding gardens with shaded deck.

Livingston Mansion • ⌂⌂⌂ $$$$ ∅

4132 Livingston Rd. (P.O. Box 1476), Jacksonville, OR 97530; (503) 899-7107. Couples and singles $90 to $100. Three units with private baths; full breakfast. Huge 1915 shingle-sided Craftsman country home, furnished with English oak and other period pieces. Landscaped yard, pool, view of the surrounding countryside. A short distance from downtown Jacksonville.

McCully House Inn • ⌂⌂⌂ $$$$ ∅

240 E. California St. (P.O. Box 13), Jacksonville, OR 97530; (503) 899-1942. Couples $85, singles $75. Three rooms with private baths; full breakfast. MC/VISA, AMEX. Opulent Greek revival mansion furnished with museum-quality antiques. One of Ashland's oldest homes, built by a physician in 1861; listed on the National Register of Historic Places. Short walk to downtown historic district and Britt Pavilion. Restaurant listed above.

Reams House 1868 • ⌂⌂⌂ $$$$ ∅

550 E. California St. (P.O. Box 128), Jacksonville, OR 97530; (503) 899-1868. Couples and singles $75 to $90. Four rooms, two with private baths; full breakfast. No credit cards. Early American home listed on National Register of Historic Places; rooms furnished with Victorian and American antiques. Walking distance to downtown; gardens, patio, library, bicycles.

Medford

Population: 50,000   **Elevation: 1,380 feet**

To return to the community that offers hugs, follow South Fifth Street (which becomes State Highway 238) east from Jacksonville. It takes you about five miles through more orchards and farms into Medford's back door.

About two miles short of town, you might pause for a bite at a very inexpensive restaurant that's something of a local legend. **LaBurrita** at 2715 Jacksonville Highway (on your left, opposite Bi-Mart) is a Mexican deli serving hefty meals for under $5. There's another downtown (see listing below). Nearing Medford, Highway 238 becomes Main Street, although a one-way grid shifts you a block south to Eighth Street. Note the pleasantly tree-shaded **Alba Park** wrapped by Eighth, Main, Holly and Ivy. As you cross Central, you're in the heart of downtown, and a right turn will carry you three blocks to the main office of the **Medford Visitors and Convention Bureau** at 304 S. Central; (503) 779-4847. It's open weekdays 9 to 5 and you can load up on brochures and maps, in case you haven't already done so at the log cabin visitor center on the northern edge of town.

A few blocks north, at 106 N. Central near Sixth, is the **Southern Oregon Museum and History Store** (Monday-Friday 9 to 5 and Saturday 10 to 5; 773-6536). Central is one-way going south, so you'll have to drive up Front Street to reach it. Housed in an old J.C. Penney building, it offers a goodly collection of pioneer artifacts, with nicely-done exhibits on area farming, logging and mining. The downstairs History Store is one of the better museum gift shops around, with a selection of old fashioned toy replicas, folk art and other worthy curios. If you want to grab a bite while you're downtown, we'd recommend **C.K. Tiffin's** at 266 E. Main, between Bartlett and Central (listed below).

Although downtown is suffering suburban withdrawal pains as businesses flee to the malls, it's holding up reasonably well. Only a few of its 1930s and 1940s storefronts are empty. It is, incidentally, a good area for antiquing. You'll find several yesterday shops here, particularly at the **Main Antique Mall** at 30 North Riverside (779-9490).

Medford isn't a tourist town, but it needn't suffer a complex about that. It can serve as a base of operations for voyages to Ashland, Jacksonville, Grants Pass, the Rogue River and Crater Lake. It offers a goodly assortment of motels, and two covered malls, with the best shopping variety in the Rogue River Valley. Both are easily reached from I-5. **Medford Mall** is on Biddle Road, paralleling the east side of the freeway and the larger **Rogue Valley Mall** borders Riverside Avenue west of the freeway.

Medford got its start because the citizens of Jacksonville refused to grease the palms of Oregon & California Railroad officials. They wanted $25,000 to build a station there in 1883. Rebuffed by J'ville, they chose a crossing of Bear Creek and called it Middle Ford. Later, it was shortened to Midford and then Medford. A town site was platted and Medford started growing while Jacksonville fell asleep at the switch.

Ironically, the railroad no longer serves Medford. The San Francisco-Seattle Amtrak favors the Klamath Falls route instead of the steep ascent over the Siskiyous. **Greyhound/Trailways** (779-2103) offers frequent service along the busy I-5 corridor.

JACKSON COUNTY ANNUAL EVENTS

Pear Blossom Festival in Medford, early April; 734-7327.

Rogue Valley Intertribal Pow-Wow with Native American dances, songs, foods and crafts, late May; 535-6031.

Pioneer Days in Jacksonville, old time Western celebration, mid-June; 889-8118.

Jackson County Fair in Medford, third weekend of July; 779-4847.

Hometown Christmas Celebration in Ashland with caroling, tree lighting ceremony and Christmas plays, through December; 482- 3486.

Air services

Medford Airport (776-7222) is served by United Airlines, United Express and Horizon, with Budget and National rental car outlets. Because of Ashland and Jacksonville's tourist lures, it offers a surprising number of flights for a small city, particularly in summer. If you plan a Southwestern Oregon fly-drive, we'd suggest early reservations.

WHERE TO DINE

C.K. Tiffin's ● ∆∆ $

266 E. Main St.; (503) 779-0480. American; wine and beer. Weekdays only, 8 a.m. to 8 p.m. MC/VISA, DISC. Very attractive cafè with interior brick walls, ceiling fans, drop lamps and wooden booths. Menu features a health-conscious selection of chicken dishes, seafood fettuccini and several vegetarian meals. Prices are modest, between $6 and $9. The weekday-only hours are an indicator of life in downtown Medford.

Hungry Woodsman ● ∆∆ $$

2001 N. Pacific Highway; (503) 772-2050. American; full bar service. Lunch weekdays from 11, dinner nightly. Major credit cards. Medford's signature restaurant, a virtual lumberjack museum, decorated with memorabilia from the logging industry that helps support the town. Essentially American menu features hefty steaks, prime rib, chicken dishes and seafood.

LaBurrita ● ∆ $

2715 Jacksonville Highway, (503) 770-5770 and 603 S. Riverside Ave. (503) 770-2848. Mexican; wine and beer. Daily 10:30 to 8. No credit cards. Basic Mexican joint serving huge meals for a very few dollars. Fill your plate in the deli and adjourn to the adjacent cafè, decorated with a fake tile roof and fuzzy paintings. A store in the Jackson Highway cafè sells Mexican breads, LaBurrita's salsas, pastries and specialty foods; a factory elsewhere makes tortillas and chips sold throughout the state.

Mon Desir Inn ● ∆∆∆ $$ ∅

4615 Hamrick Rd. (I-5 exit 32), Central Point; (503) 664-6661. American; full bar service. Monday-Saturday 5 p.m. to 10 p.m., Sunday 10 to 2 and 4 to 9. Major credit cards. Decades-old dining room with comfortable early American dècor and traditional American dishes, served in generous portions. It's a slice of country elegance, in Central Point, just north of Medford.

The Sandpiper ● ∆∆ $$

1841 Barnett Rd. (just off I-5); (503) 779-0100. American; full bar service. Dinner nightly from 5. Major credit cards. Cozy split-level restaurant offering Medford's best seafood menu. Specialties include fresh salmon, bacon-wrapped steak in burgundy sauce and brandied pork.

WHERE TO SLEEP

Best Western Medford Inn ● ◠◠ $$ ∅

1015 Riverside Ave. (I-5 exit 27), Medford, OR 97501; (800) 528-1234 or (503) 773-8266. Couples $47 to $52, singles $42. Major credit cards. Very nicely appointed rooms in a 112-unit motel; TV, room phones; some refrigerators and some suites with spa tubs. Swimming pool; restaurants adjacent.

Best Western Pony Soldier Inn ● ⌂⌂ $$$ ∅

2340 Crater Lake Highway (I-5 exit 30), Medford, OR 97504; (800) 528-1234 or (503) 779-2011. Couples $66 to $70, singles $56 to $64. Major credit cards. Attractive motel complex with TV movies, room phones, some refrigerators. Coin laundry, pool and spa; restaurant adjacent.

Cedar Lodge Motor Inn ● ⌂ $$ ∅

518 N. Riverside Ave. (I-5 exit 27), Medford, OR 97501; (503) 773-7361. Couples $45 to $60, singles $35 to $39. Major credit cards. Well-kept 79-unit motel with TV movies, room phones, some refrigerators. Pool.

Nandel's Inn ● ⌂⌂ $$$ ∅

2300 Crater Lake Highway (I-5 exit 30), Medford, OR 97504; (503) 779-3141. Couples $66 to $71, singles $50 to $65, suites $100 to $120. Major credit cards. Nicely done rooms with TV, room phones; refrigerators in suites. Indoor pool, kids pool, rec room. **Restaurant** serves American fare 6:30 a.m. to 10 p.m.; dinners $9 to $16; full bar service.

Pear Tree Motel ● ⌂⌂ $$ ∅

3730 Fern Valley Rd. (I-5 exit 24), Medford, OR 97504; (503) 535-4445. Couples $37 to $63, singles $37. Major credit cards. Impeccably maintained motel; TV, pay movies. Coin laundry, pool, spa, playground. Restaurant and RV park (listed below) adjacent.

Windmill Inn of Medford ● ⌂⌂ $$$ ∅

1950 Biddle Rd. (I-5 exit 30), Medford, OR 97504; (800) 547-4747 or (503) 779-0050. Couples $50 to $70, singles $50 to $61. Major credit cards. Large, attractive 123-unit inn with TV movies, room phones. Pool, sauna, guest bicycles, library.

WHERE TO CAMP

Holiday RV Park ● *I-5 exit 24 (P.O. Box 1020), Phoenix, OR 97535; (800) 452-7970 or (503) 535-2183. RV sites only, full hookups $17, water and electric $13. Reservations accepted; MC/VISA.* Close-together but clean, tree-shaded sites; many pull-throughs, just off freeway. Showers, pool, laundry, play area, convenience store, rec room. Midway between Medford and Ashland.

Pear Tree RV Park ● *I-5 exit 24 (3730 Fern Valley Rd., Medford, OR 97504; (800) 645-7332 or (503) 535-4445. RV sites only, full hookups $19. Reservations accepted; Major credit cards.* New RV park adjacent to motel with access to a mini-mart, service station, pool, showers, spa and playground. Spotless layout; sites close together and unshaded (although the new trees will grow). Across the freeway from Holiday RV Park (above).

MEDFORD TO CRATER LAKE

Oregon's only national park is two hours north, and getting there is at least half the fun, since you'll travel along the scenically meandering route of the upper Rogue River. It's busy with campsites, swimming holes, fishing holes, and boating, tubing and whitewater rafting stretches. Sidetracked by this user-friendly stream, some folks headed for Crater Lake National Park have been known to arrive several days late.

From downtown, pick up Riverside Avenue, the main one-way street heading north, and follow it past Rogue Valley Mall. Just beyond, fork left, following North Medford/Central Point signs, then take a quick right onto Table Rock Road.

If it's the second or fourth Sunday of the month (April through October), look for a small green sign to **Medford Railroad Park.** It's on the right, just after you hit Table Rock Road. A group of rail buffs offer rides to kiddies of all sizes (including grown-up ones) on handsomely crafted scale model trains, from 11 a.m. to 3 p.m. Rides are free and donations are appreciated. You'll also see an old Medford Corporation logging train, several cabeese and some other full-sized rolling stock. There's a picnic pavilion here as well.

Continuing out Table Rock Road, you'll get your first glimpse of the legendary **Rogue River.** The highway crosses it at **Tou Velle State Park,** a streamside picnicking and swimming area. Beyond, you approach two of the most interesting geological formations in southern Oregon.

☺ Upper and lower **Table Rocks** are sandstone-basalt mesas rising 800 feet above the valley floor. They suggest a pair of giant aircraft carriers run aground, absolutely flat with little vegetation on top. These strange formations with near-vertical sides were formed when basaltic lava flows oozed into the valley 4.5 million years ago, covering a softer base of sandstone. As the sandstone weathered away, chunks of the harder basaltic cap rock remained.

The two tables been havens for curious hikers and rock-scramblers since man first came to this valley. They were, in fact, retreats for the Rogue Indians until they were routed during the 1850s Rogue Valley wars. Eventually becoming part of a local ranch, they were purchased by the Nature Conservancy in 1979. They're jointly managed by the conservancy and Bureau of Land Management.

From trailheads off Table Rock Road, you can hike up to their flat tops. The easiest ascent is up Lower Table Rock. A two-mile trek takes you up its steep flanks then across the broad mesa for an awesome view from its craggy ramparts. From your dizzying perch, you'll see the squiggly tree-lined course of the Rogue, patchwork farmlands and the glistening rooftops of distant Medford, all rimmed by wooded peaks of the surrounding Siskiyous. With proper courage, you can sit with your feet hanging over eternity. Hawks and buzzards circle lazily below and cliff swallows dart in and out of their basaltic niches.

To reach the trailhead, continue out Table Rock Road, following it around to the left until you see a small green sign indicating Wheeler Road (toward the Dogs for the Deaf training school). A left turn takes you to the trailhead.

Even if you aren't in a climbing mood, you'll enjoy the detour to the base of these intriguing mesas. To get back on track, retrace Table Rock Road, then turn left onto Modock Road. Follow it toward Upper Table Rock until you hit Highway 234 after three miles. Turn right and you'll encounter Route 62, the Crater Lake Highway. Logic dictates a left turn toward Crater Lake. But first, go right and backtrack to the hamlet of **Eagle Point** to visit Oregon's only working grist mill.

☺ The 1872 **Butte Creek Mill** is open Monday-Saturday from 9 to 5; (503) 826-3531. You can listen to the grunting melody of the old stones turning and inhale the heady aroma of fresh-ground wheat. At an adjacent shop, choose from among a dozen varieties of healthy stone-ground grains, homemade peanut butter and other specialty foods. The 1,400-pound grinding wheels have a history all their own. They were quarried in France, shaped in Illinois, shipped around the Horn, and then hauled by wagon over the Siskiyous.

The adjacent **Oregon General Store Museum** exhibits early day fixtures, advertising signs and other items from a 19th century general store. Unfortunately, its hours were limited when we visited: Saturdays only from 11 to 4.

From Eagle Point, Crater Lake Highway soon leaves the flat pastureland and heads toward wooded mountains. At a junction, you can follow a gently winding, tree-lined paved road 16 miles to the mountain hamlet of **Butte Falls,** and to **Willow Lake** beyond. It's popular for summer swimming and boating. This is in the foothills of the Cascade Range, and forestry roads reach from Butte Falls into the rugged heights of the **Sky Lakes Wilderness** and the Pacific Crest Scenic Trail.

Continuing up the Crater Lake Highway, you'll hit the nondescript community of **Shady Cove** on the Rogue River. From this point, the stream becomes your roadside companion most of the way to Crater Lake. It's famous here for steelhead and trout fishing. A rather calm stretch of the Rogue above Shady Cove is riffle country, popular for flatwater floats and tubing. Several local outfits rent rafts and provide shuttle service to assorted put-in points, mostly at the base of Lost Creek Dam above. Among those doing business locally are **Raft Right Rentals,** 878-4005; **Dry Dock Marina,** 878-2737; **Rapid Pleasure Raft Rentals,** 878-2500 and **Adventures West,** 878-4019.

WHERE TO CAMP

This is RV country as well. Among the campgrounds that cluster about and above Shady Cove are:

Fly Casters RV Park ● *21655 Crater Lake Highway (P.O. Box 699), Shady Cove, OR 97539; (503) 878-2749. RV sites; full hookups $20 on the river and $16 off. Reservations accepted; MC/VISA.* Older, well-maintained park with gravel roadways; most sites shaded. Cable TV, Propane, showers, coin laundry, picnic tables. Fishing guide service and raft launching area.

Rogue River Resort & RV Park ● *21800 Crater Lake Highway, Shady Cove, OR 97539; (503) 878-2404. RV sites; $14 to $22 with full hookups. Reservations accepted; MC/VISA.* Newer but less shady than Fly Casters; some paved interior roads; many pull-throughs; sites on the river. Cable TV, RV supplies and dump station, horseshoe pits and playground, rec room, convenience store, laundry and boat ramp. Guide service and river rafting.

Shady Trails on the River ● *Crater Lake Highway just north of Shady Cove; (503) 878-2206. RV and tent sites; full hookups $16, tents $10.* Older park with gravel roads, some sites on the river. Showers, groceries, Propane, fishing supplies, picnic tables, horseshoe pits and beach.

Bear Mountain RV Park ● *27301 Rogue River Highway, Trail, OR 97541; (503) 878-2400. RV sites; $10 to $14; full hookups. Reservations accepted.* Small, well-maintained park with gravel roads, some shaded sites. Showers, coin laundry, convenience store with fishing tackle, horseshoes, playground and rec field, boat dock and fishing.

Continuing upward, you pass a mix of conifers and riverside homes. Past the turnoff to the tiny hamlet of **Trail,** you encounter yet another camping area.

Rogue Elk County Park ● *RV and tent sites; $11 for electrical and $10 dry camp; day use $2 per vehicle. No reservations or credit cards.* Nice spot on a bend in the river with a grassy lawn area. Shaded campsites, coin showers, picnic tables and barbecues, raft launching area and "inflation station."

If you're a serious fisherperson or want to become one, watch on your right above Rogue Elk Park for **Pat's Hand-Tied Flies,** (878-2338) a tackle shop with proper lures to seduce the local fish. It also has beer, ice and other basic provisions, a rock shop with hand-made jewelry and lots of free fishing advice; MC/VISA.

Pressing northeast into ever-greening countryside, you encounter the region's largest and busiest recreation area. It's created by **Lost Creek Dam,** which plugged up the Rogue in 1977. The reservoir by the same name is popular for boating, water skiing and fishing. A nicely done interpretive center at **McGregor Park** below the dam has historical, geological and critter exhibits. An inviting, grassy streamside picnic area is nearby.

Just beyond the park is **Cole M. Rivers Fish Hatchery** (878-2235), at the base of a diversion dam that's a popular launching spot for rafters. One of the largest hatcheries in the West, the facility rears nearly 2.5 million salmon, steelhead and rainbow trout each year. Graphics and exhibits in the hatch house explain how all this is done. Out by the rearing ponds, you can create your own personal feeding frenzy for 25 cents with a handful of fish food from a vending machine. At a nearby fish ladder, you can watch huge and weary salmon following blind instinct by swimming into the hatchery that gave them birth.

The bulky earth and rockfill dam is a bit farther upstream, offering boat launches, picnic areas and a visitor center open weekdays from 8 to 5; (503) 472-2434. Hiking trails loop the lake and link up with the Rogue River Trail that reaches all the way to Crater Lake. If you brought your backpack, you can hoof it to several hike-in campsites on the edge of the reservoir. Hiking maps are available locally or by writing: Army Corps of Engineers, Rogue River Basin Project, Trail, OR 97541.

If you return to the highway and drive along the eastern edge of Lost Creek Lake, you'll soon find yourself at **Joseph Stewart State Park.** It offers picnic tables, recreation areas, boat launches, a marina, store and a small café. The adjacent campground has sites on attractive lawn areas at $12 for electrical and $10 for tents. It's a pleasant spot, with hot showers and a network of asphalt walking and biking trails.

Above the reservoir, the Rogue runs wild and free, prior to its collision with Lost Creek Dam. Continuing northward, take the turnoff to Prospect and pause at the **Mill Creek Falls** parking area. Short trails through a thick Douglas fir forest take you to three waterfalls and a rough Avenue of the Boulders (which is more boulder than avenue). This pleasant spot is part of Boise-Cascade's Rogue Elk Tree Farm. Markers identify the trees as you stroll. **Prospect** is a rustic town with the essentials for this part of the country: service stations, convenience stores and a sporting goods store. Take time to visit—and perhaps plan dinner at—a venerable 1889 hotel that has hosted folks such as Zane Grey (a fan of Rogue River fishing), Teddy Roosevelt and Jack London:

☺ Prospect Hotel ● △△△ $$$ ∅
391 Millcreek Rd., Prospect, OR 97536: (503) 560-3664. Hotel rooms $65, adjacent motel rooms $45 to $75. MC/VISA. It's as charming as rustic gets, featuring a wraparound porch with twig furniture and a porch swing, and vintage rooms upstairs. It offers eight small, simply furnished hotel rooms and modern motel units. A cozy **dining room** with tulip chandeliers, ceiling fans and wainscoting, serves daily from 7 a.m. to 9 p.m. The fare is American-continental mix and the kitchen is famous for its huckleberry pie. Smoking is permitted in the motel units; not in the hotel rooms or restaurant.

Above Prospect, you enter **Rogue River National Forest** and begin passing a parade of rushing rapids, campgrounds and riverside hiking trails. The stretch from here to its headwaters near Crater Lake is on the National Wild and Scenic River list. You can pick up an area map at the U.S. Forest Service ranger station in Prospect, open weekdays from 8 to 5. The highway through the forest here is arrow-straight, skimming the bends in the river.

☺ A required stop is **Natural Bridge,** where the river disappears into a lava tube, travels 200 feet underground, then thunders out the other end. At several campgrounds and trailheads, you can hike sections of the Rogue River Trail, passing massive boulders and thundering cataracts. For a short stroll along a particularly dramatic section of the river, pull off at the narrow, steep-walled **Rogue Gorge** and hike up to Farewell Bend or back to Union Creek campgrounds. They're only a mile or so away.

Take your pick of places to pitch your tent or park your RV along here— Mill Creek, River Bridge, Natural Bridge, Union Creek or Farewell Bend. Like most national forest campgrounds, they have shaded and generally uncrowded sites, with either pit or flush potties. Fees range from $8 to free. In the hamlet of **Union Creek,** you'll find a wonderful forest enclave that dates back to the early 1900s, when it hosted travelers on the old Crater Lake Trail:

☺ Union Creek Resort ● △△△ $$
Prospect, OR 97536; (503) 3339 or 560-3565. Sleeping cabins $43 to $50, lodge rooms from $35, housekeeping cabins $52 to $75. This carefully restored lodge, listed on the National Register of Historic Places, offers rustic but neat-as-a-pin accommodations. **Beckie's Café** serves hearty home-style fare for breakfast, lunch and dinner, with dinner prices ranging from $9 to $15. Its homemade pies are legendary. The next-door ice cream parlor serves old fashioned soda fountain treats.

From this point, you have choices. You can stay with the wild course of the Rogue by following State Highway 230 north, or you can remain on the Rogue River Highway (Route 62), which delivers you shortly to the gateway of Crater Lake National Park.

If you follow the river, watch for the turnoff to National Creek Falls about six miles from Union Creek. A four-mile forestry road takes you to a marked trailhead, and a half-mile hike takes you to an overlook where the Rogue—now totally wild—thunders downward.

Continuing north, you can see the shoulders of ancient Mount Mazama as you skim the edge of Crater Lake National Park. It blew its stack 7,000 years ago to form the lake's caldera. From the **crater rim viewpoint** about 16 miles above Union Creek, you can hike two miles down to **Bound-**

ary Springs. Here, the Rogue gushes full flow from a mossy webwork of stone and fallen logs. The Rogue doesn't leak from the bottom of Crater Lake, as some folks once thought. It is nourished instead by a series of springs emerging from the porous lava in these mossy slopes. From this boggy meadow, the upper Rogue River Trail follows the stream all the way back to Prospect.

Above Boundary Springs and just below **Diamond Lake**, the route joins State Highway 138. This is the Umpqua Highway, tracing a river equally as scenic and nearly as wild as the Rogue. We shall visit that stream on a side trip from Roseburg in the next chapter.

CRATER LAKE NATIONAL PARK

As you drive east from Union Creek on Highway 62, the route is relatively straight and the ascent is gradual. It doesn't seem that you're climbing the shoulders of a volcano. However, as you turn northward toward the lake, the road begins a steep spiral. There's no question that you're heading into the sleeping jaws of Mount Mazama.

If I were visiting Crater Lake for the first time, I'd arrive before dawn, head for the rim and drive to the Wizard Island overlook. I'd park, pour myself a bowl of Honey Nut Cheerios, perch on the rock wall at the viewpoint and wait for sunup.

Nine hundred feet below, the lake is a sleeping slate gray oval, cradled in steeply sloping caldera walls. As the sun breaks over the far rim, its first rays skitter across the flat surface, painting it baby blue. Shadows along the walls fall away to reveal volcanic dikes and ridges. Far to the right, the Phantom Ship emerges silently—a misplaced Loch Ness monster. With its perfect reflection, it becomes an inkblot test. As the sun climbs higher, the water color deepens until it is an unbelievable cobalt blue. Around the edges, it softens to shimmering bands of violet and turquoise, like a Caribbean shore.

Crater Lake may be the single most striking vision in the Northwest. It is certainly among Oregon's most photographed sights. When you visit, plan to spend at least a full day, to watch the colors and shadows change. Follow the 33-mile rim drive very slowly, stopping at every turnout to savor each view in the changing light. Drive the rim clockwise, since this puts you on the lake side of the roadway. You can pull into turnouts without harassing other motorists. Allow at least two hours for the trip. And to really absorb the beauty of the lake and its complex lava walls, do a morning and then an afternoon drive.

☺ The **Wizard Island** turnout offers the most impressive of the lake's views, with the near-perfect cinder cone in a fore bay and the pond beyond. Another essential stop is **Cleetwood Cove,** where you can hike the only trail down to the water's edge. This is a tough go because you're above 6,000 feet, where the air is thin. You lose nearly 700 feet on the 1.1-mile trail and have to recapture it coming back.

☺ From June through Labor Day, two-hour narrated **boat tours** depart Cleetwood Cove between 10 and 4:30. The fare is $10 for adults and $5.50 for kids under 12. Reservations aren't accepted but you can call (503) 594-2511 for information.

The boats pause briefly at Wizard Island, and you can get off for a longer visit and catch a later cruise back. A spiral trail leads to the top, offering in-

A steep quarter-mile hike to Sun Notch will give Crater Lake visitors a close-up view of Phantom Ship. Here, it's framed in the jaws of a snag.
— **Betty Woo Martin**

credible views from this volcano within a caldera. However, there's no guarantee that you'll catch the next boat back. If it's full, you may spend a good part of the day on the island, so take water, something to nibble and maybe a good book.

More than 100 miles of hiking trails fan out through the park, and some lead to rim ramparts not reached by car. Here are a couple of our favorites:

☺ **Garfield Peak Trail** is the most striking of these rim walks. Starting just behind Crater Lake Lodge, it twists steeply for 1.7 miles to the top of Garfield Peak. The view down to the lake, now nearly 2,000 feet below, is awesome. A ranger-led hike covers part of this trail, providing both views and an explanation of what you're viewing. It's one of many interpretive programs scheduled in the park between late June and Labor Day weekend.

☺ Another memorable hike, steep but only a quarter of a mile, is through **Sun Notch** to a point on the rim just above **Phantom Ship.** The "ship" is the jagged remnant of a 400,000-year-old volcanic dike. The rim is a sheer drop here, so approach it with caution—possibly even trepidation. The Sun Notch turnout is on the southern edge of the Rim Drive.

Oregon's tallest peak?

Had not Mazama blown its top, it may have been the tallest peak in Oregon. Geologists estimate its original height at 12,000 feet, topping Mount Hood's 11,237. It was born of the Ring of Fire, which circles the Pacific Rim and gives many of its residents periodic shakes. The name Mazama, incidentally, comes from a South American mountain goat. It was applied to the former volcano decades ago by a Northwest mountaineering club. And we don't know why it was named for a bleating critter.

Basaltic lavas that form the base of Mazama and the rest of the Cascade Range were laid down 200 million years ago when western Oregon was still submerged beneath the Pacific. As the Juan de Fuca oceanic plate ground under the North American Plate 60 million years ago, the early Cascades were thrust above the surface. A later range, consisting of the present-day volcanic peaks—including the headline-grabbing Mount St. Helens— emerged through cracks in the plate within the last million years.

Through carbon-14 dating, geologists have traced Mazama's big bang to precisely 7,709 years ago. Like its St. Helens sister, it erupted with a hellish roar and spewed 18 cubic miles of pumice and ash over the countryside. The volcanic cone collapsed within itself, leaving a 4,000 foot deep caldera six miles wide. Sealed at the bottom by its cooling lava, it began filling with rainwater and snow melt.

What you see today is the deepest lake in America, measured at 1,932 feet, and the seventh deepest in the world. This depth absorbs all the red, yellow and green of the light spectrum and reflects back the blue, creating the incredibly dense color. On wind-free, partly cloudy days, its still waters duplicate the sky canopy like a giant camera obscura.

Mid-summer is a good best time to catch the deepest blue (and the thickest tourist crowds.) However, the lake is most stunning in winter when a thick mantle of snow adds dazzling contrast to the indigo water. The road to Rim Village is kept open the year around, although most visitor facilities are shut down from October to early June. A 15-foot snow depth is not uncommon, although it has been considerably less during recent drought years. The most popular winter activity is cross-country skiing, and equipment rentals are available from Thanksgiving to early April (594-2511).

The essentials

Gate admission is $5 per car or $15 for an annual pass. A $25 Golden Eagle Pass provides admission to all U.S. parks and monuments for the calendar year.

General park information: Superintendent, Crater Lake National Park, P.O. Box 7, Crater Lake, OR 97604; (503) 594-2211. For concessionaire visitor services, contact Crater Lake Lodge, P.O. Box 128, Crater Lake, OR 97604; (503) 594-2511.

Visitor centers: The **William G. Steel Visitor Information Center** is in the park administration building. It's an old stone and shingled structure at the junction of the south entrance road and Rim Drive. It's open daily 8 to 5, offering an information desk, assorted brochures and publications, and a well-done 18-minute video of the national park's development. A couple of miles above, the **Rim Village Visitor Center** is open 8 a.m. to 7 p.m. from late June through Labor Day and from 9:30 to 5 the rest of the year. Stop here for schedules of ranger activities, a weather report and assorted natural history publications. Nearby **Sinnot Memorial Overlook** offers an impressive lake view, geology exhibits and a large relief model of the park and the lake. Souvenirs, gifts and other essentials are available in the **Crater Lake Gift Shop.** Hours are 8 to 8 in summer and 9 to 4 in winter. **Gasoline** is available from June through mid-October at Mazama Village, three miles below the rim.

Food: Cafè service is available at the **Cafeteria, Watchman Restaurant Deli** and **Mountain Fountain**, all at Rim Village. Call (503) 594-2511 for hours. Crater Lake Lodge will have a more formal dining room when it re-opens (see below).

Lodging: Historic Crater Lake Lodge on the rim is being rehabilitated and is expected to open for the 1995 summer season. Overnight accommodations are available (summer only) at **Mazama Village,** a few miles from the south entrance. Prices for modern motel-style rooms are $72 for singles or couples, $77 for three and $82 for four. Make reservations as early as possible through: Crater Lake Lodge, P.O. Box 128, Crater Lake, OR 97604; (503) 594-2511. MC/VISA are accepted.

Camping: It's first come, first served at the large **Mazama Village Campground**, so arrive early (preferably not on a weekend). Best times to catch a site are mid-morning as others prepare to leave, and on Sunday afternoon as weekend crowds depart. Sites are $11, with water and flush potties but no hookups. The adjacent Mazama Village Camper Services building offers coin operated showers and laundry, and a convenience store. **Lost Creek Campground,** southeast of Rim Drive toward the Pinnacles geological exhibit, has 16 spaces, water and flush toilets.

The chilly season: During winter, the only facilities open are the **Mountain Fountain**, offering light meals, and the adjacent **Crater Lake Gift Shop**. No lodging or gasoline are available in the park. And of course, roads and services can be closed temporarily by snow. Call ahead (594-2211) to check on road conditions, and *always* carry tire chains. The **Steel Information Center** near the park entrance remains open in winter, daily from 8 to 5. It offers visitor information, permits and a book sales area.

Lakes of another sort

From the north Rim Drive, you can follow State Highway 209 toward Diamond and Lemolo lakes, which are pale blue by comparison. En route, still inside the park, you'll pass through the intriguing **Pumice Desert**, nearly barren of vegetation. At a turnout on the left, you'll learn that this vast pumice field was deposited during Mazama's big blast. The resulting soil is too poor and porous to support much plant life.

Both Diamond Lake and Lemolo Lake are conventional mountain ponds, popular for boating, fishing and such. We'll visit them as a side-trip from Roseburg along the scenically rewarding Umpqua Highway in the next chapter. Meanwhile, a drive north through the park's pumice desert, then west and south to pick up Highway 62 makes a nice loop trip for your Medford to Crater Lake adventure.

MEDFORD TO GRANTS PASS

As you head northwest from Medford on I-5, the valley narrows and the mountains become greener. The *real* Rogue River Valley is much prettier than the broad agricultural Bear Creek Valley that cradles Medford and Jacksonville.

Your first town of sorts is **Gold Hill,** a one-time mining camp and now home to about 1,000 souls. It's main—and only—attraction is an odd spot of swirling magnetic energy:

House of Mystery ● *Four miles up Sardine Creek Road from Gold Hill; (503) 855-1543. Daily 9 to 6 in summer and 9 to 5 the rest of the year. Adults*

SOUTHWESTERN OREGON

N

ROGUE RIVER

Glendale
Wolf Creek

Illahe
Almeda
Ophir
Agness
Galice
5
Merlin

Wedderburn
Rogue River
Gold Hill
Gold Beach
Grants Pass

Wilderville
Wonder
99
TO MEDFORD

ILLINOIS RIVER
101
Murphy
238
Jacksonville
Pistol River
Selma

Carpenterville
199
Dryden
Applegate
Williams

PACIFIC OCEAN
Cave Junction
46

Brookings
O'Brien
Waldo
Holland

Harbor
OREGON CAVES
NATIONAL
MONUMENT
Elk Creek
Takilma

CALIFORNIA

and teens $5, kids 11 and under, $3.75. Balls roll uphill, folks tilt at funny angles and appear to grow and shrink as they move around in a tumbled-down old assay office at this attraction. The brochure talks about an above-ground, below-ground spherical field of force, gravational vortexes and electronic vortexes. You need to see it to believe it, and cameras are invited. Scientific tests apparently have proven the existence of this swirling magnetic field, which has been measured at precisely 165 feet, 4.5 inches. Incidentally, tours into this tilted world won't start until two people are present. "We can't show the phenomena with just one of you," our guide explained.

Now that you're off the freeway, you can take a more rural path into Grants Pass by staying on the Gold Hill frontage road. It becomes the old Rogue River Route. This isn't an awesome drive, but it's more leisurely, passing riverside homes, blackberry bushes, picnic waysides and boat launches. Beyond the town of Rogue River, the stream's flow is stalled by Savage Rapids Dam, creating a playground for boaters, water skiers, trollers and swimmers.

Either the river route or I-5 will take you shortly to **Rogue River,** a charming town tucked up against the legendary stream. It dates back to 1850 when one Davis "Coyote" Evans built a pair of log cabins and a cable ferry. Some folks didn't like his toll prices so they swam their horses across, holding onto their tails. From this practice, the town earned the name of Tailholt. It went through a couple of other name changes before settling on Rogue River in 1912.

Prowling its two-block business district, you'll find a souvenir shop or two and an antique store or two. The **Chamber of Commerce** on Main Street (P.O. Box 457, Rogue River, OR 97537; 582-0242) is open weekdays from 9 to 5. Nearby, at Main and Oak, is the **Woodville Museum,** with a busy if undisciplined collection of pioneer artifacts. It's open from 10 to 4, Tuesday-Sunday in summer and Tuesday-Saturday the rest of the year.

Incidentally, the tiny town has something to crow about. It's home to the annual **Rogue River Rooster Crow Contest**, held the last weekend of June. Call the chamber for details. This folksy event, with crowing competitions, down-home music and bike races, has been featured in national travel articles.

To stay with the Rogue River Route, cross the freeway and the stream and make a right turn in front of the attractive new **Inn at the Rogue,** (see listing under Grants Pass). A short distance beyond, on the left, is **Lee's Olive House,** a busy shop featuring lots of olives, Oregon specialty foods and curios.

Pressing west toward Grants Pass, you'll pass an assortment of RV parks on the river bank. Among them are, in order of appearance:

Circle W RV Park ● *8110 Rogue River Hwy. (P.O. Box 1320), Rogue River, OR 97537; (503) 582-1686. Full hookups $16, water and electric $14.50, tents $10. Reservations accepted; DISC.* Pleasant spot with grassy sites, some right over the water; riverside dock and sitting area; swimming, fishing, rafting, paddleboat rentals. Picnic area, cable TV, mini-mart and Propane, showers, laundry room. Some pull-throughs.

Riverfront RV Park ● *7060 Rogue River Hwy., Grants Pass, OR 97527; (503) 582-0985. RV sites only, full hookups $15 a night or $80 a week. Reservations accepted; no credit cards.* Small, older and well-maintained park snug against the river with showers, riverfront promenade, boat launching and water skiing.

Riverpark RV Resort ● *2956 Rogue River Hwy., Grants Pass, OR 97527; (800) 677-8857 or (503) 479-0046. Full hookups $16, tent sites $11. Reservations accepted; MC/VISA.* Older, very attractive park with mature trees and grassy sites and 700 feet of river frontage. Some sites on the water. Cable TV, showers, laundry, phone hookups, barbecues and picnic tables.

Just beyond Riverfront RV Park is **Savage Rapids County Park,** with a boat launch, picnic area, pit potties and a swimming bay. The small **Savage Rapids Dam** is just below. The rapids that were here prior to the dam weren't very savage. Their name comes from early settlers, James and Margaret Savage.

As you approach Grants Pass, you'll see some elegant riverside homes, then the Rogue River Route disintegrates into a string of small businesses, tired old motels and service stations.

Grants Pass

Population: 17,500   **Elevation: 951 feet**

Grants Pass enjoys a rather striking setting, hugging the banks of the river and cradled by surrounding hills. You'll cross the River Rogue on a low-railing bridge and enter the open, low-rise downtown area on one-way Seventh Street. Parallel is the unusual concrete arch Caveman Bridge which carries Sixth Street in the other direction. One of the few concrete arch suspension bridges around, it dates back to 1934. So do I, come to think of it— and in the same town.

If you've arrived at picnic time, drop down to **Riverside Park** before crossing the bridge. It ambles along the riverfront for about a mile, shaded by giant maples and oaks, with swimming beaches and an old fashioned bandstand. Among the park's residents—often begging for food—are friendly Canadian honkers and aggressive domestic geese. The honkers are drop-outs from the Pacific Flyway who've found the good life here in Grants Pass and stopped commuting.

The town has an ordinary history. It was named in honor of General Ulysses S. Grant in 1865 when a road-building party in the area heard that he'd captured Vicksburg. It became a stage coach stop and grew slowly and steadily as a lumbering, agricultural and provisioning center.

What is extraordinary about this town is its location on one of America's most famous rivers, and its benign, nearly wind-free climate (as heralded by a sign over Sixth Street). The local visitor's bureau calls Grants Pass "Nature's Amusement Park" and the title is appropriate.

The Rogue exercises a dual personality as it flows through Josephine County (of which Grants Pass is the seat). Its passage through town is calm and content, making it ideal for swimming, trolling and general bankside lazing. As it flows northwest, however, it becomes the Wild Rogue, the playground of kayakers, baloney-boaters, and jet boaters. More than two dozen local outfitters offer whitewater, jet boat and drift boat fishing trips.

Like Medford, Grants Pass a handy base for exploring Southwestern Oregon, within an hour or so of the Shakespeare and Britt Festivals, Crater Lake and Oregon Caves National Monument. The California redwoods and Pacific Coast are a couple of hours south on U.S. 199. We'll visit Oregon Caves shortly, but save the redwoods for our companion *California Discovery Guide.*

As you drive through town on Seventh (or Sixth if you've arrived via I-5), you might pause to explore some of the old fashioned storefronts and tree-shaded Victorian homes in the neighborhoods. For maps and guides to these sights, plus lists of outfitters, RV parks, restaurants, motels and such, stop in at the **Grants Pass Visitors & Convention Bureau** at Sixth and Midland Avenue, a few blocks north of downtown. It's open weekdays 8 to 5 and weekends 9 to 5; (503) 476-5510.

Worth checking out downtown is the **Oregon Myrtlewood Store** at 332 NW Sixth, where the tawny fine-grain wood of this native laurel is shaped into every conceivable type of souvenir. Antiquing is big in Grants Pass; visit the large **Sixth Street Antiques** at Sixth and I. If it's a hot day, duck into the vintage **Grants Pass Pharmacy** with a 1930s soda fountain. Farther down Sixth, just short of Caveman Bridge in Riverside Plaza, is the **Oregon Store,** one of those stores featuring the state's wines, foods and crafts.

Another interesting spot, rather a legend, is **Blind George's Newsstand** on G Street between Sixth and Fifth. It sells various-sized bags of the crunchiest, butteriest popcorn you'll ever eat. The shop's vintage Cretors popping machine is vented to the sidewalk, so just follow your nose. "Blind" George Spencer started a newspaper stand in a tent with a $50 investment in 1937. (I remember him scolding me for putting my popcorn nickel on the counter; since he was blind, money was to go into his *hand*. He ran the stand without assistance and folks say he could identify hundreds of his regular customers by their voices.) Although George is long gone, this newer version of his stand still thrives, selling hundreds of varieties of magazines and that awesome popcorn, which locals cart away in sacks the size of grocery bags.

This block of G street is interesting for its brick and iron front stores, some sheltering good old boy saloons dating back to the turn of the century. (As kids, we thought it was Skid Row and steered clear, but it's rustically charming and not at all grim.)

Flying the Rogue

☺ **Hellgate Jet Boat Excursions** operates out of a dock at the Riverside Inn near the downtown bridges. The ticket office is nearby, at 953 SE Seventh St., and phone numbers are (800) 648-4874 and (503) 479-7204. Trip run from May 1 through September 30 and prices vary from $18 to $34, depending on length; no credit cards but out-of-town checks are accepted. These trips can be chilly, particularly in the morning, so take a warm wrap. And don't forget binoculars for wildlife spotting.

Jet boats are powered by turbine pumps instead of props, so they draw as little as six inches of water. They can travel over almost anything except a damp street. These howling monsters, some generating nearly 1,000 horsepower, are the darling of tour groups and others in a rush. Whitewater enthusiasts find them appalling for there's no finesse here. The big flat-bottomed boats slam through the rapids instead of dancing over them.

The trips are informative and interesting, however. We signed up for a five-and-a-half hour run through Hellgate Canyon, with a lunch stop. We were impressed by the driver's knowledge of every critter, riffle and snag on the river. The wildlife apparently is used to the hellish howl of these red and blue demons. Scores of ospreys, a rare bald eagle, sunning turtles and streamside deer watched us idly as we screamed past.

At Galice Resort, several miles downstream, we had lunch on a deck overlooking the stream we'd just assaulted. After lingering over burgers and beer, we slammed back upriver. The driver did a couple of wheelies, which we grudgingly admit were a lot of fun.

Think of this outing as a whitewater trip in the fast lane.

Another operator in the area is **Jet Boat River Excursions,** P.O. Box 658 (8896-B Rogue River Hwy.), Rogue River, OR 97537; (503) 582-0800. It offers scenic excursions for $16 and dinner excursions for $32 (kids half-price on both); MC/VISA.

Running the Rogue

You have a wide choice of river-runners here. Many float and whitewater trips enter the wilderness section of the Rogue, below Galice, where the beauty of the mountains and the crags of Hellgate Canyon are part of the experience. Fishing guides take their angler guests through this area as well.

☺ If you want to be a part of the action instead of a passive baloney boat passenger, sign on with **Orange Torpedo Trips,** P.O. Box 1111-D, Grants Pass, OR 97526; (800) 635-2925 or (503) 479-5061. A couple of decades ago, Jerry Bentley came up with the idea of plunking his guests into inflatable kayaks and teaching them to run the rapids. The firm now runs seven different rivers. Despite the intimidating roar of angry water, the trips are safe, but plan on getting wet. Orange Torpedoes (named for the bright boats they use) run two-hour to two-day trips on the Rogue, with prices ranging from $15 to $195.

Here's a partial list of other river-running operations: **River Adventure Float Trips,** P.O. Box 841, Grants Pass, OR 97526, 476-6493; offers white water rafting and drift boat fishing trips. **Otter River Trips,** P.O. Box 338, Merlin, OR 97532, 476-8590; whitewater rafts and fishing trips. **Rogue Wilderness, Inc.,** P.O. Box 1647 (325 Merlin/Galice Rd.) Grants Pass, OR 97526, 479-9554 or 476-5336; rafting and fishing trips. **Galice Resort,** 11744 Galice Rd., Merlin, OR 97532, 476-3818; guided raft trips and raft rentals. **Bradbury's Gun-N-Tackle,** 1809 Rogue River Hwy., Grants Pass, OR 97526, 479-1531; inflatable kayak and raft rentals and guided trips. **River Trips Unlimited,** 4140 Dry Creek Rd., Medford, OR 97504, 779-3798; whitewater rafting and fishing trips. **Morrison's Lodge,** 8500 Galice Rd., Merlin, OR 97532-9799; (800) 826-1963 or (503) 476-3825; raft trips, some combined with stays at the lodge (listed below under "Rogue wild and scenic"). **Rogue Excursions Unlimited,** P.O. Box 2626, White City, OR 97503, 826-6222; whitewater and fishing float trips. **Vista Whitewater,** 310 Merlin Rd., Merlin, OR 97532 (474-7422), raft rentals and shuttle service.

OTHER ATTRACTIONS & ACTIVITIES

Grower's Market • *P.O. Box 573, Grants Pass, OR 97526; (503) 476-5375. March 15 through Thanksgiving, Saturdays 9 to 1; plus Tuesdays 9 to 1 starting in June. Call for location (changed in 1993).* This is Oregon's largest agricultural market, featuring farm fresh foods, baked goods, specialty foods, plants and handicrafts.

Horse racing • *Grants Pass Downs at Josephine County Fairgrounds; (503) 476-3215.* Parimutuel horse racing Friday through Sunday and holidays from Memorial Day weekend through July.

Hot air ballooning • *Rogue Valley Balloon Flights, 4640 Sardine Creek Rd., Gold Hill, OR 97525; (503) 855-1290. Flights $125 a person; MC/VISA.* Early morning trips include continental breakfast, one-hour flight and champagne picnic brunch.

Myrtlewood factory tour • *Myrtlewood Products, Inc., 1785 Dowell Rd. (on U.S. 199 southwest of town), Grants Pass, OR 97526; (503) 479-6664. Free tours by reservation on weekdays, 9 to noon and 12:30 to 4. Gift shop open Monday-Saturday 9 to 5 and Sunday 10 to 4; MC/VISA, DISC.* Watch craftspeople create the myriad of myrtlewood gifts and souvenirs sold throughout the state. Gift shop is adjacent.

Rogue Music Theatre • *Rogue Community College, P.O. Box 862, Grants Pass, OR 97526; (503) 479-2559.* This group presents Broadway-style musicals from May through mid-July at the Rogue Community College outdoor amphitheater.

Schmidt House • *508 SW Fifth St., Grants Pass, OR 97526; (503) 479-7827. Tuesday-Friday 10 to 4; free.* Home of the Josephine County Historical Society and library. While not a museum, this brick 1890 home displays many of the original furnishings of the Schmidts, a pioneer merchant family. Furnished rooms and historical library are open to the public.

Wildlife Images Rehabilitation Center • *11845 Lower River Rd., Grants Pass, OR 97526; (503) 476-0222. Daily tours by reservation 11 to 1; free; do-*

nations accepted. Picnic area and gift shop. Guides introduce visitors to injured cougars, raccoons, bears and other critters at this rehab center.

Wine tasting • *Rogue River Winery, 3145 Helms Rd., Grants Pass, OR 97527; (503) 476-1051. Tasting room open daily noon to 5.* To reach the winery, head southwest on U.S. 99 for seven miles and turn left onto Helms Road; it's six blocks off the highway. The winery offers informal tours, tastings and a gift shop with Oregon specialty products.

WHERE TO DINE

Granny's Kitchen • △△ $$
117 NE F St.; (503) 476-7185. American; no alcohol. Daily 6 a.m. to 10 p.m.; MC/VISA. Old fashioned family restaurant with rural American menu, featuring liver and onions and chicken pot pie, plus fresh fish and steaks. Many full dinners under $10. Adjacent bakery issues savory pastries.

Joy's Kitchen & Bakery • △△ $ ∅
428 SW Sixth St.; (503) 479-1814. American; no alcohol. Monday-Thursday 7 a.m. to 2 p.m., Friday-Saturday 7 a.m. to 7 p.m., Sunday 8 to 2:30. MC/VISA. Cute café with hanging plants, natural wood trim and plush booths. A good breakfast and lunch stop, featuring assorted omelettes, bakery goods, salads and sandwiches. Health-conscious menu.

LaBurrita • △ $
941 SW Seventh St.; (503) 471-1441. Mexican; wine and beer. Daily 10:30 to 8. No credit cards. A branch of Medford's locally popular cafeteria-style restaurant. The food's basic but good for the price; the most you can spend on a hearty smashed beans and rice dinner is $5.

Riverside Inn Restaurant • △△ $$
At Riverside Inn, 971 E. Sixth St.; (503) 479-2052. American; full bar service. Major credit cards. Bright, attractive dining room overlooking the river. Menu ranges from fresh seafood (including local trout) to chicken Dijon, steaks and pastas. Downstairs **Deck House** is more casual and a bit less expensive; try the $7.95 steamers. Both have outdoor decks over the river.

☺ Yankee Pot Roast • △△△ $$ ∅
720 N. Sixth St.; (503) 476-0551. American; full bar service. Monday and Wednesday-Saturday 5 to 9, Sunday noon to 8, closed Tuesday. MC/VISA. Stylish early American restaurant in a 1905 Victorian home with print wallpaper, polished woods and chandeliers. Menu is mostly rural American, with country fried steak, grilled pork chops, plus some continental dishes. Waitresses wear Victorian dress; dining room is smoke-free.

WHERE TO SLEEP

Most of the city's motels are near the north I-5 exit and along Sixth Street leading into town.

Best Western Grants Pass Inn • ⌂⌂⌂ $$$$ ∅
111 NE Agness Ave. (I-5 and U.S. 199 junction), Grants Pass, OR 97526; (800) 553-ROOM or (503) 476-1117. Couples $74 to $79, singles $64 to $74, kitchenettes $95 to $110, suites $101 to $125. Major credit cards. Attractive 84-room motel with TV movies, room phones, VCRs with movie rentals; pool, in-room coffee. **Elmer's Steak and Pancake House** serves American fare; 6 a.m. to 10 p.m.; full bar service.

City Center Motel • ◠◠ $ ∅
741 NE Sixth St. (at A Street), Grants Pass, OR 97526; (503) 476-6134. Couples $33 to $47, singles $24 to $30, kitchenettes $30 to $51.MC/VISA. Thirty rooms, most with phones, some with refrigerators and microwaves.

Grants Pass Travelodge • ◠◠ $$ ∅
748 SE Seventh St., Grants Pass, OR 97526; (503) 476-7793. Couples from $47, singles from $44. Major credit cards. A 35-unit motel three blocks from downtown and the Rogue River with in-room movies, phones and swimming pool.

Hawk's Inn Motel • ◠ $
1464 NW Sixth St. (at Midland), Grants Pass, OR 97526; (503) 479-4057. Couples $24 to $38, singles $24, suites $38 to $42. Major credit cards. A 17-room motel with TV, room phones and pool; near downtown.

Inn at the Rogue • ◠◠◠ $$$
In Rogue River at I-5 exit 48; mailing address: 8959 Rogue River Highway, Grants Pass, OR 97527; (800) 238-0700 or (503) 582-2200. Couples from $69.50, singles from $59.50, including continental breakfast. Major credit cards. Attractive new Best Western inn opposite the bridge in Rogue River. Nicely furnished rooms with TV, room phones; some spa tubs. Swimming pool, spa; short walk to beach and Rogue River shops.

Knights Inn Motel • ◠ $$
104 SE Seventh St., Grants Pass, OR 97526; (800) 826-6853 or (503) 479-5595. Couples $38 to $42, singles $30 to $35, kitchenettes $45 to $50. Major credit cards. A 32-unit motel with TV movies and room phones. Near city center and Rogue River.

Redwood Motel • ◠◠ $$ ∅
815 NE Sixth St., Grants Pass, OR 97526; (503) 476-0878. Couples $45 to $49, singles $36 to $40, kitchenettes $10 higher. Major credit cards. Older, well-maintained 24-room motel with pool, shaded grounds and children's playground. TV movies, phones.

Riverside Inn • ◠◠◠ $$$ ∅
971 SE Sixth St. (on the Rogue River), Grants Pass, OR 97526; (800) 334-4567 or (503) 476-6873. Couples $70 to $90, singles $65 to $85, kitchenettes $120 to $225. Major credit cards. Long-established, nicely appointed and well-maintained inn with 174 rooms, many with river views. TV movies, VCR rentals, room phones; two swimming pools and full health club. Hells gate Jetboat Excursions operate from here. **Riverside Restaurant and Lounge** *and* **Deck House** *listed above.*

Shilo Inn • ◠◠ $$$ ∅
1880 NW Sixth St. (I-5 exit 58), Grants Pass, OR 97526; (800) 222-2244 or (503) 479-8391. Couples and singles $59 to $67. Major credit cards. New 70-unit motel with TV movies, room phones, continental breakfast; sauna and steam room.

Bed & breakfast inns

Ahlf House • ◠◠ $$$ ∅
762 NW Sixth St., Grants Pass, OR 97526; (503) 474-1374. Couples $65, singles $55. Three rooms with shared bath; full breakfast. No credit cards. A

1902 Queen Anne Victorian—the city's largest—converted into a comfortable inn. Furnished with antiques, many accumulated by the owners.

Chriswood Inn • ⌂⌂⌂ $$$ ∅

220 NW A St., Grants Pass, OR 97526; (503) 474-9733. Couples $65, singles $45. Three rooms with semi-private baths; full English breakfast. No credit cards. A 1925 Tudor-style cottage on the city's historic building list; large suites with country English furnishings. "Pub room" with dart board.

The Clemens House • ⌂⌂⌂ $$$ ∅

612 NW Third St., Grants Pass, OR 97526; (503) 476-5564. Couples $60 to $70, singles $50 to $60. Three rooms with private baths and TV; full breakfast. No credit cards. Nicely restored and furnished 1905 Craftsman Home listed on the National Registry of Historic Places. Large rooms with antiques and family heirlooms, one with fireplace. In a quiet residential neighborhood, fronted by one of the city's more brilliant gardens.

Martha's Inn • ⌂⌂⌂ $$$$ ∅

764 N. Fourth St., Grants Pass, OR 97526; (503) 476-4330. Couples $70 to $85, singles $65 to $70. Three rooms with private baths; full breakfast. MC/VISA. Handsome two-story Victorian farmhouse furnished with American antiques. Enclosed porch; attractive gardens; hot tub.

☺ Riverbanks Inn • ⌂⌂⌂ $$$$ ∅

8401 Riverbanks Rd., Grants Pass, OR 97527; (503) 479-1118. Couples $75 to $150, singles $65 to $130. Five rooms and cabins with private baths; full breakfast. MC/VISA. Riverside hideaway with an Oriental garden and boat dock, surrounded by forest. Three rooms in lodge with eclectic furnishings; two-bedroom housekeeping cottage $175, three-bedroom $275.

Washington Inn Bed & Breakfast • ⌂⌂ $$$ ∅

1002 NW Washington Blvd., Grants Pass, OR 97526; (503) 476-1131. Couples $40 to $65, singles $30 to $65. Three units, one with private and two with shared baths; full breakfast. MC/VISA, AMEX. A two-story 1864 Victorian listed on the National Register of Historic Places; one of the city's oldest surviving homes. Rooms furnished in an "antique mix"; one with a private fireplace. Bikes available, including a tandem.

WHERE TO CAMP

Josephine County Parks Department • *For a brochure, contact Josephine County Parks, Municipal Building, Sixth and A streets, Grants Pass, OR 97526; (503) 474-5285.* The county maintains five campgrounds on the Rogue, one on Grave Creek near Wolf Creek off I-5 to the north and one at Lake Selmac. Most have showers and hookups, plus fishing, boating and swimming areas. Rates vary from $16 with full hookups to $9 for tent sites. The queen of these is Indian Mary Park on the lower Rogue, with grassy campsites under mature trees, hookups, showers and barbecues.

Rogue Valley Overnighters • *1806 NW Sixth St., Grants Pass, OR 97526; (503) 479-2208. RV sites with full hookups. Reservations accepted; no credit cards.* Some pull-throughs, showers, picnic tables, cable TV, coin laundry and rec hall. A quarter mile south from I-5 exit 58.

Valley of the Rogue State Park • *Off I-5 between Medford and Grants Pass at Exit 85-B. Full hookups $13, water and electric $12, tents $11.* One of the area's most attractive campgrounds, with grassy, tree-shaded sites, picnic tables and fire pits, at stream side across from the town of Rogue River. Bank fishing and boat launch. There's also a rest stop and picnic area here.

Also see riverside RV park listings under "Medford to Grants Pass" above.

THE ROGUE WILD AND SCENIC

We mentioned above that the Rogue gets into a partying mood northwest of Grants Pass. After clearing suburbs and agricultural fields, it cuts a jagged notch through Hellgate Canyon. Below here, a 40-mile stretch from Graves Creek through the Coast Range has been designated as a Wild and Scenic River. A hiking trail covers the full length of this portion.

Permits to run the protected section are hard to come by. Only 25 a day are issued, to keep the wild in this wilderness experience. To get in on this difficult lottery, contact the **Rand Visitors Center,** 14335 Galice Rd., Merlin, OR 97532; (503) 479-3735. Or you can sign up with one of the river runners listed above, who have commercial permits. The 14-mile stretch between Hellgate Canyon and Graves Creek can be run without a permit. You will have to contend with jet boats on this section, although their operators are painfully polite to rubber boaters and kayakers. A popular sport is to try and splash passengers as the power boats chortle slowly past. Some jet boat drivers will cheerfully threaten to swamp you, but don't you believe it.

Many of the firms listed above offer day trips on this section, and some rent rafts. Also, **Morrison Lodge** and **Galice Resort** in this area have raft rentals and guided trips. No, this part of the river does not offer a wilderness experience, although the wooded, V-shaped canyon is quite appealing. During summer weekends, you can almost walk from shore to shore on baloney boats without getting your feet wet.

You can drive to this area without getting anything wet, and it's a very scenic route. Lower River Road out of Grants Pass will get you here, although this approach isn't particularly awesome and you catch only occasional glimpses of the river until you hit Merlin. Further, the rural twists and turns are hard to follow. For a much easier approach, head north out of Grants Pass on I-5 for about three miles and take exit 61 to **Merlin.** This scatter of a country town offers small markets and a service station or two.

Beyond Merlin, you pass through a mix of woods and pastureland. You shortly pick up the Rogue and the scenery that goes with it—the steep-walled Hellgate Canyon and narrow, wooded river canyons beyond. An information kiosk just short of the **Hellgate Canyon Bridge** discusses the geology and history of the area. You learn that the section of the Rogue below here was one of the first in the nation to earn a Wild and Scenic designation, way back in 1968.

Across the bridge, the road and river wind deeper and twistier into the forested canyon. **Indian Mary Campground** alongside the stream was named in honor of an Umpqua lady who's father warned settlers of a planned massacre. About a mile beyond, you'll encounter one of the Rogue's more enticing retreats:

☺ Morrison Lodge • ⌂⌂⌂ $$$$

8500 Galice Rd., Merlin, OR 97532; (800) 826-1963 or (503) 476-3825. From $80 per person including two meals or $130 double occupancy in housekeeping cottages. MC/VISA. The lodge sits rustically at riverside, shaded by mature trees, with cabin-style units overlooking a large lawn that overlooks the river. Facilities include a swimming pool, tennis courts, plus fishing and whitewater trips on the river. Lodging/fishing packages are available. MC/VISA are accepted.

☺ A bit farther along, also perched on the river, is **Galice,** which is more of a rustic resort than a town. It's our favorite refueling stop on the Rogue, offering a river-view dining deck, hearty breakfasts, remarkably good hamburgers and pizza. Homestyle dinners range from $9 to $11, including barbecued beans, salad, veggies and bread. Strawberry pie is a specialty here; don't start home without a slice. If that doesn't tempt you, try hefty home-made ice cream sandwiches, well worth their $1 price tag. Note the old fashioned saloon with knotty pine walls and batwing doors. Galice also has a convenience mart, raft and inflatable kayak rentals with shuttle service and guided whitewater trips. Rustic accommodations range from $40 a night up to $100 for a two-bedroom house. Contact: Galice Resort, 11744 Galice Rd., Merlin, OR 97532; (503) 476- 3818.

A turnoff near Galice takes you into the Coast Range wilderness and up over a wooded mountain pass with an lofty view down to the Rogue. Ultimately, after 64 dizzying miles, you reach the Oregon Coast at Gold Beach. The route, while twistier than a stepped-on snake, is all paved. Much of it travels through Siskiyou National Forest.

If you continue along the Rogue beyond Galice, you pass the **Rand Visitor's Center** mentioned above, and then **Alameda County Park,** with picnic tables, river access and no-hookup campsites for $9. As you press onward, the road hugs a canyon shelf above the river, luring you deeper into the overlapping wedges of mountains.

At **Grave Creek,** the wild and scenic Rogue disappears into a narrow chasm. This is launch point for commercial outfitters and private groups with permits to run this section. The road ends and the **Rogue River Trail** begins here. From this point, you can retrace your route to Grants Pass. Or follow an equally twisting and scenic road north along Grave Creek and pick up I-5 at Wolf Creek. This historic hamlet and its tavern are discussed in the next chapter.

GRANTS PASS TO OREGON CAVES

To reach the "Marble Halls of Oregon," head southwest from Grants Pass on U.S. 199. Within a couple of miles, you'll see the **Oregon Myrtlewood Factory** on your left. A bit beyond is the **Rogue River Winery,** with a tasting room just off the highway in a small cottage. (Both are listed above under "Activities.")

After the highway clears Grants Pass suburbia, it travels through low wooded hills. **Wilderville,** just off the highway, consists mostly of the Wilderville Store and the charming old Jones Memorial Methodist Church, with a New England style square bell tower.

There's little to wonder about **Wonder,** which is even smaller than Wilderville; a general store offers essentials. A **KOA Kampground** is just beyond, a small operation with shaded, grassy sites; hookups from $12 to $16.50. Facilities include a mini-mart, showers, laundry, horseshoe pit, playground and rec hall; a stream is nearby. Call (503) 476-6508.

You'll top a modest pass and enter the **Illinois Valley,** named by and for early settlers from that state. Gold discoveries hereabouts brought some of southern Oregon's first residents. **Selma,** a bit larger that Wilderville and Wonder, offers a good-sized market and service station.

Just beyond Selma, you can turn left toward **Lake Selmac** if you're interested in a reservoir recreation area and campground. En route, you might pause at **Martin's Pottery,** open Monday-Saturday 9 to 5; (503) 597-4565. Potter Richard Martin (no relation, so this isn't a plug) offers hand-turned creations ranging from Raiku styles to American folk art.

Lake Selmac Resort has showers, full hookups, cable TV, a convenience mart, dump station, boat rentals and horseback rides. Sites, mostly shaded, range from $9 for tents to $13 for full hookups. To reserve a spot, contact: Lake Selmac RV Resort, 2700 Lakeshore Dr., Selma, OR 97538; (503) 597-4989.

Kerbyville, now shortened to **Kerby,** was one of southern Oregon's first towns, laid out in 1854 after gold was found in the nearby hills. It was the county seat until Grants Pass took it away in 1887.

Kerbyville Ghost Town, just east of Kerby, never was a ghost town. It's a scruffy little collection of weathered and properly sagging buildings, moved to this site as a tourist attraction. Some of the lumber was salvaged from old Kerbyville. The Eight Dollar Mining Company building, however, bears a suspicious resemblance to a double-wide trailer, painted rustic red. The "town" opens daily in summer at 9, with gold panning, donkey rides, old timey photos and some curio shops.

Kerby is just beyond, a appealing town tucked among the trees. Its offerings include a couple of antique shops, a burlwood factory, trading post mini-mart and a remarkably good country museum:

☺ **Kerbyville Museum** • *Highway 199; (503) 592-2076 or 474-5285. Open mid-May to mid-September, Monday-Saturday 10 to 5 and Sunday 1:30 to 5. Free; donations appreciated.* The complex consists of an 1871 white clapboard home and a cinder block annex. A back yard shelters a blacksmith shop, rock shop, log schoolhouse and a century-old flatbed press used to print most of the county's early newspapers. The house is a mix of furnished rooms and nicely-displayed pioneer relics. The annex is busy with a bit of everything from yesterday, ranging from World War II mementos to Indian baskets to a bottle opener collection.

Bridgeview Winery is elsewhere, although it has a tasting room in Kerby, open daily 11 to 5 from May 30 through Labor Day weekend. Just beyond Kerby is a town that has made Oregon Caves National Monument something of a cottage industry.

Cave Junction

Population: 1,100   **Elevation: 1,325 feet**

Cave Junction began life as a lumbering center. However, with the popularity of Oregon Caves National Monument, it functions primarily as gateway to the caverns, 20 miles up a twisting road. As such, it offers several places to eat and sleep, and not much else.

WHERE TO DINE

Black Forest Family Restaurant • ∆∆ $

At the junction, corner of highways 199 and 46; (503) 592-6434. American; full bar service. Daily 6 a.m. to 9 p.m. MC/VISA. New café with a bright early American look. Inexpensive Americana dinners ranging from liver and onions to chicken fried steak; meals include all-you-can-eat salad bar.

The Chocolate Retreat • Δ $

129 Caves Ave. (in the Caves Mall); 592-6723. American; no alcohol. Monday-Saturday 9 to 5:30, Sunday 10:30 to 3. Take your sweet tooth to this place and turn it loose on assorted chocoholic desserts. Espresso, cappuccino, a variety of hot stuffed potatoes, soups and sub sandwiches also appear on the busy menu.

Dragon Gate Restaurant • Δ $

240 N. Redwood Hwy.; (503) 592-3113. Chinese-American; wine and beer. Daily 11 to 9. MC/VISA. A mix of Cantonese fare and American dinners, served in a tidy space that looks more American diner than Oriental. Inexpensive combination dinners on the Chinese side of the menu; American steaks, chicken, chops and seafood on the other.

Mr. B's • Δ $

202 N. Redwood Hwy.; (503) 592-2266. American; wine and beer. Daily 7 a.m. to 9 p.m. Essentially rustic family restaurant with comfy booths and a counter. Menu offerings range from teriyaki steak to veal cutlets to liver and onions.

Red Garter Saloon & Steak House • ΔΔ $$

126 S. Redwood Highway; (503) 592-2892. American; full bar service. Lunch Tuesday-Friday 11 to 2, dinner Sunday and Tuesday-Thursday 5 to 9, closed Monday. Lively western style false front café decorated mostly with wagon wheels and good-old-boy friendliness. Menu consists of "the best steaks in the valley" plus the usual array of chicken and chops.

WHERE TO SLEEP

Oregon Caves Chateau • *See below.*

Junction Inn Motel & Restaurant • ⌂⌂ $$

406 S. Redwood Hwy. (P.O. Box 429), Cave Junction, OR 97532; (503) 592-3106. Couples $50 to $60, singles $45 to $60, suites from $50. MC/VISA, DISC. Well-kept motel across from the turnoff to the caves; TV, room phones. Early American style **Restaurant** serves from 5:30 a.m. to 11 p.m.; dinners $4 to $13; no alcohol. Thai buffet Monday-Friday 11 to 2 for $4.50.

Woodland Echoes Resort • ⌂ $$

7901 Caves Hwy., Cave Junction, OR 97523; (503) 592-3406. Couples $35. Also RV sites for $20 with full hookups and $10 for tents. MC/VISA. Rustically attractive complex in the woods, eight miles up the road to Oregon Caves, with a kids' theme park. Simply-furnished units.

WHERE TO CAMP

Shady Acres RV Park • *27550 Redwood Hwy., Cave Junction, OR 97523; (503) 592-3702. Full hookups $13, tent sites $10. No credit cards.* Older park with closely-bunched but grassy and shaded sites, just south of Cave Junction. Some pull-throughs; showers, dump station, horseshoe pits.

Woodland Echoes Resort • See listing above.

Rogue River National Forest campsites • Two campgrounds are along the road to the monument. **Grayback Campground** sits below the twisty portion of the road, a good place to stop and drop your trailer (or rig if you have a tow-along), since the final haul to the monument is very winding. Open May 15 through early fall, with shaded, creekside campsites in a thick forested setting; no hookups but with flush potties, $5. **Cave Creek** is just four miles below the monument, a mile off the main highway, also in a wooded section beside the creek; $5, with pit potties and no hookups. It opens June 1.

En route to the national monument, you might pause at the **Illinois Valley Visitor Center** in an attractive bungalow at the Highway 199 junction to the caves. It's open daily 9 to 5; (503) 592-2631. As you begin your ascent toward the caves, you'll encounter signs to a pair of wineries. **Foris Winery** is about six miles from Cave Junction; follow signs to the right onto Holland Loop Road, past the tiny town of Holland. The tasting room is sort of open daily; a sign invites you to "honk for service." Returning to the main road, you'll see the sign to **Siskiyou Vineyards** just ahead, directing you to the left for a short distance. The tasting room, occupying one end of a barn-like winery, is open daily 11 to 5.

Beyond the wineries, you'll pass **Woodland Echoes** motel, RV park and kiddie playland, then begin climbing into the steep foothills. This drive through thick forest, often beside a gurgling creek, is worth the trip even if there wasn't a limestone cavern at the end.

Oregon Caves National Monument

This is Oregon's oldest national monument, established in 1909 after Joaquin Miller, the "poet of the Sierra," extolled its virtues in sonnet. The cave (make that singular, despite the plural name) was discovered in 1874 when Elijah Davidson was deer hunting in the area. His dumb dog Bruno chased a bear into a hole and Elijah followed, armed only with his rifle and a few sulfur matches. He ran out of matches and courage, and had to crawl out of the blackness, following the gurgle of a stream (which is still running). Bruno emerged also, but the bear stayed inside.

This is not an awesome cave as limestone caverns go. However, it's worth the side-trip from Grants Pass, or a diversion if you're headed north from California up U.S. 199. Many of the formations were broken off by souvenir hunters before it became a monument, although some impressive ones remain. This is a live cave, and one can see nature still at work, adding a few millimeters of fresh deposits to the wounded stalactites. The most striking stop in the cave is Paradise Lost, with dozens of flowstone formations resembling fluted beehives.

During your 75-minute walk through a half mile of corridors, your guide will regale you with fascinating facts. You'll learn about dripping water, limestone, carbon dioxide, carbonic acid and calcite and how they all get together to form stalactites, stalagmites, columns, flowstone, soda straws and such. (Our guide kept saying stalagtite, but we appreciated his enthusiasm.)

The caves should have a nice new look by the time you visit. The old lighting system is being replaced and natural ravines and side caverns, filled with rubble when access routes were widened decades ago, are being cleaned out. Much of this work is being done by volunteers.

The essentials

Tours are conducted all year; price is $4.75 for adults and $2.50 for children. Kids under six aren't admitted, but child care is available for $2.50. Tours leave frequently, as soon as 16 people are accumulated. Hours are 8 a.m. to 7 p.m. mid-June through Labor Day weekend; 9 to 5 for the rest of

September and May through mid-June; and 10:30 to 12:30 and 2 to 3:30 from October through April. Take a wrap 'cause it's chilly in there. You must be in reasonable physical shape, since the tour covers a vertical rise of 218 feet (including scores of steps), and you're at 4,000 feet elevation, where the air is a bit thin.

There's a well-stocked gift shop where you can kill time while waiting for your tour to start, and a great old lodge offering rooms and meals, listed below. The monument's setting, in a proscenium of huge firs, is nearly as pleasant as the cave interior.

After your tour, drop out of the crowd and follow the Cliff Nature Trail back to the lodge. Longer than the regular return route, it takes you up and over a ridge with impressive views of mountains and wooded valleys. Another pleasant hike is the Big Tree Loop Trail, which takes you just under two miles through an old growth forest. If you see a spotted owl, smile and wave.

WHERE TO DINE AND SLEEP

☺ Oregon Caves Chateau • ⌂⌂⌂ $$$

P.O. Box 128, Cave Junction, OR 97523; (503) 592-3400. Couples and singles $53 to $59, larger family units $61 to $72. MC/VISA. Open mid-June through Labor Day Weekend. Handsomely rustic chalet built in 1934; tucked into a hollow and rising six stories above a waterfall. A massive marble fireplaces accents the lofty cedar-timbered lobby. The **Chateau Dining Room** matches the woodsy look of the lodge, and it has a stream flowing through it. Dinner is served from 6 to 9 p.m.; $8.50 to $29; full bar service. A 1930s style **coffee shop** serves breakfast and lunch from 7 a.m. to 6 p.m.

Back in Cave Junction, you'll find a **U.S. Forest Service** office just south of town, where you can pick up forestry maps and brochures about this attractive mountainous area. It's open weekdays 8:30 to 5.

If you continue a bit farther south, you'll find a small zoo and petting park called **Noah's Ark.** It's open weekdays 11 to 4 and weekends 10 to 5. The opportunity to make friends with llamas, zebras, goats, deer and stuff costs $4.50 for adults, $3.25 for seniors and juniors and $2.25 for kids 3 to 5. Pony rides are $1.50. The adjacent knotty pine café serves barbecued sandwiches, a tortilla special, soups and salads.

Beyond the ark, U.S. 199 winds pleasantly through steepening wooded mountains, headed for the California Coast at Crescent City. A cutoff at the Smith River southwest of Gasquet, Calif., will take you to Brookings and the southern Oregon Coast, covered in detail in Chapter 5.

JOSEPHINE COUNTY ANNUAL EVENTS

Southern Oregon Amateur Rodeo at the county fairgrounds in Grants Pass, late February; 476-1270.

Boatnik Festival on the river and off, with parades, jet boat races and such, Grants Pass, late May; 474-2361.

Southern Oregon Wine Festival at Siskiyou Vineyards, Cave Junction, mid-June; 592-3727.

Rooster Crow Festival in Rogue River, late June; 582-0242.

Wild Blackberry Festival in Cave Junction, early July; 592-2507.

White Water Races on the Rogue in Grants Pass, Labor Day Weekend; 476-5510.

TRIP PLANNER

WHEN TO GO ● The Umpqua and Willamette Valleys are good all-season destinations, since the weather is relatively benign. Unlike those in more tourist-oriented areas, museums and other attractions are more likely to be open the year around, although hours may be shorter. Here as elsewhere in the state, museums tend to close on Monday, so plan accordingly.

WHAT TO SEE ● Historic Wolf Creek and its tavern, the Douglas County Museum in Roseburg, University of Oregon campus (and particularly the art museum) in Eugene and Oregon State University in Corvallis, the Oregon state capitol and Deepwood Estate in Salem, Silver Falls State Park and Mount Angel Abbey near Mount Angel, Old Aurora Colony Museum, Clackamas County History Museum and Oregon Trail Visitors Center in Oregon City, and Champoeg State Park near Newberg.

WHAT TO DO ● Talk to the animals at the Wildlife Safari in Winston; explore recreation areas of the Umpqua; McKenzie and Santiam rivers; take your love beads to the Eugene Saturday Street Market; tour historic neighborhoods of Albany and Salem; hike the waterfalls trail at Silver Falls State Park; soak your body and psyche at Breitenbush Hot Springs and then follow the Clackamas River Canyon into Portland; walk the river bluff promenade and ride the public elevator in Oregon City.

Useful contacts

Roseburg Visitors & Convention Bureau, P.O. Box 1262 (410 SE Spruce St.), Roseburg, OR 97470; (503) 672-9731.

Eugene Convention & Visitors Bureau, 305 W. Seventh St., Eugene, OR 97401; (800) 452-3670 in Oregon or (503) 484-5307.

Albany Convention & Visitors Commission, P.O. Box 548 (300 SW Second), Albany, OR 97321; (503) 926-1517.

Salem Convention & Visitors Assn., 1313 SE Mill St., Salem, OR 97301; (800) 874-7012 outside Oregon or (503) 581-4325.

Clackamas County Associated Chambers of Commerce, P.O. Box 624, West Linn, OR 97068; (503) 655-1765.

Oregon City Chamber of Commerce, P.O. Box 26 (Washington and Abernethy streets), Oregon City, OR 97045; (800) 424-3002 or (503) 656-1619.

WINERY TOURING: Yamhill County Wineries Assn., P.O. Box 871, McMinnville, OR 97128; (503) 434-5814. South Willamette Chapter, Oregon Winegrowers Assn., P.O. Box 1591, Eugene, OR 97440. Contact the Roseburg Visitors & Convention Bureau for a brochure of Umpqua Valley wineries.

I-5 corridor radio stations

KLCC & KLCO-FM, 88.5, Roseburg—National Public Radio
KMGE-FM, 94.5, Eugene-Springfield—rock oldies
KUGN-FM, 97.9, Eugene—country
KHBE-FM, 107.9, Eugene—Christian radio & light rock
KAVE-FM, 95.3, Eugene—blues, rock, oldies, talk & news
KSND-FM, 93.1, Eugene—rock
KZEL-FM, 96.1, Eugene—classic rock
KFAT-FM, 106.1, Corvallis—country
KGEN-AM, 590, Eugene—oldies, news & sports
KUGN-AM, 590, Eugene—news & talk
KQEN-AM, 1240, Roseburg—country

Chapter Three

THE I-5 CORRIDOR

People, pines and produce

A DEMOGRAPHIC LOOK at Oregon might suggest that the folks here have more sense than their neighbors to the south. Most Californians, Nevadans and Arizonans live in the drier reaches of their states. Much of their food, water and other essentials have to be carried to them. In Oregon, most people live where the crops grow and the rivers flow.

More than eighty percent of the state's residents occupy a narrow band of foothills and farmlands between the Cascades and the Coast Range. This area doesn't offer the state's best climate or scenery. Much of it is somewhat overcast and drizzly. The scenery's off to the left and right, along the coast and in the high Cascades. Unlike Mohammed, practical minded Oregonians believe in leaving the mountains where they are. The broad, fertile Willamette Valley provides their food and level bases for their cities. Rivers flowing out of the mountains provide cheap power and irrigation.

Despite chronic "night and morning low cloudiness," residents along the I-5 population corridor enjoy the good life. Come Friday night or Saturday morning, and many head for the coast or up into the sunny Cascades. Both recreational areas are less than two hours away.

The Willamette Valley, nourished by one of America's few northward flowing rivers, was the goal of Oregon Trail pioneers. They'd had enough of sunny climates with their droughts and crop failures. They sought green grass and cooling rains. Agriculture is Oregon's second leading industry, just behind lumbering and ahead of tourism. Most of that is centered in this broad 120-mile-long valley.

So much for a lesson in Oregon economics. What does the busy I-5 corridor offer to tourists? Two university towns with their attendant cultural lures, historic sites, collections of old Victorian homes, roadside berry stands, most of Oregon's wineries and the stately marble halls of the state capitol.

Incidentally, if you have allergy problems, don't plan a spring visit to the Willamette Valley. With its agricultural lands including grass seed farms, lush flower gardens and a tendency toward air inversion, it becomes a sniffle corridor in May and June.

GRANTS PASS TO ROSEBURG

With all this talk about the Willamette Valley, we aren't even there yet. Southwestern Oregon's mix of mountains—an overlapping blend of Siskiyous, Coast Range and Cascades—extends a hundred miles north of Grants Pass before the Willamette Valley begins. I-5 cuts a broad swath through these hills, nipping edges of Canyonville, Roseburg, Sutherlin and Cottage Grove before reaching Eugene, on the southern edge of the Willamette.

Much of this area is wrapped up in the neat package of Douglas County. It offers many of the same attractions as the region to the south: a wild river (the Umpqua), historic towns, wineries and nearby mountains with fishing, camping and hiking. It doesn't offer Shakespeare, but you can talk to the animals at Wildlife Safari.

Heading north from Grants Pass, I-5 takes a long and gentle hike over Sexton Mountain Pass, then drops down into **Sunny Valley,** a pretty meadowland rimmed by wooded hills. During western Oregon's formative years, scores of **covered bridges** were built to protect the trusses and decks from rain deterioration (see box). Many still survive and one of them is within sight of the freeway here. If you like rumbling through these quaint old structures, take exit 71 and go briefly east to Graves Creek.

Back on the freeway, jump off in the townlet of Wolf Creek for a visit to Oregon's oldest roadhouse:

☺ Wolf Creek Tavern ● ⌂⌂ $$$ ∅
P.O. Box 97, Wolf Creek, OR 97497; (503) 866-2474. Couples and singles $45 to $64. Run by the state department of parks and recreation, the wood frame stage stop has resumed the services it offered more than a century ago. The rooms aren't fancy; they're styled to the era when passengers of the Oregon Stage Company stopped for a respite from their long, dusty ride. They do have modern plumbing, however. In the oldstyle **dining room,** you can try such fare as Cobb salad, Cornish pasties or chicken *almandine.* The restaurant is open Monday-Saturday 11 to 8:30 and Sunday 10 to 8; dinner prices range from $10 to $16.

If you're just passing through, you're welcome to look around the hotel a bit, and you can peek into a spartan exhibit room where Jack and Charmian London stayed while he finished writing his novel, *The End of the Story.*

Nearby is the 1880 **Wolf Creek General Store,** worth a quick peek for its eclectic décor of game trophies, farm implements and old Coke plaques. You can buy anything from groceries to alfalfa pellets for your rabbits to night crawlers for your next fishing trip. While you're off the freeway, cross back under it and drive 3.5 miles east on Coyote Creek Road to the ghost town of **Golden.** It was established as a mining camp in the 1890s. It's now owned by Roger Ramsey, whose great grandfather held the land where the town's four surviving shanties stand. You can poke into the 1892 Swiss-style church and watch a rather rambling videotape by Roger. And

GRANTS PASS TO ROSEBURG

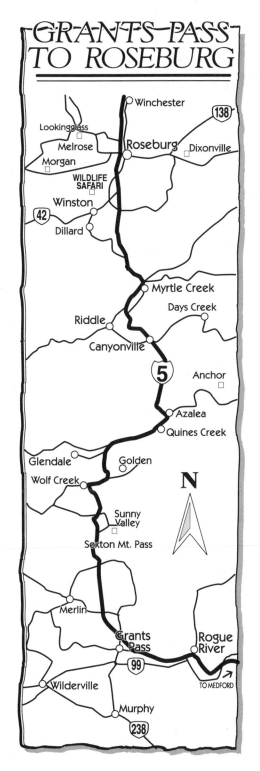

you might find the "mayor of Golden" and his wife Lynn at the 1906 general store, which they keep open on most summer weekends as a curio shop.

Moving northward on I-5, you enter Douglas County and pass the town of **Glendale,** an attractive hamlet in a wooded farming valley, then you begin a long descent into the **Umpqua Valley.** Exit 98 takes you through the old fashioned main street of **Canyonville.** Here, you can nibble free samples at the Oregon Gourmet Beef Jerky Store, and browse through a couple of antique shops. The town's **Visitor Information Center** is at the north end, sharing the combination city hall, police station and library; it's open weekdays 9 to 5.

If you like driving along old fashioned main streets just because they're there, hop off the freeway again at exit 103 and drag through **Myrtle Creek,** a town of about 3,200 folks. Signs will direct you from downtown to an old **covered bridge** on Neal Lane.

Another few miles up the freeway brings you to exit 119, where you can take Highway 42 west toward **Winston** and talk to the animals. Some of them may even answer back.

☺ **Wildlife Safari** ● *P.O. Box 1600, Winston, OR 97496; (503) 679-6761. Open daily, from 8:30 in summer and 9 in the off-season, closes around dusk. Adults $8.95, seniors $7.50, kids $5.75, plus $1 per vehicle. Rental drive-through cars available for those with convertibles or motorcycles. It may seem a bit strange driving through an elephant or camel herd in Oregon while listening to Garth Brooks on your car ra-*

dio. The wildlife safari is a drive-through zoo covering 600 acres of verdant countryside. Creatures from the dry and dusty African veldt must be startled by all this greenery, but most seem rather content with their lot. The compound is divided by country of origin, with critters from Asia, Africa and North American. (No, those cows belong to a farm across the fence.)

Best time to drive through is early in the morning before the big cats and cheetahs become too lethargic. Perhaps they'll stroll up and check out your car; keep the windows up, please. The adjacent village offers a critter-oriented gift shop, animal shows at the Safari Theater, a thought-provoking endangered species exhibit and cafeteria. The village was a bit scruffy when we visited, but a renovation plan is in the works for this non-profit park. Since it's dedicated to the study and protection of endangered species, and to public education about wildlife, it deserves your support.

If you're RVing, you can overnight at the rather basic **Safari RV Park,** just short of the main gate. It offers grassy (well, weedy) sites, pit potties and not much else; $5 with electrical hookups and $3 without.

Roseburg

Population: 16,600   **Elevation: 479 feet**

When I was growing up in Grants Pass, we kids regarded Roseburg as that hick lumbering town to the north. Actually, it's a charming little city with a well-preserved old downtown area and lush green parks. You'll discover several winery tasting rooms to the west and the Umpqua River recreation area to the east. So much for the prejudice of youth.

The town emerged early in the state's history. Its forerunner was Fort Umpqua, established by Hudson's Bay Company trappers in 1836. By mid-century, pioneers were filtering down from the north, following the Applegate Trail blazed from the terminus of the Oregon Trail in Oregon City. The Umpqua Valley became an important farming and ranching area and Jesse Applegate planted some of the state's first vineyards in 1876. The valley today is second only to the Willamette Valley for Northwest wine production.

Roseburg's biggest surprise is its outstanding museum, reached by jumping off the freeway just short of downtown at exit 123:

☺ **Douglas County Museum** ● *At Douglas County Fairgrounds, P.O. Box 1550, Roseburg, OR 97470; (503) 440-4507. Tuesday-Saturday 10 to 4, Sunday noon to 4. Free; donations appreciated.* This is one of Oregon's best county museums with professionally done exhibits tracing the Umpqua Valley's history from the rocks to the Native Americans to the fur traders and settlers. A full-scale "log pen" is typical of the first crude shelters built by settlers. Strolling through this logically arrayed museum, you can see the skeleton of a saber tooth cat attacking the skeleton of a ground sloth, follow a geological time line, view well done wildlife dioramas and learn all about early Umpqua farming, ranching, wine making and cowboying. Adjacent the museum is the restored train station of neighboring Dillard, with an intriguing photographic display of train wrecks.

If you return to the freeway and hop off at the next off ramp, you'll wind up in downtown Roseburg, which seems to be winning its battle against suburban business flight. Signs will direct you to the **Roseburg Visitor and Convention Bureau** at 410 SE Spruce St.; open weekdays 9 to 5; (503) 672-9731. It's near an attractive riverside park with picnic areas.

A walking tour of Roseburg's old houses can begin right here, since the visitor's center is on the edge of an historic district. Start with the 1866 **Lane House,** a block away at Douglas and Spruce streets, open weekends 1 to 4 and operated by the Douglas County Historical Society; (503) 459-1393 or 673-4563. Also worthy of a peek is the 1929 Federalist style **Douglas County Courthouse** at Douglas and Kane streets.

While you're hanging out downtown, stop in at the **Umpqua Brewing Company** for a sip of micro-brewed beer. It's a proper place to end a day of sightseeing, since it doesn't open until 5. This old fashioned brewpub is at 328 SE Jackson near Court Avenue; hours are Wednesday-Thursday 5 to midnight and Friday-Saturday 5 to 1 a.m.

A valley of the grape

A brochure available at the visitor center will direct you to the Umpqua Valley's seven wineries with tasting rooms. The route is a bit hard to follow, since the wineries are scattered widely across the valley's crazy quilt agricultural lands. However, this is a pleasant area in which to be lost. Just settle back and enjoy the unrolling panorama of pasturelands and orchards. Blue and white signs erected by the local vintners will help steer you along this 42-mile course.

The warm weather in this low, mountain-sheltered valley produces tasty Pinot Noir, Cabernet Sauvignon, Chardonnay, Riesling and Gewürztraminer. It's one of the few areas in Oregon warm enough to produce a decent Zinfandel which—of course—is the red wine of choice for us plebeians. Oregon's modern wine industry started here when Californian Richard Sommer planted the state's first commercial varietal grapes in 1961. His **HillCrest Winery** is still producing highly drinkable wines at 240 Vineyard Lane, open daily 10 to 5; (503) 673-3709

If you can't lay your hands on a winery tour brochure, take the Winston exit toward the Wildlife Safari, then make an immediate left down Winery Lane to **La Garza Winery,** open Tuesday-Sunday 11 to 5. You can get a map and start following those small blue and white signs from there.

DOUGLAS COUNTY ANNUAL EVENTS

Wine & food tasting, County Fairgrounds, February; (503) 440-4505.

Rhododendron garden tours, Roseburg, late April to mid-May; (503) 673-3760.

South Douglas County Rodeo, Myrtle Creek, early June; (503) 863-3171 or 863-5271.

Grand Celebration, Oakland historic festival, June; (503) 459-9435.

Roseburg Graffiti Weekend, a back to the 50s celebration, mid-July; (503) 679-8808 or 672-3703.

Douglas County Timber Days, Sutherlin, mid-July; (503) 459-2236.

Douglas County Fair, fairgrounds, mid-August; (503) 440-4505.

Umpqua Valley Wine, Art & Jazz Festival, downtown Oakland; (503) 672-2648.

WHERE TO DINE

All of the listed cafés are close together in the downtown area.

Cafè Espresso ● ΔΔ $ Ø

368 SE Jackson; (503) 672-1859. Deli; no alcohol. Weekdays 6 a.m. to 3 p.m. No credit cards. Fetching 1950s style diner with black and white checkered tile and oilcloth tables. Soups, salads, sandwiches and some creative luncheon specials; chocolate desserts are featured. All non-smoking.

Little Brother's Pub • ΔΔ $

428 SE Main St.; (503) 672-0912. American; wine and beer. Monday-Friday 8 a.m. to 9 p.m., Saturday 10 to 4. No credit cards. Oldstyle, dimly-lit pub popular with business locals for lunch; varied dinner menu.

Los Dos Amigos • ΔΔ $

537 SE Jackson St.; (503) 673-1351. Mexican; wine and beer. Monday-Thursday 11 to 10, Friday-Saturday 11 to 11 and Sunday noon to 10. MC/VISA. Cheerful café with high-backed carved chairs and bright Mexican trappings on the walls. Several Latino seafood dishes in addition to conventional tortilla-wrapped things; also American steaks and burgers.

Mr. & Mrs. M's • ΔΔ $

443 SE Jackson St.; (503) 672-5966. American; wine and beer. Monday-Friday 7:30 to 7:30, Saturday 9 to 5, closed Sunday. MC/VISA. Rural Americana look to the café and menu. Country artifacts on the walls, cozy wooden booths; chicken fried steak, breaded pork chops, and steak and onions.

WHERE TO SLEEP

Budget 16 Motel • ⌂⌂ $$ ∅

1067 NE Stephens St. (south of Garden Valley Blvd.), Roseburg, OR 97470; (503) 673-5556. Couples and kitchenettes $38 to $42, singles from $32. Major credit cards. Well-kept 48-unit motel with TV movies, room phones and pool.

Sycamore Motel • ⌂⌂ $$ ∅

1627 SE Stephens, Roseburg, OR 97470; (503) 672-3354. Couples $38 to $42, singles $27 to $30, kitchenettes $32 to $35. Major credit cards. A 12-unit motel with newly remodeled rooms; TV movies and room phones. **Restaurant** across the street, serving Chinese and American fare 11 a.m. to 10 p.m.; dinners $6 to $10.

Umpqua House Bed & Breakfast Inn • ⌂⌂ $$$

7338 Oak Hill Rd. (off Garden Valley Blvd.), Roseburg, OR 97470; (503) 459-4700. Couples $50, singles $40. Two rooms with shared bath; full breakfast. No credit cards. Country-style home on six wooded acres near town; comfortable modern furnishings. Private entrances, two sun decks, valley views; near wineries and Wildlife Safari.

Windmill Inn of Roseburg • ⌂⌂⌂ $$$ ∅

1450 NW Mulholland Dr. (I-5 exit 125), Roseburg, OR 97470; (800) 547-4747 or (503) 673-0901. Couples $68 to $80, singles $52 to $60, kitchenettes and suites from $85. Major credit cards. Attractive new 128-unit inn with TV movies, room phones; free continental breakfast. Microwaves and refrigerators available; pool. **Sandpiper** Restaurant serves 6 to noon, **Dinner House** 11:30 to 2 and 5 to 10; American fare; dinners $7 to $25; full bar.

WHERE TO CAMP

Fairgrounds RV Park • *2110 Frear St. (I-5 exit 123), Roseburg, OR 97470; (503) 440-4505. RV sites with electrical hookups, $10 for pull-throughs, $8 for back-in. No reservations or credit cards.* Grassy sites with water, showers, dump station; adjacent to museum.

Ron Sher Estates • *25 SW Manor Loop (Winston exit 119), Roseburg, OR 97470; (503) 679-7571. RV sites only, $12 to $16. Reservations accepted;*

UMPQUA RIVER RECREATION AREA

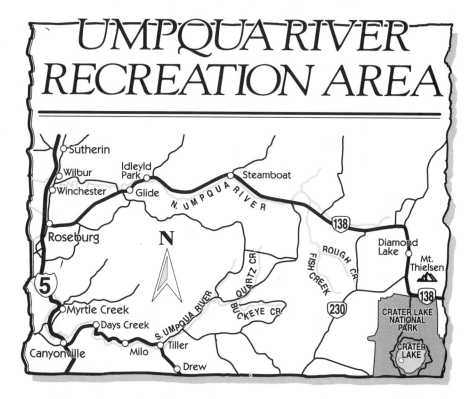

MC/VISA. Older park with paved interior roads; patios and grass areas; showers, laundry, rec room and cable TV.

Twin Rivers Vacation Park ● *433 River Forks Park Rd. (exit 125 then west six miles on Garden Valley Road), Roseburg, OR 97470; (503) 673-3811. RV and tent sites, $12 to $14. Reservations accepted.* Rather attractive park on the Umpqua River with swimming, boating and fishing. Showers, full hookups, dump station, laundry, convenience mart, playground. Some pull-throughs.

Umpqua River recreation area

Like the Rogue, the Umpqua River spills from the high Cascades, weaves through the foothills, calms down in an agricultural valley, then somehow finds a route through the Coast Range to the Pacific. Both streams have their roots near Crater Lake.

The Umpqua Highway provides easy access to the upper reaches of the North Umpqua, creating a playground for boaters, fisherpersons and other river lovers. Creek fed waterfalls tumble over cliffs to join the main stream and campgrounds and resorts line its banks. Beyond are Lemolo Lake and Diamond Lake, offering fishing, boating and swimming.

The North Umpqua is one of the premiere fishing rivers of the North-west, legendary for its trout, steelhead and salmon. Zane Grey and Clark Gable are among the luminaries who have dampened their dry flies here.

To reach this scenic river route, take exit 124 east and follow State Highway 138 signs through downtown Roseburg. You'll soon clear the burg part and pass through rolling farmlands. On the western edge of **Glide,** watch for a sign announcing the **Colliding Rivers** just beyond a bridge. Mother Nature, in a quirky mood, aimed the North Umpqua and Little River right at one another, creating a liquid head-on collision in a shallow serpentine canyon. It more resembles a merger than a crash during normal flow, although it becomes a foaming cauldron at periods of high runoff.

The **Diamond Lake Ranger District** of Umpqua National Forest is headquartered at Idleyld Park; stop in for maps and brochures of the area. If you prefer advanced planning, contact: Umpqua National Forest, HC 60, Box 101, Idleyld Park, OR 97447; (503) 498-2531.

Above Idleyld Park, the highway and river duck between the flanks of a basaltic canyon, adding further drama to the whitewater rush. Sections here are popular with kayakers and rafters. **Susan Creek Campground,** run by the Bureau of Land Management, offers cedar-shaded units for $6 a night. There are no hookups, but who cares? You're right on the river, with access to rafting and kayaking. New showers may be in place by the time you read this.

Just beyond is one of the hideaway jewels of the North Umpqua:

☺ Steamboat Inn • ⌒⌒⌒ $$$$

C/o Steamboat, OR 97447; (503) 496-3495 or 498-2411. Cabins and suites $85 to $195. A rustically immaculate resort with cabins over the river, a knotty pine dining room and carefully tended lawns and gardens. Each evening, a sumptuous fishermen's dinner is served, available only to guests and those who have made reservations. The **dining room** is open to the public for breakfast and lunch.

You're now in the thick timber of Umpqua National Forest. Road and river are lined with forest service campsites. **Whitehorse Falls Campground** and **Clear Water Falls Campground,** as the names imply, have sites within walking distance of waterfalls.

Watson Falls, the second highest in Oregon, is the most dramatic cataract along this route, plunging 272 feet down a basaltic cliff. A moderately steep half-mile hike along mossy creek-side boulders takes you to the base of this feathery veil. A further investment in huffing and puffing will elevate you to a point midway up the cataract. Plan on getting very wet if the wind comes up.

The highway leaves the river above Watson Falls and you'll shortly encounter a sign to **Lemolo Lake Resort.** On the pleasantly funky side, it offers cabins and lodge rooms from $45 to $65, plus a restaurant and lounge, store, service station and marina with boat rentals. An RV park has full hookups for $12, water and electric for $10. Showers, laundry and a dump station are available. For specifics: Lemolo Lake Resort, HC 60, Box 79-B, Idleyld Park, OR 97447; (503) 496-0900. Several national forest campgrounds are on or near the small lake as well.

From the Lemolo Lake turnoff, Highway 130 curves southward toward the large **Diamond Lake Recreation Area.** The region's most popular retreat, it offers fishing, swimming, boating, hiking, camping, resort facilities and a winter cross-country ski program. There's even an eleven-mile bicycle route, snaking among the trees and winding around the lake.

The forest service's **Diamond Lake Visitor Information Center,** at the entrance to Diamond Lake Campground, is open from Memorial Day through Labor Day, daily 9 to 5; (503) 793-3310. Interpretive programs are

ROSEBURG TO EUGENE

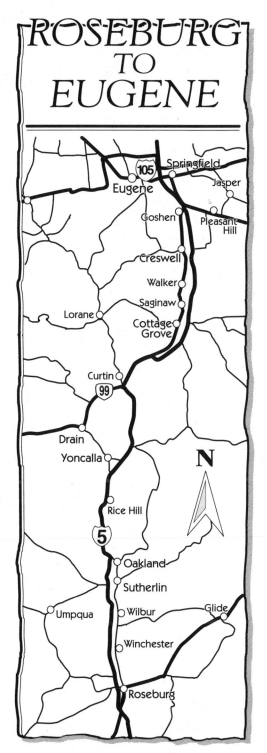

held in summer at the campground amphitheater. The forest service has 450 campsites around the lake.

Diamond Lake Resort offers the full range of lures: restaurants, convenience store, marina with boat and water play rentals, laundry, gift shop, horse rentals, and charter fishing services. A winter sports center offers snowmobile accessories and rentals, plus snowmobile tours and cross-country ski rentals.

The lodge's Thielsen dining room, open 5 to 11, issues dinners of assorted steaks, chicken and seafood for $15 to $25. Diamond Lake Café and South Shore Pizza are substantially cheaper. Modest motel-type rooms go for $51, cabins are $80 to $100. The contact for all of this is: Diamond Lake Resort, Diamond Lake, OR 97731; (800) 733-7593 or (503) 793-3333.

Whitewater & fishing outfitters

The North Umpqua is one of Oregon's more popular fishing and rafting streams. Whitewater raft trips are available through **Cimarron Outdoors,** HC 60, Box 62, Idleyld Park, OR 97447, (503) 498-2235; and **North Umpqua Outfitters,** P.O. Box 1574, Roseburg, OR 97470; (503) 673-4599.

Among the fishing guides in the area are **Bill Conners Guide Service**, P.O. Box 575, Glide, OR 97443; (503) 496-0309; **Gary's Guide Service**, 607 Fawn Dr., Roseburg, OR 97470; (503) 672-2460; and **Umpqua Angler,** 420 E Main St., Roseburg, OR 97470; (503) 673-9809.

ROSEBURG TO EUGENE

Meanwhile, back on I-5, a short drive north from Roseburg will take you to a pair of hamlets often overlooked by freeway-focused motorists. **Sutherlin,** a town of 4,300, has a goodly gathering of antique and collectible shops in its downtown area. Take exit 136 and cruise east on Central Avenue.

From here, you can follow old Highway 99 a couple of miles north to **Oakland,** one of Oregon's genuine jewels. This tiny town of 850 harbors one of the state's finest collections of 19th century brick storefronts. A two-block section brims with curio shops, antique parlors and a restaurant or two. The area, like Jacksonville, wears the mantle of national historic landmark. Each building is labeled with its vintage and its former use.

☺ Classiest establishment in town is **Tolly's,** an energetic enterprise that occupies three inter- connected store fronts. You can sip sodas and such at the old fashioned marble-topped soda fountain, where syrups are still used to build your drink. Upstairs is the classy **Tolly's Restaurant,** with a full service bar and mostly American menu ranging from seafood to grilled chicken to poached salmon for $12.50 to $23. Lunch is served 10 to 6 daily and dinner service is Tuesday-Sunday 5:30 to 9:30; (503) 459-3796. Occupying adjacent buildings and reached through Tolly's are **Tollefson Art Gallery** and **Tollefson Antiques,** both as handsomely coiffed as the restaurant/soda fountain.

Also worthy of a peek is **First Interstate Bank** in the 1892 E.C. Young building, with 19th century carved oak teller cages and such. Across the street, the **Oakland Museum** offers a pleasing if undisciplined clutter of old bottles, insulators, Edison cylinder phonograph and mockups of a tack shop and general store. It's free and open 1 to 4:30 daily.

Oakland got its start in the 1850s as a stage coach stop. The Oregon & California Railroad built a station here, so the community bustled for decades as a center for hop production, prunes and—during the Depression—as one of the country's major turkey production centers. The town declined with the railroad after World War II but, happily for visitors who love old brick, it never quite went to sleep.

If you'd like to rumble through yet another roofed bridge, drive south out of Oakland on Stearns Lane, pass under the freeway and continue south for 2.5 miles. **Rochester Covered Bridge** is on your right, a short distance up Rochester Bridge Road. As you press north on I-5, you'll pass **Cottage Grove,** a pleasant community that offers no pressing reason to pause. Just beyond the townlet of **Walker,** you cross the Coast fork of the Willamette River and thus enter the demographic heartland of Oregon. Your next stop harbors the answer to a question people rarely ask anymore:

Whatever happened to all the flower children?"

Eugene

Population: 112,700   **Elevation: 422 feet**

Assorted demographic studies have labeled Eugene as one of the most livable cities in America. Located on the lower lumpy end of the Willamette Valley with a river running through town, it offers an abundance of recreational lures. Its University of Oregon offers an abundance of cultural lures.

Further, the city is a softbed of liberalism and socio-organic-whole earth awareness. Liberal newspapers circulating about town suggest that Oregon's

Rochester Bridge near Oakland is one of the Willamette Valley's many carefully restored covered bridges. -- **Betty Woo Martin**

environmental movement is focused here. In Eugene, fitness and lifestyle are the same word here. The town has more than a hundred miles of biking/running/power walking paths. It even has a city bicycle coordinator.

If you hang around the fringes of the university or attend the Saturday Street Fair, you'll be convinced that most of San Francisco's 1960s flower children drove their VWs to Eugene and never left. Eugene is not a major tourism center. However, if you're culturally bent and/or you like public markets, theme shopping centers and riverside parks, it it can be *your* tourist town.

There isn't much drama in Eugene's founding. Yesterday, like today, folks just decided that it was a very livable area—a good place to sink roots. Early settlers worked their way south from the Willamette's upper reaches in the mid-1860s and started homesteading here. With ample forests nearby, good graze and the river for navigation, the settlement couldn't help but grow. It's still doing so, having recently passed Salem to become Oregon's second largest city.

If you approach from the south, hop off I-5 at exit 192, which puts you on Franklin Boulevard. You'll shortly brush the edge of the **University of Oregon's** extensive red-brick campus, home to the city's better museums. To explore it, turn left into a visitor parking lot at Franklin and Agate (opposite a New Oregon Best Western Motel). You can pick up a campus map at the information kiosk, open weekdays 8 to 5. If it's closed, cross Agate to the administrative center in Oregon Hall.

Beyond the university, Franklin follows the course of the Willamette River, although much of it is shielded here by businesses. Farther along, the stream is flanked by almost continuous parklands, one of the city's most appealing features. Franklin eventually carries you downtown and swings west into a one-way grid of numbered streets. Sixth (westbound) and Seventh (eastbound) are the main drags.

To load up on acclimation information, stop at the **Eugene-Springfield Visitors Information Center** at the corner of Sixth and Lincoln, open weekdays 8:30 to 5; (503) 484-5307. Sections of the downtown area have been malled and semi-malled, in an effort to stem business flight to the real malls on the edge of town. Several of Eugene's more popular restaurants are on or near the Willamette Street and Broadway pedestrian malls; many have sidewalk tables.

From downtown, backtrack on Seventh, turn left onto High Street and follow it to **Skinner Butte and Park**. From atop the butte (you can hike it or drive it), you'll see that Eugene is a virtual garden city, with lush foliage and trees embracing its urban spread. Down at the bank-side park, you can pick up a biking/pedestrian trail along the Willamette.

If you're in a shopping or nibbling mood, visit the **Fifth Street Public Market,** off High Street between Fifth and Sixth. This former feed mill has been fashioned into an atrium shopping center, nicely arranged around a courtyard and fountain. You'll find the predictable number of boutiques, cafés and food booths. A non-smoking café section offers spicy Chinese fare, Tandoori Indian, tortilla-wrapped Mexican, British bangers, Greek *dolmas* and—it had to happen in Eugene—tofu hot dogs.

A nearby spinoff to the market, **Station Square** at Pearl and Fifth, has similar sorts of shops and cafés. Our favorite here is an vintage style brewpub, **Steelhead Brewery and Café** (listed below under restaurants).

ATTRACTIONS

University of Oregon ● This brick, tree-shaded campus with its expansive parklands is an attraction within itself. Stroll its shady paths, relax on its lawns and take in its museums. The lushly landscaped campus has been used to portray typical Ivy League schools in films, including—unfortunately—*Animal House*. To sample a campus commercial fringe similar to Berkeley's Telegraph Avenue, stroll west along east 13th Avenue to Kincaid Street. The route takes you past some of the school's oldest buildings, dating back to 1876. Among the attractions on campus:

☺ **University Art Museum** ● *Wednesday-Sunday noon to 5; free; (503) 346-3027.* Easily the best art museum between San Francisco and Portland, it has an outstanding collection of Asian art, Rodin sculptures, Russian icon paintings and works from the masters of Europe. Changing exhibits range from *avant garde* to kinetic to lunatic fringe—much of it student art. Among its fine permanent displays are a black lacquer and gold Japanese palanquin, rare Chinese jade and bas relief panels from Cambodia's Angkor Wat.

Museum of Natural History ● *Wednesday-Sunday noon to 5; free; (503) 346-3024.* Look for a distinctive chalet style building with rough hewn columns, suggestive of Northwest Native American architecture. Inside, you'll find a small but impressive collection focusing on Oregon's original people, earth sciences and wildlife. Changing exhibits are particularly versatile, ranging from Indonesian puppet shows to photos of China's 20th century missionary period.

Off campus attractions

☺ **Lane County Historical Museum** ● *740 W. 13th Ave. (adjacent to Lane County Fairgrounds); (503) 687-4239. Tuesday-Friday 10 to 5, Saturday-Sunday 11 to 4. Adults $2, seniors $1, kids 3 to 17, 75 cents.* This large, barn-like structure is impressive mostly for its carriage collection and a full-sized emigrant wagon. Roseburg's Douglas County Museum is better arranged, although this one contains lots of interesting stuff. We liked its offbeat exhibits, such as the history of footware from turn-of-the- century men's pointy-toed shoes to 1960s garter belts.

Willamette Science & Technology Center • *2300 Centennial Blvd.; (503) 687-3619. Weekends 10 to 5, longer hours in summer. Adults $3, seniors and collegiates $2.50, kids 3 to 17, $2. Planetarium shows Friday at 4, weekends at 2; $3 for adults, $2.50 for seniors and students and $1 for kids. To get there, turn into the Autzen Stadium parking lot off Centennial Boulevard and head toward a rounded concrete building standing alone in a weedy field.* WISTEC is a mid-sized science center directed mostly toward youngsters, with lots of hands-on stuff relating to the physical sciences. A white-jacketed "Dr. Science" type strolls about, helping kids with the exhibits. We adults had fun making our own movie on a zoetrope machine and watching sunspots on a projected disk.

Hendricks Park and Rhododendron Garden • *East end of Summit Avenue. To get there, take Agate south past the university campus, then go east on Summit.* This wooded park has a stunning blossom show May through June when its thousands of rhododendrons and azaleas are in bloom.

Oregon Air Museum • *Boeing Drive (at Eugene Airport); (503) 461-1101. Adults $3, seniors and students $2.50, kids 6 to 17, $2.* This is a small, emerging museum that's probably worth the drive out to the airport if you're an aviation nut. The limited collection includes plane models, flight suits and pieces of planes (plus complete ones outside), focusing mostly on aviation's development in Oregon. To find it, head toward the airport on Airport Road, then bypass the terminal turn-in and continue a couple of blocks to Boeing Drive (at the Flightcraft sign), and turn right.

ACTIVITIES AND ANNUAL EVENTS

Theatrics and music • The impressive, state-of-the-art **Hult Center for the Performing Arts** downtown on Willamette between Sixth and Seventh books top-name performers, musicales and such. Experts say it has the best acoustics of any concert hall on the West Coast. Free tours of this facility are conducted Thursday and Saturday at 1; call (503) 687-5087. For performances, the box office is (503) 687-5000. Pick up a copy of the center's quarterly *On Stage* for a schedule of upcoming events; (503) 687-5087. The adjacent **Jacobs Gallery** features works of local artists.

Oregon Bach Festival • For ticket information, call the Hult Center at (503) 687-5000. This highly acclaimed festival, which runs the last two weeks of June, features more than 40 concerts at the Hult Center and the University's Beall Concert Hall. Its 80-member orchestra doesn't just go back to Bach; it features the music of Mozart, Schubert, Brahms and other classic composers, plus works of 20th century artists.

Alive and onstage • The **University Theater** offers a season of productions on campus; 346-4191. Two other local groups are **Very Little Theater,** doing a variety of comedies and dramas, 344-7751; and **Actors Cabaret,** featuring Broadway-style musicals, 687-5000.

Other cultural occurrences • For a detailed list of everything else going on in this culturally busy community, pick up a copy of *What's Happening,* issued weekly. They're in racks on the campus and all over town;

call (503) 484-0519 to find out where. The weekend edition of the *Eugene Register-Guard* also has a good rundown on local activities and events.

Millrace canoeing • *EMU Waterworks Canoe Shack, 1595 Franklin Blvd. (at Onyx Street, opposite the university); (503) 346-4386 or 346-3711. Open Monday-Friday 12:30 to dusk and Saturday-Sunday 11 to dusk, March through October (weather permitting). Canoe and kayak rentals $3.65 an hour or $14 a day, plus deposit.* Looking for something that's *really* different? Rent a canoe and paddle it down the Millrace, a somewhat murky channel paralleling the Willamette River along Franklin Boulevard. You'll paddle through flotillas of ducks, past hanging blackberry bushes and willows on this curious outing within earshot of the city's traffic rumbles.

☺ **Saturday Street Fair** • *Weekends at Oak and Eighth streets downtown.* If you miss the Sixties, head for this weekend arts and crafts market with a strong hippie counter- culture accent. Shoulder among booths offering American folk crafts, joss sticks, dulcimers, tarot cards and herbal flea collars. Food booths issue the predictable fajitas, curries, fried tofu and earthy grains. I bought a huge earth-grain organically correct cookie that tasted more like earth than grain.

☺ **Oregon Country Fair** • *Late July, off Highway 126 near the hamlet of Noti, west of Eugene. Contact Oregon Country Faire, P.O. Box 2972, Eugene, OR 97402; (503) 343-4298.* Blend together a renaissance crafts fair, a hippie love-in, an environmental awareness exhibition, an outdoor music festival and season it with yogurt, feta, earth grains and tofu and what've you got? One of the largest outdoor events in the Northwest. The annual affair, in perfect tempo and temperament for nearby Eugene, is the Saturday Street Fair multiplied. Slip into your tie-dyed T-shirt and flops and get involved.

Winetasting • The *Wineries of Oregon's South Willamette Valley* brochure directs you to a dozen vintners with tasting rooms. Pick up a copy at the visitor center or write: South Willamette Chapter, Oregon Winegrowers Assn., P.O. Box 1591, Eugene, OR 97440.

Transportation services

Eugene airport (687-5430), 20 minutes northwest off Highway 99W, is served by **Alaska Airlines,** (800) 426-0333; **American** (800) 547-7000; **Horizon Air,** (800) 547-9308; **Northwest,** (800) 692-7000); **United Express,** (800) 241-6552; and **USAir,** (800) 428-4322. The **Amtrak** station is at Fourth and Willamette; call (800) USA-RAIL or (503) 344-6265.

WHERE TO DINE
Downtown

☺ **Ambrosia** • ∆∆∆ **$$**

174 Broadway (at Pearl); 342-4141. Italian; full bar service. Monday-Thursday 11:30 to 10:30, Friday-Saturday 11:30 to 11:30, Sunday 4:30 to 10. MC/VISA. Handsome café with dark woods and beveled glass; in one of downtown's old brick buildings. Creative menu features prawns sautéed with shallots and garlic, boneless chicken breast stuffed with goat cheese, assorted pastas, grilled lamb and fresh seafood. Outdoor seating.

Zenon Cafè • ∆∆∆ $$ ø

898 Pearl (at Broadway); 343-3005. Eclectic; wine and beer. Monday-Thursday 8 to 11, Friday-Saturday 8 to midnight, Sunday 10 to 11; MC/VISA.

Creative menu that dances from pasta to salmon to rabbit to vegetarian; changes weekly with specials such as lamb curry with braised apple and vegetarian endive *au gratin* with goronzola cream sauce. Nicely simple interior with bentwood chairs and marble topped tables.

Fettuccini & Co. • Δ $
901 Pearl (at Broadway); (503) 485-6480. Greek-Italian; wine and beer. Monday-Thursday 8 a.m. to 9 p.m., Friday 8 to 10, Saturday 9 to 10, closed Sunday. Cozy deli serving pastas and light entrèes such as spana kopita (spinach, feta, green onions and mint), stuffed chicken breasts and assorted sandwiches. Good duck-in spot for a quick bite.

Huson's Seafood Grotto • ΔΔ $$
Willamette and Seventh (opposite Hult Center); (503) 343-2006. Seafood; full bar service. Monday-Thursday 11 to 9:30, Friday 11 to 11, Saturday 4 to 10 and Sunday 4 to 9. MC/VISA. Serious seafood parlor displaying blackboard menu with daily catch, so you know what's fresh. Inexpensive small dinners $5.50 to $8.50. Steak and prime rib in addition to fish and shellfish. Nautical dècor consists mostly of commercial fishing photos.

Pape's Anatolia • ΔΔ $$
992 E. Willamette (on the mall at Tenth); (503) 343-9661. Mideastern; wine and beer. Monday-Thursday 11:30 to 9, Friday 11:30 to 10, Saturday 11:30 to 2 and 5 to 10 and Sunday 11:30 to 3:30. MC/VISA. Small, pleasantly funky cafè with exposed beams, dark woods and mideastern rugs. Menu features Greek *moussaka, gyros,* chicken curry and halibut *psito.*

☺ Steelhead Brewery and Cafè • ΔΔ $
199 E. Fifth Ave. (in Station Square); 686-BREW. American; wine and beer. Daily 11:30 to 11. MC/VISA. Microbrewery and brewpub with old fashioned fixtures, exposed beams and a bright red London phone booth. Copper and stainless steel workings of the brewery visible behind the bar. Brewpub fare such as sausage platter, calzone and cheese steak. Outdoor tables.

☺ Willie's on Seventh • ΔΔΔ $$
388 W. Seventh St. (at Lawrence); (503) 485-0601. American; full bar service. Lunch weekdays 11 to 2, dinner Monday-Thursday 5 to 9 and Friday-Saturday 5 to 10, closed Sunday. MC/VISA. Early American style restaurant in a refurbished house on the edge of downtown; natural woods, striped wallpaper, plate rails and such. Creative entrèes include pepper steak, chicken and scallops, honey glazed pork loin and pecan chicken.

University district

China Blue • Δ $
879 E. 13th Ave. (Kincaid); (503) 343-2832. Chinese; wine and beer. Monday-Thursday 11 to 9:30, Friday 11 to 10, Saturday 5 to 10, Sunday 11 to 3 and 5 to 9:30. MC/VISA. Basic formica cafè serving good portions of straightforward Chinese food; mostly Cantonese with some spicier Mandarin; *dim sum* (Chinese tea lunch) on Sunday.

Excelsior Cafè • ΔΔΔ $$$
754 E. 13th Ave.; (503) 485-1206. American regional; full bar service. Dinner Sunday-Thursday 5:30 to 9 and Friday-Saturday 5:30 to 10, continental breakfast 7:30 to 11 and lunch 11:30 to 2:30 weekdays, Sunday brunch 10 to 2. MC/VISA, AMEX. Fashionable spot with a black and white Ascot look,

set in an old colonial house. Changing menu focuses on whatever's fresh, ranging from spring lamb to Chinook salmon to Yaquina Bay oysters.

Guido's Restaurant & More • △△ $

801 E. 13th Ave. (at Alder); (503) 343-0681. Italian-American; full bar service. Monday-Saturday 11 to 10 (later on weekends). MC/VISA, AMEX. Popular student hangout; spacious, high-ceiling café with sunken dining area and brick walls. The usual calzones, pizzas, chicken cacciatores, plus burgers and other sandwiches, served to the tune of Sixties jukebox tunes.

For quick bites, duck into the **Fall Creek Bakery** (881 E. 13th; 484-1662) for espresso and diet-spoiling bakery goodies. Or hit **Espresso Roma** (825 E. 13th; 484-4848) for croissants and tasty king-sized muffins to compliment your espresso or cappuccino.

WHERE TO SLEEP

Barron's Motor Inn • △△ $$ ∅

1859 Franklin Blvd., Eugene, OR 97401; (800) 444-6383 or (503) 342-6383. Couples $46 to $64, singles $36 to $65, suites $60 to $68. Major credit cards. A 60-unit motel with TV movies, room phones, continental breakfast; hot tub, sauna, free newspapers and free use of bicycles.

Eugene Motor Lodge • △ $$ ∅

476 E. Broadway, Eugene, OR 97401; (800) 876-7829 or (503) 344-5233. Couples $36 to $44, singles $28 to $32. Major credit cards. A 49-unit motel with TV movies and pool; most rooms non-smoking.

Red Lion Inn • △△△ $$$$ ∅

205 Coburg Rd. (downtown I-5 exit), Eugene, OR 97401; (800) 547-8010 or (503) 342-5201. Couples $79 to $87, singles $64 to $72. Major credit cards. Large, recently remodeled rooms with TV movies, phones; pool. Near downtown. **Coffee Garden** and **Misty's** restaurants serve American and continental fare; 6 a.m. to 10 p.m.; dinners $7 to $20; full bar service.

Shilo Inn • △△△ $$$ ∅

3350 Gateway (I-5 exit 195), Springfield, OR 97477; (800) 222-2244 or (503) 747-0332. Couples $60 to $68, singles $52 to $60, kitchenettes $68 to $76. Major credit cards. A 143-unit hotel with TV movies, room phones, continental breakfast; mini-suites with kitchens; pool; guest laundry; *Confetti's Lounge* and *The Diner* restaurant.

Timbers Motel • △ $$ ∅

1015 Pearl St., Eugene, OR 97401; (800) 643-4167 or (503) 343-3343. Couples $41 to $47, singles $30 to $40. Major credit cards. A 57-room motel with TV, pool and sauna.

Travelers Inn Motel • △△ $$ ∅

540 E. Broadway (at Patterson), Eugene, OR 97401; (800) 432-5999 or (503) 342-1109. Couples $39 to $43, singles $31 to $33. Major credit cards. A well-kept 34-unit motel with TV movies, room phones, in-room coffee makers and some refrigerators; pool.

Bed & breakfast inns

☺ Duckworth Bed & Breakfast • △△△ $$$$ ∅

987 E. 19th Ave., Eugene, OR 97403; (503) 686-2451. Couples and singles $65 to $75. Three rooms with TV and room phones; one private, two shared baths; full breakfast. No credit cards. English Tudor style inn with English and American antiques. In-room VCRs with 600-movie library; player piano in living room; English gardens; bikes available. Near university campus.

The Lyon & The Lambe Inn ● ⌂⌂⌂ $$$ ∅

988 Lawrence at Tenth, Eugene, OR 97401; (503) 683-3160. Couples $60 to $83, singles $55 to $78. Four units with room phones and private baths; full breakfast. MC/VISA. New two-story home built in 1930s style with wrap-around porch; extensive library and fireplace in living room. Designer rooms with a mix of contemporary furnishing and European antiques; one with spa tub. Pets accepted. Near downtown.

WHERE TO CAMP

Eugene KOA ● I-5 exit 199 (Route 2, box 353), Eugene, OR 97401; (800) 621-6628 or (503) 343-4832. RV and tent sites, $12.50 to $17.50. Reservations accepted; MC/VISA. Grassy sites, full hookups, some pull-throughs. Laundry, showers, rec room, miniature golf course, cable TV, mini-mart.

Eugene Mobile Home Village ● 4750 Franklin Blvd. (I-5 exit 189), Eugene, OR 97403; (503) 747-2257. RV sites, $13 to $14. Reservations accepted; MC/VISA. Forest setting, some pull-throughs. Showers, cable TV, laundry, mini-mart, recreation area, playground and rec room.

Sherwood Forest KOA ● 298 E. Oregon Ave. (nine miles south, exit 182), Cresswell, OR 97426; (503) 895-4110. RV and tent sites, $12 to $17. Reservations accepted; MC/VISA. Tree shaded sites and some pull-throughs. Showers, laundry, mini- mart, pool and spa, rec room and playground.

McKenzie River recreation area

We've established that you're never far from surf or pine-cloaked mountains along the I-5 corridor. A westward run along State Highway 126 carries you to the coast at Florence, and the **Oregon Dunes National Recreation Area,** which we explore in detail in Chapter 5. Heading east on 126 and you'll discover some of the reasons that Eugenites enjoy the good life. Like the Umpqua and Rogue below, the **McKenzie River** is the heart of a major recreation area, offering fishing, lazy floats and whitewater rafting.

We'll explore the McKenzie area as part of a loop drive, returning on U.S. Highway 20 to Albany. From downtown Eugene, head southeast on Franklin Boulevard, which becomes Route 126 and steers you through the suburb of **Springfield.** This ordinary looking community of 45,000 functions primarily as a handy bedroom for Eugene. The downtown area, while not deteriorating, has a lot of thrift shops and discount stores, occupying handsome brick and masonry buildings. A mustard-yellow former railroad station housing the **Springfield Chamber of Commerce** is the brightest thing around. You'll see it at Second and A streets; open weekdays 8:30 to 5; (503) 746-1651.

Two attractions are worthy of a Springfield pause. The **Springfield Museum** occupies a storefront at Sixth and Main streets, open Wednesday-Friday 10 to 4 and Saturday noon to 4; (503) 726-2300. It offers a nicely arrayed display of pioneer artifacts and photos tracing the town's lumbering and agricultural heritage. **Dorris Ranch** at 151 N. Fourth Street is an old 250-acre filbert ranch operated as a living history museum by the area parks and recreation district. Call (503) 726-4335 to arrange a tour.

McKENZIE RIVER RECREATION AREA

Beyond Springfield, the McKenzie flows calmly through a lush agricultural valley. The road stays with the river much of the way, with frequent picnic sites, swimming holes and boat launch areas. Between **Leaburg** and **Vida**, you can swing right and cross the 1938 **Goodpasture Covered Bridge.** Above Vida, the river becomes a bit more frisky, offering gentle whitewater for rafters, canoeists and kayakers.

At **Blue River,** you can buy detailed recreational maps of the area at the U.S. Forest Service's **Blue River Ranger District Office,** open weekdays 8:30 to 5; (503) 822-3317. To reach it, take Blue River Road off Highway 126. Just beyond, where the road rejoins the highway, is **Forest Glen Restaurant** (822-3714), an attractive oldstyle American dining room with lace curtains, wagon wheel décor and such. It's open Monday-Saturday 5 to 10, serving hearty American fare; dinners from $7.50 to $18. Champagne brunches are popular hereabouts, served Sunday 10 to 2. It takes MC/VISA.

To stay close to the river, take McKenzie River Drive, which guides you through the hamlet of **Rainbow.** Just beyond is a noted hideaway where folks such as President Herbert Hoover and Victor Bergeron of Trader Vic fame have found sanctuary.

☺ **Holiday Farm** ⌂⌂ **$$$$$** ∅

C/o Blue River, OR 97413; (503) 822-3715 (call collect). Rooms and cottages $100 to $185. No credit cards. Elegantly rustic farm style retreat, noted for its simple elegance and excellent nearby fishing. There are two lakes on the property and golf is half a mile away. The **restaurant** serves excellent

American fare from 7 a.m. to noon and 5:30 to 10; dinners $10.50 to $25; full bar service.

Up the road a bit is **Rainbow Park RV Resort** (822-3928) in a woodsy setting across the road from the river, near a covered bridge. Facilities include a coin laundry, cable TV and shaded sites; rates are $11 for water and electric; no reservations or credit cards. **Belknap Bridge** here is new as covered bridges go, rebuilt in 1966 after the Christmas Flood of 1964 destroyed an earlier version. Another RV spot along McKenzie River Drive is **Patio RV Park** (822-3596), right on the river with hookups for $15. It's a pleasant spot with shaded sites, cable TV, showers, coin laundry and a rec hall with a fireplace.

You'll soon merge back onto Highway 126 at the village of **McKenzie Bridge,** consisting of a two-gas-pump general store. You're about to enter Willamette National Forest and this is the last place you can gas up for 50 miles. A ranger station here offers a second chance to pick up maps and hiking trail brochures on the area; it's open daily 8:30 to 5; (503) 822-3381.

From this point, the river remains your roadside companion, offering campgrounds, picnic sites and fishing spots. State Highway 242 branches to the right here, heading for McKenzie Pass and Bend, which we've saved for Chapter 8. Stay with 126 as it swings north through tumbled foothills and picks up the **Smith River.** A few miles above **Trail Bridge Reservoir,** pause at the turnout for **Sahalie Falls.** This impressive cataract crashes 60 feet over a lava flow into a mossy ravine. Then hike downstream a quarter of a mile to **Koosah Falls** at **Ice Cap Campground.** This dazzling multiple cataract drops a hundred feet over a lava face.

☺ Just beyond is **Clear Lake Resort,** a neat retreat on a rowboat-only lake with a small cafè, woodsy cabins and boat launch. A forest service picnic area is nearby, above the lake shore. You're on the edge of the **Mount Washington Wilderness** here and hiking trails lead therein. Occasionally, you catch a glimpse of Washington's craggy, snowcapped volcanic tip.

At the juncture with U.S. 20 (the South Santiam Highway), swing west and climb to **Tombstone Summit,** named for a square monolith jutting from a forested ridge. You then begin a long downhill spiral into the Willamette Valley. You'll soon join the **South Santiam River,** little more than a creek at this point. The usual national forest campgrounds dot it banks.

The town of **Sweet Home** marks your transition from forest to field. At the south end, look for the **East Linn Museum** in a paint-peeling red and white 1905 church building. It's open Tuesday-Saturday 11 to 4 and Sunday 1 to 4. Several rooms are filled with an undisciplined clutter of pioneer artifacts. Highway 20 carries you past filbert orchards, barkey and hay fields, through the towns of **Waterloo** and **Lebanon** and rejoins Interstate 5 opposite Albany.

McKenzie River outfitters

If you want to play in the water, contact **McKenzie Pontoon Trips,** 378 S. 69th Place, Springfield, OR 97478, (503) 741-1905, for whitewater raft trips; **Jim's Oregon Whitewater,** 56324 McKenzie Hwy., McKenzie Bridge, OR 97413, (503) 822-6003, for rafting and fishing trips; **Mountain View Guide Service,** 90485 Mt. View Lane, Leaburg, OR 97489, (503) 896-3348 for fishing trips; and **Brad Edwards,** 90497 Mt. View Lane, Leaburg, OR 97489, (503) 896-3547, for fishing trips.

Albany

Population: 29,500   **Elevation: 210 feet**

Assuming you've taken our loop trip from Eugene, cross over I-5 and head toward U.S. 99-E, watching for signs to Albany's downtown and the historic district. The **Albany Visitors' Association** is inside a shopping mall called the Market Place, carved from several old stores at 300 SW Second Ave.; (503) 928-0911. It's open Monday-Saturday 8 to 5 and Sunday noon to 5; off-season hours are 8 to 5 weekdays. At most other times, you can enter the mall and pick up stuff from brochure racks in the hallway.

Albany is one of those early-day towns that was bypassed and thus preserved. It dates back to 1849 when it was settled by farmers and became an important shipping center for the Willamette Valley's wheat and produce. By the turn of the century, it was a busy railroad hub. Later, commerce shifted elsewhere, sending the local economy adrift.

Today, the town has nearly 350 historic houses, dating from the Victoria era. If you like to see an assortment of old homes—Carpenter Gothic, gingerbread Victorian, turn-of- the-century Craftsman and Eastlake—you'll get your fill here. Few are elaborate; most are sturdy family cottages that have survived. Some are nicely restored; others await attention.

The Albany Visitors' Association works hard to lure lovers of old homes, with walking and driving tour maps and brochures. It also issues a driving map to area covered bridges, lists of Albany antique dealers and other helpful stuff. The town sponsors lots of historic functions, such as homes tours and Gibson Girl horse-drawn carriage tours in July and August. (See "Salem-Albany area events" under Salem, below.)

ATTRACTIONS

Monteith House ● *518 SW Second Ave.; (503) 928-0911. Open June through September, Wednesday-Sunday noon to 4.* This simple two-story colonial, built in 1849 by the founding Thomas Monteith family, is one of the oldest structures in Oregon. Its rooms are furnished to the period, staffed by costumed docents.

Albany Regional Museum ● *302 SW Ferry St.; (503) 967-6540. Open June through September, Wednesday-Sunday noon to 4; the rest of the year on Wednesday and Saturday noon to 4.* You can browse through an old-timey general store, doctor's office and barber shop and see specialized historic exhibits at this indoor-outdoor museum.

Albany Fire Museum ● *120 SE 34th St.; (503) 967-4302. Call for appointment.* The local fire department has preserved memorabilia from its yesterdays, including a 1907 horse-drawn, steam-operated fire engine.

Salem

Population: 107,800   **Elevation: 171 feet**

Oregon's capital city, 25 miles up the freeway from Albany, wears its mantle of leadership well. It's a nicely groomed community for the most part, with a well-preserved downtown area. The capitol building is one of the more attractive in the country, with its distinctive cylindrical tower. Oregon's third largest city, it offers a a good number of museums and historic sites. The name is proper for a capital city. "Salem" comes from the Hebrew word *shalom,* meaning peace.

OREGON'S ROOFS OVER RIVERS

Among Oregon's most endearing survivors are its many covered bridges. Back in the old days, they were called "kissing bridges," since they were great places to pull up the buggy and steal a smooch. Covered bridge-building dates from the 1850s and by the 1930s, the state had more than 300. They were designed not so much to protect the decks from Oregon's damp climate, but to protect the more expensive trusses. The roofs weren't intended to keep the floor dry. In fact, in winter, residents would shovel snow onto the bridge planking so sleighs could pass through more smoothly.

Sadly, many of these charming relics were replaced by colorless steel and concrete spans. This "modernization" has been stopped in recent years as communities—spurred by interest groups—recognize their aesthetic and visitor appeal. Thanks to efforts of organizations such as The Covered Bridge Society of Oregon, 53 of these spans survive. That's more than any other state west of the Mississippi. Oregon ranks fourth in the covered bridge count, after Pennsylvania's 228, Ohio's 141 and Indiana's 92.

Willamette: the valley of the bridges

Many travelers, including the authors of this book, will venture far off course for the privilege of driving through these dim and cozy bridges to the past. We visit several on the pages ahead. The Willamette Valley has the state's greatest concentration, and several area chambers of commerce offer driving guides. Although some of the bridges are merely showpieces, many have been reinforced or reconstructed, and are open to regular traffic.

Lane County has the state's largest number of bridges. About 20 can be visited during drives around the Eugene-Springfield-Cottage Grove area. Another good concentration is along Highway 228 in the Brownsville-Sweet Home area, east of Albany in Linn County. A covered bridge in Sunny Valley, north of Grants Pass, is within view of the I-5 freeway, and a handy off-ramp gets you to it.

For driving maps and other information on these old charmers, contact the **Covered Bridge Society of Oregon**, 9070 SW Rambler Lane, Portland, OR 97223; (503) 246-2953. The book, *Roofs Over Oregon* by Bill and Nick Cockrell (Oregon Sentinel Publishing), is a detailed guide to these bridges; it's available at many bookstores in the state. Another good source is the **Cottage Grove Chamber of Commerce,** P.O. Box 587, Cottage Grove, OR 97424; (503) 942-2411. It produces a brochure featuring all 53 of the state's roofed spans, and the community sponsors a covered bridge festival in September.

Other organizations with material on area bridges include the **Roseburg Visitors Information Bureau,** P.O. Box 1262, Roseburg, OR 97470, (800) 444-9584 or (503) 672-9731; **Albany Visitors Association,** P.O. Box 965, Albany, OR 97321, (800) 526-2256 or (503) 928-0911; **Grants Pass Visitors Information Center,** P.O. Box 970, Grants Pass, OR 97526, (800) 547-5927 or (503) 476-7717, and the **Lincoln County Historical Society,** 545 SW Ninth St., Newport, OR 97365, (503) 265-7509.

Some of the state's earliest roots were put down here. Jason Lee, the first Protestant missionary in the Oregon Country, arrived in 1834 to teach the Calapooyan Indians "to cultivate the ground...and as they do this, teach them religion." However, the Native Americans didn't take to the plow or the Bible. After years of effort and only limited success, Lee built a flour mill, platted a town and set the foundations for the Oregon Institute. It prevails to this day as Willamette University, the oldest school of higher learning west of the Rockies.

In 1843, the first overland migration arrived in the Willamette Valley and Salem began growing in earnest. When the Oregon Territory was established in 1849, Oregon City was picked as the capitol. However, it was shifted to Salem when statehood was achieved ten years later.

Approaching on I-5, take exit 253 (Highway 22), and head west toward downtown Salem. After a mile, take the University/City Center sign to the right (99E), then right again for 12th Street/state offices. This takes you to a good starting spot, the **Mission Mill Village,** a theme shopping center and museum in an old woolen mill. It houses the **Salem Convention & Visitors Association**, open Monday-Saturday 8 to 5 and Sunday noon to 5; (503) 581-4325.

☺ The museum portion of the mill is certainly worth a prowl, with its pioneer village exhibits. You'll see several historic houses including the 1841 Jason Lee home and his parsonage, the 1896 woolen mill, a machine shop, a water-powered turbine and the Marion County Museum of History. Hours are Tuesday-Saturday 10 to 4:30 and Sunday 1 to 4:30; adults $2.50, seniors and teens $2 and kids six to 11, $1. It's closed on Monday. In fact, much of tourist Salem is closed that day, so plan your visit around this gap.

Now, you're ready to attack the rest of Salem. A logical place to start is the capital complex, reached by continuing north on 12th street and following the signs.

ATTRACTIONS

☺ **Oregon state capitol** ● *Between Court and State Streets; (503) 378-4423. Building open weekdays 8 to 5, Saturday 9 to 4 and Sunday noon to 4. Guided tours from June through Labor Day, Monday-Saturday, hourly 9 to 3.* This striking creation of Vermont marble is easily the most distinctive public building in the state. It was completed in 1936 after fire destroyed an earlier version, although it looks much more modern than that. Instead of the conventional Corinthian columns and copper dome, it has a fluted cylindrical tower, topped by a generic gold-plated pioneer. Massive bas relief sculptures flank the main entrance, depicting the Lewis and Clark epic and covered wagons on the Oregon Trail. The marble and polished wood interior is imposing, yet not overdone. A giant state seal is set in mosaic tile on the floor. Chambers of the Senate and House of Representatives occupy two wings, richly detailed in Oregon woods and theme carpeting—trout for the senators and evergreens for the reps.

A velvety green park surrounds the capitol, staffed by some of the most brazen squirrels you'll find anywhere. Take some peanuts to avoid getting mugged. The grounds contain the usual statues, including a bronze of a circuit-riding preacher with his nose in his Bible, presumably trusting his horse to get him where he's headed. Most of the other governmental buildings here are rather institutional.

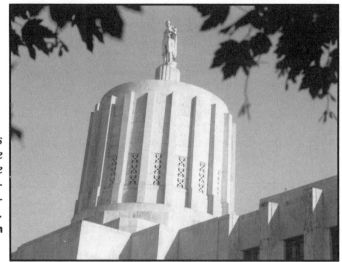

Although it dates from 1936, the cylindrical dome of Oregon's capitol has a very contemporary look.
– Don W. Martin

☺ An attractive exception is the **Supreme Court** at State and Waverly. The oldest structure in the capital complex, it's rather ornate, with fluted marble columns and a barrel arch ceiling. Hike up three flights of a curving stairway to the handsome walnut-paneled court chambers, under a canopy of leaded glass that contains the state seal.

Across State Street from the capitol is **Willamette University,** a dignified collection of old brick in a park-like setting, shaded by century-old trees. A campus stroll provides a fitting finish to this capital visit.

☺ **Deepwood Estate** ● *1116 SE Mission St.; (503) 363-1825. Tours Sunday-Friday noon to 4:30. Adults $2, seniors and students $1.50 and kids 75 cents.* Salem's most ornate home, this Victorian study in gingerbread trim, turrets and cupolas was built in 1894. Even if you aren't there during tour hours, you can wander the elaborate formal gardens with their ivy-entwined and moss-coated trees. Note particularly the monstrous 25-foot tall holly.

☺ **Bush Pasture and Mansion** ● *600 Mission St.; (503) 363- 4714. Tuesday-Sunday noon to 5 in summer and 2 to 5 the rest of the year. Adults $2, seniors and students $1.50, kids 75 cents.* A pasture in the middle of Salem? Bush Pasture, one of the city's finest parks, was fashioned from the estate of Asahel Bush, a wealthy banker and founder of Oregon's first newspaper. His Italianate Victorian, completed in 1878 and occupied by the family for 75 years, contains many original furnishings. Also in the area are the **Bush Barn Art Center** with works of mostly local artists, and the **Bush Conservatory** greenhouse, blooming with orchids and other tropical plants. The "pasture" is rimmed by a neighborhood of restored 19th century homes.

Enchanted Forest ● *8462 Enchanted Way; I-5 exit 248, seven miles south; (503) 363-3060. Open mid-March through September, daily 9:30 to 6. Adults and juniors $4.25, kids 3 to 12, $3.75. Bobsled and haunted house, $1 each.* This is a good place to park the kids while you explore Salem's historic lures. Or you can go in with them if you like soggy bobsled runs, scary houses and dancing waters. The park's theme is eclectic, to say the least—a Western mining town set in a fairy tale forest. The Old Ranger meets the Seven Dwarfs?

Antique Powerland ● *3995 NE Brooklake Rd.; (503) 393-2424. Daily 9 to 6. Equipment fired up the last weekend of July and first weekend of August.* This museum features a goodly gathering of power-driven farm equipment, including kerosene tractors, steam engines and such. The adjacent **Pacific Northwest Museum of Transportation** features a collection of antique trucks and other early cargo carriers.

Honeywood Winery ● *1350 SE Hines St.; (503) 362-1111. Daily 9 to 5; guided tours 10 and 2.* Since it started with fruit wines, Honeywood claims to be the oldest winery in the state, dating from 1934. It has since added the essence of the grape to its wine line, giving you a good sipping variety. It's easy to find since it's within a block of Mission Mill Village. Several other wineries are tucked among the farmlands east of Salem. The Convention & Visitors Association can provide a tour map.

Gilbert House Children's Museum ● *116 NE Marion St.; (503) 371-3631. Monday-Saturday 10 to 5 and Sunday noon to 4. Admission $2.* This small kiddie museum is tucked into an attractive scallop-shingled 19th century home. Youngsters can enclose themselves in a giant bubble and fiddle with assorted hands-on games and experiments.

Touring Salem

The Visitors Association's **Historic Salem** tour map will steer you through most of the city's points of interest, including its historic neighborhoods and the downtown area. It's relatively easy to follow as tour maps go. Blue and white "Historic Salem" street markers along the route will help guide you.

The driving tour begins at the capitol grounds, takes you downtown, thence to the Pioneer Cemetery, Bush Pasture, Deepwood Estate, Mission Mill, and finally to a nice collection of old residences in the Court-Chemeketa district just east of the capitol. *Chemeketa* was the Native American name for this region, which meant "place of rest."

The downtown area is a nicely preserved gathering of low-rise brick and masonry. You'll find no skyscrapers and no parking meters. Some of the town's more interesting restaurants are here (and listed below), catering to business folk and tourists like yourselves. If you're in a shopping mood, step into the former **Reed Opera House** at Court and Liberty streets. This ornate 1870 brick structure encloses an atrium sheltering boutiques and restaurants. The adjacent waterfront cries for development and hopefully, something is in the works. But for now, it offers only a small and rather scruffy park between Marion and Center streets. The above-mentioned Gilbert House Children's Museum is in this area, tucked between twin bridges over the Willamette.

SALEM-ALBANY AREA EVENTS

Salem's Oregon State Fairgrounds is the site for dozens of local and regional events. The biggie, of course, is the **Oregon State Fair** starting in late August and continuing through Labor Day Weekend. Call (503) 378-3247 for specifics on this and other fairgrounds events. Other area activities:

Tour de Vin, late May, tour of area wineries; (503) 362-4111.

World Champion Timber Carnival, Albany, July 4; (503) 928-0911.

Salem Art Fair and Festival, third weekend of July; (503) 581-4325.

Victorian Days with dress-up and horse-drawn carriage rides, Albany, late July; (503) 928-0911.

Great Balloon Escape & Wine Fest, July, Albany; (503) 928-0911.

Great Oregon Steam-up at Antique Powerland, last weekend of July and first weekend of August; (503) 393-2424.

Salem Art Fair & Festival in Bush's Pasture, August; (503) 581-2228.

Oregon State Championship Chili and Barbecue Cook-off in Albany, early September; (503) 928-0911.

Northwest Hot Air Balloon Championships, Salem Airport, mid-September; (503) 581-4325.

Linn County Fair in Albany; (503) 928-0911.

Victorian Christmas with home tours, costumed shopkeepers and carriage rides in Albany; (503) 928-0911.

Transportation services

Salem Airport (588-6314) just east of town is served by **Horizon Air;** (800) 547-9308. The **Amtrak** station is downtown at 13th and Oak streets; (800) USA-RAIL or (503) 588-1551.

WHERE TO DINE

☺ Casa Juanita • ΔΔ $

In the Reed Opera House at Court and Liberty; (503) 364-9265. Mexican; full bar service. Monday-Saturday 11 to 9. MC/VISA, DISC. Appealing cafè with a surprisingly inexpensive menu; on a mezzanine with a view down to the Reed Opera House shops; Spanish courtyard entrance. *Polo picado* (chicken with bell pepper and onions), chimichangas and chili verde are menu specialties.

Cheema's Indian & Pakistani Cafè • Δ $$

Court and Liberty streets; (503) 371-4808. Mideastern; wine and beer. Lunch daily 11:30 to 2:30, dinner Tuesday-Sunday 5 to 9 MC/VISA. A simply-attired, inexpensive diner serving spicy fare such as *murgh do peyaja* (chicken sautèed in vinegar with spices), and fish or prawn curry. The seven-course buffet luncheon is a good buy.

Dairy Lunch • Δ $

347 Court St.; (503) 363-6433. American; no alcohol. Weekdays 7 a.m. to 2 p.m. No credit cards. Good cafè for a legendary lunch, featuring fresh cheeses, cottage cheese dishes and other dairy products, plus meatloaf sandwiches and chili. The Naugahyde and wood-paneled cafè dates back to 1929 and is now run by third generation of the founders.

La Casa Real • ΔΔ $$

698 SE 12th St.; (503) 588-0700. Mexican; full bar service. Daily 11 to 10:30; MC/VISA. Cheerfully decorated adobe-style cafè with *pinatas*, tropical birds and other Mexican predicables. A good array of Mexican menu specialties and lots of *hors d'oeuvres* at the lively bar. Convenient to Mission Mill Village and the capitol.

☺ Night Deposit Restaurant • ΔΔΔ $$

Commercial and Court streets; (503) 585-5588. American; full bar service. Lunch weekdays 11 to 2, dinner Monday-Thursday 5 to 10, Friday-Saturday 5 to 11 and Sunday 5 to 9. MC/VISA. Handsome high ceiling dining room with wood paneling and beveled glass; one of Salem's more attractive restaurants. Creative menu includes salmon teriyaki, raspberry pistachio chicken and a Cajun medley of fish, scallops and prawns.

Pilar's Restaurant & Pasta Factory • △△ $$ ∅
In the Reed Opera House at Court and Liberty; (503) 371-1812. Italian; full bar service. Monday-Thursday 11 to 8, Friday-Saturday 11 to 9, closed Sunday. MC/VISA, AMEX. Attractive place with several dining rooms; some smoke-free. Interesting green and white décor against exposed brick, with a display of old pasta machines—some still being used. Obviously, fresh pasta is a feature here, along with the usual items *Italiano.*

WHERE TO SLEEP

Best Western Pacific Highway Inn • ◠◠ $$$ ∅
4526 NE Portland Rd. (I-5 exit 258), Salem, OR 97305; (800) 528-1234 or (503) 390-3200. Couples $53 to $63, singles $49 to $54. Major credit cards. Well-appointed 52-room motel with TV movies, room phones, refrigerators available; pool, spa, continental breakfast, kids' play area.

City Center Motel • ◠◠ $$ ∅
510 SE Liberty St. (at Highway 22), Salem, OR 97301; (800) 289-0121 or (503) 364-0121. Couples $45 to $55, singles $38 to $45. Major credit cards. A 30-room motel with TV movies; continental breakfast, coin laundry; photocopy and FAX service available.

Execulodge • ◠◠◠ $$$ ∅
200 SE Commercial (downtown at Trade and Ferry), Salem, OR 97301; (800) 452-7879 or (503) 363-4123. Couples $60 to $70, singles $50 to $60, suites $70 to $135. Major credit cards. Attractive 114-unit inn with TV movies, room phones; pool, sauna and spa, free continental breakfast and limo service. **Stuart Anderson's Black Angus** serves from 11:30 to 10; American fare $7 to $19; full bar service.

Lamplighter Inn • ◠◠ $$ ∅
3195 Portland Rd. NE, Salem, OR 97303; (503) 585-2900. Couples $40 to $48, singles $28 to $35. Major credit cards. A 40-unit motel with TV movies, room phones and swimming pool; some rooms with refrigerators.

Quality Inn Motel • ◠◠◠ $$$ ∅
3301 NE Market St., Salem, OR 97301; (800) 248-6273 or (503) 370-7888. Couples $64 to $110, singles $59 to $100. Major credit cards. Attractive 156-room motel with TV movies, phones and indoor pool. **Steamers** restaurant serves from 6:30 a.m. to 2 and 5 to 10; dinners $6 to $15; full bar.

Shilo Inn • ◠◠◠ $$$$ ∅
3304 Market St. (I-5 exit 256), Salem, OR 97301; (800) 222-2244 or (503) 581-4001. Couples and singles $74 to $79, suites $79 to $89. Major credit cards. A new 89-unit mini-suite motel with TV movies, phones, free continental breakfast; indoor pool, spa, sauna, fitness room and laundry.

WHERE TO CAMP

Salem KOA • *3700 NE Hagers Grove Rd. (I-5 exit 253), Salem, OR 97301; (800) 826-9605 or (503) 581-6736. RV and tent sites $11 to $16. Reservations accepted; MC/VISA.* Large RV park with some shady sites. Showers, laundry, mini-mart, playground, game room.

Salem RV Park • *4490 NE Silverton Rd. (exit 256 east, then north on Lancaster to Silverton and right), Salem, OR 97301; (503) 364-5490. RV sites, full hookups $18. Reservations accepted; MC/VISA.* New park with pull-

Hikes into the Mount Jefferson Wilderness will reward travelers with close-up vistas of the majestic snow-patched peak. -- **Don W. Martin**

throughs, showers, laundry, rec room with kitchen, picnic-barbecue area, shuffleboard and horseshoe pits.

North Santiam recreation area

Like the other Willamette cities, Salem has its escape route to the Cascades. In this case, it's State Highway 22 along the North Santiam River. The usual green farmlands blend into the usual greener woods as you follow the North Santiam and Little North Fork Santiam rivers eastward.

Beyond the scruffy hamlet of **Gates,** you pass **Big Cliff Dam** with a small reservoir behind it. You then encounter the more substantial **Detroit Dam,** impounding a large recreational lake with swimming, boating and fishing lures. From a parking area, you can walk atop the dam for a dizzying look to the powerhouse, 436 feet below. A visitor center at mid-span provides a windowed view, potties and a brochure rack with information on Detroit Lake's recreational lures. You learn that you're standing on a concrete gravity dam (gravity, indeed) that holds back 3,500 acre feet of water in nine-mile-long Detroit Lake.

Detroit Lake State Park offers lakeside campsites with full hookups for $13, electrical for $12 and tent sites for $11. Most are shaded, with barbecue and picnic areas. The town of **Detroit,** handsome in a rustic sort of way, is just up the road, with a couple of small motels and restaurants. Should you want to linger, **Detroit Motel** offers spartan rooms for $28 and kitchenettes for $38; check in at Cook's Market or call (503) 854-3344.

The sawed-off butte you see to the north as you approach Detroit is aptly named **Table Rock.** To the southeast, you can catch occasional glimpses of snow-streaked **Mount Jefferson,** one of the Cascades' most dramatic volcanic steeples. Beyond Detroit, you can follow Highway 22 to trailheads that lead into the **Mount Jefferson Wilderness.** Before you do that, stop at the **Willamette National Forest Visitor Center,** on the left just before you reach the town. It's one of the forest service's better-equipped centers, open weekdays 7:45 to 4:30, plus weekends and holidays 7:45 to 11:45 and 12:30 to 4:30.

Ultimately, Route 22 will take you over **Santiam Pass,** into Bend and Chapter 8. Instead of doing that, we're going to suggest an interesting way to reach Portland. From downtown Detroit, turn left and follow a gently-curving paved forest service highway northeast through thick forest along the **Breitenbush River.**

After ten miles, turn right just beyond **Cleator Bend Campground** and follow a dirt road a mile and a half to **Breitenbush Hot Springs and Conference Center.** This place of internal peace and soothing mineral springs is tucked into a glen trimmed with rhododendrons and azaleas. It's one of those search-for-inner-self yin/yan hideaways where guests walk around in heavy-lidded contentment, smiling benignly. You almost expect someone to flash the peace sign. You can rent *very* rustic cabins for a day or week's worth of retreat and contemplation ($40 to $70), and attend spiritually uplifting lectures, seminars and such. Or you can pay a smaller fee and rent space in one of the mineral spring hot tubs. For lodging reservations, contact: Breitenbush Hot Springs, P.O. Box 578, Detroit, OR 976342; (503) 854-3314. The folks accept MC/VISA for lodgings.

☺ Now spiritually correct, you're ready to fully appreciate one of Oregon's hidden jewels—an exceptionally scenic route along this little traveled yet paved forestry road. It takes you through old growth spotted owl havens that somehow escaped the woodsman's ax. Eventually, you pick up the **Clackamas River** and descend through a steep-walled canyon. At some point, your unmarked road becomes State Route 224. The road and river are one as they twist through the narrow canyon, where campgrounds, picnic areas, trailheads and scenery abound. This area is a favored weekend haunt of the Portland crowd.

Reluctantly, you leave the river canyon and enter a foothill area of woods and farmlands. Still following the winding Clackamas, you encounter the town of **Estacada,** gateway to the area you just left. The **Chamber of Commerce,** P.O. Box 298, Estacada, OR 97023, (503) 630-3483, will send you lots of information about the river canyon and forested wilds above. The **Estacada Ranger District** office is here, too, at 61431 E. Highway 224; (503) 630-6861.

The highway, often canopied by trees, now slows with local traffic as it passes through a succession of small communities. And suddenly, there's a howling freeway ahead of you—Interstate 205. If you head north to I-84 and then go west, you'll be in downtown Portland before you can spell Breitenbush. It isn't too late to turn back...

SALEM TO PORTLAND HISTORIC ROUTE

The reason this book is called a discovery guide is because it offers you lots of options. The most direct route between two points is a straight line, also known as an interstate freeway. We prefer detours, and this one will take you into the historic heart of Oregon.

Head southeast from Salem on State Highway 22 for ten miles, then branch left onto Highway 214. It takes you through contoured farmlands

EUGENE TO PORTLAND
& NORTH SANTIAM
RECREATION AREA

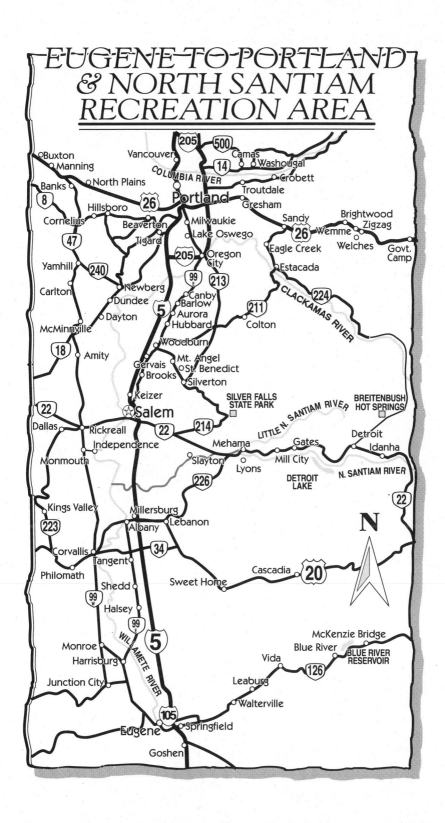

and past hundreds of acres of Christmas tree farms. Then you round a bend, climb a rise and suddenly you're in the forests of the largest and one of the most attractive of Oregon's 200 state parks.

☺ **Silver Falls State Park** • *20024 SE Silver Falls Highway, Sublimity, OR 97385; (503) 873-8681. Day use fee $2, tent sites $11; water and electric $12.* Other park facilities include picnic areas, miles of biking and hiking trails, a small swimming lake and a snack bar. From a high point in the park, a trail takes you past—and often behind—the ten waterfalls of serpentine **Silver Creek Canyon.** It's a great retreat on a hot day, particularly when you're standing in the mist behind one of these silvery cataracts. It's so lush, cool and humid here that you might imagine you're in a Hawaiian jungle. A long day's round trip hike will take you to all the falls and back. If there's a non-hiker in your crowd, you might convince them to drop you at the top and meet you at the bottom.

Continuing through the park, you emerge into more Christmas tree farms (mostly noble fir) and head toward **Silverton,** a tidy farm community of 5,700. The **Silverton Country Museum** occupies a 19th century home and an adjacent railroad station at 428 Water St.; (503) 873-4766. Its exhibits, busy but not too cluttered, are open Thursday and Sunday 1 to 4.

☺ **Mount Angel** is one of the Willamette Valley's most attractive small communities. Follow signs from Silverton to this picturesque hamlet of 2,950 presumably contented souls. With its shady streets and orderly homes behind carefully-tended gardens, it has a look of bucolic prosperity. Note the **Mount Angel Railroad Depot** with a ridiculously oversized clock tower. It now houses an antique shop. The old fashioned main street with brick and masonry stores is as prim and trim as the rest of the town.

Note the touches of Bavarian architecture, which offer a clue to the town's founding. It was established in 1880 by German immigrants. (Their descendants keep the old world spirit alive by staging Oregon's largest Oktoberfest in late September.) Swiss Benedictine monks followed on the heels of the German settlers in 1883 to build Mount Angel Abbey, which crowns a low hill nearby. To reach it, follow Church Street northeast through town. Note on your right the imposing, spired **St. Mary's Catholic Church,** dating from 1910. The turnoff to the abbey is a few blocks beyond.

☺ **Mount Angel Abbey** is indeed an angelic haven—a beige brick and tile roofed complex around immaculate lawns, sheltered by towering evergreens. The views are nice—across checkered farmlands to the snow-capped crowns of Mount Hood, Mount Adams and what's left of Mount St. Helens. Head for the far right corner of the compound to the **Retreat House and Gift Shop** and pick up a walking map. It will direct you to the chapel with its oak pews and high arched ceilings, and the Lobby Gallery and rare book room. The gallery, open daily 10:30 to 4:30, has changing art exhibits and the book room stores a priceless collection of illuminated manuscripts. One can arrange stays at the retreat house by contacting: Mt. Angel Abbey, St. Benedictine, OR 97373; (800) 365-5156 or (503) 845-3025.

From Mount Angel, follow Highway 214 north to **Woodburn,** where it merges with U.S. 99-E. Driving north toward Portland, you'll pass through **Hubbard,** a former Mennonite farm community and now just an ordinary town. Beyond, across the Pudding River, is **Aurora,** whose roots are still very much evident. In fact, the downtown area has been declared a national historic district. Aurora was established in 1855 by visionary William Keil as the first religious commune on the Pacific Coast. It was named for Keil's daughter who, appropriate to his thinking, was named for the new dawn.

"From each according to his ability, to each according to his need." Keil's communal colony prospered until his death in 1877. Aurora today, not much bigger than it was then, preserves its past in an interesting museum-village complex:

☺ **Old Aurora Colony Museum** • *Second and Liberty streets. Tuesday-Saturday 10:30 to 4:30, Sunday 1 to 4:30. Adults $2.50, students $1. (Admission includes tour.)* Knowledgeable and enthusiastic docents conduct visitors through the huge 1862 ox barn, an 1865 farmhouse with a feather tick bed and other simple furnishings, a communal shed (for washing, cooking and gossiping) and a rough-hewn squared log cabin. The barn, one of the original structures, first served as an animal shelter for the colony, then as a storage facility with apartments on the second floor.

Tours are animated and interesting. Your guide may play a few bars of *Amazing Grace* on an antique organ, then describe how the communal wives made applesauce, sauerkraut and sausages with their simple appliances. Tools for butter-making, spinning, cobbling and other frontier skills are demonstrated.

Just below the museum, you might pause at the **Pacific Hazelnut Factory** at Highway 99 E and Ottaway Avenue (south end of Aurora) for an introduction to Oregon's favorite nut. You can sample hazelnuts (filberts, if you prefer) and candies made from them. Watch them being processed and candied through viewing windows, then pick up a few to take home, along with other Oregon specialty foods. Hours are Tuesday-Friday 10 to 5 and Saturday 10 to 4; (503) 687-2755.

Continuing north from Aurora, you encounter the attractive farming community of **Canby,** called the "Garden spot of Clackamas County." At the first signal, turn left onto Elm Street, then right onto Third Avenue and follow it past downtown to the **Canby Depot Museum,** housed in an old railway station at the Clackamas County Fairgrounds. It's open Tuesday-Sunday 1 to 4; (503) 266-9421. Among its typical pioneering memorabilia are nicely done models of an old steam tractor and thresher. If you'd like to cross one of only three remaining cable ferries on the Willamette River, reverse your route on Third Street, then go right onto Holly Street and follow signs. The tiny **Canby Ferry** crosses the Willamette just above its junction with the Mollalla. On the other side, the road leads to Wilsonville and West Linn. However, do a U-turn, come back to Canby and continue north on 99-E to one of the places where Oregon began.

Oregon City

Population: 14,700   **Elevation: 55 feet**

In an ironic twist of history, a Canadian-born British subject was responsible for establishing the first incorporated U.S. city west of the Mississippi. Dr. John McLoughlin, chief factor for the Hudson's Bay Company based in Fort Vancouver (now in Washington state), sent a party south to build three cabins near Willamette River Falls in 1829. Native Americans, not caring much for this intrusion, burned them. In 1832, he ordered construction of a sawmill and flour mill, powered by water from the falls. Protected by armed settlers, they survived to form the nucleus of the future town.

McLoughlin remained in Fort Vancouver, and he encouraged Oregon

Trail pioneers to move southward, figuring the area below the Columbia would become U.S. territory when the border issue was settled. (Vancouver was considered the trail's end since most pioneers completed the trek by rafting their wagons down river from The Dalles.) In 1841, McLoughlin laid out the town of Oregon City. Two years later a group of American settlers meeting in nearby Champoeg (pronounced Sham-pooey) set up a provisional government, with McLoughlin's new town as its headquarters. It was given a charter of incorporation in 1844 and became the official territorial capital in 1849.

Meanwhile, the overland Barlow Road was blazed from The Dalles, and Oregon City became the terminus of the Oregon Trail. "Here at Abernethy Green in the fall of 1845, members of the Barlow-Palmer-Rector wagon train entered Oregon City as best they could," reads a marker at Highway 99-E and Abernethy Street.

Oregon City today has preserved much of its history, with some of the finest 19th century buildings in the state. The town's focal point is Willamette Falls, a horseshoe-shaped mini-Niagara that dumps over a basaltic cliff in the middle of the river. You'll note when you pause at the falls viewpoint on 99-E that most of the water is now diverted into paper mills crowded around the cataract. Only during spring runoff do the falls fall.

Oregon City is a split-level community, with most of its homes perched on 80-foot bluffs above the river; its narrow business district is crowded at the base. The **Oregon City Municipal Elevator,** rather loosely described as "America's only vertical street," connects the two levels. The current version was built in 1954 and is electrically powered. The 1913 original was water-powered—the only one of its kind in America.

A good starting point for your Oregon City exploration is the outstanding **Clackamas County History Museum,** on the bluff just above the falls viewpoint, at 99-E and Tumwater Drive. If you enjoy walking, you can park here, hike up to a promenade at bluff's edge and follow it northward to the town's sundry historical sites, including the **McLoughlin house.** Maps available at the museum will help guide your way. Later, you can ride the elevator downtown and stroll along Main Street. Although the area is quite tidy, many of the old brick and masonry buildings are empty. You can poke into an antique shop or two. Make it a point to see the elaborate 1936 brick **Clackamas County Courthouse** at Eighth and Main streets. You can catch a **street fair and market** downtown on summer Saturdays.

The **Tri-City Chamber of Commerce** is on the north edge of town at Washington and Abernethy, across from the Oregon Trail marker. Hours are Monday-Friday 9 to noon and one to 5, and Saturday 10 to 2; (503) 656-1619. It's several blocks up from the museum, so you might want to retrieve your car. Here, you can pick up additional walking and driving tour maps.

THE ATTRACTIONS

☺ **Clackamas County History Museum** ● *211 Tumwater Dr.; (503) 655-5574. Monday-Friday 10 to 5, weekends and holidays 1 to 5. Adults $3, seniors $2, kids 6 to 12, $1 and family groups $7.50 (includes admission to Stevens-Crawford House).* This brand-new cast concrete and wood facility, with picture windows overlooking river and falls, is one of the state's best small museums. Nicely done exhibits follow a logical course from Native Americans to fur traders to pioneers and merchants. Particularly impressive is a full-sized immigrant wagon loaded for the trail. America's first long-distance electrical transmission began at the falls below, and a fine exhibit discusses this. It's intriguing to read the graphics and then look through a picture window, down to the source.

Oregon Trail Visitor Center ● *Fifth and Washington streets; (503) 657-9336. Tuesday-Sunday 10 to 4. Adults $2, seniors $1.50, kids $1.* Plans are afoot to build an Oregon Trail National Historic Park at the end of the trail marker opposite the Tri-City Chamber of Commerce. In the meantime, this small but well-done museum in the town's senior center serves the purpose. A full-sized wagon, a wheel barrel full of buffalo chips, sunbonnets, rubbings from trail-side graves and costumed mannequins help tell the story of this hazardous crossing.

☺ **McLoughlin House National Historic Site** ● *713 Center St.; (503) 656-5146. Tuesday-Saturday 10 to 4 and Sunday 1 to 4; closed Monday and all of January. Adults $3, seniors $2.50 and students $1.* When Dr. McLoughlin was forced out of the Hudson's Bay Company in 1845 for being too pro-American, he retired to Oregon City and built this white clapboard home. Entry is by guided tour, which begins at the adjacent 1850 Dr. Forbes Barclay House. You'll see much of the McLoughlins' original furniture and a monumental four-poster bed that once belonged to the Meriwether Lewis family of Lewis and Clark fame. Furnishings range from elegant pieces that came around the Horn to simpler stuff crafted locally.

Stevens-Crawford House ● *Sixth and Washington streets; (503) 655-2866. Tuesday-Saturday 10 to 4 and Sunday 1 to 4. Adults $3, seniors $2, kids 6 to 12, $1.50 and family groups $7.50 (includes admission to the Clackamas County History Museum).* This three-story 1907 clapboard home was owned by the original family until 1968, so many furnishings are intact. The interior is a mix of furnished rooms and historic museum, with displays ranging from Indian baskets to souvenir plates to children's toys.

Heading north toward Portland on 99-E, you'll see an old roadhouse on your left with several wood carvings out front. It's worth a stop for its rustic interior and ample entrées:

Pearson's Tavern ● ∆∆ **$**
20890 S. Highway 99-E, Canby; (503) 622-8862. Mexican-American; full bar service. Sunday-Thursday 11 to 9, Friday-Saturday 11 to 10, closed Monday. MC/VISA. This woodsy knotty pine roadhouse, dating back to 1934, serves whopping chimichangas and other ample Mexican dinners, plus American steaks and hamburgers. Note the large wood carvings outside, worth a stop even if you aren't hungry. It's on the east side of 99-E, about midway between Canby and Oregon City.

EUGENE TO PORTLAND VIA 99-W

Before the advent of Interstate 5, we natives used Highway 99 to get from south to north. Above Eugene, it split into 99-East and 99-West. Today, most of 99-E has disappeared under I-5 asphalt. We've take you over some of the sections that haven't, through Albany, Aurora and Oregon City. Much of old 99-W survives. This 140-mile stretch, from Junction City above Eugene to Tigard just below Portland, passes through a string of friendly farm communities on the western flank of the Willamette Valley. You might enjoy it as an alternative to swift I-5, or you can return this way just variety.

We aren't suggesting that it's a major tourist route. Mostly what you see are ordinary towns populated by ordinary folks like us. However, the rolling farmlands, orchards and vineyards are attractive, often backdropped by wooded foothills of the Coast Range. You'll find most of Oregon's winery tasting rooms within a short drive of 99-W, plus a few community museums, and recreation areas along the small rivers that feed into the Willamette.

The best area guide is the **99W Scenic Route** brochure, available at visitor centers in Eugene and Portland and at towns along the way. From chambers of commerce in **Corvallis** (334-8118), **Monmouth** (838-4268), **Dallas** (623-2564), **McMinnville** (472-6196) and **Newberg** (538-2014), you can get more detailed material on the area.

You won't be impressed by the first leg north from Eugene, which passes through a sprawl of light industry and commerce, with an aggravating number of stoplights to impede your progress. At **Junction City,** named for the separation of the routes, 99-W splits to the left and the Eugene megasprawl yields finally to attractive farm country.

A few miles north is **Corvallis,** home to Oregon State University. With students comprising nearly a third of its 43,000 population, it is the penultimate American college town. It's handsome to a fault with wide, tree-sheltered streets, red brick and gleaming white masonry buildings downtown and a general look of scholastic contentment. It was in fact Bernard Malamud's model town for his novel, *A New Life.*

Take a pause to view the **OSU campus,** which we feel is as attractive as Eugene's University of Oregon. To reach it, follow Jefferson Way or Madison Avenue west from downtown. The route takes you through neighborhoods of elegantly landscaped old homes. Jefferson leads into the campus and you can pick up a map at a kiosk at a large parking area, or from the adjacent administrative center. The campus is closed to traffic, making it all the more pleasant to stroll its pathways between old brick, over billiard green lawns roofed by century-old trees. The adjacent university commercial area, with its predictable coffee houses, bookstores and small cafès, is northwest on Monroe Avenue, beyond 14th Street.

As you return downtown and resume your northward trek, note the white masonry **Benton County Courthouse** with its distinctive three-tiered clock tower. Cradled between Fourth, Fifth and Monroe streets, it's the tallest object in this primly neat low-rise downtown area.

Beyond Corvallis, 99-W is mostly two-lane, often slowed by local traffic. Settle back and enjoy the panoramic passage of fields, orchards and timbered foothills. The towns thin out considerably in rural Polk County; you'll pass through only two of note: **Monmouth** and **Rickreall**. In Monmouth, you might take a side trip to **Western Oregon State College** to explore an interesting specialty archive:

☺ **Paul Jensen Arctic Museum** ● *On campus at 590 W. Church Street; (503) 838-8468. Tuesday-Saturday 10 to 4; free.* A mixed-media display presents the sights and sounds of a typical day in the great northland in this well done theme museum. Exhibits include an extensive collection of Eskimo art and Arctic artifacts gathered by Jensen and other Arctic explorers.

Yamhill County calls itself the heart of Oregon's wine country, and that may be a fair claim. Sixteen wineries have tasting rooms open to the public and most are within a short drive of 99-W. The climate here, often compared with that of France's Burgundy, is ideal for such classic wine varieties as Pinot Noir, Chardonnay and White Riesling.

The knolls around **Dundee** indeed suggest those of Burgundy. Although most of Oregon's vineyards are rather scattered, hundreds of acres are concentrated near this small town, dancing over the hills like green hooked rugs. A turn westward onto SW Ninth Street (Worden Hill Road) takes you into this scenic vineland and to **Knudsen Erath,** one of the state's largest wineries; the tasting room is open daily. If it's noonish, buy a bottle and have a picnic on the patio, or at the nearby Crabtree Park, which has barbecue facilities. Two other wineries, **Elk Cove** and **Argyle,** have tasting rooms in Dundee, alongside 99-W. At wineries and tasting rooms, you can pick up a free copy of "Discover Oregon Wineries" or local wine guides.

Yamhill County also has several bed & breakfast inns and some appealing country restaurants to complement its wine industry. For lists of these, plus a directory of the county's wineries, contact: Greater McMinnville Chamber of Commerce, McMinnville, OR 97128; (503) 472-6196 or Yamhill County Wineries Assn., P.O. Box 871, McMinnville, OR 97128; (503) 434-5814. In **Newberg,** pick up State Highway 219 and follow signs southeast to a spot along the Willamette River with deep Oregon roots:

☺ **Champoeg State Park** ● *Champoeg Road (Highway 219); (503) 678-1251. Visitor center open weekdays 8 to 4 and weekends 9:30 to 5:30.* It was at Champoeg on the banks of the Willamette River that a group of American settlers and French-Canadian trappers voted in 1843 to start a provisional government. This set the stage for the establishment of the Oregon Territory. The barn-style visitor center has excellent graphics and displays heralding this event and tracing the state's development. Several historic buildings, some moved from other sites, stand nearby. The **Campground** has tent and RV sites with water and electric hookups and showers, from $12; no reservations. Other park facilities include picnic areas, river access for boating and fishing, hiking and biking trails.

From Champoeg, you can continue east to I-5 for a quick run to Portland or return to 99-W to complete this route. The highway is four-lane above Newberg but it doesn't exactly brim with visitor attractions, and you'll hit a lot of local traffic and stoplights.

Historic Oregon events

The *Champoeg!* history pageant is held during July in the park's outdoor amphitheater. For information, contact: Champoeg Tickets, Mid-Valley Arts Council, 265 NE Court St., Salem, OR 97301; (503) 245-3922.

The annual *Oregon Trail Pageant* is held during the last three weeks of July at the Clackamas Community College amphitheater south of Oregon City. For ticket information, contact: Oregon Trail Pageant, P.O. Box 68, Oregon City, OR 97045; (503) 657-0988.

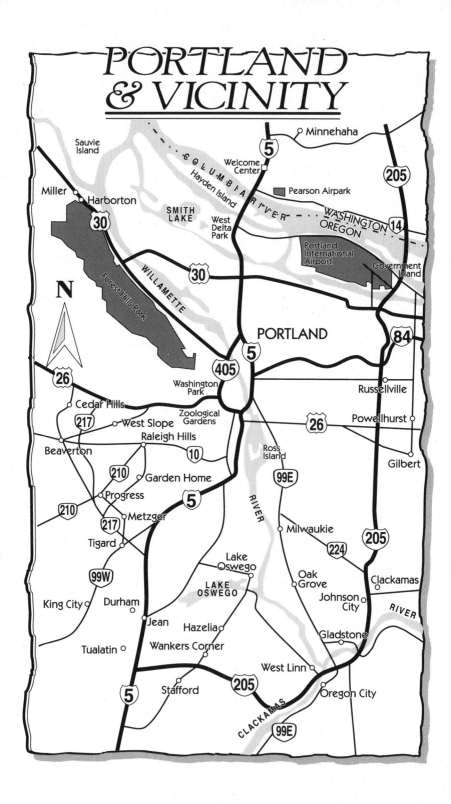

PORTLAND & VICINITY

N

Minnehaha

Sauvie Island

COLUMBIA RIVER

Welcome Center

Hayden Island

Pearson Airpark

Miller
Harborton

SMITH LAKE

West Delta Park

WASHINGTON
OREGON

205

14

30

Portland International Airport

Government Island

WILLAMETTE

Forest Hills Park

30

PORTLAND

84

405

5

Russellville

Washington Park

26

Powellhurst

Cedar Hills

Zoological Gardens

217

West Slope

Raleigh Hills

26

Beaverton

10

Ross Island

Gilbert

210

Garden Home

Progress

99E

210

Metzger

217

Milwaukie

Tigard

224

205

Lake Oswego

99W

LAKE OSWEGO

Oak Grove

Clackamas

King City

Durham

Johnson City

RIVER

Jean

Hazelia

Gladstone

Tualatin

Wankers Corner

West Linn

205

Stafford

Oregon City

5

CLACKAMAS

99E

Chapter Four

PORTLAND

Roses, rain and renewal in Rip City

IF THERE'S A CLOUD hanging over Portland—and there often is—it has a silver lining and it's probably wearing a grin. Because it's looking down on one of the cleanest, safest and most appealing metropolitan centers in America.

Portland is what a city should be—vibrant, attractive, culturally alive and ethnically diverse. It's beautifully maintained, from its kelly green parklands to its revitalized waterfront to its clean-swept streets. Graffiti, that progenitor to urban decay, is rare here. On the other hand, public art is abundant. Local codes require that a percentage of all new construction funds go to art works and landscaping.

Simply put, Portland is a city that has its act together.

For the visitor, we rate it second only to San Francisco as the best urban destination west of the Rockies. With 37,000 acres of parks, 50 galleries and museums, 23 theater companies, an historic old town, a lively street market and a grand new waterfront park, it could keep you busy for weeks.

And don't forget them Blazers. It's difficult to get a ticket when the hot NBA basketball team is in town, but televised games turn every pub into an instant sports bar. The Trailblazers are responsible—courtesy of local sports writers—for Portland's "Rip City" nickname.

City-watchers confirm Portland's appeal. It has been rated as America's most livable city by the U.S. Conference of Mayors, one of America's ten hottest cities by *Newsweek* and number three in Quality of Life by the 1990 Cushman and Wakefield study. Rand McNally's best cities index always has it near the top and the American Public Transit Association gave its "Amer-

TRIP PLANNER

WHEN TO GO ● If you're planning a fall-through-spring Oregon vacation, this is the place! Most of Portland's tourist lures remain open during the off-season. May through mid-June is the prettiest time of the year, when roses, rhododendrons and azaleas are blooming in this city of flowers. You'll catch the Portland Rose Festival then, so make early reservations. Fall offers the best weather; you'll get stellar views of that grand Portland guardian, Mount Hood, and other Cascade peaks. Winter is the peak of the cultural season, and the city dresses beautifully for Christmas.

WEATHER OR NOT ● Call (503) 275-9292 for a seven-day weather forecast, updated daily.

TRANSIT INFORMATION ● Call Tri- Met at (503) 233-3511, or stop in at the office on Pioneer Courthouse Square, 701 SW Sixth Ave., open weekdays 9 to 5.

WHAT TO SEE ● The brand-new Oregon Museum of Science and Industry; the lures of Washington Park—Japanese Garden, International Rose Test Gardens, Hoyt Arboretum, World Forestry Center and Metro Washington Park Zoo; Tom McCall Riverfront Park; Portland Art Museum and Oregon Historical Center; the Grotto off Sandy Boulevard and the Carousel Museum near the convention center.

WHAT TO DO ● Ride MAX to the end of the line and back for a quickie Portland tour; explore the downtown buildings, parks and fountains from Pioneer Courthouse Square; attend an Oregon Shakespeare production or other play or concert at the Portland Center for the Performing Arts; hit the Saturday Market in Old Town; catch a Trailblazers game at the Coliseum or on TV in a lively bar; stroll the waterfront along Riverfront Park and maybe walk onto one of the bridges for a view of busy river traffic; take the sternwheeler *Columbia Gorge* up the Willamette River; prowl the farm roads and hiking trails of Sauvie Island.

Useful contacts

Portland/Oregon Visitors Association, 26 SW Salmon St., Portland, OR 97204; 222-2223. Visitor center is at the foot of Salmon at the riverfront, open weekdays 8:30 to 5 and weekends 9 to 3.

Portland South Visitor Information Center, 9400 Sunnyside Rd., Clackamas, OR 97015; (800) 432-1205 or (503) 659-5540.

Washington County Visitors Association, 10172 SW Washington Square Rd., Portland, OR 97223; (800) 537-3149 or (503) 684-5555. Weekdays 9 to 5.

Portland area radio stations

KOPB-FM, 91.5—National Public Radio
KUFO-FM, 101—rock
KISN-FM, 91.7—rock
KWJJ-FM, 99.5—country
KXL-FM, 95.5 —light hits, oldies.
KINK-FM, 102—new wave & light rock
KXL-AM, 750—news, sports & talk.
KWJJ-AM, 1080—country.
KOPB-AM, 550—National Public Radio
KXL-AM, 750—talk radio
KISN-AM, 910—rock
KKEY-AM, 1150—talk radio
KEX-AM, 1190—top 40, news & sports
KBBT-AM, 970—rock

ica's best transit system" award in 1990. The core of this system—take notice, you cities of rising fares and subway dungeons—is a 300-square-block free ride zone downtown.

A flipoff

Had a coin landed the other way in 1845, we'd be talking about Boston, Oregon.

As pioneers straggled into the Oregon Country, it was inevitable that a town would be established here. Although it's 110 miles from the Ocean, the deep water Columbia and Willamette Rivers provide easy access, and protection from ocean storms. Chinook Indians appreciated this spot, using it as a trading camp that became known as "The Clearing." Settlers Amos Lovejoy and Francis Pettygrove saw its potential in 1844 and filed a 640-acre claim under the Organic Act. As trees were cut to erect cabins, it earned the inglorious name of Stumptown.

Needing something classier than that, they flipped a penny to see who got to name it for his hometown. Maine's Lovejoy won the toss over Pettygrove of Massachusetts.

The town was incorporated in 1851, although it initially was overshadowed by bustling Oregon City to the south. After all, it had Willamette River Falls to power its mills and fuel its economy. However, as the region prospered, Portland's potential as a deep water port was realized. Unlike boom towns of San Francisco and Seattle, it took shape slowly, crafted of sturdy brick and masonry, with cast-iron façades. The New England influence of Lovejoy and Pettygrove is still evident in its Gothic architecture and many Cape Cod style homes.

Except for its deep water advantage, Portland is oddly located for Oregon's metropolitan center, tucked into the northwest edge of this large state. It's as if someone tilted a pool table and rolled everything into a corner pocket. Indeed, more than half of Oregon's 2,800,000 residents live in the greater Portland area. The population of the city proper is around half a million. Water remains the key to its success. This is the West Coast's third busiest port and home to hundreds of smokeless industries that rely on cheap hydroelectric power. Included among them are some household brand names—Nike shoes, Jantzen swimwear and Pendleton woolens.

Getting there

A dozen airlines serve PDX, **Portland International Airport**, about 20 minutes northeast of downtown. It's one of the West's most attractive air terminals, with a new Northwest-style terminal and a shopping mall featuring Oregon specialty items. Dozens of hotels offer airport shuttle service, in addition to the usual fleet of taxis and limos. The RAZ Downtowner runs between the airport and Greyhound terminal with hotel stops, for $5. Cab fare downtown is about $20. For budget travelers, Tri-Met bus #12 stops just outside the baggage claim, leaving for downtown every 15 minutes. Half a dozen rental car agencies maintain booths at the airport. Call (503) 231-5000, extension 411 for airport information.

Amtrak's Coast Starline runs north to Seattle and south to San Francisco once a day. The Pioneer and Empire Builder trundle through Columbia River gorge, headed for Salt Lake City and other points east. The reservation number is (800) USA-RAIL. The handsome old fashioned **Union Station** is at the northern end of Sixth avenue, near the river.

The **Greyhound** terminal is at 550 NW Sixth Avenue at Glisan Street; (503) 243-2313. The **Green Tortoise,** a semi-funky and reasonably reliable "alternative" bus service, operates from the University Deli at Sixth and College. It runs to Seattle and San Francisco via I-5; phone (503) 225-0310.

Interstate 5 is the main highway corridor. I-405 splits off at Marquam Bridge to pass through the edge of downtown. Highway 5 also is the direct route from Washington and British Columbia. Interstate 84 arrives from the east, following old Highway 30's Columbia River Gorge route. Freeway 26 from the coast skirts the western edge of Washington Park's and links with 405 near downtown. Interstate 205 splits from I-5 several miles south at Tualatin, offering a bypass of the heart of Portland. But why would anyone want to do that?

Visitor Services

The Portland/Oregon Visitors Association operates a **Visitors Information Center** at the foot of Salmon Street, just up from the riverfront; phone (503) 222-2223. It's open weekdays 8:30 to 5 and weekends 9 to 3. Although it's is easy to find once you get there, you might want to request maps and stuff in advance by writing: Portland/Oregon Visitors Assn., 26 SW Salmon St., Portland, OR 97204.

If you're bringing I-5 from the north, pause at the **Jantzen Beach/Oregon Welcome Center** at 12345 N. Union; (285-1631); take the Hayden Island exit and keep curling around to the right. May through October hours are Monday-Saturday 8 to 6 and Sunday 9 to 5. The rest of the year, it's open weekdays 9 to 5, Saturday 9 to 4 Saturday and Sunday 10 to 3.

Visitor information also hits the streets. **Portland Guides** walk about the downtown area, willing and ready to answer tourists' questions. Look for them in their kelly green jackets with yellow and red "Portland Progress" patches on their sleeves or caps. When it's rainy, they don bright yellow capes. They can direct you to Nike Town, Chinatown, or tell you the best street to take to get anywhere in town. To find out what's happening where, call the **events hotline** at (503) 233-4444. The *Oregonian,* Portland's only surviving daily, prints a hefty "Arts and Entertainment" section on Fridays, thoroughly covering the night life and cultural scenes.

Finding your way

The city's suburban sprawl along both sides of the Willamette River may look intimidating to a map-clutching visitor. However, many of its attractions are focused in the downtown section. They can be reached easily and cheaply by foot, bus or the MAX light rail system, since this is the Fareless Square area. A freeway system that rarely suffers Los Angeles-style congestion will get you to out-of-town attractions in a hurry. A lacework of 11 bridges hops across the river.

Portland divides itself into five neighborhoods, and streets are labeled by points of the compass. Thus, any address will give you a quick clue to its location. The river separates east from west and Burnside Street—running through the north side of downtown—divides north from south. The sections and their reasons for visiting are:

Northwest: The **Skidmore Old Town District** along the waterfront is in this section, along with **Chinatown,** and the **Greyhound** and **Amtrak** terminals.

Southwest: This quadrant includes the heart of downtown, with most of the city's urban museums, shops and restaurants. **Tom McCall Waterfront Park** is a wonderful greenbelt and shopping area along the river. Burnside Street, the upper border of Portland SW, takes you west to **Washington Park,** that lush forest within a city. It contains **Metro Washington Park Zoo, Hoyt Arboretum,** the **Japanese Garden** and the noted **International Rose Test Garden.**

Southeast: Across the river, this is mostly residential area with little to offer visitors. However, the new **Oregon Museum of Science and Industry** is located here, on the riverfront just across from downtown. The region also contains **Mount Tabor Park** with an extinct volcano (the only one within an American city); it offers nice views of the countryside.

Northeast: The **Portland Convention Center, Memorial Coliseum, Carousel Courtyard** and **Lloyd Center** shopping mall are clustered close together in this area. They're served by MAX light rail from downtown. **Portland International Airport** also is in this quadrant, several miles northeast alongside the Columbia River.

North: This is Portland's upper wedge, an industrial and residential area. You'd go in this direction to get to **Jantzen Beach Mall, Sauvie Island Wildlife Refuge** and Washington state.

The right approach

If you're approaching Portland from the south on I-5, follow City Center signs to the left, which direct you onto Front Avenue, leading to the waterfront area and the core of downtown. This avoids the Marquam Bridge, which carries I-5 across the river and often is congested. (Marquam is the second bridge you'll see, after the Ross Island Bridge.)

Coming from the north, switch from I-5 onto I-405 at exit 302-B, cross the Willamette River on Fremont Bridge and go south to Burnside. This puts you in the old town area, just above downtown.

RV folks can find two places to stay north of town, **Portland Meadows** and **Jantzen Beach** RV parks. Others are to the east in Troutdale and Gresham; see "Where to camp" toward the end of this chapter.

Once you've abandoned your vehicle, find your way to **Pioneer Courthouse Square,** bounded by Broadway, Sixth, Morrison and Yamhill. This is a good area to begin an exploration of downtown Portland. MAX, or Metropolitan Area Express, loops around the square, while nearby Sixth and Seventh avenues are transit malls, where the greater Portland bus system spins off into its neighborhoods.

MAX is a swift light rail system that travels east from downtown through Old Town, across Steel Bridge, past the Portland Convention Center and Lloyd Center shopping complex. It continues on to Gresham, 15 miles from downtown, and plans are afoot to expand it. MAX is part of Tri-Met, the 770-mile bus system that serves the three counties of greater Portland. Basic fares are 90 cents outside the free zone and maximum rates are $1.20 both for Max and Met; seniors ride for 40 cents. Tickets are available at handy vending machines. For information, call (503) 233-3511 or stop in at the Tri-Met office on Pioneer Courthouse Square, 701 SW Sixth Ave., open weekdays 9 to 5.

Downtown Portland is a very walkable city and **Powell's Bookstore** offers a free map that will guide your feet to and through most of its highlights. One of the outlets, Powell's Travel Store, is at Sixth and Yamhill, bordering Pioneer Courthouse Square. Copies also are available at the **Portland/Oregon Visitors Association** at the foot of Salmon Street.

Portland walk-about

The walking route is a bit complicated and it covers about six miles. However, it's easy to follow with map in hand. We'll touch on some of the highlights, but don't try this without the map.

Pioneer Courthouse Square is a handsome sunken brick plaza with landscaping, floral displays and benches for lounging—a focal point of downtown. Before you depart, note the whimsical bronze of a businessman with an umbrella, trying to hail a cab (a common sight in Portland).

From the square, the walking map takes you south along the Sixth Avenue transit mall, and then drops down to Fifth and Main for a look at the **Portland Building,** designed by Michael Graves and built in 1982 as America's first post-modern highrise. Note the monumental bronze of **Portlandia,** clutching a trident and kneeling above the front entrance. She's the second largest hammered copper statue in the world, outweighed only by the Statue of Liberty.

You next walk through the ornate cut stone **Portland City Hall** at Fifth and Madison Street. It squats like a hunched little old man amidst the city's highrises. Crossing **Chapman Square,** you're directed through the modern **Justice Center** at Madison and Third Avenue with its striking galleria-style entrance. Pass through the building to the police department on the lower level facing Second Avenue and take an elevator to the 16th floor **Police Historical Museum.**

Portland's various urban renewal projects, started in the 1970s, have gained international attention for creating attractive public spaces. A good example of this is **Portland Center,** several city blocks of fountains, parks, plazas and businesses cradled by Second and Third avenues and Columbia and Hall streets. A focal point is **Ira Keller Fountain** at Third and Clay, a full city block of terraced, cascading fountains, patios and lawns. It's a favorite retreat of downtowners.

☺ Next, head for the river to our favorite downtown haven, **Tom McCall Waterfront Park.** Forward- thinking planners ordered the demolition of a four-lane expressway to create this mile-long strip of lawns, marinas and river walks. Its focal point is **RiverPlace** on the south end, with a marina, boutiques and outdoor cafès with river views. Pause for a glass of wine or lunch on the floating dock of **Newport Bay** restaurant and watch the busy river parade of cargo liners, tug- pushed barges, pleasure boats and water skiers.

If it's a hot day and you want to feel like a kid again, join the fun at **Salmon Street Springs** on the waterfront at the foot of Salmon Street. Built flush to the sidewalk, it's an inviting walk-in fountain with dozens of jets that create a dancing waters effect. They douse those bold enough to skip through them. For a stunning sunset view, stand just up Salmon Street from the fountain and watch the snowcap of **Mount Hood**—framed directly behind it—fade to pink as it catches the last rays of the day.

The **World Trade Center,** across Front Avenue from the fountain, is an ultra-modern greenhouse tied together by glass catwalks. Next door at Second Avenue and Taylor is **Yamhill Marketplace** on the edge of the **Yamhill Historic District.** Within this old masonry building, you'll find a

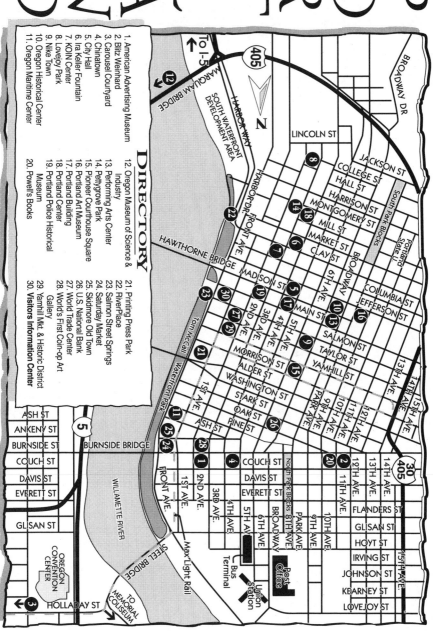

farmers' market abrim with fresh produce, fruits and meats. Its atrium interior also houses a collection of boutiques and a score of ethnic cafès and food booths.

This completes your transition from today to yesterday. The Yamhill Historic District blends into **Skidmore Old Town** in the heart of the original city. It was here that Stumptown became Portland at the flip of a coin. The first log and whipsaw board homes and businesses were replaced by sturdier structures as the new city prospered. Then a few decades ago as growth shifted southward, this became Portland's skid road. Today, its venerable brick, masonry and iron-front buildings shelter boutiques, antique stores and art galleries. Oldstyle lamp posts are hung with flower baskets, adding splashes of color.

Focal point is **Skidmore Fountain** plaza, festooned with bronze plaques that talk about the old days. The adjacent **Skidmore Fountain Building** is an impressive space, with boutiques and cafès tucked about its hanging staircases and bold brick-arch walls.

☺ Oregon's largest public market happens in the Skidmore district every weekend from March through December. Never mind that it's called the **Saturday Market.** This happy melee of artisans, musicians and food booths happens on Saturday *and* Sunday. It's conducted in and around Skidmore Fountain and spilling under the anchorage of the Burnside Bridge. Browse among more than 250 booths and maybe pick up a macrame pot hanger, a tie-dyed T-shirt or hand-made baubles, bangles and beads. Fill your tummy with a pita sandwich, skewered *yakitori* or barbecued chicken, perhaps with an elephant ear for dessert. (It looks like a giant sugar-dusted fritter that was run over by a truck.)

A couple of blocks up from the waterfront, stop in at the **American Advertising Museum** at Second Avenue and Burnside, then walk two blocks up Burnside to the **Chinatown Gate** at Fourth Avenue. (Actually, the walking map has you coming in Chinatown's side door.) This isn't as elaborate or colorful as San Francisco's Chinatown, but it has a good array of restaurants and the requisite dragon-entwined lampposts. From Chinatown, the walking map weaves you into downtown, through the shadow of some of Portland's tallest structures.

☺ Be sure to walk through the neo-classical **U.S. National Bank** building at Sixth Avenue and Stark, with its squared marble columns and high, floral coffered ceilings. Follow Stark west to Tenth Avenue, then turn right to an amazing retreat for bibliophiles.

☺ **Powell's City of Books** is the world's largest bookstore, with more than *one million* titles. Should you grow weary of browsing through this warehouse of new and used volumes, you can select a title and retire to the adjacent coffee shop.

You next hike south along Tenth Street to the **Portland Art Museum** at Madison, then drop down to Ninth and the **South Park Blocks.** This is another area that makes the city so livable—a twelve-block park strip of lawns, benches and sheltering trees. Although this suggests the work of urban renewalists, the Park Blocks date from 1852. Clustered at the north end of the blocks are the **Oregon Historical Center, Schnitzer Concert Hall** and **Performing Arts Center.**

One might also call these the "Church Blocks," since several of the city's more imposing preaching parlors are in this area. Note the ornate Gothic

First Congregational Church shaded by giant elms at Park Avenue and Madison, the fortress-like **Christian Science Church** and yellow brick **First Christian Church,** on Park between Columbia and Jefferson. Walk from the Park Blocks up Clay Street to the ornate 1879 steepled edifice at Clay and Tenth (this isn't on your map). This former Protestant sanctuary is now home to the **Korean Church.** A block beyond at Eleventh and Clay is the 1882 former **Cavalry Presbyterian Church,** now a non-profit community center known simply as the "Old Church." Step inside to admire its semi-circular sanctuary with curved wooden pews and vaulted arch ceilings beneath a witch's hat spire.

If you hike uphill through the Park Blocks, you'll enter the attractively landscaped campus of **Portland State University,** a noble collection of interconnected brick buildings. From this neighborhood, you can retreat to Yamhill Street and follow it downhill to Pioneer Courthouse Square, where all this began.

ATTRACTIONS DOWNTOWN & NEARBY

☺ **Oregon Museum of Science and Industry** • *1945 SE Water Ave.; (503) 797-4000. Saturday-Thursday 9 to 7, Friday 9 to 9. Adults $5.25, seniors $4.25, kids 3-17, $3.50, planetarium shows $1.50; MC/VISA.* One of America's best science museums got even better in the fall of 1992. That's when it moved from Washington Park to a 210,000 square foot glass and brick pyramidal atrium on the east bank of the Willamette, across from downtown. It can be reached via I-5 across the Marquam Bridge. The beautiful new $40 million 18-acre site houses a state of the art science center, the Northwest's only Omnimax theater with a giant screen four stories high, the Sky Theater laser-art planetarium, labs and a restaurant with a riverside patio. One large wing of the science center is reserved for traveling exhibits, which are always exceptional. The new OMSI is rated among the top ten science museums in the country.

☺ **Oregon Historical Center** • *1230 SW Park Ave.; (503) 222-1741. Monday-Saturday 10 to 4:45, Sunday noon to 4:45; free.* This large museum with skillfully done, uncluttered exhibits covers three floors. A time-line called "Land of Promise, Land of Plenty" discusses the seafarers, the Native Americans who met their boats, the immigrants, the lumbermen, the fishermen and the industrialists. Artifacts range from old navigational instruments to a cut-away Nike (the shoe, not the rocket). Among other exhibits are models of ships significant to Oregon's history, a nice collection of children's antique toys and a cut-away immigrant prairie schooner. It has an excellent museum gift shop with an extensive collection of books.

☺ **Portland Art Museum** • *1219 SW Park Ave.; (503) 226-2811. Tuesday-Saturday 11 to 5, Sunday 1 to 5, closed Monday. Adults $4, students $2, kids 6 to 12, $1.* The museum's collection is broad-based, ranging from Asian jade to early Italian religious art. The best stuff is in the Northwest Coast Gallery, with a fine assortment of regional Native American carvings, house posts and a totem, of course. Particularly striking is a 12-foot-long ceremonial potlatch dish carved from a log into the shape of a reclining woman. The small and select European masters collection includes bronzes by Rodin and paintings by Renoir, Degas and Monet. Japanese Hokusai prints and Han dynasty statues highlight the extensive Asian collection.

☺ **American Advertising Museum** ● *9 NW Second Ave.; (503) 226-0000. Wednesday-Friday 11 to 5, weekends noon to 5. Adults $3, seniors and kids 6 to 12, $1.50.* America's only museum dedicated to hype informs you that the first recorded ads were inscribed on Babylonian bricks in 3000 B.C. From there, the exhibits are more contemporary: Mobil's flying red horse, the Philip Morris midget's costume and Burma Shave signs. You can park before a TV set and watch now-forbidden Marlboro man commercials and listen while the guy reaches for the Alka-Seltzer and groans: "I can't believe I ate the whole thing."

☺ **Carousel Courtyard and International Museum of Carousel Art** ● *710 NE Holladay St.; (503) 235-2252. Daily 11 to 5; admission $1, including carousel ride. It's near the Portland Convention Center; easiest way to get there is to take MAX to the Seventh Avenue station.* Duane and Carol Perron have turned a love for old carousels into a vocation and a passion. Their collection includes a beautifully restored 1895 Charles Looff carousel, and enough carousel animals and other odds and ends in the adjacent museum to build more than a dozen more. Portland, incidentally, is known as the "city of carousels" because seven of them operate within the municipality. The Perrons have been responsible for acquiring and restoring five of them.

Portland Police Historical Museum ● *1111 SW Second Ave., 16th floor of the Justice Center; (503) 796-3019 To get there, enter through the police department on the lower floor; only one elevator goes to the 16th floor, so be selective. Tuesday-Friday 10 to 3; free.* Push a button to hear an anti-crime message from Mr. McGruff, then peruse the memories of Portland's men and women in blue. You'll see an early police bike with a sidecar, unusual confiscated weapons, old police badges and uniforms and a rogue's gallery of Portland's shady characters from the past.

Oregon Maritime Center and Museum ● *113 SW Front Ave.; (503) 222-2828. Wednesday-Sunday 11 to 4 in summer and Friday-Sunday 11 to 4 the rest of the year. Adults $2, seniors and kids $1.25.* Artifacts from the battleship *U.S.S. Oregon,* which distinguished itself in two world wars, are a feature of this seagoing archive. Other exhibits—targeted to Northwestern maritime history—include ship models, figureheads, seagoing paintings and lots of brass from old ships.

☺ **Nike Town** ● *920 SW Sixth Ave. (at Salmon); (503) 503-221-NIKE. Monday-Thursday 10 to 7:01, Friday 10 to 8, Saturday 10 to 6:52, Sunday 11:25 to 6:23; free.* See mannequins of Michael Jordan slam-dunk and Bo Jackson cross-train in their Nikes at this high-style sports store and jock museum. Andre Agassi's here, too, and he's not even scolding a linesman. This attractive space, representing the leading edge of retail design, has the look and feel of a sports disco. It sells the full line of Nike sports shoes and assorted logo items, from "just do it" T-shirts to shorts and sweats.

Printing Press Park ● *Morrison and First streets.* This tiny wedge of a park in the Yamhill District features copper plates of front pages from the *Oregonian* newspaper. They include the paper's first edition on December 4, 1850, the end of World Wars I and II, JFK's assassination, the moon landing and the eruption of Mount St. Helens.

World's First 24-Hour Coin Operated Art Gallery & Church of Elvis ● *219 SW Ankeny (near Second Avenue); (503) 226-3671. Admission—as many quarters as you want to waste.* This store-window contrivance gets mixed re-

The U.S. Coast Guard pays a visit to Portland's attractive downtown water-front during the annual Rose Festival. **— Don W. Martin**

views from other guidebooks. Our impression was that it's pointless and silly. By feeding quarters into a slot and pushing buttons, you get computer activated foolishness ranging from psychic counseling to utterings from the spirit of Elvis.

WASHINGTON PARK & ITS ATTRACTIONS

One of America's most attractive forests-within-a-city, the 332-acre Washington Park contains some of Portland's best attractions. It also offers striking vistas, including that often-photographed view of the city's flowers and highrises with Mount Hood glowing in the background. Plan most of a day here, particularly if you have kids in tow, and bring a picnic. There are dozens of areas to enjoy outdoor lunch with a view.

To get there, follow Burnside west from downtown. Before going into the heart of the park, continue about a mile beyond, to a sign directing you to **Pittock Mansion** on the right. Then return and follow brown directional signs into the park on Kingston Street. The tourist lures below are listed in order of appearance as you follow the park's winding roads southwesterly.

Parking near the Japanese Garden and rose gardens may be a problem on summer weekends. You can park on one of the attractive neighborhood streets just outside and walk in. As you drive on to the zoo and forestry center, parking won't be scarce, since the popular Oregon Museum of Science and Industry has moved from there to its new riverfront home.

Incidentally, once you get parked, you can ride the narrow-gauge **Washington Park Train** between the rose gardens and zoo. Tickets (adults $2, kids $1.50) are good for a round-trip, allowing stops at attractions along the way. Catch it either at the zoo or at Washington Park Station above the rose gardens. It runs between the two areas only in the summer, and operates within the zoo the rest of the year.

☺ **Pittock Mansion** ● *3229 NW Pittock Dr.; (503) 248-4469. Home tours daily 1 to 4; adults $3.50, seniors $3, kids 6 to 18, $1.50. Grounds open* *daily until dark; free. Located in Pittock Acres Park, just beyond Washington Park.* This 1914 French Renaissance castle was home to Henry Pittock, founder of the Portland *Oregonian.* It remained in the family until 1964 when it was sold to the city. The hour and a half tour thus offers an intimate look at the man and his furnishings. It's a virtual treasure house of museum quality antiques. The park-like grounds, high above Portland, offers stellar views.

☺ **Japanese Garden** ● *611 SW Kingston Ave.; (503) 223-1321 or 223-4070. Daily 9 to 8 in summer, 10 to 6 in spring and fall and 10 to 4 in winter. Adults $4.50, seniors and students, $2.50; MC/VISA.* The garden is 500 feet up a winding path, although a shuttle makes the trip every few minutes and wheelchair drop-offs are permitted at the top. This is actually many gardens within a garden, terraced into a sloping, wooded hillside of Washington Park. Their names provide obvious clues: the Strolling Pond Garden, Tea Garden, Natural Garden and Sand and Stone Garden. Stone paths lead to shady niches with places to sit and relax. Best time to see this beauty in bloom is from March through early April when the cherry blossoms emerge.

☺ **International Rose Test Gardens** ● *400 SW Kingston Ave.; (503) 796-5193 or 248-4302; free.* City of roses, indeed! Thousands of bushes issue hundreds of thousands of blooms from late May through October, filling the air with their delicate perfume. America's oldest agricultural test plot, the rose gardens date back to 1917. This four and a half acres of terraced rose bushes may be the most interesting space in the city. When you aren't sniffing and examining the 400 varieties, you can glance down to the Portland skyline, and across the river to distant Mount Hood. The bushes are labeled so you can tell Sunday's Best from Prairie Fire from Crimson Tide. The beds of roses are widely spaced, with plenty of room between to spread a picnic lunch. We *told* you to bring one!

Hoyt Arboretum ● *4000 SW Fairview Blvd.; (503) 228-8732. Visitor center open daily 10 to 4; free.* In this land of evergreens, it's appropriate that Oregon's finest arboretum specializes in trees. More than 700 varieties of trees and shrubs fill this 214-acre garden, with seven miles of strolling trails. You'll see everything from bristlecone pines to redwoods, and they're all labeled. Oregon's **Vietnam Memorial** is located here as well, beneath a cathedral of conifers.

☺ **World Forestry Center** ● *4033 SW Canyon Rd.; (503) 228-1367. Daily 10 to 5. Adults $3, seniors and kids $2.* Douglas, the fir, greets you in the center's main exhibit hall, and tells you how a tree works. Having learned this, you can peruse displays on logging yesterday and today, fire fighting and reforesting. You'll learn how a sawmill, plywood mill and pulp mill work. Particularly interesting is a collection of sample slices from virtually every tree on the planet. It will come as no surprise that this exhibit is *very* pro lumber industry.

☺ **Metro Washington Park Zoo** ● *4001 SW Canyon Rd.; (503) 226-1561. Adults $5, seniors $3.50 and kids $3; also combination zoo- train ride tickets.* This is one of the West's best zoos, featuring several thematic "total environment" exhibits. In the Alaska tundra, you'll hear wails of lonely wolves, learn about the midnight sun and see assorted critters from that area. Humidifiers and heaters set a properly damp mood for the African Rainforest, which has an outstanding display concerning efforts to curb poaching of endangered animals. The Antarctic domain will transport you to a shoreline penguin colony, complete with the aroma. The zoo's grounds are a virtual garden of landscaping, and several animal statues make inviting jungle gyms for kids.

ATTRACTIONS ELSEWHERE

☺ **The Grotto** ● *NE 85th Avenue at NE Sandy Blvd.; (503) 254-7371. Open daily, 10 to 8 in summer, 10 to 5 in the off-season. Elevator ride $2 for adults and $1 for seniors and students. To reach it from downtown, cross the river on the Burnside Bridge, then pick up NE Sandy Boulevard (business route 30) and follow it northeast about five miles.* This jewel of a botanical garden and religious shrine is often overlooked, even by longtime Portland residents. Its focal point is the National Sanctuary of Our Sorrowful Mother, a shrine set into the base of a cliff with a replica of Michelangelo's *Pieta.* The shrine is cloaked in ferns and ivy and sheltered by towering conifers. From this hushed enclave, you can take an elevator up the face of a 110-foot cliff to a lush botanical garden, with impressive views northward across the Columbia River. Founded in 1924 as a Catholic retreat, the Grotto is a scene of quiet reflection that attracts folks of all faiths.

Mount Tabor Park ● *SE 60th Avenue and Salmon Street. To reach it from downtown, drive east across the Hawthorne Bridge. Then follow Hawthorne Boulevard about three miles east to SE 60th Avenue, go left two blocks to Salmon, then right into the park.* Portland is the only city in America that can claim an extinct volcano within its limits. An asphalt road and hiking trails reach the top of Mount Tabor, offering predictably impressive views of the city surrounding you.

Other parks ● Portland claims to have more parks and park acreage than any other city of its size in the world. A total of 280 parks contain more than 37,000 acres of "urban wilds." They range from 4,683-acre **Forest Park** in northwest Portland, which is basically wooded hills that happen to be surrounded by a city, to 24-square-inch **Mill Ends' Park** at SW Front Avenue and Taylor Street, which is basically a gimmick. The largest wooded urban park in the world, Forest is reached from downtown by NW Lovejoy, which becomes NW Summit and skirts the park's lower end. Several miles of trails and lanes wander through this huge woodland.

May through early June is a good time to explore the city's parks, when rhododendrons and azaleas are in bloom. The best of these are in **Crystal Springs Rhododendron Garden,** where more than 2,000 of these beautiful blooming shrubs thrive. It's just off SE McLoughlin Blvd. (99-E), near Reed College, southeast of downtown. **Laurelhurst Park** offers splashes of rhododendrons and a duck-busy lake at SE 39th Avenue and Stark Street. As a bonus, it's in one of Portland's noble old residential districts. Drive east on Burnside to 39th and go right for a short distance.

Kelley Point Park in north Portland, at the merger of the Willamette and Columbia rivers, is a good place to watch the ship traffic pass.

For information on the city's parks and their attractions, contact the **Portland Parks Bureau** in the Portland Building, downtown at Fifth Avenue and Main Street, fifth floor; (503) 796-5193.

Sauvie Island Wildlife Area ● *Northeast of Portland on the Columbia River. From downtown, take I-405 north, then U.S. 30 northwest for ten miles. For a brochure, contact: Oregon Fish & Wildlife, P.O. Box 59, Portland, OR 97207; (503) 229-5400.* Sauvie is a large, low-lying island hugging the Oregon shore of the Columbia, just above its confluence with the Willamette. Its northern end has been set aside as a 12,000-acre sanctuary operated by the Oregon Fish & Wildlife Department. For a $2.50 daily parking fee, you can view blue herons, sandhill cranes, an occasional bald eagle and 250 other varieties of winged things. Permits are available at various businesses on the island and at the visitor center on the west side drive, about a mile from the bridge. You can pick up a map and brochure there as well.

The reserve is interlaced with walking trails and it's busy with sandy swimming and fishing beaches and inland lagoons. **Walton Beach** off the east side drive on the Columbia River has some good swimming areas. The island's level roads are ideal for biking. **Sauvie Cove** here offers RV and tent sites for $12 a day, plus a mini-mart and marina (see camping listing below). Much of the island is in farmland noted for blueberries, strawberries, raspberries and apples. During springtime, you can pick your own berries or pick up fresh baskets at roadside stands. The most complete selection is at **The Berry Basket,** north of the bridge that links the island to the mainland. The **James Y. Bybee House** just beyond is an 1858 clapboard farmhouse with period furnishings. It's open for tours in summer Wednesday-Sunday noon to 5.

A minor negative note: the island is plastered with black and yellow signs telling you what you can and can't do and where you can and can't park. They detract from the spirit of discovery and exploration.

ACTIVITIES & TOURS

GETTING TICKETED ● Portland's major charge-by-phone ticket outlet is **Ticketmaster,** (800) 745-0888 or (503) 224-4400. It has outlets at all **GI Joe Stores** in the area as well.

Auto racing ● **Portland Speedway**, 9727 N. Martin Luther King Jr., Blvd., (503) 285-2269; and at **Portland International Raceway**, N. Victory in West Delta Park, (503) 285-6635.

Brewpub hopping ● Portland has nine micro-breweries producing "hand-tailored" beers and ales, and four are linked to brewpubs. A $1 directory/map is available at Bridgeport Brewery and Brew Pub, 1313 NW Marshall St., (503) 241-7179, and at Powell's and other bookstores about town.

☺ **Brewery Tour** ● **Blitz-Weinhard Brewing Company**, 1133 W. Burnside St.; (503) 222-4351. Free tours weekdays at 1, 2, 3 and 4 p.m., June through October and at 1, 2:30 and 4 the rest of the year. You'll learn how beer is brewed at this century-old home of Henry Weinhard's. If you're old enough, you'll get a sip of Henry's at tour's end.

Coliseum events ● In addition to hosting the Trailblazers, the Memorial Coliseum and Civic Stadium present a variety of concerts, headliners, circuses and sports events. Call (503) 248-4496 for ticket information.

Greyhound racing ● **Multnomah Kennel Club**, P.O. Box 9, Fairview, OR 97024; (503) 667-7700. The doggie stadium is at NE 223rd and Glisan and the season is May through September; MC/VISA.

Guided tours ● **Gray Line of Portland**, P.O. Box 17306, Portland, OR 97217; (800) 422-7042 or 285-9845; MC/VISA. City tours plus bus tours of Mount Hood, the Columbia River Gorge, historic Astoria and nearby coastal areas. **Taste of Oregon Tours**, 7406 SE 28th St., Portland, OR 97202; (503) 235-3260. Tours of nearby scenic areas with a focus on Oregon foods and wines.

Guided hikes ● **Friends of the Columbia Gorge**, P.O. Box 40820, Portland, OR 97240, (503) 241-3762. The group offers a variety of conducted hikes around the gorge, Multnomah Falls and other nearby scenic areas.

Hiking in the city ● The classic is a 14-mile trail from **Hoyt Arboretum** to **Forest Park**. You'll find several miles of trails in Forest Park as well. **Macleay Park**, wedged between Forest Park and Washington Park, also has a good trail system. For books and maps on urban hiking, check out the **Portland Audubon Society Bookstore** near the Macleay Park trailhead at 5152 NW Cornell Rd., Portland, OR 97210; (503) 292-6855. The society's maps cover 200 wildlife sites within the city. Another good guide, available at the society bookstore, at Powells and other local outlets, is *A Pedestrian's Guide to Portland* by Karen and Terry Whitehill.

The **Forty-Mile-Loop Land Trust** is working on a 140-mile trail system that will encircle the city. Some sections are now in place; call (503) 241-9105 for an update. One of the longest routes covers 33 miles on the west side of the Willamette. A good starting point is **Marquam Nature Park,** a semi-developed area south of Marquam Bridge. From here, the trail continues south through Willamette Park. Maps of completed sections of the 140-mile trail are available at Powell's Travel Bookstore off Pioneer Courthouse Square and at the Portland Parks Bureau in the Portland Building, downtown at Fifth Avenue and Main Street, fifth floor; (503) 796-5193. The Parks Bureau also has information on other city park trails.

Horse racing ● **Portland Meadows**, 1001 N. Schmeer Rd., Portland, OR 97217; (503) 285-9144. This modern glass-enclosed race facility has dining and cocktail service; the season is October through April.

☺ **Live and onstage** ● **Portland Center for the Performing Arts** at 1111 SW Broadway, Portland, OR 97205, offers a year- around season of 800 dramas, concerts and such in four theaters. Call (503) 248-4495 for ticket information. The **Oregon Shakespeare Festival-Portland**, presents a November-April season of five classic and modern plays at the Portland Center, (503) 274-6588; MC/VISA, AMEX. **Portland Opera**, 1516 SW Alder, Portland, OR 97205, offers for traditional operas and a classical American musical during its season; MC/VISA. **Portland Repertory Theater,** 25 SW Salmon, Portland, OR 97204, (503) 224-4491, is a professional Equity group presenting a variety of contemporary dramas and comedies; MC/VISA. **Oregon Symphony,** 719 SW Alder, Portland, OR 97205; (503) 228-1353, offers a season of classic, pops and kids concerts at the Portland Center; MC/VISA, AMEX, DISC.

NBA basketball ● **Portland Trailblazers**, 700 NE Multnomah, Portland, OR 97232; (503) 231-8000. Home games are at Memorial Coliseum; ticket office hours are weekdays 8:30 to 5:30 October-April; MC/VISA, AMEX. Blazer tickets go quickly, so get yours early.

Other pro teams ● The AAA farm club for the Minnesota Twins is the **Portland Beavers,** P.O. Box 1659, Portland, OR 97207; (503) 248-4496; MC/VISA, AMEX. The **Winter Hawks** ice hockey team, 1401 N. Wheeler, Portland, OR 97229; (503) 238-6366, plays at the Memorial Coliseum.

☺ **River tours** ● **Sternwheeler** *Columbia Gorge*, 1200 NW Front Ave., Suite 110, Portland, OR 97209; (503) 223-3928 or 374-8427. The paddlewheeler has a variety of Willamette and Columbia river voyages, including trips through the Columbia River Gorge, dinner, lunch and brunch cruises and dance cruises. It operates from The Dalles in the summer (see Chapter 7) and from the Portland waterfront during the off- season.

Yachts-O-Fun, (503) 289-6665, offers dinner, brunch and harbor cruises on the Willamette; major credit cards. **Sternwheeler Rose,** 6211 M Ensign, Portland, OR 97217; (503) 286-ROSE, features Willamette sight-seeing and harbor cruises; MC/VISA.

Vintage trolley ride ● The **Willamette Shore Trolley,** 333 S. State St., Suite 500, Lake Oswego, OR 97034; (503) 222-2226, offers 90-minute nostalgia rides on its 1913 electric trolley between Portland and Lake Oswego. The trip follows the riverbank, ducks through an old tunnel, and underneath forest canopies as it clickity-clacks past stately homes.

Winery tours ● Many of Oregon's wineries are located within a short drive of Portland (see driving tours below). A map/guide, **Wineries of Washington County** is available at the visitor information center and at various wineries.

ANNUAL EVENTS

Portland Rose Festival is the biggie—one of the largest and liveliest urban parties in the West. This 24-day celebration, dating from 1907, begins in late May and continues well into June. Features include selection and coronation of the Rose Queen from local high schools, fireworks, an international marketplace, festival of flowers, air show, special concerts and plays, tours of Navy and Coast Guard ships and a non-stop carnival along the riverfront. The highlight of it all is the Grand Floral Parade, the world's second largest flower procession, after Pasadena's Tournament of Roses on New Year's Day. (At least Portland does it in the right season, to celebrate the blooming of the city's millions of roses; most of Pasadena's flowers are hothouse grown.) Call (503) 227-2681 for a complete schedule of events.

For updates on events listed below and a more extensive calendar, contact the Portland/Oregon Visitors Association, 26 SW Salmon, Portland, OR 97204-3299; (503) 222-2223. Or call the Events Hotline at (503) 233-4444.

Pro-Rodeo Classic, January at Memorial Coliseum; (503) 235-8771 .

International Film Festival in February and March at the Oregon Art Institute, 1219 SW Park Ave.; (503) 221-1156.

Northwest Chili Cook-off in February at the Portland Expo Center, to benefit the zoo; (503) 226-1561 or 285-7756.

Shamrock Run, on the weekend near St. Patrick's Day, 8K run and four-mile walk at Waterfront Park; (503) 226-5080.

Mother's Day Annual Rhododendron Show in Crystal Springs Rhododendron Garden, May; (503) 777-1734.

Peanut Butter and Jam Noon Concerts all summer, Tuesdays and Thursdays at Pioneer Courthouse Square; (503) 223-1613.

Fox 29 River Grand Prix in June, on the Willamette River between Hawthorne and Ross Island bridges; (503) 222-2715.

Waterfront Blues Festival, July at Waterfront Park; (503) 282-0555.

Oregon Brewers Festival, July at Waterfront Park, described as "America's largest beer party"; (503) 241-7179 or 281-2437.

Artquake, August and September; outdoor art, music, theater and dance festival at Pioneer Courthouse Square; (503) 227-2787.

A Taste of Portland, August at Waterfront Park; food booths from Portland's leading restaurants; (503) 248-0600.

Oktoberfests are held during September at Holladay Park and Lloyd Center, (503) 235-3138; Oaks Amusement Park, (503) 232-3000 and of course at Mount Angel (see previous chapter), (503) 845-9291.

Meier & Frank Holiday Parade, November in downtown Portland to launch Christmas shopping season; (503) 241-5328.

Tree lighting ceremony, late November in Pioneer Courthouse Square; (503) 223-1613.

Harvest Festival, November, featuring handmade gifts, food booths and entertainment, Oregon Convention Center; (503) 235-7575.

Christmas activities during December include the Festival of Trees with gingerbread houses and trains at the Memorial Coliseum, (503) 235-8771; skating on a frozen outdoor rink at Pioneer Courthouse Square, (503) 222-7425; Winterlights Festival at Metro Washington Park Zoo, with night-lighted exhibits, (503) 226-1561 and the Portland Parade of Christmas Ships, cruising the Willamette and Columbia rivers nightly; (503) 222-2223.

SHOPPING UNTIL YOU'RE DROPPING

☺ **Lloyd Center** (282-2511) at NE Broadway and NE Multnomah, tops our list of areas to shop for historic reasons. Built in 1960, it was the world's first covered shopping mall and it ruled as the largest for several years. Sparkling from a $100 million renovation, it offers several "anchor" stores, more than 170 shops and restaurants, a ten-screen theater and a domed ice rink. It's easy to reach; just hop on MAX and hop off at the center.

The heart of **downtown shopping** is along Morrison Street between SW Fourth and Tenth avenues. The **Galleria** at Morrison and Ninth is a complex of boutiques built around a five-story atrium in an old masonry building. Major department stores in this area include **Meier & Frank** at Sixth and Morrison, **Fred Meyer** at Sixth and Alder, **Nordstrom's** at Broadway and Morrison and **Sak's Fifth Avenue** at Fifth and Yamhill. For a lunch break with a view during your shopping spree, try **Rene's Fifth Avenue** (241-0710) on the 21st floor of the First Interstate Bank Tower at Fourth Avenue and Jefferson.

The ultimate bookstore, in Portland and the rest of the world, is **Powell's City of Books** at 1005 W. Burnside (800) 878-READ or (503) 228-4651. With a million titles in a warehouse-store the size of a city block, it is easily the largest bookstore on the globe. **Powell's Travel Store** off Pioneer Courthouse Square at SW Sixth Avenue and Yamhill (228-1108) has an extensive selection of travel books and related items.

If you're interest in art or antiques, head for old town and the **Yamhill** and **Skidmore** historic districts. They're on the MAX line, or hike north along Waterfront Park which, incidentally, is a proper place for buying curios. The **Saturday Market,** held weekends in the Skidmore area from March through December, features more than 200 arts and crafts booths. Several buildings in this area have been converted into boutiques and galleries, including **Yamhill Marketplace, New Market Village, Import Plaza** in the old Globe Hotel and the **Skidmore Fountain Building.**

The ultimate outlet for antiquers is the **Sellwood District** in southeast Portland, just across the Sellwood Bridge. More than two dozen antique shops occupy this old section on a ridge above the river, blended in with century-old homes. For a bit of "1960s Berkeley meets Second Hand Rose," tour the **Hawthorne District** immediately west of Mount Tabor Park.

Hawthorne Boulevard is lined with cafès, used clothing stores, galleries, antique shops and book stores. Most are between 32nd and 40th avenues.

North of the city, hop off I-5 at Interstate Bridge for the **Jantzen Beach Center,** a shopping complex with five department stores and 100 other shops and restaurants. Its focal point is a huge 72-horse carousel, yours to ride for 50 cents a whirl.

Most of the other major shopping centers are in the suburbs to the south of downtown. Go south on I-5 then northwest on Freeway 217 to SW Canyon Road and **Washington Square** on the edge of **Beaverton.** A bit farther along, off SW Walker Road, is **Beaverton Mall**; look for the clock tower. **Clackamas Town Center** has more than 180 stores and a skating rink in its mall at I-205 and SE Sunnyside Road. Also off the freeway is the **I-205 Mall** at the Stark Street exit, just northeast of **Mount Tabor Park.**

WHERE TO DINE

Portland's rich ethnic mix naturally results in an interesting blend of restaurants. The city has no "restaurant row" as such, although visitors will find several cafès along the waterfront. Most combine dining—usually with a seafood emphasis—with river views. Some examples are **Newport Bay** and **HarborSide Restaurant** at RiverPlace and **Esplanade Restaurant** at the RiverPlace Alexis Hotel. **Salty's On the Columbia** is opposite the airport at 3839 NE Marine Drive.

Other view restaurants, off the waterfront, include **Rene's Fifth Avenue** (241-0710) in the First Interstate Bank Tower at Fourth Avenue and Jefferson; and **Atwater's** (275-3600) on the 30th floor of US Bancorp Tower, 111 SW Fifth Avenue.

Naturally, the emphasis is on seafood in this city rimmed by water. **Dan and Louis' Oyster Bar** (227-5906) between Second and Third on Ankeny in the Skidmore District is a legendary spot, dating from 1907. Others with good shellfish and swimfish menus are **Couch Street Fish House** at 105 NW Third (223-6173), **McCormick & Schmick's Seafood** (224-7522) at 235 SW First Avenue and **Jake's Famous Crawfish Restaurant** (226-1419) at 401 SW 12th Avenue.

The **Yamhill Marketplace** offers a large concentration of restaurants and international cafès. You can have lunch while browsing for arts and crafts at the **Saturday Market,** which features many international food stalls. Incidentally, despite the often drizzly weather, many of Portland's optimistic restaurateurs offer outdoor dining. Most of our selections are clustered around the downtown area, where most of you visitors will be. For more listings, written more for locals, consult the **Portland Best Places** book or **The Menu: A Restaurant Guide to Oregon,** which lists sample menus and hours. Both are available at local bookstores.

American, including seafood

☺ **Atwater's** ● ∆∆∆∆ $$$$

US Bancorp Tower, 111 SW Fifth Ave.; (503) 275-3600. American regional; full bar service. Sunday-Thursday 5:30 to 9:30, Friday-Saturday 5:30 to 10. Major credit cards. Sleekly modern restaurant in proper peach and salmon with stunning views of the countryside. Northwest menu includes savories such as halibut in macadamia nut crust and veal with crab legs in brandied crayfish sauce. In menu and view, it's Portland's top restaurant.

Couch Street Fish House • △△△ $$$

105 NW Third Ave.; (503) 223-6173. Seafood and Northwest regional; full bar service. Monday-Thursday 5 to 10, Friday-Saturday 5 to 11. MC/VISA, AMEX. Old European atmosphere with dark woods, linen nappery and formally attired waiters bearing whisk brooms. Good selections of fresh fish, particularly local shellfish, plus regional chop, steak and chicken dishes.

☺ Dan & Lois Oyster Bar • △△ $$

208 SW Ankeny St.; (503) 227-5906. Seafood; wine and beer. Sunday-Thursday 11 to 10, Friday-Saturday 11 to midnight. Major credit cards. Rich nautical dècor with lots of polished woods and brass trim in this 1907 legend. Yaquina Bay oysters are a specialty here, and you can order assorted shrimp, scallop and oyster fry combinations, plus calamari and steamed fresh fish. If you must, there's steak on the menu.

Denny King's Veritable Quandary • △△ $$

First and Madison (near the waterfront); (503) 227-7342. American; full bar service. Daily 11:30 to 11. MC/VISA. Attractive old fashion decor, with lofty ceilings and high-backed booths that give it a men's club look. Eclectic menu wanders from curried vegetables to seafood specials to chicken fettuccini. Popular with the business lunch crowd; outdoor dining.

☺ Esplanade • △△△△ $$$$

At the RiverPlace Alexis Hotel, 1510 SW Harbor Way; (503) 295-6166. American nouveau; full bar service. Breakfast daily 6:30 to 10:30, lunch weekdays 11:30 to 2:30, dinner nightly 5:30 to 10, Sunday brunch 11 to 2:30. Major credit cards. Posh restaurant with river views and a busy, pricey menu. A full soup-to-dessert dinner will send you toward $50. Try steamed lobster medallions in napa cabbage or grilled swordfish with lemon grass sauce, or one of the duck, veal chop or lamb dishes. When the check comes, remember—it's *your* vacation.

Hamburger Mary's • △ $

847 Park Ave.; (503) 223-0900. American; wine and beer. Daily 7 a.m. to 2:30 a.m. MC/VISA, AMEX. A copy of the San Francisco original, with a wood-paneled interior, cluttered dècor and huge, gloppy hamburgers. It's a good breakfast or lunch stop for downtown explorers, and a handy spot to grab an inexpensive bite before or after the theater or concert, considering its crazy hours. Versatile breakfast omelettes are a specialty. Outdoor dining.

HarborSide Restaurant • △△ $$$

On the waterfront at 309 SW Montgomery; (503) 220-1865. American, mostly seafood; full bar service with microbrewery adjacent. Monday-Thursday 11 to 10, Friday-Saturday 11 to 11, Sunday 10 to 10. Major credit cards. You can tell it's a stylishly new joint because of the capital "S" in the middle of its name. The menu is primarily seafood, plus an eclectic selection that wanders over much of the globe. The best features of this cafè are the new **Pilsner Room** brewpub next door, and outdoor tables with a river view.

Heathman Bakery & Pub • △△ $$

901 SW Salmon St.; (503) 227-5700. American bistro; wine and beer. Sunday-Thursday 7 a.m. to 11 p.m. Friday-Saturday 8 a.m. to midnight. Major credit cards. Lively vintage pub with a mixed grill menu. Breakfasts include corned beef and hash and salmon Benedict. Lunch and dinners bounce from smoked chicken gazpacho salad and game patè to beef stroganoff, plus Italian fare and wood oven pizza. Specialty beers featured.

☺ Jake's Famous Crawfish Restaurant • ∆∆∆ $$

401 SW 12th Ave.; (503) 226-1419. American, mostly seafood; full bar service. Monday-Thursday 11:30 to 11, Friday-Saturday 11:30 to midnight, Sunday 5 to 10. Major credit cards. Artistic 19th century dècor and versatile menu are highlights of this popular, long-established hangout. In addition to crawfish done in assorted ways, the menu features other local shellfish, catch of the day and chicken, chops, steaks and a couple of pasta dishes.

McCormick & Schmick's Seafood Restaurant • ∆∆∆ $$$

235 SW First Ave.; (503) 224-7522. Seafood; full bar service. Weekdays 11:30 to 2 and 5 to 11, Saturday 5 to 11, Sunday 5 to 10. Major credit cards. Another local institution, housed in a yesterday building with turn-of-the-century dècor. The accent is more on fish filets here, although local shellfish is featured as well, along with a few chops, steaks, chickens and remarkably good 'burgers and fries.

Newport Bay Restaurant • ∆∆ $$$

Waterfront pier off RiverPlace (245 SW Montgomery); (503) 227-3474. Mostly seafood; full bar service. Monday-Thursday 11 to 11, Friday-Saturday 11 to midnight, Sunday 9 to 11. Major credit cards. Modern nautical restaurant whose river pier site with its attendant views are better than the menu. The adjacent outdoor floating dock is more casual and quite pleasant on a sunny day. Menu is contemporary, with the predictable Cajun and blackened things, plus some seafood pasta dishes.

☺ Paddy's Bar & Grill • ∆∆ $$

Yamhill and First Avenue; (503) 224-5626. American; full bar service. Weekdays from 11, weekends noon to 1:30 a.m. MC/VISA. Great old fashioned bar with high ceilings and a towering glass back bar with a library ladder to reach the seven-high rows of booze. Simple fare includes Irish stew, cannelloni, buckets of clams and such. Good lunch stop on the edge of the old town districts.

Rafatti's Restaurant • ∆∆∆ $$$

In the World Trade Center at 25 SW Salmon St.; (503) 248-9305. American-continental; full bar service. Daily 11 to 10:30. Major credit cards. Bright, sunny restaurant built into the glasswork of the World Trade Center; river views and outdoor tables. Mostly seafood, plus mesquite barbecued pork loin, shish kabob and teriyaki steak.

☺ Rene's Fifth Avenue • ∆∆∆ $$

First Interstate Bank Tower, Fourth Avenue and Jefferson, 21st floor; (503) 241-0710. American; full bar service. Lunch only, 11:30 to 2:30, cocktail lounge open until 7:30. MC/VISA. This sleek restaurant is a favorite spot for business folk to impress clients with a 240-degree view of the city—north, west and south. It's a pity the restaurant doesn't serve dinner, for the night light view is awesome. Go for a sunset cocktail.

☺ The Ringside • ∆∆∆ $$$

2165 W. Burnside (at 22nd Avenue); (503) 223-1513. Mostly steak; full bar service. Monday-Saturday 5 to midnight, Sunday 4 to 11:30. Major credit cards. This has been *the* Portland steak house since 1944, where thick slabs of beef are served by tuxedo-clad waiters in a clubby dining room. Go for the pound and a half Porterhouse if you're a serious steak eater, with Walla Walla onion rings on the side. Prime rib is excellent, too.

Salty's ● ΔΔ $$

3839 NE Marine Drive on the Columbia, (503) 288-4444; and 513 SE Clatsop on the Willamette, (503) 239-8900. American with seafood priority; full bar service. Monday-Saturday 11 to 11, Sunday 10 to 11. Major credit cards. Informal diners with river views; conventional menu with surf and turf, seafood fettuccini and sautéed prawns. Fresh salmon is featured—broiled, baked or blackened. Steak and poultry dishes also are on menu.

International

Bush Garden ● ΔΔΔ $$$

900 SW Morrison; (503) 226-7181. Japanese; full bar service. Lunch weekdays 11:30 to 2, dinner Monday-Saturday 5 to 10 and Sunday 5 to 9. Major credit cards. Excellent sushi bar is a highlight of this tasteful restaurant in a Japanese garden setting. The food is typical—the usual tempuras, sukiyakis and nabès, plus some combination dinners providing a broad sampler of fare *Nippon*. Live Japanese music in the adjacent lounge.

☺ Chang's Yangzte ● ΔΔΔ $$

921 SW Morrison, third floor; (503) 241-0218. Chinese; full bar service. Monday-Thursday 11:30 to 10, Friday-Saturday 11:30 to 11, Sunday 4 to 10. MC/VISA. A cheery, not quite garish interior sets the mood for spicy Hunan and Szechuan dishes in Portland's best Chinese restaurant. Start with potstickers, try a spicy or subtle vegetable dish (whatever's fresh), and then move on to lively Kung Pao Chicken, Mu Shu Pork or Mongolian beef.

Greek Cusina ● ΔΔ $$

SW Fourth Avenue and Washington; (503) 224-2288. Greek; full bar service. Monday-Thursday 7 a.m. to 11 p.m., Friday-Saturday 7 to 2:30 a.m., Sunday 11 to 11. MC/VISA, AMEX. Lively Greek deli and cafè with music and belly dancers. Typical menu features lamb, beef or chicken kabob, *moussaka* (eggplant, zucchini and ground meat), lamb with pita, and shrimp with feta. Greek "munchies" menu is handy for an inexpensive lunch, including dolmas to go if you're in a rush.

House of Louie ● ΔΔ $$

331 NW Davis (at Fourth Avenue, in Chinatown); (503) 228-9898. Chinese; full bar service. Daily 11 to 11. MC/VISA. Classic example of Chinese garish, with Naugahyde red and gold booths, lacquered gold grillwork and red and gold decorative ceiling tiles. It'll make you blink as you sample the busy Cantonese, Szechuan and Hunan menu; there are a few American dishes as well.

Marrakesh ● ΔΔ $$$

121 NW 23rd Ave. (northwest of downtown); (503) 248-9442. Moroccan; full bar service. Tuesday-Saturday 5 to 10, Sunday 5 to 9, closed Monday. MC/VISA, AMEX. Sit among silken pillows inside a tapestried tent and try the spicy lamb, chicken and beef dishes with *couscous* and lentil soup. Best way to enjoy this typical Moroccan dining experience is to order a combination dinner and turn the chef loose. Try the royale feast at $17 a person or *mechoui* with spit-roasted sheep for $28.

Martinotti's Deli & Restaurant • ∆ $
402 Tenth St.; (503) 224-9028. Italian; wine and beer. Weekdays 8:30 to 6, Saturday 10 to 6, closed Sunday. MC/VISA. Huge deli with Italian savories stuffed into cases, stacked on shelves and hanging from the ceiling. Settle down at a blue- checkered oilcloth table for a quick and inexpensive lunch.

Pazzo Ristorante • ∆∆ $$
627 SW Washington; (503) 228-1515. Italian; full bar service. Breakfast weekdays 7 to 10:30 and weekends 8 to 10:30, lunch daily 11:30 to 2:30. dinner Sunday-Thursday 5 to 10 and Friday-Saturday 5 to 11. Major credit cards. This is where you go for your *antipasti, insalata, zuppa* and main course, even for breakfast. The Italian menu is huge, with fare ranging from veal *saltimbocca* and roast duck in *grappa* to calzones and a long list of pastas.

WHERE TO SLEEP
Portland has several affordable downtown lodgings, plus the usual luxury hotels. Since most of the city's attractions are near downtown, our list focuses on lodgings in or near this southwestern quadrant. A motel row of sorts rambles along SE 82nd Avenue, paralleling I-205 east of downtown. Other motel clusters are located along Sandy Boulevard, immediately northeast of downtown and Interstate Avenue, paralleling northbound I-5 between Portland and Vancouver.

Rooms for $100 or more a night

☺ The Benson Hotel • ⌂⌂⌂⌂ $$$$$ ∅
309 SW Broadway (downtown at Oak), Portland, OR 97205; (800) 426-0670 or (503) 228-2000. Couples $170 to $205, singles $145 to $180, suites $325 to $600. Major credit cards. One of America's grand old hotels, built by Simon Benson in 1912 and impeccably restored to its original elegance. Large, luxuriant rooms with TV movies, honor bars and all resort amenities; some with fireplaces and spa tubs. Two restaurants: **Trader Vic's** serves Polynesian and **London Grill** serves continental fare; food service 6:30 a.m. to 2 a.m.; dinners $19 to $36; full bar service.

☺ The Heathman Hotel • ⌂⌂⌂⌂ $$$$$ ∅
1009 SW Broadway (downtown at Salmon), Portland, OR 97205; (800) 551-0011 or (503) 241-4100. Couples $155 to $205, singles $135 to $185, suites $265 to $375. Major credit cards. Exquisitely restored 1927 hotel with Italian Renaissance façade and classic tea court; adjoining Performing Arts Center. Luxury amenities; elegant rooms with polished woods, modern artworks and marble baths; TV and VCR with library of 250 films. European style concierge service; twice-daily maid service. Health club adjacent with gym, pool, sauna and steam room. **Heathman Restaurant** noted for its Pacific Northwest cuisine; 6:30 a.m. to 11 p.m.; dinners $18 to $35; full bar.

Portland Marriott • ⌂⌂⌂⌂ $$$$$ ∅
1401 SW Front Ave. (downtown, at the riverfront), Portland, OR 97201; (800) 228-9290 or (503) 226-7600. Couples $147 to $160, singles $137 to $150. Major credit cards. Sleekly modern, luxurious 503-room hotel on the waterfront; TV movies, room phones, all amenities. Many rooms with river views; pool, saunas, spa, health club. **Fazzio's Café** and **King's Wharf** serve American fare (seafood at King's); 6:30 a.m. to 11:30 p.m.; dinners $7 to $20; full bar service.

Red Lion Hotel • ⌂⌂⌂ $$$$$ Ø

310 SW Lincoln (at Fourth Avenue), Portland, OR 97201: (800) 547-8010 or (503) 221-0450. Couples $100 to $118, singles $95 to $110, suites $275 to $375. Major credit cards. Attractive 235-room downtown hotel with TV movies, room phones; health club, pool. **Cityside Dining Room** serves American fare 6 a.m. to 10 p.m.; dinners $17 to $25; full bar service.

☺ RiverPlace Alexis Hotel • ⌂⌂⌂⌂ $$$$$ Ø

1510 SW Harbor Way (downtown, on the waterfront), Portland, OR 97201; (800) 227-1333 or (503) 228-3233. Couples $165 to $180, singles $145 to $180, kitchenettes $250 to $350, suites $180 to $500; rates include continental breakfast. Major credit cards. Portland's most elegant new hotel, built into a modern European style rotunda with tall French windows and a courtyard opening onto Waterfront Park. The 84 rooms have full resort amenities; all with river or downtown views, some with fireplaces. Spa and sauna; shopping esplanade, jogging path and nearby athletic club. **Esplanade** dining room listed above.

Shilo Inn Portland Airport • ⌂⌂⌂⌂ $$$$$ Ø

11707 NE Airport Way (I-205 exit 24B), Portland, OR 97220; (800) 222-2244 or (503) 252-7500. All suite hotel with rooms from $115 to $130. Major credit cards. Two hundred suites with three TVs, VCRs, in-room movies, two-line phones, microwaves, refrigerators and wet bars. Continental breakfast, indoor pool, spa, sauna, steam room and fitness center. **Shilo Restaurant** serves American regional fare, Sunday-Thursday 6 a.m. to 10 p.m. and Friday-Saturday 6 to 11; full bar service.

Rooms $50 to $99 a night

Best Western Heritage • ⌂⌂⌂ $$$ Ø

4319 NW Yeon Ave. (northwest, near Montgomery Park), Portland, OR 97210; (800) 528-1234 or (503) 497-9044. Couples $58 to $65, singles $51 to $58, kitchenettes $63 to $83, suites $87. Major credit cards. Well-kept 65-room inn with TV movies, phones, some room refrigerators; free continental breakfast, FAX service, indoor pool, sauna and spa.

Cypress Inn • ⌂⌂⌂ $$$ Ø

809 SW King Ave., Portland, OR 97205; (800) 445-4205 in Oregon, (800) 225-4205 elsewhere, (503) 226-6288 locally. Couples $60 to $90, singles $48 to $83, includes continental breakfast. Major credit cards. Attractive 82-room lodge near downtown with TV movies, room refrigerators, many mini-suites, guest laundry.

Imperial Hotel • ⌂⌂ $$ Ø

400 SW Broadway (at Stark Street downtown), Portland, OR 97205; (800) 452-2323 or (503) 228-7221. Couples $44 to $70, singles $45 to $60. Major credit cards. Older, well-maintained hotel undergoing renovation. TV, room phones. Newly remodeled **Dining Room** serves American fare daily 6:30 a.m. to 8 p.m., dinners $3.50 to $12.95; full bar service.

☺ Mallory Hotel • ⌂⌂⌂ $$$

729 SW 15th (at Yamhill downtown), Portland. OR 97205; (800) 228-8657 or (503) 223-6311. Couples $50 to $85, singles $45 to $75. Major credit cards. Very well maintained smaller hotel with TV movies, phones, room refrigerators; quiet location near downtown. **Mallory Dining Room** serves American fare 6:30 a.m. to 9 p.m., dinners $11 to $16; full bar service.

Portland Inn ● ⌂⌂⌂ $$$ ∅
1414 SW Sixth Ave. (at Clay), Portland, OR 97205; (800) 648-6440 or (503) 221-1611. Couples $72 to $82, singles $62 to $72. Major credit cards. Nicely maintained downtown hotel; 175 rooms with TV, phones; pool. **Portland Bar & Grill** serves American fare 6:30 a.m. to 10 p.m., dinners $7 to $14; full bar service.

Red Lion Lloyd Center ● ⌂⌂⌂ $$$$
1000 NE Multnomah (opposite Lloyd Center), Portland, OR 97232; (800) 547-8010 or (503) 281-6111. Couples $79 to $160, singles $79 to $140, suites $199 to $485. Major credit cards. Sleekly modern 576-room hotel with TV movies, phones and other amenities; some rooms with wet bars and spa tubs. Pool, exercise room; airport shuttle. Three **restaurants** serving American and Mexican fare, 6 a.m. to midnight; full bar service.

Shilo Inn Lloyd Center ● ⌂⌂ $$$ ∅
1506 NE Second Ave. (I-5 exit 302A), Portland, OR 97232; (800) 222-2244 or (503) 231-7665. Couples $61 to $69, singles $53 to $61. Major credit cards. A 44-room motel with TV movies, room phones, continental breakfast; sauna, laundromat.

Rooms under $50 a night

Cameo Motel ● ⌂ $$ ∅
4111 NE 82nd Ave. (at Sandy), Portland, OR 97220; (503) 288-5981. Couples $34 to $42, singles $29. Major credit cards. Well-kept 40-unit motel with TV, room phones and refrigerators. Adjacent **Cameo and Sirloin Restaurant** serves from 6:30 a.m. to 8 p.m.; dinners $8 to $10; no alcohol.

Midtown Motel ● ⌂ $
1415 NE Sandy Blvd. (at 14th Avenue), Portland, OR 97232; (503) 234-0316. Couples $30 to $41, singles $22 to $32, kitchenettes $34 to $41. Major credit cards. A 40-unit motel with TV movies and room phones; some rooms with refrigerators and microwaves. Near Convention Center.

St. Francis Hotel ● ⌂ $ ∅
1110 SW Eleventh Ave. (at Main downtown), Portland, OR 97205; (503) 223-2161. Couples $30 to $48, singles $28 to $35. MC/VISA. Simply furnished 25-room residence hotel that takes overnighters. No room TV or phones. **Dining Room** serves breakfast, lunch and dinner, no alcohol. Smoke-free lobby and dining area.

Downtown Value Inn ● ⌂ $$ ∅
415 SW Montgomery (between Fourth and Fifth), Portland, OR 97201. Couples $36 to $46, singles $33 to $40. MC/VISA. A 22-unit motel with TV and room phones; near Civic Auditorium.

WHERE TO CAMP
Obviously, you won't find a lot of campgrounds in Oregon's metropolitan core (despite its urban forests). However, several parks on the outskirts provide places to plant your RV.

Jantzen Beach RV Park ● *1503 N. Hayden Island Dr., Portland, OR 97217; (503) 289-7626. RV sites from $16 to $22. Reservations accepted;*

MC/VISA. Full hookups, some shaded sites and pull-throughs; showers, laundry, pool, rec room and playground. On an island in the Columbia River; take exit 308 off I-5 north of Portland.

Oxbow Park • *3010 SE Oxbow Parkway, Gresham, OR 97080; (503) 663-4708. RV and tent sites, $7. No reservations or credit cards.* County park in a wooded area with swimming, boating, shore fishing and nature trails. Mostly shaded sites; no hookups or showers; pit potties. East of Portland; take Lewis & Clark/Division Street exit from I-205 and go east 13 miles on Division to Oxbow Parkway.

Portland Fairview RV Park • *21401 E. Sandy Blvd. (U.S. 30), Troutdale, OR 97060; (503) 661-1047. RV sites; full hookups $18. Reservations accepted.* All pull-throughs, some shaded. Showers, laundry, creek, pool, horseshoe pits, lawns. East of Portland; take Sandy Boulevard exit 15 from I-84 and go northwest on Sandy a third of a mile.

Portland Meadows RV Park • *222 NE Gertz Rd., Portland, OR 97211; (503) 285-1617. RV sites, full hookups $20. Reservations accepted.* Some pull-throughs and shaded sites; showers, mini-mart, laundry. North of Portland; take Columbia Boulevard exit off I-5 and follow signs.

Rolling Hills Mobile Terrace • *20145 NE Sandy Blvd., Troutdale, OR 97060; (503) 666-7282. RV and tent sites; from $16. Reservations accepted.* Some pull-throughs and shaded sites; showers, cable TV, lounge, pool, laundry; restaurant and mini-mart adjacent. East of Portland, take Sandy Boulevard exit 15 from I-84 and go northwest just under a mile.

Sauvie Cove • *31421 NW Reeder Rd., Sauvie Island, Portland, OR 97231; (503) 621-9741. RV and tent sites; $12 a day for water and electric. Reservations accepted.* Small campground near marina, just off Columbia River, ten miles northwest of Portland. Coin laundry, showers,'mini-mart.

Town & Country RV Park • *9911 SE 82nd Ave., Portland, OR 97266; (503) 771-1040. RV sites with full hookups $14.75, water and electric $12.50. Reservations accepted.* Some pull-throughs; some shaded spaces. Showers, coin laundry, some supplies. Take exit 14 from I-205, go west .7 mile on Sunnyside Road, north on SE 82nd for 1.3 miles.

Trailer Park of Portland • *6645 Nyberg Rd., Tualatin, OR 97062; (503) 692-0225. RV sites; full hookups $16.50. Reservations accepted; MC/VISA.* Grassy sites, some shaded; showers, laundry, RV supplies, playground and horseshoe pits, fishing on adjacent Tualatin River. South of Portland, take Nyberg Road exit 269 from I-5, just north of I-205 interchange.

Side tripping

If you're interested in an urban vacation with rural fringes offering lots of scenery, Portland is an ideal base of operations. The city is rimmed with woods, wineries, historic spots and other lures, reached within an hour or so by outbound freeway.

The most famous route out of Portland is the **Mount Hood/Columbia Gorge Loop.** It's required driving for just about anyone vacationing in Portland with the family sedan, an RV or a rental car. You can get a detailed driving map at the **Portland/Oregon Visitors Association** at 26 SW Salmon St., or contact **Hood River County Chamber of Commerce,** Port Marina Park, Hood River, OR 97031; (503) 386-2000 or the **Mt. Hood Area Chamber of Commerce,** P.O. Box 158, Welshes, OR 97067; (503) 622-3017. The **American Automobile Association** also puts out a

Mount Hood Loop Highway map for its members. The Portland office (the Automobile Club of Oregon) is at 600 SW Market Street at Broadway.

We cover this noted loop in detail as we travel the Columbia River Corridor in Chapter 7. Meanwhile, here are several other interesting loop drives out of the City of Roses:

Urban forest tour • *About 15 miles; allow a morning or an afternoon. It's best to get a detailed city map to help guide you.* This tour follows a wooded ridge along Forest Park and through Washington Park, offering some nice views of the city.

From downtown, head west on NW Lovejoy, which becomes Cornell Road. Turn right at a stop sign (remaining on Cornell), pass through a couple of tunnels and you emerge onto a high ridge with tree shrouded homes and occasional glimpses of the city. As you enter **Macleay Park,** you'll see the **Audubon Nature Store** (5151 NW Cornell Rd., 292-6855), which we mentioned in the hiking section above. Here, you can pick up maps and trails into Macleay and other parks, and visit the **Wildlife Restoration Center** where wounded critters are nursed back to health.

Forest Park, the world's largest urban woodland, extends eight miles from here. To enter this realm, turn left onto NW 53rd Drive, just beyond the Audubon center. Otherwise, stay on Cornell until you hit a four-way stop. Turn right onto Skyline Boulevard and follow it along the southwestern edge of the park. **Skyline Memorial Gardens** on you left offers some fine city views westward, toward Hillsboro.

If you stay on Skyline Drive, you'll drop down out of the hills, so do a U-turn at **Skyline Tavern** and return to the four-way stop. Continue straight ahead, remaining on Skyline and perhaps pause at a turnout on your right for the **Surveyor's Monument.** A short hike takes you to this marker, from which all the lands of Oregon were sectionalized. It was established in 1851. Continue on Skyline to the road to **Pittock Mansion,** which is certainly worth a visit if you haven't already done so.

Beyond the mansion, follow the **Washington Park** sign to the right for all of the attractions we described above: the Japanese Garden, International Rose Test Gardens, Hoyt Arboretum, World Forestry Center and Metro Washington Park Zoo. The main park road passing between the zoo and forestry center deposits you on Freeway 26, which provides a quick return to downtown Portland. Or you can blend into our next tour.

Willamette River and historic Oregon tour • *About 80 miles; plan a full day for this one. A detailed Portland area map will be useful in steering you through this course.* From downtown, follow one-way Broadway south and fork to the right (Barbur Boulevard/Ross Island Bridge sign) as you cross Freeway 26 overpass. Within two blocks, swing to the right, following the Terwilliger Boulevard sign. After a quarter of a mile, turn left at a stoplight onto Terwilliger and follow it up through wooded **Terwilliger Boulevard Park,** past the strikingly modern structures of the **Oregon Health Sciences University** buildings.

From this winding, wooded hillside drive, you'll catch nice views of the Willamette River and the spreading suburbs beyond. You'll have to stay alert to stay with Terwilliger because it take a couple of tricky turns. Its passage across Barbur Boulevard about three miles from the park is rather kinky, for instance; stay in the center lane to stay with it. Just beyond, you cross over I-5, then after a mile, you must veer to the left to avoid getting peeled off

Chugging out of yesterday, the old Canby Ferry carries travelers across the Willamette River below Portland.
— Don W. Martin

onto Boones Ferry Road. A short distance beyond, fork right to avoid being funneled into Lewis and Clark College. Through all of this, you drive through a mix of suburb and attractive parklands, with occasional river glimpses. Large **Tryon Creek State Park** offers miles of hiking trails in a virtual wilderness surrounded by suburbia.

Just below the park, Terwilliger bumps into State Highway 43 (State Street), which delivers you to the attractive residential community of **Lake Oswego.** A left turn onto A Avenue will take you to the **Lake Oswego Country Club** and some of the nicest homes in the Portland area. To loop the lake, turn left onto Mountain Boulevard, left again onto Lake View Boulevard, and then another left onto South Shore Boulevard.

Back on the main road, keep pressing south along Highway 43, which is now Willamette Drive. You go through wooded suburbs, past **Mary S. Young State Park.** Cross under I-205 and veer to the left into the heart of historic **Oregon City.** We explored Oregon's oldest city in detail in the last chapter. You'll cross an old bridge over the river, headed directly for Oregon City's famous cliff face elevator. Turn right down Main Street, then left at the 99-E sign at Fifth Street. From here, head south on Highway 99-E, past **Willamette River Falls** to the attractive country town of **Canby.** Midway between the two towns on your left is a good lunch stop, **Pearson's Tavern,** a Mexican-American restaurant housed in a 1934 bungalow. We describe it in the Canby section of the previous chapter.

Approaching Canby, look for the **Clackamas County Fairgrounds** sign and turn right onto A Street for the **Depot Museum,** also covered in the previous chapter. It's an attractive small archive housed in the old Canby railroad depot. Just beyond is **Aurora,** whose colony museum we visited in the chapter before. Before continuing on to Aurora, you may want to cross one of two remaining Willamette River cable ferries. To reach it, take Third Street a few blocks south from the Canby Museum, turn right onto Holly Street and follow signs past dahlia fields and blackberry vines to the free, five-car **Canby Ferry.** Then return to Highway 99-E for your Aurora visit.

Your last stop on this lengthy tour is **Champoeg State Park**, where the political foundations of Oregon were laid. We visited it in the "Eugene to Portland via 99-W" section of the previous chapter. To get there from Aurora, follow signs to I-5, cross over the freeway and follow more signs to the park.

Washington County Winery Tour ● *About 70 miles; allow a day.* This tour is best done with the *Wineries of Washington County* brochure, available at the visitors bureau. If you don't have it, don't blame us when you get lost, since these wineries are widely scattered. Also, the tour is best taken on a weekend, since a couple of the tasting rooms are closed weekdays.

This route takes you through some of state's most attractive farming areas, over wooded ridges and past U-pick orchards, berry patches and roadside stands. To begin, head west from Portland on Freeway 26 (the Sunset Highway). After about 25 miles, turn left onto Highway 6, heading toward the farm hamlet of **Banks.** From here, blue and white directional signs point the way to the wineries. However, there are some gaps, so plan on getting lost a couple of times. Have patience and enjoy the countryside.

In Banks, turn left onto Highway 47, then right on Greenville Road, left on Thatcher Kansas City Road and quickly right onto Clapshaw Hill Road— all the while being aimed by those blue signs. With luck, you'll wind up at **Tualatin Vineyards** on Seavy Road (357-5005); it's open weekdays 10 to 4 and weekends noon to 5.

Return now to Thatcher Kansas City Road and turn right, headed toward **Forest Grove.** Watch for a sign to David Hill Road to the right, which you'll follow up a wooded hill, offering sweeping views of this patchwork farm country. Your destination is **Laurel Ridge Winery,** (359-5436), open daily noon to 5. Retrace your route on David Hill, turn right, go south toward **Forest Grove** and pick up Highway 47 on the edge of town. Continue south for about a mile until a sign directs you toward **Montinore Vineyards** at 3663 SW Dilley Rd. (359-5012). It's open daily noon to 5 May through October and weekends only the rest of the year.

From Montinore, reverse yourself, heading back toward Forest Grove. Short of the town, fork right onto a bypass, following signs toward Highway 8 and **Hillsboro.** Pass through this attractive suburb of 37,000, and go right onto Highway 219. Head south for about five miles, watching for Burkhalter Road and signs directing you to **Oak Knoll Winery** at 29700 SW Burkhalter (648-8188). It's open daily noon to 5.

Continue beyond the winery, go right onto Rood Bridge Road at a stop sign, then left onto Highway 10 toward **Beaverton.** After about five miles, you'll reach the tiny town of **Hazelton.** Turn right onto Grabhorn Road and follow it south to **Cooper Mountain Vineyards** (649-0027), open weekends noon to 5. This takes you over a high ridge with stellar views of this attractive countryside.

Driving south on Grabhorn, you drop down off the ridge and go left at a T-intersection onto Tile Flat Road. After less than a mile, go left again onto Scholls Ferry Road (Highway 210), then right after a mile or so onto Vandermost Road. With luck, you're at **Ponzi Vineyards,** (628-1227), open weekends noon to 5. From here, Highway 210 takes you to **Tigard,** and I-5 will return you quickly to Portland.

Chapter Five

THE SOUTH COAST

State parks, seagulls and sand dunes

ONE MUST REACH deeply into the drawer of adjectives to adequately describe the Oregon Coast. Basaltic sea cliffs, wooded mountains, river estuaries, old lighthouses and even older towns, and curious weather patterns combine to create the state's most varied region.

If you don't like the weather, wait a few minutes and it will change.

If you're tired of the scenery, drive a short distance and it, too, will change.

Nature was generous in the creation of this coast. Colliding plates rumpled the land and built mountain ranges at water's edge. The offshore Japanese current brought warm, moisture-laden clouds to soak and cloak the mountains with thick conifer stands and lush undergrowth. A dozen rivers cut deep canyons through the mountains, then slowed to form tidal estuaries rich with wildlife. River sand, washed to sea and then back to land, formed miles of sensuously curved sand dunes. Basaltic plugs of old volcanoes marched into the surf to form irregular colonnades of seastacks.

Men have been less generous, contributing saltwater taffy shops, dinosaur parks, petting zoos, wax museums and buzzing squadrons of dune buggies. However, they've been environmental heroes as well as villains, setting aside many parcels for parks and wild areas. Oregon has preserved the entire shoreline for perpetual public use and created the greatest concentration of parklands in the world.

A glimpse at an Oregon map will reveal a coastline wonderfully cluttered with state parks. The dozens of preserves offer campgrounds, picnic sites, vista points, hiking and fishing areas. The parks shelter rainforests, river es-

TRIP PLANNER

WHEN TO GO ● September through mid-October is a good time to explore the southern Oregon Coast. You'll suffer a few museum closings but what the hey. There are no exceptional ones here, anyhow. Fall offers some of the coast's best weather, with crisp, clear and occasional wind-free days. It's also dungeness crab season and low tides provide fine clamming. If you're a salmon fisherman, you can get in on the fall runs up the estuaries.

WHAT TO SEE ● The 26-mile scenic coastal stretch between Brookings and Gold Beach, particularly Natural Bridge Cove and Cape Sebastian viewpoint, Prehistoric Gardens above Gold Beach, charmingly weathered old Port Orford, Cape Blanco light and state park, Old Town Bandon, formal gardens at Shore Acres State Park and the view from Cape Arago.

WHAT TO DO ● Hike or bike some or all of the Oregon Coast Trail and the Oregon Coast Bike Route; ride a jet boat up the Rogue River to Agness; haul in a salmon at one of the river estuaries; scope out the sea birds at Oregon Islands National Wildlife Refuge off Cape Blanco. Also, nibble Cajun cheddar at the Bandon Cheese Factory; watch the fall cranberry harvest near Bandon; hike the nature trails of South Slough National Estuarine Preserve below Charleston; walk the seacliff trail between Cape Arago and Sunset Bay state parks near; take a sand hike at Oregon Dunes NRA's Oregon Dunes Overlook north of Winchester Bay.

Useful contacts

Bandon Chamber of Commerce, P.O. Box 1515, Bandon, OR 97411; (503) 347-9616.

Brookings-Harbor Chamber of Commerce, P.O. Box 940, Brookings, OR 97415; (503) 469-3181.

Bay Area Chamber of Commerce, P.O. Box 210, Coos Bay, OR 97420; (800) 824-8486 or (503) 269-0215.

Charleston Information Center, P.O. Box 5735, Charleston, OR 97420; (503) 888-2311.

Gold Beach Chamber of Commerce, 1225 S. Ellensburg Ave., Gold Beach, OR 97444; (800) 525-2334 or (503) 247-7526.

Lower Umpqua Chamber of Commerce, P.O. Box 11-B, Reedsport, OR 97467; (800) 247-2155 in Oregon only, and (503) 271-3495.

North Bend Information Center, 1380 Sherman Ave., North Bend, OR 97459; (503) 756-4613.

Oregon Dunes National Recreation Area, 855 Highway Ave., Reedsport, OR 97467; (503) 271-3611.

Southern Oregon Coast radio stations

KURY-AM, 910, Brookings—top 40, oldies and news
KINX-AM, Eureka, Calif.—News and sports
KRED-AM, 1480, Eureka, Calif.—country and some pops
KRED-FM, 92.3, Eureka, Calif.—rock and pops
KVO-FM, 97.9, Crescent City—country
KYCT-FM, 105.5, Coos Bay—pop music, Christian music
KHAQ-FM, 90.5, Arcata, Calif.—National Public Radio
KGBR-FM, 92.7, Gold Beach—country, easy listening, oldies
KOOS-FM, 94.9, Coos Bay—country, including oldies
KYTT-FM, 98.7, Coos Bay—Christian radio
KBBR-FM, 107.3, North Bend—light rock & oldies
KSBA-FM, 88.5, Coos Bay—National Public Radio
KBBR-AM, 1340, Coos Bay—country

tuaries, endless miles of beaches and sand dunes, lighthouses, forts and other historic sites.

The federal government is involved, too. Its Siskiyou and Siuslaw (*Sigh-OOS-law*) national forests cover the coastal mountainous, offering camping, hiking and fishing. Two other federal reserves have been established here—Oregon Dunes National Recreation area along the central coast and the lesser known South Slough National Estuarine Sanctuary below Coos Bay.

All of these visitor lures are stitched together by a remarkable piece of engineering called the Coast Highway, and several slender bridges that stride across wide estuaries and harbors. Highway 101 reaches from Mexico to Canada and Oregon's section was the most difficult to build. It is therefore the most dramatically interesting to drive.

Although much of the coastline is preserved in parks, it is by no means a wilderness. Its parklands are among the most used in the state. Between them, small towns line much of the highway, with strung-out business districts of motels, RV parks, curio shops and restaurants.

You'll find some unpopulated stretches between the towns, offering awesome vistas of crescent beaches with their scalloped surf and seastacks. Further, a short drive inland will almost instantly remove you from civilization. Towns are scarce and usually small on the many highways extending into mainland Oregon.

The weather

When you come to the coast, come dressed for anything. Although freezing is rare and snowfall is almost nonexistent, it's often chilly, foggy and blustery. When we began researching this chapter, our first day dawned cloudy, then it was sunny until mid-afternoon. The clouds, which lurked offshore like restless ghosts, returned in the company of a howling, cold wind. By sunset, the wind and clouds vanished and we were admiring a starry sky. The next morning, our campsite was wrapped in a silent, dripping fog.

This is the wettest part of Oregon, with rainfall ranging from more than 100 inches in Port Orford on the central coast to around 75 in Brookings. Inland rainforests get as much as 150 inches. Most coastal rain falls in the winter, with sunny dry spells between storms. Weatherwise, the best times to visit are spring and fall.

Summer weather is difficult to predict. Sunny days are common, although cloud banks often stand offshore. When summer temperatures rise in the Willamette and Rogue valleys—not an uncommon event—the clouds are drawn inshore, caressing the coast. Generally, you can escape this gloom with a short drive inland.

Incidentally, if you plan to swim on in coastal waters, bring a wetsuit. Although the offshore Japanese current is rather warm, the surf at the beach is in the chilly 40s to 50s. However, the calm water in many estuaries is quite swimmable, and several riverside parks offer swimming areas.

Dining

Not surprisingly, the coast abounds with seafood restaurants. Most seem stamped from the same mold, with similar menus—fish and chips, shrimp, scallops and clam strips, often fresh from the freezer and deep fried. Seafood linguine is a popular number, as well. Of course, most offer freshly-caught fish, usually salmon, sole, red snapper and halibut. If you like your fish lightly done, it couldn't hurt to mention this to your server.

If you're a shellfish fan, come between October and March when succulent dungeness crabs are in peak season. World-famous Yaquina Bay oysters, grown commercially, are available in restaurants the year around and you often can get razor clams, small and tasty bay shrimp and large and tasty crayfish. Fresh salmon is a specialty, since the big fish caught in many of the rivers and estuaries.

We like some of the smaller seafood cafès, which often are tied to fish markets. They offer fresh fish with low prices and ambiance to match. You won't get an ocean view, but you often get good food for the price. Our first coastal meal, a fish and chips lunch at the small Wharfside Restaurant at Brookings Harbor, was one of the best we've had.

Incidentally, blackberries ripen in abundance on the coast from mid-July through August. Many restaurants and bakeries feature them in pies, tarts, shortcake and turnovers. You can pick your own dessert fresh from roadside vines, even in some of the small towns. We took frequent blackberry breaks during our slow cruise up the coast.

Lodging

Most of the digs along the coast are small motels, many with ocean views. There are a few luxury resorts, such as the AAA five diamond rated Salishan Lodge at Gleneden Beach, the elegantly rustic Tu Tu' Tun Lodge upriver from Gold Beach and the Inn at Spanish Head in Lincoln City.

Obviously, summer reservations should be made early, particularly on weekends. However, there is a startling abundance of motels and inns along the coast, and we always saw vacancy signs, even on weekends. Of course, selections will be more limited without reservations.

Camping

The Oregon Coast is the happy campers' dream. It boasts the largest concentration of campgrounds and RV parks in the state. Further, there are scores of turnouts where RVers can pull over and enjoy lunch with a view.

State park campgrounds fill up very fast, and sites are difficult to find on summer weekends. Reservations are accepted from Memorial Day weekend through Labor Day weekend at these beach parks: Fort Stevens, Cape Lookout, Devil's Lake, Beverly Beach, South beach, Beachside, Jessie M. Honeyman, Sunset Bay and Harris Beach.

If you seek access to these pleasant places—most with widely-spaced, sheltered campsites—make reservations well in advance. They must be made by mail or in person, directly with the individual parks. Pick up forms at chambers of commerce, tourist information centers, state parks, motor vehicle and state police offices. Or contact the **State Parks & Recreation Department,** 525 Trade St. SE, Salem, OR 97310, (503) 378-7488, for a parks brochure and reservations form. A call to the state's **Campsite Information Center** at (800) 452-5687 (within the state, in summer from 8 to 4:30) will provide up-to-the-minute information on campsite availability. However, you can't reserve a site by phone.

If you don't have a spot reserved, hit the campground of your choice early in the day and hope, since some sites are withheld from the reservation system. Also, you can find sites at the many national forest campgrounds, which are usually a bit inland. Further, the coast has so many commercial RV parks that you generally can find space, even late in the day. Don't expect tree-shaded, tucked-away sites, however. Most commercial parks are little more than glorified parking lots, but you already know that if you're an RVer.

Here's a bit of irony: Many commercial RV parks are right on the beach or at least offer ocean views, while the more desirable state park campgrounds are rarely on the water.

Biking & hiking

This is probably the best biking area in the state, as well as one of its best hiking regions. Many communities have bike routes, and hiking trails abound in the state parks and national forests. Further, special biker and hiker routes extend the full length of the coastline.

The **Oregon Coast Bike Route** travels 367 miles from Astoria to Brookings—mostly on the shoulder of Highway 101. Although the bike lane isn't separated from traffic in most areas, the Department of Transportation is working to widen the shoulder every year. If you want to pedal the full length, officials recommend riding north to south because of prevailing northwest winds. Most of the scenic turnouts are on the ocean side, and most bike lane improvements are being made on that shoulder.

If you're in good shape, you can probably pedal the length of the coast in six to eight days. Motels are plentiful, and several state park campgrounds have hiker-biker sites with showers for just $2 a night. Reservations aren't needed, since these are essentially tent-pitching areas. Free copies of the *Oregon Coast Bike Route Map* are available at various visitors bureaus, or by contacting the Bikeway Program Manager, Department of Transportation, Room 200, Transportation Building, Salem, OR 97310; (503) 378-3432.

Roughly paralleling the bike route but off the highway is the **Oregon Coast Trail**, stretching 360 miles—with a few urban interruptions. It's a beautiful route, traveling through thick forests, climbing into lofty headlands and swinging down to the beach. The *Oregon Coast Trail Guide* also is available at various visitor centers, or contact the Trails Coordinator, Oregon State Parks, 525 SE Trade St., Salem, OR 97310; (503) 378-5012. Like the bike map, it details routes and shows locations of hiker-biker campgrounds. It also points out urban bypasses, which generally direct hikers down to the beachfront of coastal communities.

Fishing

Many coastal towns offer deep sea charter boats, and we list these in the paragraphs ahead. However, you don't have to bounce about the briny to catch fish here. Harbor and jetty fishing or surf-casting may produce your dinner of rockfish, ling cod, snapper, bass and—with luck—possibly even a salmon. Bays, estuaries and upriver streams are popular for salmon, trout and steelhead fishing. Many communities offer boat rentals and fishing guide service. We list some of these, and you can check local chambers of commerce for others.

Clamming

Clamming is permitted the year-around on Oregon's coast, unlike California, which has a closed summer season because of a toxin that may develop in mollusks in warm water. You're undoubtedly aware that clamming is a low-tide sport. Most fishing and sporting goods stores have tidal books, which also offer tips on catching assorted mollusks.

A license isn't required for clamming, but there are daily limits: 24 razor clams, 36 softshell varieties and a total of 20 bay clams including a maximum of 12 gapers. The bay clam list includes butter and littleneck, cockles and gapers. Other limits are 72 mussels, 24 scallops and three dungeness crabs. You can rent crab rings or pots at some harbor bait and tackle shops.

These limits and the year-around season may change, so check before you dig or dip. For specifics on fishing and clamming, get a copy of *Oregon Sportfishing Regulations* from the **Department of Fish and Wildlife**, 2501 SW First St. (P.O. Box 59), Portland, OR 97207; (503) 229-5400.

Whale watching

Watching the magnificent gray whales migrate each year is one of the more pleasantly benign sports along the coastline. With a good pair of binoculars, or an alert naked eye, you can witness this annual rite of passage from several sites.

The whales migrate in a gentle arc from Alaska to the lagoons of Baja California. They come closest to the coast at promontories such as the **Port Orford Harbor, Paradise Point Wayside** just below **Cape Blanco**, the cape itself, off **Cape Foulweather, Depoe Bay** and below **Umpqua Lighthouse** north of Winchester Bay. Graphics at a whale-watching station near Umpqua Light discuss whale specifics and tell you how to spot them. Some commercial outfits offer offshore whale-watching cruises for a closer look; inquire at chambers of commerce, harbors and tackle shops.

Best whale-watching periods are December through mid-January, when they head south to Mexico, and mid-March through April on their return leg. Nearly extinct a few decades ago, the great and gentle beasts now number about 20,000. Longer than a Greyhound bus and weighing a sprightly 45 tons, they are among the most intelligent of nature's beasts. Their 12,000-mile round trip is the longest migration of any mammal.

What to watch for? The vapory "spout" as whales surface to exhale. You'll see their shiny backs as they cruise along the surface between dives, and catch a glimpse of their giant flukes when they sound. With luck, you might see one breach, leaping almost clear of the water and then falling back with a mighty splash. Occasionally they "spy hop," thrusting their immense conical heads above water briefly—presumably for a look around.

However, most of these antics occur when they reach their winter breeding grounds in Mexico. For the most part, they glide gracefully along, traveling solo or in pods of as many as a dozen. Scientists say they don't eat during this long migration. On the return leg, you'll likely see mothers traveling with their young. With a 12-month gestation cycle, the whales conceive during their Mexico vacation, give birth there the following year, then repeat the process. Presumably, a frisky female stays perpetually pregnant.

Bird watching

Many offshore seastacks and mini-isles are part of **Oregon Islands National Wildlife Refuge,** providing nesting sites and shelter for hundreds of thousands of sea birds.

At various promontories and waysides along the coast, you'll see signs that indicate these preserves and identify the critters living thereon. With binoculars, you can bring in cormorants, terns, western gulls, murres, tufted puffins and pigeon guillemots. Sea lions likely will be lounging at the base of these offshore sanctuaries. Incidentally, you should know that state law forbids climbing on all offshore promontories. Among the better sea bird-watching areas are **Cape Blanco** above Port Orford, **Sea Lion Caves** above Florence and **Yaquina Head** just north of Newport.

Go fly a...

With the coast's near constant winds and open beaches, kite flying is a popular pastime. Many communities have kite shops, where you can buy everything from the standard diamond-with-tail to elaborate Asian dragon and box kites. A firm called Catch the Wind has outlets in several coastal towns. Need to vent your frustrations? Learn to manipulate a fighting kite and see if you can sever the string of your companion's flyer.

Several communities have annual kite festivals, including Yachats, Newport, Lincoln City, Rockaway Beach, Manzanita and Cannon Beach.

Beachcombing

Oregon's restless beaches yield a rich trove of sunbleached driftwood, washed-ashore coral and sea fossils and—in areas near stream outlets—agates, jasper and other semi-precious stones. Driftwood may be gathered for artistic purposes or for fires in many areas, although fires are *never* allowed within driftwood piles.

Local chambers of commerce can direct you to the best beachcombing and driftwood-collecting areas.

Now that we've thoroughly introduced you to this wonderland called the Oregon Coast, let's begin exploring it, traveling south to north. Because there was so much to compile and thus so much for you to read, we've divided the coast into two chapters. Each can easily occupy a one or two-week vacation.

We begin where Oregon's section of the coast begins, at Brookings just north of the California border. We'll break this chapter north of Oregon Dunes National Recreation Area, near the geographic middle of the Emerald State's seashore.

Brookings

Population: 4,465   **Elevation 129 feet**

Approaching on U.S. 101 from California, you'll lose the ocean at Crescent City. Smith River, the last California town, calls itself the Easter lily capital of the world—a claim that is either disputed or shared by Brookings. From 70 to 90 percent of the world's commercial supply is produced on the broad coastal plain between them.

At **Last Chance Liquors,** a couple of miles short of the border, you might want to stock up on the hard stuff to avoid paying state-inflated Oregon booze prices. After crossing the border and before reaching Brookings, the first item of interest is the **world's largest cypress tree.** It's on your right, behind a real estate office. A sign offers its impressive statistics—a 30-foot girth and 107-foot crown. Behind it is the **Chetco Valley Museum** in an 1857 clapboard cottage; (503) 469-6651. Open Wednesday-Sunday, noon to five, the small facility offers the usual pioneer artifacts and a nicely-furnished living room and kitchen setup. The area's oldest structure, it once functioned as a way station operated by one Harrison Blake. Admission is $1 for adults and 25 cents for kids.

Your Oregon Coast far has not been particularly dramatic thus far—except in spring when the lilies are in bloom. Brookings, on the upper edge of the coastal plain, is an ordinary-looking town with its business district strung out along the highway.

What *is* impressive here is the climate; it's the mildest along the coast. Warm air drawn from the often hot Rogue River Valley mixes with cool ocean breezes to produce what the chamber of commerce gleefully calls a "banana belt." The climate is temperate the year around, with 70s common in January and July. It does rain its brains out, however, about 90 inches a year.

A few locals have planted palm trees, which are doing quite well. No bananas, however. Not surprisingly, nearly half the population is comprised of retirees lured from less benign climes.

Brookings had a simple beginning. The seat of Curry County and shopping hub of the south coast started life as the Brookings Box Company in 1914. With its location at the mouth of the Chetco River, it was bound to thrive. It grew quietly and contentedly, pretty much ignored by the rest of the world until a bold Japanese aviator put in a brief appearance. On September 9, 1942, Nobuo Fujita flew a submarine-launched seaplane a short distance inland and dropped a pair of incendiary bombs (see box). They singed only seven trees but the event put the town briefly in the world spotlight. It was the first time mainland America had been hit by an "air raid."

Twenty years later, in an event that seemed scripted for a movie, Fujita was invited to Brookings' annual Azalea Festival. He presented the town with his personal samurai sword, which he had carried in his plane for good luck. The bombing site, marked by a monument, is about an hour's drive inland, off the South Bank Chetco River Road. For directions, pick up a brochure from the Brookings-Harbor Chamber of Commerce or from the Chetco Ranger District in Brookings.

Before you hit town, you'll encounter the unincorporated hamlet of **Harbor** which is essentially that—a harbor complex at the mouth of the Chetco River. Follow signs down to the harbor at Harbor and load up on brochures at the **Brookings-Harbor Chamber of Commerce** visitor information center. It's at 16330 Lower Harbor Road; (503) 469-3181; open weekdays 9 to 5, plus 9 to 1 on Saturday in summer. The harbor is a pleasant spot, with the usual small-craft basin, seafood restaurants, a tackle shop and markets featuring fresh-caught fish. During crab season, October through March, you can buy a steaming dungeness fresh from the pot. You can book deep sea fishing trips here as well.

Continuing across the Chetco River, you'll be greeted by a small botanical garden, added in the summer of 1992 to brighten Brookings' entry. Just to your right on North Bank Road is **Azalea State Park,** a picnic area rimmed by huge wild azaleas; their peak bloom is April through June.

Downtown Brookings is just beyond, rimming Highway 101. Although most of its buildings are ordinary, the large, weathered **Central Mall** on the left should catch your eye. This structure was built in 1915 as administrative headquarters for the firm that started the box company here. It now houses several shops, a restaurant and a rather casual **museum** in the basement. Located adjacent to a Coldwell Banker real estate office, it's open whenever the office is staffed, which is during most daylight hours. The rather cluttered, undisciplined collection includes old newspapers, type cases, drag saws and early day photos.

OREGON'S SILENT SIEGE

Everyone knows that America was catapulted into World War II by Japan's surprise bombing of Pearl Harbor. However, one rarely hears about several nuisance attacks directed at the American mainland during the war. Most were centered on the Oregon coast, aimed at burning our forests and disrupting our morale. The strikes ranged from comical to tragic. Three of these attack sites are marked—two on the coast and one between Klamath Falls and Lakeview.

The shelling of Battery Russell

Commander Meiji Tagami's *I-25* was one busy submarine. Cruising off the Oregon Coast during the war, it sank two U.S. tankers and a Russian sub. *That* was a mistake, since Japan wasn't yet at war with the Soviet Union. It also sailed boldly into the mouth of the Columbia River, following a fishing fleet to avoid mine fields, and shelled Battery Russell at Fort Stevens. The attack occurred at first light on Sunday morning, June 21, 1942.

The sub fired 17 rounds, all of which missed their targets, then it submerged and scuttled out of there. Army defenders scrambled out of bed to return fire. Much to their disgust, they were ordered not to shoot because the sub was beyond the range of their antiquated 1903 artillery pieces.

Visitors to present-day Fort Sevens State Park can tour the Battery Russell shelling site. A marker erroneously states that this was the first foreign attack on the U.S. mainland since the War of 1812. It was the second, since another sub, the *I-17*, fired on an oil field near Santa Barbara in February of that year.

The great forest raid

Later, the peripatetic *I-25* launched the first and only air raid against the U.S. mainland in our history. Like several other large Japanese subs, it carried a disassembled seaplane in a special enclosure in its hull. These Yokosuka E-14Y1 float planes normally were used for scouting, but pilot Nobuo Fujita was instructed to fly over the forest near Brookings and drop incendiary bombs.

Fujita made two runs, on September 9 and 29, but the forests were wet with recent rains and no serious fires were started. The first attack burned only seven trees and the second was never located. A monument marks the first site, reached by a short trail. For directions, contact the Chetco Ranger District of Siskiyou National Forest, 555 Fifth Street in Brookings; (503) 469-2196.

The wicked "Windship Weapons"

The third Oregon incident ended in tragedy. During the closing days of the war, a desperate Japan launched 6,000 "balloon bombs" that caught the jet stream and floated over North America. The devilish devices were hung with fragmentation and incendiary bombs to be released by pressure-sensitive aneroid barometer triggers, activated by a change in altitude. They were supposed to explode on impact, starting wildfires.

When U.S. authorities intercepted the first of them, they spread the alarm by word of mouth through schools and churches. By keeping the news out of the press, they hoped Japan would assume the bombs weren't reaching our shores. I recall a scary afternoon in 1944 when the teacher at my small country school near Grants pass warned us to watch for the lethal contraptions.

Although several "Windship Weapons" reached the U.S., none started fires. Most settled to the ground without dropping their payloads, and were disarmed by bomb squads. Others where shot out of the sky by our warplanes. However, one bomb killed five children and a minister's wife after they found it during an outing on Gearhart Mountain in south central Oregon. It exploded after they apparently kicked or dropped it. The site of the only mainland casualties of World War II is marked by a monument. To find it, contact the Bly Ranger District of Fremont National Forest at (503) 353-2427. Bly is midway between Klamath Falls and Lakeview on Highway 140.

Brookings' beachfront is graced with a rather dramatic set of seastacks, which aren't that evident from the town. There is no beachfront drive, although several downtown streets will get you to the surf. Follow Tanbark Avenue, Wharf Street or Mill Beach Road if you feel an urge to beach comb.

Exploring inland

Drives inland along the Chetco River will take you to thick Douglas Fir woodlands, campgrounds and hiking trails of Siskiyou National Forest. North Bank Road delivers you to **Loeb State Park** with camping, picnicking and swimming areas. About half a mile beyond the park is a trailhead for the one-mile **Redwood Nature Trail** through one of America's northernmost groves of Big Trees. Signs mark the rich trove of flora in this rainforest wilderness. If you continue up the road, you can loop over to the Chetco River's south bank for the return to Brookings. The forest service office at 555 Fifth Street will supply you with brochures and maps, including directions to the famous bomb site. It's a couple of blocks east of Highway 101; hours are 7:30 to 4:30 weekdays; (503) 469-2196.

The **Kamiopsis Wilderness,** Oregon's largest primitive area, covering 180,000 acres, can be reached by forest service roads from Brookings. Once an offshore island, this high Klamath Mountains rainforest is virtually unchanged from the last Ice Age. It's a rich repository of rare plants including the insect-eating Darlingtonia, plus old growth stands of Port Orford cedar, redwoods and giant Douglas fir. Roads—and rough ones at that—only nibble at the edges. Rarely-trod hiking trails penetrate further into Oregon's least-disturbed wilderness. If you're game to explore a primeval forest, the Brookings forestry office can provide maps and details.

Immediately north of town, the coastal plain rumples into mountains, and you begin seeing the dramatic seacoast of postcard fame.

☺ **Harris Beach** is the first major state park you'll encounter and one of the more attractive along the coast. Crescent sandy beaches are broken by ranks of craggy seastacks. Picnic tables are terraced above the strand for splendid outdoor dining views. The campground (see below) is just up from the beach. Across the road is the **Oregon Welcome Center,** with pounds of material on the coast and the rest of the state. It's open May through October, Monday-Saturday 8 to 6 and Sunday 9 to 5; (503) 469-4117.

ACTIVITIES

Fishing guides • **Bob Brown's Professional Guide Service,** P.O. Box 443, Brookings, OR 97415, (503) 469-5717; **Dick's Sporthaven Marina,** P.O. Box 2215, Harbor, OR 97415, (503) 469-3301; **Lee Myers Guide Service,** operating out of the Great American Smokehouse, 15657 S. Highway 101, Harbor, OR 97415, (503) 469-6903; **Leta-J Charters,** 97448 North Bank Rd., Harbor, OR 97415; (503) 469-3452.

Guided hikes • The **South Coast Interpreters** conduct walks along the Riverview Nature Trail and Redwood Nature Trail at Loeb State Park. The walks are free but you must register in advance. Contact the Chetco Ranger District office at 555 Fifth Street in Brookings; (503) 469-2196.

ANNUAL EVENTS

For specifics on these, call the Chamber of Commerce at (503) 469-3181.

Beachcombers' Festival in March; exhibits of arts and crafts created from beach flotsam.

Azalea Festival on Memorial Day weekend; the community's major annual event with a parade, floral displays and art exhibits.

Log Show by the Sea in October; loggers' competitions at the harbor.

WHERE TO DINE

Chetco River House • ∆∆ $$

241 Chetco Ave.; (503) 469-7539. American, mostly seafood; wine and beer. Tuesday-Saturday 5:30 to 9. MC/VISA. Attractive old structure on the north bank of the Chetco River, reached by a tree-sheltered lane. The dining room is rather austere, although it offers pleasant river views. Fresh fish is the focus of the menu, plus the usual oysters, scallops prawns and fried fisherman's platter, and a few chickens and chops.

Great American Smokehouse • ∆∆ $$

15657 S. Highway 101; (503) 469-6903. American, mostly seafood; wine and beer. Daily 11 to 9. MC/VISA. Knotty pine nautical café with adjacent shop offering smoked and fresh fish and Oregon specialty foods. The usual seafood entrées, properly poached or broiled, plus a few steaks and chops. Generous dinners include chowder, salad and garlic bread.

Mama's Ristorante Italiano • ∆∆ $

In Central Mall at 703 Chetco Ave. (Highway 101); (503) 469- 7611. Italian; wine and beer. Daily 11 to 11. MC/VISA. Cute bistro with red-checkered table cloths, lace curtains and ceiling fans. Typical Italian fare with several hearty meals under $10, plus a range of pizzas. Specialties include primavera and seafood pastas.

Rubio's Mexican Restaurant • ∆ $

1136 Chetco Ave. (Highway 101); (503) 469-4919. Mexican; wine and beer. Tuesday-Thursday 11 to 9, Friday-Saturday 11 to 9:30, closed Sunday-Monday. MC/VISA. Garish red, yellow and green café with the usual smashed beans and rice dishes; locally known for its home-made salsa. Full meals under $10; umbrella-shaded outdoor patio.

Sporthaven Restaurant • ∆ $$

At the Harbor; (503) 469-3301. American, mostly seafood; full bar service. Sunday-Thursday 5 a.m. to 9 p.m., Friday-Saturday 6 to 10. MC/VISA. Typical family-style café with a few nautical touches, dark woods and Naugahyde booths. Menu is mostly standard seafood, plus a few steaks, prime rib, chicken and chops and some Mexican dishes.

☺ Wharfside Restaurant • ∆∆ $

16362 Lower Harbor Road; (503) 469-7316. Seafood; wine and beer. Tuesday-Sunday 11:30 to 9 (to 9:30 Friday-Saturday), closed Monday. MC/VISA. Small, casual café serving huge portions at low prices. The specialty is deep-fried calamari, prawns or cod with chips, served hot and perfectly crisp. Also several fresh fish entrées and sandwiches. Cozy interior tables and outdoor dining patio.

WHERE TO SLEEP

Beaver State Motel • ⌒⌒ $$$ ∅

437 Chetco Ave. (P.O. Box 7000), Brookings, OR 97415; (503) 469-5361. Couples $52 to $64, singles $45 to $55. MC/VISA. A 17-unit motel on the highway (north end); nicely appointed rooms with TV movies and phones.

Best Western Beachfront Inn • ⌂⌂⌂ $$$

Lower Harbor and Boat Basin roads (P.O. Box 2729), Brookings, OR 97415; (800) 468-4081 or (503) 469-7779. Couples $59 to $84, singles $54 to $74, suites $95 to $160. Major credit cards. Modern, attractive inn at the harbor; all rooms with ocean view. TV movies, room phones, microwaves and refrigerators; swimming pool and spa. Short walk to the beach.

Best Western Brookings Inn • ⌂⌂⌂ $$ ∅

1143 Chetco Ave. (P.O. Box 1139), Brookings, OR 97415; (800) 822-9087 or (503) 469-2173. Couples $42 to $52, singles $37 to $47. Major credit cards. A 68-unit motel; large, attractive rooms with TV movies and phones; some with refrigerators, wet bars and spa tubs. Spa; lobby bar. **Restaurant** serves American fare, 6 a.m. to 10 p.m.; dinners $5 to $13; full bar service.

Bonn Motel • ⌂⌂ $$ ∅

1216 Chetco Ave. (P.O. Box 639), Brookings, OR 97415; (503) 469-2161. Couples $42 to $55, singles $35 to $42, kitchenettes $48 to $75. Major credit cards. A 37-room motel with TV movies, room phones; indoor pool and sauna. Within walking distance of the beach.

Chetco Inn • ⌂⌂ $$

417 Fern St. (P.O. Box 1386), Brookings, OR 97415; (503) 469-5347. Couples $37 to $39 and singles $34 to $36 with private bath; couples $30 to $32 and singles $27 to $29 with shared bath. A 1915 lumber company inn undergoing restoration. Rooms with period furnishings, folk crafts and prints; many with ocean views. Bicycles, horseshoes and croquet.

Pacific Sunset Inn • ⌂⌂ $$$

1144 Chetco Ave. (P.O. Box AL). Brookings, OR 97415; (503) 469-2141. Couples $47 to $62, singles $37 to $47, kitchenettes $62 to $80. Major credit cards. A 40-unit motel with TV movies, phones. **O'Hollowran's Restaurant** serves steak and seafood dinners; $5 to $15; 2 p.m. to 2 a.m.; full bar.

Spindrift Motor Inn • ⌂⌂ $$$ ∅

1215 Chetco Ave. (P.O. Box 6026), Brookings, OR 97415; (800) 292-1171 or (503) 469-5345. Couples $55 to $65, singles $49 to $59. Major credit cards. A 35-unit motel on the highway, north side; attractive rooms with TV movies and phones; fish freezer available. Near the beach.

Westward Motel • ⌂⌂ $$ ∅

Fifth and Moore streets (P.O. Box 1079), Brookings, OR 97415; (503) 469-7471. Couples $38 to $80, singles $28 to $60. Major credit cards. New 32-unit motel with TV movies and room phones; near downtown.

Bed & breakfast inns

☺ Chetco River Inn • ⌂⌂⌂ $$$$ ∅

21202 High Prairie Rd. (17 miles up Chetco River), Brookings, OR 97415; (503) 469-8128. Couples $85, singles $75. Three rooms, private baths; full breakfast. MC/VISA. Secluded "alternate energy" home on the river; 35 acres with swimming, hiking, darts, archery and horseshoes. Attractive cedar interior with Oriental rugs; modern eclectic furnishings.

☺ Holmes Sea Cove Bed & Breakfast • ⌂⌂⌂ $$$$ ∅

17350 Holmes Dr., (two miles north) Brookings, OR 97415; (503) 469-3025. Couples $80 to $95, singles $75 to $90. Three rooms with private baths;

continental breakfast. MC/VISA. Attractive cedar beach house with path to private creekside park and to the nearby beach. Furnished with a mix of antique, nautical and modern; all have ocean view. Guest TV and refrigerator.

Ward House Bed & Breakfast ● ⌂⌂⌂ $$$ ∅
516 Redwood St., Brookings OR 97415; (503) 469-5557. Couples $65 to $75, singles $60 to $70. Three rooms with private baths; full breakfast. Imposing 1917 Craftsman home built by Brookings Lumber Mill president. It features mix of antique and modern furnishings with TV in each room. Parlor with fireplace; spa and sauna; gazebo with an ocean view.

WHERE TO CAMP

Beachfront RV Park ● *16035 Boat Basin Rd., Brookings, OR 97415; (800) 441-0856 (Oregon only) or (503) 469-5867. RV sites only, full hookups $14, water and electric $12, no hookups $7. Reservations accepted; MC/VISA.* Large facility on spit between harbor and ocean; many water-view sites. Not fancy, but it offers laundry, showers, convenience mart and small café.

Harris Beach State Park ● *1655 Highway 101 (two miles north), Brookings, OR 97416; (503) 469-2021. RV and tent sites, full hookups $13, water and electric $12, no hookups $11. Mail reservations accepted (see "Camping" in the introduction above).* Well-spaced, shaded sites in grassy lawn area; barbecues, picnic tables and showers. Short walk to beach.

Loeb State Park ● *Eight miles up North Bank Road on the Chetco River; (503) 469-2021. RV and tent sites, water and electric $12. No reservations.* Attractive riverside spot with sheltered sites, showers, fire pits and barbecues; fishing, swimming and boat ramp.

Portside RV Park ● *16219 Lower Harbor Rd., Harbor, OR 97415; (503) 469-6616. RV sites only, hookups $12 to $14. Reservations accepted; MC/VISA.* New, well-maintained park at the harbor with showers, cable TV, laundry, rec hall, RV supplies; some pull-throughs.

Siskiyou National Forest ● A drive up the Chetco River takes you to several nicely wooded national forest campsites, ranging from $4 to free; some have flush potties but no hookups; most have pit toilets.

Whaleshead RV Park ● *19921 Whaleshead Rd., seven miles north off Highway 101 (P.O. Box J), Brookings, OR 97415; (503) 469-7446. RV sites, full hookups $18 to $20, water and electric $15. Reservations accepted; MC/VISA.* Attractive wooded and terraced sites with decks, some with ocean views; beach access via tunnel. Restaurant, mini-mart, showers, fee cable TV, rec hall, horseshoe pits.

BROOKINGS TO GOLD BEACH

The 26-mile stretch north from Brookings is one of the most dramatically beautiful segments of the entire coastline. Other than Whaleshead RV Park seven miles north (listed above), it's virtually free of commercial development. Various viewpoints, turnouts and picnic pauses along here are segments of **Samuel H. Boardman State Park,** named for the father of Oregon's park system. He served as its first superintendent and acquired many parklands during his tenure from 1929 until 1950.

The highway hugs the ocean along this route, alternately brushing the coast and then climbing to high ridges for awesome vistas. From **Rainbow Rock** viewpoint above Brookings, dozens of offshore nubs poke from the water like the heads of giant stone seals. **Whales Head Beach** just below the RV park, offers surfside picnicking at a sheltered cove. A short distance beyond, **Thomas Creek Bridge** leaps across a steep-walled side canyon. At 354 feet, it's the highest bridge in the state.

☺ At the risk of overdoing superlatives, **Natural Bridge Cove** is one of the coast's most striking viewpoints. A short walk takes you to the **Oregon Coast Trail** and to a footbridge, from where you can see a beautiful, sheltered cove far below with natural arches cut into three monoliths. A *very* steep goat trail, branching from the Coast Trail, takes you through a thick ferny forest down to the arches. Take care here; the cliffs are sheer, the trail is narrow and it's a long drop to the briny.

Pistol River State Park offers a beach access and picnic area framed by more of those dramatic seastacks. A monument discusses one of the last battles in the Rogue Indian War. Several skirmishes occurred here in March of 1865 when the Rogues besieged a settlers' log stronghold—without success. The hamlet of **Pistol River**, offering little more than a general store, is a mile inland.

Beyond Pistol River, basaltic pinnacles rise from the sea like a flooded Stonehenge. **Meyer Creek Beach,** another shore access and picnic area, is tucked among them. From here, U.S. 101 climbs steeply to the headlands of **Cape Sebastian State Park.** A short drive off the highway takes you to a pair of parking areas, both offering impressive views up and down the coast. The vista from the south parking lot is best. If you have lots of time on your hands, you can follow a switchback trail from here, about two miles down to the surf.

The first major promontory on the south coast, Cape Sebastian was named by Spanish navigator Sebastiano Vizcaino when he sailed past this point in 1603. A dizzying 700 feet above the surf, it's one of the Pacific Coast's highest headlands served by a road, rivaled only by the Cape Perpetua lookout to the north (see next chapter).

BROOKINGS TO BANDON

Incidentally, if you long for the deep woods, you can turn inland onto **Carpenterville Road**, a couple of miles north of Brookings, and follow it 20 miles to Pistol River. However, the road travels through inland foothills and you'd miss that stunning coastal scenery. Also, the road is steep, twisting and often bouncy, although paved. It *is* a pretty drive through lush forest. You might do it as a loop, emerging at Pistol River and then heading south on U.S. 101 back to Brookings. That would put you on the proper side of the highway for all of turnouts and ocean vistas.

Gold Beach

Population: 1,585   **Elevation: 60 feet**

The name refers not to the ocean shore, but to the sands of the Rogue River estuary, which were sifted for gold in the middle of the last century. Fifty years later, it was the site of Robert Hume's salmon cannery, one of the largest operations on the coast and for decades the backbone of the town's economy.

The mighty Rogue, which undergoes many personality changes during its trek from the high Cascades, is a tame tidal flat here. The river, not the ocean, is the area's chief attraction. Salmon and steelhead fishing in the Rogue estuary and upriver is legendary—made so by Zane Grey, Jack London, Herbert Hoover, Winston Churchill, Jimmy Carter and a handful of film stars.

Thousands come here each year not to fish, but to ride the jet boats that growl and hammer upstream to the village of **Agness,** and to rapids of the wild and scenic section of the Rogue beyond. Upriver boating started as a mail and passenger service back in 1895, when only the Rogue linked Agness to the outside world. In fact, roads didn't reach the town until well into this century.

As you enter Gold Beach from the south on Highway 101 (which becomes Ellensburg Avenue), you'll note a handy visitor center combo on your right. The **Siskiyou National Forest** and **Gold Beach Chamber of Commerce** share the same office, at 510 S. Ellensburg Ave.; (503) 247-7526. It's open weekdays 8 to 5 and weekends 8 to 4.

A few blocks farther along, at the downtown Curry County Fairgrounds, is the town's archive:

☺ **Curry County Historical Museum** ● *920 S. Ellensburg Ave.; (503) 247-6113. Wednesday-Sunday noon to 5 in summer and Thursday-Sunday noon to 4 the rest of the year. Free; donations appreciated.* This is a rather nicely done archive, tucked into a barnboard building behind the Chowderhead Restaurant. Wall graphics and neat display cases trace the area's history from Native Americans to gold miners, trappers, settlers and salmon catchers and canners. A mock-up miner's cabin is a focal point of the museum, and a photo exhibit recalls ships that once called here (and occasionally ran aground).

The **Gold Beach Summer Theater** is beside the museum, offering a season of comedies and dramas (see "Activities" below). The **Port of Gold Beach** harbor is just beyond downtown, with a small craft marina, seafood cafès, a boat launch and a couple of fishing outfitters. This also is home to one of two major jet boat operators in the area, **Jerry's Rogue Jets.**

☺ The ticket office houses the small **Rogue River Museum,** which traces the stream's history from its geologic formation to the pioneer boaters

Driftwood creates scattered sculptures along the southern Oregon Coast.

—Betty Woo Martin

who first challenged its rapids. Among its exhibits are photos of avid fisherman Zane Grey and a woodland diorama of stuffed critters one might encounter in the Rogue wilderness upstream. The museum is free, and open during office hours, 7 a.m. to 9 p.m. (shorter hours in the off-season).

Returning to Highway 101, you'll cross the **Isaac Patterson Bridge,** built in 1932 to span the wide Rogue estuary. It's one of only two concrete block arch bridges of this design in the world; the other resides in France. An obvious presence here is **Jot's Resort,** a large facility at the bridge's north anchorage that offers lodging, dining, fishing guide service and a boat launch. See listings under "Where to sleep" and "Activities."

You're now in the unincorporated town of **Wedderburn.** A right turn onto Rogue River Road will take you to the second major jet boat operator, **Rogue River Mail Boats.** This was the original firm, which started carrying the U.S. Mail to Agness in 1895. It was a tough two-day haul back then. The 1,000-horsepower jet boats now make the trip in less than three hours, and they still deliver the mail to the tiny Agness post office.

Beyond the jet boat dock, Rogue River Road takes you upstream to a wooded fishing, swimming and camping area and eventually to Agness, 30 miles inland. You can do a loop of the lower section of the river by driving about nine miles to **Lobster Creek Campground** on the edge of **Siskiyou National Forest.** The road crosses the river just beyond, and you can return to Gold Beach on the south bank. Or you can press on to Agness, another 20 or so miles. From there, a paved but *very* twisty and winding road travels through the Coast Range wilderness, inland to Grants Pass.

The drive to Agness is quite pleasant, often brushing the wooded shoreline of the river and climbing an occasional canyon wall. However, you may prefer to visit Agness the way the pioneers did—by way of the water.

Flying the Rogue...again

☺ We won't recommend one jet boat operator over the other. They offer nearly identical trips and—when we last checked—identical prices. For specifics, contact **Rogue River Mail Boats,** P.O. Box 1165, Gold Beach, OR 97444 (800) 458-3511 or (503) 247-7033; or **Jerry's Rogue Jets,** P.O. Box 1011, Gold Beach, OR 97444; (800) 451-3645 or (503) 247-4571. Both take MC/VISA and they'll pick up guests at shoreside motels and RV parks.

Trips run May 1 through October 31 and come in three packages:

● A 64-mile run to Agness and back, six hours including a two-hour lunch or dinner break. Adults $27.50, kids $10, not including the meal.

● An 80-mile white water run, beyond Agness to lower rapids in the Rogue's wild and scenic section. Six to seven hours, including a lunch or dinner break in Agness. Adults $40, kids $15, not including the meal.

● A 104-mile run through more and rougher rapids to the highest point that jet boats are permitted. About eight hours, with a lunch break at a riverside lodge. Adults $65 and kids $30, including lunch.

The trip begins rather calmly as the water turbine-powered boat chortles quietly past small fishing boats, shoreside homes and RV parks along the estuary. At **Lobster Creek,** you leave the wide delta with its civilization, and enter a thickly wooded vee canyon in the river's lower wild and scenic area. Basaltic cliffs jut from the shore and the once-calm river begins offering riffles and—as you fly past Agness—some serious rapids.

If you read our first installment of "Flying the Rogue" in Chapter 2 (from Grants Pass to Hellgate Canyon), you'll recall that these big, howling boats slam through the rapids, offering a jolting ride that most folks find exciting. (Whitewater rafters and kayakers don't necessarily agree.)

As in the upper river trip, the lower run offers an abundance of wildlife sightings, and the critters aren't set fleeing by the roaring engines. Displaying an uncanny ability to spot a distant critter and dodge a boulder at the same time, our driver pointed out ospreys, a pair of bald eagles, deer and an entire beaver. All of the trip wasn't slam bam through the rapids, ma'am. We spent several pleasant moments with the big boat at idle while we watched a mama river otter and her two kids at play.

After the whitewater run, we returned to Agness with a choice of three resorts for lunch—Cougar Lane, Singing Springs and Lucas Lodge. Of these, Lucas is the most attractive, an oldstyle resort with turn of the century dècor. The appeal of Cougar and Singing Springs is that both offer outdoor dining decks over the river. (See listings below, under Agness.)

Returning to Gold Beach, our driver—apparently feeling as frisky as those otters—did at least a dozen wheelies. This is always the high point of a jet boat trip for the kids, including some well beyond their sixties.

OTHER GOLD BEACH ACTIVITIES

Deep sea fishing • **Wild Bill's,** (503) 247-2671; **Briggs Charter,** (503) 247-7150; **Jot's Resort,** (800) 367-5687 or (503) 247-6676; **Shamrock Charters,** (503) 247-6676.

Rogue fishing guide service • At last count, 12 licensed fishing guides were operating in the area. For a list, contact the Gold Beach Chamber of Commerce, 1225 S. Ellensburg Ave., Gold Beach, OR 97444; (800)525-2334 or (503) 247-7526.

Summer theater • **Gold Beach Summer Theatre** at the fairgrounds, P.O. Box 1324, Gold Beach, OR 97444-1324; (503) 247-2721.

ANNUAL EVENTS

For specifics, call the Gold Beach Chamber of Commerce at (800) 452-2334 inside Oregon, (800) 542-2334 outside and locally (503) 247-7526.

Whale of a Wine Festival in January, whale watching and wine.

Rogue River Jet Boat Marathon in June.

Curry County Fair in July, at the fairgrounds in Gold Beach.

Calico Country Bazaar and **Festival of Lights** in November.

WHERE TO DINE

Captain's Table • Δ $$

1295 S. Ellensburg Ave.; (503) 247-6308. American, mostly seafood; full bar service. Dinner nightly 5 to 10. MC/VISA. The restaurant is housed in an old cottage that's bright red outside and rather drab within, but with ocean views. Menu offerings include broiled fresh seafood, salmon teriyaki, midwestern beef and interesting combos such as rabbit teriyaki and crab.

The Chowderhead Restaurant • ΔΔ $$

910 S. Ellensburg Ave.; (503) 247-7174. American, mostly seafood; full bar service. Daily 11 to 10. MC/VISA, AMEX. Simple family-style café with ocean-view tables; reasonably priced and locally popular. Salmon with dumplings is a specialty, plus properly-done sole almandine and fresh-caught fish.

The Crow's Nest • Δ $

565 N. Ellensburg Ave.; (503) 247-6837. Mexican-American; wine and beer. Daily from 7 a.m.. MC/VISA. Despite the name, the fare in this modest café is mostly Mexican; note that the crow is wearing a serapè. The usual chimichangas, quesadillas and fajitas, plus some chicken, steak and fried fish dishes; most dinners under $10.

☺ Nor'Wester Seafood Restaurant • ΔΔΔ $$$

Port of Gold Beach; (503) 247-2333. American, mostly seafood; full bar service. Dinner nightly from 5. MC/VISA. Attractive "upscale fishing shack" style restaurant at pier side on the harbor. Several fresh broiled fish dishes from the high teens on down, plus snapper *meuniere* and Florentine, seafood fettuccini, Coquille St. Jacques and several steak and seafood combos.

Rod 'n' Reel Tavern Company • ΔΔ $$

At Jot's Resort on the estuary in Wedderburn; (503) 274-6823. American; full bar service. Open daily, breakfast-lunch 6 to 2, dinner from 5. Major credit cards. Rustically attractive café with harbor-view dining. Balanced menu ranging from seafood, beef, chicken and chops to Italian. Most dinners from $10 to the mid-teens; steak and seafood combos higher.

Wong's Café • ∆ $
280 N. Ellensburg Ave.; (503) 247-7423. Chinese-American; wine and beer. Monday-Saturday 11:30 to 9:30, Sunday 4 to 9:30. Simple, attractive wood-paneled dining room; a good spot to fill up cheaply on well-prepared food. Both spicy and mild Chinese dishes, plus American steaks, chicken fried steak, fish and chips and grilled halibut.

WHERE TO SLEEP

Gold Beach Resort • ⌂⌂⌂ $$$$ ∅
1330 S. Ellensburg (Highway 101), Gold Beach, OR 97444; (800) 541-0947 or (503) 247-7066. Couples $79 to $89, singles $69 to $79, suites $105 to $165. Major credit cards. Ocean-view 39-unit resort with TV, room phones, refrigerators, some fireplaces; indoor pool, spa. **Beach House** restaurant serves American fare 7 a.m. to 10 p.m.; dinners $9 to $12, with full bar service.

Ireland's Rustic Lodges • ⌂⌂ $$ ∅
1120 S. Ellensburg Ave. (south end); (503) 247-7718. Couples and singles $35 to $61, kitchenettes $40 to $80, suites $40 to $120. No credit cards. Nicely landscaped 40-unit resort lodge units and rustic cabins with fireplaces; some units with ocean views; all with TV.

Jot's Resort • ⌂⌂⌂ $$$
P.O. Box J (on the estuary, north side of the bridge), Gold Beach, OR 97444; (800) 367-5687 or (503) 247-6676. Couples $65 to $95. Major credit cards. Full-service resort with 140 modern harbor-view rooms and condo suites with kitchenettes. Two pools, sauna, spa, jogging track. Marina with boat and fishing gear rentals, tackle shop, boat launch, deep sea charters and river fishing guides.

Rogue Landing • ⌂ $
94749 Jerry's Flat Rd., Gold Beach, OR 97444; (503) 247-6031. Couples and singles from $25. MC/VISA. Four units with TV; basic accommodations on the south bank of the Rogue. Also 25-space RV park (see below). **Rogue Landing Restaurant** serves seafood and continental fare; dinners $12 to $16; full bar service; river-view dining.

☺ Tu Tu' Tun Lodge • ⌂⌂⌂⌂ $$$$$
96550 North Bank Rogue, Gold Beach, OR 97444; (503) 247-6664. Couples $118 to $128, singles $105, suites $169 to $179, cottage with fireplace from $189. One of the coast's finest resorts; a rustically exquisite 19-unit hideaway with river-view balconies and patios. Comfortably elegant rooms, library-sitting room with fireplace. Pool, boat dock and ramp, pitch and putt golf, fishing, library, spacious wooded grounds. **Dining Room** for guest only, serves from 7:30 a.m., *prix fixe* dinners $25; full bar service.

Bed & breakfast inns

Heather House Bed & Breakfast • ⌂⌂ $$$ ∅
190 Eleventh St., Gold Beach, OR 97444; (503) 247-2074. Couples $55 to $70, singles $50 to $65. Four rooms, two with private baths; full breakfast. MC/VISA. Craftsman style cottage with Scottish theme; above the beach with ocean views; within walking distance of downtown. Rooms have theme décor: Scottish, Victorian, paisley and Oriental; three have ocean views.

☺ **Inn at Nesika Beach** ● △△△ **$$$$** ∅
33026 Nesika Rd., Gold Beach, OR 97444; (503) 247-6434. Rooms $75 to $85; four units with private baths; full breakfast. New Victorian-style inn above the Pacific, furnished with antiques. All rooms have spa tubs and feather beds; three have fireplaces and two have private decks.

WHERE TO CAMP

Most RV parks are located along the river instead of the ocean, taking advantage of the Rogue's fishing fame. Farther upriver are several Siskiyou National Forest campgrounds; also see listing under Agness below.

Four Seasons RV Resort ● *96526 North Bank Rogue, Gold Beach, OR 97444; (800) 248-4503 or (503) 247-4503. RV and tent sites; $11 to $21.50. Reservations accepted; major credit cards.* Well-tended but close-together grassy sites at water's edge, seven miles upriver. Showers, cable TV, boat dock and ramp, fishing tackle and guide service, on-site trailers available, mini-mart.

Indian Creek Recreation Park ● *94680 Jerry's Flat Rd., Gold Beach, OR 97444; (503) 247-7704. RV and tent sites; $11 to $17. Reservations accepted; MC/VISA.* Attractive, well-maintained park on the south bank, half a mile from town. Campsites across road from the river. Showers, coin laundry, rec room, mini-mart. Restaurant and riding stables adjacent.

Kimball Creek Bend RV Resort ● *97136 North Bank Rogue, Gold Beach, OR 97444; (503) 247-7580. RV and tent sites; $16.50 to $23.50. Reservations accepted; MC/VISA.* Well-run full-service resort on the banks of the Rogue, eight miles upriver. Showers, fire rings, rec room and adult lounge, kids' play area, rental trailers, mini-mart, boat launch and dock, fishing and guide service.

Oceanside RV Park ● *South Jetty Road (P.O. Box 1107), Gold Beach, OR 97444; (503) 247-2301. RV sites only, full hookups $17, water and electric $15. Reservations accepted; no credit cards.* It's not at the ocean despite the name, but it's a short walk to the beach. Close-together spaces; facilities a bit scruffy but reasonably clean. Showers, coin laundry, picnic tables, mini-mart with fishing gear.

Rogue Landing RV Park ● *94749 Jerry's Flat Rd., Gold Beach, OR 97444; (503) 247-6031. RV sites, full hookups $14, water and electric $11. Reservations accepted.* Older, rather basic park on the south bank of the river, half a mile from town. Some sites over the water; showers, picnic tables, coin laundry, cable TV; restaurant and motel adjacent (see above).

Agness

An all-weather road finally linked Agness to the outside world in 1960, although it is still among the most pleasantly isolated villages in Oregon. The entire town consists of a small wooden general store and a smaller post office, plus a few rustic riverside resorts and homes.

Fishing, swimming, blackberry picking and loafing in the sun are favorite pursuits. Since it's several miles inland, summers can get toasty. There's plenty of shade, since the town is tucked into a thick forest.

Where to dine and sleep

If you want to stay in Agness overnight, you can arrange to be delivered and retrieved by one of the jet boats, instead of driving.

Cougar Lane Resort ● △ $$

04219 Agness Rd., Agness, OR 97406; (503) 247-7233. Couples $35 to $55. Simple lodge units, store and rustic cocktail lounge. **Restaurant** with outdoor and indoor seating serves a lunch and dinner buffet for $8.95, other American dinners from $8 to $13, and sandwiches. Full bar service.

☺ Lucas Lodge ● △△ $$

P.O. Box 37, Agness, OR 97406; (503) 247-7443. Lodge rooms and housekeeping cabins $30 to $60. Charming turn-of-the-century lodge on 150 acres near the river. **Dining room** noted for its $8.50 chicken dinners, plus other rural American-style chops, fish, ribs, turkey and chicken. Wine and beer.

Singing Springs Resort ● △ $$

P.O. Box 68, Agness, OR 97406; (503) 247-6162. Sleeping units from $40, housekeeping cabins $45 to $65. Pleasant old resort shaded by huge fir and myrtlewoods; large lawn area. **Restaurant** offers a dining deck over the river, with an $8.95 roast beef and chicken buffet; or dinners of steak, shrimp, scallop or salmon from $9 to $14. Wine and beer.

WHERE TO CAMP

Agness RV Park ● *04215 Agness Rd., Agness, OR 97406; (503) 247-2813. RV and camp sites, $10 to $12; full hookups. Reservations accepted; MC/VISA.* Wooded campground near the river; showers, laundromat, picnic tables, rec room; boat ramp.

GOLD BEACH TO BANDON

As you continue north on Highway 101, pause at a vista point just beyond Wedderburn for a nice look at where you've just been. From this high vantage point, you can see an overview of the Rogue, cradled between rock jetties of the harbor, and the usually-misty headlands beyond.

The route swings inland for a few miles, passing through a corridor of Douglas fir and spruce. Then it returns to the surf at **Nesika Beach**, a scruffy hamlet that offers little reason to leave the highway. Just beyond is a rest area with easy access to a nice long seashore. You again curve inland and enter a land of—dinosaurs?

☺ **Prehistoric Gardens** ● *36848 S. Highway 101, Port Orford, OR 97465; (503) 332-4463. Open daily 8 to dusk; adults $4.50, students and seniors $3.50, kids 5 to 11, $2.50; MC/VISA.* This well-maintained park offers several life-sized gunnite dinosaurs set in a lush forest. With as much as ten feet of rainfall a year in this sheltered valley, common ferns and even skunk cabbage grow to huge size. This provides a convincing "primeval forest" for the garden's critters. Among its residents are a long-necked *brachiosaurus* peeking over the treetops to check for highway traffic, and a 46-foot *stegosauras* with dragon-like armor plate on its back and a brain the size of a walnut. The brochure says everything is "scientifically correct" and the critters looked pretty convincing to us—if a bit vividly colored. This well-maintained, uncluttered attraction is worth the price. We particularly liked an excellent exhibit on the transition of plant life from primeval times. The only thing really hokey is the gift shop.

Of course, if you *want* to take home a plastic dinosaur...

A few miles beyond is **Arizona Beach Campground**, one of the better-located private RV parks on the coast. It sits down near the water, about midway between Gold Beach and Port Orford. This attractive park has tent and RV sites, a creek, wooded areas, mini-mart and laundromat. Rates are $12 to $18; MC/VISA. Contact: Arizona Beach, P.O. Box 621, Gold Beach, OR 97444; (503) 332-6491.

The coast is quite attractive through here, with tiny islands and basaltic spires scattered along the surf. Just ahead on the right is **Humbug State Park** with a campground, picnic area and hiking trails at the base of Humbug Mountain. This wooded peak is one of the coast's more impressive high rises. A three-mile trail leads to the top, with predictably impressive views. The large campground, a bit crowded for a state park, has full hookups for $13, no hookups for $11. It's across the road from the strand, and a trail leads under the highway to the attractive black sand Humbug Beach.

It was this beach that gave the area its odd name. Prospectors rushed here in the 1850s, spurred by a false rumor that the sand contained gold. Perhaps the disgruntled miner who named the area had been reading Charles Dickens.

Port Orford

Population: 1,000   **Elevation: 60 feet**

Occupying a wooded shelf above the Pacific, Port Orford is one of the coast's more photogenic hamlets. Weather-darkened false front businesses line its tiny downtown area. Old fishing boats add proper nautical touches to the small harbor. The town looks like a movie set for Rogers and Hammerstein's *Carousel*. **Battle Rock**, a ridge-like promontory just offshore, adds drama to the setting.

The major local industry—logging and shipping Port Orford cedar—has been shut down for decades, so the town is in an economic slumber. Despite its charm, tourism hasn't blossomed here. Offerings are limited to a couple of motels and several restaurants—most of them ordinary. *Forbes Magazine* once called Port Orford a sleeper waiting to be discovered. However, the new immigrants will have to contend with a 108-inch annual rainfall, the most on the coast.

Port Orford is the westernmost town on the American mainland. It's also among Oregon's oldest, dating back to June 9, 1851, when Captain William Tichenor landed a party of nine settlers. The Native Americans didn't care for the intrusion and chased them to Battle Rock, where they were able to hold out until Tichenor returned with reinforcements.

The **Chamber of Commerce** maintains an information kiosk at a small park just opposite Battle Rock. This dramatic promontory will certainly catch your eye as you enter town. It's variously a peninsula and an island, depending on the mood of the tides. Clambering about its rough ramparts is a popular visitor sport.

At the information kiosk, you can pick up a walking tour map of historic structures, which will consume about twenty minutes. You might spend a few more strolling among the dramatic seastacks of the beachfront, starting at **Battle Rock State Park**. And that's about it, other than poking into a couple of curio and antique shops, and perhaps choosing lunch or dinner at one of several restaurants—mostly seafood, of course.

WHERE TO DINE

The Truculent Oyster • ΔΔ $$$
236 Highway 101; (503) 332-4461. Seafood; full bar service. Daily 8 a.m. to 10 p.m. Major credit cards. The best of a handful of local seafood restaurants; cozy nautical interior with dark woods and votive candles. Salmon in season is excellent; several other fresh-caught entrèes appear on the menu, plus a few Mexican dishes. Finish with locally-famous blackberry pie, then pause for a nightcap next door at the Western-style Peg Leg Saloon.

☺ Whale Cove • ΔΔΔ $$$
190 Highway 101; (503) 332-7575. Continental-nouveau; wine and beer. Wednesday-Monday 5 to 9, Sunday brunch 11 to 2:30, closed Tuesday. MC/VISA. One of the coast's better restaurants, set in an elegantly simple French style cafè. Multi-course $18.50 *prix fixe* dinners are crafted by chef-owner Christophe Baudry, late of Mark Antony's in Ashland and Christophe's in Sausalito. Try prawns Shelton with white wine, prosciutto and English cheese, scallops with leeks and champagne sauce or duck Magret with poached oysters. The menu changes with the caprice of the chef and the availability of fresh fish and local produce.

WHERE TO SLEEP

Castaway by the Sea • ⌂⌂ $$$ ∅
545 W Fifth St. at Oregon (P.O. Box 844), Port Orford, OR 97465; (503) 332-4502. Couples $45 to $60, singles $45, kitchenettes $60 to $70, suites $70 to $100. MC/VISA. Attractive 13-unit motel on coastal bluff with private glass sun porches overlooking the Pacific. All rooms have ocean view; some kitchens and electric fireplaces. Two blocks from Battle Rock.

Sea Crest Motel • ⌂⌂ $$ ∅
P.O. Box C, Port Orford, OR 97465; (503) 332-3040. Couples $35 to $54, singles $29 to $37. MC/VISA. Well-tended 18-unit motel with attractive grounds and sea view rooms; TV movies, room phones.

Shoreline Motel • ⌂ $ ∅
Highway 101 at Jefferson (P.O. Box 426), Port Orford, OR 97465; (503) 332-2903. Couples $28 to $40, singles $24 to $36, kitchenettes $32 to $44, suites $38 to $50. MC/VISA, DISC. A 13-room motel with TV, and room phones; some room refrigerators. Across highway from the beach.

Bed & breakfast inns

☺ Floras Lake House • ⌂⌂⌂ $$$$ ∅
92870 Boice Cope Rd., Langlois, OR 97450; (503) 348-2573. Couples $90 to $125, singles $80 to $115. Four rooms with private baths; continental breakfast. MC/VISA. Classy country home with open- beam ceilings, 12 miles north of Port Orford and three miles west of U.S. 101 on Floras Lake. Modern, comfortable rooms with private deck entries and views of the lake and the nearby ocean. Two rooms have fireplaces; all are bright and airy.

Gwendolyn's Bed & Breakfast • ⌂⌂ $$
735 Oregon St. (P.O. Box 913), Port Orford, OR 97465; (503) 332-43743. Couples $45 to $55, singles $35. Four rooms, two with private baths; full breakfast. MC/VISA. A 1921 Victorian style cottage with comfortable parlor

The 59-foot tower of Cape Blanco Light is the focal point of one of the coast's most interesting state parks.
—Betty Woo Martin

and fireplace; surrounded by attractive garden; near downtown. Rooms done in early American and nostalgic 1920s to 1940s dècor.

Home By the Sea Bed & Breakfast ● ⌂ $$$ Ø

444 Jackson St. (P.O. Box 606-B), Port Orford, OR 97465-0606; (503) 332-2855. Couples and singles $65 to $75. Two units with private baths, TV and room phones; full breakfast. MC/VISA. Contemporary wood frame home on a spit with outstanding ocean view; short walk to harbor and Battle Rock. Modern furnishings with queen-sized myrtlewood beds; laundry facilities.

WHERE TO CAMP

Two state campgrounds, **Humbug** (listed above) and **Cape Blanco** (listed below) are within a short drive of Port Orford. Close to town are:

Madrona-101 RV Park ● *63 Madrona, Port Orford, OR 97465; (503) 332-4025. RV sites, $12 to $14. Reservations accepted.* New park with some pull-throughs and shaded sites; showers, cable TV, coin laundry. In town, near shops and restaurants.

Camp Blanco RV Park ● *2011 Oregon St., Port Orford, OR 97465; (503) 332-6175. RV and tent sites, $8 to $12.* Older park with mostly pull-throughs, cable TV. North end of town on the highway, near shops and restaurants.

Cape Blanco State Park

☺ Nine miles northwest of Port Orford, this park is so versatile that it earns its own listing. To reach it, drive five miles from Port Orford to the hamlet of **Sixes,** and then five miles west through woods and English-style moors to the cape.

Located on a windswept headland, Cape Blanco is the most westerly point in mainland America, jutting out to sea to meet the storms and seagulls. Not surprisingly, **Cape Blanco Light** occupies this promontory. It's been at work since December 20, 1870, making it the oldest in continuous use on the coast. With a 59-foot tower perched 425 feet above the sea, it's the highest light in Oregon. Further, it may be the windiest; gales have been clocked here at 184 miles an hour. Now automated and still using its original French-made fresnel lens, it's closed to visitors. You can walk around its base and follow trails through grasslands to the dizzying edge of the promontory for awesome views of seastacks and coastal panoramas.

Offshore rocks and reefs are part of **Oregon Islands National Wildlife Refuge** and signs along the walk to the lighthouse help you identify sea birds and mammals that occupy them.

Cape Blanco Campground (332-6774) offers sites sheltered by wind-bent Sitka spruce, with water and electric hookups for $12. It's not on the state reservation system, so get there early. A steep road leads to a nearby picnic area with views of a rocky, driftwood- littered beach just below. A steeper road leads to the beach itself and you're permitted to drive thereon if you have a four- wheel drive. *Don't* try it in the family Belchfire Six. Of course, you can walk down to the beach, which is excellent for bundling and tidepooling. Somewhat sheltered, it's not as windy as the headland.

Yet another park attraction is the **Hughes House,** a wood-framed Victorian that you passed on the way in. It's impeccably restored and furnished to its 1898 era, when it was built by wealthy dairyman Patrick Hughes. Admission is free; donations are appreciated. Friends of Cape Blanco volunteers conduct tours during the summer on Monday, Thursday, Friday and Saturday 10 to 5 and Sunday noon to 5; it's closed Tuesday and Wednesday.

In addition to these specific lures, Cape Blanco State Park has several miles of hiking and riding trails. There's a horse camp here, in case you brought Silver or Trigger along.

Since Highway 101 skirts Cape Blanco, the route to Bandon takes you through a mix of woodlands and farm country. The teeny town of **Langlois** has the courage to offer a restaurant called the **Greasy Spoon,** (348-2515) billeted in a weathered house. It's open Monday-Saturday 6 a.m. to 3 p.m. and homemade pies are a specialty. You'll pass an occasional roadside fruit stand in this area, offering locally grown blackberries, marionberries, blueberries, huckleberries and gooseberries transformed into jam.

West Coast Game Park • *P.O. Box 1330, Bandon, OR 97411; (503) 347-3106. Adults $5.75, kids 7 to 12, $5 and 1 to 6, $3.25. March through November, daily from 9 to dusk, with shorter hours the rest of the year; MC/VISA.* Seven miles short of Bandon, it claims to be the world's largest wild animal petting park, and who are we to question it? Inside the wooded compound, you'll walk through herds of deer, aromatic goats and other pettable creatures. You and the kids also can become friendly with baby chimps, leopards, tigers and bears—under the supervision of handlers. Several other critters are caged, and animal shows are held periodically.

North of the walk-through zoo, the roadside myrtlewood shops, glass-blowing studios and galleries begin to thicken. You just know you're in serious tourist country.

Bandon

Population: 2,770   **Elevation: 55 feet**

Like Port Orford, Bandon is a charming village with a history stretching well back into the last century. Unlike Port Orford, it has caught the magic ring of tourism. Old Town on the estuary of the Coquille River has been transformed from weathered to deliberately rustic, and Bandon's rocky coastline is lined with resort motels.

The town is evolving into something of an art colony, with several galleries and theater groups. Despite its touristic preoccupation, it retains much of its early-day innocence. It's one of the Oregon Coast's most likable communities.

The highway misses most of what's interesting here, so turn left at the sign indicating the scenic **Beach Loop Drive** and **Bandon Beach State Park.** This is one of the most attractive *populated* beaches on the coast—an impressive strip of strand broken by rocky sea crags, including some spectacular vertical columns. Motels and homes are tucked above and about the shoreline, but you can ignore them and marvel at promontories such as **Garden of the Gods, Elephant Rock** and the immense basaltic monolith, **Face Rock.** The state park provides adequate beach access between the homes and resort motels.

Beyond the shorefront, Beach Loop Drive swings around to the right onto southwest Fourth Street and eventually to Jetty Road, where you have choices. A left takes you out to the **South Jetty** of the Coquille River, with a couple of antique shops, nautical firms and a restaurant. Across the way, on the north jetty, you can see **Bandon Light** (more properly called the Coquille River Lighthouse). You can't get there from here, but stay with us.

Re-trace your route on Jetty Road and follow signs to **Old Town Bandon.** En route, you'll pass the imposing two-story white and green wood frame **Coast Guard Facility,** built in 1939. It now houses the **Bandon Historical Society Museum** and a few shops.

Old Town Bandon is an attractive wedge, tucked between the boat basin and Highway 101, which has curved back into the picture here. Its streets are lined with restaurants, curio shops and galleries, tucked mostly into renovated 19th century buildings. The **Bandon Chamber of Commerce** tourist information center is at Chicago Avenue and Second Street, just up from the waterfront; (503) 347-9616. It's open daily 9 to 5.

Once you've finished with Old Town and resumed driving north, you'll see the **Bandon Cheddar Cheese Factory,** at the edge of town on your right. Continue north on Highway 101 for a couple of miles, then turn left into **Bullards Beach State Park,** which offers picnicking and camping (listed below). A road through a coastal flat takes you three miles to the earlier-mentioned lighthouse.

Settled by Irish immigrants in the middle of the last century, Bandon got its name from a town in County Cork. It thrived as a center for fishing, lumbering, dairying and cranberry bogging (see below). During the turn-of-the-century heyday of coastal steamers, it became an important stop on the San Francisco to Seattle run. Bandon thus enjoyed its first flush of tourism. A mere $10 would get you passage on the *S.S. Elizabeth* for the 40-hour cruise to San Francisco.

Two major fires—in 1914 and 1936—wrecked Bandon and its tourist industry. After "Black Saturday" in 1936, the town went to sleep. The few buildings that survived the fire remained almost unchanged, to form the nucleus for old town.

It's the cranberries

Before leaving town, drive past some of the 900 acres of **cranberry bogs** nearby, near Highway 101 north of town. Folks at the visitor center will tell you where to look. They may be able to arrange for a visit to a cranberry farm during harvest, which occurs in late fall. Easterner Charles McFarlin introduced the berries here in 1885, when he transferred his operation from Cape Cod. Oregon is now one of only five states producing this necessary adjunct to Thanksgiving dinner. All of the state's 1,340 acres of cranberries are on the coast, since they need soggy bogs to flourish, and most of these are around Bandon. They're quite picturesque when the bogs are flooded to facilitate the harvest, turning them into liquid carpets of red.

Cranberries are one of only three commercially-grown fruits native to America, along with blueberries and Concord grapes. They were growing wild in Oregon when Lewis and Clark hit the coast at the mouth of the Columbia River nearly 200 years ago. The name, in case you never wondered, comes from "craneberry." During the flowering stage, the white petals fold back to reveal a dark, pointed stamen, resembling the head of a crane.

If you'd like to learn more, contact (we love this name) the Oregon Cranberry Farmers' Alliance, P.O. Box 1737, Bandon, OR 97411.

ATTRACTIONS

☺ **Bandon Historical Society Museum** • *Coast Guard building on First Street; (503) 347-2164. Tuesday-Saturday noon to 4; adults $1, kids free.* The museum and the building that houses it are equally interesting. The impressive two-story, green-shuttered former Coast Guard headquarters catches your eye as you pass. Inside, artifacts and graphics recall Bandon's yesterdays, with the usual photos of ships that came calling and sometimes came apart on the rocks. Other displays include pioneer relics, a large presentation concerning the Coquille Indians and a nicely done exhibit on the Bandon Marsh Wildlife Refuge.

☺ **Bandon Cheddar Cheese Factory and Store** • *Highway 101, just north of Old Town; (503) 347-2456. Monday-Saturday 8:30 to 5:30, Sunday 9 to 5; MC/VISA.* Oregon's second largest cheese plant, after the huge Tillamook operation to the north, Bandon Cheddar Cheese factory dates from 1939, when local dairymen formed a co- op. You can watch cheese being made and try a startling variety of cheddar samples, including onion, Cajun, jalapeno, pimento, Baja (which will clear your sinus if the jalapeno didn't) and garlic. These varieties are all for sale, of course, along with a large assortment of other Oregon specialty foods and giftwares.

Bullards Beach State Park • *Two miles north on U.S. 101 (P.O. Box 25), Bandon, OR 97411; (503) 347-2209. This attractive park covers 1,226 acres, occupying much of the north side of the Coquille River estuary. Facilities* include a campground and Coquille River Lighthouse (both listed separately below), swimming, picnicking, boat launch, hiking and nature trails.

Coquille River Lighthouse ● *At Bullards Beach State Park; (503) 347-2209.* This rather squat edifice helped steer ships up the Coquille River from 1896 until 1939. Now inactive, the shell of the structure has been carefully restored. There was little inside when we last visited, other than a few wall plaques. They discuss the history of local shipping, and point out that some of the vessels failed to heed this guiding light. One ran into the lighthouse itself!

Cranberry Sweets ● *At First and Chicago in Old Town; (503) 347-9475. Monday-Saturday 9 to 5:30, Sunday 9 to 5; MC/VISA.* The sweet thing about this shop, which is Oregon's largest retail candy store, is that you can sample a dozen different kinds of goodies. Most are tasty nougats, including several cranberry specialties.

Driftwood museum ● *In Big Wheel Farm Supply and General Store, First and Baltimore in Old Town; (503) 347-3719. Monday-Friday 5 to 9, Saturday 5 to 9:30, Sunday 11 to 5.* The "museum," in a side room of the store, consists of a large collection of locally-gathered driftwood, and objects made from it. This is the place for that tacky driftwood slab wall clock you've always wanted. There are some nice wood carvings here, as well. The rest of this large old town structure is occupied by a curio, Western supply and farm supply store.

ACTIVITIES

Fishing charters and gear ● **Coquille River Charters,** Route 2, Box 1080, Bandon, OR 97411, (503) 347-9093 or 347-4313, will take you fishing. **Bandon Bait Shop,** 110 First Street at the Boat Basin, (503) 347-3905, has fishing tackle and crab trap rentals.

Horseback riding ● **Bandon Beach Loop Stables** on the loop drive south of Old Town, near Crooked Beach State Park, (503) 347-9342, rents nags for beach rides; also pony rides for kiddies and riding lessons.

Nature seminars ● **Bandon Stormwatchers,** P.O. Box 1693, Bandon, OR 97411; (503) 347-2144 or 347-7246. From January through April, the group conducts seminars about local flora and fauna at the Bandon Community Center in the city park on Beach Loop Drive opposite Face Rock. Gatherings generally are Saturdays at 3 p.m.

River cruise ● **Dixie Lee** is a charming little sternwheeler offering daylight and dinner cruises up the Coquille River; Route 2, Box 2485, Bandon, OR 97411; (503) 347-3942.

Theater ● **Encore Presenters** is a semi-pro group that features light comedies, musicals and skits at Harbor Hall, 325 Second St.; (503) 347-4404. Check the Chamber of Commerce for lists of Bandon's several **amateur theater groups**. The **Sawdust Theater** in neighboring Coquille (145 E. Second St.; 396-3947) presents old "meller-drammers" in summer; the audience is expected to cheer the good guys and hiss the bad ones.

ANNUAL EVENTS

Contact the Chamber of Commerce at (503) 347-9616 for details.

Stormwatchers' Seafood and Wine Festival and sand castle competition, over Memorial Day Weekend.

Native American Salmon Bake conducted by the Coquille Tribe, the weekend before the Fourth of July.

Cranberry Follies, the big annual event, in late September or early October; features queen contest, parade, exhibits, food booths and music.

Festival of Lights during Christmas season with lighted boats and buildings in Old Town.

WHERE TO DINE

☺ Andrea's • ∆∆∆ $$

160 Baltimore Avenue in Old Town; (503) 347-3022. Eclectic menu; wine and beer. Breakfast and lunch Monday-Saturday from 9 a.m., dinner nightly, Sunday brunch 10 to 3. No credit cards. Dinner in this cheerfully funky and cozy place is whatever strikes chef-owner Andrea Gatov-Beck's fancy. It can range from home-grown lamb to fresh seafood done with interesting seasonings to Russian entrées. Excellent pizzas, earth-grain breads, pastries and cheese cakes also emerge from her busy kitchen.

Bandon Boatworks • ∆∆ $$

On the South Jetty; (503) 347-2111. American; wine and beer. Lunch Tuesday-Saturday 11:30 to 2:30, dinner 5 to 9, Sunday noon to 8:30, closed Monday. Major credit cards. Simple, attractive dining room with maple furniture, burgundy napery and a nice harbor view through large windows. Busy menu ranges from locally fresh seafood and steaks to veal cordon bleu, chicken Marsala and a couple of pasta dishes.

Bandon Fish Market • ∆ $

249 First Street on the boat basin in Old Town; (503) 347-4282. Seafood take-out. Daily 10 to 8 in summer, 11 to 7 the rest of the year. No credit cards. Handy spot for a quick meal while you're exploring Old Town. Pick up fish and chips, fried shrimp, fried fresh local fish, clam chowder or a seafood cocktail, and pack it all out to dockside tables.

Bavarian Bakery and Coffee House • ∆ $

170 Second St.; (503) 347-9812. Light snacks and bakery goods. Daily 7 to 5; no credit cards. Pleasant bakery-café with bright Bavarian décor, offering interesting cranberry creations. They're prepared nicely tart so you can taste the fruit. Try cranberry muffins, breads, tarts and such. Soups, salads and other light fare to take out or eat in.

Harp's Restaurant • ∆∆ $$

130 Chicago Avenue near First Street in Old Town; (503) 347-9057. American; wine and beer. Nightly 5 to 10, Sunday brunch 10 to 2:30. MC/VISA. Pleasantly funky café with driftwood décor to match the weathered look of Old Town. Locally popular and winner of a couple of regional dining awards. Small, versatile menu ranges from teriyaki chicken and marinated halibut to scampi Montezuma. Start off with the cream of shrimp soup spiced with tarragon.

☺ Lord Bennett's Restaurant • ∆∆∆ $$$

1695 Beach Loop Road; (503) 347-3663. American, mostly seafood; full bar service. Daily 11 to 3 and 5 to 10. MC/VISA, AMEX. Exceptionally attractive restaurant on a bluff with ocean views. Starkly modern interior has pastel artworks on white walls, drop lamps and potted plants. Blackened fish, broiled catch of the day and sole stuffed with mushrooms, artichokes and cream cheese occupy the seafood side of the menu. It also features veal dishes, fettuccini and several steak selections.

Wheelhouse • ΔΔ $$

Over the boat harbor, Old Town; (503) 347-9331. American, mostly seafood; full bar service. Lunch from 11, dinner from 5. MC/VISA. Attractive nautical English pub dècor with exposed beam ceiling, dark woods and fireplace. Typical seafood menu features the daily catch, shellfish and seafood fettuccini, plus chicken and brandied pepper steak. Adjourn to the upstairs lounge for a nice view of the boat basin.

WHERE TO SLEEP

Harbor View Motel • ⌂⌂ $$$ ∅

Highway 101 at the harbor (P.O. Box 1409), Bandon, OR 97411; (800) 526-0209 or (503) 347-4417. Couples $54 to $69, singles $50 to $63. Major credit cards. Attractive motel with 59 harbor-view rooms; TV movies, room refrigerators and phones; spa; continental breakfast. Adjacent to Old Town.

Sunset Motel • ⌂⌂ $$ & $$$ ∅

1955 Beach Loop Rd., Bandon, OR 97411; (800) 842-2407 or (503) 347-2453. Couples $40 to $100, singles $30 to $80, kitchenettes $70 to $115, suites $115 to $195. Major credit cards. A 56-unit motel above the beach with basic to luxury rooms; TV, room phones; spa, beach access. Opposite **Lord Bennett's** restaurant (see above).

Table Rock Motel • ⌂ $$

Beach Loop Drive near Eighth (P.O. Box 236), Bandon, OR 97411; (503) 347-2700. Couples $37.10 to $47.10, singles $28.62 to $37.10, kitchenettes $58.30 to $74.20. MC/VISA, DISC. A simple 15-unit motel with TV; not far from the beach.

Windermere Motel • ⌂⌂ $$$

3250 Beach Loop Rd., Bandon, OR 97411; (503) 347-3710. Rooms $50 to $65, kitchenettes $60 to $85. MC/VISA. A 17-unit motel right above the beach with ocean-view rooms; TV and room phones.

Bed & breakfast inn

Lighthouse Bed & Breakfast • ⌂⌂⌂ $$$$ ∅

650 SW Jetty Rd. (P.O. Box 24), Bandon, OR 97411; (503) 347-9316. Couples $80 to $105. Four rooms with private baths; continental breakfast. Not in a lighthouse, this B&B is opposite it, across the estuary. This modern, woodsy bungalow is perched above the harbor with views of the estuary. Dècor is light and airy, with potted plants.

WHERE TO CAMP

Bandon RV Park • *935 E. Second St. (U.S. 101), Bandon, OR 97411; (503) 347-4122. RV sites only, full hookups $14. Reservations accepted; MC/VISA.* Just above Old Town; close-together spaces, some pull-throughs. Showers, cable TV, laundromat.

Bullards Beach State Park • *Two miles north on U.S. 101 (P.O. Box 25), Bandon, OR 97411; (503) 347-2209. RV and tent sites, full hookups $13, electrical $12, hiker-biker $2. No reservations or credit cards.* Well-spaced sites, some shaded; showers, barbecues and picnic tables. Details on other park facilities listed above.

Driftwood Shores RV Park • *935 E. Second St., Bandon, OR 97411; (503) 347-4122. RV sites only, $12 to $14. Reservations accepted; MC/VISA.*

North end of town, a block off U.S. 101; small park with full hookups, laundry, RV supplies and cable TV.

BANDON TO COOS BAY/NORTH BEND

If you'd like an inland diversion, follow State Highway 42 northeast from Bandon. It will take you 17 miles to **Coquille,** the seat of Coos County. This sturdy old town of 4,100 is noted for its Victorian homes and Sawdust Theater Gay Nineties revue (listed under "Activities" above). If you'd like to learn more about this woodsy version of small town Americana, contact the **Coquille Chamber of Commerce**, 119 N. Birch St., Coquille, OR 97423; (503) 396-3414. If you stay with Highway 42, you'll wind through a scenic stretch of the Coast Range and wind up in Roseburg.

Meanwhile, back on Highway 101, a sign 13 miles north of Bandon directs you west to the **Charleston Recreation Area.** This is our preferred route to Coos Bay/North Bend. You'll follow a ridge through forests and former forests, since much of this area has suffered under the brutal hand of clearcutting. Side roads from here will take you to **Seven Devils** and **Whiskey Run** state parks, two remote and rarely visited beach areas.

Continuing along the route toward Charleston, you'll encounter an intriguing new idea in nature sanctuaries:

☺ **South Slough National Estuarine Preserve** • *Daily 8:30 to 4:30. Free guided trail walks Wednesday 9 to noon and Friday 1 to 4.* What this sanctuary preserves is a distinctive ecological niche known as a river estuary—part flowing stream and part tidal flat. South Slough, which joins several other streams to form Coos Bay, is America's first such federal reserve. The visitor center occupies a wooded rise above the slough. Exhibits and a nicely done video explain that a tidal estuary is one of nature's richest habitats. You can follow an assortment of trails for more indoctrination into the world of the tidal river.

Pressing onward, you see a few rural homes as you approach the trio of cities on Oregon's largest bay—Charleston, Coos Bay and North Bend. Before surrendering to their civilization, however, turn left onto Cape Arago Highway and drive to a trio of state parks—Sunset Bay, Shore Acres and Cape Arago. Side-by-side on coastal bluffs, they're among the coast's more appealing preserves. The beauty of this short drive will rival any vistas you've thus far seen.

☺ You first encounter **Sunset Bay**, a lush, green park that encloses a delightful small crescent bay peppered with offshore seastacks. Sheltered from wind and surf by high sea walls, its calm waters are excellent for tidepooling, seaweed scuffing and lazing in the sand. Bring your teeny bikini, since this is one of the coast's few places where sheltered waters are warm enough for a dip. Optimistic park officials have erected a bathhouse here, and picnic tables, of course. **Camping** is available along a shallow ravine up from the beach (see listing below).

☺ A drive through a luxuriant rainforest canopy takes you to **Shore Acres** which, for a state park, is something of a surprise. It contains the former estate of Louis J. Simpson, a lumber and shipping baron who established the town of North Bend. The family mansion is gone, burned in a spectacular fire on the Fourth of July, 1921. What remains is the extensive grounds, including beautiful English Gardens and an Oriental garden, and the notable coastal view that was enjoyed by the Simpsons. You can learn about the Simpson family and its estate at an information kiosk. Step to a grassy bluff for a view down to a tilted stair-step strata of seastacks, then tour the elegant gardens, immaculately maintained by the park staff. A gift and information center at the gardens is open daily noon to 5. We were struck by the contrast here: the formal English gardens with their brick patios and carefully trimmed hedges, the free-form yet orderly Oriental Garden and the view down to a coastal wilderness just a short walk away.

☺ **Cape Arago State Park** completes this attractive trio. It's essentially a viewpoint atop a narrow coastal promontory, offering impressive vistas at this seastack seashore. If you'd like lunch with a stunning view, you'll find picnic tables terraced into the bluffs. For more viewing, follow a two-mile cliffs-edge trail from Cape Arago to Sunset Bay. Other trails lead down to the beach.

Charleston/Coos Bay/North Bend

Charleston, about 700   Coos Bay, 15,100   North Bend, 9,600

At the risk of being unkind to these sturdy towns, they are not tourist meccas. Charleston is rather charming—a small fishing village tucked between the bay and the ocean. Coos Bay and North Bend, however, are ordinary working class communities. Among them, they comprise the largest and most industrialized urban center on the coast. The three towns and their attendant lumber mills and cargo docks line the shores of the largest natural harbor between San Francisco and Seattle.

We don't suggest that you bypass what locals call the "Bay Area" (sorry about that, San Francisco). The region offers a couple of interesting museums and it's rimmed by scenic beaches. Oregon Dunes National Recreation Area, the world's longest stretch of aquatic sand piles, is just to the north.

Asa Simpson, sea captain and shipbuilder, settled here in the 1850s, establishing a sawmill and a shipyard. His son Louis took over the operation in 1899 and platted the town of North Bend. Meanwhile, J.C. Toleman arrived in 1854 to establish the port of Coos Bay, which he called Marshfield, after his hometown in Massachusetts. It went by that name until citizens voted in 1944 to name it after the bay.

Out near the ocean, South Slough estuary provided a good site for a small boat harbor, and Charleston developed as a commercial fishing and canning center. Through the generations, the trio became roughneck lumbering, shipping and canning towns, busy with saloons and bawdy houses. They're tough towns to this day, made of sturdy old brick and masonry. However, harlots no longer hang out second-story windows to entice horny seamen and lumberjacks.

North Bend claims a tiny piece of history not related to shipping, logging or harlots. In 1925, local flying enthusiast Vern Gorst formed Pacific Air Lines to carry mail and an occasional passenger, who had to share cramped cargo space with the mail sacks. Large Coos Bay was the "airstrip" for Gorst's float planes. Six years later, Pacific merged with several other firms to form United Airlines.

Today, this industrialized heart of the coast is suffering economic doldrums wrought by a cutback in lumber production. Some of the giant mills lining Highway 101 and the bayfront around Coos Bay and North Bend are silent. However, Coos Bay still can claim to be the world's largest shipper of

BANDON TO FLORENCE

Heceta Head
Minerva
Swisshome
Mapleton
Heceta Beach
126 Tiernan
Florence
Cushman
Glenada
Canary
HONEYMAN STATE PARK
Dunes City
Siltcoos
Sulphur Springs

N

OREGON DUNES NATIONAL RECREATION AREA

Gardiner
Reedsport
38
Winchester Bay
UMPQUA LIGHT STATE PARK
TUGMAN STATE PARK
Lakeside
101
Hauser
Allegany
North Bend
Coos Bay
SUNSET BAY STATE PARK
SHORE ACRES STATE PARK
Charleston
Sumner
CAPE ARAGO STATE PARK
Coquille
COQUILLE RIVER
Riverton
BANDON BEACH STATE PARK
Prosper
Norway
Bandon
Gravelford
Myrtle Point

wood products. Much of this cargo is chips, headed to Japan for paper production. You'll see great heaps of it along the waterfront highway.

Start with Charleston

To accomplish your tour of this area, follow Cape Arago Highway from the state parks into Charleston. It's a pleasant old waterfront town, the most picturesque of the three, with one of the coast's largest commercial fishing fleets. It consists of a couple of restaurants, a general store, a curio shop or two and a boat basin.

The **Charleston Information Center** is on your right as you enter town, at Cape Arago Highway and Boat Basin Drive; (503) 888-2311. It's open daily 10 to 5. Here, you can load up on brochures and maps that will direct you through the two other communities. You can book charter boats at Charleston, poke through the shops or just relax with a seafood cocktail and watch the drawbridge rise over South Slough.

Bastendorff Beach, at the ocean two miles southwest of town, is a county park with camping (listed below), a kids' playground and lots of beach for strolling, clamming and surf-casting; (503) 888-5353. To reach it, head toward Sunset Bay State Park on Cape Arago Highway, and turn right at the county park sign.

For an impressive seaward view of the Bay Area, follow Boat Basin Drive northwest for about half a mile. Then turn left onto an unmarked road and follow it to a parking area on a bluff above the jetties of

Coos Bay. Beyond, closed to the public but visible for your camera, is the **Coast Guard Tower.** From your high perch, you may see a Japanese lumber freighter lumbering into port, along with assorted fishing boats and pleasure craft.

From Charleston, Cape Arago Highway wanders along the channel, offering alternate views of water, woodlands, waterfront homes and businesses. Although the route goes through several name changes, it eventually takes you to Coos Bay. There's not a lot to explore in the old downtown area, which is putting up a good fight against a sagging economy. You can park and go walkabout, admiring some of the early 20th century storefronts and an occasional Victorian home in the neighborhoods.

The **Coos County Art Museum,** on Anderson between Second and Third, is among the town's more interesting structures, occupying an attractive federalist style former post office building. It's open Tuesday-Friday 11 to 5 and weekends 1 to 4. Exhibits focus mostly on art and photos of Coos Bay Area and other Oregon artisans. It is, incidentally, the only community art museum on the Oregon Coast.

Follow any of the named avenues (as opposed to numbered streets) to the bayfront, and you're back on Highway 101. The **Bay Area Chamber of Commerce** visitor center is here, at the base of the Central Avenue shopping mall; (503) 269-0215. It's open Monday-Friday 8:30 to 6:30, Saturday 10 to 4 and Sunday noon to 5. Oregon Dunes National Recreation Area and Siuslaw National Forest visitor facilities share the structure.

From the visitor center, Bayshore Drive (Highway 101) will send you north toward North Bend. Before you go too far, watch on your right for the a bit of publishing yesterday, tucked among the bayfront cargo sheds. It's opposite Timber Inn Motel at the upper edge of downtown Coos Bay:

☺ **Marshfield Sun Printing Museum** • *Bayshore Drive at Front Street; (503) 7656-6418. Tuesday-Saturday 1 to 4 from Memorial Day through Labor Day.* Housed in a small white board and batten structure, it preserves relics of the paper that reported the local news from 1891 until 1944. It's not so much a museum as an old newspaper office and job shop frozen in time. The *Sun* was one of the last newspapers in the state to use hand-set type, and its 200 type cases survive. You'll also see dusty printing presses, galley proofers and typewriters. For a kid like me, who started out as a printer's devil, this is a marvelous archive!

Between Coos Bay and North Bend, the highway and bayfront are lined with lumber mills and freight docks. Vessels flying flags of international shipping stand at dockside, loading their cargoes of forest products. Downtown North Bend, like Coos Bay, is in need of economic refueling. Earlier prosperity is evident in its sturdy brick and masonry buildings. However, they now house second hand shops, antique stores, used book stores and other secondary businesses. Some stand empty.

To learn of their past, stop by the **North Bend Information Center** in Simpson Park. It's at 1380 Sherman Ave., on the left side of the highway just beyond downtown; (503) 756-4613. Pick up a walking map for guidance through the historic old town section and nearby neighborhoods.

☺ **Coos County Historical Museum** • *In Simpson Park near the visitor center. Monday-Saturday 10 to 4 and Sunday noon to 4 in summer and Tuesday-Saturday 10 to 4 the rest of the year; (503) 756-6320. Adults $1, kids 5 to 11, an entire quarter.* The museum's most eye-catching exhibit—parked outside, of course—is a black and bold Baldwin steam locomotive. It hauled logs for the Coos Bay Lumber Company from 1923 until 1954. Inside, the fair-sized museum contains the usual pioneer artifacts and bottle collections, more or less neatly arranged. Expect to find lots of photos and artifacts concerning shipping and logging. Particularly intriguing is a display of "myrtlewood money," issued by the city in 1933 to pay salaries when it ran out of cash. The city will still redeem them, although they're obviously more valuable as collector pieces.

ACTIVITIES

Fishing charters • **Charleston Charters**, 5100 Cape Arago Hwy. (P.O. Box 5032), Charleston, OR 97420, (503) 888-4846; **Betty Kay Charters,** P.O. Box 5020, Charleston, OR 97420, (503) 888-9021; **Bob's Sport Fishing,** P.O. Box 5018, Charleston, OR 97420, (503) 888-4241.

Music festival • **Oregon Coast Music Association** holds its music festival in late July, featuring classical and contemporary works in Coos Bay and other communities. It also stages year-around concerts; offices at the Coos Art Museum, 235 Anderson St., (503) 267-0938.

Theater • **Little Theatre on the Bay,** 756-4336; **Playwrights American Conservatory Theatre** in the Broadway Theatre at 226 S. Broadway, (503) 269-2501; **Dolphin Players,** (503) 269-0215. **Southwestern Oregon Community College** also has an active drama department; (503) 888-2525.

ANNUAL EVENTS

Fourth of July Celebration with fireworks over the bay; (503) 269-0215.

Oregon Coast Music Festival in July, at various communities; (503) 267-0938.

Bay Area Fun Festival, downtown Coos Bay and on the bay with parade, games, booths, boating events, mid-September; (503) 269-0215.

Scandinavian Day, Nordic festivities, North Bend, (503) 756-4613.

WHERE TO DINE

☺ Blue Heron Bistro • △△△ $$

North Broadway at Commercial, downtown Coos Bay; (503) 267-3933. American-continental; wine and beer. Daily 8:30 to 10. MC/VISA. A chef-owned café noted for culinary creativity, ranging from Indonesian grilled chicken to chicken scaloppine, plus fresh local seafood, homemade croissants and breads. It's all served up in a pleasant bistro space of beamed ceilings, lace curtains and drop lamps. Outdoor dining patio.

Café Français • △△ $$

Cape Argo Highway and Roosevelt, Charleston; (503) 888-9977. French country, seafood; wine and beer. Tuesday-Saturday 5 to 9:30. Charming café with a French country look; wainscotting, light woods and floral décor. The chef-owner's menu ranges from chicken Dijon and beef fillets in cognac to salmon in lemon butter, scallops, scampi and whatever's just been caught.

☺ Portside Restaurant & Lounge • △△△ $$

At the boat basin, Charleston; (503) 888-5544. American, mostly seafood; full bar service. Daily 11:30 to 11. Major credit cards. The Bay Area's best seafood café, serving fish fresh off the boat, which is owned by the restaurant's proprietors. Extensive seafood menu, properly cooked and subtly seasoned by the Chinese owner-chefs. Small-plate dinners under $10, plus full dinners with chowder and salad up to the mid-teens. Attractive nautical décor with dockside views.

Broadway, paralleling Coos Bay's waterfront, is something of a mini-restaurant row, offering these three places. Two are next door; the third is a few blocks away.

Benetti's Italian Restaurant ● △△ $$
260 S. Broadway, Coos Bay; (503) 267-6066. Italian; full bar service. Sunday-Thursday 5 to 9, Friday-Saturday 5 to 10. MC/VISA. Hearty Italian fare served with soup, salad and garlic bread, plus special calzones and vegetarian lasagna. Attractive café with red carpeting, burgundy booths and an aquarium for a conversation piece. Upstairs dining room has bay views.

El Patio del Puerto ● △△ $
252 Broadway, Coos Bay; (503) 269-7754. Mexican and Southwestern; wine and beer. Monday-Thursday 11:30 to 9, Friday-Saturday noon to 10, Sunday noon to 8. MC/VISA. A cut above the usual Latino fare. Specials include sole stuffed with chili, Veracruz shrimp, spicy Santa Fe filet and Monterey chicken. The narrow, high ceiling restaurant is brightened with Latin doo-dads; some tables have bay views; outdoor patio.

Kum Yon's ● △△ $
836 S. Broadway, Coos Bay; (503) 269-2662. Asian; wine and beer. Daily 11 to 10. MC/VISA. Chef-owned café serving a tasty variety of Chinese, Japanese and Korean food—plus an occasional American-style fish filet. Chinese fare is mostly spicy Szechuan, such as Mongolian beef and hot and sour soup. The busy menu also has Japanese entrèes such as shrimp tempura and beef teriyaki, plus specialties from the owner's native Korea. Also featured are dim sum lunches and American-style desserts.

WHERE TO SLEEP
Bay Bridge Motel ● △△ $$$ ∅
33 Coast Highway (at East Bay Drive), North Bend, OR 97459; (503) 756-3151. Couples $49 to $59, singles $40 to $50, kitchenettes from $62. Major credit cards. A 16-unit motel on Russell Point with views of Coos Bay; rooms with TV and phones.

Bayshore Motel ● △ $$ ∅
1685 N. Bayshore Dr. (U.S. 101), Coos Bay, OR 97420; (503) 267-4138. Couples $46 to $68, singles $36 to $48. MC/VISA. Basic 32-unit motel with TV and room phones.

Captain John's Motel ● △△ $$ ∅
8061 Kingfisher Dr. (P.O. Box 5005), Charleston, OR 97420; (503) 888-4041. Couples $35 to $65, singles $30 to $60, kitchenettes $12 extra, suites from $85. MC/VISA. A 46-unit motel near the boat basin with TV, room phones; some refrigerators. **Portside Restaurant** adjacent, listed above.

City Center Motel ● △ $$ ∅
750 Connecticut Ave. (at S. Highway 101), North Bend, OR 97459; (503) 756-5118. Couples $38 to $48, singles $28 to $38. MC/VISA, DISC. An 18-unit motel with TV and room phones.

Pacific Empire Motel ● △ $
155 S. Empire Blvd., Coos Bay, OR 97420; (503) 888-3281. Couples and singles $32, kitchenettes $37. MC/VISA. Basic 40-unit motel with TV and room phones. **Restaurant** serves American fare; dinners $4.50 to $14.

Terrace Motel ● △ $$ ∅
1109 S. First St., Coos Bay, OR 97420; (503) 269-5061. Couples $38 to $48, singles $32 to $35, kitchenettes $38 to $48. MC/VISA. A 15-unit motel with TV and room phones.

Bed & breakfast inns

Coos Bay Manor Bed & Breakfast ● △△ $$$ ∅
955 S. Fifth St. (Ingersoll), Coos Bay, OR 97420; (503) 269-1224. Couples and singles $55 to $65. Five rooms, one private and four share baths; continental breakfast. No credit cards. Colonial style home built in 1911, with imposing columned entry. Each room has a decorator theme: Victorian, Western, American country, Colonial and a garden room with wicker and potted plants.

Itty Bitty Inn ● △△ $$
1504 Sherman Ave. (Highway 101), North Bend, OR 97459; (503) 756-6398. Couples $34 to $38, singles $31 to $35, add $2 per person for full breakfast; private baths. MC/VISA, DISC. Former motel remodeled into a B&B with Southwestern décor. Five rooms with private entrances, phones, TV movies and refrigerator.

This Olde House Bed & Breakfast ● △△ $$$ ∅
202 Alder Ave. (two blocks off 101), Coos Bay, OR 97420; (503) 267-5224. Couples $65 to $75, singles $55. Three rooms, one with private bath; full breakfast. No credit cards. A restored 1893 Victorian with a a bay view. Lofty ten-foot ceilings and a double stairway provide a proper setting for the owners' collection of antiques. Downtown, close to shops.

Upper Room Chalet ● △△ $$$ ∅
306 N. Eighth St. (Commercial), Coos Bay, OR 97420; (503) 269-5385. Couples $55 to $65, singles $35 to $60. Four units; one private, three share baths; full breakfast. No credit cards. Early 20th century home with Victorian and American antiques, surrounded by evergreens and rhododendrons. Comfortable sitting room with fireplace, large library, piano and Victrola.

WHERE TO CAMP

Bastendorff Beach County Park ● *Just off Cape Arago Highway; (503) 888-5353. RV and tent sites, water and electric $12, no hookups $10. No reservations or credit cards.* Wooded, fairly well-spaced sites with barbecues, picnic tables and showers. Swimming, horseshoes, kids playground.

Charleston Travel Park ● *Downtown Charleston, on Kingfisher Drive next to the marina; (503) 888-9512. RV and tent sites, $6 to $11.50. Reservations accepted.* Some pull-throughs; showers, kids' play area, adult lounge, laundry, cable TV, ice and RV supplies; crab rings and clam shovels for rent.

Oceanside RV Park ● *9838 Cape Arago Hwy., Charleston; (503) 888-2598. RV sites, full hookups $14, water and electric $12, no hookups $10. No credit cards.* Small, simple spot with grassy sites, some pull-throughs, showers and laundry. Path to nearby beach.

Sunset Bay State Park ● *10965 Cape Arago Hwy.; (503) 888-4920. RV and tent sites, full hookups $13, water and electric $12, no hookups $11, hiker-biker $2. Part of the state park reservation system (see intro above under "Camping").* Nicely spaced tree-sheltered sites with fire pits, barbecues, picnic tables and showers.

As you continue north on U.S. 101, the concrete arch and steel girder **McCullough Bridge** carries you across a wide expanse of Coos Bay. For a scenic side trip, turn right just beyond the bridge, following signs to **Mc-Cullough Wayside** along the bay's north shore. You soon leave lumber mills, log piles and shipping docks behind, and enter a lush green woodland. With the wide blue estuary on your left, you may think you've been transported to Alaska's Inside Passage.

Oregon Dunes National Recreation Area

North of North Bend, the Pacific disappears behind the shapely curves of the world's largest collection of coastal sand dunes. They stretch more than 40 miles along Highway 101 between the Bay Area and Florence. Much of this area has been preserved in Oregon Dunes National Recreation Area (271-3611), headquartered in Reedsport at the junction of highways 101 and 38.

"Preserved" may be too generous a word, since a popular recreation here is roaring over the dunes in sputtering sand buggies. On weekends, great squadrons of these little growlers occupy campgrounds and other staging areas. These folks often trailer in their toys on a Friday night. Then they greet the dawn with grinning faces as they tune their engines for the day's play. Staging areas sound like lawn mower conventions.

About half of the 14,000 acres of "unvegetated" dunes are open to all-terrain vehicles. However, only a third of the area's two million annual visitors are dune-buggiers, according to rangers. You can avoid ATV areas and campgrounds that are used as staging areas. Or you can join the sand party and rent your own rig. We list several outlets at the end of this section.

If you'd prefer to hike in the dunes instead of racing over them, many areas are restricted to foot traffic, and some offer hiking trails. One of the better spots is **The Oregon Dunes Overlook** just north of Reedsport. Graphics describe the nomenclature of sand dunes, and trails lead through them to the distant beach. Another good spot is **Eel Creek Campground** near Lakeside. Here, a short trail takes you to the crest of the dunes, then it's dead-reckoning to the shore.

It's easy to lose your sense of direction in sand dunes, so orient yourself to a high landmark before starting out, and carry a compass, like a good Scout. Since dunes are piled up by the wind, the windward side is gently inclined, while the leeward side, called the "slipface" is often quite steep. The ritual of dune hiking is to trudge up the windward side, then slide or roll merrily down the slipface. Since the wind erases footprints and tracks, access isn't restricted to specific trails.

You'll discover that hiking through sand dunes is akin to walking through sifted flour (although the fine, clean sand doesn't stick). Some folks do it only for the novelty, and usually only once. However, your kids probably will want to spend the day in the dunes.

Oregon's dunes, like nearly all beach sand, was washed to the sea from rivers, starting about a million years ago. The Umpqua River is a primary contributor here, carrying glacial material from the Cascades and Coast Range. Once this refined sand reaches the sea, it's shifted along the coastline by currents and deposited on the beaches by wave action. The broad two-mile wide plain between Florence and Coos Bay provides a natural depository for these so-called "ocean dunes." Wind shapes them into constantly changing curves, and the dunes migrate inland at the rate of six to 12 feet a year. In many areas, they march into coastal woodlands, gradually suffocating the trees. You'll see several "ghost forests" as you drive north.

However, the rapid spread of European beach grass, introduced farther north at the turn of the century to anchor the sand, may eventually eradicate the unvegetated dunes. It has gained footholds in many areas, allowing Sitka spruce and shore pines to re-establish. Some experts speculate that the open dunes may vanish within a couple of centuries because of the tenacious grass.

To learn more about sand dunes, sign up for one of the summer interpretive programs, held between Memorial Day and Labor Day at several places around the NRA. A publication called *Sand Tracks* lists these interpretive programs, overlooks, campgrounds, dune buggy staging areas, hiking areas and other information. A handy strip map helps guide you through the region. The publication is available at the visitor center at the Reedsport Chamber of Commerce.

NORTH BEND TO REEDSPORT

A couple of miles north of North Bend, a left turn takes you into the first section of Oregon Dunes NRA, on Horsfall Dunes and Beach Access Road. Drive past the North Bay Marine Industrial Park, then follow signs to several campgrounds among the dunes, including **Horsfall, Horsfall Beach** and **Bluebill. Horsfall** and **Bluebill** have flush potties and Horsfall has showers (no hookups). **Horsfall Beach** is essentially a tarmac for self-contained units only, with flush potties but no showers. Bluebill is the most secluded of the three, with sheltered sites. Horsfall and Horsfall Beach are primarily dune buggy staging areas. Rates at Oregon Dunes NRA campgrounds range from $6 to $8.

Continuing north on U.S. 101, you'll soon see the first of several dune buggy rental outfits, **Far West ATV Rental**, on your left. Nearby is the **Myrtlewood Factory Store** open daily 8 to 5; it gives tours on weekdays. About four miles farther is **Spinreel Campground**, with attractive if snugly-spaced units; flush potties but no showers or hookups. You next encounter the small community of **Lakeside** and **Tugman State Park.** This attractive campground is a good refuge if you want to avoid the buzz of dune buggies. Water and electric hookups are $12 a night and showers are available. You can swim, boat and picnic here on **Eel Lake.**

Four miles north of Tugman, go left on Old Lighthouse Road through lush forests to **Umpqua Lighthouse State Park**. It's on the summer reservation system (see "Camping" in the introduction above), with full hookups for $13, water and electric $11, no hookups $10. **Umpqua Lighthouse** crowns a hill just beyond; it's closed to the public. The original lighthouse was the first in the Oregon Territory, built at the mouth of the Umpqua River in 1857. The present one, still in operation, was erected in 1894.

☺ Opposite the light is the **Umpqua River Whale Watching Station,** with nice views down to the beach and the mouth of the Umpqua.

This is a good spot for watching the annual migration of the gray whale, and graphics tell you about their antics and habits. The migration occurs from December through April. The best whale spotting times are December to early January and mid-March to mid-April. Just beyond is an interesting gathering of coastal memorabilia:

Coastal Visitor Center • *Old Lighthouse Road, Winchester Bay; (503) 440-4500. May through September, Wednesday-Saturday 10 to 5 and Sunday 1 to 5. Free; donations appreciated.* Occupying the administration building and barracks of the old Umpqua River Coast Guard Station, this attractive museum contains photos and artifacts of the early days of Umpqua River settlement. Exhibits include a scale model of an 1863 lumber mill, items from the sternwheeler *Eva* that once plied the river and lots of stuff on the U.S. Life Saving Service, the forerunner of the Coast Guard. A special exhibit focuses on the gray whale and its remarkable 12,000-mile round trip past the Oregon Coast.

From here, drive downhill toward Winchester Bay, turn left at a stop and follow an estuary road south between sand dunes and surf to **Ziolkowsky Beach County Park.** It offers beach and sand dune access and picnic areas. Beyond, you re-enter Oregon Dunes National Recreation Area. As you drive, you'll enjoy views of the dunes, thatched here and there with clumps of trees and dune grass. Then head north to the mouth of—forgive us—the mother river of the Oregon dunes.

Although it's less famous than the Rogue, the Umpqua is the largest West Coast river between the Columbia and the Sacramento in central California. Starting high in the Cascades, it gathers a dozen tributaries as it wanders between the Willamette and Rogue valleys, cuts through the Coast Range, widens into a sizable estuary at Reedsport and finally meets the Pacific in Winchester Bay. Steamers once chugged 20 miles inland to Scottsburg, where wagons picked up lumber, produce and salmon for delivery to the Willamette Valley.

Winchester Bay/Reedsport

Winchester Bay: 900   **Reedsport: 5,030**

Sitting beside Salmon Harbor near the mouth of the Umpqua, tiny Winchester Bay is one of the coast's real charmers. More of a boat basin than a town, it occupies an attractive niche at the base of a wooded bluff.

It's a compact and handsomely weathered collection of seafood cafès, fish markets, canneries and curio shops. You can snack on fish kebobs from a small stall, book a fishing trip, sample smoked salmon and poke around the shops. At **Sportsmen's Cannery and Gift Shop** (271-3293), sample smoked fish with interesting seafood dips, and pick up a cup of cioppino or shrimp cocktail to go. It also sells fresh fish, Oregon specialty foods and curios. Although the harbor's commercial area is small, the marina is quite large, with 900 slips cradling the coast's largest sportfishing fleet.

Following Salmon Harbor Boulevard from Winchester Bay, you re-join Highway 101 and drive four miles to Reedsport. Larger and more prosperous, it lacks the rustic charm of the smaller town. However, the **old town** section to the right of the highway has a few shops, galleries and antique stores in sturdy old structures. **The Mercantile Company** at 495 Fir Avenue is done up in vintage dècor, featuring antiques, gifts and Oregon specialty foods.

Reedsport is a good place to stock up on provisions and grab a motel room or campsite for the night. If you haven't already done so, you can load up on information about Oregon Dunes and other area lures. The visitor centers of **Oregon Dunes National Recreation Area** (271-3611) and **Lower Umpqua Chamber of Commerce** (271-3495) sit at the junction of U.S. 101 and State Highway 38, in the middle of town. ODNRA hours are Monday-Friday 8 to 6 and weekends 9:30 to 6 in summer and 8 to 4:30 the rest of the year.

The estuary between Winchester Bay and Reedsport is one of the finest salmon fishing areas on the state's coast. Its mud flats and nearby coastal beaches are good for clamming.

ACTIVITIES

Dune buggy rentals ● Most rentals are four-wheel all-terrain vehicles, and rates range from $20 to $35 an hour. Among firms on the edge of Oregon Dunes NRA are **Sandland Adventures Inc.,** 85366 S. Highway 101, Florence, OR 97439, (503) 997-8087; **Dunes Odyssey Rentals,** Highway 101, Winchester Bay, OR 97+67, (503) 271-4011; **Far West Rentals,** Hauser (North Bend), OR 97459; (503) 756-2322 or 756-4274; **Dune Quad Runners,** HC 4, Box 245, Reedsport, OR 97467, (503) 271-3443; **Pacific Coast Recreation**, 4121 U.S. 101, Hauser (North Bend), OR 97459; (503) 756-7183; and **Spinreel Dune Buggy Rentals,** 9122 Wildwood Dr., North Bend, OR 97459; (503) 759-3313.

Dune buggy tours ● If you'd rather leave the driving to others, these firms offer sand dune tours: **Sandland Adventures,** 85366 S. Highway 101, Florence, OR 97439, (503) 997-8087; **Pacific Coast Recreation**, 4121 U.S. 101, Hauser (North Bend), OR 97459; (503) 756-7183; and **Oregon Dune Tours,** 9122 Wildwood Dr., North Bend, OR 97459, (503) 759-4777.

Fishing charters ● **Krista-J Charters,** Salmon Harbor, Winchester Bay, OR 97467, (503) 271-5698 or 271-3293; **Gee Gee Charters,** 465 Beach Blvd., Winchester Bay, OR 97465, (503) 271-3152 or 271-4134; **The Main Charters,** Salmon Harbor, Winchester Bay, OR 97467, (503) 271-3800.

WHERE TO DINE

Salmon Harbor Cafè ● ∆ $

196 Bay Front Loop, Winchester Bay; (503) 271-5523. American, mostly seafood; wine and beer. Daily 5 a.m. to 3 p.m. MC/VISA. Cozy, simple spot for an inexpensive lunch. The menu features seafood—mostly fried—plus good old chicken fried steak, liver and onions and such. You can carbo-load on breakfast pancakes before your early morning fishing trip.

Seafood Grotto Restaurant ● ∆∆ $$

Eighth and Broadway, Winchester Bay; (503) 271-4250. American, mostly seafood; full bar service. Daily 11 to 9. MC/VISA. Attractive old fashioned cafè with wainscotting, print wallpaper and ceiling fans. Menu features several salmon dishes, seafood calamari, clam strips and oysters, plus the usual steak, chicken and pork.

Windjammer Restaurant ● ∆∆ $$

1281 Highway Ave., Reedsport; (503) 271-5415. American, mostly seafood; full bar service. Daily from 6 a.m. MC/VISA. Typically nautical diner, popular with locals; balanced menu of fresh seafood and American steaks, chicken and chops. Malibu chicken topped with ham and cheese is tasty. Fish, scallop, prawn and oyster dinners come in three sizes to fit various appetites and wallets.

WHERE TO SLEEP

Best Western Salbasgeon Inn ● △△ $$$ ∅
1400 Highway Ave., Reedsport, OR 97467; (800) 528-1234 or (503) 271-4831. Couples $71 to $120, singles $66 to $105, kitchenettes $88 to $120, suites $105 to $120. Major credit cards. Attractive 42-room motel with TV movies, room phones; some units with spa tubs and fireplaces. Indoor pool, spa, exercise room.

Douglas Country Inn ● △△ $ ∅
1894 Winchester Ave. (Highway 101 at 19th Street), Reedsport, OR 97467; (503) 271-3686. One bed (one or two people) $28 to $42, two beds $38 to $48, three beds $48 to $52, kitchenettes $45 to $55. MC/VISA. Refurbished 23-unit motel with TV and room phones; some refrigerators.

Salbasgeon Inn of the Umpqua ● △△ $$$
45209 Highway 38 (7.5 miles east), Reedsport, OR 97467; (503) 271-2025. Couples $66 to $86, singles $61 to $81, kitchenettes $76. Major credit cards. Small, attractive 13-room inn with TV movies, room phones; at river's edge with boat ramp; all rooms have river views.

Tropicana Motel ● △ $$ ∅
1593 Highway Ave., Reedsport, OR 97467; (503) 271-3671. Couples $32 to $80, singles $28 to $55, kitchenettes $40 to $80. Major credit cards. A 41-unit motel with TV, room phones and pool.

Western Hills Motel ● △△ $$ ∅
1821 Winchester Ave. (Highway 101), Reedsport, OR 97467; (503) 271-2149. Couples and singles $36 to $98. Major credit cards. Well-kept 21-room motel with TV movies, phones and swimming pool.

Winchester Bay Friendship Inn ● △△ $$$ ∅
390 Broadway (P.O. Box 1037), Winchester Bay, OR 97467; (800) 424-4777 or (503) 271-4871. Couples $58 to $75, singles $45 to $85, kitchenettes $55 to $85, suites $53 to $85. Major credit cards. A 52-unit motel with TV movies and phones. Free continental breakfast; harbor view rooms; some rooms with spa tubs. Quiet, off-highway location.

Winchester Bay Motel ● △△ $$ ∅
P.O. Box 37, Winchester Bay, OR 97467; (503) 271-4871. Couples $45 to $48, kitchenettes $55. MC/VISA. Fairly tidy units with TV, phones. Within walking distance of boat basin restaurants and shops.

WHERE TO CAMP

Harbor RV Park ● *75325 Highway 101, Winchester Bay, OR 97467 (503) 469-2222. RV units; $8 to $15. Reservations accepted.* Clean but closely packed sites across U.S. 101 from Winchester Bay; full hookups, showers.

Surfwood Campground ● *75381 Highway 101 (Route 4, Box 268), Reedsport, OR 97467; (503) 271-4020. RV and tent sites with full hookups; $10 to $14. Reservations accepted.* Complete, well-maintained facility with pull-throughs, mini-mart, pool and sauna, recreation pavilion, fish cleaning station, kids play area and horseshoes.

Windy Cove Campgrounds ● *Off Salmon Harbor Boulevard (P.O. Box 265), Winchester Bay, OR 97467; (503) 271-5634. RV and tent sites, $8.40 to $10.50. No reservations or credit cards.* Two Douglas County park campgrounds near the beach; some shaded sites; water and electric, showers. Marina, boat rentals, boat launch, fishing, swimming.

REEDSPORT TO FLORENCE

North of Reedsport, you'll cross the **Umpqua Estuary** on a sturdy old concrete arch bridge and pass through the tiny town of **Gardiner.** It consists mostly of a large lumber-loading dock and the Gardiner Wood Products division of International Paper Company. You might like to pause and watch a giant pincer-jaw crane heft logs around.

Tahkenitch Campground, seven miles north of Reedsport, is another Oregon Dunes NRA facility. It's adjacent to Tahkenitch Lake, with nicely wooded RV and tent sites for $8. Nearby is the **Tahkenitch Landing Archeological Site,** an ancient Native American encampment. Ask for directions at the campground.

☺ Another three miles takes you to **Oregon Dunes Overlook,** with two viewing platforms offering graphics detailing the life of a sand dune. A ranger or volunteer may be on duty to further enlighten you. The hike through the dunes to the beach and back is about two miles. The least painful approach is to take the south trail over Big Dune to the surf, then return on the much firmer forest trail to the north viewpoint. North of the overlook, **Siltcoos Dune and Beach** access road takes you west from Highway 101 into the dunes and several more NRA campgrounds.

☺ You then emerge from the national recreation area and arrive at **Honeyman State Park** (997-3641). Surrounding Cleowax Lake, it's one of the most complete—and heavily used—parks on the coast. Campsites, which are on the summer reservation system, are $13 with full hookups, $12 water and electric, $11 no hookup and $2 for hiker-biker. Other facilities in this attractive, thickly wooded park include a swimming area, boat and paddle boat rentals, mini-mart and even a light meal restaurant open daily 7 a.m. to 9 p.m. Sand dunes crawl down to the opposite shore of Cleowax Lake, reached by hiking trail or by paddling your boat across.

Beyond Honeyman, you approach the town of **Florence** and the northernmost element of Oregon Dunes National Recreation Area. This puts you at mid-point on the Oregon Coast—a perfectly logical place to end this chapter.

TRIP PLANNER

WHEN TO GO ● As with the southern half, the northern coast offers its best weather in the fall. It's the best clamming and crabbing season as well, and anglers can catch the fall salmon and steelhead runs in the estuaries. If you have a moody artists' soul, go during winter and watch the storms. Yachats and Oceanside are excellent winter hideaways.

WHAT TO SEE ● The northern reaches of Oregon Dunes National Recreation Area, the excellent visitor center at Cape Perpetua Scenic Area and the viewpoint above, Alsea Bay Bridge Interpretive Center in Waldport, the new Oregon Coast Museum and Yaquina Bay Lighthouse in Newport, Yaquina Head Natural Area north of Newport, Cape Meares Lighthouse and the Octopus Tree, the Blimp Hangar Museum near Tillamook, coastal highway views from Oswald West State Park.

WHAT TO DO ● Prowl the riverfront streets of old towns in Florence, Yachats, Newport and Garibaldi; drive the Three Capes Scenic Route; watch the dory "surf launch" at Pacific City; nibble some cheddar at the Tillamook Cheese Factory; hike to the secluded beach below Oswald West walk-in campground; hike to Tillamook Head from Cannon Beach or Seaside; browse the shops and galleries of Cannon Beach; walk the Prom at Seaside.

Useful contacts

Cannon Beach Chamber of Commerce, 201 E. Second St. (P.O. Box 64), Cannon Beach, OR 97110; (503) 436-2623.

Cape Perpetua Visitor Center, Siuslaw National Forest, P.O. Box 274, Yachats, OR 97498; (503) 547-3289.

Depoe Bay Chamber of Commerce, P.O. Box 21, Depoe Bay, OR 97341; (503) 765-2889.

Florence Chamber of Commerce, 270 Highway 101, Florence, OR 97439; (503) 997-3128.

Lincoln City Visitor & Convention Bureau, 801 SW Highway 101, Lincoln City, OR 97367; (800) 452-2151 or (503) 994-8378.

Greater Newport Chamber of Commerce, 555 SW Coast Highway, Newport, OR 97365; (800) 262-7844 or (503) 265-8801.

Pacific City Chamber of Commerce, P.O. Box 331, Pacific City, OR 97135; (503) 965-6161.

Seaside Chamber of Commerce, Seven N. Roosevelt Dr. (P.O. Box 7), Seaside, OR 97138-0007; (800) 444-6740 or (503) 738-6391.

Tillamook Chamber of Commerce, 3705 N. Highway 101, Tillamook, OR 97141; (503) 842-7525.

Waldport Area Chamber of Commerce, P.O. Box 669, Waldport, OR 97394; (503) 563-2133.

Yachats Area Chamber of Commerce, P.O. Box 728, Yachats, OR 97498; (503) 547-3530.

Northern Oregon Coast radio stations

KYLE-FM, 102.7, Newport-Lincoln City—light rock, easy listening
KLCO-FM, 90.5, Newport—National Public Radio
KCRF-FM, 96.7, Lincoln City—classics and easy listening
KCRO-FM 104.1, Tillamook—top 40 oldies
KKEE-FM, 94.3, Long Beach, Wash.—rock, including oldies
KBCH-AM, 1400, Newport-Lincoln City—top 40, news
KCRO-AM 1590, Tillamook—top 40 oldies
KSWB-AM, 840, Seaside—talk and news

Chapter Six

THE NORTH COAST

Seastacks, sea lions and "say cheese"

WHEN MOTHER NATURE crafted the Oregon Coast, she saw no need to differentiate between the southern and northern sections. Both ends are wet, windy and equally attractive. Vegetation and climate are similar and those dramatic seastacks are rather uniformly scattered.

There are differences, however, and most have been wrought by man. The towns, although small, are more concentrated in the northern end. This is demographically logical since settlement began in this area. Further, most of the coast's weekend visitors are drawn from the Portland-to-Eugene population corridor. Thus, north coast towns are more geared to commercial tourism. This is particularly true of Newport, Lincoln City, Cannon Beach and Seaside.

We aren't suggesting that the north coast is one long Coney Island, however. It offers many of the same beautiful coastal panoramas as the southern section. Cape Perpetua near Yachats may be the single most striking viewpoint on the entire coastline. The Three Capes Route below Tillamook rivals any scenic byway to the south. Siuslaw (*Sigh-OOS-law*) National Forest and Tillamook State Forest offer quick and easy escapes inland to evergreen wilds.

Since we left Reedsport in the previous chapter, Highway 101 has traveled inland, buffered from the ocean by the Oregon dunes. The Pacific remains out of sight as you approach Florence. However, the old town's location on the Siuslaw River estuary provides ocean access and a salt water port. The rain-rinsed terrain around Florence is noted for its wild and cultivated rhododendrons and the town honors them with two annual celebrations.

Florence

Population: 5,200   **Elevation: 11 feet**

Florence is a pleasant community that is at once tied to its past and headed for the future. It dates back to the 1850s when it was developed as a lumbering port at the mouth of the Siuslaw River. Like other coastal cities of the day, it grew close to the waterfront, relying on the river for personal transit, commerce and fresh fish for dinner. History has muddled the source of its name. Take your pick from two versions:

• It was named for Lane County representative A.B. Florence, which sounds perfectly logical.

• It was named for the French ship *Florence* which went aground here and a board bearing her name was washed ashore. This makes a much better story, and most folks prefer it.

Yesterday's Florence is still rooted in the river, literally. Her once-shabby pier piling buildings along Bay Street are being fashioned into boutiques and seafood restaurants. With its board and batten buildings and an occasional Victorian, it's a natural lure for visitors. Modern Florence is a growing retirement community, with nondescript new businesses and suburbs spreading northward along the coast.

Approaching town from the south, you'll see the **Siuslaw Pioneer Museum** on your left (listed below). Just beyond, a grand concrete and steel bridge with Art Deco accents spans the broad estuary of the Siuslaw River. It's one of several created by Oregon's master bridge builder Conde B. McCullough in the 1930s. (See box under Waldport below.) As you cross the bridge, you'll see Old Town to the left, on the estuary's north bank. Before dropping down there, stop at the small visitor center of the **Florence Chamber of Commerce** on Highway 101 just beyond the bridge; (503) 997-3128. It's open daily 9 to 5.

The northernmost section of Oregon Dunes National Recreation Area ends at the south jetty of the Siuslaw River. To reach these undulating dunes and the beach beyond, take South Jetty Road just below the bridge and follow it coastward. You'll pass interesting extremes of mixed use—dune buggy staging areas and marshy lakes that are havens for shorebirds and bird watchers. At the far end of the road, a dock over the jetty is popular for crabbing and fishing. (See the previous chapter for more details on Oregon Dunes NRA.)

ATTRACTIONS & ACTIVITIES

☺ **Siuslaw Pioneer Museum** • *85294 S. Highway 101; (503) 997-7884. Tuesday-Sunday 10 to 4; donations appreciated.* Housed in a curious structure with a curved gabled roof, the museum offers the typical pioneer and Indian artifacts. Among its more interesting lures are displays on logging, homesteaders relics and documents proving that the federal government conned the Siuslaw Indians out of their land.

Indian Forest • *88493 N. Highway 101 (four miles north), Florence, OR 97439; (503) 997-3677. Summers 8 a.m. to dusk, the rest of the year 10 to 4. Adults $3; MC/VISA.* We haven't taken a poll, but some Native Americans might be put off by this tourist gimmick, with its cigar store Indian out front and rubber tomahawks and head dresses for sale in the gift shop. Out back, proprietors have assembled several full-scale Indian dwellings that are accurate in detail, if a bit stereotyped. They range from plains teepees to coastal Indians' rough board structures. A few buffalo roam among the trees.

Horseback riding • C&M Stables, 90241 N. Highway 101 (eight miles north), Florence, OR 97439; (503) 997-7540 or 997-3021. Conducted and independent beach and mountain rides; horse boarding.

River trips • Siuslaw River Jet Boat Excursions, 1441 Bay St., Florence, OR 97439, (503) 997-7308; MC/VISA; upriver trips every two hours in summer. **Frontier Riverboat Rides,** Highway 126 Milepost 9, Florence, OR 97439; (503) 268-4017; excursions and dinner cruises up the Siuslaw River aboard the *Westward Ho!,* an old fashioned sternwheeler.

ANNUAL EVENTS

Rhododendron and Azalea Show, March; (503) 997-8697.

Rhododendron Festival, late May; (503) 997-3128.

National Stilt Walking Championship, part of Fourth of July celebration; (503) 997-3128.

Community Salmon Barbecue, August; (503) 997-3128.

WHERE TO DINE

☺ Bridgewater Seafood Restaurant • ▲▲▲ $$

1297 Bay Street at Laurel (in Old Town); (503) 997-9405. Seafood and continental; full bar service. Lunch and dinner daily from 11 a.m. MC/VISA. Handsome vintage décor restaurant housed in a 1901 Italianate storefront; high ceilings and wicker furniture. Creative menu ranges from honey-mustard halibut and seafood sauté to jambalaya and chicken cacciatore.

Fisherman's Wharf • ▲ $

1341 Bay Street at Laurel (in Old Town); (503) 997-2613. American, mostly seafood; full bar service. Open 24 hours. Simple barnboard café with standard American menu ranging from steamer clams and fried and sautéed seafoods to steak, chicken and pork chops.

Mo's • ▲ $

1436 Bay St. (Old town); (503) 997-2185. Seafood; wine and beer. Lunch and dinner daily from 11 a.m. MC/VISA. Mo's is something of a local institution with several basic, inexpensive cafés along the central Oregon Coast. It was started years ago in Newport by Native American Mohava Niemi of the Siletz tribe. The Florence version is built on a pier over the estuary. The large seafood menu ranges from steamer clams, oysters and other shellfish to salmon and halibut; most dinners under $9.

In addition to the above, you'll find a couple of basic walk-up cafés in Old Town: **Travelers' Cove** open 11 to 7:30, with tables on the estuary and light fare; and **Harbor House,** open 7 to 7 daily except Wednesday, issuing mostly fried seafood through a take-out window, up to $7; seating on a dock over the estuary.

WHERE TO SLEEP

Best Western Pier Point Inn • ⌂⌂⌂ $$$ ∅

U.S. 101 at south end of bridge (P.O. Box 2235), Florence, OR 97439; (800) 528-1234 or (503) 997-7191. Couples $45 to $85, singles $40 to $79. Major credit cards. Nicely furnished 49-unit motel; balconies with bay views; TV movies and room phones; Spa, sauna. **Restaurant** serves 7 a.m. to 2 and 5 to 9 p.m.; dinners $8 to $16; full bar service.

Driftwood Shores Surfside Resort ● △△ $$$$ ∅
88416 First Ave. (Haceta Beach Road), Florence, OR 97439; (503) 997-8263. Couples $72 to $98, singles $55 to $66. Major credit cards. Well-kept 120-unit apartment resort with studios, one and two-bedroom units, many with sea views. TV, pay movies, room phones, refrigerators, many kitchens. Pool, sauna, spa, coin laundry; beach nearby. **Restaurant** serves 8 a.m. to 9 p.m.; dinners $7 to $16; full bar service.

Le Chateau Motel ● △ $$ ∅∅
Highway 101 near Route 126 (P.O. Box 98), Florence, OR 97439; (503) 997-3481. Couples $36 to $60, singles from $30. Major credit cards. Neatly kept 48-unit motel with TV, pay movies and room phones; pool, sauna and spa.

Money-Saver Motel ● △ $$ ∅
170 Highway 101 (a mile south), Florence, OR 97439; (503) 997-7131. Couples $34 to $48, singles $30 to $42. Major credit cards. A 40-unit motel with TV and room phones.

Park Motel ● △△ $ ∅
85034 Highway 101 (1.25 miles south), Florence, OR 97439; (503) 997-2634. Couples $32 to $44, singles from $24, kitchenettes from $58. Major credit cards. Older, well-kept 15-unit motel with TV and room phones.

Bed & breakfast inn

Oak Street Bed & Breakfast ● △△ $$ ∅
394 Oak Street at Fourth (P.O. Box 2799), Florence, OR 97439; (503) 997-4000. Couples and singles $50 to $75. Six rooms; private and shared baths; full breakfast. MC/VISA. Early American style sea captain's home built in 1904; rooms done in American and Victorian antiques. In Old Town section, just up from the riverfront.

WHERE TO CAMP

C&D Dock ● *09634 Highway 126 (P.O. Box 7), Mapleton, OR 97453; (503) 268-9950. RV sites, water and electric $10.* Basic, well-maintained park with sites on the Siuslaw River, ten miles up from Florence. Showers, with marina adjacent.

Heceta Beach RV Park ● *04636 Heceta Beach Rd. (three miles north), Florence, OR 97349; (503) 997-7664. RV sites, full hookups, $12.50. Reservations accepted; MC/VISA.* Fairly well-spaced sites near beach; some pull-throughs; showers, cable TV, rec hall, laundry.

Woahink Lake RV Resort ● *83570 S. Highway 101, (four miles south), Florence, OR 97439; (503) 997-6454. RV sites, full hookups $14. Reservations accepted; MC/VISA.* Very attractive facility by a small lake adjacent to Oregon Dunes National Recreation Area. Pull-throughs; showers, coin laundry, cable TV. Sand dune observation platform, boat dock, hiking trails.

Side trip upstream to Mapleton

Highway 126 ties Florence to Eugene, 61 miles inland. Expect it to be a busy corridor on summer weekends. It's also a rather pleasing drive as it twists gently through the Coast Range, following wooded banks of the meandering Siuslaw River. Even if you aren't Eugene-bound, you might enjoy a side-trip to the upriver hamlet of Mapleton.

The Florence waterfront on the Siuslaw River estuary retains its rustic charm despite rapid suburban growth.
-- Betty Woo Martin

The first few miles take you through a stretch of Siuslaw National Forest, decorating the roadside with thick groves of Douglas fir and Sitka spruce. The river, a slow tidal estuary at this point, is rarely out of view. It's navigable for fishing boats and thus popular for seekers of salmon, perch and the occasional sturgeon. A couple of marinas and RV parks stand along its banks. (C&D Dock is listed above.)

You'll pass the home port of the paddlewheeler *Westward Ho!* (listed above, under Activities) about eight miles upstream from Florence. Fifteen miles inland, you encounter semi-charming **Mapleton,** with a one-block oldstyle business district and a few homes along both sides of the river. Its primary lures are two restaurants, so distinctive that they draw diners from Florence and Eugene.

☺ Alpha Bits ● △ $ ∅
Downtown Mapleton; (503) 268-4311. American; meals $4 to $9. No credit cards. A book and craft store and café, serving whole-grain, whole-earth and probably organic fare such as "grainburgers," pita sandwiches, holistic juices and excellent muffins. Properly rustic and funky, it was started in 1972 by the Alpha commune from nearby Deadwood.

☺ Gingerbread Village ● △△ $
Two miles east of Mapleton, State Route 126; (503) 268-4713. American; dinners $6 to $9. Monday-Saturday 6 a.m. to 9 p.m., Sunday 8 to 9. MC/VISA. The opposite of Alpha Bits; a very attractive Bavarian-style café with warm woods, wainscoting and cheerful flower trim. Despite the old world look, the menu is essential American: steak, chicken and chops, all very inexpensive. The café's namesake gingerbread is outstanding, worth a special trip for the sweet-tooth set.

FLORENCE TO NEWPORT
The north end of Florence is a booming and rather ungainly commercial strip that marks the old community's current prosperity. Beyond the upper edge of town, you'll see some of the most northerly of the Oregon dunes.

Here, the shifting sands are drowning an old woodland. Let your imagination flow and you can picture a coral forest rising from the sandy floor of the ocean.

A couple of miles beyond **Indian Forest** (listed above), you encounter **Sutton Lake Recreation Area** of Siuslaw National Forest with attractive, shaded campsites (flush potties, no hookups) for $8 a night. The highway is still off the coast here, although trails lead to the beach.

☺ Watch on your left for **Darlingtonia Wayside,** just beyond Sutton. This state park shelters the rare and intriguing *darlingtonia californica,* the insect-eating pitcher plant. It devours bugs by luring them into its deep throat with nectar and trapping them inside. Graphics tell their unusual botanical-carnivorous story. The best time to watch them lunching on a bug is during the May to June blooming period. Unlike the Venus flytrap, they're passive eaters, so there isn't much to watch.

Above the wayside, highway and ocean again merge, and they do so in dramatic fashion. The ten-mile stretch between here and Yachats rivals the Brookings-to-Gold Beach strip as the most striking panorama on the coast. Seastacks march out to sea, forests cloak lofty headlands and hideaway inns offer seclusion and dramatic views. The road alternately brushes driftwood-littered beaches, then climbs to the heights for stunning vistas. Along this stretch, you encounter one of the coast's senior tourist lures.

☺ **Sea Lion Caves** ● *91560 Highway 101, Yachats, OR 97498; (503) 547-3111. Daily 8 a.m. to dusk. Adults $5, kids 3 to 15, $3.* One of the world's largest sea caves, this large cavern has been sheltering sea lions for thousands of years, and hosting visitors since 1932. The tourist facility perches on a lofty headland and an elevator cut through solid basalt whisks folks 205 down feet to the grotto. Visitors peer through screened windows to the dimly-lit lower level, where sea lions may or may not be lounging on the rocks, engaged in *a Capella* barking. You may see scores of the critters, a handful or none. However, a visit to this grotto is worth the trip even if it's empty. Nicely done displays inform you that this 125-foot-high complex was carved by wave action from a basaltic fracture. Another grotto window offers views of the distant coastline and nearby seacliffs draped with cormorants, guillemots and other sea birds. You also have a nicely framed view of one of the coast's most photographed sites—the white and red tile-roofed **Heceta Head Lighthouse.** It's tucked into a coastal niche to the north.

☺ A short distance up the highway, a turnout offers a closer view of Heceta Head Light, then you encounter **Devil's Elbow State Park.** It's a delightful sheltered bay and picnic area rimmed by basaltic seacliffs. A trail leads from here to Heceta Head Light. You then drive past the lighthouse without realizing it because it's shielded from the highway. A short drive north takes you to a couple of coastal campgrounds:

Washburne State Park ● *(503) 547-3416. RV and tent sites, $13 to $11, hiker-biker sites $2. No reservations or credit cards.* Attractive, well-spaced wooded sites with picnic tables and barbecues. A trail leads to a small tidepool beach.

Sea Perch RV Park ● *95480 Highway 101, Yachats, OR 97498; (503) 547-3505. RV and tent sites, full hookups, $14 to $16. Reservations accepted; MC/VISA.* Well-maintained facility with sites just off the beach; cable TV, showers, mini-mart, deli, shell museum, rec room and RV supplies.

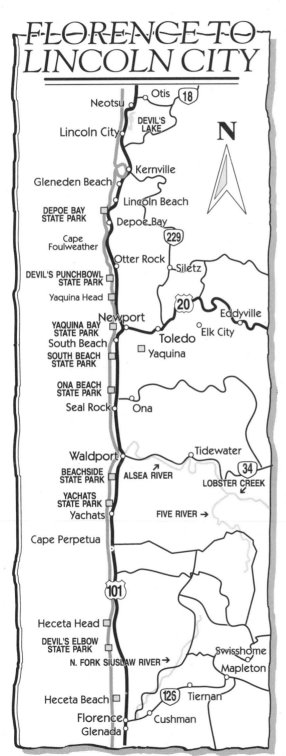

FLORENCE TO LINCOLN CITY

Otis · 18
Neotsu
DEVIL'S LAKE
Lincoln City
N
Kernville
Gleneden Beach
Lincoln Beach
DEPOE BAY STATE PARK
Depoe Bay
Cape Foulweather · 229
Otter Rock
Siletz
DEVIL'S PUNCHBOWL STATE PARK
Yaquina Head · 20
Newport · Eddyville
YAQUINA BAY STATE PARK · Elk City
South Beach · Toledo
SOUTH BEACH STATE PARK · Yaquina
ONA BEACH STATE PARK
Seal Rock · Ona
Waldport · Tidewater
BEACHSIDE STATE PARK · ALSEA RIVER · 34
YACHATS STATE PARK · LOBSTER CREEK
Yachats · FIVE RIVER →
Cape Perpetua
101
Heceta Head
DEVIL'S ELBOW STATE PARK · Swisshome
N. FORK SIUSLAW RIVER → · Mapleton
Heceta Beach · 126 · Tiernan
Florence · Cushman
Glenada

☺ A few miles north, the highway winds past the base of **Cape Perpetua,** one of the coast's most dramatic spots, soaring 800 feet from the Pacific. It's the focal point of the 2,700-acre Cape Perpetua Scenic Area, managed by Siuslaw National Forest. Begin your exploration with a stop at the Cape Perpetua Visitor Center on the right, just above the highway. It's open daily from 9 to 5. Graphics and displays teach you about the geology, flora, fauna and Native Americans of the cape.

A glance out a large picture window reveals postcard views of seastacks and scalloped surf. A nearby forest service **campground** has well-spaced, tree-shades sites for $8 a night. Trails from the visitor center lead down to the beach and up to the spectacular Cape Perpetua Viewpoint.

You don't have to hike it, however. From the visitor center, you can drive two miles up to the viewpoint, which is on the site of an old Coast Guard lookout station. To reach it, take a road to the right just north of the visitor center, follow it a mile up into the woods, then make a sharp left at a Y-intersection and spiral upward for another mile.

As you can see from our cover photo, the views from here are *very* impressive. On a good day, you can see 150 miles up and down the coast. A short trail loops the cape summit, offering a changing panorama of the world below. A trail leads from here back down to the visitor center.

Driving back to the Y-intersection, you can swing to the left and pursue a winding paved logging road 19 miles inland. It rejoins Highway 101 near Yachats. It's not as scenic as the coast route, although much of the drive is through thick rainforest, which should appeal to lovers of wooded solitude. As you drive, watch carefully for another fork 13 miles from Yachats, where you must turn left. If you continue straight ahead, you'll probably encounter more solitude than you ever wanted!

If you follow Highway 101 from Cape Perpetua to Yachats, pause at **Devil's Churn Wayside,** about two miles below. Incoming waves rush up a coastal trench and crash into a basaltic rock, sending thunderous sprays high into the air. It's particularly dramatic during a storm or incoming tide.

Yachats

Population: 560   **Elevation: sea level**

Yachats (make that "YAH-hots") is a special jewel in the necklace of small towns strung along the Pacific Coast. This tiny charmer is perched at the edge of an inlet where the Yachats River meets the Pacific. It's a likable little place, cradled by lush woodlands of Siuslaw National Forest. The name is appropriate; it's a variation on *Yahuts,* the Chinook term for "dark waters at the base of a mountain."

The tiny old fashioned business district houses a few boutiques, a coffee shop and a couple of restaurants. Several motels, including attractive ocean-view resorts, attest to Yachats' popularity. Yet, there is no tourist rustle and bustle here; no inland highway to bring large weekend crowds. Folks come to Yachats to stroll stony beaches and scuff at seaweed, to peer into tide-pools and walk woodland trails inland. In winter, they come to marvel at storms that dance offshore like fairy demons, crashing the surf against basaltic headlands.

And certainly they come here to fish! Unlike streams that have carved large tidal estuaries, the Yachats River is a creek-sized affair, noted for fresh-water salmon and trout fishing. Also, the ocean beach here is one of the few areas in the world where silver smelt come ashore to spawn. Between May and September, hundreds of fisherfolk come to snare these sardine-like fish with special hand-held triangular nets.

To reach **Yachats State Beach,** sheltering part of the town's rocky and sandy shoreline, follow signs down Second Street. Also, note the **Little Log Church,** built in 1927 in the shape of a cross; it's just off the highway on Third Street. No longer active, it's owned by the Lincoln County Historical Society and was being converted into a museum when we visited. If you're inclined to pause in Yachats—an easy temptation—pick up information at the **Chamber of Commerce** visitors' bureau in a small shopping center at Highway 101 and Third Street; (503) 547-3530. It's open weekdays 9 to 5.

ANNUAL EVENTS

Call the chamber at (503) 547-3530 for details on these functions:

Arts and Crafts Fair in March.

Yachats Smelt Fry, mid-July; hundreds of pounds of smelt are served to the public on the grounds of Yachats School.

Yachats Kite Festival, Late October or early November.

WHERE TO DINE

☺ La Serre Seafood Restaurant • ∆∆∆ $$

Second and Beach (Highway 101); (503) 547-3420. American; full bar service. Dinner nightly from 5, Sunday breakfast 9 to noon. MC/VISA, AMEX. One of the coast's more appealing restaurants, with early American décor beneath a vaulted greenhouse ceiling. Potted plants and stark white walls add to the spacious garden atmosphere. Adjacent bar is furnished like a comfortable living room. Local seafood, clams, oysters, bouillabaisse, cioppino, steaks and roast chicken are featured on the menu.

Landmark Restaurant • ∆∆ $$

Highway 101, south end; (503) 547-3215. American, mostly seafood; full bar service. Daily 8 a.m. to 10 p.m. MC/VISA. Small, select seafood menu featuring steamer clams, halibut, salmon and other fresh fish in season. Simple interior with curved greenhouse glass offering bay views.

New Morning Coffee House • ∆ $

Highway 101 at Fourth Street; (503) 547-3848. American; no alcohol. Breakfast and lunch Wednesday-Sunday. No credit cards. Tasty baked goods, soups, salads and sandwiches, plus several vegetarian selections are specialties. They're served in a cheerful space with beamed cathedral ceilings, plants and folk crafts. An outdoor deck is a pleasant lunch spot.

Yachats Crab and Chowder House • ∆∆ $$

Highway 101, south end; (503) 547-4132. Seafood; wine and beer. Tuesday and Tuesday-Thursday 11:30 to 9, Friday-Saturday 11:30 to 9:30, closed Monday. MC/VISA. Attractive café with upholstered booths, windows on the harbor and an outdoor patio. Busy seafood menu has the usual fried clams, shrimp and such, plus cod, perch, halibut and salmon.

WHERE TO SLEEP

Of the lodgings listed below, the Oregon House and Sea Quest are south of Yachats, in the scenic area between Cape Perpetua and Heceta Head.

Fireside Resort Motel • ⌒⌒ $$$ ∅

1881 N. Highway 101 (P.O. Box 313), Yachats, OR 97498; (800) 336-3575 or (503) 547-3636. Couples $55 to $75, singles $50 to $70, suites from $115. MC/VISA, DISC. A 43-unit inn just above the beach with TV, room phones and refrigerators, some with wood-burning stoves; most rooms with ocean views.

Ocean Cove Inn • ⌒ $$$ ∅

Highway 101 at Prospect, downtown (P.O. Box 593), Yachats, OR 97498; (503) 547-3900. Rooms $50 to $60. MC/VISA. Small four-unit motel with TV; all rooms have ocean views.

☺ Oregon House • ⌒⌒ $$$ ∅

94288 Highway 101 (eight miles south), Yachats, OR 97498; (503) 547-3329. Couples and singles $40 to $95, suites $60 to $95. MC/VISA. Intriguing hideaway on a coastal headland, with a creek and lighted trail to the nearby beach. Ten rooms fashioned from a 1930s estate; nine have kitchenettes, one is a B&B unit. Some have fireplaces and spas; most have ocean views. The complex is on three and a half acres of woods and lawns, midway between Cape Perpetua and Heceta Head.

Rock Park Cottages ● △ $$
Adjacent to Yachats State Park (P.O. Box 77), Yachats, OR 97498; (503) 547-3214. Couples and singles $34 to $48. Simple, basically furnished housekeeping cabins, just up from the beach.

Shamrock Lodgettes ● △△ $$$ ∅
106 S. Highway 101 (P.O. Box 346), Yachats, OR 97498; (800) 845-5028 or (503) 547-3312. Couples and singles $61 to $90, kitchenettes $79 to $90, suites $85 to $90. Major credit cards. Attractive 19-unit resort in quiet, landscaped area off the highway. Lodge rooms and rustic cabins with TV movies, room phones and fireplaces; some with spa tubs. Sauna and hot tub.

Bed & breakfast inns

☺ Sea Quest Bed & Breakfast ● △△△ $$$$ ∅
95354 Highway 101 (seven miles south), Yachats, OR 97948; (503) 547-3782. Couples and singles $95 to $300; private baths; full breakfast. MC/VISA. Modern coastal hideaway with handsomely furnished rooms; all have spa tubs and private entrances, views of the ocean and forest. On a two and a half acre wooded bluff above Ten Mile Creek, between Heceta Head and Cape Perpetua. A common room offers a library and wood-burning stove.

Serenity Bed & Breakfast ● △△ $$$$ ∅
5985 Yachats River Rd. (six miles inland), Yachats, OR 97498; (503) 547-3813. Couples and singles $69 to $145. Four rooms with private baths; full breakfast. MC/VISA. European-style hideaway on ten acres surrounded by Siuslaw National Forest. Colonial Ranch style home is finished in rich woods and furnished with European antiques; some rooms with spa tubs.

WHERE TO CAMP: Check **Sea Perch Campground** listed above and **Tillicum Beach** and **Beachside State Park** campgrounds below.

Waldport

Population: 1,610   **Elevation: sea level**

North of Yachats, the coastline goes flat—literally—and loses much of its scenic appeal. The roadside is dotted with motels, shell shops and small beaches. Two public campgrounds between Yachats and Waldport provide nice interruptions to this string of flatland businesses. **Tillicum Beach Campground** of Siuslaw National Forest has sites right on the beach, with flush potties, for $9. Just beyond, also on the coast, is **Beachside State Park** with full hookups for $13.

Although Waldport (German for "Forest Port") is in a nice setting on Alsea Bay, the town itself is little more than a compression of the small businesses you've been seeing along the highway. Once an Alsi Indian encampment, it datesfrom the 1880s when gold miners, loggers and dairymen came seeking their fortunes. It became an important shipping center for upstream communities.

All that is gone now; the lumber mills have closed and the dairy cattle have moved to greener pastures. What remains is a small modernized business district with a few motels. They're occupied mostly by latter-day Isaac Waltons drawn by the outstanding fishing in the Alsea River.

Upstream, one can find more fishing, plus camping and hiking in Siuslaw National Forest's **Alsea River Recreation Area.** Offering a mix of

THE BRIDGES SO FAR

Driving the Oregon Coast Highway, one is struck by the bold Art Deco look of several concrete arch bridges crossing the wide river estuaries. Those spanning the Umpqua River at Reedsport, Coos Bay, the Siuslaw River at Florence and Yaquina Bay at Newport appear to have a common design.

They should. All were crafted by the same man, and all were completed in 1936, along with Waldport's Alsea Bay bridge, which has since been replaced. Total price tag for the bridges: $5,208,825.50. An excellent new visitors center at the south anchorage of the Alsea Bay bridge tells the intriguing story of Oregon's coastal spans.

When settlers began trickling down the coast from Astoria and crossing the mountains from the Willamette Valley, they saw the need to tie their communities together. This, however, was a mean task. Tidal estuaries extended far inland, isolating the towns from one another. Engineering of the day lacked the skills to span a mile or more of water with bridges high enough for ship clearance. At the turn of the century, when many coastal cities were at their economic peak, only scattered sections of roads ran along the coastline. Ferries chugged across estuaries and paddlewheelers served upriver towns.

Then in 1917, Congress decided to build the Coast Military Highway that would stretch from the Puget Sound to Mexico. Construction began in 1919, and 400 miles of the Oregon coast section were completed by the early 1930s, when it became known as the Roosevelt Highway. However, only one of the coast's six major estuaries had been spanned. The Isaac Patterson Bridge across the Rogue at Gold Beach was completed in 1932.

Conde B. McCullough, bridge designer for the Oregon Highway Department, was given the task of closing the final five gaps in the coastal roadway. Both an engineer and an artist, he borrowed the latest technology from Europe, fashioning a series of concrete tied-arch bridges and decorating them with sculpted pylons and obelisks.

Four of his works still stand. The Alsea Bridge was replaced in 1991 because saltwater had penetrated the concrete and reached the re bar within. As a memorial to the state's remarkable bridge builder, McCullough's obelisks and some pylons and railing from the original bridge have been incorporated into the new structure. The Alsea Bay Bridge Interpretive Center was built at its south anchorage to tell the story of trans-coastal travel. It's operated by the Oregon State Parks and Recreation Department.

forest service facilities and commercial fishing lodges, inns, small marinas and woodsy restaurants, it borders Highway 34, which links Waldport to Corvallis. As a diversion from the coast, you might enjoy this pleasantly winding drive along the river's thickly wooded banks. To learn about the area and other nearby forest lures, stop in at the **Waldport Ranger Station** downtown; (503) 563-3211; open weekdays 8 to 5. Also, pick up an *Alsea River Recreation Area Map/Guide* at the **Waldport Chamber of Commerce.**

In addition to surrounding forests, beaches and fishing spots, Waldport has one authentic tourist attraction, opened in the early 1990s:

☺ **Alsea Bay Bridge Interpretive Center** ● *South anchorage of Alsea Bay Bridge; (503) 563-2002. Free; daily 9 to 5; historic bridge walks 2 p.m. weekends (more often in summer).* This excellent museum traces the history of transportation on the Oregon Coast, from Native American game trails to the present chain of bridges over coastal estuaries (see box). Displays focus on various types of bridges, early road development and settlements on the coast. The center is operated by the State Parks Department. A ranger conducts walks across the new Alsea Bay Bridge (completed in 1991), and gives crabbing and clamming demonstrations.

Waldport Chamber of Commerce (563-2133) visitor's bureau is incorporated into the new interpretive center, with the same hours.

North of Waldport, the highway rarely leaves the ocean or civilization. Several state parks, mostly beach accesses and picnic areas, offer respite from the string of businesses. Among the more curious tourist lures is **Sea Gulch,** near the village of **Seal Rock,** where a quarter-mile trail is lined with chain saw art. The saw blade artisan has created assorted Western, fairy tale and animal characters from tree trunks. It's open daily from 8 a.m. to dusk and admission is $3.50; (503) 563-2727.

Newport

Population: 8,710   **Elevation: 68 feet**

From Newport north, commercial tourism leaves many footprints in the coastal sands. Thousands of inland Oregonians make weekend pilgrimages to the boutiques, seafood restaurants, shell shops, wax museums and other lures of Newport, Lincoln City, Cannon Beach and Seaside.

Certainly, tourism is not new to Newport. As far back as the 1860s, beach-seekers endured a 12-hour stagecoach ride from Corvallis to Elk City, then caught a mail boat down the Yaquina River to the coast. Small and succulent oysters from Newport's Yaquina Bay became world famous, providing the base for the town's earliest industry.

Now scarce in the wild but grown commercially, Yaquina Bay oysters remain the shellfish of choice for many gourmet restaurants. You can buy Yaquinas and watch them being processed at the **Oregon Oyster Company** at 6878 Bay Road, eight miles inland. This oyster farm is open to the public daily from 9 to 4; (503) 265-3078. The bay also is famous for Dungeness crabs and you can rent or buy crab rings and traps at local tackle shops. Its mud flats yield an abundance of clams and other shellfish, so pick up a shovel and a tidal chart and start digging for your dinner.

Newport rivals Seaside as the Oregon's most-visited coastal playland, and it has the suburban sprawl and tourist gimmicks to prove it. However, it occupies a more attractive setting, on a wooded peninsula between Yaquina Bay and the Pacific. The Old Bayfront section is particularly appealing, with its false front stores and Victorians tucked into a northside cove of the bay.

How to do Newport

This driving route will take you to the town's lures. Just beyond the south city limits sign, before you cross the Yaquina Bay Bridge, follow signs east and north to the impressive new **Oregon Coast Aquarium.** It occupies a peninsula across the bay from Old Bayfront. From the aquarium parking lot, continue north past the **Newport Marina** to the **Mark O. Hatfield Marine Science Center** of the University of Oregon. It has several exhibits open to the public.

Return to Highway 101, cross the bridge and follow signs to **Yaquina Bay State Park**, on a bluff overlooking the bay entrance. The route curls under the bridge anchorage, going west toward the ocean. **Yaquina Bay Lighthouse** is the primary lure here. The state park also offers nice coastal and bay views, picnic areas and trails to the beach. Then retrace your route under the bridge anchorage, following the northbound arrow, and peel off to the right at the **Bayfront** sign. You'll pass the white and green board and batten structures of the old **Yaquina Bay Coast Guard Station**, and wind up at the Bayfront.

This area is both a working waterfront and a tourist attraction. A couple of canneries are still in operation and a commercial fishing fleet keeps local seafood markets stocked. You can peek through a window to watch fresh-caught shrimp being processed and stroll the docks and watch the catch of the day being unloaded.

Naturally, the area has its share of curio shops, seafood restaurants and markets where you can buy fresh and smoked fish. Step into the **Newport Candy Shoppe** at 440 SW Bay Boulevard and load up on dozens of flavors of saltwater taffy, made on the premises and arrayed in row upon row of bins. It's a great way to give your bridgework a workout. With salt water taffy, can other tourist gimmicks be far beyond? Bayfront's eastern end is occupied by **Undersea Gardens, The Wax Works** and a **Ripley's Believe It or Not!** museum. Your amusements can thus range from downing an oyster shooter at a seafood café to staring at a waxen green Yoda.

Having survived all this tourism, return to the highway, drive a few blocks north through "new" Newport and you'll see the **Greater Newport Chamber of Commerce,** housed in a Cape Cod style building on your left; (503) 265-8801. Its hours are 8:30 to 5 weekdays, plus 10 to 4 on summer weekends. Among other things, you can pick up a driving map to Lincoln County's historic sites and four covered bridges. A block behind the visitor center, at Fall and Ninth streets, are the **Log Cabin Museum** and **Burrows House Museum.**

ATTRACTIONS
(In order of appearance)

☺ **The Oregon Coast Aquarium** • *2820 E. Ferry Slip Rd. (P.O. Box 2000), Newport, OR 97365; (503) 867-3474 or 867-3123. Daily 9 to 6 in summer and 10 to 4:30 the rest of the year. Adults $7, seniors and teens $5, kids 4 to 11, $3.* While it doesn't have the impact of California's Monterey Bay Aquarium with its giant kelp tank, this new facility is easily the best of its kind in the Northwest. Opened in the summer of 1992, it invites you to follow a raindrop from the upland tributaries of the Yaquina River to the ocean. Scores of fish tanks, state of the art exhibits, fine graphics, hands-on displays, videos and interactive computers take you to estuary wetlands, sandy and rocky shores and Oregon's coastal waters. You and the kids can grope about a tidepool, watch a well-done film on the gray whale migration and walk through a sea bird aviary. The museum's best attraction is the outdoor "rocky coast" exhibit, where harbor seals, sea lions and sea otters splash about in realistic cast concrete grottoes.

☺ **Mark O. Hatfield Marine Science Center** • *2030 Marine Science Dr., Newport, OR 97365; (503) 867-3011. Daily 9:30 to 6 in the summer and 10 to 4 the rest of the year; free.* The University of Oregon's marine center is smaller and rather more political than the Oregon Coast Aquarium. While the aquarium teaches you about life in rivers and oceans, the science center warns that we're hell-bent on destroying it. Several aquarium tanks and a touchy-feely tidepool are interesting, although the environmental exhibits are much more stimulating. Particularly provoking is a display damming the giant drift nets of Japan and Korea that destroy every sea creature in their paths while decimating the world's albacore population. You're likely to come away mad, wanting to kick a Toyota and maybe even a Hyundai.

☺ **Yaquina Bay Lighthouse** • *Yaquina Bay State Park; (503) 867-7451. Daily 11 to 5 in summer, weekends noon to 4 the rest of the year.* This chubby board and batten structure was a combination lighthouse and residence, one of the few of its kind in the world. It now serves as a museum, with furnished rooms and exhibits concerning the Coast Guard and its predecessor, the U.S. Life Saving Service. You can poke about the living quarters and climb up to the watch room just below the light tower. On a quiet day, you can sit in this small room and listen for the footsteps of Muriel, the lighthouse's official ghost. Having communed with her spirit, you can adjourn to the basement to browse about a gift shop and watch a video concerning her mysterious demise.

Yaquina Bay Light was short-lived, the victim of bureaucratic boondoggelry. In 1869, the government decided to build two light houses—at the mouth of the harbor and another at Cape Foulweather, about ten miles north. Yaquina was completed on schedule and lit in late 1871. However, builders couldn't get materials to the remote Cape Foulweather, so they decided to build the second light on Yaquina Head, right across the bay from the first one! It made the Yaquina Bay Light redundant, so it was extinguished in 1874. Now comes the ghost story: Around the turn of the century, teenager Muriel Trevenard and several friends decided to explore the abandoned light's empty rooms. They poked around a bit, found the crumbling old place to be a bit spooky and left. Then Muriel discovered that she'd left her handkerchief inside, so she went back to retrieve it. She failed to emerge, and her friends returned to look for her. After a search that became increasingly frantic, they found only her hankie, now stained with blood.

Muriel Trevenard was never seen again.

Meanwhile, down at the bayfront, the long-established Undersea Gardens has been joined by two other attractions: The Wax Works and Ripley's Believe It or Not! museum. All three are under the same management and have identical hours and prices: Daily 9 to 6; adults $5, kids 5 to 11, $3.

☺ **Undersea Gardens** • *250 SW Bay Blvd.; (503) 265-2206.* The best of the lot, it's housed in a double-walled sunken chamber just off the bayfront. More than 5,000 sea creatures swim and function freely just outside viewing windows, held captive by an imperceptible double chamber. Divers appear periodically to pluck a tangly octopus, indignant wolf eel and assorted starfishes from their resting places and show them off to the glassed-in audience.

The Wax Works • *Mariner Square; (503) 265-2206.* Waxen images of Mr. Spock, busty mermaids, Yoda and assorted film and TV stars populate this tourist trap, along with some animated beasts. Is it "so astonishing you'll want to return again and again," as the brochure says? Probably not.

Ripley's Believe It or Not! • *Mariner Square; (503) 265-2206.* Are you ready to come face-to-face with a real shrunken head or stare into the four eyes of a Chinese emperor? Do you want to trek through a bone-chilling graveyard and talk to a ghost? (No, it isn't Muriel.) And do you really want to part with $5 to see this foolishness?

Log Cabin Museum • *579 SW Ninth St.; (503) 265-2013. Tuesday-Sunday 10 to 5; adults $2, kids $1.* Built of half-round timbers salvaged from a sunken logging ship, the museum offers the usual displays on Newport's yesterdays. Unprofessional but interesting exhibits include old cans of Oregon products, a large seashell collection, various items maritime and a gathering of Native American baskets, tools and willow baby-packers.

Burrows House Museum • *545 SW Ninth St.; (503) 265-7509. Tuesday-Sunday 10 to 5; admission included with Log Cabin Museum.* Furnished rooms in this 1895 boarding house recall the era when one could get room and board for a dollar a night. It offers nicely preserved examples of old furniture, children's toys, glassware and a Victorian kitchen. You Ghostbusters will want to know that this is where Muriel lived.

ACTIVITIES

Boat rentals • **Embarcadero Marina,** 1000 SE Bay Blvd., (503) 265-5435; **Newport Marina,** 600 SE Bay Blvd., (503) 867-3321; **Riverbend Moorage,** 5262 Yaquina Bay Rd., (503) 265-9243.

Clamming and crabbing • **Newport Water Sports** on South Jetty Road (867-3742) can tell you where to find clams and crabs, and and sell or rent you the proper equipment for catching them. For a list of other outfits offering clamming and crabbing gear, check with the chamber.

Fishing charters • Most of these are at the Newport Marina or in the Old Bayfront area: **Fish On! Charters,** Port Dock 3, SE Bay Boulevard; (503) 265-8607; **Newport Marina,** 600 SE Bay Blvd., (503) 867-3321; **Newport Sportfishing,** 1000 SE Bay Blvd., (503) 265-7558; **Newport Tradewinds,** 653 SW Bay Blvd., (503) 265-2101; **Sea Gull Charters,** 343 SW Bay Blvd., 265-7441.

Performing arts • **Newport Performing Arts Center** offers live entertainment in a 400-seat theater at Nye Beach; (503) 265-9231.

Riverboat cruises • *The Belle of Newport*, P.O. Box 1224, Newport, OR 97365; (503) 265-BELL; MC/VISA. Oldstyle sternwheeler offers scenic and dinner cruises from the Bayfront up the Alsea River.

ANNUAL EVENTS

Seafood and Wine Festival, Bayfront, February; (503) 265-8801.
Loyalty Days with boat races and a parade, May; (503) 265-8801.
Red, White and Blue Kite Festival in June; (503) 994-9500.
Lincoln County Fair and Rodeo in July; (503) 265-6237.
Siletz Powwow at the Siletz Reservation, inland near Toledo, early August; (503) 336-3183.
Whale-watching week in December; (503) 867-3011.

WHERE TO DINE

We've focused our dining choices on the Bayfront, since it's the most interesting part of town.

☺ Bayfront Brewery • ∆∆ $
748 SW Bay Blvd.; (503) 265-ALES. Brewpub; beer and wine. Daily 11 a.m. to 10 p.m. MC/VISA. Microbrewery housed in an old storefront, with a properly rustic interior. The home of Rogue Ale, it features a brass and wood brewpub on one side and a family dining room on the other. The menu focuses on seafood and offerings suitable for hearty brews.

Mo's and Mo's Annex • ∆ $
622 SW Bay Blvd. (263-9411) and 657 SW Bay Blvd. (265-7512). Seafood; wine and beer. Daily 11 to 9. MC/VISA. The original Mo's and an extension are across the street from one another at the Bayfront. Both have the spartan dècor and cheap prices typical of this central coast chain. Think of them as nautical pizza parlors. Specials include steamer clams, cioppino, Hangtown Fry (stolen from Placerville, California) and the usual fried seafoods. Original Mo's is a small and scruffy cafè; the annex is basic but more tidy, offering bay views.

Port Dock • ∆∆ $$
325 SW Bay Blvd., (503) 265-2911. American and Italian, mostly seafood; full bar service. Daily 11 to 10. MC/VISA. Simply attired nautical dining room with bay views; menu features fettuccini *primavera*, steak and oysters, scallop sautè, steamer clams and fresh seafood. The upstairs bar has better vistas—a good spot for drinks before or after dinner.

☺ Whale's Tale • ∆∆∆ $$
452 SW Bay Blvd., (503) 265-8660. American, mostly seafood; wine and beer. Breakfast through dinner daily. MC/VISA, AMEX. Possibly Newport's best restaurant, with creative touches applied to fresh seafood. Entrèes range from mussels marinara and grilled Yaquina oysters to seafood sautè and a German sausage plate. It's also noted for an award-winning clam chowder and lively breakfast omelets. Very reasonable prices; woodsy, pub-like nautical interior with beam ceilings.

WHERE TO SLEEP

☺ Embarcadero Resort Hotel & Marina ⌂⌂⌂ $$$$ ∅
1000 SE Bay Blvd. (Highway 20), Newport, OR 97365; (800) 547-4779 or (503) 265-8521. Couples $66 to $162, singles $58 to $162, kitchenettes and suites $85 to $162. Major credit cards. Nicely appointed hotel with extensive beachfront grounds; TV movies, room phones. All rooms with private patios offering Yaquina Bay views; some apartment units with full kitchens. **Embarcadero Seafood Restaurant** serves from 7 a.m. to 9 p.m. (to 10 on weekends); dinners $13 to $25; full bar service.

Hotel Newport • ⌂⌂⌂ $$$$ ∅
3019 N. Coast Highway, Newport, OR 97365; (800) 547-3310 or (503) 265-9411. Couples and singles $72 to $96. Major credit cards. Very attractive 146-room hotel with direct beach access; TV, room phones; pool, game room, spa. Many rooms with ocean views. **Beachhouse Restaurant and Pub** serves American fare 7 a.m. to 9 p.m.; dinners $9 to $16; full bar.

Ocean House Bed & Breakfast • ⌂⌂⌂ $$$$ ∅
4920 NW Woody Way, Newport, OR 97365; (503) 265-6158 or (503) 265-7779. Couples $65 to $100, singles $60 to $95. Four rooms with private

baths; full breakfast. MC/VISA. Ocean-view country home above Agate Beach, with terraced gardens and a trail to the surf. Contemporary and antique furnishings; art gallery; sitting room with fireplace; sea-view decks.

Puerto Nuevo Inn • ⌂⌂ $$ ∅

544 SW Coast Highway (Fall Street, north of bridge), Newport, OR 97365; (800) 999-3068 or (503) 265-5767. Couples $42 to $54, singles $40 to $45, kitchenettes $80 to $100, suites $60 to $100. Major credit cards. Attractive units, all with microwave/refrigerator kitchen galleys; TV and VCRs, room phones; some suites with spas. Free continental breakfast; indoor spa.

Shilo Inn Newport • ⌂⌂⌂ $$$$ ∅

536 SW Elizabeth St. (west on Falls Street, off Highway 101), Newport, OR 97365; (800) 265-5687 or (503) 265-7701. Couples $85 to $132, singles $74 to $85. Major credit cards. Inviting inn with 179 ocean-view rooms; TV movies, room phones; two indoor pools, laundromat. **Restaurant** and **Café** serve American regional cuisine, 7 a.m. to 10 p.m.; full bar service.

Surf 'n' Sand Motel • ⌂⌂⌂ $$$

8143 N. Coast Highway (three miles north), Newport, OR 97365; (503) 265-2215. Couples $65 to $75, singles $52 to $65, kitchenettes $58 to $62, suites $75 to $85. MC/VISA, DIN. Attractive motel with 18 ocean-view rooms; TV, room phones, refrigerators; some rooms with fireplaces. Path to nearby beach.

Val-U Inn • ⌂⌂ $$$$ ∅

531 SW Fall St. (a block off Highway 101), Newport, OR 97365; (800) 443-777 or (503) 265-6203. Couples from $80, singles from $70, kitchenettes $85 to $120, suites from $120. Major credit cards. Nicely furnished suites with TV, fee movies and room phones; continental breakfast included. Some units with spas. Coin laundry.

The Whaler • ⌂⌂⌂ $$$$ ∅

155 SW Elizabeth St. (near SW Second), Newport, OR 97365; (800) 433-4360 in Oregon, (800) 433-9444 elsewhere and (503) 265-9261. Couples and singles $75 to $90, including continental breakfast. Major credit cards. Very attractive ocean-front motel; 61 units, all with sea views; TV movies, phones; laundry, free popcorn. Some efficiencies and rooms with fireplaces.

WHERE TO CAMP

Beverly Beach State Park • 198 NE 123rd St., Newport, OR 97365; (503) 265-9278. RV and tent sites, $11 to $13. On the state park reservation system; see "Camping" in previous chapter intro. Well-spaced, shaded sites just off Highway 101, seven miles north. Full hookups, showers, fishing, swimming, nature trails, beach access.

Harbor Village RV Park • 923 SE Bay Blvd., Newport, OR 97365; (503) 265-5088. RV sites, full hookups $12.60. Reservations accepted; MC/VISA. Closely spaced but wooded sites in attractive area near Newport Marina, adjacent to Yaquina Bay. Showers, coin laundry, horseshoes, RV supplies.

Newport Marina RV Park • 600 SE Bay Blvd., Newport, OR 97365; (503) 867-7200 or 867-3321. RV sites only, full hookups $12.50, no hookups $10. MC/VISA. An asphalt parking area near the Oregon Coast Aquarium and Hatfield Marine Science Center; coin showers, mini-mart and full marina facilities adjacent.

Pacific Shores RV Resort • *6225 N. Coast Highway, Newport, OR 97365; (503) 265-3750. RV sites, $16 to $28. Reservations accepted; MC/VISA.* Full service RV resort two miles north of town with paved sites, some pull-throughs and some with ocean views. Clubhouse, game room, exercise room, indoor pool and sauna, cable TV, mini-mart.

South Beach State Park • *5580 S. Coast Highway, South Beach, OR 97366; (503) 867-4715. RV and tent sites, $11. On the state park reservation system; see "Camping" in previous chapter intro.* Well-spaced, shaded sites just off Highway 101, two miles south of Newport. Water and electric, showers, fishing, nature trails, beach access.

NEWPORT TO LINCOLN CITY

About the time you've decided that Oregon's coastline is getting too busy with development, you encounter an absolute jewel, such as Yaquina Head.

☺ The **Yaquina Head Natural Area,** operated by the Bureau of Land Management, is just beyond the reach of Newport's business sprawl. Its centerpiece is the 1873 **Yaquina Head Light,** second oldest on the coast and still operating. It's closed to visitors, although the surrounding nature preserve is well worth an extended pause.

Colony Rock and other craggy seastacks here are aflutter with Western gulls, pigeon guillemots, puffins and cormorants. Signs help you identify them. Part of the **Oregon Islands National Wildlife Refuge**, the promontories are just a few dozen feet offshore, offering some of the best bird watching on the coast. Paths lead down to a tidepooling area. Interpreters are sometimes on hand in summer to assist those who wouldn't know a sea cucumber from a zucchini.

Continuing north, the highway follows a low tableland, dipping in and out of the shoreline, which is marked by low sandstone bluffs, sandy beaches and seastacks. It then drifts away from the beach, but Otter Crest Scenic Drive keeps you close, looping around **Cape Foulweather**. It's a particularly pleasant meander through thick forests, which separate occasionally to reveal dramatic slices of rocky shoreline.

Shortly after leaving the highway, the scenic drive takes you to **Otter Rock,** a tiny, shabby coastal town, and **Devil's Punchbowl State Park.** Here, incoming tides are funneled into a collapsed sea cave and churned into a witch's cauldron. Combine tides and an offshore storm, and the thundering spray can jet skyward in a spectacular display.

A viewpoint, just a few feet above the cauldron, is occupied by yet another Mo's seafood cafè and a few curio shops. With picnic tables nearby, this makes a nice lunch stop. A nearby path leads to a nice collection of tidepools at **Marine Gardens,** just north of the punchbowl.

☺ **Otter Crest State Park**, a spectacular viewpoint atop Cape Foulweather, is two miles beyond. (It was named by Captain James Cook when he was having a bad day with the weather in 1778.) Standing 500 feet above a crashing surf, you'll enjoy magnificent coastal vistas. Also on Otter Crest Scenic Drive, you pass one of the coast's more desirable resorts, perched on a bluff above the sea:

☺ **The Inn at Otter Crest** • △△△ $$$$ ∅
P.O. Box 50, Otter Rock, OR 97369; (800) 452-2101 or (503) 765-2111. Couples and singles $81 to $172, suites $145 to $222. Major credit cards.

Beautifully situated condo resort with studios and apartments, many with fireplaces; balconies with ocean views. Tennis courts, trail to beach, miniature golf, spa, nature trails, recreational program. **Flying Dutchman** restaurant serves 8 a.m. to 9 p.m.; dinners $9 to $24; full bar service.

Just beyond the inn, you'll return to Highway 101 at **Rocky Creek State Park,** offering beach access and a picnic area. You then pass **Whale Cove Inn,** a restaurant with one of the coast's best views (listed below). Just beyond is a hamlet that's more reputation than substance.

Depoe Bay

Population: 900 **Elevation: sea level**

Misspelled name and all, this teeny town works at being terribly cute. It offers the world's smallest harbor (six acres) and a deliberately rustic shopping area consisting mostly of curio shops, yogurt shops and seafood restaurants. Depoe Bay's position on a particularly striking section of the coast fortifies its quest for cuteness.

As you approach, watch for the teeny **Chamber of Commerce**, on your right just south of the bridge over the teeny harbor; (503) 765- 2889. It's open weekdays 10 to 3. Ask directions to the **Spouting Horns** near the harbor mouth. Here, inrushing tides slam into basaltic fissures and send spumes skyward. Depoe Bay obviously is a good place for storm-watching. Whale-watching is a favored pastime as well, since the noble beasts past close to Cape Foulweather to the south.

The town came into being in the late 1920s when the coastal highway reached this piece of shoreline. The inlet was named for a Siletz Indian known as Charlie Depot because he worked for a nearby Army supply depot. Somewhere along the line, Depot Bay got misspelled.

Writers have been drawn to this area, including William Least Heat Moon of *Blue Highways* and Oregon's man of the radical pen, Ken Kesey. This region served as the model for Kesey's fictitious Wakonda lumbering town in *Sometimes a Great Notion*. Scenes from the movie version, called *Never Give an Inch* with Paul Newman and Lee Remick, were filmed in this area. Jack Nicholson took fellow inmates salmon fishing from Depoe Bay in Kesey's *One Flew Over the Cuckoo's Nest*.

Tourists are drawn here, too, by the swarms on weekends, so you might want to schedule your visit accordingly.

ATTRACTIONS & ACTIVITIES

Depoe Bay Aquarium and Shell Shop • *Highway 101 at Bay St.; (503) 765-2259. Daily 10 to 8 in summer, 10 to 5 in the off-season. Adults $2.25, kids 6 to 12, $1.75.* This teeny aquarium features an entire octopus, a few performing sea lions and a fish tank or two.

☺ **Siletz Tribal Smokehouse** • *Highway 101, south end of town; (503) 765-2286. Monday-Saturday 10 to 6, Sunday 10 to 3.* Nibble samples of spicy "hot-smoke" salmon cured by a centuries-old coastal Indian process, and take some home. The attractive gift shop sells tinned and foil-pouched smoked fish, unsmoked canned fish and authentic Native American curios.

Fishing & whale watching trips • The teeny Depoe Bay harbor is stuffed with a remarkable number of boats, and many are available for fishing charters. Whale watching trips also are scheduled from winter through spring. Among charter outfits are: **Deep Sea Trollers,** (503) 765-2705;

Depoe Bay Sportfishing, (503) 765-2382; **Dockside Charters,** (503) 765-2545; and **Tradewinds,** (503) 765-2345.

Sightseeing flights • **Sunset Scenic Flights,** P.O. Box 427, Depoe Bay, OR 97341; (503) 764-3304 or 765-2672. The firm offers scenic and whale-watching flights from Siletz Bay airport at Gleneden Beach, five miles north.

ANNUAL EVENTS

Celebration of the Whales in January; (503) 765-2889.

Fleet of Flowers on Memorial Day, to honor those lost at sea; (503) 765-2345.

Depoe Bay Salmon Bake, third Saturday of September, Fogarty Creek State Park; (503) 765-2889.

WHERE TO DINE

Sea Hag Food & Grog • ∆∆ $$

5757 U.S. 101 (north end); (503) 265-2734. American, mostly seafood; full bar service. Breakfast, lunch and dinner daily. MC/VISA. Popular with locals, particularly when they line up for the Friday night all-you-can-eat seafood buffet. The Hag also is noted for its chowder, well-prepared fresh local fish and fried seafood *hors d'oeuvres.* The décor is typically nautical.

☺ Whale Cove Inn • ∆∆∆ $$

Two miles south on Highway 101; (503) 765-2255. American, mostly seafood; full bar service. Daily 6 a.m. to 11 p.m. MC/VISA. Perched above rock-ribbed Whale Cove, the restaurant offers the most spectacular dining vista on the coast. The food's good, too, served in generous portions. Menu items include Norfolk prawns, fresh crab, creatively seasoned fresh fish and scallops in butter, garlic and lemon. Both the dining room and bar offer views.

Whale Watch Inn • ∆∆ $

221 SW Highway 101; (503) 763-2623. American; wine and beer. Breakfast, lunch and dinner. MC/VISA. Small family café noted mostly for its view, since it's cantilevered over the channel to the harbor. Basic American menu features local seafood plus creative breakfast omelettes.

WHERE TO SLEEP

Channel House Bed & Breakfast Inn • ⌂⌂⌂ $$$$ ∅

35 Ellingston St. (P.O. Box 56), Depoe Bay, OR 97341; (800) 447-2140 or (503) 765-2140. Couples $75 to $200, singles $55 to $75. Twelve units with private baths; full breakfast. MC/VISA. Very attractively appointed B&B with private baths, personal spas and fireplaces in each ocean view room. Modern décor with nautical touches.

Holiday Surf Lodge • ⌂⌂ ∅

P.O. Box 9 (Highway 101), Depoe Bay, OR 97341; (800) 452-2108 or (503) 765-2133. Couples $59 to $89, singles $38 to $55, kitchenettes $55 to $120, suites $89 to $93. MC/VISA, DISC. Well-maintained 84-unit oceanfront inn with TV, room phones; indoor pool, video game parlor.

Inn at Arch Rock • ⌂ $$$

P.O. Box 21, Depoe Bay, OR 97341; (503) 765-2560. Couples and singles $50 to $70, kitchenettes $58 to $69. MC/VISA. Well-tended eight-unit motel with room TV; near shops and restaurants.

Trollers Lodge ● ⌂ $$ ø

P.O. Box 66 (Highway 101 just south of bridge), Depoe Bay, OR 97341. Couples from $45, singles from $42, kitchenettes $59 to $65, suites $75. Major credit cards. Recently renovated ocean-view 12-unit motel with TV, room phones, some kitchens; near harbor and shops.

Boiler Bay State Park is two miles north of town, offering a bird watching vantage point and picnic tables. It earned its name because the boiler of the steamship *Marhoffer*, which ran aground in 1910, is sometimes visible at low tide.

Like Depoe Bay, much of the coast from here to Lincoln City has surrendered to the cash register call of commercialism. The highway is lined with curio shops, small motels and chowder houses. A refreshing break in these miracle money miles is the hamlet of **Gleneden Beach** on Siletz Bay, five miles north of Depoe Bay. It consists primarily of the upscale **Salishan Market Place,** a skylighted shopping complex. Just inland is Oregon's only AAA Five Diamond resort.

☺ Salishan Lodge ● ⌂⌂⌂⌂ $$$$$

P.O. Box 118, Gleneden Beach, OR 97388; (800) 452-2300 or (503) 764-2371. Couples $98 to $220. Major credit cards. Luxurious resort just inland from the ocean, on elaborately landscaped grounds. Rooms have full resort amenities, including TV movies, VCRs, fireplaces, refrigerators and balconies. Several suites and two-bedroom units. Indoor pool, saunas, spas, putting green, tennis courts, 18-hole golf course, running track, workout room, kids' playground, plus nature trails and beach access. **The Dining Room** serves American-continental fare from 7 a.m. to 10 p.m. (Friday-Saturday to 11); dinners $10 to $20. Two other restaurants in complex. Adjacent cocktail lounge features live entertainment.

If you grow weary of the strip commercialism along this route, turn southeast onto State Highway 229 and slip into a comfortable forest beside the Siletz River. A few miles inland, look across the river for a sturdy, ornate Victorian home; it starred in *Never Give an Inch*. From here, the road winds southward along the banks of the small, sparkling Siletz, toward the old and rather weary-looking former lumber town of **Toledo.** Here, you can pick up U.S. Highway 20 and go west to Newport for a loop trip.

Lincoln City

Population: 7,000 and growing   **Elevation: 114 feet**

Your next stop on Highway 101 is an inelegant seven-mile sprawl of strip commercialism. Lincoln City has all the grace and style of a car wash. One wonders if it were planned by characters from *One Flew Over the Cuckoo's Nest.*

Actually, it wasn't planned. Five nondescript coastal hamlets joined forces in 1964 to seek some sort of communal identity. They soon ran together like melting ice cream in a gutter, forming a one-block- wide string city that quickly *lost* its identity.

This is the fastest growing town on the coast, recently passing northern neighbor Seaside in population. What ties String City together? Its major lure is a seven-mile beach, one of the longest uninterrupted strands along the coast. Many of the town's motels, hotels and rental condos are perched on a bluff above. They wisely turn their backs on the city and offer sea views to their tenants. Thousands flock here every weekend from nearby Portland and Salem, filling all these rooms and filling the salt sea air with sounds of beach play.

Passersby on Highway 101 miss all this. The attractive beach is hidden behind a commercial Berlin Wall of taco shops, service stations, chowder houses, shell shops, motels, real estate offices and real estate signs. Since the town is caught between the seacliff and Siuslaw National Forest's wooded hills, it grows long and skinny, like a stepped-on tube of Aqua-fresh.

If you have a family in tow, the kids will like cavorting on that endless strand, where they can scamper along the surf and fly their kites with abandon. Looking up at sculpted sandstone cliffs, the place begins to look appealing, even as thousands of eyes from hotel and motel rooms look down on you. Another local lure is **Devils Lake** on the northern end of town, which offers boating, swimming, picnicking and camping (listed below).

Lincoln City has a genuine claim to fame—the world's shortest river with the shortest name: "D". However, the *Guinness Book of Records* may be stretching a point to give the title to the 440-foot-long D River. It looks suspiciously like a tidal channel between Devils Lake and the ocean.

If the River D is a rather tenuous attraction, this one is more legitimate: **North Lincoln County Historical Museum** ● *1512 SE Highway 101; (503) 994-6614. Tuesday-Sunday noon to 4. Free; donations appreciated.* Housed in a storefront next to a BP gasoline station, the small museum does a good job of recalling earlier days. Mannequins of a school marm, a wool spinner and an early telephone switchboard operator add dimension to its displays. Rounding out the exhibits are a pioneer bedroom, turn of the century kitchen and samples of Native American beadwork and basketry.

Since it's just a hop, skip and a sip to the wineries of Yamhill County, you'll find a couple of tasting rooms in Lincoln City. The sample parlor for **Honeywood Winery** is at 30 SE Highway 101 (994-2755) and **Oak Knoll Winery** is at 3521 SW Highway 101 (996-3221). If you drive inland on State Highway 18, you'll find their mother wineries, along with several others in the Yamhill Valley near **McMinnville**. The Lincoln City tasting rooms have winery touring maps of this area.

Should you want to linger here, pause at the **Lincoln City Visitors Information Center** (994-8378) in a green two-story city office complex on your left in the middle of town. It's at 801 SW Highway 101, adjacent to Price n' Pride Food Center. Hours are weekdays 8 to 6, Saturday 8 to 5 and Sunday 10 to 4. You can pick up names of restaurants, curio shops and galleries, of which there are many, to meet the rising tide of tourism.

ANNUAL EVENTS

Oregon Wine Festival in April; (503) 994-8293.
Spring Kite Festival in May; (503) 994-3070.
Flower and Garden Show in August; (503) 994-2131.
International Kite Festival in September; (503) 994-3070.

WHERE TO DINE

☺ The Bay House ● △△△ $$

5911 SW Highway 101; (503) 996-3222. Northwest regional and continental; full bar service. Dinner nightly 6 to 10 in summer, Wednesday-Sunday in the off-season. MC/VISA. Warmly modern restaurant with soft lights, crispy white nappery and excellent views of Siletz Bay. Northwest menu focuses on locally fresh seafood and shellfish, such as Dungeness crab in dill sauce and crisp salads mounded with bay shrimp, plus other specialties such as lamb, Tuscan brochettes and roast duckling. Desserts are excellent.

Lighthouse Brew Pub • △△ $

4157 N. Highway 101; (503) 994-7238. Microbrewery; beer and wine. Daily 11 to 11. Typically woodsy and brass brewpub featuring several locally brewed ales and stouts, plus a couple of dozen others on tap. Fare is proper for a microbrewery—pizza, deli sandwiches and such.

Mo's • △ $

860 SW 51st St.; (503) 996-2535. Seafood; wine and beer. Daily from 11 a.m. MC/VISA. Naturally, there's got to be a Mo's seafood parlor in booming Lincoln City. Like the rest, it's spartan of look, heavy of plate and cheap of price, serving heaps of mostly fried seafood.

☺ Road's End Dory Cove • △ $

5819 Logan Cove; (503) 994-5180. Basic American; wine and beer. Daily from 11 a.m. MC/VISA. Rustic beachside cafè popular with local hamburger and fish 'n' chip fans, plus other simple American entrèes. Save room for homemade pies. It's missed by most passersby, north of town and off the highway, near Roads End State Wayside. The beach is within easy reach, so plan lunch before or after a stroll on the strand.

WHERE TO SLEEP

Dozens of lodgings offer 1,800 rooms, more than any other city on the coast. We list a select few here.

Best Western Lincoln Sands Inn • △△△ $$$$ ∅

535 NW Inlet (a block off U.S. 101 at NW Sixth), Lincoln City, OR 97367; (800) 528-1234 or (503) 994-4227. Couples $75 to $130, singles $65 to $120. Major credit cards. Very attractive 33-unit beachfront inn with mini-suites featuring kitchens and balconies or patios; TV movies, room phones. Indoor pool, spa; short walk to the beach.

Coho Inn • △△ $$$

1635 NW Harbor (three block off 101 at N 17th), Lincoln City, OR 97367; (503) 994-3684. Couples $58 to $80, singles $48 to $66. Major credit cards. A 50-unit motel near the beach; many rooms with ocean views, balconies and patios, some kitchenettes. TV movies, room phones.

☺ The Inn at Spanish Head • △△△△ $$$$ ∅

4009 S. Highway 101, Lincoln City, OR 97367; (800) 452-8127 in Oregon, (800) 547-5235 elsewhere or (503) 996-2161. Couples and singles $86 to $133. Major credit cards. Modern 118-unit condo resort dramatically notched into a seacliff above the ocean. Units have kitchens, TV movies, room phones; most with ocean-view balconies. Coin laundry, recreation room, pool, spa and sauna. Tenth-floor **dining room** offers American fare and impressive views; dinners $12 to $25; full bar service.

Nordic Motel • △△ $$$ ∅

2133 NW Inlet (four blocks off 101 at NW 21st), Lincoln City, OR 97367; (503) 994-2329. Couples $44 to $72. Major credit cards. A 52-unit ocean-view motel with TV, room phones; some kitchenettes and fireplaces. Indoor pool, sauna, spa; short walk to beach.

Shilo Inn Oceanfront Resort ● △△△ $$$$ Ø

1501 NW 40th St. (on the beach, north end), Lincoln City, OR 97367; (800) 222-2244 or (503) 994-3655. Couples $79 to $132, singles $74 to $102. Major credit cards. Attractive new resort on bluff overlooking the beach; 187 rooms, many with ocean views; TV movies, room phones, some refrigerators. Indoor pool, sauna and spa, gift shop, laundromat. **Shilo Restaurant** serves American and Northwest regional fare 7 a.m. to 10 p.m. (to 11 Friday and Saturday); full bar service.

Bed & breakfast inns

Coastwood Inn ● △△△ $$$ Ø

843 SW 50th St. (off Highway 101, south end), Lincoln City, OR 97367; (503) 994-4014. From $60 to $75. Four rooms with private baths; full breakfast. MC/VISA, AMEX. Modern country style inn tucked among trees, near Siletz Bay and the ocean. Bright, spacious rooms have contemporary décor; two with fireplaces Indoor pool, sun deck; short walk to beach. Five-course dinners by appointment, billed separately.

The Rustic Inn ● △△ $$

4507 NE Holmes Rd. (at Highway 101 near Devils Lake), Lincoln City, OR 97367; (503) 994-5111. Couples $40 to $70. Three rooms with TV and private baths; full breakfast. MC/VISA. Contemporary log structure half mile from beach; large front porch and sun deck. Rooms have a mix of antique and modern furnishings; two have private entrances; one with spa tub.

Salmon River Lodge ● △△ $$ Ø

5622 Salmon River Hwy. (State Route 18), Otis, OR 97368; (503) 994-2639. Couples $40 to $50, singles $35 to $50. Four rooms, some private and some shared baths; full breakfast. MC/VISA, DISC. Ranch style home on wooded riverbank with a mix of antique and country furnishings. Sitting room with fireplace, TV and VCR.

WHERE TO CAMP

Devil's Lake State Park ● *1452 NE Sixth St., Lincoln City, OR 97367; (503) 994-2002. On state campground reservation system. Tent and RV sites; full hookups $13, water and electric $12, no hookups $11. No credit cards.* Situated near the lake, the campground offers a wooded retreat at the north edge of town. Appropriate to Lincoln City's popularity, it fills up quickly, even on weekdays in the summer.

LINCOLN CITY TO TILLAMOOK

As you leave Lincoln City, you leave the seacoast and travel through a wooded lowland. Instead of staying with U.S. 101, you might prefer a scenic byway through a lush rainforest just inland. Turn east onto State Highway 18 and follow it five miles to **Otis,** then turn left onto **Scenic Old U.S. 101** which winds through **Siuslaw National Forest.** At an experimental forest site, you're invited to pause and watch the trees grow. Signs along this winding paved route discuss coastal forest ecology.

After eight miles, you re-join "new" Highway 101 at the resort hamlet of **Neskowin** *(ness-COW-in)* It's comprised of a small business district with a

LINCOLN CITY TO ASTORIA

Ilwaco
Chinook
FORT STEVENS STATE PARK
COLUMBIA RIVER
Hammond
Astoria
Warrenton
FORT CLATSOP NATIONAL MEMORIAL
Svensen
30
Camp Rilea
Gearhart
LEWIS & CLARK RIVER
Seaside
Tillamook Head
ECOLA STATE PARK
Cannon Beach
26
HUG POINT STATE PARK
Arch Cape
NEHALEM RIVER
OSWALD WEST STATE PARK
53
Cape Falcon
NEAHKAHNIE MOUNTAIN
Manzanita
Nehalem
Mohler
NEHALEM BAY STATE PARK
Wheeler
N
Brighton
Rockaway Beach
Barview
Kincheloe Point
Garibaldi
Tillamook Bay
Bay City
CAPE MEARES STATE PARK
Oceanside
Tillamook
Netarts
6
Netarts Bay
101
CAPE LOOKOUT STATE PARK
Sandlake
Beaver
CAPE KIWANDA STATE PARK
Hebo
Pacific City
Cloverdale
Nestucca Bay
NESTUCCA RIVER
STRAUB STATE PARK
Neskowin
18
Cascade Head
Otis
Rose Lodge
Neotsu
DEVILS LAKE
Lincoln City

resort and café and a collection of homes in a wooded grove beside the beach. The narrow lanes of these coastal homes (no RVs, please, a sign advises) may remind you of California's coastal Carmel. Two golf courses suggest that folks come here to play and not much else. There's an old money ambiance about this community, although some of the homes are modest. You'll find a resort and an interesting café up by the highway:

Neskowin Resort ● ⌂
$$$$ ∅

P.O. Box 728, Neskowin, OR 97149; (800) 827-3191 or (503) 392-3191. Couples $45 to $60, ocean-view studios $59 to $105, ocean-view suites and condos $79 to $135. MC/VISA. Modest-looking resort with a nice location, at the edge of a beach that extends for seven miles. All rooms non-smoking. **Raku Grill** offers ocean-view dining and full bar service.

☺ Hawk Creek Café ●
△△ $$ ∅

Adjacent to Neskowin Resort; (503) 392-3838. American; wine and beer. Daily 7 a.m. to 9 p.m. with a 2 to 5 siesta. MC/VISA. Exceptionally nice wood-paneled diner with benches and oilcloth tables, lots of plants and an outdoor deck. Menu focuses on breakfast, burgers and other sandwiches for lunch, plus evening steak, halibut and shrimp entrées for $11 to $15.

Cape crusader?

A mile beyond Neskowin, a left turn toward Cape Kiwanda recreational beaches puts you on the 36-mile **Three Capes**

Scenic Route. This is one of the most appealing byways on the coast. Although the route itself isn't particularly scenic for the most part, each of the three capes is strikingly attractive. The road travels mostly through dairy country and small towns.

After a few miles you encounter the tiny village of **Pacific City**, home of one of the Oregon Coast's two rocks named Haystack. This **Haystack Rock** towers 327 feet, a few hundred yards offshore. (The second is at Cannon Beach to the north.)

Pacific City also is home to an intriguing ritual, which dates back to the 1920s. Commercial fishermen launch their dories directly into the pounding surf from a flat sandy beach, without benefit of a launch ramp or pier hoist. They put to sea from boat trailers hauled by fat-tired (and usually four-wheel-drive) pickups. When they return with the day's catch, they head for shore at full throttle until they skid onto the beach, like a chase scene from a Hollywood comedy. The pickups pull them higher and drier with long ropes, then winch them onto the trailers. Incidentally, some of these boats are available for charter fishing trips, permitting visitors to take part in the launch and retrieve ritual.

You'll have to be up before dawn to see them launch, although you can catch their return from late morning until afternoon. What's a dory? A small, open fishing boat with a flat bottom and wide beam designed to handle heavy surf. It was developed for the rough seas off Newfoundland and New England. The flat bottoms that allow the boats to launch *au natural*.

Overlooking the dory launch is **Cape Kiwanda**, popular for another kind of launching—hang gliders from its near-vertical face. Both bold and masochistic, the participants drag their awkward wings up to the north face, then launch over the restless sea. Mere mortals can make the hike without the Icarus rigs, and enjoy awesome coastline views from the top.

You can buy what the dorymen caught at a couple of fish marts, along with chilled drinks and other goodies for a beach picnic. **Doryman Fish Company** offers fresh-cooked crab and shrimp, pre-made sandwiches and chilled drinks. The larger **Kiwanda Fish Company** has a more extensive selection, including pickled and smoked fish and oysters, and fish sandwiches—salmon, crab or shrimp. The firm also has RV parking.

South of town at the end of a narrow spit is **Bob Straub State Park**, with a beach access. If you want to linger in Pacific City, there's a restaurant and an RV park just across from the dory launching site:

Hungry Harbor Seafood Restaurant ● ▵▵ $$

Pacific City; (503) 965-6245. American, mostly seafood; wine and beer. Sunday-Thursday 8 to 8, Friday-Saturday 8 to 9. MC/VISA. Good seafood menu of razor clams, shrimp, scallops, oysters and what's fresh from the dory fleet. The interior is simple and vaguely nautical and the view through large windows to Haystack Rock is exceptional.

Cape Kiwanda RV Park ● *P.O. Box 129, Pacific City, OR 97135; (503) 965-6230. RV sites, $13.50 to $14.50. Reservations accepted; MC/VISA.* Snugly-spaced sites with full hookups, showers, some pull-throughs; coin laundry, rec room, horseshoes.

From Pacific City, the highway climbs wooded Cape Kiwanda, drops down the other side and passes the beachside community of **Tierra del r** (a name so logical it seems almost pointless). Eight miles from Pacific a left turn takes you just over two miles to Siuslaw National Forest's

In one of the Oregon Coast's more interesting rituals, dorymen land their flat-bottom boats with pickups on the beach at Pacific City. — **Betty Woo Martin**

Sand Lake Campground, with a beach access beyond. The campsites, shaded by shore pines, are near a small inland lake; $8 a day with no hook-ups. It's a popular dune buggy hangout on weekends.

☺ Driving northward on the scenic drive, follow a sign to the left to **Cape Lookout State Park** for the second of the three promontories. This large preserve encompasses the finger-like cape, its wooded headlands and the skinny sandspit of Netarts Bay to the north. The road doesn't reach the cape itself. To get there, follow the highway to a high point on the headland and stop at a turnout marked "wildlife viewing area." (It would be more helpful if the sign said "Cape Lookout trailhead.") From here, it's a 2.5-mile hike out to land's end. The trail isn't difficult and the awesome views up and down the coastline are worth the effort. If you're not up to the hike, a 15-minute walk will reward you with views southward to Cascade Head. Walk a bit farther and you see the large inland puddle of **Netarts Bay** to the north. It's a landlocked lagoon clinging to the mainland by the thread of its skinny sandspit.

As the highway spirals down the north side of the headland, pause mid-way at **Anderson Viewpoint** for a nice vista of Netarts Bay. At the bottom of the bluff, you encounter Cape Lookout State Park's campground, with full hookups for $13 and none for $11. It's on the reserved campsite system; send a completed form and payment to: 13000 W. Whiskey Creek Rd., Til-lamook, OR 97141; (503) 842-4981. From here, you can hike five miles back up to Cape Lookout, enjoying ocean vistas as you pant skyward.

Continuing northward, the highway rims the eastern edge of Netarts Bay, which is a good clamming spot, and passes through the small town **Netarts**, where the lagoon opens to the sea. It offers a motel and a camp-ground, and not much else. They're both located right on the bay.

Terimore Motel ● ⌂⌂ $$

5105 Crab Ave. (P.O. Box 250), Netarts, OR 97143; (800) 635-1821 or (503) 842-4623. Couples, singles and kitchenettes $30 to $68. MC/VISA. Sev-

eral simply-furnished rooms, mini-suites and kitchen units, all with TV movies and phones. Some units with ocean and bay views and fireplaces.

Happy Camp RV Resort ● *P.O. Box 823, Netarts, OR 97143; (503) 842-4012. RVs only, water and electric $15, three nights for $30 midweek special. MC/VISA.* Asphalt RV parking area adjacent to Netarts Bay with showers, boat rentals, fish cleaning station and crab cooker.

A short drive beyond, you'll encounter one of the most fetching little towns on the entire coast.

Oceanside

Population: 250   **Elevation: sea level**

This tiny hamlet's homes, luxurious and otherwise, are cantilevered into a steep headland overlooking the dramatic spires of **Three Arch Rocks**. The seastack wildlife refuge, busy with bird varieties and sea lions, stands just offshore from a wide, sandy beach. With its narrow switch-back streets, Oceanside brings to mind some of the terraced villages of Switzerland's lakes district. Drive up one of those skinny streets to the **House on the Hill,** a motel clinging tenaciously to a narrow saddle above the beach. From here, follow Maxwell Mountain Road's switchbacks to the top of the headland. Park, catch your breath and absorb views of Three Arch Rocks, a sweep of Pacific blue and the town terraced at your feet.

If you're looking for a hideaway, this town has the essential ingredients: no through traffic, lots of blackberry bushes, a couple of lodgings, a restaurant, tavern, post office and *no* souvenir shops. The broad beach, just a step down from town, is sandy and smooth, a fine place to stroll, scuff at seaweed and commune with the gulls.

WHERE TO EAT & SLEEP

☺ **Roseanna's Cafè** ● △△ **$$**

NW Pacific Street; (503) 842-7351. American, mostly seafood; wine and beer. Daily 8 a.m. to 9 p.m. Charming shingle-sided Mystic Seaport sort of cafè perched above the beach, with nautical touches, knotty pine walls and great views. Well-prepared entrèes include Tillamook oysters, salmon *meuniere*, rock cod Veracruz, ginger prawns and seafood fettuccini.

☺ **House on the Hill** ● △△△ **$$$$**

P.O. Box 187, Oceanside, OR 97134; (503) 842-6030. Couples and singles $75 to $90, kitchenettes $80 to $95. MC/VISA. A 16-unit motel perched dramatically on a narrow ridge 250 feet above the sea. TV, phones; all rooms have ocean views. Nicely landscaped grounds; small nautical and shell museum adjacent to office.

Oceanside Inn ● △ **$$$** ∅

1440 NW Pacific St. (P.O. Box 142), Oceanside, OR 97134; (800) 347-2972 or (503) 842-2961. Double rooms and mini-suites, all with kitchenettes, $45 to $75. MC/VISA. Recently renovated eight-unit motel just above the beach; cable TV, ocean views.

Ocean Front Cabins ● △ **$$$**

NW Pacific Street (P.O. Box 203), Oceanside, OR 97134; (503) 842-6081. ʻenettes $50 to $85, sleeper with no kitchen $45. MC/VISA. Modestly furʻnicely maintained old beach cabins; TV. A few steps from the beach.

Three Capes Bed & Breakfast ● ⌂⌂⌂ $$$$ ∅

1685 Maxwell Mountain Rd. (P.O. Box 93), Oceanside, OR 97134; (503) 842-6126. Couples $75 and $85, singles $70 and $80. Two rooms with private baths; full breakfast. No credit cards. Refurbished 1938 home tucked into the hills above the Pacific. Rooms have pink and blue country decor; both have windows on the ocean. Breakfast served on view deck in good weather.

Continuing north from Oceanside, the scenic route travels along the seaward side of a sandspit that forms large **Tillamook Bay.** You're headed for the last of the three headlands at **Cape Meares State Park.** This scenic promontory is home to a restored lighthouse open to visitors and a natural curiosity called the Octopus Tree.

☺ **Cape Meares Lighthouse** is recessed into a niche, offering an eyelevel view of the glittering fresnel lens as you approach from the parking area. From the tower, you get impressive views of coastal seastacks and odd views of other visitors, distorted through the prismatic lens. Docents often are on hand to chat about its workings. They'll tell you that the light was lit in 1890 and de-activated in 1963, replaced by an automated version higher on the cape. Some will chuckle that the light was *supposed* to have been built at Cape Lookout, although the state park brochure insists otherwise.

Follow a dizzying seacliff path from the lighthouse to the **Octopus Tree,** a mixed-up Sitka spruce that branched into six separate trunks. Take your pick of impressions: a wooden tarantula, an upside-down candelabra or—of course—an evergreen octopus. Native American legends say it was shaped that way to cradle the burial canoes of dead chieftains. Scientists don't know how it got into that condition. Walk a few paces from the wooden octopus to the edge of a seacliff for a smashing coastal vista. Then follow a path inland back to the parking lot, through giant—and normal—spruce trees.

The Three Capes Scenic Route loops southward from Cape Meares, around the bottom of Tillamook Bay. Following directional signs toward Tillamook, you begin seeing—and smelling—the cows that made this homely town famous.

Tillamook

Population: 4,000   **Elevation: 22 feet**

There's nothing photogenic about this ordinary community that's built on the mud flats of Tillamook Bay. Of course, when folks here say "cheese," they mean cheddar. Tillamook cheese, shipped at the rate of 40 million pounds a year, is so well known that the factory is among Oregon's top three tourist attractions. Each year, more than 750,000 visitors watch the cheese-making process from galleries and nibble free samples in a huge, crowded gift shop.

At the risk of blasphemy, we prefer the Bandon Cheese Factory down south, since it's less crowded and offers a greater variety of samples. Of course, it doesn't have the sophisticated videos and displays of the huge Tillamook factory. And who are we to question the tastes of 750,000 people?

Tillamook (originally Killamook) is a local tribal name, meaning "people of the land of many waters." Settlers were drawn to this flat, lush grassland late in the last century and saw its potential for dairy herds. The Killamooks

212 — CHAPTER SIX

were pushed aside and the area soon became the land of many dairies, most of them producing salted butter for trade.

In 1894, a dairyman hired Canadian Peter McIntosh, who possessed the skills for "cheddering," a cheese-making process from 14th century England. Cheddar cheese, easier to preserve and ship than butter, soon became Tillamook's main export. Ten cheese factories got together in 1909 to form the Tillamook County Creamery Association. Although nearly 30 individual cheesemakers operated in the county at one time, most were absorbed into the association, which still functions.

If you approach Tillamook from the Three Capes Scenic Route, you'll blend onto Third Street, which carries you into the old town area. Before heading north for your free sample of cheddar, you might want to see a couple of other lures. From downtown, head south on Highway 101 two miles to the former **Tillamook Naval Air Station** for a visit to the **Blimp Hangar Museum.** The cliche: "You can't miss it" was never more appropriate. Two gigantic lighter-than-air hangars dominate the horizon to your left as you draw near. They're the largest unsupported wooden structures in the world. Signs direct you to the nearest one—the only blimp hanger in America now serving as a museum.

From the hangar, follow U.S. 101 back into Tillamook; it becomes Pacific Street downtown. Turn right onto Second Street and you're in front of the **Tillamook County Pioneer Museum,** housed in the former courthouse. Then continue north on Highway 101 and watch for the **Blue Heron French Cheese Company,** in a Pennsylvania Dutch structure on your right. Another mile brings you to the imposing blue and white **Tillamook Cheese Company.** Across the parking lot is the visitor information center of the **Tillamook Chamber of Commerce**; (503) 842-7525. It's open weekdays 9 to 5, Saturday 10 to 4:30 and Sunday 10 to 2.

ATTRACTIONS
(In order of appearance)

☺ **Blimp Hangar Museum** ● *4000 Blimp Blvd.; (503) 842-2413. Adults $2, kids 6 to 12, $1. Open 10 to 6, daily in summer and weekends and holidays the rest of the year.* Step through the door and start reaching for superlatives. This monumental inner space measures 1,080 by 300 feet, covering seven acres, enough for a dozen football fields. A 15-story building could fit beneath its 195-foot arched ceiling. Everything inside is dwarfed. A deflated hot air balloon hanging from the ceiling, a 65-foot-long advertising blimp and a World War II barrage balloon look like toys. Which proves, if nothing else, that everything is relative.

Naval Air Station Tillamook was built at the beginning of World War II as a base for anti-submarine blimps to escort Pacific shipping. The two giant hangars, simply called "A" and "B," were among 17 identical wooden structures built around the country. The base was de-commissioned after the war and now is an industrial park operated by the Port of Tillamook Bay. The port, assisted by volunteers, also runs the museum, which opened in 1992. It contains assorted balloons, photos, drawings and other artifacts relating to lighter-than-air travel.

Tillamook County Pioneer Museum ● *2106 Second St., (503) 842-4553. Monday-Saturday 8 to 5, Sunday noon to 5; closed Mondays in the off-season. Adults $1, families $5.* This 1905 masonry structure became the county's museum in 1935 after the court house moved to a "new" federalist style building just across the way. It has amassed a sizable collection of curiosities, some associated with Tillamook County, some not. You'll see a replica of the tree bark shelter built in 1851 by the area's first settler, a large international doll collection, a 19th century kitchen, a Victorian parlor, a pioneer barn and workshop, a selection of stuffed critters and bird dioramas.

Blue Heron French Cheese Company ● *Blue Heron Drive; (503) 842-8281. Daily 8 to 8 in summer, 9 to 6 the rest of the year. Major credit cards.* Visitors can sample *brie* and other French cheeses, not cheddar, in this attractive tasting room and gift shop. Oregon specialty foods also are sampled, and you can sip Oregon wines at $1 a pour. You can buy picnic fixin's from a well-stocked deli, and adjourn to tables out front. Blue Heron draws only a fraction of the crowds converging on the Tillamook factory down the road. This may or may not be a commentary on *brie* versus cheddar.

☺ **Tillamook Cheese Company** ● *4175 N. Highway 101; (503) 842-4481. Daily 8 to 8. MC/VISA.* A self-guided tour with videos, graphics and old dairy equipment tells visitors how the cheese-making business began here. During working hours, you can see cheese being made through gallery viewing windows. As you watch, on-going videos explain what's happening. Below you are enough stainless steel vats and pipes, dials and levers to equip a nuclear sub. At a large gift shop and deli, you can sample mild, medium and sharp cheddars, plus smoked cheddar, jalapeno and cheese curds. Two locations dispense Tillamook-made ice cream cones, which seems to be more popular than the cheese. Apparently, visitors are intent on getting their cholesterol one way or the other.

Other culinary venues ● In addition to cheese factories, several other nearby outfits specialize in good things to eat and drink. You can visit them by following the *Tillamook County Cheese, Seafood and Winery Tour.* Flyers are available at the visitors center, cheese factories and other spots where tourists converge.

Around Tillamook

Seven miles south of town is **Munson Creek Falls,** the highest in the Coast Range, cascading 266 feet. To reach the site (which you missed by following the Three Capes Scenic Route) drive south on Highway 101 and watch for a small sign. It points you west, a mile and a half up a narrow, steep road to the falls parking area. A short stroll takes you to the base of the cataract, and a steeper path takes you up a bluff for an eye-level view.

Continuing south on 101, you'll encounter western America's only artichoke fields outside of California. A produce stand, **Bear Creek Artichokes** (398-5411), stocks local 'chokes, other produce and Oregon specialty foods. It's about four miles south of the Munson Falls turnoff.

A drive east from Tillamook on State Highway 6 takes you through the luxuriant fir and spruce woodlands of **Tillamook State Forest** along the banks of the **Wilson River.** This pleasantly winding route deposits you on U.S. Highway 26 expressway for a quick run into Portland.

TILLAMOOK TO CANNON BEACH

North from Tillamook, Highway 101 wraps around Tillamook Bay, passing the small towns of **Bay City** and **Garibaldi.** A nice old village of 1,060, Garibaldi wraps around a bayside inlet and crawls up into nearby hills. **Lumberman's Park** on the left offers a couple of picnic tables and a turn-of-the-century steam engine. From here, follow the seagulls to the **Port of Garibaldi,** a working waterfront. It's a vision from a John Steinbeck novel, with a couple of fish canneries, fish markets, small seafood cafes— and not a souvenir stand in sight.

Continuing north, you'll clear the mouth of Tillamook Bay and pick up the ocean. Near the bay entrance, note the delightful white and red trimmed Victorian **Tillamook Harbor Coast Guard Station.** As you drive along the inner edge of Tillamook Bay, you'll pass teeny **Barview,** consisting mostly of a general store.

Rockaway Beach, a resort hamlet popular with inland Oregonians, has a few beach homes, motels and an occasional curio shop. The highway swings inland north of here, following the tidal estuary of the Nehalem River. A one-mile drive up Highway 53 just beyond **Wheeler** will take you to **Nehalem Bay Winery,** the closest vintner to the coast; (503) 368-5300. Housed in a European-style cross-timbered building, the tasting room/gift shop is open daily 10 to 5.

Back on Highway 101, you'll encounter **Nehalem,** an old fashioned town snuggled beside its namesake river. False front stores shelter a couple of antique and curio shops and little else of visitor interest. A road leads a mile and a half south to **Nehalem Bay State Park.** It's perched on the tip of a skinny spit that separates **Nehalem Bay** from the Pacific. A short hike over grass- anchored dunes takes you to a long, flat and sandy beach. Facilities include a bike trail, equestrian trail and meeting hall. The bay side offers good clamming and crabbing. (See "Where to camp" below.)

A bit farther north on Highway 101 is **Manzanita,** a charming town tucked among shore pines. The shorefront residential area reminds one of the quiet streets of California's Carmel, although it lacks Carmel's tourist facilities.

Beyond Manzanita, the highway climbs **Neah-kah-nie Headlands,** a wooded promontory that provides sudden respite from the string of small coastal towns. Named for the Tillamook fire god, Neah-kah-nie is one of the coast's highest headlands, at 1,631 feet. Much of its thick forest and the coastal ramparts of **Cape Falcon** are enclosed in the 2,474-acre **Oswald West State Park.** From the loftiest Highway 101 turnouts on the Pacific Coast, 700 feet above the sea, you'll enjoy exquisite vistas of Nehalem Bay and the shoreline.

If you'd like to get even higher, a steep switchback trail leads to Neah-kah-nie's peak. Pick it up opposite the Neahkanie Golf Course, 2.6 miles south of the **Short Sands Beach** parking area. Another trail from the parking area leads out to Cape Falcon for more stirring coastal views.

☺ As you follow Highway 101 down Neah-kah-nie's north slope, you'll encounter one of the coast's jewels at **Oswald West walk-in campground.** Only tenters can use the campsites, since they're half a mile down a steep trail; wheelbarrows are provided to trundle one's gear. Even if you don't have a tent handy, you should take time to explore this area. A trail delivers you to a delightfully secluded beach, sheltered by low seacliffs. To reach it, start toward the campground, then fork to the left. Your hike takes you through old growth forest, alongside a rocky creek bed and across a swinging bridge to the cove. You'll have to pick your way across a breastwork of driftwood to reach the beach. (Try not to think about those scenes from *Pet Sematary*.)

Continuing your drive north, you'll pass more turnouts with more trails leading to more secluded beaches. Several provide access to the **Oregon Coast Trail**. You'll exit the state park via Arch Cape Tunnel, which deposits you on the doorstep of the hamlet of **Arch Cape**. Ahead lies Oregon's northwestern most wedge—Clatsop County of Lewis and Clark fame.

TILLAMOOK COUNTY ACTIVITIES

Deep sea fishing ● **Garibaldi Charters,** 606 S. Commercial St. (P.O. Box 556), Garibaldi, OR 97118, (503) 322-0007; **Siggi-G Ocean Charters,** P.O. Box 536, Garibaldi, OR 97118, (503) 322-3285; and **Troller Deep Sea Fishing,** P.O. Box 605, Garibaldi, OR 97118, (503) 322-3343. For boat rentals, fishing, clam-digging and crabbing gear, contact **Jetty Fishery** at 27550 N. Highway 101, Rockaway Beach, OR 97136, (503) 368-5746.

Freshwater fishing ● The 14-mile-long Tillamook River, reached by eastbound State Highway 6, is popular for steelhead, salmon and trout fishing. Farther north, the Trask River is noted for spring and fall salmon runs. Among local fishing guides are **Dean's Guide Service,** P.O. Box 199, Netarts, OR 97143, (503) 842-7107; and **Rick Howard's Guide Service,** 52122 SE Third Place, Scappoose, OR 97056, (503) 743-7372.

TILLAMOOK COUNTY ANNUAL EVENTS

Swiss Festival, March at Tillamook County Fairgrounds; (503) 842-7525.

Pacific Northwest Crab Races and Clam Fritter Feed, February in Garibaldi; (503) 322-3380.

Rockaway Beach Kite Festival, May at Rockaway Beach; 355-8108.

Blessing of the Fleet, May in Garibaldi; (503) 322-3380.

Dairy Parade, June in Tillamook; (503) 842-7725.,

Tillamook County Rodeo, June in Tillamook; (503) 842-7525.

Garibaldi Days, July in Garibaldi, celebrating the founding of the city; (503) 322-0301.

Tillamook County Fair, August in Tillamook; (503) 842-7525.

Cheese and Seafood Festival, September in and around Tillamook; (503) 842-7525.

Autumn Festival and Sand Castle Contest, October in Rockaway Beach; (503) 355-8108.

WHERE TO DINE IN TILLAMOOK COUNTY

Not a tourist town, Tillamook attracts few overnighters. A look at the blimp hangar, a peek into the historical museum, a bite of cheese and most folks move on. Small towns to the north in Tillamook County have a few small motels, patronized mostly by Oregon weekenders and fisherfolk.

Cedar Bay Restaurant ● ΔΔ $$

2015 First St., Tillamook; (503) 842-8288. American; full bar service. Sunday-Monday 4 to 9, Tuesday-Thursday 11 to 9, Friday-Saturday 11 to 9:30. MC/VISA. Oldstyle dining room with upholstered chairs, wainscotting and chandeliers, in a venerable brick building. Grilled and deep-fried seafoods, tiger prawns and a few steaks, chicken and chops.

McClaskey's Restaurant • ∆∆ $$

2102 First St., Tillamook; (503) 842-5674. American, mostly seafood; wine and beer. Monday-Thursday 7 a.m. to 8:30 p.m., Friday-Saturday 7 to 9, Sunday 7:30 to 8. Vaguely early American décor with high-backed booths, ceiling fans and drop lamps. Versatile seafood menu ranging from batter fried halibut and prawns to Tillamook Bay oysters, plus several chicken dishes and some steaks and chops.

Troller Restaurant & Lounge • ∆∆ $$

Port of Garibaldi on Mooring Basin Road, Garibaldi; (503) 322-3666. American, mostly seafood; full bar service. Open 24 hours a day in summer, shorter hours the rest of the year. MC/VISA. Pleasantly rustic seafood parlor featuring local fresh fish, Bay City oysters, steamer clams, fish and chips, plus a few steak, chicken and chop entrées. Try trout and eggs or fried oysters and eggs for breakfast.

WHERE TO SLEEP

☺ The Inn at Manzanita • ⌂⌂⌂ $$$$ Ø

67 Laneda Ave. (P.O. Box 243), Manzanita, OR 97130; (503) 368-6754. Couples $90 to $120, singles $80 to $110. MC/VISA. A nice eight-room inn tucked among pines just off the beach. Each room has a theme décor, with a TV and VCR, stocked refrigerator, wet bar and view deck.

Shilo Inn Tillamook • ⌂⌂⌂ $$$ Ø

2515 N. Main St. (south of cheese factory), Tillamook, OR 97141; (800) 222-2244 or (503) 842-7971. Couples and singles $62 to $79, kitchenettes $79 to $90. Major credit cards. Attractive 100-unit inn on the Wilson River; all mini-suites with TV movies, phones, microwaves, refrigerators and wet bars. Indoor pool, sauna, spa, steam and fitness room, laundry. **Restaurant** serves American fare 6 a.m. to 10 p.m., Friday-Saturday to 11; full bar.

Bed & breakfast inns

Blue Haven Inn • ⌂⌂ $$$ Ø

3025 Gienger Rd., Tillamook, OR 97141; (503) 842-2265. Couples $50 to $60, singles $45. Three rooms, one with private bath; full breakfast. No credit cards. Country-style American home surrounded by a two-acre garden. Croquet and lawn tennis, old-fashioned front porch with swing, game room with antique radio and Gramophone. Bedrooms decorated in family heirlooms and other collectibles.

Hill Top House • ⌂⌂ $$$ Ø

Holly Avenue at Third (P.O. Box 145), Garibaldi, OR 97118; (503) 322-3221. Couples $62 to $83.50, singles $52 to $73. Three rooms with private baths; full breakfast. MC/VISA. Attractive cedar home on the highest street in town, with nice views of Garibaldi, the harbor and ocean; garden with spa. Rooms furnished with an eclectic mix of antiques and "comfy modern."

WHERE TO CAMP

Barview Jetty County Park • *On Tillamook Bay at Barview, north of Garibaldi; (503) 322-3477. RV and tent sites; full hookups $12, water and electric $10, no hookups $9. No reservations or credit cards.* Showers, picnic tables. Large park with sites near sand dunes; some shaded and well-spaced.

Nehalem Bay State Park • *Nehalem, three miles south of Manzanita junction; (503) 368-5943. RV and tent sites, full hookups $13, water and electric $11, no hookups $9. No reservations or credit cards.* Attractive sites sheltered by shore pines. Showers, picnic tables and barbecues. Beach activities, biking, hiking; horse camping and fly-in camping (airport adjacent).

Tillamook KOA • *11880 S. Highway 101 (six miles south), Tillamook, OR 97141; (800) 345-8352 or (503) 842-4779. RV and tent sites, $12 to $17.50. Reservations accepted; MC/VISA.* Close-together sites in well-maintained park near river; some pull-throughs. Showers, coin laundry, mini-mart; fishing, horseshoes, rec hall, kids' playground, rec field.

Cannon Beach

Population: 1,260   **Elevation: sea level**

As you emerge from Cape Arch Tunnel, you're still several miles from the woodsy-*chic* art colony of Cannon Beach. An historical marker here will tell you how it got its name. It explains that the U.S. Naval survey schooner *Shark* ran aground on September 10, 1846, while trying to leave the mouth of the Columbia River. It had been charting the area during those testy days when America and England were fussing over division of the Oregon Country. A chunk of the *Shark's* wooden deck, with a cannon and capstan still attached, drifted southward along the coast and washed ashore near Arch Cape. A settler tugged it from the surf and set the cannon in concrete.

Earlier, William Clark of the Corps of Discovery had gazed down upon this pretty shoreline, which is highlighted by the coast's second Haystack Rock. His diary reports that he led a party 20 miles south from Fort Clatsop in 1806. They climbed what likely was Tillamook Head and saw a "butifull Sand Shore" to the south.

Despite these early visitations, the community is a latter-day creation. A Cannon Beach post office had been opened in 1891 near the spot of the cannon discovery, but it was closed ten years later. The present Cannon Beach, several miles north, wasn't settled until early in this century. A few artists from the crowded resort of Seaside sought refuge here. They built raw wood shacks at the beach near Ecola Creek, set up their easels and painted seagulls flitting about the seastacks. The highway bypassed the town, and the artists-in-residence and other settlers were content in their self-exile.

The name Cannon Beach was applied to this Haystack Rock-Ecola Creek settlement in 1922, and the town was incorporated in 1955. Some of the artists opened galleries to peddle their paintings, tourists began discovering the hideaway town and the inevitable happened.

Cannon Beach is being discovered to pieces.

Thousands of visitors swarm through its quaint shops, boutiques and galleries. On summer weekends, one is hard-pressed to find a parking place. Signs warn rec vehicles *not* to park on the streets. (We saw a young parking patrol officer ticketing a pickup camper, although it fit easily into its space. RV's *are* accommodated, however, in a special parking area.

Like Carmel, Cannon Beach fights to remain quaint. Strict planning regulations prohibit neon and free-standing signs. The charming mix of chalet-style, pseudo-Cape Cod and woodsy-rustic buildings are painted in muted colors. Service stations and fast food outlets are banished to the outskirts.

Yet, even as it battles excess tourism, it surrenders to it. The Cannon Beach Chamber of Commerce passes out pounds of literature and offers benches for sitting while you browse through your brochures. The chamber's thick *Cannon Beach Magazine*—free to visitors—is filled with ads for galleries, import shops, kitchenware shops, yogurt shops, cookie companies, toy shops, candy shops, jewelry boutiques, bike rental shops and an "art shirt" shop. They line Hemlock, the main street; they're crowded into mini-arcades and tucked into cul-de-sac shopping alleys.

Certainly the beach is here, just a block or so off Hemlock. It's a particularly inviting one, wide and sandy with seastacks offshore and headlands onshore. There is no beachfront drive, although any of a dozen cross streets will take you to the strand. Here, you can stroll idly and scuff seaweed and fly a kite and poke about tidepools. You can admire through binoculars the shorebirds and sea birds that swarm around Haystack Rock and its neighboring pinnacles called The Needles.

You'll have plenty of room to enjoy the attractive beach of Cannon. Most of the other visitors are strung out along Hemlock Street, frozen yogurt cones in hand, shopping until they're dropping.

To reach this loved-to-death art colony, turn left onto the **Cannon Beach-Tolovana Park beach loop,** just beyond Arch Cape. You first encounter the small village of **Tolovana Park**. It offers a large shingle-sided resort (listed below), a few motels and **Tolovana State Park,** a beach access near yet another Mo's seafood parlor.

Just beyond, you pick up Hemlock Street and enter Cannon Beach. Although the heart of boutique row is compact and walkable, peripheral businesses are strung out for a couple of miles. In the middle of downtown, turn right onto Second Street, drive one block and you'll hit the **Chamber of Commerce**, (503) 436-2623. It's open Monday-Saturday 11 to 5 and Sunday 11 to 4. The RV parking area is a block beyond.

☺ Handsome **Ecola State Park** is Cannon Beach's neighbor to the north. To reach it, follow the loop drive across Ecola Creek and turn left onto Fifth Street, which becomes Ecola Park Road. Before reaching the state reserve, pause at the attractive **Les Shirley City Park** beside Ecola Creek on your left. Local historians say this may have been the southernmost reach of the Lewis and Clark expedition. Their diaries recount an encounter with a whale carcass, which may have been at this spot. Later, they bought blubber from local Indians and reported it to be a welcome change in their diet.

From Les Shirley, the road winds upward through a thick evergreen canopy and ends at a T-intersection in Ecola State Park. A left turn takes you to a viewpoint and picnic area at **Ecola Point,** offering striking vistas southward to Haystack Rock and Cannon Beach's beach. A right turn takes you—via a long downward spiral through a ferny forest primeval—to **Indian Beach** in a sheltered cove. Squint seaward from Ecola Point and you may see **Tillamook Rock Light,** which guided ships from 1881 until 1957. Now a columbarium for preserving cremated ashes, it's called—appropriately—Eternity at Sea. A two-mile trail links Ecola Point with Indian Beach, and a six-mile trail leads to **Tillamook Head.** The latter is part of the **Tillamook Head Recreation Trail** that leads all the way to Seaside.

ACTIVITIES

Bike rentals ● Three-wheel "recliner " bikes are available at **Manzanita Fun Merchants,** 1235 S. Hemlock (436-1880); **Mike's Bike Shop** (436-1266) rents bicycles and three-wheelers.

Drama • **Coaster Theater Playhouse** at 108 N. Hemlock (P.O. Box 643) Cannon Beach, OR 97110; (503) 436-1242, presents dramas, comedies, concerts and other entertainments the year-around.

Horseback riding • **Sea Ranch Stables** at Sea Ranch Resort off Highway 101 at the north end of town (436-2815), rents horses for beach riding from mid-May through Labor Day weekend.

ANNUAL EVENTS

Kite Festival in April; (503) 436-2623.

Sandcastle Day in May; largest sand castle contest on the coast, drawing hundreds of participants and thousands of spectators; (503) 436-2627.

Stormy Weather Festival in November, with art, music and exhibits; (503) 436-2627.

Dickens Festival in December at the Coaster Theater, plus **Victorian Christmas decorations** about town; (503) 436-1242 or 436-2627.

WHERE TO DINE

☺ **Café de la Mer** • ∆∆∆∆ **$$$**

1287 S. Hemlock St.; (503) 436-1179. Continental-Northwest regional fare; wine and beer. Dinner Wednesday-Sunday. MC/VISA, AMEX. Trendy-rustic and expensive café with a wood-paneled dining room, a greenhouse dining patio, and an open kitchen between. Menu includes hearty and rich bouillabaisse, oysters tarragon, veal, crab *Dijon* and tasty presentations of fresh local fish. Extensive and rather expensive wine list.

☺ **The Bistro** • ∆∆∆ **$$** ∅

263 N. Hemlock St.; (503) 436-2661. French with Northwest accents; full bar service. Dinner nightly, various hours. MC/VISA. More rural Northwestern than French, it occupies a small beach house trimmed with window boxes, with a cozy and rustic dining parlor. Lightly seasoned salmon and halibut, shrimp Dianne, veal scaloppine and steak are among its varied entrées. The restaurant is smoke-free.

Lazy Susan Café • ∆ **$** ∅

126 N. Hemlock; (503) 436-2816. American; wine and beer. Wednesday-Monday 7:30 to 2:30. No credit cards. Cheerful spot with natural wood paneling, hanging plants and oilcloth tables. It's in a board and batten building off the street, behind the Wine Shack. The health-conscious menu features breakfast omelets and yogurt-topped oatmeal waffles, plus quiche, salads and creative sandwiches for lunch. Try the turkey sandwich with curried mayo and chutney. Smoke-free.

Mo's at Tolovana • ∆ **$**

3400 S. Hemlock at Tolovana Park, opposite Tolovana Resort; (503) 436-1111. Seafood; wine and beer. Sunday-Thursday 11 to 9, Friday-Saturday 11 to 10. MC/VISA, DISC. Like the others Mo's, this simple café serves ample portions of cheap fish and shellfish. As a bonus, it offers an outstanding view of the Tolovana coast.

Morris' Fireside Restaurant • ∆∆ **$$**

3400 S. Hemlock; (503) 436-2917. American; full bar service. Daily 6 a.m. to 9:30 p.m. MC/VISA, AMEX. What's the Old West doing in trendy Cannon Beach? This curious log house restaurant with a fieldstone fireplace serves hearty portions of steak, the usual fried and grilled seafoods and other typical American fare.

☺ Pulicci's Restaurant • ∆∆∆ $$

988 S. Hemlock St. (a few blocks south of downtown); (503) 436-1279. Italian and seafood; wine and beer. Daily 5 p.m. to 10 p.m. MC/VISA. Very attractive cafe in a bright yellow house with carefully-tended flower beds out front. The dining area is partitioned with leaded glass panels. Italian side of the menu includes chicken cacciatore, lasagna and fettuccini. From the seafood side emerges garlic prawns, smoked mussels and various fresh fish filets.

The Whaler Restaurant • ∆ $$

200 Hemlock; (503) 436-2821. American, mostly seafood; wine and beer. Daily 8 a.m. to 9 p.m. MC/VISA, AMEX, DISC. Typical American seafood cafè: Naugahyde nautical with booths and bartop tables. Offerings include halibut and chips, lobster, scallops and various fish dishes fried, baked or sautèed, plus an occasional steak and chicken.

WHERE TO SLEEP

Best Western Surfsand Resort • ⌒⌒⌒ $$$$$

Hemlock and Gower streets (P.O. Box 219), Cannon Beach, OR 97110; (800) 547-6100 or (503) 436-2274. Couples $109 to $169, singles $109 to $145, suites $129 to $199. Major credit cards. Luxury 75-room oceanfront resort; all rooms with refrigerators, TV movies, VCRs and room phones; many with tub spas and fireplaces. Indoor pool and spa. **Wayfarer Restaurant** serves seafood and steaks; 8 a.m. to 1 a.m.; dinners $12 to $18; full bar.

☺ Cannon Beach Hotel • ⌒⌒⌒ $$$ ∅

1116 S. Hemlock St. (P.O. Box 943), Cannon Beach, OR 97110; (503) 436-1392. Couples and singles $49 to $119. MC/VISA. Turn-of-the-century boarding house refurbished into a small European-style hotel. Nine rooms with TV, phones; some with fireplaces and spa tubs. Attractive early American style lobby with fireplace. All rooms smoke-free. **JP's at Cannon Beach** is a European style bistro with a mixed menu focusing on seafood and pasta; dinners $10 to $16; wine and beer.

Hallmark Resort • ⌒⌒⌒ $$$$

P.O. Box 547 (Hemlock and Sunset), Cannon Beach, OR 97110; (800) 345-5676 or (503) 436-1566. Couples $95 to $199, singles $65 to $159, suites with kitchens $139 to $185. Major credit cards. Very attractive 130-unit resort on a bluff overlooking the Pacific; room with TV, phones, refrigerators and coffee makers; some with spa tubs and kitchens. Indoor pool, sauna, spa, coin laundry; easy beach access.

Haystack Resort Motel • ⌒⌒ $$$ ∅

3339 S. Hemlock (P.O. Box 775), Cannon Beach, OR 97110; (800) 547-6100 or (503) 436-1577. Couples $94 to $134, singles $69 to $104, kitchenettes and suites $104 to $134. Major credit cards. Well-equipped 23-room motel near the beach; TV, room phones; swimming pool.

Land's End Motel • ⌒⌒⌒ $$$$ ∅

263 Second St. (P.O. Box 475), Cannon Beach, OR 97110; (503) 436-2264. Rooms $95 to $150. MC/VISA, AMEX. Small, well-kept beachfront resort with 14 rooms; all have ocean views, fireplaces and refrigerators; some with full kitchens. Small spa and meeting room.

Quiet Cannon Lodgings • ⌂⌂ $$$$

372 N. Spruce St. (P.O. Box 174), Cannon Beach, OR 97110; (503) 436-1405. Kitchenettes $75 to $85. No credit cards. Fully-furnished apartments on the beach with TV, kitchens and other amenities.

Stephanie Inn • ⌂⌂⌂ $$$$$ ∅

2740 S. Pacific St., (P.O. Box 219) Cannon Beach, OR 97110; (800) 633-3466 or (503) 436-2221. Couples and singles $109 to $299. Major credit cards. Small ocean-front luxury inn with 46 smoke-free rooms; TV and VCRs, balconies, refrigerators and fireplaces; free breakfast. Social hour with complimentary wine. **Restaurant** for guests only with full bar service.

Tolovana Inn • ⌂⌂⌂ $$$$

3400 S. Hemlock (P.O. Box 165), Tolovana Park, OR 97145; (800) 333-8890 or (503) 436-2211. Couples $54 to $101, suites $140 to $181. Major credit cards. Resort just off the beach with studios (starting at $93) and suites with ocean views, plus smaller rooms ($54 to $67) with mountain views. TV, pay movies, room phones, refrigerators; many with kitchens, some with fireplaces. Pool, sauna, spa and coin laundry.

Bed & breakfast inn

Tern Inn Bed & Breakfast • ⌂⌂⌂ $$$$ ∅

P.O. Box 952 (a block south of Tolovana Park Inn), Cannon Beach, OR 97110; (503) 436-1528. Rooms $75 to $95. Two units with TV, room phones and private baths; full breakfast. MC/VISA, AMEX. Modern European-style home with an ocean view; modern furnishings in the rooms; one with fireplace, one with spa tub. Kitchenette with microwave for guests' use.

WHERE TO CAMP

RV Resort at Cannon Beach • *345 Elk Creek Rd. (P.O. Box 219), Cannon Beach, OR 97110; (800) 547-6100 or (503) 436-2231. RV sites only, $18 to $26. Reservations accepted; MC/VISA.* Full-service RV resort just east of Highway 101. Landscaped grounds, shaded sites, some pull-throughs. Picnic tables, showers, cable TV, mini-mart, coin laundry, rec center, indoor pool and spa, kids' playground, bicycle rentals, gasoline.

Sea Ranch Resort • *Highway 101, north exit (P.O. Box 214), Cannon Beach, OR 97110; (503) 436-2815. RV and tent sites, $12 to $14. Reservations accepted.* Older, well-maintained park with some shaded sites; full hookups and showers; creek adjacent for swimming and fishing. Horseback riding and salmon charter boat available.

CANNON BEACH TO SEASIDE

After picking up Highway 101 on Cannon Beach's north side, you begin climbing the wooded slopes of **Tillamook Head.** A roadside marker discusses William Clark's exploratory trek, during which his group found the whale carcass and picked up some dinner blubber from the Native Americans. It indicates that this headland was their furthest point south, although Cannon Beach historians like to think they made it to Ecola Creek.

The highway travels inland as it climbs Tillamook Head, depriving you of one of the most dramatic vistas on the coast. Wrote Clark in 1806:

I beheld the grandest and most pleasing prospect which my eyes ever surveyed. Immediately in front of us is the ocean breaking in fury. To this boisterous scene (is the distant) Columbia with its tributaries, and studded on both sides with the Chinook and Clatsop villages...

You can view this boisterous scene by hiking the Tillamook Head Recreation Trail between Cannon Beach and Seaside, mentioned above. The villages are a bit different today, although the one called Seaside is as boisterous as Clark's breaking surf.

Seaside

Population: 5,400   **Elevation: 15 feet**

Another guidebook calls Seaside the "quintessential family beach resort" and it certainly is that. Stand on the concrete promenade and you could be at the beach fronts of Santa Cruz, Coney Island or Atlantic City. It's all here—the cotton candy, the saltwater taffy, the corn dogs, the carousel and the penny (now a quarter) arcades. One thing is missing: a surf warm enough for swimming. The place is thus aptly named. You lie in the sand beside the sea.

At the risk of affronting the local chamber, we'll guess that out-of-staters are probably drawn more to Oregon's beautiful wilderness shores than to Seaside's carny beachfront. Of course, many Oregonians love the place, because it's *their* Coney Island, Santa Cruz or Atlantic City. Certainly, it's a nice weekend escape for families, with its amusements, pedicycles, fried seafood takeouts and the two-mile-long beach promenade.

Seaside was Oregon's first beach resort and it was the largest until runaway Lincoln City ran past it in recent years. However, long and skinny Lincoln City lacks the compactness and the old fashioned promenade and carny atmosphere. Entrepreneur Ben Holladay built Seaside's first resort hotel in the 1870s. It was patronized by wealthy Portlanders who ferried down the Columbia River to Astoria, then caught a stagecoach south. Later, a railroad made the trip easier. Today, folks breeze out here on the Sunset Highway (U.S. 26), an 80-mile jaunt from the City of Roses.

The town's shops and assorted tourist gimmicks are focused along a T-formation, consisting of Broadway running east and west and a concrete promenade running north and south along the beach. This promenade was completed in 1921 as a protective sea wall and walkway to replace a rotting boardwalk.

As Highway 101 enters Seaside, it becomes Roosevelt Drive, paralleling the beach half a mile away. If you plan to do the town, stop first at the **Seaside Chamber of Commerce** at Roosevelt and Broadway; (503) 738-6391. This large and well-equipped visitor center is open weekdays 9 to 6 and weekends 10 to 6. Pick up two walking tour maps, since compact Seaside is a good strolling city. The *Million Dollar Walk* is a sidewalk tour of Broadway's tourist lures and old buildings, and the *Walking Tour of Historic Seaside Prom* is just what it says. Another map, the *Scenic Driving Tour*, takes you past the town's excellent collection of Victorian and early 20th century homes.

From the chamber, drive west on Broadway, cross the Necanicum River, go about five more blocks and you'll hit the **Turnaround** at the beachfront. Swing around this traffic circle and—while dodging herds of pedicycles—start looking for a parking place. That's no easy task on a summer weekend, although several downtown blocks have been scrubbed free of old buildings and turned into parking lots.

A plaque on the Turnaround suggests that this was the end of the Lewis and Clark Trail. This appears to contradict that highway plaque on Tillamook Head and the display in Cannon Beach's Les Shirley Park. But never mind. If you follow the "Prom" south eight blocks to Lewis and Clark Way, then go a block inland to Beach Drive, you'll see the **Lewis and Clark Salt Cairn.** At this site, now reconstructed, expedition members boiled seawater to make salt for their trip back across the country.

The Prom offers the best views in town, and it's lined with grand old Victorians built by the wealthy. Many of these homes are described on the historic walking tour map. A short walk north from the Turnaround takes you to **Seaside Aquarium** at the corner of Second Avenue. If you then walk east on Second to Necanicum Drive and follow it north along the river, you'll encounter the **Seaside Museum** at Necanicum and Fifth Avenue.

And that about covers Seaside's walkable highlights. You can next fetch your wheels and follow that Seaside Driving Tour past historic homes. Or, if you drive south of town to the end of Sunset Boulevard, near an area known as the **Cove,** you can pick up the six-mile **Tillamook Head Recreation Trail.** On the other hand, perhaps you've worked up an appetite for a lunch of cotton candy, a corn dog and a few pieces of salt water taffy. Hold onto your dental work.

THE TWO ATTRACTIONS

Seaside Aquarium ● *200 N. Promenade; (503) 738-6211. Daily from March through October, Wednesday-Sunday the rest of the year; open at 9 a.m., various closing hours. Adults $4.50, kids 6 to 11, $2.25; MC/VISA.* Looking a bit weathered, the aquarium offers the usual sea creatures residing behind glass, from moray eels to leopard sharks. You can grope for starfish in a touchy-feely tank and feed excessively friendly seals. The brochure says you can "follow the teetering tentacles of a wily octopus." I wonder who writes their copy?

Seaside Museum and Historical Society ● *570 Necanicum Dr.; (503) 738-7065. Daily 10:30 to 4. Adults $1, kids 50 cents.* Modest yet nicely arranged, the museum offers exhibits on Native Americans, the Lewis and Clark expedition and of course on Seaside's development as Oregon's first beach spa. You'll see historic photos of the original boardwalk, the Prom's construction and naughty bathing beauties in neck-to-ankle swim costumes.

ACTIVITIES

Bike rentals ● Among outfits renting various things with pedals are **The Prom Bike Shop,** 325 S. Holladay Dr., (503) 738-8251; **Manzanita Fun Merchants,** 332 S. Columbia, (503) 738-3733; and **Seaside Arco,** 231 S. Holladay Dr., (503) 738-7105.

Pedi-cab tours ● If you'd rather have someone else do the peddling, contact **North Coast Pedi-Cabs,** 1021 Broadway, (503) 738-0433.

ANNUAL EVENTS

Trail's End Marathon and **Beachcomber Festival,** February; (503) 738-6391.

Miss Oregon Pageant in July; (503) 738-8326.

Beach Volleyball Tournament in August; (503) 738-6391.

Lewis and Clark Historical Drama, mid-July through late August, a pageant tracing the Corps of Discovery's journey west, held outdoors in Broadway Park; (800) 444-6740 or (503) 738-0817.

Cruisin' the Turnaround nostalgia celebration, September; (503) 738-6391.

WHERE TO DINE

Mostly, visitors dine on corn dogs, fish and chips and other takeouts. A culinary center Seaside isn't. Among its few offerings:

Channel Club ● △△ $$
521 Broadway; (503) 738-8618. American, mostly seafood; full bar service. Breakfast, lunch and dinner daily. MC/VISA. Family restaurant noted for its breakfasts and for its large seafood menu at dinner. Entrées include the usual fresh local fish, plus frogs legs, sea bass and shark, along with steak, chicken and chops.

Christiano's ● △△ $
412 Broadway; (503) 738-5058. Mexican; full bar service. Daily from 11 a.m. MC/VISA, AMEX. This inviting *cantina* features several Mexican seafood dishes in addition to the typical things in tortillas. Specialties include garlic prawns and spiced halibut, plus fajitas and other Mexican-California items. Dine amidst cheerful Latin trappings, with soft guitars in the background.

Doogers Seafood Grill ● △△ $$ ∅
505 Broadway; (503) 738-3773. American, mostly seafood, wine and beer. Daily from 11 a.m. MC/VISA. Nautical café specializing in crab, halibut and oyster halibut for lunch, plus a variety of fishy dinner entrées and excellent clam chowder. In addition to fresh locally-caught fish, the menu offers a few steaks and chops.

WHERE TO SLEEP

Dozens of motels are crowded into popular Seaside, and many are along the Prom, offering sea views. Also, the town's numerous Victorians lend themselves to bed & breakfast conversions.

Ambassador by the Sea ● △△△ $$$$ ∅
40 Avenue U (at Beach Drive), Seaside, OR 97138; (503) 738-6382. Studios $49 to $54, kitchenettes $75 to $90. MC/VISA. Oceanside condominiums; studios and one or two bedrooms with TV and room phones, refrigerators or full kitchens. Courtyard with tables and barbecue; 50 feet from the beach.

Best Western Ocean View Resort ● △△△ $$$$ ∅
414 N. Prom, Seaside, OR 97138; (800) 234-8439 or (503) 738-3334. Couples and singles from $69.50, kitchenettes $86.50 to $149, suites $165 to $240. Major credit cards. Very attractive units in a 105-room oceanside resort. TV, room phones, refrigerators; all with ocean-view decks; some with spa tubs and fireplaces. **Breakers Restaurant** serves Northwest regional fare, 7 a.m. to 10 p.m.; dinners $10 to $20; full bar service.

☺ Colonial Motor Inn ● △△△ $$$
1120 N. Holladay Dr. (between 11th and 12th), Seaside, OR 97138. Couples $61 to $73, singles $49 to $79. Major credit cards. Colonial style motel with very enticing rooms, furnished in Queen Anne style with rolltop desks

and four-poster beds. On the Nacanicum River, three blocks from the beach, with river-view gazebo. Adjacent **restaurant** serves American fare, mostly seafood; 7 a.m. to 10 p.m.; dinners $7 to $15; full bar service.

Hi-Tide Motel • △△△ $$$$ ∅
30 Avenue G, Seaside, OR 97138; (800) 621-9876, (503) 738-8414 or 738-8371. Couples $90 to $120, singles $75 to $85, kitchenettes $80 to $155. Major credit cards. Very attractive motel near the beach; 83 rooms with TV, room phones. Heated pool, spa and steam room.

Inn on the Prom • △△ $$$ ∅
361 S. Prom, Seaside, OR 97138; (503) 738-5241. Couples and singles $60 to $125 in summer, $40 to $90 off-season. Major credit cards. Well-kept 24-unit motel on the Prom with TV and room phones; many units have ocean views.

Sand & Sea Condominiums • △△△ $$$ ∅
The Prom and B Street (P.O. Box 945), Seaside, OR 97138; (800) 628-2371 or (503) 738-8441. Condo units from $42.80 (off-season) to $214. MC/VISA. Luxury units on the Prom, fully furnished with kitchens and two bedrooms and two baths, gas fireplaces and private decks. **Restaurant** serves 9 a.m. to 3 a.m.

Seashore Resort • △△ $$$
60 N. Prom (at First Avenue), Seaside, OR 97138; (503) 738-6368. Couples and singles $68 to $88, kitchenettes $98 to $108, suites $140 to $170. Major credit cards. Well-maintained 53-unit inn with TV, room phones; indoor pool, spa and sauna. On the Prom.

☺ Shilo Inn Seaside Oceanfront Resort • △△△ $$$$$ ∅
30 N. Prom, Seaside, OR 97130; (800) 222-2244 or (503) 738-9571. Kitchenettes and suites $126 to $172, singles $75 to $125. Major credit cards. A 112-room luxury beachfront hotel with many resort amenities. Oceanfront rooms with TV movies, phones, kitchens and balconies. Indoor pool, spa, sauna, steam and fitness room. **Restaurant** serves Sunday-Thursday 7 a.m. to 10 p.m. and Friday-Saturday 7 to 11; ocean-view dining; full bar service.

Shilo Inn East • △△ $$$ ∅
900 S. Holladay, Seaside, OR 97130; (800) 222-2244 or (503) 738-0549. Couples $63 to $90, singles $49 to $79, kitchenettes $73 to $100. Major credit cards. A 58-unit inn with TV movies and phones; most rooms are mini-suites with refrigerators and microwaves. Indoor pool, spa, sauna, steam room, coin laundry, free continental breakfast.

Bed & breakfast inns
Beachwood Bed & Breakfast • △△△ $$$$ ∅
671 Beach Dr., Seaside, OR 97138; (503) 738-9585. Couples $69 to $94, singles $64 to $89. Three rooms with private baths; full breakfast. Attractive turn-of-the-century craftsman home surrounded by extensive gardens. Rooms furnished with American antiques; Holladay suite has a fireplace, canopy bed and spa. Sitting room with TV and VCR.

Custer House Bed & Breakfast • △△ $$$ ∅
811 First Ave., Seaside, OR 97138; (503) 738-7825. Couples $60 to $70, singles $55 to $65. Three rooms, one with private bath; full breakfast.

MC/VISA. Turn-of-the-century Victorian with early American decor, accented by dark woods; nicely done guest rooms with wicker and queen beds. The inn is four blocks from the Pacific.

Rita Mae's Bed & Breakfast ● ⌂⌂⌂ $$$$ ∅
486 Necanicum Dr., Seaside, OR 97138; (503) 738-8800. Couples $65 to $75. Three rooms, one with private bath; full breakfast. MC/VISA. Two-story modern home with a mix of American antique, contemporary and African art and artifacts. Guest spa, 4,000-volume library and music collection. Bright and airy rooms with American, Egyptian or Polynesian décor. On the Necanicum River, a short walk to the beach.

Riverside Inn ● ⌂⌂⌂ $$$ ∅
430 S. Holladay Dr., Seaside, OR 97138; (800) 826-6151 or (503) 738-8254. Couples $39 to $80, singles $35 to $75. Eleven rooms with private baths and TV; full breakfast. MC/VISA, DISC. A 1907 inn refurbished and decorated in American country style. Rooms in original inn and a two-story annex; some units with full kitchens. On the Necanicum River, with a deck, gardens and barbecue area. Two blocks from Broadway and three from the beach.

Summerhouse Bed & Breakfast ● ⌂⌂ $$$ ∅
1221 N. Franklin, Seaside, OR 97138; (800) 745-BEST or (503) 738-5740. Couples $55 to $75, singles $50 to $70. Four rooms with private baths; full breakfast. MC/VISA. Contemporary home done in Southwestern colors; bright and cheerful rooms with queen beds; one with fireplace. A block from the beach.

Seaside and a suburban nub called **Gearhart** are the northernmost towns on Oregon Coast, so we end this chapter here. North of Gearhart, Highway 101 swings inland to **Warrenton** and **Astoria,** the historic city on the Columbia River.

The coast's final landfall is about 18 miles north of Gearhart at Point Adams, on the tip of a narrow jetty marking the mouth of the Columbia River. Fort Stevens was built here in 1864 to discourage Confederate ships from sailing into Oregon waters. It's now a state park. Not far away is Lewis and Clark's winter camp, Fort Clatsop National Memorial. Since these relate more to the Columbia River than the coast, we will visit them in the next chapter.

Chapter Seven

THE COLUMBIA CORRIDOR

Fur traders, falls & fields of grain

BY EVERY MEASURE, the Columbia is the grand river of the American West. Of all the streams on the North American continent, only the Mississippi, St. Lawrence and Mackenzie have a greater water volume.

The mighty river has its roots in Columbia Lake in the western foothills of British Columbia's Rockies, 2,700 feet above sea level. It meanders for 1,210 miles south through Canada and eastern Washington, then it heads west to form the Oregon-Washington border. Just beyond Portland, it swings north in search of a low spot in the Coast Range, then it turns west again to meet the Pacific at Astoria.

Gathering tributaries and strength as it flows, it carries 180 million acre feet of water into the sea each year. Its largest tributary is the Snake, which drains Wyoming's Yellowstone-Grand Teton area, then flows west through southern Idaho. The Columbia is the largest river flowing into the Pacific, and it drains 85 percent of northwestern America's land area. At its mouth near Astoria, it's nearly five miles wide, more resembling a sea than a river. In fact, early sailors missed this noble stream, thinking it to be an inlet.

It's also the largest producer of hydroelectric power in America, generating 80 percent of the Northwest's juice and 40 percent of the country's total hydroelectric output. Dozens of dams check its flow, creating a virtual chain of lakes from Bonneville east and north toward its source in Canada. (See box on page 248.)

Although it cascades sharply down from the Colorado Rockies, the Columbia becomes placid by the time it reaches Oregon. Even before dams impeded its progress, it flowed slowly through a mile-wide, almost level channel. The site of Bonneville Dam, 140 miles upstream, is only 52 feet

TRIP PLANNER

WHEN TO GO ● Since snowfall is rare, the Columbia Corridor is a year-around vacation area. Plan on getting wet in Astoria and the Columbia River gorge from late fall through late spring. East of Hood River, it's sunny most of the year, and it can get hot in summer.

WHAT TO SEE ● Fort Clatsop National Memorial, Fort Stevens State Park and Columbia River Maritime Museum in Astoria; the Portland Women's Forum viewpoint and Vista House in the Columbia Gorge; the major waterfalls—Latourell, Bridal Veil, Wahkeena, Multnomah and Horsetail; the major downriver dams—Bonneville, The Dalles and John Day; Columbia Gorge Hotel and gardens in Hood River; Timberline Lodge on Mount Hood; Rowena Crest lookout east of Mosier; Maryhill Museum of Art and Stonehenge in Washington, across from Biggs.

WHAT TO DO ● Climb to the top of Astoria Column; drive to Larch Mountain lookout above Columbia River Gorge; hike through Oneonta Gorge; hike to the top of Horsetail Falls; cruise aboard the sternwheeler *Columbia Gorge* from Cascade Locks; watch the windsurfers play, and take the Mount Hood Scenic Railroad in Hood River; prowl the pretty fruit orchards of Hood River Valley; ride the work train at The Dalles Dam.

Useful contacts

Greater Astoria Chamber of Commerce, Marine Drive at Hume Avenue (P.O. Box 176), Astoria, OR 97103; (800) 535-3637 or (503) 325-6311.

Cascade Locks Tourism Committee, Port of Cascade Locks (P.O. Box 355), Cascade Locks, OR 97014; (503) 374-8619.

Columbia Gorge National Scenic Area: Columbia Gorge Ranger Station, Mount Hood National Forest, 31520 SE Woodard Rd., Troutdale, OR 97060; (503) 695-2276.

The Dalles Convention & Visitors Bureau, 901 E. Second St. (P.O. Box 1053), The Dalles, OR 97058; (800) 255-3385 or (503) 296-6616.

Hood River County Chamber of Commerce, Port Marina Park, Hood River, OR 97031; (800) 366-3530 or (503) 386-2000.

Mount Hood Information Center, 65000 E. Highway 26 (P.O. Box 819), Welshes, OR 97067; (503) 622-4822.

Mount Hood Recreation Association, P.O. Box 342, Welshes, OR 97067; (503) 622-3162.

Mount Hood Recreation Area: Mount Hood National Forest, Zig Zag Ranger Station, 70220 E. Highway 26, Zigzag, OR 97049, (503) 622-3191; and Hood River Ranger Station, 6730 Highway 35, Parkdale, OR 97041, (503) 352-6002.

Columbia corridor radio stations

In addition to stations listed below, many Portland broadcasters reach west toward Astoria and east into the gorge (Chapter 4). Also, north coast stations serve the Astoria area (Chapter 6).

KNUN-FM, 91.9, Astoria—National Public Radio
KVAS-AM, 1230, Astoria—country
KACI-FM, 97.7, The Dalles—light rock and top forty
KQMC-FM, 104.5, The Dalles—rock, light to heavy
KACI-AM, 1300, The Dalles—light rock and top 40
KODL-AM, 1440, The Dalles—country

above sea level. Above Bonneville, an occasional brace of rapids once disrupted its downstream flow, much to the consternation of Lewis and Clark. Those rapids have since been inundated by dams.

The most impressive section of the stream is the Columbia Gorge, where it has cut a mile-wide course through near-vertical basaltic walls of the Cascades. A series of prehistoric cataclysms called the Missoula Floods created this amazing channel. Geologists speculate that the Columbia has been flowing for at least 26 million years, picking and choosing its way through lava flows and other basaltic upheavals. When the Cascades began their slow rise about six million years ago, the Columbia cut a V-shaped canyon. Then, within the last hundred thousands years, ice age glaciers alternately dammed upstream flows and then broke loose. These Missoula Floods sent massive walls of water downstream, scouring away the Oregon side of the Cascades to create the 1,000-foot-high basaltic cliffs that remain today.

The mother of Western Rivers flowed unnoticed by the outside world until Spanish sea captain Bruno de Heceta spotted its mouth from the deck of his *Santiago* on August 17, 1775. However, he thought it was a large inlet. Other explorers bypassed it until America's Captain Robert Gray sailed his fur-trading ship, the *Columbia Rediviva* across the dangerous bar on May 11, 1792. The inlet "extended to the NE as far as eye cou'd reach," Gray wrote in his log, realizing that he'd found a great river. He named it for his ship.

The Columbia and its streamside highways offer an intriguing and varied journey for the Oregon visitor. From historic Astoria, one travels through thick forest, past the metropolitan scatter of Portland, up the legendary gorge, past the fruit orchards of Hood River to the arid wheat country of eastern Oregon. No other contiguous route in the state provides so much variety.

We begin at the river's mouth. The Columbia ends where American settlement of Oregon began, more or less.

Astoria

Population: 10,100   **Elevation: 16 feet**

To call Astoria the oldest American settlement west of the Mississippi River—which most history books and brochures do—one must rely on a technicality.

Meriwether Lewis and William Clark built Fort Clatsop nearby in the winter of 1805-06, but that was intended as temporary quarters. (See box below.) Boston trader John Jacob Astor, after hearing of Lewis and Clark's exploits, sent agents of his Pacific Fur Company west to establish a trading post near their campsite. It was led by one Wilson Price Hunt.

Construction of Fort Astoria began in 1811. Then a year later, its occupants were intimidated by the sight of British gunboats sailing up the Columbia. Aware that the United States and Britain were engaged in the War of 1812, they sold out to the Canadian North West Company and abandoned the settlement. The captain of a British ship claimed the fort for his country. By 1818, British and Americans had agreed on joint occupancy of the Oregon Country and Astoria was restored to the U.S. However, no attempt was made to reestablish the settlement for 30 years.

Incidentally, Astor apparently never visited his namesake city. He sent only his men, his money and his influence to begin America's first—although short-lived—western settlement. By the time Astoria was re-occupied, Oregon City, established in 1841, rightfully claimed to be the West's first *permanent* town.

During the Civil War, Fort Stevens was built at the mouth of the Columbia to forestall an imagined Confederate invasion, or possible incursion by the British. Astoria remained a sleepy village until later in that century, when it began to boom as a major salmon canning, lumber exporting and shipbuilding center. A brawling, wicked waterfront town, it gained notoriety for the "requisitioning" of unwilling seamen on ships bound for Shanghai and other points east. Astoria soon became Oregon's second largest city, after Portland. Despite the usual Depression-era slump, it claimed 20,000 residents by the end World War II.

Since then, cuts in lumber and fishing industries have cost the riverfront city half of its population. However, Astoria is no derelict. It's still the largest Oregon city along Highway 101. The town is surviving—if not thriving—on tourism and what's left of its fishing and lumbering industry.

Today, it offers a mixed appearance—partly Victorian, partly riverfront industrial and partly ordinary American community. One of its most inviting attributes is its location, on a steep, wooded hillside overlooking the Columbia. Many Victorian homes, survivors of grander days, have been beautifully restored. One is a fine museum and a few others shelter bed and breakfast inns. Plan at least a couple of days here, to visit forts Clatsop and Stevens, the outstanding Columbia River Maritime Museum, Astoria Column and sundry other attractions.

Driving Astoria

If you've dutifully followed our route up the Oregon Coast (previous chapter), you'll encounter Fort Stevens State Park and Fort Clatsop before you hit Astoria itself. As you drive north on Highway 101 from **Seaside-Gearhart,** a sign will point you to the left toward **Fort Stevens State Park.** It's a very large facility with several points of interest scattered about, so pick up a map once you get there. From Fort Stevens, head northeast through **Hammond** and **Warrenton** on Warrenton Drive toward Astoria. You'll cross the **Skipanon River** and merge onto east Harbor Drive, where another sign will direct you to **Fort Clatsop National Memorial.**

If you're starting your area exploration from Astoria, a sufficiency of directional signs will get you to these two major attractions. Marine Drive is Astoria's main drag, paralleling the waterfront. The **Greater Astoria Chamber of Commerce** is at the west end of town near the anchorage of the Astoria Bridge at Marine and Hume Avenue; (503) 325-6311. Housed in an attractive Nantucket style building, it's open Monday-Saturday 8 to 6 and Sunday 9 to 5. Off-season hours are weekdays 8 to 5 and weekends 11 to 4.

☺ Incidentally, the lofty, 4.1-mile- long **Astoria Bridge** is an attraction of itself. Many travelers cross it just for the views down to the Astoria waterfront, since its southern span was built high enough to admit the tallest ships. This impressive span was completed in 1966 to fuse the last link in Highway 101's lengthy journey from San Diego to Canada. Until then, this crossing was accomplished by ferry. If you'd like to take a curiosity drive over the bridge, it'll cost you a $1.50 toll each direction.

☺ After your pause at the chamber, stop at **Josephson's Smokehouse,** just beyond at 106 W. Marine Drive (on the left, at First Street). It has a savory selection of smoked fish, cubed pickled fish fillets, smoked scallops and clam chowder to go. Housed in the clapboard 1898 Fishermen's Protective Association building, it has been a smoked fish place since 1920. It's open weekdays 8 to 6, Saturday 9 to 5 and Sunday 10 to 5; (503) 325-2190.

Continue five blocks up Marine Drive to Sixth Street (at the MacDonald's sign), turn and drive a block to a **river viewing tower.** You can watch the big cargo ships, tugs and barges pass, then stop at the adjacent **Salmon Kotale Gift Shop.** Run by a salmon fishermen's protective association, it has all sorts of salmon-theme curios, cookbooks and T-shirts. Hours are Monday-Friday 8 to 5, Saturday 10 to 3 and Sunday noon to 4.

Drive two more blocks east on Marine Drive, and go right two blocks to the **Flavel House Museum** at Eighth and Duane streets. The old **Clatsop County Jail** is across Duane to the left, beside the **County Courthouse.** You can step inside this grim calaboose, although there are no exhibits.

From here, follow Duane east through the old fashioned downtown area to **Fort Astoria Park,** on your right at the corner of Duane and Fifteenth. A small model blockhouse marks the site of the original Astor fort. Continue uphill on 15th, following signs to **Astoria Column** atop Coxcomb Hill. The view of Astoria, the Columbia River and the Lewis and Clark River toward Fort Clatsop are awesome. They're even better if you commit yourself to the 164-step spiral staircase to the top. (As I stood on the view platform, staring down between my toes at Astoria, I had a funny thought: "What if there's an earthquake?")

Returning downtown, go right on Duane and follow it to the **Clatsop County Heritage Center,** housed in the former county courthouse at 16th. Across Duane Street is the tasting room of **Shallon Winery,** (325-5978) open "most days" from noon to 6 (although it was closed mid-afternoon when we stopped by).

From here, you can see the imposing roofline sweep of the **Columbia River Maritime Museum** on the riverfront. One of Oregon's penultimate theme museums, it will provide a fine introduction to the river you are about to follow. Continuing east on Marine Drive (U.S. Highway 30) toward Portland, you'll encounter the **Uppertown Fire Fighters Museum** at 30th Street.

Astoria is a good walking city as well, since its neighborhoods shelter dozens of Victorian and early 20th century American homes. Most are in the slopes above downtown, so wear comfortable shoes. A detailed walking tour map is available from the chamber for $2.50, or you can merely wander the upper slopes, zig-zagging among the numbered streets off Franklin. Start at the Flavel House and work eastward, along the brow of Coxcomb Hill.

ATTRACTIONS
(In order of appearance)

☺ **Fort Stevens State Park** ● *Hammond, OR 97121; (503) 861- 2000. Museum and War Games building open daily 10 to 6; free. For camping information, see "Where to camp" below.*

Fort Stevens is tucked into Oregon's northwestern tip, on a peninsula between the Columbia River and the Pacific, about ten miles northwest of Astoria. One of the most diverse of the state's parks, it comes in three major pieces, all reached from Ridge Road in Hammond. To the north, just opposite Hammond and overlooking the Columbia River is the Museum/War

Look carefully and you'll see people framed in the rusting hulk of the schooner Peter Iredale *on the beach at Fort Stevens State Park.*   **— Betty Woo Martin**

Games Building and former headquarters area. A bit south is Battery Russell, famous as the "victim" of a Japanese submarine attack during World War II. Farther south is the campground and beyond it, the wreck of the Peter Iredale, a ship that's disintegrating into the sand. All of this is tied together by several miles of hiking and biking trails, picnic areas and a long sandy beach.

The white masonry **Museum\War Games Building** traces the history of Fort Stevens, with assorted artifacts, costumed mannequins and old photos. A banner scrawled by fort personnel after the sub's shelling of Battery Russell reads: "Nine shots fired, nine shots missed; to hell with Hirohito." Actually, 17 shots were fired and all of them missed. Submarine *I-25*, which spent much of World War II prowling along our coastline, surfaced on June 21, 1942, and lobbed its shells toward the battery. Shore crews didn't fire back because the enemy was out of range of its antiquated guns. Although the *I-25* did no damage here, it sank several merchant ships off the coast, and launched the airplane that dropped incendiary bombs on the southern Oregon forest. (See box in Chapter 5.)

Outside the museum, you can prowl about the former headquarters compound and nearby gun emplacements. Some structures remain, although the area is comprised mostly of empty foundations. A few have been put to use as platforms for picnic tables. You can pick up a walking tour map of the area in the museum. Archaeologists are excavating and reconstructing the original Civil War era earthworks, which will be ready for viewing toward the end of this century.

Battery Russell is relatively intact, although all armament has been removed. From the concrete bunker, troops had a view of the Pacific, now obscured by drifting sand and vegetation. A "Pacific Rim Peace Memorial" was unveiled here on June 21, 1992, marking the 50th anniversary of the shelling. It's dedicated to personnel of the fort and the crew of the *I-25*. From Battery Russell, you can drive north to the very tip of Oregon at Point Adams, where a narrow jetty separates the Pacific from the Columbia. A platform offers nice views of sea and stream.

The **Peter Iredale**, a British schooner that went aground in 1906, is nearly buried in the beach sand about a mile from the campground. All that remains are a few hull ribs and a some barnacle-encrusted pieces of the deck. It has the look of a rusting whale skeleton. The adjacent parking area provides a handy beach access, and there are picnic tables nearby.

The original Fort Stevens was born of Civil War paranoia, or perhaps bureaucratic boondoggling. Even as the conflict was coming to a close, the fort was built to protect the mouth of the Columbia from a possible Confederate attack. The original was a classic five-sided earthwork, with a moat and even a drawbridge—the only one of its kind in the West. Fort Stevens remained on alert through World War II, never firing an angry shot. It even blew its one chance to do battle with an enemy sub.

☺ **Fort Clatsop National Memorial** • *Route 3, Box 604-FC, Astoria, OR 97103; (503) 861-2471. Daily 8 to 8 in summer, 8 to 5 the rest of the year. Adults $1, families $3.* If you're a fan of the Corps of Discovery, this is your place. Lewis and Clark's winter quarters have been faithfully restored, right down to the chinked-log fort, crude wooden furniture, bunks with animal skin coverlets and tallow candles. A trail leads to their canoe landing and spring at the mouth of the Netual River (now called the Lewis and Clark). It's a small tributary of the Columbia. Here, hollowed-out canoes await launch. Except for the well- groomed wood chip path, the thickly wooded site has probably changed little since Lewis and Clark's winter stay.

During the summer, park rangers in period costume present living history demonstrations, from candle-making to musket shooting. "We call these Fort Clatsop spitwads," says a ranger as she fires a blank into the air.

The adjacent visitor center is an encyclopedic museum of the Lewis and Clark expedition, with maps of their route, displays of the kinds of implements they used, slide shows and videos. A book store stocks just about everything ever written concerning the Corps of Discovery.

☺ **Flavel House Museum** • *441 Eighth Street at Duane; (503) 325-2203. Daily 10 to 5. Adults $4, kids 6 to 12, $2 (includes admission to the Heritage Center).* Built by George Flavel, owner of a shipping and pilot boat company, this three- story 1883 Queen Anne is a showplace of Victorian opulence. The lower floor is particularly striking, with carved mahogany and cherrywood wainscotting and door frames, Oriental rugs and marble fireplaces. Many of the elegant furnishings are original, since the mansion was given to the Clatsop County Historical Society by Flavel's granddaughters. Tours are self-guiding, permitting a leisurely, envious stroll through its palatial rooms.

☺ **Astoria Column** • *Atop Coxcomb Hill; (503) 325- 6311. Daily 8 a.m. to dusk; free.* Each time we visit Astoria, the spiral frieze around this 125-foot high column has faded a bit more and we keep hoping that someone will restore it. The column was erected in 1926 by the Northern Pacific Railway and descendants of John Jacob Astor to commemorate the settlement of the Northwest. The fading frieze depicts events of the westward movement. The column itself is patterned after a structure erected by Roman Emperor

THE JOURNEY OF JOURNEYS

The object of your mission is to explore the Missouri River, and such principal stream of it, as, by its course and communications with the Pacific Ocean, and offer the most direct and practicable water route across this Continent for the purpose of commerce.

With this excessively wordy pronouncement, President Thomas Jefferson launched his private secretary Meriwether Lewis on one of history's epic wilderness trips. Lewis, who had spent several years in the army, chose longtime friend William Clark as his lieutenant. Clark, age 33, was the oldest member of the group; Lewis was but 29. The pair selected for their Corps of Discovery "good hunters, stout, healthy, unmarried young men, accustomed to the woods," along with Clark's black servant, York.

The group spent the winter of 1803 at Camp Wood River near the mouth of the Missouri, north of St. Louis. Here, they trained and stocked up for their journey into the unknown. The cross-country trek began on May 14, 1804. They spent a second winter near the present site of Bismark, North Dakota, constructing temporary quarters they called Fort Mandan. Here, they enlisted the services of half-breed French interpreter Toussaint Charbonneau, his wife Sacagawea and their infant son.

Not a guide as some history books suggest, Sacagawea served more as a liaison and peace symbol for the troupe. Native peoples they encountered along the way assumed that a group traveling with an Indian woman meant no harm. They only time she was asked to guide the group, she chose the wrong route over Bozeman Pass in Montana. As Clark's diary recalled, her choice was "an intolerable rout caused by beavers daming the stream; a muddy wet rout."

The explorers followed the Missouri River to its source, and then forged through unknown country, making several attempts before successfully crossing the Continental Divide in present-day Idaho. They picked up the Clearwater, followed it to the Snake and finally to the Columbia, arriving at the Pacific on November 15, 1805.

Wet Washington lost out

Washington state might have laid claim to hosting the Corps of Discovery, for the travelers first made camp on the Columbia's northern shore. However, the weather was so wet and windy that they crossed south to the Oregon side. Here, they found a more sheltered spot on a small tributary the local Indians called the Netul River. This site wasn't much better, for it rained 94 of the 106 days of their stay.

Fighting colds, flu and general miseries, the men built Fort Clatsop, explored the area, traveled south down the coast to make salt for the return trips, traded with friendly Indians and took copious notes. Lewis and Clark and several other members of the group kept detailed journals. If they didn't feel well, they apparently ate and dressed well. The group traded with the Indians for otter and seal skins, seal and elk meat and edible roots. The explorers were adept hunters as well, bagging 131 elk, 20 deer and assorted smaller animals.

The Corps of Discovery departed Fort Clatsop on March 23, 1806, for the long voyage home, arriving in St. Louis that September. Amazingly, the group suffered only one casualty during this epic journey. A Sergeant Charles Floyd died within the first few days of the out-bound trip, probably from appendicitis.

When the group arrived triumphantly in St. Louis, their leaders "suffered the party to fire off their pieces as a Salute to the Town." The men had good reason to celebrate. They carried with them a treasure of information about this vast, unknown land. Their remarkable expedition opened the door for more exploration and ultimate settlement of the American Northwest.

Trajan in 114 A.D. An inner stairway takes hearty hikers 164 steps to a platform for dizzying views of the countryside.

Heritage Museum ● *1618 Exchange Street at 16th; (503) 325-2203. Daily 10 to 5. Adults $4, kids 6 to 12, $2 (includes admission to the Flavel House).* The Clatsop County Historical Society museum is housed in the 1904 neo-classic former courthouse and library. While not professionally done, exhibits are attractively arrayed, telling the story of yesterday Astoria. A special display focuses on the Chinese and other immigrants to the north coast. Others relate to logging, salmon canning and shipping.

☺ **Columbia River Maritime Museum** ● *1792 Marine Drive; (503) 326-2323. Daily 9:30 to 5. Adults $4, seniors $3, kids over 6, $2.* If you've always want to go down to the sea in ships, plan the better part of a day for this elaborate, beautifully done 37,000 square foot museum. Excellent exhibits celebrate the Columbia River and seafaring in general, from man's earliest nervous ventures into the briny to today's Navy.

With a towering roof in the sweeping shape of a cresting wave, the museum is built around the navigational bridge of the *USS Knapp* World War II destroyer. This, however, is only a small part of the extensive complex. You'll see exhibits of scrimshaw, ship models and paintings, fish canneries and handicrafts made by men at sea. Step into the pilot house of the *Achiever,* a mock-up of a typical Columbia River sternwheeler. Study the wicked-looking 90mm whaling gun with its explosive harpoon, and the giant surgical instruments used to carve its victims. Outside, you can tour the lightship *Columbia* to get a feel for life in the crowded, bobbing confines of a "seagoing lighthouse." The working U.S. Coast Guard cutter *Resolute* shares the museum's dock with the lightship. It's open for public tours Sundays from 1 to 4.

Uppertown Fire Fighters Museum ● *30th Street at Marine Drive; (503) 325-2203. Daily 10 to 5. Adults $4, kids 6 to 12, $2.* Operated by the Clatsop County Historical Society, this facility exhibits fire engines ranging from horse-drawn 1877 models to 1951 motorized rigs. The display of smoke-eaters' gear isn't extensive, but it'll interest fans of fire laddies and ladies. You'll learn about Astoria's historic conflagrations, including a spectacular burn that leveled the town in the late 1800s.

WHERE TO SHOP

Astoria's appealingly rustic riverfront hasn't developed its potential as a theme waterfront shopping area, which some folks probably prefer. It's still a working waterfront with fish canneries, towboat firms and such. One rather attractive "mini-mall" has been developed at **Pier 11**, a block off Marine Drive between Tenth and Eleventh streets. It offers a couple of curio shops, an excellent bookstore and the river-view **Feed Store Restaurant** (listed below). Stop in at the **Pier 11 Lounge** with a bar in the shape of curving sea serpent. Within the same neighborhood, you'll find a few modest galleries and antique ships. Most are along Tenth, between the waterfront and Commercial Street.

ACTIVITIES

Fishing charters ● **Warrenton Deep Sea,** 45 NE Harbor Place (Route 1), Warrenton, OR 97146, (503) 861-1233, offers deep-sea and Columbia river fishing, including angling for Columbia sturgeon. Other firms are **Tiki**

Fleet, 897 Pacific St., Hammond, OR 97121; (503) 325-7990 and **Thunderbird Charters,** (503) 325-7990.

Historical tours • For personalized tours of the town's significant sites, contact **Historical Tours of Astoria,** 612 Florence St., Astoria, OR 97103, (503) 325-3005.

History cruises • **Executive Charters,** 352 Industry St., Astoria, OR 96103, (503) 325-7990, offers river cruises with historic narratives.

Live theater • The **Astor Street Opry Company** (503-325-6104) presents an old-fashioned musical melodrama, *Shanghaied in Astoria* in the lobby of the classic J.J. Astor Hotel. It's downtown at 14th and Commercial.

ANNUAL EVENTS

Astoria Crab Feed & Seafood Festival, late April; (503) 325-6311.

Astoria Scandinavian Festival in late June, a major celebration relating to the town's Scandinavian heritage; (503) 325-6311.

Astoria Regatta on the Columbia River, mid-August; (503) 325-6311.

Clatsop County Fair in August; (503) 325-4600.

Christmas Holiday Program, Fort Clatsop; (503) 861-2471.

WHERE TO DINE

Despite its popularity with visitors, Astoria is curiously short on restaurants, other than the usual franchise diners along Marine Drive. These three are pleasant alternatives to Denny's and MacDonald's:

Little Denmark • △ $

125 Ninth near Marine Drive; (503) 325-2409. Scandinavian; wine and beer. Daily 8 a.m. to 2 p.m. MC/VISA. It's one of those cafés that's so basic and simple it's cute—sort of a Danish coffee shop. Little Denmark is a popular breakfast and lunch stop for the predominately Scandinavian locals, serving *aebleskiver* (small pancake globes) and Danish open faced sandwiches. Try the *stegesild* for lunch, a concoction of pickled herring with sour cream, chives and onion rings; much tastier than it sounds.

☺ Pier 11 Feed Store Restaurant • △△ $$

Pier 11; (503) 325-0279. American; full bar. Daily 7 a.m. to 10 p.m. MC/VISA, DISC. Oldstyle nautical cafe with beam ceiling, simulated Tiffany lamps and Columbia River views. Seafood menu features the usual freshly caught local flippers and shellfish, plus a few steak and chicken items. A specialty is the King Neptune casserole with shrimp, scallops and crabs legs.

Ship Inn • △△ $$

One Second Street at Marine Drive; (503) 325-0033. American, mostly seafood; full bar service. Daily 11:30 to 9:30. MC/VISA, DISC. A basic chowder house with a spartan dining room, but with a nice view over the Columbia. The prices are right: well-prepared, good-sized entrèes of halibut, prawns, oysters, salmon and such from the low teens down.

WHERE TO SLEEP

Bayshore Motor Inn • ◠◠ $$$ ∅

555 Hamburg, Astoria, OR 97103; (503) 325-2205. Couples $50 to $60, singles $40 to $50. Major credit cards. Well-tended 36-unit motel with aquatic views; TV movies, room phones; some rooms with refrigerators; coin laundry.

Crest Motel ● ⌂ $$$

5366 Leif Erickson Dr., Astoria, OR 97103; (800) 421-3141 or (503) 325-3141. Couples $45.50 to $78.50. Major credit cards. A 40-unit motel on two and a half landscaped acres with TV movies, phones, views of the Columbia and Astoria waterfront. Spa, coin laundry, continental breakfast for a fee.

Red Lion Inn ● ⌂⌂ $$$$ Ø

400 Industry St., Astoria, OR 97103; (800) 547-8010 or (503) 325-7373. Couples $78 to $83, singles $62 to $68. Major credit cards. Very attractive 124-unit complex with river views, TV movies, room phones; balconies. **Seafare Restaurant** offers view dining, American/seafood, dinners $12 to $16; weekdays 6 to 10, Saturday 6 to 11, Sunday 6 to 9; full bar service.

Shilo Inn ● ⌂⌂ $$$ Ø

1609 E. Harbor Dr., Warrenton, OR 97146; (800) 222-2244 or (503) 861-2181. Couples and singles $64 to $90, kitchenettes $74 to $100. Major credit cards. Nicely-done mini-suite inn with TV movies, phones, microwaves and refrigerators. Indoor pool, spa, sauna, steam and fitness room, guest laundry. **Shilo Restaurant** serves American and regional fare 6 a.m. to 10 p.m. Sunday-Thursday and 6 to 11 Friday-Saturday; full bar service.

Bed & breakfast inns

Astoria Inn Bed & Breakfast ● ⌂⌂ $$$$ Ø

3391 Irving Ave., Astoria, OR 97103; (503) 325-8153. Couples $70 to $85, singles $65 to $80. Three rooms with private baths, TV and room phones; full breakfast. MC/VISA. Restored 1890 farmhouse with a wrap-around veranda, furnished in country French and American antiques. Located in the historic Uppertown area, with views of the Columbia.

Columbia River Inn Bed & Breakfast ● ⌂⌂ $$$$ Ø

1681 Franklin Ave., Astoria, OR 97103; (503) 325-5044. Couples $70 to $80, singles $65 to $75. Five rooms with private baths; full breakfast. MC/VISA. An 1870 home built by a wealthy businessman, fashioned into a Victorian inn with a mix of American and English antiques. Attractive garden with sitting areas; some rooms have a view of the Columbia. Short walk to downtown points of interest.

Grandview Bed & Breakfast ● ⌂⌂ $$ Ø

1574 Grand Ave., Astoria, OR 97104; (800) 488-3250 or (503) 488-3250. Rooms $39 to $88, suites $79 to $102. Seven rooms, available singly or in combination with baths between. Some private, some shared baths; continental breakfast. A large shingle-sided home built in 1896 for local cannery owners; with a bullet turret, balconies, bay windows and open staircase. It's furnished with American country and Victorian antiques.

ASTORIA TO PORTLAND

As you head east from Astoria, you'll follow historic U.S. 30, one of America's first transcontinental highways. The drive takes you through thick woodlands, some of it soggy enough to be rainforest. Initially, you see little of the river, since the highway swings inland through the tip of Clatsop State Forest.

When you do catch glimpses of the Columbia, you'll see that it has become a huge tidal estuary, more than a mile wide and dotted with wooded

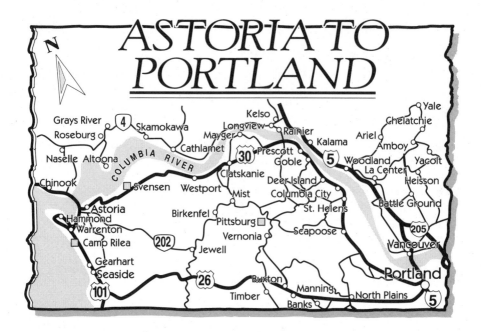

ASTORIA TO PORTLAND

N

Grays River 4 Skamokawa
Roseburg
Naselle Altoona
COLUMBIA RIVER
Chinook Svensen Westport
Astoria
Hammond
Warrenton
Camp Rilea 202
Gearhart
Seaside
101

Cathlamet
Clatskanie
Birkenfel Pittsburg
Vernonia
Jewell

26
Buxton
Timber
Banks

Kelso
Longview
Mayger Rainier
Kalama
Prescott 30
Goble
Deer Island
Columbia City
Seapoose
Mist
St. Helens

Manning
North Plains

Yale
Chelatchie
Ariel
Amboy
5 Woodland Yacolt
La Center
Heisson
Battle Ground
205
Vancouver
Portland
5

islands. The views are nice, across the broad river to the green hills of Washington. Although the area is lushly beautiful, there is little civilization here, perhaps because of the wet weather.

The Oregon State Park's **Bradley Wayside,** 22 miles from Astoria, offers a picnic area and pleasant vistas. Another dozen or so miles beyond, you encounter your first town of sorts, a hamlet called **Westport.** Here, you can catch a ferry across the Columbia to Cathlamet, Washington.

Beyond Westport, you lose the river until you reach **Rainier,** 48 miles from Astoria. It's appropriately named. Driving this route, you often have clear views of Washington's **Mount Rainier**, and what's left of the headline-grabbing **Mount St. Helens**. If you feel the need for speed in getting to Portland, you can cross the river at Rainier and pick up I-5 at **Longview, Washington,** for a quick trip south.

If you remain on the Oregon shore, you'll pass through a string of riverside blue-collar towns—**Prescott, Columbia City, St. Helens** and **Scappoose**—none offering travelers much cause to pause.

Beyond Scappoose, at a traffic signal in the middle of Highway 30, you'll see the bridge entrance to **Sauvie Island.** Its interesting for its bird sanctuary and fertile berry farms. (See details in Chapter 4.) From here, you enter Portland's suburban-industrial edge, where strip businesses and stop lights will slow your approach.

Below Sauvie Island, your streamside companion has become the **Willamette River.** If you aren't planning to get off in Portland and you want to stay close to the Columbia, cross the Willamette on St. John's Bridge, following the U.S 30 bypass. It becomes Lombard Street, which you follow about 3.5 miles to I-5. Take this north toward Vancouver and watch for the Marine Drive turnoff just before the freeway crosses the Columbia.

After a certain degree of twisting and turning, Marine Drive begins skimming along the riverbank. Watch for the proper road signs to stay your course. It passes through riverfront industrial areas, then nips the edge of **Portland International Airport.** Here, it becomes a levee highway, providing clear views of traffic both on the river and on the landing field. If you're in need of a lunch stop, **Salty's on the Columbia** is a locally popular seafood café perched right over the river. (See "Where to dine" in Chapter 4 for details.)

On a clear day, you can see **Mount Hood,** lofty and aloof from other crests of the Cascade Range. It's Oregon's tallest peak at 11,239 feet and you can set your directional compass by it for the next several miles. Beyond the airport, Marine Drive tucks under I-205 and continues eastward. It follows the Columbia's South Channel below **Government Island.**

Beyond Government Island, the route veers southeast away from the river, skimming the edge of the suburban communities of **Gresham** and **Troutdale.** As you enter the latter, Marine Drive blends onto Interstate 84. However, you jump off again in less than a mile, taking exit 18 toward **Lewis and Clark State Park.** You've begun your journey up the Columbia's legendary chasm.

COLUMBIA GORGE-MOUNT HOOD LOOP

As you pause at Lewis and Clark State Park, you're on the western end of one of the most famous loop drives in America. Two historic routes have been linked by tourist promoters to create the **Columbia Gorge-Mount Hood Loop.** Both started as private roads that later became part of the state highway system.

The first Oregon Trail immigrant trains couldn't negotiate the narrow Columbia Gorge by land, so they completed their trek to Fort Vancouver and on to Oregon City by ferrying down river. It was a costly and sometimes dangerous experience. In 1846, a group led by Samuel Barlow hacked out a toll road from The Dalles, along the south flank of Mount Hood. The Barlow Road provided the first overland link to the end of the Oregon Trail. Somewhat altered and now starting from the town of Hood River, this route is now State Highway 35 and U.S. 26. It forms the inland link to the Columbia Gorge-Mount Hood loop.

The gorge highway is of more recent vintage. It's the 20th century creation of Samuel Hill, an idealistic entrepreneur, Quaker pacifist and railroad heir. He wanted to build a road through the gorge to his Washington state mansion at Maryhill. In doing so, he created America's first scenic highway. His efforts were aided by several Portland interests, including lumber baron Simon Benson, who saw the value of a highway east along the Columbia.

Construction began in 1913 and was completed two years later. This was no mere highway, but a work of engineering art in the classic European style. It featured Florentine viaducts and beautiful mortar-free stonework in its bridge railings, arches and retaining walls. Five years earlier, Hill and his construction engineer Samuel Lancaster had toured Europe. They found inspiration in the mortarless stonework of Charlemagne's roads through the Rhine Valley, which had stood for 12 centuries.

Built for the views

Instead of avoiding curves and dizzying drops, Hill and Lancaster's highway was cantilevered high into the basaltic cliffs, with frequent turn-outs to afford the finest views. It was routed past the many waterfalls spilling into serpentine canyons that led to the river.

The first paved road in the Northwest, this 73.8-mile route later became part of U.S. Highway 30. Of course, with its great popularity and its hairpin

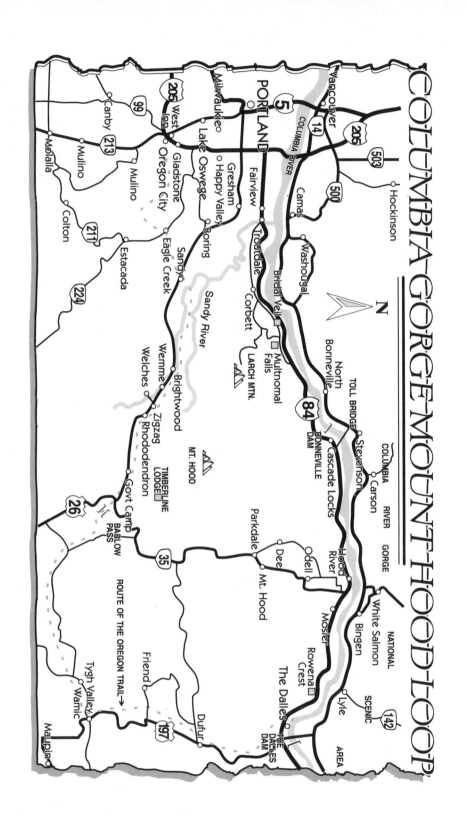

turns, it soon became hopelessly congested. When engineers replaced the old Highway with I-84, they abandoned much of the original twisting route in favor of a straightaway at river's edge.

Only about 14 miles of Sam Hill's road is still in use, from Crown Point east to Dodson. However, it's linked by later additions, permitting an uninterrupted 22.5-mile scenic drive from Lewis and Clark State Park to Dodson. You can hike other sections of the original road, giving yourself ample time to admire the fine (and often moss-covered) stonework.

The Columbia Gorge is one of Oregon's most popular recreation areas, containing its highest waterfalls, lush woodlands, those sheer basaltic cliffs, that fine "Charlemagne stonework" and dazzling river vistas. With major climate and elevation extremes—from mossy rainforests to semi-arid desert and from near sea level to the high flanks of Mount Hood—it shelters a tremendous variety of plants. It's also one of the windiest areas of the state. Great howling gusts are drawn from the cool ocean to the warm prairie beyond the gorge. This isn't bad news if you're a windsurfer; the area has become the windsurfing center of the globe. As you drive this scenic route, you'll see dozens of their bright triangular sails on the water below.

Much of this area is part of Mount Hood National Forest, offering one of the finest networks of hiking trails in Oregon. Paths lead to the ferny basins and to the tops of the larger waterfalls. Others continue above the falls into the north flanks of Mount Hood, and to the top of Larch Mountain for one of the area's most impressive views.

A 60-mile swath of the Columbia River, from Troutdale to Biggs, was set aside in 1986 as **Columbia River Gorge National Scenic Area.** This further protects its resources and natural attractions for visitors.

Mapping things out

The *Mt. Hood/Columbia Gorge Loop* map, somewhat commercialized because it's co-sponsored by American Express, is available at various chambers of commerce along the route, including Sandy, Hood River and Cascade Locks. Also, the Hood River Chamber of Commerce's *Hood River County* brochure includes a loop map. Serious hikers should pick up a Mount Hood National Forest *Trails of the Columbia Gorge* map. It shows hiking trails and sections of the old scenic highway that are closed to traffic but open to hikers. See the Trip Planner at the beginning of this chapter for addresses of these map sources.

The American Automobile Association issues one of the most informative and detailed Columbia Gorge and Mount Hood Loop maps, but you have to be an AAA member to get one. The Portland office is at 600 SW Market Street near Broadway; (503) 222-6734.

Driving the gorge

A sign at Lewis and Clark State Park advises that the group camped here after canoeing past the precipitous walls of the gorge. They noted that a small tributary of the Columbia "throws out emence quantities of sand and is very shallow," so they named it Sandy River.

Continue inland from the park, following a mix of woods and farmlands along the shoreline of the Sandy toward the small village of **Springdale**. En route, a "Historic Columbia River Highway" sign will direct you to the left. The Sandy is a good fishing, wading, swimming and splashing river, so you may want to linger. At **Dabney State Park,** you can pause for a picnic and pick up a 1.5-mile hiking trail along the banks.

You leave the Sandy at Springdale and head through more forests and farmlands to **Corbett,** another rural community. You've had not a glimpse of the Columbia since leaving I-84. Beyond Corbett, you climb steeply to the **Portland Women's Club Forum State Park** for your first—and very impressive—view of the Columbia River Gorge. It's the highest viewpoint on the Columbia River Scenic Highway. Far below is the famous cut-stone Crown Point Vista House, perched on a rocky peninsula above the gorge.

Just beyond the Women's Forum site, a right turn will take you 14 twisting miles, through thick fir forest up to **Larch Mountain Viewpoint** and picnic area in Mount Hood National Forest. The curves are semi-gentle, so even large RVs should have no problem with the climb. To see the promised view, walk to the right side of the parking lot and follow an asphalt path about a quarter mile to **Sherrard Point** on the rocky tip of Larch Mountain. Hold onto your camera and your adjectives!

On a clear day, this 4,056-foot perch offers dramatic sweeps of Oregon and Washington and the now-minuscule Columbia River Gorge below. Markers point your eyes to the monarchs of the Cascades: Mounts Hood, Jefferson, St. Helens and Adams. A sign on the left side of the parking lot marks various hiking trails in the area, including a 6.8-mile jaunt down to Multnomah Falls.

☺ Returning to the scenic highway, you encounter **Crown Point Vista House,** that legendary and lovable viewpoint that's been drawing in Model-T's and tour buses since 1917. The circular stone structure is perched 725 feet above the river. Built just after the completion of the scenic highway, it's the jewel in Lancaster's engineering crown. He envisioned an observatory from which the vista "both up and down the Columbia could be viewed in silent communion with the infinite." Frequent winds and tour buses may disturb your silent communion, but the view is awesome. The observatory and its vista comprise one of the most photographed spots in America.

Open daily from 9 to 6, it contains a gift shop, a U.S. Forest Service interpretive center (695-2230) and lots of big windows for Columbia Gorge viewing. This is a good place to pick up forest service maps and other guides to the area. Pictures and graphics recall the building of America's first scenic highway. On a good day, you can see 30 miles up and down the gorge.

The trail of cataracts

Beyond the Vista House, the route becomes an eleven-mile trek past a parade of waterfalls. Most are brushed by the wandering road, as intended by engineer Lancaster. This is the greatest gathering of waterfalls in America. They spill down sheer cliffs, crash into ferny grottoes, then snake their way to the Columbia through serpentine ravines. The grottoes are particularly inviting—misty, green emeralds. I like to think that leprechauns come out to play in the moonlight, after all the tourists have left.

After driving beneath a lush forest canopy, you encounter your first cataract, **Latourelle Falls,** about three miles from Crown Point. It's the second highest in the gorge after Multnomah, dropping 249 feet in a thin, silvery veil. A quarter-mile trail leads into the forest beside the falls, offering views from several levels as you climb. Another trail reaches the fern-laced dell at Latourelle's base.

Crown Point Vista House has been the proper place to pause in the Columbia River Gorge since its completion in 1917. **— Don W. Martin**

☺ **Shepherd's Dell,** often bypassed because of limited parking, is a pretty sheltered grotto less than a mile from Latourell. Look for the slim parking area on the right, just across a bridge spanning Young's Creek below the dell.

Bridal Veil, fed by a stream passing almost unnoticed beneath a highway bridge, is the only major waterfall north of the highway. From a parking area, a one-mile round trip trail leads down to the attractive two-level cataract. Another trail wanders across a camas lily meadow and past blackberry vines to a river overlook. Save some time for pickin' if you're there in July or August; the berries are big and plentiful. **Bridal Veil Lodge Bed & Breakfast** (listed below) also is reached from this parking area.

☺ **Wahkeena Falls,** just under four miles from Bridal Veil, is one of the more dramatic of the local cataracts. It does a triple jump down through a steep, moss-covered gorge of its own making. The cascade is reached by a quarter-mile trail that seems to be headed the wrong direction, but then it switches back.

☺ **Multnomah Falls** is Oregon's tallest cataract and one of its most famous landmarks. It thunders down a double drop for 620 feet, more than twice the height of Latourelle. It's the fourth highest in cascade America. While the other falls are attractions, Multnomah is an event—a requisite stop on this trail of cataracts. Expect crowds, particularly on summer weekends. It's easy to shake the mob by hiking up to and beyond a stone bridge at the falls' mid- point. A heavy investment in shoe leather will carry you 6.8 miles up to **Larch Mountain** viewpoint.

The historic **Multnomah Falls Lodge** sits near the base of the cataract. It houses a handsome restaurant (listed below), large gift and souvenir shop, a snack bar and a Forest Service information center (695-2376). The bold stone structure was built by the City of Portland in 1925. It's now operated as a concession of Mount Hood National Forest. Plan lunch or dinner in the atrium dining room, so you can admire at leisure the Depression-era WPA paintings of the gorge and the Cascade Range. The dining room and lodge are open Monday-Saturday 8 to 10 and Sunday 8 to 9.

About two miles beyond Multnomah, **Oneonta Gorge Botanical Area** offers a rich collection of rock-dwelling, aquatic and woodland plants. They grow in profusion in this narrow basaltic side canyon to the Columbia. If you're an accomplished rock-hopper and/or you're willing to get your feet wet, you can scramble far into this serpentine chasm. It's so narrow in areas that the walls almost touch. Upstream, you'll encounter **Triple Falls,** a visual treat not seen from the road.

☺ **Horsetail Falls,** often overlooked in Multnomah's limelight and thus rarely crowded, is our favorite. It's the most user-friendly waterfall in the gorge. Picnic tables are parked at the base, right beside the ferny dell that catches this 176-foot drop. A half-mile switchback trail takes you to **Upper Horsetail Falls,** offering impressive gorge views as you climb. The trail passes behind the falls, through an undercut so deep that you stay dry—unless it's a very windy day. The view from behind the water is intriguing—like looking at the world through marbled glass.

For an exhilarating visual and physical workout, follow the two- mile **Horsetail-Oneonta Loop Trail** which takes you high up the gorge's basaltic slope, then down into Oneonta Gorge. You can then hike north through the gorge and stroll along the highway back to Horsetail. Or if you're feeling terribly ambitious, you can continue west on a trail to Multnomah Falls.

East of Horsetail Falls, you'll leave the parade of cataracts and encounter **Ainsworth State Park,** offering camping (listed below), picnicking and hiking. Just beyond, the Columbia River Scenic Highway blends onto I-84. You can stay on a frontage road and pass through **Dodsworth** and **Warrendale,** although neither hamlet offers any visitor interest. Beyond Warrendale, there are no options; the old highway is buried under the freeway.

Across the river from Warrendale, you'll see the towering lava face of 848-foot **Beacon Rock.** It's supposedly the world's second largest exposed promontory, after the Rock of Gibraltar.

About five miles east of Warrendale, freeway exit 40 will deliver you to Bonneville, the first and most westerly of the Columbia's many dams. From this point east, the river becomes a chain of reservoirs, beginning with 48-mile-long Lake Bonneville.

If your vision of hydroelectric dams was influenced by the imposing concrete wedges on the Colorado and other canyon-carving rivers, prepare yourself for a different look on the Columbia. These are low-rise dams, much wider than they are deep. Those on the lower Columbia have fish ladders and navigational locks to allow the flow of natural and man-made river traffic. Most dams have viewing windows where one can watch salmon pass on their way to spawn. Lock-watching is interesting, too, although usually only once. It takes about half an hour for one of the huge concrete boxes to fill or drain and send the freighters, barges and pleasure boats to the next level.

☺ **Bonneville Dam, Lock and Fish Hatchery** ● *Cascade Locks, OR 97014-0150; (503) 374-8820. Visitor center open daily 9 to 8 in summer and 9 to 5 the rest of the year.* Completed in 1937, Bonneville has been around for so long that it has acquired national historic landmark status. It's actually three separate dams, set in a staggered line across two midstream islands. The main visitor facility and fish hatchery are on Bradford Island, reached by a bridge from the southern shore. A new $331 million navigation lock between the south shore and Bradford Island, was completed in 1993 to speed river traffic through the complex.

Like many of President Franklin D. Roosevelt's New Deal projects, the facility was crafted carefully, with Art Deco touches and with tourism in mind. For instance, the hatchery on the western end of the island more resembles a park than a fish nursery. Landscaped paths take you past special viewing ponds, where you can see the usual trout and steelhead, plus smaller versions of the giant Columbia sturgeon, which can attain lengths of 18 feet. This is one of the few hatcheries where this fish is reared.

The dam visitor center, at the island's eastern end, is spread over four levels served by elevators. Self-guiding tours begin at parking lot level. Here, a nicely-done museum focuses on the history of the Columbia, starting with the Native Americans and working through the development of hydroelectric power. You learn that the dam was named for Capt. Benjamin L.E. de Bonneville, a West Pointer who took leave of the army to engage in the Northwest fur trade. Traveling about the area from 1832 to 1835, he pioneered much of the Oregon Trail.

From the main visitor center, you can elevate to a rooftop viewing area or descend to a theater level to see movies and slides about the dam. Next stop is the fish viewing room, where assorted salmon and trout swim lazily past. Best viewing season is during the fall and spring spawning runs.

Incidentally, being a salmon is no piece of cake. For every 8,000 born in upstream hatcheries, only five make it back for a final spawning fling. And then they die. As if their lives weren't tough enough, a small gift shop at the hatchery sells smoked and canned salmon, salmon jerky and salmon leather.

As you follow the course of the Columbia eastward, you often catch glimpses of Mount Hood to the southeast. Approaching Cascade Locks and Hood River, you'll start seeing another snowcapped majesty on the Washington side. It's **Mount Adams,** heftier and taller—12,326 feet, compared with Hood's 11,239. Despite its height, Mount Adams isn't Washington's tallest peak. That honor goes to 14,408-foot Mount Rainier, often visible to the far northwest.

A mile north of Bonneville is the small **Cascade Fish Hatchery,** reached by exit 41. Above the hatchery, tucked into a wooded ridge, is **Eagle Creek Campground** of the U.S. Forest Service (listed below). Another three miles along the freeway takes you to a village that thrived during Bonneville's construction. However, its history goes back much further than that.

Cascade Locks

Population: 900   **Elevation: 102 feet**

Cascade Locks is a quiet, likable community with an impressive view of the river and a fascinating past. For eons, this was the site of the final brace of major rapids on the Columbia. It was a favorite fishing spot for Native Americans, who netted spawning salmon as they leaped high to struggle over the cataracts.

Lewis and Clark took the chicken route here, roping their canoes down the rapids and portaging their gear around. The process took them three days. Wrote Lewis:

This great chut of falls is about one half a mile. With the water of this great river compressed within the space of 150 paces...foaming and boiling in a horriable manner.

The town began as a construction camp, not for Bonneville Dam, but for a set of navigational locks around the rapids. Work started in 1874 and dragged on until 1896 because of funding and weather problems. Obviously, the small village later became a boom town during the construction of Bonneville.

At the west end of town, the Bridge of the Gods, named for an Indian legend, was built across the Columbia in 1926. It was raised in 1938 to clear the rising waters of Lake Bonneville. The lake also drowned the rapids and ruined the Indians' fishing grounds, a cruel event that gained national publicity. Their sons still practice the art of dip-netting at the base of Bonneville Dam's fish ladder.

Before you drive along Wa Na Pa Street through Cascade Locks, cross over to the Washington side for a visit to Bonneville's newest facility, simply called the Second Powerhouse. The gorge view is gorgeous as you cross; unfortunately, there's no pedestrian path.

☺ Completed in 1983, the **Second Powerhouse** is open daily from 9 to 5. Visitors can take a self-guided tour past rows of humming generators, then down into one of the turbine pits to watch the 62-inch spinning shafts. Graphics designed to boggle minds point out that each 32-foot- high generator weighs 1.5 million pounds, and has a 433-foot rotor. About 624 tons of water per second pass through the turbines to produce 105,000 horsepower. Finally, you'll probably want to know that these monsters are called alternating current synchronous generators. Are you boggled yet?

An escalator reaches yet another fish viewing room, with nicely done displays about fish migratory habits. A particularly interesting exhibit here concerns fish wheels, contraptions that resembled a combination water wheel and net. These devices could snatch as many as 4,000 salmon a day from the Columbia. Once in common use to feed the hungry canneries, they were outlawed early in this century.

The new powerhouse more than doubles Bonneville's output to over a million kilowatts. It cost $662 million, compared with the main dam's $83 million in the 1930s. That inflationary jump included relocating the Washington town of North Bonneville two miles downstream—lock, stock and public park. Only a bit of terracing above the parking lot betrays the town's original location.

Back in Cascade Locks, drive along the main street and turn left at the information sign to the **Port of Cascade Locks.** The port building houses the ticket office of the sternwheeler *Columbia Gorge,* which offers two-hour cruises to Bonneville Dam during the summer. These cruises don't include a trip through the locks, although some of the longer voyages do. Outings range from the basic trips to dance, dinner, lunch, breakfast and brunch cruises, plus voyages between Cascade Locks and Portland. During the off-season, the ship operates out of Portland, offering Willamette River cruises. For information, contact: Sternwheeler *Columbia Gorge,* 1200 NW Front Ave., Suite 110; (503) 223-3928 or 374-8427.

The **Visitor Center** of the Cascade Locks Tourism Committee also is located at the port; (503) 374-8619. A short distance away, in the former locktender's house, is the town's yesterday repository:

☺ **Cascade Locks Historical Museum** • *Open May through September, Monday-Thursday noon to 5 and Friday-Sunday 10 to 5. Free; donations appreciated.* This is an attractive small museum, with some rooms of the locktender's house furnished to the turn-of-the-century period when the locks were active. Among other displays are Native American exhibits and items concerning the construction of the locks and Bonneville Dam. Outside, you can greet the Oregon Pony, a tiny steam engine that tugged freight cars along a portage around the rapids before the locks were built. Employed in 1862 to replace mules on the portage, it was the first steam engine in the Oregon Territory.

WHERE TO DINE IN THE GORGE

☺ **Multnomah Falls Lodge** • ∆∆∆ **$$**
Multnomah Falls; (503) 695-2376. American; full bar service. Monday-Saturday 8 a.m. to 10 p.m., Sunday 8 to 9. MC/VISA, AMEX. Exceptionally attractive galleria dining room with views of the falls through high arched windows. Walls are decorated with Depression-era paintings of the Columbia Gorge and Cascades. Menu ranges from steaks and chops to fresh seafood. Try the seafood sautèe with prawns, scampi, halibut and salmon.

Cascade Inn Restaurant & Lounge • ∆ **$**
Downtown Cascade Locks; (503) 374-8340. American; full bar service. Sunday-Thursday 7 a.m. to 10 p.m., Friday-Saturday 7 to 11. Major credit cards. Ordinary Naugahyde family cafè offering ample servings of halibut and salmon, steak, chickens and chops. Most entrèes under $10.

WHERE TO SLEEP

Bridge of the Gods Motel • △ **$$**
630 Wa Na Pa St. (P.O. Box 98), Cascade Locks, OR 97014; (503) 374-8628. Couples $40 to $44, singles $30 to $33, kitchenettes $40 to $44. Major credit cards. Simple motel with queen beds, TV, room phones and refrigerators; some kitchens. RV park adjacent; listed below.

Scandian Motor Lodge • △△ **$$** ∅
P.O. Box 217 (downtown, I-84 exit 44), Cascade Locks, OR 97014; (503) 374-8417. Couples $38 to $48, singles $32 to $35. Major credit cards. Nicely maintained 30-unit motel with attractive rooms done in Scandinavian dècor. TV, room phones; sauna. **Cascade Inn Restaurant** adjacent; listed above.

Bed & breakfast inns

Bridal Veil Lodge • △△ **$$$** ∅
At Bridal Veil Falls (P.O. Box 87), Bridal Veil, OR 97010; (503) 695-2333. Couples $60, singles $52. Two units with a shared bath; full breakfast. No credit cards. This rustic 1926 lodge in a wooded setting, a short walk from Bridal Veil Falls, was recently reopened as a B&B. It has a knotty pine interior with simply furnished country-style rooms and a comfortable "English country" parlor with an antique player piano.

Shahala at the Locks • △△ **$$$** ∅
1280 Forest Lane, Cascade Locks, OR 97014; (503) 374-8222. Couples $50 to $75, singles $45 to $70. Seven units, two with private baths; full breakfast. MC/VISA. Modern ranch style home on 16 wooded acres overlooking the Columbia River; contemporary furnishings. Rec room with pool table, games,

A RIVER BE DAMMED

The mighty Columbia, once the greatest free-flowing river west of the Rockies, is now one of the most harnessed streams in the world. Millions of people have come to rely on it for electricity, irrigation, flood control and transportation.

A total of 202 dams and other diversions slow the river's 1,210-mile flow from its source in British Columbia to Astoria. The lower river impediments are lock and dam combinations, creating a 270-mile navigable waterway from the Pacific Ocean to Lewiston, Idaho.

The power potential of these dams is phenomenal. The Columbia produces 40 percent of America's hydroelectric output. Eventually, it may generate more than 50 percent as more power plants are put on line. In fact, America's four largest hydroelectric dams are on the Columbia—the Grand Coulee, John Day, Chief Joseph and The Dalles. All of the major dams are linked by a massive super-power grid with a total capacity of more than *twelve million kilowatts.*

Most of the dams were constructed and are operated by the U.S. Army Corps of Engineers. The corps is thus America's largest—pardon the pun—power broker. Most of the electricity is wholesaled to local power companies, although several riverside aluminum plants buy their juice directly from the government.

Harnessing the Columbia began in 1934 when the first bucket of concrete was poured for **Bonneville Dam,** about 40 miles upstream from Portland. It was part of President Franklin D. Roosevelt's program to create public works jobs during the Depression. FDR himself dedicated the completed dam on September 20, 1937, although it didn't go into service until June 6, 1938.

One of the world's largest dams when it was completed, Bonneville has since been dwarfed by the **Grand Coulee** in eastern Washington. Completed in 1951, it's the world's largest concrete structure and America's largest producer of hydroelectric power. Grand Coulee is 550 feet high and it produces more than two million kilowatts of juice, compared with Bonneville's 197 feet and one million-plus kilowatts.

Traveling west to east along the Oregon side of the Columbia, you'll encounter these other major lock and dam projects:

The Dalles Dam, near The Dalles, rises 260 feet and it can produce 1,806,800 kilowatts. Its completion in 1957 flooded Celilo Falls, an early impediment to navigation—and an historic Indian fishing area. Before the dam and locks were built, the Dalles-Celilo railroad and later Dalles-Celilo canal permitted upriver navigation.

John Day Dam, 25 miles upstream from The Dalles, went on line in 1971. The 219-foot-high structure boasts the world's second largest powerhouse, with room for enough generators to eventually produce 2.7 million kilowatts. Present output is 2.16 kilowatts, making it a close second to Grand Coulee.

McNary Dam, northwest of Pendleton near the point where the Columbia joins the Oregon-Washington border, was finished in 1957.

TV and VCR; licensed for beer and wine; living room with fireplace and chandeliered dining room. Large view windows.

WHERE TO CAMP

State Park and national forest campgrounds in the gorge fill up early in the summer, particularly on weekends.

Ainsworth State Park ● *Columbia Gorge, I-84 exit 35. RV and tent sites, full hookups, $13. No credit cards or reservations.* Many pull-throughs; terraced sites, a bit snugly spaced for a state park. Showers, picnic tables and hiking trails.

Bridge of the Gods RV Park ● *630 Highway 30 (P.O. Box 98), Cascade Locks, OR 97014. RV sites, $12 to $16.* Small park with grassy sites, full hookups, showers and coin laundry. Adjacent to Bridge of the Gods Motel.

Cascade Locks KOA ● *I-84 exit 44 east of town, Star Route, Box 660, Cascade Locks, OR 97014; (503) 374-8668. RV and tent sites, $13.50 to $17, "Kamping Kabins" $25. Reservations accepted; MC/VISA.* Tree-shaded sites, some pull-throughs. Showers, coin laundry, mini-mart, pool, spa, recreation room, playground, horseshoes.

Eagle Creek Campground ● *Columbia Gorge, I-84 exit 41; (503) 695-2276. Tent and RV sites, $5. No reservations or credit cards.* Attractive national forest campground above Eagle Creek Fish Hatchery; some sites with views of the river. Flush potties, water, no hookups.

Hood River

Population: 4,600   **Elevation: 154 feet**

The Columbia Gorge loses some of its grandeur and the forests begin to thin as you press eastward, although its basaltic walls remain impressive. About 18 miles from Cascade Locks, you encounter once-sleepy Hood River.

This rural riverside town has long been noted as the eastern apex of the Columbia Gorge/Mount Hood Loop and the center of one of America's largest apple and winter pear producing regions. Because of a recent invasion of baby-boomers with time and money on their hands, it has a curious new claim to fame, as the windsurfing capital of the world.

This is hardly a yuppie Lahaina or Malibu, but to an increasing number of "board-heads," it's *the* place to hang out. Spending their days riding the aquatic winds and their evenings in coffee houses that appear to be transferred from Berkeley, they contribute $25 million a year to the local economy. This, according to a study by the University of Oregon. Two major windsurfing events (or sail-boarding, if you prefer) lend credence to the town's claim as the global center for this sport—the Columbia Gorge Pro-Am and the Gorge Blowout.

As you approach Hood River, take exit 62 and visit the exquisitely-restored Spanish-Moorish style **Columbia Gorge Hotel**, on the west side of town. Spend time admiring the lobby chandeliers and fireplace, the formal gardens and river views. Perhaps stay for lunch or make reservations for dinner in the elegant 19th century European-style dining room.

Continue into town, perhaps pausing to admire the vintage downtown area along Oak Street. The tidy look of the businesses and the tidy homes terraced into the hills above reflect the modest affluence brought by its tourist-and-fruit economy. And in what other rural Oregon town will you find a sushi bar? (Kampai at Third and Oak, listed below.)

If you want to watch the sailboards at play, you have two choices. Follow **Second Street** to the waterfront, where you can park for $2 and walk to river's edge. Or continue on Oak to **Columbia Gorge Sailpark** and **Port Marina Park** the eastern edge of town, just west of a bridge across the Columbia. If you want to give this sport a go, Oak Street is lined with shops that'll sell or rent you the gear and give lessons. Others are at the marina.

Also at the Marina, you'll find the **Hood River County Visitors Center,** sharing space with the local office of **Mount Hood National Forest** and the **Port of Hood River.** Obviously, this facility can provide plentiful information about the town, the loop drive and sailboarding. It's open weekdays 9 to 5 and weekends 10 to 4. A quarter-mile west of the visitor center is the town's house of memories:

Hood River County Historical Museum ● *Port Marina Park; (503) 386-6772. Open April to October, Wednesday-Saturday 10 to 4 and Sunday noon to 4. Free; donations appreciated.* This is an attractive small museum with neatly arrayed displays of Hood River County's past. You'll see the usual spinning wheels, Edison cylinder phonograph and early day costumes, plus a nicely done Victorian living room, tools of the lumbering trade, Hood River apple box labels and an interesting collection of 19th century kitchen appliances. An enclosed courtyard contains native plants.

ACTIVITIES

Bicycle rentals ● Available at **Discover Bicycles,** 10210 Wasco St., Hood River, OR 97031; (503) 386-4820.

Scenic flights ● Fly the Columbia Gorge and flanks of Mount Hood with **Mid Columbia Water Sports**, based at the Marina, (503) 386-3321.

Reservation services ● **Gorge Central Reservations**, 1220 Eugene St., Hood River, OR 97031, (503) 386-6109, can arrange lodgings, rental cars, sailboard rentals, lessons and other recreational activities.

☺ **Scenic railway** ● Trips through the apple and pear orchards into the flanks of Mount Hood are offered by **Mount Hood Scenic Railroad** at the Amtrak station, 110 Railroad Ave., Hood River, OR 97031; (800) 872-4661 or (503) 386-3556. Following the route of an old fruit train line, diesel locomotives tug 1910 railcars up one of America's last switchback railroad grades. Two runs are scheduled daily—a 44-mile round trip to Parkdale and 17-mile run to Odell and back. The Parkdale run is best, since it reaches higher into Mount Hood's wooded flanks for better valley views.

Windsurfing ● Nearly a dozen shops can set you up for seeking Columbia breezes. They're listed in *Northwest Sailboard,* available locally or write to: P.O. Box 918, Hood River, OR 97031. Call 387-WIND for weather and windsurfing information.

Winetasting ● Hood River Valley's German-style climate produces fine Chardonnays and Gewürtztraminers. You can sip the essence of the grape at **Three Rivers Winery,** 275 Country Club Road (386-5453), open Monday-Saturday 11 to 5 and Sunday 1 to 5; and **Hood River Vineyard,** 4693 Westwood Drive (386-7772), daily 10 to 5. Brochures and directions are available at the visitor center.

ANNUAL EVENTS

Hood River Blossom Festival, late April, with arts, crafts and orchard blossom tours; (503) 386-2000.

Columbia Gorge Pro-Am windsurfing competition, early July; (503) 386-5787.

Gorge Cities Blowout windsurfing race, mid-July; (503) 667-7778.

Hood River County Fair in early August; (503) 354-2865.

Apple Jam Music Festival, mid-August at Port Marina Park; (503) 387-7529.

Hood River Harvest Fest, late October with entertainment, crafts and fresh fruit treats to celebrate the harvest; (503) 386-2000.

Light Up the Gorge, Christmas season, with 65,000 lights on the grounds of the Columbia Gorge Hotel; (503) 386-5566.

WHERE TO DINE

☺ Horsefeathers • ΔΔ $$

State and Second streets; (503) 386-4411. American; wine and beer. Sunday-Thursday 5 p.m. to 9:30, Friday-Saturday 5 to 10. MC/VISA. Typical of the Berkeley-style *nouveau-rustic* Hood River restaurants, fashioned into an old house with oak interior, wainscotting and lofty ceilings. A deck offers river views. Busy menu features fresh fish, pizza, pasta, burgers, calamari, rack of lamb and sirloin. Nine Northwest micro-brews are poured, along with a large selection of international beers.

Kampai • ΔΔ $$

113 Third at Oak; (503) 386-2230. Japanese; wine and beer. Daily 11:30 to 2 and 5 to 9. MC/VISA. Cozy cellar restaurant with a sushi bar; also features *bunto* box-lunch style meals and the usual tempura shrimp, teriyaki, fresh seafood and some Hawaiian-Japanese fare with tropical accents. Simple *Nippon* décor with natural woods and ricepaper screens.

Yaya's International Café • ΔΔ $

207 Oak Street (between Second and Third); (503) 386-1996. International; wine and beer. Sunday-Thursday 8 a.m. to 9 p.m., Friday-Saturday 8 to 10. MC/VISA. Another Berkeley transplant with simple Mediterranean décor and wooden booths. Busy menu is mostly Greek, with the usual *gyros, spanakopoita* and *slovaki.* It also touches several other bases, from New England clam chowder to *gaspacho.*

WhiteCap BrewPub • ΔΔ $ Ø

506 Columbia (near Fourth); (503) 386-2247. Micro-brewery/café; wine and beer. Summer, Tuesday-Sunday from noon; off-season, Thursday-Friday from 4:30 and weekends from 2. MC/VISA. Typical brewpub fare, including barbecued burgers, chicken wings and Cajun oysters. Casual atmosphere, with view deck. Naturally, the locally-brewed suds are called Full Sail Ale.

WHERE TO SLEEP

Windsurfers and watchers take up many of the medium and low-priced motel rooms in spring and summer, so plan accordingly.

☺ Columbia Gorge Hotel • ◠◠◠◠ $$$$$

4000 Westcliff Dr., Hood River, OR 97031-9970; (800) 345-1921 or (503) 386-5566. Rooms $175 including breakfast. Major credit cards. Beautifully restored 1921 hotel with extensive landscaped grounds, pools and creeks above the Columbia River. Elegant European-style furnishings in common areas. The 46 rooms are exquisitely furnished with European and American antiques, some with canopy beds and fireplaces. **Columbia River Court**

dining room, voted best restaurant in Oregon, serves Northwest cuisine; 8 a.m. to 2:30 and 4 to 9; dinners $15 to $30; full bar service. Also noted for elaborate four-course breakfasts.

Inn at Cooper Spur • ⌂⌂⌂ $$$ ∅

10755 Cooper Spur Rd., Parkdale, OR 97041; (503) 352-6692. Couples $64 to $72, singles $54 to $64, suites $98, cabins $108. MC/VISA, AMEX. Distinctive 14-unit country-style inn off the Mount Hood Loop highway, about 16 miles south of Hood River. TV, room phones; several rooms with hot tubs, eight kitchen units; tennis court. **Restaurant** serves 5 to 9 Monday-Saturday and 9 a.m. to 9 p.m. Sunday; steak and seafood with homemade soups and pies; dinners $9 to $27; full bar service.

Love's Riverview Lodge • ⌂⌂ $$

1505 Oak Street (13th), Hood River, OR 97031; (503) 386-8719. Couples $42 to $67, singles $39 to $65, kitchenettes $52 to $79. Major credit cards. Well-kept 15-unit all-suite motel; TV movies, room phones; river views.

Vagabond Lodge • ⌂⌂ $$ ∅

4070 Westcliff Dr. (I-84 exit 62), Hood River, OR 97031; (503) 386-2992. Couples $39 to $59, singles $35 to $48, kitchenettes and suites $69. Major credit cards. A 40-unit motel with nicely landscaped grounds; some rooms overlooking the Columbia. TV, room phones; playground.

Bed & Breakfast inns

☺ The Beryl House • ⌂⌂⌂ $$$ ∅

4079 Barret Dr., Hood River, OR 97031; (503) 386-5567. Couples $65, singles $55. Four rooms with shared baths; full breakfast. MC/VISA. Large 1910 farm house fashioned into a country-style inn. Wraparound porch, gardens, volleyball and badminton courts, surrounded by 150 acres of orchards. A mix of antique and contemporary furnishings, accented by artworks from the owners' world travels.

Hackett House • ⌂⌂⌂ $$$ ∅

922 State St. (at 10th Street), Hood River, OR 97031; (503) 386-1014. Couples $60 to $70, singles $40 to $50. Four rooms, some private, some shared baths; full breakfast. MC/VISA, DISC. Turn-of-the-century Dutch Colonial home surrounded by extensive gardens. Common areas and guest rooms done in country-style décor; deck with old-fashioned swing; views of Columbia and Mount Adams. Short walk to downtown.

Inn at the Gorge • ⌂⌂⌂ $$$$ ∅

1113 Eugene St. (near 12th), Hood River, OR 97031; (503) 386-4429. Couples from $78, singles from $59. Four units with private baths; full breakfast. MC/VISA. A 1908 Victorian-style home with a mix of antique and modern furnishings. Kitchen available with cooking utensils; large yard; within walking distance of downtown. Innkeepers are windsurfers, offering rentals, lessons and their knowledge of local conditions.

WHERE TO CAMP

Port of Hood River RV Park • *Port Marina Park. No hookups, $5. No reservations or credit cards.* Basically a scraped-off parking area overlooking the harbor, near the museum. Campers have access to the harbor's nicely-maintained coin showers and other marina facilities.

Viento State Park ● *I-84, eight miles west; (503) 374-8811. RV and tent sites; water and electric, $9 to $11. No reservations or credit cards.* Nicely-spaced shaded sites, with showers, picnic tables and barbecues.

Mount Hood loop

The inland leg of the Columbia Gorge/Mount Hood Loop begins opposite Port Marina Park, heading south from I-84 on State Route 35. Two things generally happen quickly as you leave the gorge and drive inland: you leave the wind and—if it's cloudy on the river—you enter the sunshine.

Hood River Valley is one of Oregon's prettiest farming areas, rimmed with wooded hills, abloom with apple and pear petals in spring and glistening with ripening fruit in the fall. Mount Hood peeks over a far ridge, as if keeping an eye on the crops. If you're fortunate enough to make this drive in the fall, you can pick up fresh fruit at numerous roadside stands. Some operate in summer, too, offering winter storage apples and assorted Oregon specialty foods.

We're going to suggest a deviation from the classic Mount Hood Loop by turning left after the first quarter of a mile, following signs to **Panorama Point.** This Hood County park is aptly named, offering a postcard vision of Mount Hood, with orderly ranks of fruit orchards at its feet. Instead of returning immediately to Highway 35, take a right at the base of the viewpoint, following "Hood River County Tour Route" signs. The course meanders through orchard lands, past handsome 19th century farm homes, old red barns and weathered packing sheds.

The county tour route signs will return you to Highway 35 at the teeny town of **Pine Grove.** As you continue south from here, Mount Adams often flirts with you from your rearview mirror. About eight miles beyond, in the hamlet of **Mount Hood,** you might pause at the **Mount Hood Country Store,** which offers deli items, groceries and country crafts. We were hoping for some apple treats, but were surprised to find none.

Beyond the town, you leave the orchards and begin climbing Mount Hood's wooded flanks. **Tollbridge** near **Parkdale** is the first of a succession of Forest Service campgrounds. Most offer the usual woodsy sites with either flush or pit potties, for $5 a night. While passing Parkdale, you might pause at the **Hood River Ranger Station**, 6730 Highway 35. It offers information on the upcoming **Mount Hood Recreation Area**, with its miles of hiking trails and scores of campsites and picnic areas. If you'd like to seek out Barlow Road landmarks as you drive around the mountain, ask for the special map and guide. Hours are weekdays 8 to 5; (503) 352-6002.

During much of this trip, Mount Hood has hidden behind its own foothills. Then it appears dramatically as you round a bend just beyond **Mount Hood Meadows** ski area. It's now a massive presence, a glistening white-capped sentimental towering over its foothill realm. Commanding this otherwise low point in the Cascade Range, it's one of the most isolated promontories in America.

With the mountain practically in your lap, you see that it's not the smooth Fujiyama-like cone that appeared from afar. Its profile is ruggedly handsome, marked by rough volcanic dikes. The noble brow, high above the tree line, is dressed the year around in snow patches and glaciers. The first outsiders to see this crest were crewmen of a British Royal Navy ship, sailing up the Columbia in 1792. It was named for a British admiral.

A few miles beyond Mount Hood Meadows, you top **Barlow Pass** at the **Pacific Crest Trail,** where the immigrant road crossed its high point en route to Oregon City. A side loop takes you to the **Pioneer Woman's Grave,** a monument honoring those who perished in this difficult crossing.

You're now on the south side of the mountain, affording your passenger the best views. Turning right at the proper sign, you make the steep, squiggly six-mile climb to one of Oregon's most cherished landmarks.

The grand lodge at Timberline

☺ **Timberline Lodge,** a grand edifice of rough-cut stone, shingles and immense logs occupies a niche at the 6,000 feet elevation, less than a mile from the summit. It was hand-made during the Depression by hundreds of master craftsmen of the Works Progress Administration and Civilian Conservation Corps. One of FDR's most glamorous New Deal job corps projects, the lodge was completed in 1937.

Subsequent decades took their toll on this noble structure until a group called Friends of Timberline came to its rescue, beginning in 1975. The non-profit organization started raising funds for a meticulous restoration, right down to the solid handmade tables and chairs, the WPA pastels and the Navajo-style textiles.

It is today a living museum of Depression era art and craftsmanship. It's also the social center of the Mount Hood Recreation Area. The lodge offers refurbished rooms, a fine dining room and mountain-view bar, ski area and special summer programs. More than a million people a year pause to pay homage to this national historic landmark.

Even if you're passing through, take time to admire its massive rough-cut beams, hardwood floors and hand-carved paneling. Its focal point is a three-level octagonal fireplace with thick beams radiating outward to hold up the ceiling. Plan lunch or dinner in the rustically-formal **Cascade Dining Room,** or a drink or light snack in the **Ram's Head Bar** on the mezzanine level. The massive crown of Mount Hood fills its windows, like a framed picture come alive.

A lower lobby museum recalls the days of the lodge's construction, with photos, tools, early-day dining service and other artifacts. The sonorous voice of FDR crackles in a recording that was made when he dedicated the lodge in 1937.

The specifics

Dining: Cascade Dining Room serves breakfast from 8 to 10, lunch from noon to 2:30 and dinner from 6 to 8:30 (until 9 Saturday and Sunday). Reservations are required and most credit cards are accepted. Dinners are $16 to the mid-$20s and the menu is Northwest-continental, featuring savories such as broiled *entrecôte* of lamb, maple-cured salmon and smoked chicken Cascade with mushrooms. You dine amidst woven tapestries, hooked rugs and Depression-era watercolors. The **Rams Head** above serves light fare such as croissants, nachos and plowman's lunch.

Lodging: Rooms are faithfully restored to their original look, with knotty pine walls, pine floors, throw rugs and hand-crafted furniture. Some have fireplaces. Rates are $52 to $140.

Summer activities: Audio-visual program, nature walks and talks are conducted by Mount Hood National Forest rangers. Several hiking trails radiate from the lodge, and some lead to the top. The 3.6-mile **Hogsback**

Patrons at the Rams Head Bar in Timberline Lodge are treated to a great picture-window view of Mount Hood.
– Don W. Martin

trail is the most popular. It's not a technical climb, but it's difficult and it can be dangerous, crossing over glaciers and snow fields. Hikers should be properly equipped and should check with a ranger for conditions before starting out.

Skiing and ski-lifting: With its perpetual snowfields and glaciers, skiing is possible the year-around, although winter obviously is the peak season. The **Wy'east** day lodge adjacent to Timberline is the ski center, with equipment sales and rentals, ski clothing, accessories, gifts and lift tickets. **Palmer** and **Magic Mile** chairlifts generally operate in summer. Lift tickets for skiers are $22 all day; round-trip sightseeing tickets are $4 for adults and $2.50 for kids. The original Magic Mile lift (since replaced) was the world's second chairlift when it was opened in 1939.

Information: For room reservations, call (800) 547-1406 or write: Timberline Lodge, Timberline Ski Area, OR 97028. For skiing and other general information, write to the same address or call (503) 272-3710. The snow phone is (503) 222-2211. For forest service information, contact Hood River Ranger Station, 6730 Hwy. 35, Parkdale, OR 97041; (503) 352-6002.

Completing the loop

Continuing west on Route 35, you encounter the alpine hamlet of **Government Camp,** just off the highway. Rather scattered and shabby despite its pleasant mountainside location, it offers little for the casual traveler. It's mostly a winter ski hangout. You can grab a bite to eat or a place to sleep.

WHERE TO DINE

Huckleberry Inn Restaurant ● Δ $
Government Camp Loop; (503) 272-3325. American; wine and beer. Open 24 hours. MC/VISA. Simple American café with knotty pine and wooden booths, offering chicken fried steak, liver and onions and huckleberry specialties. The adjacent **Spirit Steak House** is more attractive, in a woodsy-cozy fashion, offering steaks and other entrèes from the mid-teens down. It's open only during the winter ski season.

Charlie's Mountain View Restaurant ● Δ $
Government Camp Loop; (503) 272-3333. American; full bar service. Food service daily 11 to 9:30. MC/VISA. A scruffy pub with a nice view of Mount Hood. Steaks, burgers and other light fare in a bare-bones back room. Hearty servings for the price; steaks from $10 down.

Below Government Camp, you practically fall off the mountain, reeling downhill on a five to six-percent grade. For the most part, the recreational and scenic offerings of the loop are behind you. At Zigzag, you leave Mount Hood National Forest.

If you're going *up* the mountain, stop at the **Zig Zag Ranger Station** for your ration of Mount Hood Recreation Area information. It's open daily except holidays from 7:45 to 4:30; (503) 622-3191. Just to the south is the town of **Welshes,** with a **Mount Hood Information Center** at 65000 E. Highway 26; (503) 622-4822. Operated by the Mount Hood Area Chamber of Commerce, it offers stuff on dining, lodging and other commercial facilities in the area. Ask for the booklet, *Mount Hood Guest Guide.*

Below Welshes, a succession of small towns flash past—**Wemme, Brightwood, Alder Creek** and **Firwood**. They offer restaurants, motels and mountain lodges that are popular mostly with Portland area residents seeking weekend retreat. Judging from the plethora of facilities, most Oregonians run the loop drive from this direction, or they simply go up to Mount Hood to play for a few days.

By the time you reach **Sandy,** the terrain has flattened into farm country that is dissolving into Portland suburbs. If you intend to continue eastward on I-84, head north to **Roslyn Lake County Park**, and then follow the Sandy River to **Springdale.** The turnoff from Sandy isn't well-marked, so ask locally for the right road. A right turn in Springdale gets you to **Corbett**, then you follow signs to an I-84 interchange at **Corbett Station.** Again before you is that glorious gorge! You'll have the privilege of a rivers' edge view as you resume your route east. The freeway runs alongside the railroad tracks at the base of the gorge. Of course, we wouldn't blame you if you decided instead to retrace your tracks along Sam Hill and Sam Lancaster's handsome Columbia Gorge Highway.

If you're returning to Portland, stay with Highway 26 until you reach **Gresham.** Then leave the highway by going straight ahead onto Burnside Road, avoiding the Route 26 fork to the left. After a few blocks, go right onto 242nd Drive at the I-84 sign and follow it to the freeway. Highway 26 will get you into Portland as well, but the freeway avoids that long suburban crawl.

HOOD RIVER TO THE DALLES

As you drive eastward from Hood River on I-84, you'll notice a drying of the terrain and a thinning of the trees. The rainshadow of the Cascade Range is beginning to take effect.

At **Mosier,** with only 260 people and yet a sailboard shop, you can leave the freeway and pick up the final segment of the Columbia Gorge Scenic Route. You'll climb a couple of hundred feet into what's left of the forest, then pass apple orchards separated by winrows of slender poplars—nice visions in the fall. You're losing the trees, but certainly not the gorge.

☺ The highway spirals upward along sheer-walled basaltic cliffs to **Rowena Crest,** one of the most dramatic viewpoints along the Columbia. With its absence of tour buses and crowds, we almost prefer this to Crown Point. The river takes a sharp bend here, so Rowena offers an awesome panorama upstream and down. From this transition zone, you see the lush forest leading westward to Mount Hood and the arid rolling prairies of eastern Oregon.

Sit on the Romanesque cut-stone wall and study the river below. You'll likely see a grain barge headed downstream, a cargo ship going up and most certainly windsurfers going every which way. Also occupying this crest is the 2,300-acre **Tom McCall Nature Preserve,** with hiking trails wandering about the nearby slopes. With luck, you'll find trail and plant guides in a drop box. Although brown much of the year, the area sparkles with blooms in the spring, particularly during May. Across the river is the Washington town of Lyle, spilling toward the Columbia along the mouth of the Klikitat River. Mount Adams huddles in the far distance.

The highway does a snake-dance down from the crest, clinging precariously to the irregular cliffs. At the townlet of **Rowena,** it parallels the freeway, and then swings inland again. It soon takes you to a most historic town on the Oregon Trail, occupying a sweeping bend in the Columbia.

The Dalles

Population: 11,100   **Elevation: 96 feet**

The largest Columbia River city east of Portland, The Dalles marked the end of the wagon road portion of the Oregon Trail. Faced with the steep cliffs of Rowena Crest, pioneers built or hired rafts and barges and braved a nasty brace of rapids to continue their journey.

Those rapids were named *Les Dalles* (the long narrows or the trough) by early French trappers. Here, the river was jammed into a 175-foot-wide basaltic trench, where it churned downstream at 30 feet per second. Unwilling to face the rapids or pay the high tolls charged by rivermen, Samuel Barlow and his family and friends began hacking an inland road from this point in 1846. Of course, the trough and rapids have disappeared under the backwaters of Bonneville Dam.

Industry and agriculture, not tourism, account for The Dalles' size. Aluminum and lumber production provide local payrolls, and this is a major shipping point for grain from northeastern Oregon's extensive wheatlands. Don't expect quiche, sushi or croissants in this area. They're downstream with all those yuppie windsurfers. The history-rich community is certainly worth a browse, however. And you'll want to cross the river to Sam Hill's remarkable **Maryhill Museum of Art** and latter-day **Stonehenge.**

Lewis and Clark camped at this bend in the river on their way west. They commented in their journals that it was "the great Indian mart of all this country." Settlement began with the arrival of the first Oregon Trail immigrants in 1843. Fort Dalles, the only stronghold on the Oregon Trail between Fort Laramie and Fort Vancouver, was established here in 1850. That firmly secured the community's place on the map. Nine years later, The Dalles became the seat of Wasco County, the largest ever formed in America. It covered 130,000 square miles, containing a good chunk of Oregon, plus parts of present-day Idaho, Montana and Wyoming.

As you approach The Dalles on the final leg of the Columbia Gorge Scenic Highway, your route becomes Sixth Street, which leads to the working-class downtown area. Old but not really weather-worn, the city center contains some fine examples of early-day stone, brick and clapboard architecture. Several Victorian home stand in the uphill residential district.

Doing The Dalles

On the west edge of town, Sixth Street swerves and blends into the one-way grids of Second and Third streets. Just prior to this point, look for the large **historical sign** that discusses The Dalles' yesterdays. Continuing east, note the brick 1881 **Wasco County Courthouse** at Third and Union, with its distinctive domed four-faced clock tower.

If you want to pick up a map before starting your exploration, continue through town to **The Dalles Convention & Visitors Bureau** at 901 E. Second Street. Occupying a large quonset where the one-way grid merges, it's open weekdays 9 to 6, Saturday 10 to 5 and Sunday 10 to 4. Even if it's closed, you can get maps and brochures from a rack in the foyer. You can get a driving map that directs you over the old Barlow Road and to other scenic rural environs, and a walking map of The Dalles' historic buildings.

From the visitor center, return to the courthouse and follow Union Street up into the residential area, noting the nice Victorians along your route. At Union and Fifth, a monument at **The Dalles City Park** designates the end of the Oregon Trail. Note the filigreed **Victor Trevitt Victorian** in the park. It was undergoing restoration but not opened when we visited. Continue uphill and turn left at 12th Street, following the **Pulpit Rock** sign. This hunk of stone, smack dab in the intersection at 12th and Court, marks the site of a Methodist Indian Mission, founded in 1838. It was one of the first in the Northwest.

Go uphill on Court for a block, then turn right onto 14th and follow signs to the fort and historic museum:

☺ **Fort Dalles Museum** ● *15th and Garrison streets; (503) 296-4547. March to October, weekdays 10:30 to 5 and weekends 10 to 5; the rest of the year, Wednesday-Friday noon to 4 and weekends 10 to 4. Adults $2, kids free.* All that remains of the fort is the board and batten surgeons' quarters, which houses the area's historic museum. The usual pioneer artifacts, weapons and old photos recall the town's rich history. A carriage shed outside is filled with yesterday rigs. The fort was built following a tragic event that occurred several miles northeast, on the Washington side of the river. In 1847, Missionary Marcus Whitman, his family and more than a dozen others were massacred during an uprising of the Cayuse Indians, who blamed them for an outbreak of smallpox among their tribe.

From the museum, swing to the right around a corner on Garrison, then turn left onto Scenic Drive. Follow its winding course to **Sorosis Park** for some nice views of the town and the Columbia River at its feet. Retrace your route downtown, if you can do so without getting lost (we *did* get lost), and check out a couple of other attractions. They're easily found with the help of a city map.

The **Lewis and Clark Memorial,** near the riverfront and railroad tracks, on the west side of town at Second and Mount Hood streets, recounts the pause here by the Corps of Discovery. Not far away, beside the Chamber of Commerce at 406 W. Second Street, is the wood clapboard **Original Wasco County Courthouse.** Open Tuesday-Saturday 10 to 5, it contains a few history exhibits; (503) 296-4798. Maps are available for self-guiding walking tours, which start here.

Continue east on Second and turn right onto Lincoln to admire **St. Peter's Landmark Church** at Third and Lincoln. It's an 1897 red brick Gothic affair with a 176-foot steeple, a Madonna crafted from a ship's keel and lots of stained glass windows. Another worthy structure is **The Dalles Art Center**, 220 E. Fourth at Washington. It's housed in a brick Grecian-style 1910 Carnegie Library building; hours are Tuesday-Saturday 10 to 4.

☺ Also well worth seeing—if it's completed—is the **Gorge Discovery Center,** on a site overlooking the Columbia off River Road, northwest of town. Write P.O. Box 998, The Dalles, OR 97058 or call (503) 296-8600 to check on its progress. It is to be a state-of-the-art heritage center focusing on the geology, flora, fauna and human history of the Columbia Gorge. We can hardly wait.

The Dalles is on the outer edge of the Hood River orchard district, and **Rasmussen Farms** has two fruit, produce and flower stands in the area. One is downtown at 3000 W. Sixth Street and the other is out in the country, off Highway 35. Drive six miles south and watch for signs; it's at 3020 Thomsen Road. Both are open daily 9 to 6; call 298-5463 or 386-4622 for directions.

The area's' largest attraction, literally and figuratively, is east of town:

☺ **The Dalles Lock and Dam** ● *P.O. Box 564, The Dalles, OR 97058; (503) 296-1181. Tours available weekdays 9 to 4, April through September. Visitor center open daily 9 to 5 the rest of the year.* This is a dam tour with a couple of twists. You reach the structure by riding a converted work train, which departs every half hour from a visitor center in Seufert Park. A guide regales you with statistics as you travel. This is the world's fourth largest hydroelectric dam, capable of lighting 18 million 100-watt light bulbs with the 22 generators in its half- mile-long turbine room. Once on the other side, you can wander about on your own, or stay with your chatty tour guide.

Another distinctive feature of this tour is that you can watch a live telecast of the fish viewing area, the same one that the fish counters view for monotonous hours. They must determine the type, sex and origin (hatchery or natural) of each of the hundreds of fish that pass each day. Hatchery fish can be identified because their rear dorsal fin is clipped before they're released. Dorsal-clipping must be about as boring as fish-counting.

The visitor center offers a fine little museum concerning the Native American and new American history of the Columbia. Photos recall the days when Indians used dip-nets to catch spawning salmon struggling up Celilo Falls above the dam. In a repeat of the Bonneville incident, the falls were drowned during the filling of The Dalles Dam in 1957. If you'd like a close-up view of a boat lifter and dropper in action, cross the river on the bridge just east of town and follow signs to **The Dalles Lock.** A small park here is open daily from 9 to 5. Visitors can stare right down into the giant rectangle of water to watch its slow-motion filling or draining, and then marvel at the opening of the massive gates. Plan on 20 minutes.

WHERE TO DINE

Casa Del Rio ● ∆∆ $

1240 W. Sixth St.; (503) 298-4661. Mexican; full bar service. Sunday-Thursday 11 to 9, Friday-Saturday 11:30 to 10. MC/VISA, DISC. Charming Latino *casa* brightened by lots of Mexican doo-dads with a busy, cheerful *cantina* adjacent. Menu offers typical tacos and related fare, plus several northern Mexico entrees. Large portions at modest prices, with full dinners ranging from $5 to $11.

☺ Cousins Restaurant ● ∆∆∆ $$ ∅

2114 W. Sixth St.; (503) 298-2771. Rural American; full bar service. Daily 6 a.m. to 10 p.m. Major credit cards. A delightfully charming red and white farm-style restaurant decorated with implements, mooing plastic cows and even farm tractors. The menu is American Gothic as well—pan-fried chicken, roast turkey, country ribs, steak, pot roast and salmon. Entrèes are served with cornbread and other rural essentials. Slip into one of those Holstein black and white Naugahyde booths and get ready to go country. The restaurant is part of the Tillicum Inn (listed below).

Dobre Deli ● ∆ $ ∅

308 E. Fourth St. (downtown); (503) 298-8239. American; wine and beer. Weekdays 7 to 7, Saturday 9 to 5, closed Sunday. MC/VISA. Handy lunch stop with typical deli fare to eat there or to go. They'll even rent you a picnic basket for $2, and pack it with goodies for not much more. Smoke-free inside; outdoor tables with smoking permitted.

The Wasco House ● ∆∆∆ $$$

515 Liberty St.; (503) 296-5158. American, continental; full bar service. Lunch weekdays 11 to 2, dinner nightly except Tuesday from 5, Sunday brunch. MC/VISA. Elegant dining room housed in an 1892 Italianate mansion with high-backed chairs, scalloped drapes and crisp white nappery. Menu ranges from well-prepared steaks, chicken and continental fare to hamburgers and snacks, which are served on an outside deck.

WHERE TO SLEEP

Inn at The Dalles ● ◠◠ $$ ∅

3350 SE Frontage Road (at Highway 197), The Dalles, OR 97058; (800) 777-3221 or (503) 296-1167. Couples $45 to $50, singles $29 to $32, kitchenette apartments $60 to $75. Major credit cards. A 45-unit motel with TV movies and room phones; pool.

Shamrock Motel ● △ $ Ø

118 W. Fourth St., The Dalles, OR 97058; (503) 296-5464. Couples $28 to $35, singles $25 to $30. Major credit cards. A 25-unit motel with TV and room phones; some room refrigerators.

Shilo Inn ● △△△ $$$ Ø

3223 Frontage Rd. (I-84 exit 87), The Dalles, OR 97058; (800) 222-2244 or (503) 298-5502. Couples $53 to $83, singles $51 to $58, suites $62 to $94. Major credit cards. New 112-unit motor hotel overlooking The Dalles Dam. TV movies, room phones; some mini-suites and full suites, with microwaves, refrigerators and wet bars. Pool, spa, sauna, fitness room and laundromat; free continental breakfast. **O'Callahan's Restaurant & Lounge** serves American fare, 6 a.m. to 10 p.m.; full bar service.

Tillicum Inn ● △△ $$$ Ø

2114 W. Sixth St. (P.O. Box 723), The Dalles, OR 97058; (800) 848-9378 in Oregon only or (503) 298-5161. Couples $52 to $67, singles $45 to $49, kitchenettes $60 to $71. Major credit cards. Well-kept 85-room motel with TV movies, room phones and refrigerators. Pool and spa. Free use of adjacent fitness club. **Cousins Restaurant** listed above.

EAST FROM THE DALLES

As you press eastward, you pass between dry, wrinkled and gently-rounded hills and steep basaltic slopes. Some of these monoliths suggest Easter Island statues if you let your imagination wander. Over all of this, Mount Hood keeps silent watch.

At exit 97, **Celilo Falls Park** offers picnicking, river access and camping, with flush potties but no hookups. It's a popular windsurfers' hangout. This is the site of the former Indian fishing falls, now a flat lake where yuppie sailboarders play. If you're struck by this irony, you'll be saddened by a short drive westward on the southside frontage road. It takes you to the shabby **Celilo Indian village** whose residents, deprived of their ancestral fishing grounds, must seek other ways to eke out a living.

Just beyond, you cross over Deschutes River and at that moment leave the Columbia Gorge National Scenic Area. However, if you like beige hills broken by dark brown cliffs, cut by a deep blue river, it's still scenic. Twenty miles from The Dalles, you approach the small town of **Biggs,** which doesn't offer much to visitors. However, two lures across the river, reached by taking exit 204, are worth abandoning Oregon for an afternoon. And never mind that this isn't a Washington guidebook.

What the Sam Hill?

We've already met Sam Hill, the man who conceived and helped fund the Columbia Gorge Highway. Across the river, we enter Sam Hill Country, 7,000 acres of tawny, rolling hills once owned by the wealthy idealist. On these slopes, he laid out a 34-acre town center with a church, hotel, offices, garages and shops. He hoped to create a utopian Quaker farm community. His venture failed; the town was abandoned and most of the buildings eventually burned.

However, Sam left two legacies. He built a replica of England's Stonehenge at the townsite, and he donated his river-view mansion four miles west for an art museum. It's remarkable for its beauty, its fine collection and its remote location. The nearest town is Biggs, not exactly a bastion of culture.

Once you've crossed the river, a right turn will take you a mile east to Stonehenge and a left will take you three miles west to Maryhill.

☺ **Stonehenge** ● *Grounds open daily 7 a.m. to 10 p.m.; free.* This replica is in much better shape than the original, built in 1350 B.C. on the Salisbury Plain of England. Commissioned by Hill as America's first World War I monument, it honors Klikitat County's 13 men who died in that conflict. This circle of massive stone columns was started on July 4, 1918, and completed in 1929. A pacifist, Hill thought the original Stonehenge was built as a temple of human sacrifice. (More likely, it was a primeval observatory.) He decided to replicate it on the site of his utopian town to honor those sacrificed in the war.

If you feel the need for a Stonehenge U.S.A. T-shirt, the Sam Hill Country Grocery is adjacent.

☺ **Maryhill Museum of Art** ● *35 Maryhill Museum Dr., Goldendale, WA 98620; (509) 773-3733. Open daily March 15 to November 15, 9 to 5. Adults $4, seniors $3.50, kids 6 to 16, $1.50.* Sam Hill commissioned his mansion in 1914, then when his town failed, he decided to turn it into a museum. It was dedicated by Queen Marie of Rumania in 1926, but not opened to the public until 1940. *Time Magazine* called it the "loneliest museum in the world." However, with its excellent collection of 19th century French decorative arts, Rodin

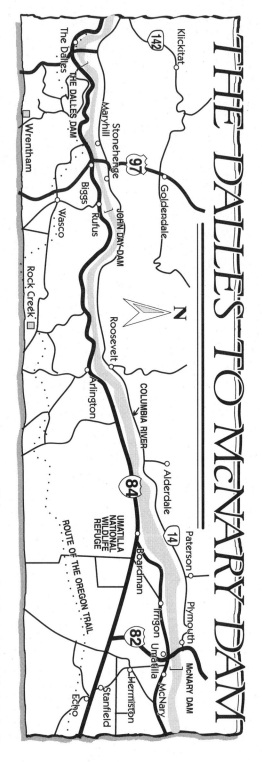

sculptures and working figures, Queen Marie memorabilia and Native American artifacts, it out-draws the major art museums of Portland and Seattle. The elaborate mansion and extensive grounds with a sweeping Columbia view are certainly worth the drive over from Biggs. It's apparently worth the drive from Portland and Seattle, as well.

Getting back on the I-84 track, you see yet another concrete blockage of the Columbia, about eight miles east of Biggs. It's reached by I-84 exit 109:

John Day Lock and Dam ● *P.O. Box 564, The Dalles, OR 97058; (503) 295-1181. Open for self-guiding tours daily 9 to 5.* Although it's not imposing in size or visitor facilities, John Day Dam is impressive in its output. Its 16 generators can crank out 2.16 million kilowatts of electricity—enough to power Seattle and Portland, with some left over. Following a self-guided tour, you enter over the fish ladder, pass the fish viewing windows, and wind up in the giant generator room. The big hummers are multi-colored, adding a nice touch. A few graphic panels in the power room discuss Native Americans of the area, power transmission and suggested side trips.

Several miles beyond the dam, the John Day River enters the Columbia. **John Day Recreation Area,** in a park-like setting at its mouth, has picnicking, swimming, fishing and a boat launch. This green wedge—obviously irrigated—offers a nice change from the tawny countryside.

As you press ever eastward, let your mind wander again and some of the basaltic monoliths lining the gorge begin to resemble fragments of Stonehenge. As you approach **Arlington,** the canyon widens into a shallow beige valley. Hop off the freeway at exit 137 for a quick peek at the town. Although it has no visitor lures, it's a nice little place, tucked into a tree-shaded side canyon. A huge grain loading facility at riverside betrays its *raison d entre.*

Beyond Arlington, the steel gray of sage joins the beige landscape as you enter the Eastern Oregon desert. The only thing green out here, other than planted trees, is the wetland of **Umatilla Wildlife Refuge** near Boardman. You are now 165 miles from Portland. As an indicator of the desolation of this area, just to the south is the **Boardman Bombing Range.**

Interstate 84 and the Columbia finally come to a parting as the freeway heads southeast toward Pendleton and into our Chapter 9. The river starts its swing northward into Washington.

If you'd like to see the last of Oregon's Columbia River dams—worth the trip only for curiosity's sake—take exit 168 and follow U.S. 173 northeast. You depart the desert and enter irrigated farmlands, passing through the drab towns of **Irrigon** and **Umatilla.** Just beyond Umatilla, follow a sign to the left to the Rodney Dangerfield of the Columbia's dams:

McNary Lock and Dam ● *Umatilla; (503) 922-3211. Visitor center open April through mid-September, 8:30 to 7.* Statistically impressive, with its 14 blue and white generators cranking out 1.12 kilowatts, McNary doesn't get much respect as a tourist attraction. Visitor facilities on the Oregon side are limited, consisting of the usual fish viewing windows, a few exhibits and the usual look down the long generator hall. A small bonus here: You can peek through windows into the dam's command center, looking a bit like Mission Control. Five other dams on the Snake and Clearwater rivers are monitored from here.

There are fish viewing windows on the Washington side as well. But then, you've probably already counted an awful lot of salmon.

TRIP PLANNER

WHEN TO GO ● Central Oregon is a year-around vacation area, with the best weather from late summer through early fall. Snow may temporarily close some of the mountain passes, and most of the Cascade Lakes Drive and Newberry Crater facilities are closed in winter. Summer comes late in the heights, so don't plan Cascade hiking much before mid-July.

WHAT TO SEE ● Old Shantiko; Smith Rock State Park; High Desert Museum in Bend; Newberry Volcanic National Monument attractions of Lava Butte, Lava River Cave, Paulina Peak and Big Obsidian Flow; the view from Dee Wright Observatory at McKenzie Pass; the headwaters of the Metolius; Fort Rock State Monument; Flavel Museum in Klamath Falls.

WHAT TO DO ● Prowl about old downtown Bend and Western-style Sisters; visit the planned resort community of Sunriver; Drive the Cascade Lakes and High Cascades loops; take the summer Summit Lift at Mount Bachelor Ski Area; hike along the Pacific Crest Trail from McKenzie Pass; watch the birdies at the Klamath National Wildlife Refuges.

Useful contacts

Bend Chamber of Commerce, 63085 N. Highway 97, Bend, OR 97701; (503) 503-382-3221.

Central Oregon Recreation Association & Reservation Center, P.O. Box 230, Bend, OR 97709; (800) 800-8334 outside Oregon or (503) 382-8334.

Deschutes National Forest, 1645 E. Highway 20, Bend, OR 97701; (503) 388-2715.

Klamath Falls Chamber of Commerce, 507 Main St., Klamath Falls, OR 97601; (503) 884-5193 or **Klamath County Department of Tourism,** 1451 Main St., Klamath Falls, OR 97601; (503) 884-0666.

La Pine Chamber of Commerce, 51470 Highway 97, Suite 5-A, La Pine, OR 97739; (503) 536-9771.

Madras/Jefferson County Chamber of Commerce, 366 Fifth St. (P.O. Box 616), Madras, OR 97741; (503) 475-2350 or 475-6975.

Newberry Volcanic National Monument, 58201 S. Highway 97, Bend, OR 97707; (503) 593-2421.

Redmond Chamber of Commerce, 106 SW Seventh St., Redmond, OR 97756; (503) 923-5191.

Sisters Area Chamber of Commerce, P.O. Box 476, Sisters, OR 97759; (503) 549-0251.

Central Oregon radio stations

KNOR-FM, 97.5, Bend—Christian music
KICE-FM, 100.7, Bend—country
KQAK-FM, 105.7, Bend—rock
KLRR-FM, 107.5, Redmond-Bend—light rock, top 40 and oldies
KCFC-FM, 90.3, Bend—National Public Radio
KSJJ-FM, 102.9, Redmond—country
KLAD-FM, 92.5, Klamath Falls—country
KAGO-FM, 99.5, Klamath Falls—adult contemporary
KSKF-FM, 90.9, Klamath Falls—National Public Radio
KRCO-AM, 690, Bend—country
KBMB-AM, 1110, Bend—talk radio and news
KBRB-AM, 1240, Redmond—country
KAGO-AM, 1150, Klamath Falls—adult contemporary
KLAD-AM, 960, Klamath Falls—country

Chapter Eight

THE MAGNIFICENT MIDDLE

Lakes, Lava Lands and luxury resorts

SNOW-CRESTED MOUNTAINS, lands of lava, pine forests, sparkling lakes and streams, and tourism promoters. They've all gotten together to create one of Oregon's most popular outdoor vacation destinations.

At a glimpse, the central Oregon playland may seem oddly located—off the main highways, away from the economic stream of things, on the far side of the Cascade Range. However, folks come to play, not to work. And they don't seem to mind the commute over mountain passes to get here.

Central Oregon occupies a wide swath extending south from the Columbia River to Klamath Falls, along the eastern slope of the Cascades. However, most of its visitor lures are focused around the communities of Bend, Redmond, Sunriver and Sisters. We shall focus our efforts there as well, while not neglecting the perimeter.

Topographically and climatically, central Oregon is a special place. It lies in the rainshadow of the Cascades, so the climate is clear and dry most of the year. In fact, the area receives so little precipitation—about 12 inches annually—that it's technically a desert. However, the eastern Cascade watershed supports a playland of lakes, streams and pine forests. Elevation around Bend is about 3,500 feet, providing cool summers and mild winters.

We like to call this wooded tableland at the foot of the mountains a "tree plain." Unlike the Coast Range and western Cascade forests with their thick undergrowth, central Oregon's woods are open and park-like. Don't expect much old growth forest. Easily accessible, this wooded tableland has been harvested in years past and virtually all of today's stands are second-growth.

Tree plains are nice for aimless strolling in summer and cross-country skiing in winter. Snowfall isn't heavy on the plains, but there's generally enough for a Nordic ski workout. Around Bend, annual snowfall is about three feet. It usually comes in two to three-inch layers and then melts before the next storm. If you want more, the snow-crested Cascades are next door. Mount Bachelor, rated as one of America's top ski resorts, has both downhill and cross country areas.

From Bend, just about any kind of climate and terrain are a short drive away. Head west and you're in a land of lakes, trout streams and high mountain passes. Go east a few miles and you're in a sagebrush desert, on the northwestern edge of the Great Basin. In the middle is the tableland mix of golden-barked ponderosa pines and gray sage. Scattered through it all are black lava flows, cindercones, lava tubes and imposing calderas.

COLUMBIA RIVER TO BEND

Central Oregon's Main Street is U.S. Highway 97, which runs south from Biggs on the Columbia River, through Redmond and Bend to Klamath Falls. From Bend south, it spends a good part of its time in the 1.6 million-acre Deschutes National Forest.

However, there's little forest in evidence as you head south from **Biggs** on Highway 97. This region is quite far from the eastern Cascade foothills, so the terrain is dry, suited more to wild grasses than ponderosa pines. After passing through the hamlets of **Wasco, Moro** and **Grass Valley,** you enter the near-ghost town of **Shantiko.** Those grasslands figure very much into its past.

These vast prairies were home to thousands of cattle and sheep late in the 19th century. Here, some of the West's last—and most violent—range wars were raged. Unlike the plot of many old Western movies, the sheepmen won.

Shantiko dates from 1900, when a spur of the Columbia Southern Railroad was extended down from the gorge to haul all those woolies to market. Until then, the only settlers in the area were at nearby Cross Hollow. A tent city emerged at the rail terminus and Cross Hollow was abandoned. Shantiko's name comes from the Native Americans' pronunciation of the last name of August Scherneckau. He was the operator of a Cross Hollow store and stage stop. Shantiko bustled for a spell, with several stores, a school, city jail and at least 13 saloons. From the turn of the century until 1911, this was the largest wool shipping center in America. Then the railroad was extended south to Bend, which grabbed most of the shipping business, and Shantiko began to fade.

It faded almost to nothing until Jean and Dorothy Farrell from Eugene took a fancy to the town in 1985. They purchased the tired old **Shantiko Hotel** in 1985 and began restoration. A few other folks have come to open boutiques and shops in the handful of weathered wooden buildings that still survive. Although hardly a boom town, this hamlet of 25 people offers a rustic break from the otherwise uneventful drive through this area. The Shantiko Hotel's lobby has been handsomely restored, with a round settee and a couple of chandeliers adding nice touches. A gift and antique shop occupies one side of the lobby and a polished oak bannister leads to several upstairs rooms.

☺ Shantiko Hotel ● ⌒ $$

P.O. Box 115, Shantiko, OR 97057; (503) 489-3441 or (503) 489- 3415. Couples $55, singles $45, attractive bridal suite at $85. MC/VISA. While not

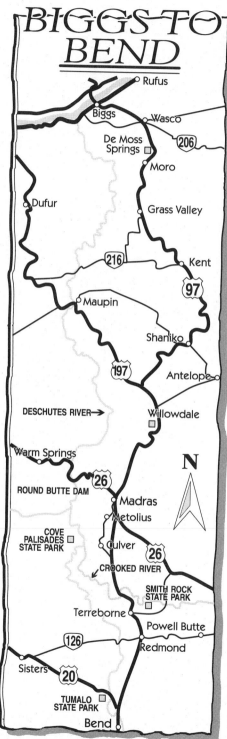

elegant, rooms are spotlessly clean with period furnishings, thick carpeting and new drapes. The **Shantiko Hotel Café** serves old timey American fare such as chicken fried steak and pork chops, daily from 7 a.m. to 10 p.m. A few farm implements decorate the walls.

Just down the street is the **Shantiko Corral RV Park,** with a few unshaded gravel sites, water and electric hookups, showers and a laundromat. Sites are $13 with hookups and $8 without; make arrangements at the hotel.

Ron and Mary Oens have located their stagecoach-building firm in town, and they give rides in the summer; $3 for adults and $2 for kids under 12. Contact them at P.O. Box 126, Shantiko, OR 97057; (503) 489-3431.

The dry prairie country continues for some distance south. Watch for a turnout on your right, where a sign identifies the far-away peaks of the Cascades, which are beginning to come into view. As you top a crest outside the town of **Madras,** their snow-streaked heights begin to dominate the western horizon. As you continue southward, you'll learn to identify this procession of volcanic peaks: Mount Jefferson, Mount Washington, the Three Sisters, the craggy remnants of Broken Top and the conical flanks of Mount Bachelor.

Madras is a tidy farming community with an old fashioned business district lining the highway. The **Madras-Jefferson County Chamber of Commerce** occupies a downtown storefront at Fifth and D streets, open weekdays 9 to 5; (503) 475-2350. You'll need to shift east a block on D to reach it, since southbound 97 is on one-way Fourth Street. You can pick up information on the **Mount Jefferson Wilderness** to the west.

The **Jefferson County Museum** is located upstairs in the brick Jefferson County Courthouse, around the corner at 503 D Street. Hours are Wednesday-Friday 2 to 5, summers only; (503) 475-3808. The museum is something of a clutter, with old kitchen appliances, farm tools, slot machines and furnished room displays. One is a combination lawyer's office and optometrist. Does this suggest that justice isn't blind?

A drive northwest from Madras on U.S. 26 will take you through the **Warm Springs Indian Reservation**. You can learn about the tribe and buy authentic Native American gifts and other curios at the **Warm Springs Visitor Information Center and Gift Shop,** (503) 553-1161. You might like to spend the night at an attractive resort run by the tribe:

☺ Kah-Nee-Ta Resort ● ⌒⌒⌒ $$$$

P.O. Box K, Warm Springs, OR 97761; (800) 831-0100 or (503) 553-1112. Couples $80 to $120, singles $80 to $95. Major credit cards. Attractive natural-wood resort set against a bluff in dry, wooded hills. Comfortable rooms have classic Indian motif, and feature TV movies, room phones, and balconies with mountain views. Some rooms have spa tubs and fireplaces. Pool, sauna, spa, lighted tennis courts, putting green and miniature golf, playground, exercise room, jogging track and rental bicycles.

About 18 miles south of Madras, pause at **Ogden Scenic Wayside,** just across a bridge that spans the narrow, steep-walled canyon of the Crooked River. From a stone wall built right on the edge, you can stare dizzily down into the 200-foot crevasse. Just beyond, you enter **Deschutes County,** which encloses much of the central Oregon recreation area.

☺ If you look east from here, you'll see the craggy palisades of **Smith Rock State Park,** which occupies a particularly dramatic section of Crooked River Canyon. To reach it, turn east at the tiny town of **Terrebone**, then follow park signs through farm country, around a couple of twists and turns. Stay alert, or you might overshoot. The final turn to the park is a left onto Crooked River Drive at the **Juniper Junction** sign. Before entering the preserve, stop at Juniper Junction and pick up a park map. It's a rustic shop devoted mostly to climbing gear, since Smith Rock is a major rock climbing area. You can get a Gatorade and light snack here; try the excellent huckleberry ice cream.

Inside the park, trails run alongside the Crooked River that flows past the base of the broken, craggy canyon wall. Some paths crawl up the wall itself. For a good afternoon workout, follow the aptly-named Misery Trail two miles up to a ridge for awesome views of the countryside. It's so steep that it consists mostly of a series of steps. As you huff and puff upward, you'll likely see rock-climbers defying gravity as they crawl spider-like up sheer faces. If you want to join them, you can sign up for the **Smith Rock Climbing School** here; (503) 548-0749.

South of Smith Rock, you enter **Redmond** (population 8,000), 16 miles north of Bend. Although Redmond is the home of the airport that brings the visitors to central Oregon, Bend gets most of the tourist glory. However, it suffers no inferiority complex. While most visitors hop off their planes, pick up their rental cars or resort shuttles and hurry south, Redmond does quite nicely as a farming and wood products manufacturing community.

The town offers another advantage: You often can find less expensive motel rooms here. And it's a handy alternative if you can't find a room in Bend—not an unusual condition on a summer weekend. It's also a good staging area for planning your approach to the recreation areas, since you can load up on brochures and maps at the **Redmond Chamber of Commerce** at 106 SW Seventh St. It's open weekdays 8 to 5; (503) 923-6442. To reach it, turn right from Highway 97 (Sixth Street) onto Angler Street and drive a block to Seventh.

From Redmond, you can follow State Highway 126 west to the cowboy-style mountain town of **Sisters,** or continue south on U.S. 97 to Bend. If you choose the Sisters route and you have kids aboard, pause at **Operation Santa Claus** reindeer farm. It's three miles west at 4355 W. Highway 126, Redmond; (503) 548-8910; free admission. As the name suggests, it's a Christmas-theme reindeer park, so say "hello" to Rudolph.

If you choose the Bend route, your diversion is the **World Famous Fantastic Museum,** on the southern edge of Redmond at 3290 S. Highway 97; (503) 923-0000. It's open daily 10 to 5; adults $5 and kids under 12, $2. Behind the Western façade and the over-stated name is a collection of antiques, assorted artifacts, sports memorabilia and stuff from the stars. Note the Bing Crosby collection, Liz Taylor's *Cleopatra* dressing room and JFK's 1938 Cadillac.

Continuing southward, you'll soon enter the spreading suburbs of Bend. Just beyond the Highway 97-20 junction is the **Oregon Welcome Center,** housed in a modern curved-roof building on your right. It's open Monday-Saturday 9 to 5 and Sunday 11 to 3; (503) 382-3221. Operated by the Bend Chamber of Commerce, it's one of the most efficiently run and well equipped visitor centers in the state. Walk among the nicely displayed brochure racks, watch the ongoing videos, chat with the friendly folks at the desk and learn all about it. This area is *serious* about tourism.

The region's visitor lures can be divided into three segments:

Cascade Lakes Drive: An 87-mile drive into the Cascade foothills takes you past a string of lakes and reservoirs, popular for swimming, boating, fishing and shore-hiking. It also passes the Mount Bachelor Ski Area, which runs a summer sightseeing lift.

Newberry National Volcanic Monument: The cindercones, lava tubes and other volcanic attractions south of Bend recently were gathered into America's newest national monument.

High Cascades loop: This drive takes you from Sisters over two mountain passes, to trailheads of the Pacific Crest Trail and to the Metolius River Recreation Area.

Before we begin, let's have a look at Bend and its two neighbors, Sunriver and Sisters. Sunriver is a planned community about 16 miles south. It offers a lodge, restaurants, shopping center and extensive recreational facilities. Sisters is a rustic-chic wanna-be-cowboy town 21 miles northeast of Bend, enjoying a dramatic location at the base of its namesake peaks.

Bend

Population: 22,000   **Elevation: 3,628 feet**

Forget the spotted owl. Business is booming in this former lumbering town, thanks to its growing reputation as a leading recreational and retirement center. Bend's prosperity is evident in the gentrification of the downtown area with its boutiques, galleries and restaurants, and in the nearby luxury resorts. During the 1980s, Deschutes was the state's fastest-growing county, and it shows little sign of slowing. Greater Bend has 48,000 residents and Deschutes County has nearly 80,000; they're the largest town and county east of the Cascades.

If there's a negative to all this, it's the growing string of service stations, fast food cafès, motels and mini-malls extending two miles in either direction along Highway 97. Driving from one side of the business end of Bend to another is becoming a chore. But never mind that. You aren't here to poke along the highway, looking for a Big Mac or hot wings. You're here to enjoy a wooded, volcanic, lake-studded recreation area.

Although Bend's suburbs are suffering new-age spread, the old downtown area is prim, compact and walkable. Many of its structures date back to the turn of the century and most are nicely preserved. The town was founded by rancher A.M. Drake on a kink in the Deschutes River in 1900. It was named for "Farewell Bend Ranch" that served as a hospitality center for travelers. The post office department dropped "Farewell" when it was incorporated in 1905. The coming of the rails in 1911 and lumber mills a few years later assured the town's future prosperity.

Exploring downtown

After leaving the welcome center, fork to the right at the Bend floral display, which puts you onto Division Street. By following Business 97 signs, you end up on Wall Street. About the time you cross Oregon Street, start looking for parking because you're in the middle of downtown.

The jewel of downtown is **Drake Park** with its **Mirror Pond,** a small lake created by a diversion dam on the Deschutes River. It's a placid place of green grass, quacking ducks and geese (watch where you step), a playground and an occasional picnic table. The park hosts an arts, crafts and food market the third Saturday of the month, from May through October; (503) 382-7906.

Bend's 12-block-square business area is clustered around the park, so everything is within an easy walk. Old masonry and brick buildings house a good assortment of boutiques, specialty shops, galleries and restaurants. Bond Street, two blocks up and parallel to the pond, is something of a restaurant row. A bright colored brochure, *Downtown on Mirror Pond,* available at the chamber and from some merchants, is a handy guide to this area.

☺ A required stop in your exploration is the **Great Harvest Bread Company** at 835 NW Bond St., (503) 389-2888. This unusual bakery features an open kitchen, where you can see and smell the savory multi-grain creations a-baking. If you *really* want fresh bread or rolls, a chalkboard indicates when the next batch is emerging from the oven. When it does emerge, one of the friendly bakers slices off chunks and passes them out to customers. Talk about sealing a sale! Try the marionberry cinnamon rolls, one of Bend's more savory creations.

The area's repository of yesterday sits on a grassy knoll at the corner of Wall and Idaho streets, on the southwest side of downtown:

Des Chutes Historical Center ● *129 NW Idaho St.; (503) 389-1813. Wednesday-Saturday 1 to 4:30. Free; donations appreciated.* The museum is housed in the three-story cut stone Reid School, built in 1914. Although displays aren't professionally done, they're uncluttered and carefully arranged.

Downtown Bend, viewed from Pilot Butte, is spread over a broad tree plain, with the snowy crests of the Three Sisters on the horizon.   **— Betty Woo Martin**

You'll see the typical pioneer artifacts, a large doll collection, some interesting turn-of-the-century appliances, early-day photos and such.

For a nice overview of Bend and a heroic panorama of all those volcanic peaks, head for **Pilot Butte.** It's a volcanic cindercone on the eastern edge of town. To reach it, follow Greenwood (Highway 20 East) from downtown, crossing Highway 97. After about a mile, watch for the Pilot Butte sign, peel off to the left and spiral to the top. From here, the views gallop off in all directions. You'll see the Cascades on the western horizon, the flat tree plain and the townsite of Bend at your feet, lava flows and wooded cindercones of Newberry National Monument to the south and the Great Basin desert to the east.

Six miles south of town, just off Highway 97, is one of the finest museums in Western America:

☺ **The High Desert Museum** ● *59800 S. Highway 97, Bend, OR 97702; (503) 382-4754. Daily 9 to 5. Adults $5.50, seniors $5, kids 5 to 12, $2.75.* This is what a museum should be—a place to learn, to enjoy and to relax. Located on 150 wooded acres adjacent to Deschutes National Forest, the state-of-the art facility is devoted to the study of the Columbia River Plateau and the Great Basin Desert. Started just over ten years ago, it has become one of the best indoor-outdoor museums in the nation. Think of it as a Northwest version of the famous Arizona-Sonora Desert Museum in Tucson.

Exhibits cover the geology, geography, flora, fauna and human history of the region. Focal point of the indoor section is the recently-opened Earle A. Chiles Center. Its Spirit of the West exhibit takes you on a sunrise to sunset stroll through the settlement of the West. History comes alive with realistic dioramas and sound effects symbolizing the Native Americans, fur traders, wagon train pioneers, gold miners, cowboys and community builders. Other indoor displays cover the geology, history, flora and fauna of the area, including exceptionally well-done changing exhibits.

Outside, you can stroll along shady paths and watch river otters at play, porcupines at rest and birds of prey on the alert. Wildlife programs are presented several times a day. Also, you can greet scores of volunteer chipmunks and ground squirrels who feel right at home in this realistic habitat. Other exhibits include a chuckwagon, 19th century lumber mill, logging displays and a settlers cabin where costumed docents may be carding and spinning wool.

If you'd like to admire the area's wide-open desert sky, drive 30 miles southeast on Highway 20 to Millican, and follow signs to **Pine Mountain Observatory.** Operated by the University of Oregon, it has several telescopes, including the largest in the Northwest. Public viewing often is permitted, so call (503) 382-8331 to see what's on tap in the heavens.

WHERE TO DINE

☺ **Café Paradisio** ● ΔΔ $

945 NW Bond St.; (503) 385-5931. American; wine and beer. Monday-Thursday 9 to 11, Friday 9 to midnight, Saturday 10 to midnight, closed Sunday. Very appealing coffee house in a grand old building; overstuffed chairs and sofas, wood paneling and ceiling fans. Light fare ranges from vegetarian manicotti and quiche to various salads and sandwiches. It pours usual range of espressos and mochas, plus several wines by the glass; sidewalk tables available.

Café Sante ● ΔΔ $

718 NW Franklin; (503) 383-3530. American; no alcohol. Daily 7 a.m. to 3 p.m. Smart, modern deli café in teal blues and beiges, across from Mirror Pond. The menu focuses on natural fare, including low fat and sugar-free items. It's good lunch stop; try the New Zealand patties with egg whites and hash browns, or nachos and fresh salads.

☺ **Deschutes Brewery & Public House** ● ΔΔ $

1044 Bond St.; (503) 382-9242. Brewpub; Monday-Thursday 11 to 11:30, Friday-Saturday 11 to 12:30 a.m., Sunday noon to 10. MC/VISA. Lively brick-front pub featuring its own hearty beers and ales; a popular local hangout. Spicy "brew food" includes German sausages and garlic burgers.

East Wind ● Δ $

1600 NE Third St. (Highway 97); (503) 389-6236. Chinese-American; wine and beer. Daily 7 to 2:30 and 4:30 to 9. MC/VISA. Good spot for a cheap fill-up; typical Formica café that looks more American diner than Chinese. Menu ranges from spicy Szechuan and mild Cantonese to American salads and sandwiches.

Guiseppi's Ristorante ● ΔΔΔ $$

932 NW Bond St.; (503) 389-8899. Italian; full bar service. Tuesday-Thursday 5 to 9:30, Friday-Saturday 5 to 10, Sunday 5 to 9. Major credit cards. Classy looking cafe with brick interior walls and candle-lit tables; very popular locally. Start your meal with mozzarella bread sticks, then try Northern Italian specials such as baked fish filets in cream sauce and vermouth, bay shrimp and artichokes or sautéed chicken breasts with sherry, rosemary and artichokes. *Bueno appetito!*

☺ McKenzie's Bar & Grill • ∆∆∆ $$
1033 NW Bond St.; (503) 388-3891. American; full bar service. Monday-Thursday 5:30 to 9:30, Friday-Saturday 5:30 to 10, Sunday 5 to 9. Major credit cards. A handsome fugitive from San Francisco's financial district with dark woods, curved decorative ceiling and a proper men's club atmosphere. Versatile menu ranges from steaks to smoked chicken breast and salmon.

McGrath's Publick Fish House • ∆∆ $$
Bend River Mall (north end, off Highway 97); (503) 388-4555. American, mostly seafood; full bar service. Monday-Thursday 11 to 10, Friday-Saturday 11 to 11, Sunday 9 to 10. Major credit cards. Nautical cafè specializing in mesquite broiled seafood, plus pasta and steak/seafood or chicken/seafood combo dishes. Large salad bar; seafood market.

Mexicali Rose • ∆∆ $
301 NE Franklin Ave.; (503) 389-0149. Mexican; full bar service. Sunday-Thursday 5 to 10, Friday-Saturday 5 to 10:30. MC/VISA. Very stylish cafè with carved woods and modern Mexican paintings within a bold lava rock building. It offers the usual Mexican dishes, plus more contemporary Southwestern fare. Very highly regarded locally.

☺ Pine Tavern Restaurant • ∆∆∆ $$
967 Brooks St.; (503) 382-5581. Varied menu; full bar service. Lunch Monday-Saturday 11:30 to 2:30, dinner nightly 5:30 to 10. Major credit cards. A local institution since 1919, housed in a woodsy chalet-style building near Mirror Pond; clubby English-American interior. Eclectic menu wanders from pork kabobs and Kona chicken teriyaki to "Ragin' Cajun" and prime rib. Sourdough scones are a specialty.

☺ Tumalo Feed Company • ∆∆∆ $$
64619 W. Highway 20, Tumalo (3.5 miles west of Bend); (503) 382-2202. American; full bar service. Monday-Saturday 4 to 10, Sunday 9 to 1 and 3 to 9. MC/VISA, DISC. Western-style steak house and saloon in a bright yellow and white false-front building on the highway to Sisters. Meals are enough to dent your saddle; entrèes include onion rings and salsa, fried potatoes, beans, garlic bread and dessert.

Yoko's • ∆∆ $
301 NW Bond St.; (503) 382-2999. Japanese; wine and beer. Lunch Tuesday-Friday 11:30 to 2, dinner Tuesday-Saturday 5 to 9:30, closed Sunday-Monday. MC/VISA, DISC. A rather attractive, modestly priced cafè with Japanese-modern dècor. Try the *tonkatsu* (lightly breaded pork cutlet in teriyaki sauce); also the usual teriyakis and tempuras, plus a sushi bar.

WHERE TO SLEEP

Bend Riverside Motel • ⌂⌂⌂ $$ ∅
1565 NW Hill St., Bend, OR 97701; (800) 284-2363. Sleeping rooms from $45, mini-suites $65 to $75, suites from $95. Major credit cards. Attractive motel on the Deschutes River; suites have river views, full kitchens, some microwaves. All units have TV movies, room phones. Pool, spa and sauna.

Bend Super 8 Motel • ⌂⌂ $$$ ∅
1275 Highway 97, Bend, OR 97701; (800) 800-8000 or (503) 388-6888. Couples $51.88 to $59.88, singles $42.88 to $46.88. Major credit cards. Well-

maintained 79-unit motel with TV movies and room phones; indoor pool and spa.

Best Western Entrada Lodge • ⌂⌂ $$$$ ∅

19221 Century Dr., Bend, OR 97702; (800) 528-1234 or (503) 382-4080. Couples and singles $55 to $75, suite $69 to $89. Major credit cards. Extremely inviting lodge on highway to Cascade lakes; TV movies, room phones; pool, spa, coin laundry, ski lockers. **Restaurant** serves breakfast only from 7 to 10 a.m.

☺ Black Butte Ranch • ⌂⌂⌂ $$$$

Highway 20 (P.O. Box 8000), Black Butte Ranch, OR 97759; (800) 452-7455) or (503) 595-6211. Couples $70 to $130, kitchenettes $115 to $170. MC/VISA, AMEX, DISC. Elegantly rustic resort set on a mountain-rimmed meadow off Highway 20 between Bend and Sisters. Eighty rooms and condos with TV, room phones and all resort amenities. Two 18-hole golf courses, tennis courts, four swimming pools, riding stables, children's rec center, basketball court, paved bike paths and hiking trails. **Dining Room** and informal **Honkers Cafè** serve American fare from 8 a.m. to 8 p.m,; dinners $12.45 to $25; full bar service.

Chalet Motel • ⌂ $$ ∅

510 SE Third St. (Highway 97), Bend, OR 97702; (503) 382-6124. Couples $40 to $45, singles $28 to $35, kitchenettes $35 to $50. MC/VISA, AMEX, DISC. A 22-unit motel with TV and room phones.

Hampton Inn-Bend • ⌂⌂ $$$ ∅

15 NE Butler Rd., Bend, OR 97701; (800) 426-7866 or (503) 388-4114. Couples $60 to $64, singles $52 to $56. Major credit cards. Attractive 99-unit inn with TV movies, room phones, free continental breakfast. Pool and spa.

Holiday Motel • ⌂⌂ $$ ∅

880 E. Third St. (Highway 97), Bend, OR 97702; (800) 252-0121 or (503) 382-4620. Couples $32 to $38, singles $28 to $32, suites $65 to $95. Major credit cards. Simple, well-kept 25-room motel with TV movies, room phones; spa, free continental breakfast.

☺ Inn of the Seventh Mountain • ⌂⌂⌂ $$$$

19717 Mt. Bachelor Drive (P.O. Box 1207), Bend, OR 97709; (800) 452-6810 or (503) 382-8711. Couples and singles $64 to $106, suites and efficiencies $94 to $148. Major credit cards. Full-service luxury resort seven miles west of Bend on the Cascade Lakes Highway. Rooms and condos with TV, VCRs, phones and all amenities; several efficiencies. Two pools, kids' pool, sauna, spa, 18-hole golf course, playground, tennis courts, jogging track. Extensive recreation program (see "Activities" below) including rental bikes, horseback riding and whitewater rafting. It's the closest major inn to Mount Bachelor ski area, and it offers a winter ski shuttle.

The Riverhouse • ⌂⌂ $$$ ∅

3075 N. Highway 97, Bend, OR 97701; (800) 547-3928 or (503) 389-3111. Couples $52 to $63, singles $46 to $55, kitchenettes $65 to $75, suites $75 to $150. Major credit cards. Attractive 220-room resort with TV movies, room phones; two pools, spas, saunas; coin laundry. Eighteen hole golf course adjacent. **Riverhouse Restaurant, Tito's Mexican Restaurant** and **Poolside Cafe** serve American and Mexican fare from 7 a.m.; dinners $11.50 to $20; full bar service; live entertainment.

Rock Springs Guest Ranch ● ⌂⌂⌂ $$$$$ ∅

64201 Tyler Rd., Bend, OR 97701; (800) 225-DUDE or (503) 382-1957. Weekly rates in summer from $1,195 per person double occupancy including all meals, daily rates during certain off-season periods from $170 for two, including two meals. Major credit cards. A handsomely rustic guest ranch nine miles northwest of Bend, offering extensive riding program, swimming pool, spa, tennis, volleyball, hiking and fishing. Guest accommodations are 26 private cabins with fireplaces, refrigerators and wet bars. Western and regional Northwest fare served to guests in the lodge.

Sonoma Lodge ● ⌂⌂ $$ ∅

450 SE Third St. (Highway 97), Bend, OR 97701; (503) 382-4891. Couples $32 to $52, singles $26 to $36, kitchenettes $30 to $69. Major credit cards. Nicely-landscaped 18-room motel with TV, room phones; free continental breakfast; some mini-kitchens with microwaves.

Bed & breakfast inns

Farewell Bend B&B ● ⌂⌂ $$$ ∅

29 NW Greeley (near Division), Bend, OR 97701; (503) 382-4374. Couples $65 to $75, singles $55. Three units with private baths; full breakfast. MC/VISA, AMEX. A 1920s Dutch Colonial home with light contemporary furnishings; handmade quilts and terry robes. TV, VCR with film library and stereo in living room. Four blocks from downtown historic area.

☺ Laura House Bed & Breakfast ● ⌂⌂⌂ $$$ ∅

640 NW Congress (at Louisiana), Bend, OR 97701; (503) 388-4064. Couples $60 to $65, singles $50 to $55. Five units with private baths; full breakfast. MC/VISA, AMEX. Bend's first bed & breakfast, fashioned from a large, three-story turn-of-the-century home overlooking Mirror Pond. Rooms individually decorated, with theme furnishings; one with a waterbed. Within walking distance of Bend's historic district.

Mill Inn Bed & Breakfast ● ⌂⌂ $$ ∅

642 NW Colorado (at Bono Street), Bend, OR 97701; (503) 389-9198. Couples $35 to $44, singles $15 to $50. Ten rooms with private baths; full breakfast. MC/VISA, AMEX. Renovated 1917 lumber mill boarding house done in rustic white pine; individual décor in guest rooms. Common area fireplace, outdoor spa, ski and bike storage; laundry, refrigerator privileges.

WHERE TO CAMP

Bend KOA ● *63615 N. Highway 97 (three miles north), Bend, OR 97701; (503) 382-7728. RV and tent sites; full hookups $15. Reservations accepted; major credit cards.* Some shaded sites and pull-throughs, grassy tent area; full hookups, cable TV, showers, coin laundry, pool, fishing pond, mini-mart and deli, game room, horseshoes.

Crown Villa RV Park ● *60801 Brosterhous Rd., Bend, OR 97702; (503) 388-1131. RV sites only; $15 to $22. MC/VISA.* New RV park with attractively landscaped grounds, paved streets, covered barbecue area. Full hookups, some pull-throughs, showers, coin laundry, fishing pond, horseshoes, rec room and rec field, playground. Two miles east of Highway 97 in south Bend (turn onto Brosterhous Road opposite Division Street).

Deschutes National Forest ● *c/o 1645 E. Highway 20, Bend, OR 97701; (503) 388-2715.* Dozens of campgrounds are scattered throughout the national forest; sites are $6 to $8 a night, with flush or pit potties. Most are to the west and south, along the Cascade Lakes Highway.

Tumalo State Park ● *Highway 20 (five miles northwest); (503) 388-6055. RV and tent sites, from $13. No credit cards or reservations.* Shaded sites near the Deschutes River; full hookups, picnic tables and barbecue pits, swimming areas, fishing and hiking trails.

Sunriver

Population: 1,000   **Elevation: approx. 3,500 feet**

Sunriver ranks as one of the most idealistic planned communities in America, and it is certainly Oregon's most complete resort. Development began several decades ago when a visionary-investor picked up several thousand acres of forest land from the Army's Camp Elliott. It had been used to train combat engineers during World War II.

However, don't look for empty quonset huts. Sunriver has evolved into an independent community with its own zip code, water and sewer system, fire department, shopping center, a prep school and private airport with a 5,500-foot paved, lighted runway. Thirty miles of walking and biking trails weave among the trees, linking wooded lots where hundreds of vacation and year-around homes have been built. To ensure environmental correctness, residents must use materials and colors that blend into the forest.

Sunriver has become one of Oregon's most popular year-around vacation spots. Lodge rooms and condos are listed below, and vacationers can rent individual homes as well.

From a recreational standpoint, there isn't much that Sunriver *doesn't* offer. Resort facilities include swimming pools, spas, saunas, tennis courts, jogging track, racquetball, fishing, nature programs and tours, bicycles rentals, a new miniature golf course and two 18-hole courses. The North Course has been rated among the top 25 in the country by *Golf Digest*. The **Sunriver Nature Center** offers exhibits, programs and tours.

Sunriver Village shopping center has a large supermarket, sixty shops, boutiques and restaurants, professional offices and—of course—several real estate offices. In winter, the walking/biking trails become cross-country ski trails. A patio in Sunriver Village shopping center is flooded to form an outdoor skating rink, and a ski shuttle is provided to the Mount Bachelor winter sports area.

WHERE TO SLEEP & EAT

☺ Sunriver Lodge ● △△△△ $$$$

At Sunriver Resort, P.O. Box 3609, Sunriver, OR 97707; (800) 547-3922 or (503) 593-1221. Bedroom units $87 to $110, suites $141 to $170, suites with kitchens $141 to $375; also family condos. MC/VISA. Central Oregon's classiest resort facility. Lodge rooms, suites and condos with TV, some VCRs, phones. Some units with balconies, loft bedrooms and fireplaces.

☺ The Meadows Restaurant ● △△△△ $$$

In Sunriver Lodge; (503) 593-1221, ext. 4487. American; full bar service. Dinner nightly 6 to 10. Major credit cards. Elegant lodge dining room with wood paneling, plush seats and tall picture windows offering views of forest

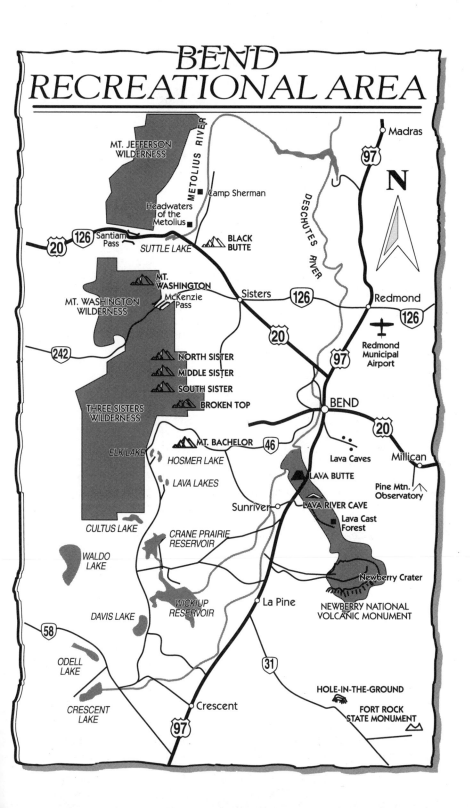

BEND RECREATIONAL AREA

and meadow. Menu offerings include fresh seafood, lamb with feta crust, prawns with spicy tomato chutney and various wild game dishes.

The Provision Company • ΔΔΔ $$

In Sunriver Lodge; (503) 593-1221, ext. 4487. American; full bar service. Daily 6:30 a.m. to 10 p.m. Major credit cards. Creative dècor, fashioned as an upscale general store with old canned goods displayed on stylized grocers' shelves; bright and airy with picture window views. The menu is a mix of basic American and pasta dishes. Outdoor deck seating is available.

Marcello's Italian Cuisine • ΔΔΔ $$

Sunriver Village at N. Ponderosa Road and Beaver Drive; (503) 593-8300. Italian; full bar service. Nightly 5 to 9:30. MC/VISA. The best of several restaurants in Sunriver Village shopping center. Lofted ceilings and brick dividers create a kind of "forest modern" look. It features a wide range of Italian entrèes, plus an active pizza oven.

Sisters

Population: 700   **Elevation: 3,100 feet**

Sisters was established in the 1880s as a way station on the old Santiam Wagon Road over the Cascades. Occupying a transition zone in the foothills of its namesake mountains, it enjoyed moderate prosperity as a lumbering and ranching area.

In recent years, it has become a Cowboy Carmel, with boutiques, galleries, Western wear stores, restaurants and the requisite yogurt shops. They're housed in Western style buildings, fronted by board sidewalks. Shops bear the usual cutesy names—Plumb Pretty, Wild Hare, Kitchen Post, True Confections, Scents & Non-Scents and Log Cabin Grocery, which is housed in one.

Although the town appears to be a survivor of the old West, most of the buildings are new. Only Hotel Sisters hearkens back to earlier days; it's now a country style restaurant. The **Sisters Area Chamber of Commerce** occupies one of these Old West store fronts. It's on the left as you approach from Bend, half a block beyond Hotel Sisters. Hours are 9 to 5 weekdays; (503) 549-0251 or 549-4253.

Sisters may be deliberately touristy and maybe even corny, but one can't fault the setting. It presents a particularly pleasing picture with its Western-style architecture and surrounding meadows and forests, backgrounded by the snow-streaked Three Sisters. Several working ranches and a couple of ranch resorts occupy the surrounding hills. Visitors can hire riding horses or sign on for pack trips into the high Cascades. (See "Activities" below.)

WHERE TO DINE

Gallery Restaurant and Bar • Δ $

230 Cascade (at Ash); (503) 549-2631. American; full bar service. Daily 6 a.m. to 9 p.m. MC/VISA. Simple family-style cafe serving large portions of down-home entrèes such as chicken fried steak, breaded veal cutlets and pork chops.

☺ Sisters Hotel Restaurant • ΔΔΔ $$

Fir and Cascade; (503) 549-7427. American; full bar service. Weekdays 11 to 9:30, weekends 11 to 10. MC/VISA. Oldstyle restaurant housed in a wood frame 1914 hotel, with wainscotting, tulip chandeliers, bentwood chairs and such. The menu is typical American steak, salmon, chicken and items barbe-cued, plus a few Mexican dishes. The adjacent saloon is a watering hole right out of the Old West. You expect the guys in black hats to push through the bat wing doors at any moment.

Southern Lites Mexican Restaurant ● △△ $

Spruce and Cascade; (503) 549-8940. Mexican; wine, beer and margaritas. Daily 11 to 9. MC/VISA. Simple, appealing cafe with knotty pine walls and a few Latino trappings. Creative menu offers specialties such as Yucatan chicken with cinnamon, tomatoes and molè, tamale pie with cornmeal crust, and chicken enchilada casserole. Most dinners under $12. Outdoor dining.

York's Cattle Crossing Restaurant ● △△ $$

497 W. Highway 20 (in Threewinds Shopping Center); (503) 549-9514. American; full bar service. Daily 7 a.m. to 10 p.m. MC/VISA. Bright, open res-taurant with Western-modern dining room, just west of downtown. Basic American menu lists steaks, chops and chickens. Dinners from mid-teens down; several under $10.

For quick bites, try the country style **Ranch House Deli** with indoor and outdoor tables at 310 E. Hood St. (549-8911); the **Depot Deli** at 351 W. Cascade (549-2572); and for you early risers, **Sisters Bakery** at 120 Cascade, open from 5 a.m. to 6 p.m.

WHERE TO SLEEP

Sisters appears to be primarily a day-use area. For all of its shops and such, it has curiously few lodgings.

Best Western Ponderosa Lodge ● △△ $$$

505 W. Highway 20 (P.O. Box 218), Sisters, OR 97759; (800) 528-1234 or (503) 549-1234. Couples $55, singles $50. Major credit cards. Nicely-land-scaped wooded grounds; large rooms with TV, phones; pool, spa.

Silver Spur Motel ● △ $$

West Cascade St., P.O. Box 415, Sisters, OR 97759; (503) 549-6591. Cou-ples $35. MC/VISA. Small motel with TV and room phones; just beyond downtown shops.

Sisters Motor Lodge ● △ $$

600 Cascade St. (P.O. Box 28), Sisters, OR 97759; (503) 549-2551. Cou-ples $39 to $45, singles $35.50. MC/VISA. Small, well-kept motel at west end near shops; TV and room phones.

WHERE TO CAMP

Circle Five RV Park ● *East edge of town on Highway 20 just west of Highway 126 junction (P.O. Box 1360), Sisters, OR 97759; (503) 549-3861. RV and tent sites; $15.50. Reservations accepted.* Small park with full hook-ups, shaded sites, some pull-throughs, coin laundry, barbecues.

Deschutes National Forest ● *c/o Sisters Ranger Station, P.O. Box 249, Sisters, OR 97759; (503) 549-2111.* Campgrounds abound in the Cascades above Sisters, for $6 to $8 a night, with flush or pit potties. The nearest is **Cold Spring**, on the McKenzie Highway (Route 242), two miles west.

Sisters City Park ● *Off Highway 20, east side of town; (503) 549-6022. RV and tent sites; no hookups $8. No reservations or credit cards.* Small park with some shaded sites; flush potties. On the eastern edge of town; stream adjacent.

280 — CHAPTER EIGHT

Sisters KOA • *67667 W. Highway 20 (three miles east of Sisters), Bend, OR 97701; (503) 549-3021. RV and tent sites; $14.75 to $18.75. Reservations accepted; MC/VISA.* Attractive wooded park with some shaded sites, some pull-throughs. Full hookups; pool, spa, lake with trout fishing, horseshoes, game room, rec field, mini-mart, coin laundry.

ACTIVITIES AND SERVICES
(The greater Bend-Redmond-Sisters area)

Airline service • Redmond Municipal Airport is served by **United Express,** (800) 241-6522, and **Horizon Air,** (503) 923-5012. Rental car agencies with offices at the airport include **Hertz,** (800) 654-3131; **Budget/Sears,** (503) 923-0699; **National,** (800) 227-7368); and **Thrifty,** (503) 389-7434.

Airport shuttle • **CAC Transportation,** (800) 955-VANS or (503) 382-1687, provides van and limo service from Redmond-Bend Airport, plus sightseeing trips; MC/VISA, AMEX.

Bicycling • For a copy of the *Deschutes County Bicycling Guide,* contact **Deschutes County Public Works,** 61150 SE 27th St., Bend, OR 97702; (503) 388-6581.

Bicycle rentals • **High Cascade Descent,** 333 Riverfront, Bend, (503) 389-0562; **Inn of the Seventh Mountain,** Cascade Lakes Highway, Bend, (503) 382-8711, extension 595; **Mount Bachelor Ski & Summer Resort,** (503) 382-2607; **Odell Lake Resort,** Highway 58, (503) 433-2540; **Skjersaa's Ski Shop,** 130 SW Century Dr., Bend, (503) 382-2154; **Four Seasons Recreational Outfitters,** Country Mall Suite D, Bend, (503) 593-2255.

Bicycle tours • **High Cascade Descent,** 333 Riverfront Dr., Bend, OR 97701, (503) 389-0562, offers mountain bike tours including scenic descents from the heights after uphill van shuttles.

Excursion train • **Crooked River Dinner Train,** O'Neil Road, Redmond and 115 N. Oregon St., Suite 24, Bend, (503) 388-1966; scenic 38-mile train ride along the Crooked River from Redmond to Prineville; dinner, brunch or excursion trips; MC/VISA, AMEX.

Fishing • Rivers and lakes abound with fish and fisherfolk and we mention many of the prime angling areas below. The local office of the **Department of Fish and Wildlife** is at 101020 Paulina Hwy., Bend, (503) 447-5111.

Fishing guides • **Central Oregon Guide Service,** Box 61, Hackett Dr., La Pine, OR 97739, (503) 433-2753; **Elliot's Guide Service,** 61612 Summer Shade Dr., Bend, OR 97702, (503) 389-6068; **Garrison's Guide Service,** P.O. Box 4113, Sunriver, OR 97707, (503) 593-8394; **Lacy's Whitewater & Wild Fish, Inc.,** (503) 389-2434; **Mickey Finn Guide Service,** P.O. Box 1171, Bend, OR 97701, (503) 382-2787 or 385-2173; **Rapid River Outfitters,** (800) 962-3327 or (503) 382-1514; **Sunriver Guides and Outfitters,** Box 3012, Sunriver, OR 97707, (503) 593-1292.

Horseback riding • **Blue Lake Corrals,** near Sisters, (503) 595-6681 or (503) 595-6671; **Eagle Crest Resort,** Redmond, (503) 923-2072; **Nova Stables** at Inn of the Seventh Mountain, (503) 389-9458 or 382-8711; **Sunriver Stables** at Sunriver Resort, (503) 593-1221, ext. 4420.

Horse packers • **Black Butte Stables,** P.O. Box 402, Sisters, OR 97759, (503) 595-6211; **Blue Lake Corrals,** P.O. Box 283, Sisters, OR

97759, (503) 595-6671; **High Cascade Stables,** 70775 Indian Ford Rd., Sisters, OR 97759, (503) 549-4972.

Hot-air ballooning • **Morning Glory Balloon Company,** 7843 SW 77th St., Redmond, (503) 389-8739; and **Rebel Sports Bungee,** which also offers bungee jumping, 1340 NE Dempsey Dr., Bend, (503) 389-1676.

Kayaking • **Bend Whitewater Supply,** (503) 389-7191 (lessons, rentals and trips).

Live theater • **Community Theatre of the Cascades,** 148 NW Greenwood, Bend, (503) 389-0803; **Magic Circle Theatre,** 2600 NW College Way, Bend, (503) 385-5511.

Rock climbing • **Smith Rock Climbing School & Guide Service,** P.O. Box 464, Terrebonne, OR 97760, (503) 548-0749.

Water sports rentals • **Bend Rental,** 353 SE Third St., Bend, (503) 382-2792 (canoes); **Bend Whitewater Supply,** 2245 NE Division St., Bend, (503) 389-7191 (canoes, kayaks and inflatables); Bill's Bobcat Rentals, Sunriver, (503) 593-5227 (canoes, ski boats and jet skis).

Whitewater rafting • The Deschutes is an excellent whitewater river. Some of these outfits also offer trips on other Oregon streams: **Bend Whitewater Supply,** (503) 389-7191; **High Cascade Descent,** 389-0562; **Hunter Expeditions,** 389-8370 or 593-3113; **Inn of the Seventh Mountain,** (503) 382-8711, extension 595; **Rapid River Rafters,** (800) 962-3327 or (503) 382-1514; **Sun Country Tours,** (503) 593-2161.

Winter sports

Ice Skating • **Blue Lake Resort,** 595-6675 or 595-6671; **Inn of the Seventh Mountain,** 382-8711, extension 595; **Shelvin Park Pond,** Shelvin Park Road in Bend, 389-PARK; **Sunriver Resort,** (503) 593-1221.

Ski areas: alpine • **Mount Bachelor Resort,** (503) 382-2607, ski report (503) 382-7888, lessons (503) 382-2442. See details below, under "Cascade Lakes drive." **Hoodoo Ski Bowl,** 25 miles west of Sisters, (503) 342-5540. See details below, under "High Cascades loop."

Ski areas: cross-country • **Mount Bachelor,** (503) 382-2607; also **Dutchman's Flat, Edison Butte, Meissner, Santiam Pass** and **Swampy Lakes** in Deschutes National Forest; call (503) 388-5664 in Bend or (503) 549-2111 in Sisters.

Ski/snowboard rentals • **Blue Lake Nordic Center,** (503) 595-6675 or 595-6671; **Mount Bachelor,** (503) 382-2607; **Odell Lake Resort,** (503) 433-2540; **Powder House Ski Shop,** 311 SW Century Dr., Bend, (503) 389-6234; **Randy Barna's Ski Shop,** 354 SW Century Dr., Bend, (503) 389-0890; **Skjersaa's,** 130 SW Century Dr., Bend, (503) 382-2154; **Stowell's Ski Haus,** 926 NE Greenwood, Bend, (503) 382-5325.

Snowmobile rentals & tours • **Bill's Bobcat Service,** Sunriver, (503) 593-5227; **Inn of the Seventh Mountain,** 382-8711, ext. 595.

ANNUAL EVENTS
(Including the greater Bend-Redmond-Sisters area)

Two major music festivals feature top stars of classical, jazz, pops and contemporary sounds: **Cascade Festival of Music,** Bend in late June; (503) 382-8381; and the **Sunriver Music Festival,** Sunriver Resort in August; (503) 593-1084.

Winter Carnivals, Mount Bachelor/Sunriver in January; (503) 382-7888 and (503) 593-1084 and in Sisters in February; (503) 549-0251.

Snowboarding World Championships, Mount Bachelor in early April; (503) 382-7888.

Sisters Rodeo, Sisters in mid-June; (503) 549-0251.

Sunfest Wine and Food Festival, Sunriver in June; (503) 593-1084.

Food, Wine and Art Festival, downtown Bend in mid-July; (503) 382-3221.

Jefferson County Fair, late July in Madras; (503) 475-2350.

Deschutes County Fair, late July to early August in Redmond; (503) 923-6442.

All-Oregon Bluegrass Festival, September at Central Oregon Community College, Bend; (503) 382-6112.

Indian Arts and Crafts Show, October at Warm Springs Reservatioin; (503) 553-1161.

Cascade Lakes Drive

This 87-mile paved route winds through the foothills of the Cascades, offering panoramas of the Three Sisters and Broken Top as it passes some of the area's most inviting lakes. Many have rustic resort and campgrounds and most are noted for their bass and lake trout fishing. If Bend area campsites are booked, you generally can find a spot at the lakes, particularly in the forest service campgrounds. Most are attractive tree-shaded camping areas close to the lakes. At some of the smaller lakes, tenters can pick their spot and camp informally right on the shoreline.

The Sisters and Broken Top are four side-by-side volcanic peaks that form the nucleus of the Three Sisters Wilderness, one of the largest primitive areas in Oregon. "Three Sisters" is a latter- day appellation. The volcanic triplets originally were named Faith, Hope and Charity, a biblical reference to the three virtues in First Corinthians. An unimaginative legislature later changed them to North, South and Middle Sister.

Trails lead into the Sisters Wilderness from the Cascade Lakes Highway and from McKenzie pass above the town of Sisters. This is a ruggedly spectacular area of sawtooth peaks, high meadows, jeweled lakes and perpetual ice. The Sisters are among the most glaciated peaks in the lower 48 states.

You can pick up a *Cascade Lakes Tour* map and guide at Deschutes National Forest offices and at the Oregon Welcome Center. Not surprisingly, the route has been designated as a National Forest Scenic Byway. The road to Mount Bachelor is kept open the year around; beyond, it's closed by winter snow. Most of the lake resorts operate from April through October.

To begin this exceptionally pretty drive, follow signs southwest on Franklin Avenue or Riverside Boulevard from the downtown area, or pick up Franklin from Highway 97 (Third Street). After passing the resorts of **Mount Bachelor Village** and **Inn of the Seventh Mountain,** you'll enter Deschutes National Forest and leave civilization behind. Turnoffs along the way invite you to picnic along the Deschutes River and enjoy vistas of the area's 6,000-year-old lava flow.

You then begin a steady and straight climb as the tree plain tilts into the Cascades foothills. You round a bend and stare at the conical mass of **Mount Bachelor,** sitting moodily off to one side of his Three Sisters. For a stunning countryside view, turn in at the **Sunrise Lodge** entrance and catch the summer ski lift to the 9,065-foot summit.

☺ **Mount Bachelor Ski & Summer Resort** ● *P.O. Box 230, Bend, OR 97709; (503) 382-2607; vacation packages (800) 800-8334 or (503) 382-8334; ski school and rentals (800) 829-2442 or (503) 382-2442; ski phone (503) 382-7888.* Rated by ski magazines as one of America's top ten winter resorts, Mount Bachelor also has a summer program. Its biggest draw is the Summit Lift, which runs daily from 10 until 4. At the top, you can enjoy awesome views, attend ranger programs and—if you choose—follow a marked trail back down to Sunrise Lodge. Lift prices are adults $8, seniors $6 and kids 7 to 12, $4. Forest service programs at the top are at 11:30 and 2:30. A snack bar and convenience shop also are open at Sunrise lodge during the summer.

The largest ski area in the Northwest, Bachelor has ten lifts ranging from beginning to expert. Vertical drop is 3,100 feet, with 54 runs covering the entire perimeter of the mountain. A cross-country area has nearly 40 miles of groomed trails. There are six day lodges on the mountain. Nearest large overnight resorts, all within half and hour and all offering ski shuttles, are Inn of the Seventh Mountain, Mount Bachelor Village and Sunriver Lodge.

Beyond Mount Bachelor, the parade of lakes begins. **Todd Lake** is a small jewel a short walk from a parking area, offering tent camping, picnicking, swimming, hiking and fishing (no motors). **Sparks Lake,** reached by a short, bumpy road from the highway, offers a fine example of a lake turning into a marsh and a meadow. The past years of drought are hastening its demise, although it still has a sizable pond, framed by a rough lava flow and backdropped by the craggy spires of Broken Top.

A bit beyond, tiny **Devil's Lake** must have been named for Satan's eyes, for it's a deep green instead of the typical blue. Informal tent camping is allowed on the shore of this 30-acre emerald. **Elk Lake** is one of the larger in the area, offering rustic kitchen cabins for $58 a night, a lake cruise for $6, somewhat shabby mini-mart and a marina with canoe, paddleboat, rowboat and motorboat rentals. The lodge was for sale when we visited, so it may be in new hands and spruced up by the time you get there, or it might be closed. It's reached by mobile phone, (503) YP-7 3954.

Lava Lake has both forest service campsites at $8 a night and an RV resort with full hookups for $16. Facilities include showers, a coin laundry, boat and fishing gear rentals. Contact Lava Lake Lodge, P.O. Box 989, Bend, OR 97709, (503) 382-9443 or 382-7857. Adjacent **Little Lava Lake** offers informal shoreline camping.

Signs will direct you to the left off Cascade Lakes Highway to the large reservoir of **Crane Prairie Lake.** It has a forestry campground with sites for $8 a night, a commercial RV park with full hookups for $15, no hookups for $12, cabins for $30 and $40, motor boat, rowboat and canoe rentals. Contact Crane Prairie Resort, Box 1171, Bend, OR 97709; (503) 383-3939.

☺ **Twin Lakes Resort,** between Crane Prairie and Wickiup reservoirs, is the best maintained of the commercial facilities along Cascade Lakes Drive. Cabins are neatly kept and a rustic restaurant goes beyond the basic menu to serve German sausages, smoked pork chops, weinerschnitzel and poppy seed chicken breasts. Food is served from 7 a.m. to 8 p.m. Tent sites are $8, RV hookups $12 and housekeeping cabins $50 to $75. Other facilities include fishing gear, boat, kayak and paddleboat rentals; a marina; convenience mart and gasoline. Contact Twin Lakes Resort, P.O. Box 3550, Sunriver, OR 97707; (503) 593-6526.

Incidentally, Crane Prairie, Twin Lakes and Wickiup are reservoirs on the Deschutes River. Twin Lakes are water-filled craters from earlier volcanic activity.

From Twin Lakes and Wickiup, you can follow paved Forestry Road 46 south to **Davis Lake,** which has several forest service campgrounds. The route eventually joins Highway 97 at **Crescent,** 34 miles south of Bend. Or you can take Forestry Road 42 east from Twin Lakes and hit 97 south of Sunriver, about 18 miles below Bend.

Newberry National Volcanic Monument

One of America's newest federal preserves, Newberry National Volcanic Monument was established in November, 1990. It covers more than 50,000 acres of lava lands touched by eruptions of Mount Newberry, a huge shield volcano covering 500 square miles. Within the monument are cindercones, lava tubes, lava casts, ash flows, pumice, an unusual obsidian flow and rhyolite domes—more than 95 percent of the world's volcanic features.

The caldera, and thus the new national monument, are named for Dr. John Strong Newberry, a physician and geologist. He explored its volcanic features when he accompanied a party looking for a railroad route through the area in 1855.

Newberry's hot breath has been felt over hundreds of square miles, leaving a thousand cindercones, craters and other volcanic disturbances. The huge shield volcano erupted thousands of times over a period of half a million years. It finally caved in on itself, leaving Newberry Crater, which is four to five miles wide and harbors two lakes.

The new volcanic national monument extends about 25 miles northwest from Newberry Crater toward Bend. Several volcanic attractions, originally designated as Lava Lands, are within the new preserve, which is administered by Deschutes National Forest.

To see all of this, simply head south from Bend on Highway 97. The first volcanic points of interest are several lava caves in the desert to the east, outside the monument's boundaries. To find them, turn east onto China Hat Road (at the Mountain High Golf Villages sign with its flying flags). The turnoff is just a mile or so south of Bend. It becomes Forestry Road 18, taking you into Deschutes National Forest and four lava tubes—**Boyd, Skeleton, Wind** and **Arnold.** Signs mark them as you approach.

Overlooked by tourist crowds, these ☺ special places are never crowded. So if you get lost in one, you'll stay lost for a long time. In exploring lava caves, **always** take two light sources. These aren't complex caverns, but you won't know which way is up if you lose your illumination. We generally explore caves with a Propane lantern, and have a flashlight tucked into a pocket. Some of these caves are so far underground and well insulated that trickling water has formed frozen lakes and ice floes. They're intriguing, but watch your footing. And take a warm jacket.

Back on Highway 97, a short drive south will take you to Newberry Crater National Monument's main visitor center and an interesting cindercone:

☺ **Lava Lands Visitor Center and Lava Butte** ● *58201 S. Highway 97; eleven miles south of Bend; (503) 593-2421. Daily 9 to 5; free. Summer shuttle to Lava Butte daily 9 to 4:30; adults $1, seniors and kids 50 cents.* The visitor center, on the edge of a 6,000-year-old lava flow, has several nicely done exhibits on area volcanism, flora and fauna, including videos, periodic films

A forestry lookout is perched atop Lava Butte in the recently-created Newberry National Volcanic Monument.
– Betty Woo Martin

and interesting light-and-sound displays. The center also offers a good selection of natural history books and info about the new national monument.

Lava Butte is a reddish 500-foot cindercone that fed the surrounding flow six centuries ago. It provides a handy platform for a forest service lookout, which has been perched on the crater lip since 1928. Visitors can step inside to chat with the ranger on duty, then step into an exhibit room below the lookout, which has a locator map of the surrounding landmarks.

Naturally, you get an impressive view of the countryside from here, particularly of the lava flow and some of the hundreds of fissures and cindercones fed by Mount Newberry. Lava Butte's flows swept into the nearby forest, leaving *kipukas*, islands of trees surrounded by a petrified sea.

On perfectly clear days, it's possible to see from California's Mount Shasta to Washington's Mount Adams. You can follow a rim trail around Lava Butte's crater, providing a slow-motion change of scenery. This area is particularly nice in late summer and fall, when yellow-blooming rabbit brush adds flashes of color to the broken black lava flows.

Since parking is limited up here, a shuttle runs every half an hour from the visitor center during the summer months. Get there early on busy weekends, since the bus holds only 25 passengers.

Benham Falls ● *Four miles from Lava Lands Visitor Center on forestry road 9702.* A dusty cinder road leads to a pleasant picnic area, shaded by huge ponderosas. After a one mile hike, you'll reach this good-sized cataract on the Deschutes River. The hike along the whitewater section of the river is as appealing as the falls themselves.

Lava River Cave ● *About 13 miles south of Bend; (503) 593-2421. Daily 9 to 5 in summer; shorter hours the rest of the year. Adults $1.50, kids 3 to 17, $1 and lantern rental $1.50. If you're in a fairly large group, it's a good idea to rent two lanterns.* Lava River Cave is the longest uncollapsed lava tube in Oregon, extending for nearly a mile. You probably know that lava tubes are formed when a river of fast-flowing *pahoehoe* basalt begins to crust over. This insulates the liquid lava beneath, which flows out from under the crust and leaves a cavern.

With a curved ceiling and rather smooth walls, Lava River Cave is unusually large, resembling a subway tunnel that was completed under budget. Your one-mile hike will take you through Echo Hall, Low Bridge Lane, Two Tube Tunnel and Sand Gardens, all of which are self-explanatory. A brochure available at the office will provide more detail. The ceiling is low in areas, so a bump hat is a good idea.

Remember to carry two sources of light into any cave, and wear a warm jacket. Only Propane lanterns and flashlights are permitted in Lava River Cave; no kerosene. If you get there between 9 and 5, you can rent a Propane lantern. The cave never closes but the office and parking lot do, so you'll have to hike in from the highway and bring your own light after hours.

Lava cast forest ● *About 15 miles off Highway 97 on Forestry Road 9720.* From Lava River Cave, drive about three miles south, then turn east onto a forestry road opposite the Sunriver sign. After winding through the pine tree desert for a few miles, you'll reach the parking area for Lava Cast Forest. A one-mile trail will take you past the casts. This isn't a "forest" by any stretch, but a series of molds formed when flowing lava incinerated trees, leaving hollows where the stumps had been. In some, you can still see the imprints of the bark.

Newberry Crater ● *About 23 miles south of Bend on Highway 97, then 14 miles east Forestry Route 21.* A new information kiosk at the Highway 97 turnoff tells you what you'll see in this section of the newly-designated national monument. Newberry Crater—really a giant caldera—cradles two lakes with small resorts, a glossy black obsidian flow and one of the best viewpoints in central Oregon. **Paulina** and **East** lakes are probably the best trout-fishing ponds in the area, and East Lake is particularly noted for trophy-sized brook and German brown trout. The two lakes have been stocked with salmon as well.

Under its new national monument status, the area offers guided hikes, ranger talks and a growing number of marked trails and interpretive signs. Schedules of summer activities are posted at trail heads and campgrounds.

A long, gently winding climb takes you into the caldera. It's so immense that visitors often aren't aware that they're in the throat of an old volcano. Only the precipitous **Paulina Peak,** visible to your right, reveals some of the original crater wall.

Your first encounter is **Paulina Lake,** with a somewhat scruffy resort offering a store, boat rentals, a small café and lodgings in assorted log cabins. The restaurant is open daily 11:30 to 7:30 and it's smoke free. Knotty pine housekeeping cabins range from $57 to $114; no credit cards. Contact Paulina Lake Resort, P.O. Box 7, La Pine, OR 97739; (503) 536-2240.

☺ Just beyond is the turnoff to **Paulina Peak,** a craggy remnant of old Mount Newberry, rising 1,500 feet above the caldera. The view from the top is simply awesome. This aerie rivals Cape Perpetua as the greatest vantage point in the state. In a panoramic sweep, you see the two lakes below, dozens of forest-clad cinder cones and far-away peaks—as far away as California and Washington. Getting there requires a grueling four-mile climb up bumpy switchback roads. As you churn ever upward, it seems as if you'll never reach the top. And if your car has worn tires and a bad cooling system, you may be right!

After surviving the Paulina drive, continue eastward through the caldera. You'll reach a kiosk that serves several forest service campgrounds beyond. Sites are the usual $8 per night with flush potties. Non-campers simply pick up a free pass at the kiosk and continue on their way.

☺ Your first stop, about a mile past the kiosk and to the right, is the **Obsidian Trail.** This one-mile path winds through Big Obsidian Flow, one of the state's more remarkable lava formations. A tumbled mass of lava is laced with glossy black obsidian, as sharp and hard as glass. In fact, as you follow the trail through the flow, it'll sound like you're walking on crushed glass. Needless to say, you won't want to stroll through here wearing flops. The varied shapes and sizes of shining obsidian are intriguing; some could pass for *avant garde* sculptures.

For centuries, Native Americans used this unusual flow as a mine for their projectile points. They fashioned arrow and spear tips and knives and traded obsidian with tribes for hundreds of miles. Their bartered goods have been found as far away as western Canada and California. Peter Skene Ogden was likely the first outsider to visit here, on November 16, 1826. He wrote in his journal: "We had for some distance not a stony road, but a flinty one, of very large size."

Beyond the Obsidian flow, the road ends at **East Lake Resort.** Although essentially rustic, it was better maintained than Paulina Resort when we visited. Facilities are more extensive, consisting of an RV park with full hookups ($12 per night), camping rooms $29 to $34, sleeping cabins $54 to $59 and housekeeping cabins $69 to $79. Other facilities include a general store, kids' playground, boat rentals, fishing gear and fishing guide service. The restaurant serves breakfast and lunch weekdays except Tuesday, and dinner on Saturday and Sunday. MC/VISA are accepted. For information: East Lake Resort, P.O. Box 95, La Pine, OR 97739; (503) 536-2230.

High Cascades Loop

This 88-mile trip, designated as the McKenzie-Santiam Scenic Byway by the U.S. Forest Service, carries you over two mountain passes and past the Metolius River Recreation Area. Sisters is the launching pad for this tour into the high Cascades. Before starting out, you can stock up on maps and brochures at **Sisters Ranger Station**. It's at the west edge of town, near the Highway 20-242 junction; daily in summer, 7:45 to 4:30; (549-2111).

At the junction, fork to the left and head west on State Highway 242. Initially a straight, steep incline, the route soon begins to twist and turn into the high Cascades. You round a horseshoe bend and stare at a remarkable sight: a fractured lava sea that seems to have spilled into the forest only yesterday. This is the outer edge of the **Yapoah Lava Flow,** which is actually 2,700 years old. It's still one of the newest lava fields in mainland America.

☺ After a few more twists and turns, the highway tops out at 5,325-foot **McKenzie Pass,** the most interesting highway summit in the Cascades. Black, fractured lava completely covers this saddle through the mountains, like a giant coal mine that exploded.

The first wagon road was hacked through this 65-acre lava field between 1866 and 1872. The CCC boys came along during the Depression, improved the road and built the lava rock **Dee Wright Memorial Observatory.** It was named for their supervisor, who died before it was completed. Inside this bold structure, reached by lava steps, slotted windows line up the high promontories of the Cascades—Mounts Hood, Jefferson, Three-Fingered Jack, Washington and the North and Middle sisters. The half-mile **Lava River Trail** snakes through a swatch of these black badlands. Signs discuss the intricacies of *a-a* lava and the geology of the area.

The **Pacific Crest Scenic Trail** crosses the highway near here, offering access to **Three Sisters Wilderness** to the south and **Mount Washington Wilderness** to the north. The borders of both wild areas nudge the highway. Even if you aren't set up for an overnight hike, day treks will take you into a beautiful area of high meadows, lava flows and alpine peaks. For the best scenic assortment, head south toward the North Sister. A tough, uphill five or six miles will take you to the lower edge of **Collier Glacier,** the largest icefield in Oregon.

A drive over the pass will carry you on a downhill spiral through the thicker Douglas fir forests of the Cascades' western slopes. After 22 miles, turn north onto Highway 126 at **Belknap Springs** and follow the McKenzie River through **Willamette National Forest.** This route takes you along the backside of the **Mount Washington Wilderness,** with occasional peeks through the trees at the 7,794-foot peak. Pause along the way to admire **Koosah** and **Sahalie** waterfalls (covered in more detail under "McKenzie River Recreation Area" in Chapter 3).

After 19 miles, turn east onto U.S. 20 (the Santiam Highway). One of the most popular routes into the Cascades from the Willamette Valley population center, the route will carry you over **Santiam Pass** and back into this chapter. Near the top of the pass is the weathered old **Santiam Lodge,** built as a Civilian Conservation Corps project during the Depression. It's still active, catering to winter skiers and summer visitors with basic and inexpensive dormitory-style lodge rooms and hearty meals; call (503) 342-5540.

Nearby **Hoodoo Ski Bowl** also dates back to the 1930s. This small family-oriented ski area offers a mix of beginner, intermediate and advanced runs and a vertical drop of about a thousand feet. Lift tickets are quite nominal for the three chair lifts and a real bargain for the rope tow. Call (503) 342-5540 for details and (503) 585-8081 for snow conditions.

As you drop back into eastern central Oregon from Santiam Pass, watch for the turnoff to the **Metolius River Recreation Area;** it's about 16 miles below the summit. The river's name comes from *mytl-lr-as,* the Native American term for whitefish. However, it's trout fishing that brings thousands of anglers here each year. This fly-fishing-only river yields regular catches of Dolly Varden, Kokanee, rainbow, brook and brown trout. Although small, the Metolius is one of the largest spring-fed rivers in America, burbling abruptly from the ground.

☺ Signs will direct you to the parking area of the **Headwaters of the Metolius,** and a short trail takes you a gently sloping mossy bank. Here, the river emerges full flow, as if from a broken water main. Geologists suspect that it reaches the surface through a fault, which accounts for its volume. Although attractive, sparkling and free-running, the Metolius is not a wilderness river. One shore is lined with U.S. Forest Service campgrounds and the other is dotted with woodsy resorts and RV parks. Forestry campsites are $7 each, with flush and pit potties. The string of campgrounds is linked by an attractive riverside trail.

Camp Sherman is the "business district" of the Metolius River Recreation Area. It consists of a shingle-sided general store, post office and several summer homes, clustered around a bridge crossing. At the bridge, you can buy fish food from a vending machine and possibly create a moderate feeding frenzy. Obviously, this spot is closed to fishing.

Although the river is too chilly for swimming, folks often take the plunge in nearby **Blue** and **Suttle Lakes,** to the southwest, just below Highway 20. **Blue Lake Resort** offers lodging, an RV park and tent sites, a marina, store, riding horses and a winter Nordic center with cross-country trails and ski rentals. Contact: Blue Lake Resort, 13900 Blue Lake Drive, Sisters, OR 97759; (503) 595-6671.

The Metolius has been luring vacationers since 1916, when wheat farmers from neighboring Sherman County began building summer homes, so they could fish and relax after the harvest. For a list of resorts and fishing lodges, contact: **Metolius Recreation Association,** P.O. Box 64, Camp Sherman, OR 97730; (503) 595-6117.

As you complete your loop trip by driving east toward Sisters on U.S. 20, you'll notice a bold Fujiyama-like peak filling the northern horizon. That's 6,415-foot **Black Butte,** one of the most nearly-symmetrical cindercones in central Oregon. Black Butte Ranch, a rustically elegant mountain resort is located at its base (listing on page 274).

SOUTH TO KLAMATH FALLS

Highway 97 follows a straight-arrow course south from Bend through the wooded tableland of Deschutes National Forest. If you feel the need to explore more forest and stream, and you're curious to see Oregon's largest ponderosa, turn west about two miles below Lava River Cave and follow signs to **La Pine State Park** (503) 388-6055. In addition to the king-sized pine, it offers camping (full hookups $13), picnicking, hiking, plus boating and fishing on the Deschutes River.

A few miles below is **La Pine,** a lumbering town with several small motels that catch some of the overflow from the Bend area. They're generally less expensive than rooms to the north. For a lodging list and other information, contact: **La Pine Chamber of Commerce,** 51470 Hwy 97, La Pine, OR 97739; (503) 536-9771.

From this point, the 80-mile drive to Klamath Falls is uneventful but pleasant, carrying you through a tableland of ponderosas and lodgepole pines. The small towns of **Gilchrist, Crescent** and **Chemult** offer little reason to stop.

To break your boredom, we'll suggest a triangular side trip to some interesting geological formations. Just south of La Pine, take State Highway 31 southeast toward Lakeview. After about 25 miles, look for signs to **Hole in the Ground**, reached by a one-mile road to the left. It's a curious 500-foot deep crater that probably was caused by a volcanic blast after lava came into contact with water.

Back on the highway, you begin dropping out of the forest and into a silver sage desert. Look far to your left and you'll see what appears to be a high rectangular ridge. Turn left at the Fort Rock turnoff; as you drive past the still-distant formation, it reveals itself as a huge natural amphitheater. Before reaching this unusual geologic shape, you'll hit the tiny farming town of **Fort Rock.**

Most of the town has withered and faded away. However, local folks have gathered several old wooden structures into a kind of mini-pioneer village at **Fort Rock Valley Museum.** Hours are Friday through Sunday and on holiday weekends 10 to 4; free; donations appreciated. It's surprisingly well done for a small-town archive, featuring three furnished homesteaders houses and the rough board Bridget's Catholic Church. Make sure you peek into the outhouse out back.

☺ From the town, a one-mile drive will fetch you to **Fort Rock State Monument,** that curious arena-shaped stone formation. Scientists theorize that it was formed during the last Ice Age, when molten lava came into contact with water-saturated rocks beneath a shallow sea. It exploded into steam, hurling material into the air, which fell into a circular pattern around the volcanic vent to form a "tuff ring" 500 feet high. Erosion washed out one side, leaving the present amphitheater shape.

Facilities here are limited to a few picnic table and a half-mile hiking trail around the arena. Interpretive signs will tell you what we already told you, and a lot more.

You can follow a dusty road directly south from Fort Rock, or back-track seven miles to Highway 31 and take it south. Both will lead you to the dusty town of **Silver Lake,** which no longer has a lake to justify its name. The former lake, now an alkaline flat, is about six miles east. From the town, you can follow a twisting paved road west to Highway 97. Or, if

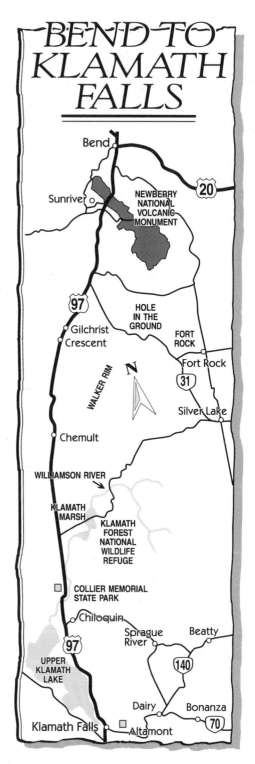

BEND TO KLAMATH FALLS

you're in a hurry to reach our last chapter, which covers Southeastern Oregon, continue on to Lakeview. The Highway 31 route is an interesting desert drive past more alkaline flats and salty lakes.

If you head west toward 97, you'll enter thinning ponderosa woodlands and pass through the marshy meadows of **Klamath Forest National Wildlife Refuge.** It's one of a series of bird sanctuaries in an extensive wetlands area around Klamath Falls. A few miles beyond, you pick up Route 97 and continue south. **Thunderbeast Park** is a roadside primeval critter attraction with big-as-life replicas of beasts that inhabited this area 50 million years ago. The focus here isn't dinosaurs, but early mammals such as saber-toothed cats, split-toed horses, camels and pre-dawn rhinos. Adults $2.50, students $1.50.

Ten miles south is **Collier Memorial State Park,** which preserves an early logging operation. Exhibits in this open-air Pioneer Village museum include steam "donkeys," a steam train, log-haulers with wheels made from cross-cut tree slices, a homesteaders' cabin and lumber camp blacksmith shop. Other facilities include a campground (full hookup and tent sites, from $13), a playground, picnic areas, fishing in the Williams River and hiking trails.

South of Collier State Park, the highway joins the eastern shoreline of **Upper Klamath Lake** and follows it for nearly 20 miles into Klamath Falls. The 25-mile-long, 64-square-mile lake is the largest in Oregon, despite the fact that a turn-of-the-century reclamation project has greatly reduced this area's wetlands. A 50-mile chain of lakes and marshes once extended along the Klamath River, past Klamath Falls and into northeastern California. Before "reclamation" began in 1905, the wetland network covered 185,000 acres and attracted more than five million waterfowl and other birds. It was *the* stopover on the Pacific Flyway.

Despite its shrinkage, it's still the best birdwatching area in the state. Three sections of the Klamath National Wildlife Refuge—Klamath Forest, Upper Klamath Lake and Lower Klamath Lake are in Oregon; another three are in California. During spring and fall migrations, you can see thousands of mallards, Canadian honkers, pintails, cormorants, gulls, herons, pelicans and other birds. It's also a winter home to more than 500 bald eagles. Best eagle-viewing time is December through February. Spring is a good time to see nesting marsh birds and waterfowl.

Reserves are open during daylight hours only; no camping is permitted. For information on the refuges, including self-guiding auto and canoe routes, contact the **U.S. Fish and Wildlife Service,** 1400 W. Miller Island Rd., Klamath Falls, OR 97603; (503) 883-5732. The refuge headquarters, with an excellent interpretive center, is across the California line in Tulelake; (916) 667-2231.

Klamath Falls

Population: 17,700   **Elevation: 4,105 feet**

The town of Linkville was established in 1876 on the Link River that flows between Upper and Lower Klamath Lakes. The lumbering and farming community later changed its name to Klamath Falls, after a small cataract on the river. The falls have since disappeared behind a dam.

The draining of the wetlands at the turn of the century provided rich farmland on both sides of the border. The area is still famous for its Klamath potatoes; adjacent Tulelake prides itself in being the horseradish capital of the world.

Lumbering was once an economic mainstay of south central Oregon's largest city, although you'll see few trees around the community today. The rather homely town is built against barren hills. It's not a major tourist town, but it is a handy provisioning center on the well-traveled path between northern California and central Oregon. Of course, it's a major draw for birdwatchers, as well. And it has three museums worth a pause. During the summer, a restored 1906 trolley offers free rides among them. Finding this trio of museums isn't difficult. Pick up Business 97 north of town and follow it southeast and then southwest toward the early day downtown area. Business 97 merges onto Main Street, where all three are located.

☺ **Flavel Museum** ● *125 W. Main St.; (503) 882-9996. Monday-Saturday 9:30 to 5:30. Adults $4, seniors $3, kids 6 to 16, $2.* This excellent facility houses one of the Northwest's most extensive collections of Native American artifacts, Western art and historical items. An impressive exhibit of 60,000 projectile points is the focal point of the Native American collection. It also includes fine examples of pottery, basketry and beadwork. Among highlights of the Western collection are works of more than 300 artists, ranging from paintings and bronzes to taxidermy, carvings and photography. Particularly interesting is a assortment of miniaturized rifles and pistols—the kind of guns that "won the West."

Baldwin Hotel Museum ● *31 Main Street.; (503) 883-4208. Tuesday-Saturday 10 to 4. Adults $3, students and seniors $2, families $6.* The once fashionable 1907 Baldwin Hotel has been restored and converted into a museum, with many of the original fixtures in place. During summers, tours are given through the imposing four-story structure.

Klamath County Museum ● *1451 Main St.; (503) 883-4208. Open daily from Memorial Day through Labor Day, 10 to 6. Free; donations appreciated.* More than a historical museum, it also covers the geology and wildlife of the Klamath Basin. Historical exhibits trace Klamath societies from Native Americans to the present. One exhibit concerns the Modoc Indian War of 1872-73, when a dissident named Captain Jack led his people off a reservation and holed up in Lava Beds National Monument, across the line in California. They held off the U.S. Army for months until cold weather and hunger forced them to surrender.

Another point of interest is the Art Deco **Ross Ragland Theater** at 218 N. Seventh Street. It has been restored and is thriving as a center for plays, concerts and other live entertainment; (503) 884-0651.

For more about the Klamath Basin and its points of interest, touch bases with the **Klamath Falls Chamber of Commerce**, 507 Main Street at Fifth. It's open weekdays 8:30 to 5; (503) 884-5193. Also, the **Klamath County Department of Tourism** maintains at information office in the Klamath County Museum at 1451 Main Street at Spring; open daily in summer 10 to 6; (503) 884-0666.

WHERE TO DINE

Chez Nous Restaurant ● ∆∆∆ $$

3927 S. Sixth St. (1.5 miles east on Highway 140/39); (503) 883-8719. American; full bar service. Tuesday-Friday 5 p.m. to 9 p.m. Major credit cards. Early American home converted into a comfortable, refined restaurant and cocktail lounge. The menu features ample servings of well-prepared steaks, chicken, chops and seafood. Excellent wine list.

Alice's Saddle Rock Cafè ● △△ $$

1012 Main St. (at Tenth); (503) 884-1444. American; full bar service. Weekdays 7:30 a.m. to 2 p.m., dinner Wednesday-Sunday 5 to 9, Sunday brunch 9 to 2. MC/VISA. Nice brick-walled cafè with modern artworks, tucked behind an old downtown facade. Klamath's most popular eastery, it features creatively-fashioned chicken, chops and steaks, several pastas with creative sauces and some vegetarian entrèes.

Fiorella's ● △△ $$

6139 Simmers Ave. (at South Sixth); (503) 882-1878. Italian; full bar service. Dinner Tuesday-Saturday from 5. MC/VISA. Attractive family-style cafè featuring northern Italian fare, plus tasty home-made pastas. Meals are inexpensive and hearty, including soup, salad, pasta and garlic bread.

WHERE TO SLEEP

Econo Lodge ● ⌒⌒ $$ ∅

75 Main St., Klamath Falls, OR 97601; (800) 446-6900 or (503) 884-7735. Couples $42 to $50, singles $34 to $38, suites from $75. MC/VISA, AMEX. Well-maintained 51-unit motel with TV movies and room phones; free continental breakfast.

Hill View Motel ● ⌒ $$ ∅

5543 S. Sixth St. (Homedale Street), Klamath Falls, OR 97601; (503) 883-7771. Couples $30 to $40, singles $28 to $36. Major credit cards. An 18-unit motel with TV movies and room phones.

Value 20 Motel ● ⌒ $ ∅

124 N. Second St. (at Main), Klamath Falls, OR 97601; (503) 882-7741. Couples $34, singles $29. Major credit cards. A 15- unit motel with TV movies, room phones, stoves and refrigerators; studio units available.

WHERE TO CAMP

Klamath Falls KOA ● *3435 Shasta Way, Klamath Falls, OR 97603; (800) 522-9086 or (503) 884-4644. RV and tent sites; $13 to $16.50. Reservations accepted; MC/VISA.* Grassy park with some shaded sites; full hookups, some pull throughs. Showers, coin laundry, mini-mart, pool, rec room, playground, horseshoes.

Oregon Motel 8 RV Park ● *5225 N. Highway 97 (three miles north), Klamath Falls, OR 97601; (503) 882-0482. RV sites; $12. Reservations accepted; MC/VISA.* Adjacent to motel with pull-throughs; full hookups, showers, coin laundry, pool, spa, rec room, horseshoes.

South from Klamath Falls, Highway 97 cuts through **Lower Klamath National Wildlife Refuge**, across prairie and grasslands, headed for another forest tableland. The bold peak on the horizon ahead is **Mount Shasta.** However, that's in California, so we'll retreat and move on to the next chapter.

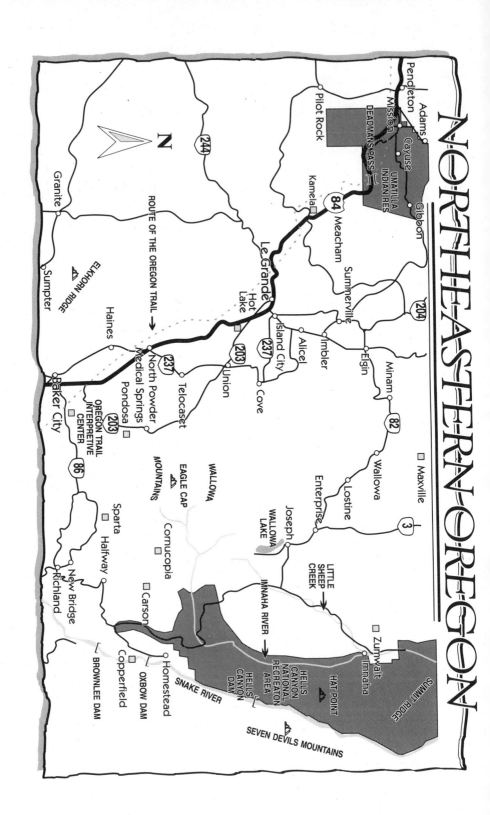

NORTHEASTERN OREGON

N

Granite

Sumpter

ELKHORN RIDGE

ROUTE OF THE OREGON TRAIL

244

Pilot Rock

Kamela

84

Meacham

Summerville

204

Le Grande

Hot Lake

Haines

North Powder

Medical Springs

Pondosa

237

Telocaset

203

Union

237

Island City

Alicel

Imbler

Elgin

Cove

Minam

82

Wallowa

Maxville

Baker City

OREGON TRAIL INTERPRETIVE CENTER

203

86

MOUNTAINS

EAGLE CAP

WALLOWA

Enterprise

Lostine

3

Sparta

Cornucopia

Joseph

WALLOWA LAKE

Halfway

New Bridge

Richland

Carson

Copperfield

OXBOW DAM

Homestead

BROWNLEE DAM

SNAKE RIVER

IMNAHA RIVER

LITTLE SHEEP CREEK

HELLS CANYON DAM

HELLS CANYON NATIONAL RECREATION AREA

HAT POINT

SUMMIT RIDGE

Zumwalt

Imnaha

SEVEN DEVILS MOUNTAINS

Pendleton

Adams

Mission

Cayuse

Gibbon

DEADMAN'S PASS

UMATILLA INDIAN RES

Chapter Nine

NORTHEASTERN CORNER

Woolies, wagon trains and the Wallowas

OREGON'S NORTHEASTERN CORNER offers an inviting mix of attractions, and an interesting past—both primeval and contemporary. Travelers will find rich fossil beds, a mountain range so rugged that it's called the "Switzerland of America," surviving ruts of the Oregon Trail and the roots to one of America's last Indian wars.

The northeast is a mix of rolling wheatlands, cattle country, mountain islands surrounded by high desert and—technically, at least—the world's deepest canyon. It's a thinly-populated area, with room to stretch out and relax, so people don't get on one another's nerves. Nor'easters are among the friendliest folks in the state. They don't even growl at Californians.

Most map-makers regard U.S. Highway 395 as the western border of northeastern Oregon. However, we're reaching a bit farther west to include the John Day Fossil Beds. The upper boundary with Washington is marked by the Blue Mountains that travel from Pendleton's rolling wheat country to Idaho. Smaller mountain ranges running west to east between John Day and Burns delineate the southern edge of this region. The rugged Wallowa Mountains, home to the legendary Chief Joseph and his people, occupy the far northeastern corner. Hells Canyon of the Snake River, now a national recreation area, separates northeastern Oregon from western Idaho, giving that boundary its irregular shape.

Interstate 84, roughly following the route of the Oregon Trail and later Highway 30, cuts a diagonal through northeastern Oregon. It links together the area's primary towns of Baker City, La Grande and Pendleton.

Northeast summers are warm and pleasant; rarely hot because of the relatively high altitude. Fall and spring days are crisp and nights are nippy.

TRIP PLANNER

WHEN TO GO ● Summer is prime time for touring northeastern Oregon, since winters can get mighty cold and much of the high country is snowed in. Spring and fall days are nice, although some of the museums are closed then.

WHAT TO SEE ● Pendleton Woolen Mill; Elgin City Hall and Opera House; Imnaha River Canyon; National Historic Oregon Trail Interpretive Center at Flagstaff Hill; Central Oregon Regional Museum in Baker City; Sumpter Gold Dredge; Kam Wah Chung Museum in John Day; the three units of John Day Fossil Beds National Monument.

WHAT TO DO ● Take the Underground Tour at Pendleton; ride the High Wallowas Tram at Wallowa Lake; drive the Idaho side of Hells Canyon to Hells Canyon Dam; hike down to the wagon ruts at the National Historic Oregon Trail Interpretive Center; ride the Sumpter Valley excursion train if it's running; float the John Day River; hike the Carroll Rim Trail in the Painted Hills unit of John Day Fossil Beds.

Useful contacts

A good overall source for area vacation information is **Northeast Oregon Vacationlands,** 490 Campbell St., Baker City, OR 97814; (800) 532-1235.

Baker County Visitor & Convention Bureau, 490 Campbell St., Baker City, OR 97814; (800) 523-1235 or (503) 525-3356.

Grant County Chamber of Commerce, 281 W. Main St., John Day, OR 97845; (503) 575-0547.

Hells Canyon National Recreation Area, 88401 Highway 82, Enterprise, OR 97828; (503) 426-4978.

John Day Fossil Beds National Monument, 420 W. Main St., John Day, OR 97845; (503) 987-2333.

Joseph Chamber of Commerce, P.O. Box 13, Joseph, OR 97846; (503) 432-1015.

National Historic Oregon Trail Interpretive Center, P.O. Box 987, Baker City, OR 97814; (503) 523-1843, extension 324.

Pendleton Chamber of Commerce, 25 SE Dorion Ave., Pendleton, OR 97801; (800) 452-9403 in Oregon, (800) 547-8911 elsewhere and (503) 276-7411 locally.

Union County Chamber of Commerce, 2111 Adams Ave., La Grande, OR 97850; (503) 963-8588.

Wallowa County Chamber of Commerce, P.O. Box 427, Enterprise, OR 97828; (503) 426-4622.

Northeastern Oregon radio stations

KZLM-FM, 97.5, Pendleton—rock and pops oldies
KWHT-FM, 103.5, Pendleton—country
KOBP-FM 90.7 and 90.9,Pendleton—National Public Radio
KTFN-FM, 99.3, Hermiston—rock
KORD-FM, 102.7, Tri-Cities, Wash.—country
KORD-AM, 87, Tri-Cities, Wash.—country
KCBM-FM, 104.7, La Grande—country
KUCL-FM, 101.1, McCall, Idaho—70s to 90s top 40, mostly rock
KKBC-FM.95.3, Baker City—country
KOPR-FM, 91.5—National Public Radio
KDJY-AM, 1400, John Day—country

Far from the tempering effects of the ocean, the area's winters can be biting cold. They're occasionally marked by howling blizzards of thin, drifting snow, like a scene from a Marlboro commercial.

Most early settlers bypassed this land in favor of more temperate climes west of the Cascades. As wagon trains traveled over the Oregon Trail, this was an area to get *through,* not *to.* Flagstaff Hill near Baker City was a welcome landmark, telling weary travelers that cool, green mountains lay ahead. That hill is now the site of one of Oregon's finest historic museums. (See box below, under "Hells Canyon to Baker City.")

Northeastern Oregon isn't regarded as a major tourist area. Most of its communities are simple working-folk towns and trading centers for farms, ranches and logging operations. By being selective, however, you'll discover that it contains some of the state's most interesting lures.

To find these, we'll take you on a grand loop through this land of far horizons. We'll hedge-hop from one attraction to the next, with smooth highways in between—for the most part. The trip begins in a town that hosts one of the world's largest rodeos.

Pendleton

Population: 15,090   **Elevation: 1,068 feet**

Northeastern Oregon's largest town, Pendleton is supported mostly by wheat, peas and its famous woolen mill. However, don't tell that to the wranglers who come into town from neighboring ranches. As far as they're concerned, this is *cowboy* country. During September, cowboys come from all over the world to take part in the famous Pendleton Roundup.

Originally, the undulating hills around Pendleton were tribal lands of the Umatilla Indians. Among the area's first outside visitors were Lewis and Clark, followed by John Jacob Astor's westbound crew. Pioneer wagons began creaking through this area in the 1840s, laying down the grooves of the Oregon trail.

Although most of these people kept on going, a few ranchers had settled in the area by the 1860s. As the region began to grow, state legislators decided to slice huge Wasco County into several smaller entities. With its seat in The Dalles, it originally occupied 130,000 square miles, including all of western Oregon and generous chunks of Idaho, Montana and Wyoming. There were no towns in the present Pendleton area, so the new Umatilla County seat went to the village of Umatilla, on the Columbia River. Then in 1868, officials decided that was too close to The Dalles, so it was moved southeast, to the banks of the Umatilla River. Its name came from a particularly obscure source—Ohio Senator George H. Pendleton, who had been picked by Oregon Democrats to run for President. Old George never got on the ticket and he never got to Oregon, but the name stuck.

The town took off quickly, becoming a major cattle and sheep-raising center and an important railway and highway stop. Like many frontier towns, it had more saloons than churches, and the downtown area boasted 18 bawdy houses by the late 1800s. City fathers decided things were getting out of hand, so they closed the bordellos and even banned drinking in 1909. Both institutions promptly went underground. The ban on booze was lifted in 1915, but national Prohibition the following year drove the saloons underground again.

"Underground" is a literal term in this old Western town. Late in the last century, Chinese laborers burrowed miles of tunnels beneath the streets of Pendleton, first at the request of merchants, and later to create their own subterranean ghetto.

Doing the town

Today's Pendleton has an early day downtown that's typical of many Oregon cities. Since wheat, farming and cattle keep the economy going, the venerable stone and brick front businesses are well maintained for the most part. Unfortunately for fans of esthetics, many have been modernized.

While hardly a tourist mecca, Pendleton offers several lures sufficient to haul you off the freeway and keep you occupied for a day. To reach the downtown area, take I-84 exit 207, which becomes Court Avenue. You'll soon pass the **Pendleton Roundup Grounds** on your left, site of the **Round-up Hall of Fame.**

Court blends onto one-way Dorion Avenue, which travels through city center. Turn right at Fourth Street and drive two blocks to the **Umatilla County Historical Museum** in an old railroad depot. From here, follow the tracks three blocks to First Street, turn left and go a block to the small store-front office of **Pendleton Underground Tours.** It's on the corner of First and Emigrant. Take First back to Dorion and continue east for a block and a half to the **Pendleton Chamber of Commerce,** in a storefront at 25 SE Dorion, across from the old red brick **City Hall.** It's open weekdays 9 to 5; (503) 276-7411.

☺ While you're downtown stop by **Hamley's Western Store** at 30 SE Court; (503) 276-2321. It's been the quintessential cowboy shop since 1883, with everything for the wrangler and his horse. Hamley custom-made saddles are world famous, and you can watch master craftsmen working weekdays from 9 to 5:30.

To reach the famous **Pendleton Woolen Mills,** follow Dorion through town and continue straight ahead onto Court Street, avoiding a right fork onto a viaduct. The mills appear on your left after a couple of blocks.

An elaborate Oregon Trail interpretive center, similar to the one near Baker, is planned for the near future. It will be located on the nearby Umatilla Indian Reservation, just east of town off I-84. That seems ironic, since it was trail that "opened" the West and forced the Indians onto reservations. Check with the chamber of commerce for progress; (503) 276-7411.

ATTRACTIONS
(In order of appearance)

Round-up Hall of Fame ● *At the Rodeo Grounds, under the south grandstand area; (503) 276-2553. Open June through mid-September Monday-Friday 1 to 4; free.* This "museum" is interesting if you're a rodeo fan or an aficionado of the Old West. Exhibits include photos and artifacts concerning the rodeo, its history and its colorful characters. Even some of the better bucking stock is honored.

Umatilla County Historical Society Museum ● *108 SW Frazer (at the railroad tracks); (503) 276-0012. Tuesday-Saturday 10 to 4. Free; donations appreciated.* The carefully restored 1909 California-style railroad station that houses the museum is as interesting as what's inside. Sheep, not cattle, are a focal point. Exhibits trace the local woolies industry and the establishment of the Pendleton Mills. Other displays concern the Umatilla Indians, the Oregon Trail and the coming of the railroad.

☺ **Pendleton Underground Tours** • *37 SW Emigrant Ave.; (503) 276-0730. Monday-Saturday 9 to 5. Underground tour and "Cozy Rooms" bordello tour are $5 each; they can be taken concurrently. MC/VISA.* This is where you *really* learn about Pendleton's wild and sinful past. In 1989, a non-profit group spent hundreds of hours cleaning and restoring some of the old Chinese tunnels, and began conducting tours. They were expanded to include an upstairs trip through one of the town's most famous bordellos, which had been boarded up since a Presbyterian minister chased the last of the "girls" out of town in 1954. The tours are conducted beneath and within the Hendricks building, built in 1897 as a brothel by one Christopher Columbus Hendricks.

As you prowl Pendleton's darkened innards, knowledgeable guides explain that 70 miles of tunnels were dug by Chinese immigrants between 1870 and 1930. Exhibits and mannequins re-create the businesses—legitimate and otherwise—that once thrived down here. Butcher shops and ice plants took advantage of the cool temperatures. Illegal saloons and opium dens, often with hidden doors and secret passages, thrived beside them.

The "Cozy Rooms" tour takes you upstairs to Miss Stella's bordello and boarding house, furnished in the 1920s to 1950s periods. Tasseled lamps, plush drapes and fainting couches recall the days when dallying with the ladies wasn't so risky. The girl's rooms had windows on the hallway, which—the guide said with a straight face—led to the term "window shopping."

☺ **Pendleton Woolen Mills tour** • *1307 SE Court Place; (503) 276-6911. Tours weekdays at 9, 11, 1:30 and 3 (or more often if crowds warrant). Sales room open Monday-Friday 8 to 4:45 and Saturday 9 to noon. The tour is free; sales room accepts MC/VISA.* If you've never been inside a textile factory, this tour can be quite fascinating. It's also done in state-of-the-art style: visitors are given individual headphones to hear the tour guides in the noisy mill. You'll see machines spinning dyed yarn into thread at the rate of half a mile a minute, and automatic looms that create the famous Pendleton geometric patterns. The machines hold 7,800 warp threads to weave these intricate designs; shuttles dart back and forth 220 times a minute. It's intriguing to watch these brilliant fabrics take form before your eyes.

The Pendleton woolen tradition began in 1909 when Yorkshireman Thomas Kay opened a mill to weave blankets for Indians. That's an interesting twist on the Navajo idea of Indians weaving blankets for whites. The firm has expanded to 14 plants around the country. It's still run by the founding family, and it's still making Indian blankets, along with an extensive line of clothing.

ANNUAL EVENTS

The event is the **Pendleton Round-Up**, of course, which turns the entire town into "The World's Round-Up City" during four days in mid-September. It's been doing so since 1910, and for several years it was the world's largest rodeo. Tickets and lodgings go fast, so if you're a rodeo fan, make arrangements early by calling (800) 524-2984. The big celebration also includes an historic pageant, parade, barbecues and large Native American encampment.

If you really want an overdose of rodeo, follow the professional cowboys to the "Big Four" of the region: Southeast Washington Frontier Days at Walla Walla, the Ellensburg (Washington) Rodeo, the Lewiston (Idaho) Round-Up and the Pendleton show. They're held consecutively from early to mid-September. High-point cowboys competing in all four win special prizes at the end of the Pendleton Round-Up.

Contact the Commerce at (503) 276-7411 for information on these other annual events:

Pendleton Arts Festival in May.
Cowboy Poet Convention in late June
Westward Ho! wagon train trek in mid-September.
Wine and Cheese Festival in mid-October.

WHERE TO DINE

Chimiyoti's Restaurant & Lounge • ∆∆ $$

137 S. Main St.; (503) 276-4314. Italian-American; full bar service. Monday-Saturday from 4 p.m. MC/VISA. Attractive, cozy cafè with dark woods and comfy booths; popular with locals. The busy menu offers an array of pastas, some Italian chicken and veal dishes, plus typical American steaks, chops, chicken and seafood. Ample servings at modest prices.

Cookie Tree Bakery and Café • ∆ $

30 SW Emigrant at Main; (503) 278-0343. American; no alcohol. Weekdays 7 a.m. to 3:30 p.m. No credit cards. A handy breakfast and lunch stop, featuring homemade soups, salads and bakery items.

Circle S Barbecue • ∆∆ $$

210 SE Fifth between Dorion and Emigrant; (503) 276-9637. American; full bar service. Tuesday-Saturday 7 to 10, Sunday 7 to 9, closed Monday. Major credit cards. Attractive Western-style cafè done up in cattle brands, wagon wheels and farm implements. The menu fits the dècor, with assorted steaks, plus barbecued chicken and ribs.

Golden Fountain • ∆ $

437 S. Main at SW Frazer; (503) 276-6130. Chinese-American; wine and beer. Daily 11 to 10. MC/VISA. A simple family restaurant with an American diner look, except for a couple of red-tasseled lanterns. Menu offers regional Chinese fare ranging from mild Cantonese to spicy Szechuan, plus American steaks, pork chops, veal cutlets and country fried chicken. Very modest prices; many dinners under $8.

Great Pacific Wine and Coffee Company • ∆ $

403 S. Main at Emigrant; (503) 276-1350. American; wine and beer. Weekdays 8:30 a.m. to 6 p.m., Saturday 9:30 to 5. MC/VISA. Pendleton's attempt at a coffee house succeeds reasonably well. It's set within brick walls with a couple of hanging plants to dress things up. The usual espresso, sandwiches and deli items are served, along with a variety of wines and a couple of microbrews.

☺ Raphael's Restaurant & Lounge • ∆∆∆ $$

233 SE Fourth between Court and Dorion; (503) 276-8500. American; full bar service. Lunch Tuesday-Friday from 11, dinner Tuesday-Saturday from 6. MC/VISA. Pendleton's best restaurant, with a good seafood menu—rare in these parts. It's attractively installed in the 19th century Raley House, with a stylish pub and a Native American art gallery. Well-prepared entrees range from fresh seafood and a good variety of steaks to chicken and pork dishes. Smoked prime rib is a specialty.

Rainbow Café • ∆ $

209 S. Main near Court; (503) 276-4120. American; full bar service. Daily 6 a.m. to 10 p.m. No credit cards. This is *the* cowboy hangout and the liveliest spot in town during rodeo. It's essentially a scruffy old bar decorated mostly with autographed rodeo cowboy photos and steer horns. The rudimentary café behind the smoky bar serves steaks, fried chicken, chicken strips and sandwiches; everything is under $7.

Westward Ho • ∆ $

Main at SW Emigrant; (503) 276-8846. American; full bar service. Monday-Saturday 6 a.m. to 8 p.m., Sunday 6 to 2. MC/VISA. Very basic family café with lots of Formica and a simple steak, chicken and chops menu. Good place for an inexpensive fill-up, since most dinners are under $10.

WHERE TO SLEEP

Chaparral Motel • ⌂ $$

620 SW Tutuilla (P.O. Box 331; I-84 exit 209), Pendleton, OR 97801; (503) 276-8654. Couples $46, singles $36 to $43, kitchenettes $49. Major credit cards. Well-kept 50-unit motel with TV, room phones, some refrigerators. **Denny's** restaurant adjacent.

Econo Lodge • ⌂ $$ ∅

201 SW Court Ave., Pendleton, OR 97801; (800) 446-6900 or (503) 276-5252. Couples $34 to $44, singles $28 to $34, suites $50 to $60. Major credit cards. Well-kept 51-room motel with TV and room phones; some refrigerators. Pool; guest laundry, VCR movie rentals.

Red Lion Inn • ⌂⌂ $$$ ∅

304 SE Nye Ave. (I-84 exit 210; P.O. Box 1556), Pendleton, OR 97801; (800) 547-8010 or (503) 276-6111. Couples $79 to $99, singles $69 to $89, suites from $175. Major credit cards. Very attractive 168-room inn with TV, pay movies, room phones; pool, hot tub. **Coffee Garden** and **Dining Room** serve 6 a.m. to 10:30 p.m.; dinners $8 to $18; full bar service.

Tapadera Inn • ⌂ $$

105 SE Court Ave. (at SE First Street), Pendleton, OR 97801; (800) 722-8277 or (503) 276-2321. Couples $36.45 to $40.50, singles $27.85 to $29.50. Major credit cards. A 47-room motel with TV, room phones, some refrigerators. Free passes to adjacent athletic club. **Steele's Bar & Grill** serves American fare Monday-Saturday 6:30 a.m. to 10 p.m., Sunday 6:30 to 2; dinners $9 to $15; full bar service.

Bed & breakfast inn

☺ Swift Station Inn • ⌂⌂ $$$ ∅

602 SE Byers, Pendleton, OR 97801; (503) 276-3739. Couples $60 to $100, singles $55 to $95. Three rooms with TV; some private and some shared baths; full or continental breakfast. MC/VISA. Imposing 1896 Victorian with gabled roofs and stone porch railing, restored and furnished with European and American antiques. Tasteful living room and parlor with fireplaces; old fashioned porch swing and carefully tended gardens.

WHERE TO CAMP

During round-up days, 1,500 RV and tent spaces are made available at the Department of Public Works area at 3920 Westgate; take I-84 exit 207. There are rest rooms but no regular hookups and no advance reservations. Just show up during rodeo week, check in at the office and find a place to park.

Brooke RV Court • *5 NE Eighth St., Pendleton, OR 97801; (503) 276-5353. RV sites; water and electric $15.* Some pull-throughs and shaded sites; showers, coin laundry, RV supplies; near the Umatilla River.

Joe DuBay's RV Park • *1500 SE Byers Ave., Pendleton, OR 97801; (503) 276-5408. RV sites only; water and electric $12. No reservations or credit cards.* Some shaded sites and pull- throughs; showers, cable TV, barbecues, playground.

Stolar's Mobile Home and RV Park • *15 SE 11th St., Pendleton, OR 97801; (503) 276-0734. RV sites only; full hookups $12.* Mostly shaded sites; TV and phone hookups, showers, coin laundry, picnic tables; near the Umatilla River.

PENDLETON TO LA GRANDE

You become one with the Oregon Trail—more or less—as you continue eastward from Pendleton on I-84. The freeway follows much of its course through here and informational kiosks mark its progress and highlights.

Immediately east of Pendleton, the highway passes through **Umatilla Indian Reservation.** It takes a graceful, sweeping climb up **Emigrant Hill,** a barren rise in the foothills of the Blue Mountains. The emigrant trail shifted northward here to avoid the sharp drop into the Umatilla River valley below. Incidentally, if your vehicle tends to overheat, avoid this long uphill grade on a hot afternoon.

Midway up, you can pause at a viewpoint for a panorama of geometrical brown and green farmlands, wheat fields and prairie country, accented here and there by the swirls of freshly tilled fields. With its old tree-lined streets, Pendleton at riverside looks remarkably green and appealing from up here.

By the time you reach the top, you're in a forest of ponderosa pine, the tree of choice in this high, arid country. At **Deadman Pass,** exit 220 takes you to a rest stop and an Oregon Trail information kiosk. The pass was named not for an emigrant mishap, but for the death of a teamster during a late 19th century Indian war.

Just beyond, the Meacham exit takes you to **Emigrant Springs State Park** with another Oregon Trail marker. You learn that John Jacob Astor's group past through here in 1812, blazing the way for the flood of immigrants that would follow in three decades. The park offers nicely shaded campsites, $13 for full hookups and $11 for none, or you can sleep in "totem bunkhouses" (bring your own sleeping bag) for $14.

The tiny town of **Meacham** is just beyond, offering gas and provisions and not much else. The 4,193-foot highway summit of the Blue Mountains is just beyond. The blue-green crests of "Switzerland of America"—the high Wallowas—appear on the far horizon, still streaked by snow in late summer. At your feet is the beige **Grand Ronde Valley**, marked by the snaking green streak of the Grand Ronde River. Cradled between the Blue Mountains and the Wallowas, it's one of the largest mountain-rimmed basins in America.

"La grande ronde!" (the great circle) exclaimed French-Canadian trappers who first laid eyes on this basin. For the tribes of the Nez Percè (*Nay Per-SAY,* meaning pierced nose), this was the "Valley of Peace," their summer gathering ground.

That name became cruel irony when the first wagons of the Oregon Trail began rolling through here. Some of the pioneers, weary of their long journey, decided this was a good place to stay. The inevitable clash between Native Americans and "new" Americans began. Initially, the intruders settled near present day La Grande and the peaceful Nez Percè withdrew farther up the valley, toward their spiritual homeland of the Wallowas.

They even yielded their land formally, signing treaties with the U.S. Army that would "guarantee" them the higher Wallowa Valley if they surrendered the Grand Ronde to the interlopers. Then the newcomers began coveting the Wallowa Valley, particularly when gold was discovered in the area.

The treaties became a shameful trail of broken promises that led to one of the last American Indian wars. The Nez Percè War of 1871 resulted in a tragedy of fame for their leader, *Hin-Mah-T-Lat-Kekht,* whose name meant "Thunder Rolling in the Mountains." Historians would know him better as Chief Joseph.

La Grande

Population: 11,800   **Elevation: 2,784 feet**

The ponderosas thin out quickly as you wind down through a shallow river canyon, following a creek-sized tributary of the Grand Ronde. Below is the community that serves as a gateway to the Wallowas and the seat of Union County.

Like Pendleton, La Grande is a tough old town that has found its economic niche in wheat, cattle and farming. Although not a tourist center, it functions as a gateway to the lakes, streams, campgrounds and other high country lures of the Wallowas and the Blues.

Its downtown area, a mix of old brick and fifties modern, appears reasonably prosperous. Some of the 19th century homes along its tree-shaded streets have been nicely restored. Overall, it has the look of a town that's content with itself.

The **La Grande-Union County Chamber of Commerce** is on the eastern edge of town, on your left in a little Spanish-style red brick building at 2111 Adams Ave.; (503) 963-8588. It's open weekdays 9 to noon and 1 to 5. Here you can pick up lodging and dining guides and driving routes through some of Union County's scenic and historic regions.

ACTIVITIES

Fishing • Little Creek Outfitters, P.O. Box 3935, La Grand, OR 97850, (503) 963-7878, offers a variety of fishing trips on the Grand Ronde and John Day rivers.

High Country pursuits • For information on hiking, camping, fishing and other recreation in the Wallowa-Whitman National forest of the Wallowa and Blue mountains, contact the **La Grande Ranger District,** Highway 30, (P.O. Box 502), La Grande, OR 97850; (503) 963-7186.

River trips • Northwest Dories runs whitewater dory trips on the Grand Ronde; contact the firm at 1127 Airway Ave., Lewiston, ID 83501, (800) 877-DORY or (208) 743-4201 or P.O. Box 16, Altaville, CA 95221 (209) 736-0805. **Little Creek Outfitters** (listed above) runs the Grand Ronde in inflatable rafts. **Tildon's River Tours**, 1610 Alder St., Elgin, OR 97827, (503) 437-9270, offers fishing and float trips on area rivers.

UNION COUNTY ANNUAL EVENTS

Call the chamber at (503) 963-8588 for details on these functions:

Raft Race and Collegiate Rodeo in La Grande, first Saturday in May.

Elgin Stampede in Elgin, mid-July; (503) 437-1971.

Union County Fair in La Grande, first weekend in August.

Oregon Trail Days Rendezvous and **Arts & Crafts Fair** in La Grande, third weekend in August.

WHERE TO DINE

☺ Centennial House • ∆∆∆ $$

1606 Sixth St.; (503) 963-6089. American-continental; full bar service. Dinner Tuesday-Saturday 5 to 9, Sunday brunch 9:30 to 2. MC/VISA, DISC. Handsomely elegant early American style dining room in a restored 1890 Victorian. Eclectic menu features egg plant Parmesan, pepper steak, veal marinara, chicken Newport in white wine and assorted pastas. Homemade dessert are a specialty. To find the restaurant, turn right from Adams onto Elm Street for a block, then do a half right onto Sixth.

Golden Crown Restaurant • ∆∆ $

1116 Adams at Elm; (503) 963-5907. Chinese-American; wine and beer. Daily from 11 a.m. MC/VISA. Basic vinyl and Naugahyde cafè with tasty Chinese food at modest prices. Mostly Cantonese, with a few spicy Szechuan entrèes and some American steaks, chickens and chops. The won ton soup is particularly generous and hearty.

Mamacita's • ∆∆ $

110 Depot near Adams; (503) 963-6223. Mexican; wine and beer. Lunch Tuesday-Friday 11 to 2, dinner Tuesday-Sunday 5:30 to 9 (until 10 Friday-Saturday). MC/VISA. Bright, cheerful and lively Mexican bistro housed in old brick, trimmed with lace cafè curtains and potted plants. Very well-prepared and properly spicy fare.

Wrangler Steak House • ∆∆ $$

1914 Adams Ave.; (503) 963-3131. American, full bar service. Monday-Friday 11 to 10, Saturday 4 to 10, Sunday noon to 9. MC/VISA, AMEX, DISC. A cowboy-modern cafè that looks right at home in northeastern Oregon, with Western decor and Naugahyde booths. It's dimly lit enough to be considered cozy. Menu focuses on steaks and seafood, with a couple of chicken dishes and an all-you-can-eat salad bar.

WHERE TO SLEEP

Broken Arrow Lodge • △ $ Ø

2215 E. Adams Ave., La Grande, OR 97850; (503) 963-7116. Couples and singles $28 to $34, suites $45 to $65. Major credit cards. A 34-room motel with TV and room phones.

Green Well Motel • ⌂⌂ $ ∅
305 Adams Ave. (at Walnut), La Grande, OR 97850; (503) 963-4134. Couples $34 to $36, singles $28 to $30. Major credit cards. A 33-unit motel with TV movies, room phones, refrigerators and pool.

Pony Soldier Inn • ⌂⌂ $$$ ∅
2612 Island Ave. (just off I-84), La Grande, OR 97850; (800) 634-PONY or (503) 963-7195. Couples $55 to $67, singles $46 to $57, suites $65. Major credit cards. Attractive 150-room motel with TV, room phones, refrigerators; guest laundry, pool, sauna and exercise room.

Stardust Lodge • ⌂ $$ ∅
402 Adams Ave., La Grande, OR 97850; (503) 963-4166. Couples $32.40 to $38.88, singles $27 to $32.40. Major credit cards. A 32-unit motel with TV movies, room phones and pool.

Bed & breakfast inn

Stange Manor Bed & Breakfast • ⌂⌂⌂ $$$ ∅
1612 Walnut St. (at Spring), La Grande, OR 97850. Couples $65, singles $60. Five rooms, two with room phones, three with private baths; full breakfast. MC/VISA. Imposing Georgian colonial mansion built in 1923 by a local lumber baron, furnished with antiques, including some originals. Beautiful woodwork in comfortable sitting room and throughout the house; spacious grounds; bicycles available for guests.

WHERE TO CAMP

Wallowa-Whitman National Forest • *C/o La Grande Ranger District, Highway 30, P.O. Box 502, La Grande, OR 97850; (503) 963-7186.* Dozens of forest service campgrounds are scattered through the Wallowa and Blue mountain ranges north, south and east of La Grande. Contact the district office for locations.

Hilgard Junction State Park • *Starkey Road, eight miles east of La Grande, off I-84. Primitive sites with no hookups, $9. No reservations or credit cards.* On the banks of the Grand Ronde River; pit toilets, barbecues and picnic tables, swimming, boating and fishing. Oregon Trail exhibit.

Hot Lake RV Resort • *65182 Hot Lake Lane (P.O. Box 1601), La Grande, OR 97850; (503) 963-LAKE. RV sites, full hookups $16. Reservations accepted; MC/VISA.* Attractive RV resort at a natural hot spring; some pull-throughs, mini-mart, coin laundry, heated pool, mineral baths and spa, steam sauna. A section of the Oregon Trail is adjacent. To reach Hot Lake, take I-84 exit 265 onto State Highway 203 and follow it five miles southeast.

ENTERPRISE TO JOSEPH

Interstate 84 travels southeast through the Grand Ronde Valley, past prairies and pasturelands between the Wallowa and Blue Mountains. You'll find Oregon Trail markers at the **Charles Reynolds Rest Stop** about 12 miles south and at the **Baker Valley Rest Stop** midway between North Powder and Baker. The trail follows the freeway quite closely through here.

We're going to suggest a different, more scenic route, however—to Joseph in the Wallowa Valley, and then on to the Hells Canyon of the Snake River. From La Grande, pick up State Highway 82 and head north through **Island City**; watch for a left turn to keep you on the right route. You'll be-

THE TRAIL OF BROKEN PROMISES

It was one of the last Indian wars in the American West, and one of the most tragic. The Nez Perce tribe of eastern Oregon and northwestern Idaho had always tried to live at peace with the intruding whites. They fed and helped pioneer groups that struggled through their lands. Even when settlers began taking their ancestral homeland in northeastern Oregon, tribal chiefs reluctantly signed treaties instead of making war.

One such treaty, drawn up in 1855, yielded considerable territory to the whites but permitted the Wallowa band of the Nez Perce to retain their summer homeland in the Wallowa Valley. Then in 1863, several Nez Perce chiefs were forced to sign a treaty that surrendered seven-eights of the land which the American government had granted them earlier.

Wallowa Chief Ta-Weet-Tuekakas (Old Joseph) had not signed that treaty and assumed his lands were safe. However, white intruders began settling in the Wallowa Valley. In a desperate move to save his summer sanctuary, he agreed to yield other tribal territory to settlers in exchange for the return of the valley. The agreement, signed on August 12, 1868, was the last treaty drawn up between Native Americans and the U.S. Government.

Intruders still swarmed into the region. The Wallowa tribe turned to President U.S. Grant, who issued an executive order barring further settlement. Then gold was discovered in the valley and the order was rescinded.

Old Joseph died in 1871 and young Joseph became chief of the tribe. He was to become one of the most eloquent Indian leaders in America, and a peacemaker who was unable to keep the peace.

Unable to reach a fair settlement with the double-talking American government, Joseph agreed in 1877 to move his people to a reservation in Idaho. However, several outspoken young warriors refused to go. They broke from the tribe and began raiding homesteads, killing several settlers.

No chance for peace

A stunned Joseph knew that peace was now hopeless. He led his tribe on an epic 1,700-mile journey across Idaho and Montana, seeking sanctuary in Canada. Maneuvering brilliantly, the tribe outflanked and outfought the U.S. Army in 13 separate engagements. Later studies indicate that other chiefs were the strategists, particularly a master tactician named Looking Glass. Joseph was more the spiritual leader and protector of the women and children. On October 5, 1877, just 30 miles short of freedom, Joseph's band was trapped in Montana's Bear Paw Mountains and forced to surrender. Facing his captors, he delivered a moving, heart-breaking plea.

"Our little children are freezing to death. My people, some of them, have run away to the hills and have no blankets, no food. No one knows where they are, perhaps freezing to death. I want time to look for my children and see how many I can find. Maybe I shall find them among the dead.

"Hear me, my chiefs. I am tired. My heart is sick and sad. From where the sun now stands, I will fight no more forever."

However, he continued his fight with eloquent words, journeying to Washington to seek fair treatment for Native Americans. In 1879 he pleaded his people's cause to the Department of Indian Affairs:

"I have heard talk and talk, but nothing is done. Good words do not pay for my dead people. They do not pay for my country, now overrun by white men. Treat all men alike. Give them the same law. Give them all an even chance to live and grow."

His pleas fell on indifferent ears. Chief Joseph died on September 21, 1904, on the Nespelem Reservation in Washington state without ever returning to his cherished Wallowa Valley.

gin a long gentle climb through attractive patchwork farming and ranching country. **Elgin,** 17 miles north of La Grande, is a farming-lumbering town of 1,701, with a prim brick and fieldstone downtown area.

☺ Pause for a look at the old brick Colonial style **Elgin City Hall and Opera house,** 100 Eight St.; (503) 437-2520. This unusual dual-function building was completed in 1912. The opera house portion has been restored to its original grandeur, with plush draperies, elaborate backdrops and a *rococo* decor, used for live performances and weekend movies.

Beyond Elgin, you'll achieve the 3,638-foot heights of **Minam Summit.** Starting downhill, you follow the Wallowa River through a shallow canyon into the ancestral lands of the Nez Percè—the Wallowa Valley.

No wonder Joseph was heartbroken! His Land of the Winding Waters is one of the prettiest valleys in all of Oregon, perhaps in all of the American West. It's a contented land today. Recalling the tragedy of the Nez Perce, you may feel a tug of sadness as your eyes travel across its grasslands to foothill woodlands and up into the snow-streaked ramparts of the Wallowas. Cows and sheep lunch on lush grass, red barns and grand old ranch homes huddle beneath stands of cottonwoods and slender poplars.

Tiny towns of **Wallowa** (population 805) and **Lostine** (207) come and go in lazy blinks of the eye. As you drive, the announcer on the local radio station invites you to the annual chamber of commerce agricultural tour, with luncheon served by the dairy wives.

Just short of Enterprise, an imposing log structure crowning a low hill houses the **Wallowa Mountains Visitor Center.** This jointly-operated facility offers information on Wallowa-Whitman National Forest, the Eagle Cap Wilderness of the Wallowa Mountains, Hells Canyon National Recreation Area and the Seven Devils Wilderness. Needless to say, it can fill all your outdoor informational needs for the area. Hours are Monday-Saturday 7:30 to 5 and Sunday 10 to 5; (503) 426-4978. The interior is impressive, with a huge ponderosa trunk sprouting through the floor, an a convincing looking stuffed cougar lurking nearby.

Just beyond the visitor center, a monument discusses the May to October 1877 war that sent Joseph and his people on their historic fighting retreat (see box).

A mile from the center is **Enterprise,** population 2,000, the seat of Wallowa County. The main highway follows North Street, turns right onto River Street and keeps going. However, before you keep going, drive down Main Street for a look at its handsome old brick, masonry and wooden false front business district. The cut stone **Wallowa County Courthouse** at River and Main is particularly attractive.

Three miles beyond is the town named in honor of the distinguished Native American leader who—in awful irony—was banished from here.

Joseph & Wallowa Lake

Population: 1,135   **Elevation: 4,400 feet**

"This little town is heaven to us; don't drive like hell through it."

Although not original, the sign at Joseph's town limits reflects the quiet, laid-back attitude of those who live in this remote corner of Oregon. Perhaps it should say: "Don't hurry, don't worry; stop to smell the flowers."

While nearby Wallowa Lake and the mountains beyond are popular tourist areas, Joseph is somewhat less disturbed by the visitor influx. Don't look for stylish boutiques among its weathered old store fronts. We couldn't even find a yogurt shop. It does offer several art galleries and is becoming something of an artists' colony. One operation, **Valley Bronze of Oregon,** is a fair-sized industry, employing 65 people. It maintains a showroom of its sculptures here and in faraway Cannon Beach. Tours of the foundry are conducted daily; write or call Valley Bronze Inc., P.O. Box 669, Joseph, OR 97846; (503) 432-7445.

This rustic art colony of a town occupies an absolute jewel of a spot, set amongst grasslands and woodlands at the base of the craggy Wallowas. Several activities keep this generally peaceful town busy in summer, including a re-enactment of the famous Joseph bank robbery on Wednesdays and Saturdays. The bank was heisted in 1896 and one of the robbers, after serving a suitable prison term, became its vice president!

Next-door Wallowa Lake has its frisky moments, too, with the occasional appearance of its own personal monster. The serpent—we'll call him Wally—has been around since Indian times and a local society has been formed to keep watch.

The **Wallowa County Museum** on Main Street at the south end of town offers the usual busy pioneer exhibits, stuff on the great bank robbery and some nice displays concerning the Nez Percè and Chief Joseph. The structure is a museum-piece as well, dating from 1888. It served as a bank (the one that was robbed), newspaper office, hospital and meeting hall. The museum is open in summers only, daily 10 to 5; (503) 432-6095.

Continuing along Main Street toward Wallowa Lake, you'll encounter the **Indian Cemetery** where Chief Joseph's father, Old Joseph, found his final resting place. His bones were moved here from an earlier burial spot that had become a settler's field. The marker makes no reference to the Nez Percè conflict. Sharing the cemetery are a few pioneers, including Frank and Martha McCully, friends of Chief Joseph's people and the founders of Wallowa County.

☺ **Wallowa Lake,** just beyond the cemetery, is a six-mile-long blue pendant hanging in a glacier-carved valley at the base of the mountains. The largest body of water in northeastern Oregon, it's a classic example of a moraine lake. It is not, however, a wilderness area. It's more of a wooded mini-Disneyland, with "Crazy Cars," bumper boats, mini-golf and burger stands. Resort cabins and summer homes line its shores. When we last visited, the area was jumpin' on a Monday night. Don't come in summer without a reservation.

A slice of the lakefront is occupied by **Wallowa Lake State Park,** offering a campground, fishing, swimming, hiking trails and other outdoor pursuits. It's one of the Oregon parks offering campsite reservations; absolutely essential in summer (see listing below).

The big attraction here, other than the lake, offers a very easy way to get high:

☺ **High Wallowas Tram** ● *Open mid-May to mid-September, 10 to 4; daily June through August, weekends in May and September. Adults $10, kids under 10, $5. MC/VISA.* Here's a quick way to escape Wallowa Lake's crowds. This is the highest and longest aerial tram in America, climbing 3,800 feet to the 8,200-foot crest of Mount Howard. Views are incredible—back down to the lake and valley, and across to the peaks of Eagle Cap Wilderness and the Seven Devils above Hells Canyon. A gentle hiking trail wanders two miles around the crest, with several marked overlooks.

If you continue past the tram base and those tourist cabins, RV parks and summer homes, you'll reach the main trailhead into the **Eagle Cap Wilderness.** With 50 alpine lakes and more than half of Oregon's peaks over 9,000 foot high, it's among the most rugged and unspoiled primitive areas in America. It also is the state's largest federal wilderness preserve, covering 364,325 acres. A nearby **Forest Service Information Center** offers maps, trail guides and advice on high-country hiking. It's open Monday-Saturday 7:30 to 5 and Sunday 10 to 5.

ACTIVITIES

Boating • **Wallowa Lake Marina,** P.O. Box 47, Joseph, OR 97846, (503) 426-4611, rents canoes, boats, paddleboats and water bikes.

Bus service and tours • **Moffit Brothers Transportation,** P.O. Box 156, Lostine, OR 97857, (503) 569-2284, offers scenic tours and daily transit between La Grande and Wallowa Lake.

Cross-country skiing • **Wallowa Lake Marina** (listed above) functions as a Nordic center from December through March, with equipment rentals and 13 miles of groomed trails around the lake; (503) 426-4611.

Horse packing • **Eagle Cap Wilderness Pack Station** at Wallowa Lake, (Box 241, Joseph OR 97846, 503-432-4145), offers guided pack trips, hunting and fishing trips and hourly trail rides. **High Country Outfitters,** Box 26, Joseph, OR 97846, (503) 432-9171, has day rides and pack trips.

Llama packing • **Wallowa Llamas,** Route 1, Box 84, Halfway, OR 97834, (503) 742-2961, runs llama trips into the mountains.

WALLOWA COUNTY ANNUAL EVENTS

Wallowa County Arts Festival, Enterprise in April; (503) 426-4611.

Lostine Flea Market in Lostine, July 4th weekend; (503) 426-4611.

Chief Joseph Days, Joseph's major community celebration with a rodeo, parades, carnival and Native American music and crafts; last weekend of July at Joseph and Wallowa Lake; (503) 432-1015.

Wallowa County Fair in Enterprise, early August; (503) 426-4611.

Wallowa Lake Monster Observation & Preservation Society Gala, Wallowa Lake, third weekend in August; (503) 432-1015.

Alpenfest, Wallowa Lake, Bavarian-Swiss festival,September; 432-1015.

WHERE TO DINE

Cactus Jack's Cowboy Bar • ΔΔ $$

Main Street at McCully, Joseph; (503) 432-6220. American; full bar service. Monday-Thursday 5 to 9, Friday-Saturday 5 to 10, Sunday noon to 9. Lively Western saloon and café housed in one of Joseph's venerable red brick buildings. Small menu features hearty servings of steaks, halibut, smoked chicken breast and chicken fried steak; prime rib on Fridays.

Russell's at the Lake • Δ $ ∅

Wallowa Lake; (503) 432-0591. American; no alcohol. Daily 9 to 9. MC/VISA. Small, informal walk-up café in a log cabin, with outdoor dining on the back lawn. Selection of $5.95 dinners with soup and salad or fries, with hamburger steak: chicken filet, chicken strips or clam strips. Non-smoking interior. Busier'n sin on summer evenings.

☺ Vali's Alpine Deli and Restaurant • △△ $

Wallowa Lake; (503) 432-5691. American and Hungarian-German; wine and beer. Tuesday-Sunday 10 to noon and 5:30 to 9; weekends only in winter. No credit cards. It starts the day as a quick-stop deli, offering homemade doughnuts and takeout items until noon. It then transforms into a German-Hungarian restaurant at night, dishing up *wienerschnitzel, shish kabob* and such, with Bavarian dècor to match.

☺ Camas Dining Room • △△△ $$ Ø

Wallowa Lake Lodge, Wallowa Lake; (503) 432-9821. American and pasta; wine and beer. Breakfast 7 to 11, dinner from 5:30 (no lunch served). MC/VISA. Spacious alpine-style restaurant with beam ceilings and wood paneled walls. Small, select menu includes grilled chicken breast, rib eye steak, halibut, salmon and pasta.

WHERE TO SLEEP

Eagle Cap Chalets • ⌂⌂ $$$ Ø

59879 Wallowa Lake Highway, Joseph (Wallowa Lake), OR 97846; (503) 432-4704. Chalet rooms $43 to $48 (singles $38 to $43), cabins $48 to $67, honeymoon suite $75, condos $55 and $65. Major credit cards. Alpine style lodgings near the lake; rooms with TV and phones. Cabins have electric kitchens; some with fireplaces. All condos have fireplaces and kitchens. Five-night minimum in cabins and condos during summer.

Indian Lodge Motel • ⌂⌂ $$ Ø

201 S. Main St., Joseph, OR 97846; (503) 432-2651. Couples $41 to $49, singles $28 to $30. MC/VISA. Rustic, well-maintained 16-unit motel with TV, room phones and refrigerators. Short walk to downtown Joseph.

Matterhorn Swiss Village • ⌂ $$$ Ø

59950 Wallowa Lake Hwy., Joseph (Wallowa Lake), OR 97846-9797; (503) 432-4071. Couples $50, three $82. MC/VISA. Rustic Swiss-style cottages with kitchens; some fireplaces. Five-night minimum during peak summer season. Other facilities include a gift and sports shops, mountain bike and water ski rentals.

☺ Wallowa Lake Lodge • ⌂⌂⌂ $$$ Ø

Route 1, Box 320, Joseph (Wallowa Lake), OR 97846; (503) 432-9821. Couples and singles $54.50 to $98.50, cabins with kitchens $85 to $115, suites $75 to $105. MC/VISA. Historic alpine lodge near the lake shore with massive fieldstone fireplace and overstuffed chairs in the lobby. It was built in 1923 and recently refurbished. Rooms individually furnished with antiques, with views of the lake or mountains; one and two-bedroom cabins also available. **Camas Dining Room** listed above. The entire lodge and dining room facility is smoke-free.

Bed & breakfast inns

Chandlers' Bed, Bread & Trail Inn • ⌂⌂ $$ Ø

700 S. Main St. (P.O. Box 639), Joseph, OR 97846; (503) 432-9765. Couples $50, singles $40. Five rooms with shared baths; full breakfast. MC/VISA. Shingle-sided "post and beam" farm style home with a sun deck, garden, gazebo and mountain views. Rooms are done in comfortable country furnishings and antiques.

Tamarack Pines Inn ● ⌂ $$$ ∅

Route 1, Box 450, Joseph, OR 97846 (60073 Wallowa Lake Highway, Wallowa Lake); (503) 432-2920. Couples $45 to $70, singles $39 to $63. Four rooms; two share and two private baths; full breakfast. MC/VISA. Ranch style B&B with antique and modern furnishings in comfortable rooms. Tucked among the pines on a landscaped half acre, a short walk from the lake. Trout pond, patio for guest barbecues, bicycles.

WHERE TO CAMP

Park at the River ● *59888 Wallowa Lake Hwy., Joseph (Wallowa Lake), OR 97846; (503) 432-8800. RV sites; full hookups $15.* Tree-shaded park with fairly snug spaces; clean restrooms and showers, cable TV, phone hookup; sun deck near office.

Scenic Meadows RV Park ● *Route #1, 59781 Wallowa Lake Hwy., Joseph (Wallowa Lake), OR 97846; (503) 432-9285. RV sites; water and electric $20. Reservations accepted; no credit cards.* New RV park opened in 1993 with showers, picnic tables, TV hookups, coin laundry. Part of Jack's complex with restaurant, mini-golf, go-carts and other facilities.

Wallowa Lake State Park ● *72214 Marina Lane, Joseph (Wallowa Lake), OR 97846; (503) 432-4185. RV and tent sites; full hookups $14, no hookups $11. It's on the summer state park reservation system; pick up forms at state tourist offices. (See "Getting camped" in Chapter 1.)* Large facility with spaces more crowded than most state parks; barbecues and picnic tables, showers, hiking trails, swimming, fishing, boat rentals and boat ramp adjacent.

Wallowa-Whitman National Forest ● *C/o Wallowa Valley Ranger District, Route 1, Box 270-A, Enterprise, OR 97828; (503) 426-4978.* Several forest service campgrounds are in the Wallowa Valley and Wallowa mountains. Contact the ranger district for locations.

Hells Canyon National Recreation Area

Joseph is a gateway to Hells Canyon, one of America's most remote and beautiful national recreation areas. Established in 1975, it sprawls over 652,488 acres of mountains, high desert and gorges along the Oregon and Idaho sides of the Snake River. It's administered by Wallowa-Whitman National Forest, with headquarters at the **Wallowa Mountains Visitor Center** just west of Enterprise.

Its centerpiece is Hells Canyon of the Snake River, said to be the deepest gorge in North America. We don't agree, although it certainly is an imposing vee-shaped ravine. The Snake River has managed to cut its way between the Seven Devils and Wallowa Mountains, and the canyon's depth is measured from the mountain tops. Many ravine aficionados—including us—insist that the Grand Canyon of the Colorado is the world's deepest ravine, since it's measured from the rim, not from some peak.

But never mind technicalities. Although it lacks the sheer grandeur of the Grand Canyon, it *is* impressive. The Snake River far below offers some of the best whitewater in America, and a long skinny reservoir impounded by Hells Canyon Dam provides fishing and flatwater sports. Most of that access is on the Idaho side.

"If the Grand Canyon is a cathedral," wrote Ric Bailey of Northwest Dories, "then Hells Canyon is a grand stadium, a vast and open chalice filled

A passing speedboat is but a speck on the vast, deep expanse of Hells Canyon Reservoir. The view is from Black Point on the Idaho side. — **Betty Woo Martin**

with wildlife, the remnants of vanished cultures, and the diverse geometry of land forms created by ancient volcanoes."

Much of Hells Canyon NRA can be reached only by foot—or by running its glorious rapids, of course. It contains nearly a thousand miles of trails.

Although few roads reach the canyon itself, you can see some very attractive countryside from the seat of your sedan or RV. We're about to take you through the Oregon side of the recreation area, into an awesome little side canyon, through thick forests and past a couple of campgrounds. You'll then cross over to the Idaho side for a drive along Hells Canyon reservoir. Even though it's partially drowned here, the crevasse is still noteworthy.

Stock up on provisions before you leave Joseph, for there are no facilities beyond the remote hamlet of Imnaha, and no gasoline for more than 80 miles. The route is partly paved, partly gravel and easily negotiable.

To begin, take Wallowa Avenue out of Joseph, heading for Imnaha. You roll through pastureland and prairie, and then begin following a brisk, sparkling stream down into wooded **Little Sheep Creek Canyon.** With the creek as your roadside companion, you descend deeper as grassy, terraced walls rise above you. The canyon narrows as you approach Imnaha, with sculpted buttes and slopes suggesting a mini-Grand Canyon.

☺ Tiny **Imnaha** occupies one of the most striking settings of any town in Oregon, tucked against the confluence of Little Sheep Creek and the Imnaha River. There's not much here—a doll house of a post office, a properly weathered general store with a tavern and café, plus a second café that once shared space with a service station. That's now gone, so we hope you followed our advice to tank up.

The **Imnaha General Store and Bar,** with a rustic, dusty Western look, has a few grocery items and other supplies. Its café serves breakfast, lunch and light suppers from 9 to 6. **Imnaha Cafè** across the street has a few steak, chicken and chop dinners, plus breakfast and lunch fare; it serves from 8 a.m. to 7 p.m.

☺ Before heading south for Hells Canyon NRA, follow the **Imnaha River Canyon** north for six miles. The route takes you through a narrow and attractive agricultural valley embraced by the terraced walls of the canyon. The rich green pasturelands, beige canyon shapes with dark outcroppings and blue river present a striking picture.

The road disintegrate after six miles, so double back to Imnaha. From here, you can drive a tough, steep and bumpy 24 miles out to **Hat Point** for a Hells Canyon overlook. The view of the tiny thread of the Snake River nearly 7,000 feet below, and the Seven Devils Mountains across the way is excellent. You'll have to decide if it's worth the bouncy ride. Plans are afoot to improve the road and erect several interpretive signs along the way, so you might inquire at the Enterprise visitor center before you sally forth.

From Imnaha, head south into the recreation area, following more of that striking river canyon. You soon lose the pavement, although the gravel road is well-maintained most of the way. If you haven't had lunch, you'll find some nice picnic spots along the river. These aren't formal picnic areas, but turnouts where you can sit on a river rock, munch a sandwich and admire the scenery.

You're not yet in the wilderness, since small farms still line the river. It's an attractive countryside—a mix of old barns, tawny meadows, grasslands and clumps of ponderosas. You're likely to see some wranglers heading their herds for the ranch.

Sixteen miles from Imnaha, the canyon narrows and the road becomes a cliff-hanger, 50 or 60 feet above the river. It begins to unkink a few miles farther, as it enters an evergreen forest. At **Imnaha Hatchery,** a weir diverts the last of the upstream spawning salmon—looking much the worse for the wear—into a holding tank. Their eggs will provide the seed for the next batch, to be released downstream. It's amazing to think that they've made it all the way from the mouth of the Columbia River!

Just beyond the hatchery, veer to the left at a fork (no sign offered directions when we passed), and you soon pick up pavement. A mile beyond are two forest service campgrounds, **Black Horse** and **Ollokoot** on either side of the river. They're nicely wooded, with paved interior roads but no plumbing. Sites are $4 a night.

Just beyond, Forestry Road 3965 leads about eight miles to a **Hells Canyon overlook.** It's graveled and in much better shape than the rocky trail to Hat Point. The river is still far below, a thin blue vein weaving through the vee-shaped canyon.

Return to the paved highway and continue south. You leave your faithful Imnaha River companion and begin a steep spiral up and over a wooded crest, then downward along the course of Pine Creek. You soon reach a townlet of the same name at the junction with State Highway 86. **Pine Creek** offers gas pumps, a general store, cafè and bar.

Head east on Highway 86, and you soon arrive at the **Oxbow Crossing** of the Snake River on the Oregon-Idaho border. **Copperfield Park** on the Oregon side is a spotlessly-maintained small RV park, picnic area and boat launch. The campground has showers, flush potties and good prices—$3 a night for full hookups and $1 for tents. It's run by the Idaho Power Company, which operates nearby Oxbow Dam and Hells Canyon Dam, 24 miles downstream. The becalmed river here is popular with power boaters, water-skiers and fisherpersons, underlining the "recreation" part of Hells Canyon National Recreation Area. The reservoirs are noted for their bass fishing, and anglers catch steelhead downstream from Hells Canyon Dam. Oxbow has no visitor facilities and Hells Canyon is open to visitors only from 1 to 2 p.m. (Mountain time, so add an hour.)

☺ However, the drive to **Hells Canyon Dam** on the Idaho side is a worthy excursion. Following a paved, winding road that clings to the side of the steep walled canyon, you'll alternately skim the edge of the reservoir and then climb high above it. After five miles, you encounter a second Idaho Power campground and picnic facility, **Hells Canyon Park.** It's an invitingly green and shady haven in this mostly-beige canyon, offering facilities and prices similar to those at Copperfield Park.

We think the views of craggy Hells Canyon—reservoir and all—are more awesome here than at Hat Point. The vista is especially awesome from Black Point, about 16 miles downstream from Oxbow Crossing. Looking at the slender, twisting reservoir several hundred feet below, one can't help wondering what a superb sight the canyon must have offered before the dam was built.

Unlike the low-lying dams of the Columbia corridor, Hells Canyon is a lofty concrete wedge. It spans this rock-ribbed ravine like a smaller version of Hoover Dam on the Colorado River's Black Canyon. Just downstream, the road leads to a favored put-in for rafters. A new seasonal visitor center and launch ramp was completed in 1993. It's part of the ongoing improvement and expansion of Hells Canyon National Recreation Area facilities.

Since there's no way to get out of the canyon for several dozen miles downstream, and since the rapids often are *huge,* the Snake is run primarily by commercial outfitters. It is, incidentally, one of the most incredible white-water trips in America. You'll note that there are no fish ladders at Hells Canyon Dam. It's so high and the canyon walls are so steep that the salmon would have to take an elevator.

ACTIVITIES & INFORMATION

For recreational information on the area, contact: **Hells Canyon National Recreation Area**, 88401 Highway 82, Enterprise, OR 97828; (503) 426-4978.

Backpacking trips ● **Hughes River Expeditions,** P.O. Box 217, Cambridge, ID 83610, (208) 257-3477; **Northwest Voyageurs,** P.O. Box 373, Lucile, ID 83542, (800) 727-9977 or (208) 628-3780.

Fishing trips ● **Hells Canyon Fishing Charters,** P.O. Box 232, Riggins, ID 83549, (208) 628-3714.

Horsepackers ● **Jeff Moore,** Route 1, Box 270, Joseph, OR 97846; **Karl Patton,** Route 1, Box 138, Joseph, OR 97846, (503) 432-4521; **Gary Marks,** Route 1, Box 454, Imnaha, OR 97842, (503) 577-3157; **Steen's Wilderness Adventures,** Route 1, Box 73, Joseph, OR 97846, (503) 432-5315; **Tri-State Outfitters,** P.O. Box 370, Joseph, OR 97846, 432-6685.

Llama packers ● **Wallowa Llamas,** Route 1, Box 84, Halfway, OR 97834; (503) 742-2961.

☺ **River runners** ● Among numerous outfits that run Hells Canyon are: **Hells Canyon Adventures** (jet boats and whitewater rafts), P.O. Box

A LONG, LONG TRAIL A-WINDING

"When the pioneers reached Flagstaff Hill, they thought they'd died and gone to heaven. And of course many of them had."

This cryptic comment in a national magazine is typical of the current interest swirling around the dusty Oregon Trail. Flagstaff Hill is just outside Baker City, where a $10 million Bureau of Land Management Oregon trail interpretive center opened in May, 1992. One of the finest exhibit centers in the West, it's among several new facilities recently completed or planned along the 2,170-mile trail that stretched from Sapling Grove near Independence, Missouri, to Oregon City.

Congress voted in 1978 to designate it as a national historic trail. Nearly 200 sites have been selected for landmark signs, monuments or interpretive centers. Much of this activity is focused in Oregon, since this is both the end of and the reason for the trail.

Interest in a cross-country wagon trail was stirred after the Lewis and Clark expedition of 1803-1806 brought back tales of rushing rivers, great forests and fertile valleys around the far-away Columbia River. Following some of the Lewis and Clark route, plus Indian game trails and mountain men's paths, the pioneers blazed a trail through Nebraska, Wyoming and southern Idaho.

The dusty trek to Flagstaff Hill

The trail entered Oregon at Farewell Bend on the Snake River, where pioneers struck out across hot, dusty prairie. Flagstaff Hill is significant, since it marked the end of a thirsty crossing and the beginning of Oregon green. From here, the Oregon Trail traveled through the lush Powder River Valley, past the foothills of the Blue Mountains and reached the Columbia River at The Dalles. There, pioneers had to brave a dangerous raft trip through downriver rapids until one Samuel Barlow built a cutoff south of Mount Hood. Interstate 84 roughly follows the Oregon Trail through most of the state, not for historic reasons but because that was the most feasible route for the freeway's predecessor, U.S. Highway 30. Oregon Trail info centers have been built at rest stops along I-84, and an interpretive center is planned near La Grande for 1994.

The epic crossing to Oregon's fertile valleys continued for just over 20 years, from the early 1840s to the 1860s. Estimates of the number who crossed vary from 250,000 to 300,000. Coupled with the argonauts of the 1848-1854 California Gold Rush—who shared the first half of the trail—this was the largest mass migration in the world's history.

Ten percent perished

One in ten died on the trail. Despite portrayals in old Hollywood films, Indians accounted for only a few casualties, while thousands of them died at the hands of the pioneers. Debilitation and disease—dysentery, smallpox and cholera—were by far the biggest killers of the Oregon-bound travelers. One historian described the trail as a 2,000-mile-long cemetery. The great majority survived, however, to become Oregon's first citizens and to ensure that this far-away territory would be a part of America.

Major celebrations were scheduled at cities and towns along the trail during 1993 to mark its 150th anniversary (although the first crossing was 1841). Much of this activity was coordinated by members of the Oregon-California Trails Association, called "rut nuts" for their zeal in seeking traces of the historic routes. The group scheduled its 1993 convention in Baker City.

If you'd like to follow the trail through Oregon, ask for a copy of the *Oregon Trail* brochure from the Oregon Tourism Division, 775 Summer St., NE, Salem, OR 97310; (800) 547-7842. Another good information source is the National Historic Oregon Trail Interpretive Center, P.O. Box 987, Baker City, OR 97814; (503) 523-1843.

159, Oxbow, OR 97840, (800) 422-3568 or (503) 785-3352; **Hells Canyon Challenge** (jet boats), Star Route, Box 25, Lostine, OR 97857, (503) 569-2445; **Hughes River Expeditions** (whitewater rafts) P.O. Box 217, Cambridge, ID 83610, (208) 257-3477; **Northwest Dories** (whitewater dory trips), 1127 Airway Ave., Lewiston, ID 83501, (800) 877-DORY or (208) 743-4201 or P.O. Box 16, Altaville, CA 95221 (209) 736-0805; **Oregon Trail Adventures** (whitewater rafts), 66716 Highway 237, La Grande, OR 97850, (503) 534-5393; **Steen's Wilderness Adventures** (whitewater rafts), Route 1, Box 73, Joseph, OR 97846, (503) 432-5315.

HELLS CANYON TO BAKER CITY

After retracing your route from the dam, head west on State Highway 83 through semi-barren hills. The hamlet of **Halfway** comes and goes in a blink. (It was Halfway between two old gold mining camps.) But before you blink, you might want to stop at Sandy Kennedy's **Wildflowers of Oregon** in the old church on Main Street. Her cottage industry makes scores of dried flower wreaths, sachets and bouquets from wildflowers gathered locally. Hours for the factory and retail outlet are Monday-Saturday 8 to 5; (503) 742- 6474.

Leaving Halfway, you'll climb steeply out of the Snake River valley, cresting at 3,653 feet. At the summit, pause for a look over your shoulder at the **Seven Devils,** squatting like hunched, weathered old men on the eastern horizon. The highway winds down into a pleasantly green farming valley surrounding the community of **Richland,** with 175 folks and a couple of stores. A few miles beyond, you cross a low summit and pick up the rocky trickle of the **Powder River.** It will lead you through bleak hills and along a dusty sagebrush plain the pioneers called Virtue Flat.

You're still several miles from Baker City and the land seems to become increasingly barren, increasingly lonely. This is a vast expanse of beige hills and silver sage, reaching from horizon to horizon. Pull over to the shoulder and listen. Is that the distant rumble of a wagon train, the shuffle of oxen feet, the squeak of leather harness? Or is it only the wind, a twig of sage brushing against an old fence post?

This lonesome land has remained unchanged since the first wagon trains passed through 150 years ago. A few days earlier, the pioneers had left the security of the Snake River at Farewell Bend and started across this dusty prairie. They had to rely on seasonal streams which often were dry when they reached here in late summer or early fall. If the country is lonely and barren now, it was desolate and foreboding then.

Listen again.

"I have just washed the dust out of my eyes so that I can see to get supper."

"Oh dear, I do so want to get there! It is now almost four months since we slept in a house."

You look ahead, squinting into the hard afternoon sun. You expect to see nothing but the narrow band of asphalt that curves and disappears over the next hill. Then you catch a glint of light atop that hill. You drive closer and see a large building up there, looking as lonely as the rest of this country. However, once you step inside this structure, the ghosts of the old Oregon Trail will come alive.

☺ **National Historic Oregon Trail Interpretive Center** • *Flagstaff Hill, near Baker City; (503) 523-1843. Daily 9 to 4; longer hours in summer; free.* Bureau of Land Management officials re-invented the museum when they completed this 23,000 square foot, $10 million museum in 1992. The facility's rather spartan barn-like exterior belies the excellence within.

You're greeted by a 100-foot long life-sized mockup of a pioneer train with loaded wagons, oxen, mules, sunbonneted women, leather-skinned men, dusty children and the straggling cows and other livestock that accompanied these trains across country. The animals are all mounted specimens, the human mannequins modeled after real people. You hear the creak of leather, the shrill cry of the women, the shouts of the wagonmaster. The crossing of the Oregon Trail lives before your eyes.

Beyond the imposing diorama, a series of graphics, artifacts and excellent videos portray various phases of the crossing. You learn what America was like in the 1840s, what moved these ordinary people to strike out across a hostile, unknown land. They piled their baggage and their hopes into a rough wooden wagon "slightly bigger than a compact car and looking like a sun bonnet on wheels." They walked while their possessions and provisions rode. They walked for two thousand miles, 20 miles a day for five months through soggy spring rains and dusty summer heat. It was a desperate slow-motion race to beat something even worse: winter. A graphic at the entrance best sums up this American saga:

No one has ever seen anything quite like it before. More than 300,000 men, women and children crossed the trail. They sensed that they were making history. While heroic, they were an imperfect people. Intolerant, prone to violence, exploitive and sometimes ill-tempered, they carried mixed baggage. Despite some tragic consequences, the story of the Oregon Trail is an epic of human endurance and reminds us of those who came as empire builders.

Outside exhibits include a wagon encampment, an amphitheater used for historical programs and a typical hardrock mine. Rangers and volunteers dressed in period garb often participate in living history demonstrations of life on the trail. A two-mile path wanders from Flagstaff Hill down into the valley, where wagon grooves of the Oregon Trail can still be seen.

Power of the Past Museum • *Highway 86, between Oregon Trail Center and Baker City; (503) 523-4003. Daily 8 to 6. Adults $2, kids under 12 free.* "Pug" Robinson has turned five acres of his ranch into an open-air museum of antique farm equipment. You'll find old threshing machines, tractors, 30 kinds of plows and other country devices. Some of his equipment dates back more than a century. The museum-farm is on the left as you approach I-84 from the Oregon Trail Center.

About three miles beyond the interpretive center, pick up I-84 and head south to the seat of Baker County, an old town whose roots had little to do with the Oregon Trail. In fact, the trail bypassed it by several miles.

Baker City

Population: 9,100 **Elevation: 3,446 feet**

Traffic on the Oregon Trail had thinned by the time gold was discovered in this valley in late 1861. A mining camp called Auburn was established the following year. In 1864, Colonel J.S. Ruckel built a gold stamp mill on the Powder River, a few miles southwest of Auburn. A settlement grew up around it, named for Colonel Edward Dickinson Baker. He was a Civil War hero, former Abraham Lincoln law partner and Oregon's first U.S. senator.

Baker City took the county seat from Auburn in 1868 and was incorporated in 1874. After the arrival of the railroad in 1884, it became the commercial hub of the entire countryside. With a population of 6,663 in 1890, it was larger than Boise or Spokane. The name was simplified to Baker after the turn of the century. Recently, as residents sensed their place in history, they voted to change it back to Baker City. The town today has the look of a sturdy midwestern community transplanted to the Oregon prairie. Brick and masonry buildings stand along Campbell Street and nice old homes line residential lanes shaded by mature trees.

The **Baker County Visitor & Convention Bureau** is near the midtown freeway interchange (exit 304) at Campbell Street, beside an old green caboose. It's open weekdays 9 to 5 and Saturday 9 to 4; (503) 523-5855. You can pick up the usual guides, lists and brochures, plus a walking tour map of the city's old buildings, and driving tour maps to nearby lures. More than a visitor center, it also has a small upstairs museum, with exhibits and photos concerning the city's early mining, cowboying and lumbering days— and the Oregon Trail, of course.

Drive down Campbell Street from the Chamber of Commerce, and browse about the oldstyle business district around Campbell and Main. It's a living architectural museum with old buildings constructed of brick, masonry, granite and even volcanic tufa. View the gold display at the **U.S. National Bank** at 2000 Main Street. Exhibits range from gold dust and leaf gold to the fist-sized 80.4-ounce Armstrong nugget, found nearby in 1913.

Continue down Campbell Street and look on your left for an imposing brick and masonry structure that covers half a city block. A surviving symbol of yesterday prosperity, it was built in 1921 as a natatorium. It boasted a swimming pool fed by nearby hot springs, a ballroom and roller skating rink. During World War II, it served as a factory for the production of munitions boxes. Today, it is a repository of yesterday:

☺ **Central Oregon Regional Museum** • *2490 Grove Street at Campbell; (503) 523-9308. Daily 9 to 5. Free; donations appreciated.* The Baker County Historical Society has been trying since the 1970s to fill this huge structure with museum exhibits. The result is a spacious, barn-like space that contains a startling variety of displays. You'll find the requisite pioneer artifacts and old photos, bug and butterfly collections, large mineral collection including a glow-icky blacklight room, an interesting selection of old tomahawks, war axes and other Native American regalia. The upstairs area, once the ballroom, still has room for a large cotillion. A pioneer bedroom and old clothing exhibit occupy one corner. The rest is used for changing exhibits and meetings.

BAKER COUNTY ANNUAL EVENTS

Sumpter Valley Country Fair, Sumpter in late May, early July and early September; (503) 894-2264.

Wagons Ho! Oregon Trail celebration in Baker City in late May; (503) 523-3356.

Miners' Jubilee in Baker, with arts and crafts, bed races and parade, mid-July; (503) 523-5855.

August Fair and 4-H Show, Baker in early August; (503) 523-1235.

WHERE TO DINE

The Brass Parrot ● ∆∆ $$

2190 Main St.; (503) 523-4266. Mexican and American; full bar service. Monday-Thursday 11 to 9, Friday-Saturday 11 to 10 and Sunday 11 to 8. Major credit cards. Attractive old fashioned dining room in the downtown historic area; decorated with antiques and yesterday photos. A good array of tortilla-based dishes and Mexican fare, plus a few American entrées.

Burrito Construction Company ● ∆ $

Second and Broadway; (503) 523-9360. American and Mexican; no alcohol. Monday-Thursday 11 to 7:30, Friday-Saturday 11 to 8. No credit cards. Good spot for a quick, inexpensive bite, specializing in "from scratch" Mexican combo dinners under $5. The café also serves American burgers, sub sandwiches and such.

Jimmy Chan's Restaurant ● ∆ $

1841 Main St.; (503) 523-5230. Chinese and American; full bar service. Daily 11 to 9. MC/VISA. Family-style café with a bit of Oriental trim. Very inexpensive Chinese menu plus a few American entrées, with dinners from $3.50 to $8.50. It's a "no MSG" place.

Sumpter Junction Restaurant ● ∆∆ $$

Campbell Street at I-5 exit 304; (503) 523-9437. American and Mexican; wine and beer. Daily 6 a.m. to 10 p.m. MC/VISA, AMEX, DISC. Attractive family restaurant with a railroading theme; watch a scale model train chug along a thousand feet of track as you dine. Typical Mexican fare plus a selection of American steaks, chicken, chops and seafood.

WHERE TO SLEEP

Eldorado Motel ● ⌂⌂ $ ∅

695 Campbell St., Baker City, OR 97814; (800) 537-5756 or (503) 523-6494. Couples $29 to $36, singles $23 to $33. Major credit cards. Spanish-style 56-unit motel with TV and room phones; spa and indoor pool.

Friendship Inn ● ⌂ $ ∅

134 Bridge St., Baker City, OR 97814; (503) 523-6571. Couples $26 to $34, singles $24 to $32. Major credit cards. Well-kept 39-unit motel with TV and room phones.

Quality Inn ● ⌂⌂ $$ ∅

810 Campbell St., Baker City, OR 97814; (800) 228-5151 or (503) 523-2242. Couples $37 to $49, singles $33 to $41. Major credit cards. Well-maintained 54-room motel with TV, room phones and refrigerators. Free continental breakfast; VCR rentals.

Royal Motor Inn ● ⌂⌂ $ ∅

2205 Broadway St. (at Third), Baker City, OR 97814; (800) 547-5827 or (503) 523-6324. Couples $33.50 to $35.30, singles $25.50 to $27.50. Major credit cards. Nicely-maintained 36-unit motel with TV, room phones and refrigerators. Pool; health club privileges.

Western Motel ● ⌂ $ ∅

3055 Tenth St. (at F), Baker City, OR 97814; (503) 523-3700. Couples $33 to $39, singles $22 to $28. Major credit cards. A 14-unit motel with TV and room phones.

Sitting in a puddle of its own making, the Fort Sumpter gold dredge sifted gravel for glitter from 1935 until 1954.　　　　　**– Betty Woo Martin**

Bed & breakfast inns

A'demain Bed & Breakfast • ⌂⌂⌂ $$$ Ø
1790 Fourth St., Baker City, OR 97814; (503) 523-2509. Couples and singles $40 to $65. One room and one suite with private baths; full breakfast. No credit cards. Nicely restored 1901 red brick Victorian in quiet older neighborhood. Furnished with antiques; down comforters, feather beds; attractively landscaped yard.

Powder River Bed & Breakfast • ⌂⌂ $$$ Ø
HCR 87, Box 500 (on Highway 7), Baker City, OR 97814; (503) 523-7143. Couples $60, singles $45 to $50. Two rooms with private baths. MC/VISA, AMEX. Modern home within city limits; antique furnishings in bedroom and modern furniture in comfortable sitting room. It offers a nice view of Eagle Cap Wilderness and Elkhorn Mountains. Guided fishing trips and local sightseeing trips available.

WHERE TO CAMP

Oregon Trails West RV Park • *Exit 302 off I-84 (Route 2, Box 48), Baker City, OR 97814; (503) 523-3236 or 523-3988. RV sites; full hookups $12. Reservations accepted; MC/VISA.* Some pull-throughs, TV hookups, showers, coin laundry, mini-mart.

Mountain View Holiday Trav-L-Park • *2845 Hughes Lane, Baker City, OR 97814; (503) 523-4824. RV and tent sites; $11 to $14. Reservations accepted; MC/VISA.* Close-together spaces, mostly pull-throughs, in a well-maintained park. Showers, coin laundry, pool, playground and mini-mart.

Union Creek Campground • *On Phillips Reservoir, 15 miles west of Baker on State Highway 7; (503) 894-2210. RV and tent sites; full hookups $12, no hookups $8, tent pads $7. No reservations or credit cards.* Sites near reservoir, with picnic tables, flush potties, paved boat ramp and swimming beach.

BAKER CITY TO JOHN DAY

To complete your loop tour of northeastern Oregon, head west on State Highway 7 from Baker City. It follows the course of the Powder River, climbing through barren hills above the city and then entering the less barren woodlands of Wallowa-Whitman National Forest.

Phillips Reservoir adds a patch of blue to the thickening forest, offering swimming, boating and camping (listed above). About 25 miles from Baker, depart Highway 7 briefly, following Elkhorn Scenic Drive signs to **Sumpter,** one of several old gold mining towns in the area. Most of those towns are empty relics, although Sumpter has survived; it's an attractive hamlet tucked among the trees. The properly rustic downtown area offers a few antique shops, cafes and other stores, housed in a mix of false-front, squared log and brick.

☺ Before reaching downtown, you'll pass the huge **Sumpter gold dredge,** one of the largest in America. Abandoned in a graveled pond of its own making, this monster operated from 1935 until 1954. Its 72 one-ton, nine cubic foot buckets could move 280,000 cubic yards of gravel a month. It was a good investment for its builders, costing $300,000 and dredging up $4.5 million in gold. The gold dredge and nearby **Sumpter Valley Railroad** recently became focal elements of Oregon's newest state park. When it's completed, at a cost of $3 million, it'll be a 200-acre day use facility with mining and railroading interpretive exhibits, hiking trails and picnic areas. Considering the condition of state budgets these days, don't hold your breath.

The railroad was established in 1890 to haul logs from the Blue Mountains to a mill in Baker City. The "Stump Dodger" carried timber, gold ore and passengers around this area for 60 years. It later was resurrected by a citizens group and gussied up to haul tourists on a brief run over its remaining six miles of track. It had ceased operation when we passed through. To see if it's steamed up again, contact: Sumpter Valley Railroad, P.O. Box 389, Baker City, OR 97814; (503) 894-2268.

From Sumpter, the **Elkhorn Scenic Byway** makes a 106-mile loop through the Elkhorn section of the Blue Mountains, passing lakes, streams and old mining camps. It's an inviting drive, all paved, and it deposits you back in Baker. For a route map, stop at the **Sumpter Ranger Station** in town; open weekdays 8 to 5.

From the Sumpter junction, Highway 7 climbs to the wooded 5,124-foot **Tipton Summit,** crosses into Grant County and blends into U.S. Highway 26 at **Austin Junction.** The route travels over **Dixie Mountain Divide** at 5,277 feet and spirals downward, heading for **Prairie City.**

The weathered old town of 1,085 is aptly named, sitting in the middle of a ranching basin. A left turn from Front Street (Highway 26) onto Main Street takes you to the **DeWitt Museum** in Depot Park. The small archive occupies a 1910 depot of the aforementioned Sumpter Valley Railroad, with the usual pioneer artifacts, rather casually arrayed. It's open in summers only, Thursday-Saturday 10 to 3. The well-tended Depot Park offers over-night camping, with showers and flush potties. Water and electric hookups are $10 and tent sites are $5.

Back on Front Street, you'll see a nice collection of yesterday architecture—wooden false front, brick, masonry and cut stone—along the three-block business district. Some merchants are fixing up old storefronts, installing antique and specialty shops to create a mini-tourist town. Pause to browse, and perhaps plan on lunch at the charming Little Diner café (listed below).

You've now reached the **Malheur National Forest** sphere of influence, and a ranger station is located in Prairie City, with the usual 8 to 5 weekday hours and usual abundance of recreation information. Just beyond town, you learn what keeps Prairie City ticking—a large lumber mill and wood chip operation.

You pick up the John Day River along here, a sure clue that you're in John Day Country. The small town of that name is 15 miles ahead, at the junction of U.S. highways 26 and 395.

John Day

Population: 2,075   **Elevation: 3,085 feet**

The largest town in sparsely populated Grant County, the community is gateway to **John Day Fossil Beds National Monument.** It is, however, a rather distant gateway. The fossil beds occur in three separate sections, and the first is a good 38 miles away. Since there's nothing out there but beautiful country and fossils, the monument's administration center is on the western end of town.

Founded as a trading center on the old Dalles Military Road in the 1860s, John Day was named for a character whose trip west was hounded by misfortune. Described as a tall man "with an elastic step as if he trod on springs," he was part of John Jacob Astor's 1810 overland trip to the mouth of the Columbia River. The party ran out of food in present-day Idaho and its leader divided the men into four hunting parties. Day's group became totally lost and all but Day and a companion perished the following winter. They resumed their journey in the spring and finally reached the Columbia. Near the mouth of a tributary called the Mah-Hah, they were confronted by unfriendly Indians, robbed and stripped naked. The pair was rescued by trappers and finally reached Fort Astoria. The river and its drainage to the south was named in honor of this luckless traveler who never set foot in John Day Country.

The **Grant County Chamber of Commerce** is mid-town at Main and Bridge Street, beside a tall-steepled 19th century church with an ornate bell tower. The chamber is open weekdays 9 to 5; (503) 575-0547. Continue a block farther on Main, then turn right onto Canton Street for one of the more intriguing small museums in the state:

☺ **Kam Wah Chung Museum** • *250 NW Canton St.; (503) 575- 0028. May to October, weekdays 9 to noon and weekends 1 to 5. Adults $2, seniors $1.50, teens $1, kids 6 to 12, 50 cents.* The museum is a cluttered and amazingly intact Chinese store and herbal shop, housed in a rough-cut fieldstone building. The structure was built in 1866 as a trading post, then purchased in 1887 by Chinese immigrants Ing Hay and Lung On. The two bachelors ran their store for decades, serving both the white and Chinese community.

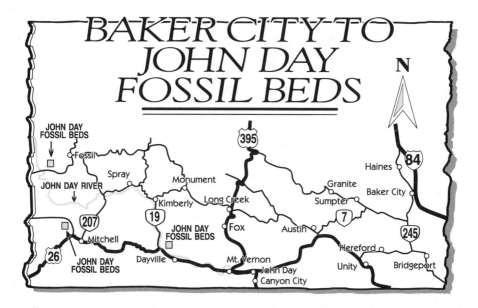

BAKER CITY TO JOHN DAY FOSSIL BEDS

N

When "Doc" Hay died in 1948, the structure was locked up his heirs. It remained padlocked for 20 years, then it was given to the city as a museum.

What a treasure-trove city officials found! Nothing had been moved since Hay's death. The place was—and still is—jammed to the rafters with American and Chinese canned goods, strings of firecrackers, notions, bootleg whisky, imported teas and more than a thousand different herbs. Nearly $25,000 in uncashed checks was found stuffed into Hay's mattress.

The hamlet of **Canyon City** is two miles south of John Day on U.S. Highway 395. It had its days of glory in the 1860s, when $26 million worth of gold was taken from the Strawberry Mountain wilderness to the south. Once bursting with a population of 5,000, it has shriveled to barely 600. However, it still serves as the Grant County seat. The small, rough stone and wood **Grant County Historical Museum** is located near the gold discovery site, with exhibits on gold mining and early settlers. The tiny Canyon City Jail and **Joaquin Miller's** cabin are next door. The complex is open to visitors June through September, Monday-Saturday 9:30 to 4:30. Adults $2, teens and seniors $1, kids 6 to 12, 50 cents; (503) 575-0362. Miller, Oregon's poet laureate, lived here during the gold rush and served as Grant County's first elected judge.

When you return to John Day and continue west through town, you'll see the fossil beds administrative center on your left, at 450 Main Street. It's open weekdays 8:30 to 6, with a few exhibits and a friendly staff that will tell you what lies down the road.

Highway 26 follows the John Day River through a narrow agricultural valley, past drab **Mount Vernon** and then **Dayville**; they're mere wisps of farm hamlets shaded by huge trees. After traveling many weary miles through this long farming strip, you'll note a couple of mesas ahead with absolutely flat caprock tops—a promise of more interesting country to come. Then you enter **Picture Gorge,** a gorgeous narrow-walled ravine cut by the John Day River. Terraced brown and ruddy walls rise 500 feet, a startling change from that 38 miles of bland farmland.

John Day Fossil Beds tour

☺ Signs direct you to the right onto State Highway 19, to the **Sheep Rock** section of John Day Fossil Beds National Monument. Sheep Rock is a multi-colored upthrust rising a couple of hundred feet from the river canyon. One of the most striking promontories in the state, it's a striated study in beiges, dark browns and pea soup green, weathered into bas relief columns, ridges and spires.

The visitor center is just beyond, housed in the former home of a well-to-do sheep ranching family named Cant. It's open daily 8:30 to 6 (closed weekends and holidays in winter). This handsome 1917 house, acquired when the national monument was established in 1975, has been meticulously restored. Some rooms are furnished to the period; others serve as offices and exhibit centers for the monument. An animated video, nicely filmed and narrated by Oregon school students, introduces you to this land of fossils. Several outbuildings occupy the carefully groomed ranch yard. In a small log cabin, you're likely to see a ranger or volunteer working on a fossil fragment.

As you explore the scattered elements of the monument, don't expect to find dinosaur bones sticking out of the ground. The fossils here are plants and mammals from six million to 50 million years ago, long after the last dinosaur perished. Lush rain forests once covered this area, and most of the fossil-bearing formations were deposited as volcanic ash. Scientists have found fragments of horses, sloths, camels, bear-dogs, rhinos, primitive elephants and various species that hit an evolutionary dead-end. More impressive than the fossil exhibits, which are relatively small, are the Technicolor formations laid down by ancient seas and volcanic ashfalls.

Plan at least one long day to see all the elements of the monument. The first area, part of the Sheep Rock unit, is **Blue Basin,** up the John Day River Canyon about three miles north of the visitor's center. A three-mile loop trail leads through sculpted rock formations to a vista point, offering a dramatic overview of the John Day Valley. The shorter Island in Time trail wanders for half a mile through a dry wash. Plexiglas-covered models of fossils have been installed at sites where the originals were found.

The **Forsee Area** is another four miles north, offering two short hikes through green mica formations. En route to Forsee, note the green **Cathedral Rock** on your left, with its precisely-cut reddish iron crest. Next to the Forsee area is the small **Asher's RV Park** on McCarty Creek, with electrical hookups for $8 and tents for $6. It offers flush potties, grassy sites and not much else.

To reach the other two elements of the fossil beds, return to Highway 26 and continue east through the narrow, rock-ribbed canyon of Mountain Creek. It's a tributary of the John Day. You'll climb through forested hills to **Keyes Summit** at 4,369 feet, then drop down into the shabby town of **Mitchell,** 31 miles from the Sheep Rock unit.

☺ Just west of town, a turnoff to the right will direct you to the **Painted Hills** unit. Here, the landscape undergoes a dramatic change. The Painted Hills are sensuously rounded mounds striped with green mica, black and red iron and buff-colored volcanic ash. The appearance is a blend of kneaded bread dough and melting parfaits, or perhaps an interplanetary set for *Star Wars.* The only facilities here are picnic tables, potties and an infor-

Color-banded formations in the Painted Hills section of John Day Fossil Beds National Monument suggest melted parfaits.
-- **Betty Woo Martin**

national kiosk. Follow a gravel road a mile to the **Carroll Rim trailhead,** then hike half a mile up a ridge for impressive views down into a prosce- nium of these mounds. A sign advises that the layers were laid down by vol- canic eruptions from the Cascades. Other short trails lead to a 30-million-year-old fossil leaf area and to Painted Cove for a close-up of more multi-colored formations.

Return with us now to Mitchell and head north on State Highway 207 toward the town of Fossil. You'll switch to Highway 19 at the Service Creek junction. The outerworldly look continues as you pass through a mixed ter- rain of low mountain ridges, shallow valleys and open grasslands, punctu- ated by occasional red and green fluted formations. They often appear unexpectedly, like beautiful open wounds on the smooth countryside.

Although the folks of **Fossil** should know better, their fading welcome sign on the outskirts bears the image of a dinosaur. The eight-square-block downtown area is interestingly shabby, a mix of old brick and wooden false front stores. **Fossil Museum,** occupying the red brick IOOF hall on First Street, offers an undisciplined scatter of pioneer artifacts, farm equipment, a fireplug, school sports trophies and a few plant fossils tossed onto a window sill. It's open daily 10 to 5. Across the street is the so-called **Asher's Car Museum,** consisting of a dusty, un-restored collection of cars of the 1920s and 1930s.

☺ Follow State Highway 218 about 20 miles from Fossil to the **Clarno Unit,** the smallest element of the national monument. The focal point here is a rugged cliff face called the Palisades, sitting in the middle of a 22-acre parcel of dusty grassland. This sculptured upthrust, resembling a fanciful temple from an Indiana Jones movie, is one of the world's richest reposito- ries of plant fossils. The Palisades' eroded shapes were formed by a mudslide of volcanic ash during a tropical rainstorm.

Like the Painted Hills unit, Clarno's facilities consist of a picnic area, information kiosk and potties. Bring your bug glass as you follow a trail from the picnic area along the base of the Palisades, since you'll be passing hundreds of plant fossils. The short hike takes you to the base of a second trail that starts at a roadside information stand. It winds steeply up through the alluvial skirt of the Palisades, ending at near-vertical walls. As you hike up this mercifully short trail, you'll be serenaded by the ghostly calls of feral pigeons that have taken refuge in the natural hollows of the cliff face.

ACTIVITIES IN JOHN DAY COUNTRY

Rafting on the John Day River is a popular summer pastime, and a few commercial outfits run its lively but short stretches of rapids. Check the outfitters listed under Hells Canyon National Recreation area above. Private groups will find rapids ranging up to class IV, which require a good bit of skill. For a brochure and map marking the rapids, contact the **Bureau of Land Management,** P.O. Box 550, Prineville, OR 97754; (503) 447-4115.

Raft rentals • John Day River Outfitters, HCR 56, Box 410, John Day, OR 97845, (503) 575-2386, rents rafts and inflatable kayaks and provides shuttles.

Cattle herding • Shades of *City Slickers*! **Cottonwood Ranch,** Box 334, Dayville, OR 97825, (503) 987-2124, conducts two-day cattle drives in the John Day River Canyon.

ANNUAL EVENTS

Call the Grant County Chamber of Commerce at (503) 575-0547 for details on these happenings.

Kam Wah Chung Chinese Festival, late April in John Day.

Cinnabar Mountain Rendezvous, Memorial Day weekend in Mount Vernon.

'62 Days to celebrate the gold discovery, early June in Canyon City.

Grasshopper Festival, third Saturday in July in Monument, a small town north of the Sheep Rock unit of John Day Fossil Beds.

Grant County Fair, third weekend of August in John Day.

WHERE TO DINE IN JOHN DAY COUNTRY

Annie Ann's Café & Lounge • ΔΔ $$

Highway 395, Canyon City; (503) 575-2426. American; full bar service. Monday-Saturday 6 a.m. to 9 p.m., Sunday 8 to 9. Old time café serving hearty steaks, chicken, and chops. A specialty is Rocky Mountain oysters and you'd better ask before you order. It's also locally popular for huge, modest-priced breakfasts.

Grubsteak Mining Company • ΔΔ $$

149 E. Main St., John Day; (503) 575-1970. American; full bar service. Lunch 11 to 2, dinner 5 to 11. Major credit cards. Handsomely rustic Western style diner with typical American menu of steaks, chops, chickens and a fairly good selection of seafood. Steaks are amenu feature.

The Little Diner • ΔΔ $$

142 Front St., Prairie City; (503) 820-4353. American; wine and beer. Wednesday-Saturday 6 a.m. to 7 p.m., Sunday 8 to 7, closed Monday and Tuesday. Cozy family-style café serving old fashioned American fare such as steaks, chicken and chops. Specialties are barbecued ribs and prime rib.

Mother Lode Restaurant ● Δ $
241 W. Main St., John Day; (503) 575-2714. American-Mexican; no alcohol. Daily 5 a.m. to 9 p.m. MC/VISA. Simple Western style café dishing up ample portions of basic American steaks, chops and chickens, plus Mexican fare on Friday and Saturday nights. Homemade pastries are a specialty.

WHERE TO SLEEP

Bed & Breakfast by the River ● ⌂ $$$ ø
Route 2, Box 790, Prairie City, OR 97869; (503) 820-4470. Couples from $50, singles from $35. Three rooms with share baths; ranch-style breakfast. No credit cards. Rustically modern ranch home on the John Day River with views of the Strawberry Wilderness. It's 2.5 miles east of Prairie City.

Best Western Inn ● ⌂ $$ ø
315 W. Main St., John Day, OR 97845; (800) 528-1234 or (503) 575-1700. Couples $40.50 to $52.50, singles $34.50 to $44.50. Major credit cards. Nicely-kept 39-room motel with TV movies, room phones and refrigerators. Indoor pool, spa; coin laundry.

Dreamers Lodge ● ⌂ $$ ø
144 N. Canyon Blvd., John Day, OR 97845; (503) 575-0526. Couples $36 to $40, singles $32 to $34. Major credit cards. Well-maintained 24-unit motel with TV movies; some suites and kitchenettes.

Fossil Motel & Trailer Park ● ⌂ $ ø
105 First St. (P.O. Box 282), Fossil, OR 97830; (503) 763-4075. Couples and singles $27 to $32, kitchenettes $30 to $35. MC/VISA. Nicely landscaped 10-unit motel; eight rooms with TV, all have refrigerators.

Sunset Inn ● ⌂ $$ ø
490 W. Main St., John Day, OR 97845; (503) 575-1462. Couples $36 to $40, singles $32. Major credit cards. A 43-unit motel with TV, indoor pool, spa. **Restaurant** serves 5 a.m. to 10 p.m.; dinners $9 to $14; full bar.

WHERE TO CAMP

Asher's RV Park ● *State Highway 19 on McCarty Creek above Sheep Rock unit of John Day Fossil Beds. RV and tent sites; water and electric $8, tents $6. No reservations or credit cards.* Grassy sites, flush potties; adjacent to Forsee section of Sheep Rock unit.

Clyde Holliday State Wayside ● *U.S. 26, seven miles west of John Day; (503) 575-2773. RV and tent sites, $11 to $9, hiker-biker sites $2. No reservations or credit cards.* Attractive, well-spaced sites with showers, picnic tables and barbecues; swimming and fishing in the adjacent John Day River.

Fossil Motel & Trailer Park ● *105 First St. (P.O. Box 282), Fossil, OR 97830; (503) 763- 4075. Full hookups $12, electric $10, tent sites $8. Reservations accepted; MC/VISA.* Twelve unit park adjacent to motel (listed above); showers, picnic tables and barbecues, TV hookups; adjacent to city park.

Shelton State Wayside ● *State Highway 19, ten miles southwest of Fossil; (503) 869-2365. RV and tent sites, no hookups; $7.* Pit potties, barbecues and picnic tables; kids' play area, nature trails and fishing in Service Creek.

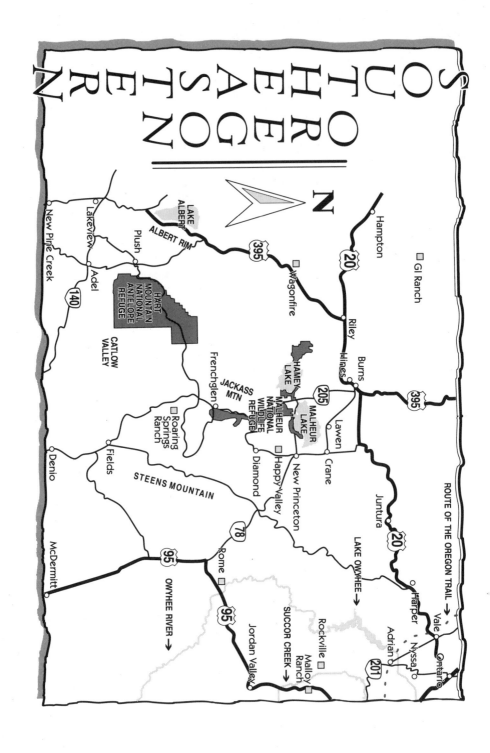

Chapter Ten

SOUTHEASTERN CORNER

Antelope asylums and awesome abysses

IF YOU LIKE THINGS REMOTE, you'll love the high deserts and sparsely timbered mountains of southeastern Oregon. Not only is it the state's least populated area, it's one of the most thinly settled regions in the entire country.

Lake, Harney and Malheur counties occupy a nearly a third of Oregon's space, yet they claim only 1.5 percent of its population. Of the 42,800 souls scattered over these 28,450 square miles, about 12,000 live in a Snake River agricultural belt around Ontario, Vale, Nyssa and Adrian. Subtract these, and you get a population density of about one body per square mile.

Harney is the largest county in Oregon—and in America—sprawled over 10,228 square miles. That's larger than Rhode Island and Massachusetts combined. Yet it's Oregon's least populated county, with 7,100 residents.

Other than the Ontario-Nyssa agricultural belt, there are only two towns of note in southeastern Oregon. Burns and Lakeview have a couple of thousand residents each, and they offer a few motels and restaurants. Beyond them, the pickin's are pretty slim. The two towns are surrounded by rough mountains and vast stretches of prairie and Great Basin desert—what some folks might describe as miles and miles of miles and miles.

Peter Skene Ogden, the Hudson's Bay Company explorer, passed through this rough country in 1826. He followed Indian and game trails through rocky ravines, between caprock buttes and across dusty alkali flats. Although this is a desert wilderness, Ogden and later travelers found enough marshy lakes and streams—notably the Owyhee River—to sustain them. Since most early settlers shunned the area, cattlemen came in the 1870s to spread their herds over thousands of unclaimed acres. They built some of

TRIP PLANNER

WHEN TO GO ● As in northeastern Oregon, summer is the best time to tour here, because of those windy, cold winters. Fall can be pleasant on the Antelope Refuge and in the Owyhee Country. Spring and fall are peak bird-watching periods at Malheur Wildlife Refuge. Because of the high elevation, access to Steens Mountain is through a very narrow climatic window, usually July through September or October.

WHAT TO SEE ● Hart Mountain National Antelope Refuge; Frenchglen Hotel; the dramatic overlooks at Steens Mountain; Harney County Museum in Burns; Owyhee Dam and various viewpoints to Owyhee Canyon.

WHAT TO DO ● Soak away the trail dust at Hunter's Hot Springs Resort in Lakeview or Hot Springs Campground at Hart Mountain Antelope Refuge; watch the birdies at Malheur Wildlife Refuge; drive and hike the volcanic show-place at Diamond Craters; pig out on a Basque dinner in Jordan Valley.

Useful contacts

Bureau of Land Management, HC 74-12533, Highway 20 West, Hines, OR 97738; (503) 573-5241 (for information on Steens Mountain wilderness).

Harney County Chamber of Commerce, 18 West D St., Burns, OR 97720; (503) 573-2636.

Hart Mountain National Wildlife Refuge, P.O. Box 111, Lakeview, OR 97630; (503) 947-3315.

Lake County Chamber of Commerce, 513 Center St., Lakeview, OR 97630-1577; (503) 947-6040.

Malheur National Wildlife Refuge, HC 72, Box 245, New Princeton, OR 97721; (503) 493-2612.

Nyssa Visitors' Information Center, 212 Main St. (P.O. Box 2515), Nyssa, OR 97913; (503) 372-3091 (for information on the Vale-Nyssa agricultural area, Jordan Valley and the Owyhee Country to the south).

Southeastern Oregon radio stations

Stations are as scarce as people out here, although many broadcasters from Klamath Falls and Boise, Idaho, reach this area. You'll note that it's hard to tune in without hearing Garth Brooks or Billy Ray Cyrus:

KKBC-FM, 95.3, Baker City—country
KLAD-FM, 92.5, Klamath Falls—country
KAGO-FM, 99.5, Klamath Falls—adult contemporary
KSKF-FM, 90.9, Klamath Falls—National Public Radio
KDJY-AM, 1400, John Day—country
KQIK-AM, 1230, Lakeview—country
KZZR-AM, 1230, Burns—country
KBOI-AM, 670, Boise, Idaho—light rock, top 40
KAGO-AM, 1150, Klamath Falls—adult contemporary
KLAD-AM, 960, Klamath Falls—country

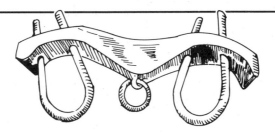

the largest ranches in the nation. They were followed later by Basque sheep-herders, sparking some of the West's more violent range wars.

The dust of those wars has long since settled, although descendants of pioneering cattlemen and sheepmen still run their herds and flocks. The iso-lated town of Burns is the commercial center for Oregon's largest ranching empire, giving the land the look of a wide-screen Marlboro commercial. Jor-dan Valley, on Highway 95 near the Idaho border, is still a Basque strong-hold.

Although hardly a major tourist area, southeastern Oregon offers a few items of note. We've outlined a driving route that touches their bases. Hart Mountain Antelope Refuge is one of the few places in America where you can see our native pronghorn. Steens Mountain offers one of the largest faulted scarps in America and Owyhee Canyon is one of Oregon's most rug-gedly handsome chasms.

Most of our route to these attractions is paved, although you'll have to suffer a dusty and often bumpy stretch between Hart Mountain and Steens Mountain, and another if you want to see the rugged beauty of Succor Creek, a tributary of Owyhee Canyon. The road up to Steens overlook is par-ticularly rough and steep. It's navigable by car or small RV, but expect a cer-tain amount of vehicular abuse.

Obviously, you should prepare yourself and your vehicle for a southeast-ern Oregon exploration. Although it's mostly high desert and doesn't get beastly hot, the thermometer often tops 100 degrees in summer and water sources are widely scattered. Make sure your car or RV is in good shape, take extra water, radiator coolant, extra food and other survival items. See the box on the next page for specifics.

Lakeview

Population: 2,810   **Elevation: 4,800 feet**

Our southeastern Oregon jumping off point can be reached via State Highway 140 from Klamath Falls or route 31 from Bend. Route 140 is an in-viting drive into Winema and Fremont national forests. Highway 31 takes you through an interesting mix of mountains, high deserts and prairie that we touched on late in Chapter 8. (See "South to Klamath Falls").

You have to be a tough old town to survive in southeastern Oregon and Lakeview has that look. Its small business district offers the usual mix of old fashioned brick and masonry buildings, some of them modernized to the 1950s. Lakeview calls itself the "tallest town in Oregon" because it has the highest elevation of any incorporated city in the state.

The **Lake County Chamber of Commerce** Welcome Center is at north Second and F streets; (503) 947-6040. It's open May 1 through Octo-ber, Monday-Saturday 8 to 6 and Sunday 9 to 5. Slightly north, at the junc-tions of U.S. 395 and State Highway 140, is the Lakeview office of **Fremont National Forest,** open weekdays 9 to 5; (503) 947-2151. A chunk of the national forest surrounds Lakeview.

The town's visitor lures consist of two side-by-each archives, both occu-pying early-day homes:

Lake County Museum ● *118 S. D Street; (503) 947-2220. Adults $1, teens 50 cents. Tuesday-Friday 10 to 5, Saturday 10 to 4.* Housed in a 1926 home of rough handmade concrete blocks, the county museum features un-cluttered exhibits nicely arrayed in glass display cases. Included are Indian

Surviving Oregon's hot and dusty wilds

Oregon's most remote corner is best explored in the spring and fall, since it can sizzle in summer and icy blizzards knife across its deserts and high prairies in winter. Any time of the year, treat this area with respect, since your travels may take you far from civilization with its mini-marts and auto parts shops.

Follow these pointers to keep yourself and your vehicle going, *particularly* if you wander off the well-traveled asphalt:

● Give your car or RV a physical before going into the boonies, to ensure that it'll get you back. Take extra engine oil, coolant and an emergency radiator sealant. Include spare parts such as fan belts, a water pump, radiator hoses—and tools to install these things. Toss an extra spare tire into the trunk, along with a tire pump, patching and sealant and that all-purpose fixer--duct tape.

● First, foremost and always, take plenty of *water*. Water to drink, to soak your clothes, to top off a leaky radiator. It's cheap, it's easily portable and it can save your life.

● Take food with you—stuff that won't spoil. If you break down, you may be out there for a while. Also pack matches, a small shovel, aluminum foil (for signaling), a can opener, a powerful flashlight and a space blanket so you can snooze in the shade of your car.

● A CB radio or cellular phone can be a life-saver. Remember that channel 9 is the emergency CB band, monitored by rescue agencies.

● *Never* drive off-road, particularly in an on-road vehicle. Loose, sandy soil can trap your car in an instant, even if the ground looks solid. We don't leave established roadways as a matter of principle, because tires are hell on the fragile desert environment. And no, we don't approve of "off-road" areas.

● Even if you keep to the roads, you might get stuck in a sand-blown area or a soft shoulder. Carry a tow chain and tire supports for soft sand, like strips of carpeting. An inexpensive device called a "come-along"—sort of a hand-winch—can get you out of a hole, if you can find something for an anchor.

● If you do become stranded in Oregon's remote reaches, stay in the shade of your car—*not* in the vehicle itself. Don't try to walk out, particularly during the heat of the day. Besides, a vehicle is easier to spot than a lonely hiker. Use a mirror or aluminum foil as a signal device, and build a signal fire. A spare tire will burn, and a douse of oil will make the fire nice and smoky. Start your blaze in a cleared area away from your vehicle. You don't want to launch a wildfire that might compound your predicament.

● If you're on a road and you know that you can reach civilization on foot, do your walking at night. Take all the water you can carry.

Avoiding "heat sickness"

Heat exhaustion and its lethal cousin heatstroke are real dangers on summer days. Both are brought on by a combination of dehydration and sun—very real risks if you're stranded in a hot and remote area.

Signs of heat exhaustion are weariness, muscle cramps and clammy skin. The pulse may slow and you may become unusually irritable. If left untreated, heat exhaustion can lead to deadly heatstroke. The skin becomes dry and hot, the pulse may quicken and you'll experience nausea and possibly a headache. Convulsions, unconsciousness, even death can follow.

At the first sign of heat sickness, get out of the sun and into the shade. Stay quiet and drink water—plenty of water. If you're near a pool, faucet or stream, douse your face and body with water, and soak your clothes. You *must* lower your body temperature quickly!

artifacts and beadwork, a large collection of early-day household goods and a mock-up 19th century school room.

☺ **Schminck Memorial Museum** • *128 S. D Street; (503) 947-2045. Adults $1, teens 50 cents. Tuesday-Saturday 1 to 5.* Operated by the Oregon State Society of the Daughters of the American Revolution, this museum in a clapboard carpenter Gothic structure has an extensive collection of clothing, furnishings and other memorabilia of early-day Lake County families. Note the beautiful "handwork" of early pioneers, a china head and bisque doll collection dressed in handmade garments, and an exhibit of American pressed glass goblets.

Another point of some interest in town is the **Indian Village** at First and E streets. This restaurant (listed below) exhibits one of the largest arrow and spearhead collections you'll find anywhere. Also, the folks at **Hunter's Hot Springs Resort** (listed below) on the north edge of town won't mind if you wander around the 47-acre grounds to check out the mineral pools. **Old Perpetual Geyser** has been erupting every 90 seconds for as long as anyone around here can remember. The resort's hot mineral pools are open to the public. The complex also has a mini-mart, trading post and health food store.

WHERE TO DINE

Indian Village Restaurant & Gift Shop • ∆∆ $
First and E streets; (503) 947-2833. American; full bar service. Daily 5 a.m. to 9 p.m. MC/VISA. The red Naugahyde booths and vinyl furnishings don't look very Indian, although the gift shop and huge arrow collection (mostly in the bar) carry the theme. Dinners are inexpensive—mostly under $8—and consist of simple American fare such as breaded veal cutlets, grilled calves liver, ham steak and cow steak.

King's Café • ∆ $
First and F streets; (503) 947-2217. Chinese-American; wine and beer. Sunday-Thursday 5 a.m. to midnight, Friday-Saturday 5 to 3 a.m. No credit cards. Lakeview's all-purpose café serves Chinese fare plus chicken-fried steak, fried chicken and other American entrées. The interior is American diner-cum-Beijing with wood paneling, paisley Naugahyde and a few Chinese lanterns.

Shamrock Café • ∆ $
E and Second streets; (503) 947-4824. American; full bar service. Daily 6 a.m. to 9:30 p.m. MC/VISA. Small, prim looking vinyl diner specializing in prime rib. The usual steaks, chickens and chops complete the menu.

WHERE TO SLEEP AND CAMP

AA Motel & Apartments • △ $$ ∅
411 N. F Street (Highway 140 and 395), Lakeview, OR 97630; (503) 947-2201. Couples $40 to $45, singles $28 to $38, kitchenettes $32 to $48. MC/VISA. Simple 14-unit motel with TV movies and room phones; some refrigerators.

Best Western Skyline Motor Lodge • △△ $$ ∅
414 N. G Street, Lakeview, OR 97630; (800) 528-1234 or (503) 947-2194. Couples $48 to $56, singles $40 to $44. Major credit cards. Nicely

maintained 38-unit motel with TV movies, VCRs and room phones; indoor pool, spa, coin laundry, free continental breakfast.

Hunters Hot Springs Resort • ◠◠ $$

P.O. Box 1189 (N. Highway 395), Lakeview, OR 97630; (503) 947-2127. Couples and singles $38 to $40; RV sites $13 for full hookups, $10.80 for water and electric. Major credit cards. A 1920s resort recently remodeled, with simple but tidy accommodations and RV park adjacent. Hot mineral pools, freshwater spa, table tennis and racquetball. **Pizza and Pasta Place** serves American and Italian fare; wine and beer; outdoor dining decks overlooking geyser ponds.

Lakeview Lodge Motel • ◠◠ $$ Ø

301 N. G Street, Lakeview., OR 97630; (503) 947-2181. Couples $40 to $84, singles $31 to $74, kitchenettes $33 to $74, suites $42 to $84. Major credit cards. Well-kept 40-unit motel with TV and room phones; new spa and fitness room. A block south of Highway 140/395 intersection.

Lakeview to Hart Mountain Antelope Refuge

No, we don't know why they call it an antelope refuge, since the native American pronghorn (*antilocatridae*) isn't an antelope. The refuge is one of the more pleasantly remote preserves in Oregon, sitting high in the concave crests of Hart Mountain above Lakeview. There are no paved roads in the refuge, so take it slow, enjoy the rugged scenery and stay alert. The odds are that you'll see a pronghorn or two, maybe a whole herd.

To reach the refuge, head north out of Lakeview on U.S. 395, then turn east after six miles onto State Route 140. You'll climb quickly into the wooded mountains of **Fremont National Forest.** After five miles, you pass the small **Warner Canyon Ski Area,** with 14 lifts and several beginner to advanced runs. It usually operates from December through March. After topping **Warner Pass** at 5,846 feet, fork to the left, following signs to Plush. You'll climb quickly onto a high juniper-sage prairie as the horizon appears to fall away. You will encounter this top-of-the-world terrain frequently as you travel through this lofty plateau country.

From your aerie, you descend steeply into **Warner Valley,** an agricultural basin flanked by rugged, terraced hills. **Plush** is a pleasantly scruffy farming hamlet shaded by thick cottonwoods and tapered poplars. Its business district consists of a single store with groceries and gas. If you forgot to tank up in Lakeview, do so here. It's the last station you'll see until you get to Frenchglen, nearly 80 miles away.

From Plush, the road takes you straight toward the terraced face of **Hart Mountain** and you may wonder what awful incline lies ahead. Then it begins taking a series of 90-degree rural turns and you realize—probably with relief—that the road is working its way around the edge of that near-vertical face. To your left, not easily seen in this flat farming terrain, are marshes of the **Warner Valley Wetlands,** which border the edge of the antelope refuge. This is an important waterfowl stop on the Pacific Flyway.

As your route swings around the northern end of Hart Mountain, you leave pavement and begin a rather washboard-rough climb. The valley drops away and ponds of the waterfowl refuge reveal themselves below, glistening in the sun. You'll soon enter the heart of the refuge, a vast and gently undulating sprawl of sage, fescue, bitterbrush and an occasional juniper.

☺ **Hart Mountain National Antelope Refuge** ● *P.O. Box 111, Lakeview, OR 97630; (503) 947-3315. Unmanned visitor center open 24 hours. Primitive tent and RV camping at Hot Springs Campgrounds; pit potties, no hookups, no fee. Sheltered hot springs bathhouse adjacent. No other services.* The 275,000- acre antelope refuge covers a huge fault block volcanic ridge on the eastern slope of Hart Mountain, rising 3,600 feet from Warner Valley. The unmanned visitor center, part of a complex of fieldstone and lava structures, offers a few exhibits on *antilocatridae* and other area wildlife, plus some pickled former living things in jars. It also has the only flush pottie within dozens of miles.

You'll learn that adult pronghorns are the fastest critters in North America, capable of short bursts at 65 miles an hour. They stand about 35 to 40 inches high and weigh 100 to 140 pounds. The name comes from their forward projecting twin horns, distinctive to this species. They prefer open high desert and prairie, between 4,000 and 6,000 feet. Before the West was "settled," 40 million of these creatures roamed free. After merciless hunting, herds had dwindled to 13,000 by the turn of the century. Now, thanks to refuges such as Hart Mountain, their numbers are approaching half a million. Most of them are in Wyoming.

Early morning and late afternoon are the best times to view wildlife on this rolling, silver-sage plateau. In addition to pronghorns (we saw several during out visit), you'll see uncounted cottontails and jackrabbits, possibly a sage grouse or two and an occasional mule deer. Bighorn sheep thrive in the crags of Hart Mountain's steep western scarp, but they're difficult to spot. We arrived in late afternoon and were startled to see literally hundreds of jackrabbits loping leisurely around the refuge headquarters. We had to slow *Ickybod*, or faithful VW camper, to a crawl to avoid dusting off the critters.

From the visitor center, a dirt road leads four miles to a primitive campground in an attractive aspen grove, along a seasonal creek. A nearby hot spring, enclosed in a concrete modesty shield, offers a chance to soak the bod and wash away the dust of that long drive. Dress or undress is optional; rules are determined by participants.

To Frenchglen and Steens Mountain

From Hart Mountain, another dusty and bumpy road leads 52 miles eastward across this high desert to the community of Frenchglen. You'll drive through 27 miles of monotonous sagebrush before you see any sign of life— that being a solitary ranch house.

Beyond the ranch, the road climbs into a pinyon-juniper belt, then spirals down toward a beige valley checked with a few green alfalfa patches. At the bottom, you hit the welcome pavement of State Highway 205. A ten-mile drive north delivers you to **Frenchglen,** a tiny community of ten, shaded by cottonwoods. Here, you'll find one of the state's more charmingly rustic accommodations, and you'd better come with reservations:

☺ **Frenchglen Hotel and Dining Room** ● ⌂⌂⌂ $$

Frenchglen, OR 97736; (503) 493-2825. Rooms $40 to $48. MC/VISA. Built in 1914 as a stage stop, this handsome wood- sided inn is now an Oregon State Park. It offers overnight accommodations in simply-furnished rooms and hearty American country fare in a basic table-and-bench dining room. Hotel and cafè are open from March to mid-November. Reservations for rooms and dinner are absolutely essential. Breakfast is served from 7:30 to 9:30 and lunch from 11:30 to 2:30, with sack lunches available. Dinner, by reservation only, hits the table at 6:30 sharp; family-style meals are $10 to $14.

If you're RVing, you can spend the night at:

Steens Mountain Camper Corral ● *Steens Mountain Loop Road, Frenchglen, OR 97736. RV sites, full hookups $10. Reservations accepted; MC/VISA.* A mile up Steens Mountain road. Some shady sites, pull-throughs, mini-mart, showers, coin laundry, TV hookups. Operators can provide fishing and hunting licenses and information on the Malheur Wildlife Refuge and Steens Mountain.

Frenchglen Mercantile, a couple of gas pumps and a post office comprise the rest of the town's business district. It was founded as a ranching center in the late 1800s by cattle baron Peter French and his father-in-law, Dr. Hugh Glenn. One of the more colorful and crusty characters of the American West, Pete French was born in Red Bluff, California, in 1849. He was hired to manage Dr. Glenn's ranch in 1873, and wound up marrying the boss' daughter. Shortly after, Glenn was murdered by his bookkeeper and French inherited the ranch. He ruthlessly shoved homesteaders and squatters off "his" land and crowded out neighboring ranchers. Within a few years, he had built the French-Glenn Livestock Company into the largest spread in American—a 100,000-acre cattle empire with 30,000 head of stock. All that ended when a neighboring rancher shot him out of the saddle on the day after Christmas in 1897.

From Frenchglen, you can head into one of Oregon's most dramatic wilderness areas, provided you have a sturdy vehicle with even sturdier tires:

☺ **Steens Mountain** ● *C/o Bureau of Land Management, HC 74-12533, Highway 20 West, Hines, OR 97738; (503) 573-5241. No services on the mountain. Loop drive map and other information available from a seasonal ranger station opposite Frenchglen general store. Camping is available at Steens Mountain Camper Corral (listed above) or at three BLM campsites— Page Springs, Fish Lake and Jackman Park, en route to East Rim Overlook. They have barbecue pits and picnic tables, pit potties and no hookups, $3 per night.*

A 30-mile long faulted block promontory, Steens Mountain rises abruptly from the Alvord Desert. Its glacier-scarred crest, capped by primeval tundra, reaches 9,773 feet into an ice-blue sky. In this high wilderness, where spring comes in July and summer ends in August, the rocky, snow-streaked terrain is carpeted with lichens and dwarf lupine. The thin blue sky appears close enough to touch. The almost sheer eastern scarp plunges dizzily to the floor of the desert, thousands of feet below.

This is one of the most dramatically beautiful places in Oregon. Although it's desert terrain, you'll pass a high country lake and serpentine streams lined with aspen groves. Alpine tundra sparkles with summer wildflowers. However, reaching all this is a chore. The Steens Mountain drive is a broken, rocky and steep road that makes a 66-mile loop into this wild high lonesome landscape. Although a carefully driven sedan with good tires can make it, the torturous road is better suited to four-wheel-drives. It is *not* recommended for large RVs. If you're reluctant to travel the entire loop, drive 27 miles up the North Loop Road to the East Rim Viewpoint, then retrace

Steens Mountain's East Rim overlook offers awesome views down the Alvord Desert and across the great expanses of southeastern Oregon. **--Betty Woo Martin**

your route. This will cover the mountain's highlights, save a few miles and avoid some of its worst bumps.

The route generally doesn't open until July, and early snows may close it by October or November. However, you may be able to reach one of the lower campgrounds in the off-season. A series of gates on the road are opened and closed as weather permits.

The first part of the route from Frenchglen is relatively smooth, taking you through the southern tip of the **Malheur Wildlife Refuge** and the surviving "long barn" of Peter French's historic **P Ranch**. A short distance beyond is **Page Springs,** an attractive campground along the aspen-lined banks of the Donner und Blitzen River. The unusual name wasn't inspired by Rudolph's teammates. The river got its name from Army Captain George B. Curry, who crossed it during a thunderstorm while in pursuit of Indians. "Donner" and "blitzen" are German for thunder and lightning.

From this point, you climb gradually and doggedly, into and beyond a pine belt, to the broad top-of-the-world tundra. About 20 miles into your drive, a sign to the left directs you to **Kiger Gorge,** a ravine carved into a perfect bowl shape by an Ice Age glacier. It curves downward from Steens' eastern face like a giant, snowless bobsled run, leading to a stream far below. After a few more miles, you cross the narrowest part of the mountain. Here, the rugged, serpentine **Little Blitzen Gorge** (which is hardly little) falls away to the right.

The **East Rim Overlook** is about a mile beyond, reached by a short side road that angles up and over the mountain's crest. Park your panting vehicle and walk carefully to the perimeter. You find yourself standing on the edge of an Oregon imitation of the Grand Canyon, except there's no opposite rim. You stare down a craggy, terraced escarpment, cut by steep ravines, to the beige and off-white Alvord Desert, several thousand feet below.

From this dizzy perch, you can see hundreds of miles in every direction, to far-away mountains and ridges that melt into a blue-gray haze. It's all too big to put inside your camera. The image simply shrivels and loses its impact in the viewfinder.

Frenchglen to Owyhee Country

Late in the last century, gold seekers traveling with a group of Hawaiians sought their fortunes in Oregon's remote southeastern corner. They disappeared into a steep-walled desert canyon and were never heard from again.

That wild ravine and its river were named in honor those natives from the islands, which locals mispronounced as "Owyhee." This farthest wedge of Oregon, a land of sculpted cliffs, deep desert canyons, badlands and "breaks," is now known collectively as the Owyhee Country.

The Owyhee River rises in the high plateau of southwestern Idaho and northern Nevada, then cuts through the desert of Oregon's Malheur County to meet the Snake River south of Ontario. A lower section of the Owyhee Canyon, north of Rome on U.S. Highway 95, is a popular spring whitewater run for several commercial river outfits. The upper section has been tamed by Owyhee Dam. It forms Owyhee Lake, Oregon's longest reservoir, stretching for more than 40 miles into the desert.

To reach Oregon's final corner, head north from Frenchglen on State Highway 205. You'll skim the desert marshlands of the 41-mile-long **Malheur Wildlife Refuge** in the Blitzen River Valley. This 183,000-acre preserve was set aside in 1908 to shelter nesting colonies of cormorants, egrets and ibis. More than 280 species of other birds have been identified here.

As you approach "the Narrows" between Harney and Malheur Lakes, you can drive a few miles east to refuge headquarters. Here, you'll learn about the birds who inhabit the marshlands, and those who pass through on their migratory flights along the Pacific Flyway. Visitor center hours are weekdays 8 to 4:30; (503) 493-2612. Next door is the **George Benson Memorial Museum** with dozens of mounted bird specimens. The facility is open daily, 6 a.m. to 9 p.m.

☺ From the visitor center, a self- guiding drive will take you through the nearby **Diamond Craters** area. Geologists say it offers the "best and most diverse basaltic volcanic features in the United States." Within a small area of this cratered complex, you'll see lava flows, cinder cones, spatter cones and other pyroclastic prototypes. Driving/hiking guides are available at the Frenchglen BLM information booth and the Malheur Wildlife Refuge headquarters.

Burns

Population: 2,920   **Elevation: 4,148 feet**

Burns and sister city **Hines** comprise the commercial hub of southeastern Oregon's cattle country. With 4,390 people between them, they contain over half the county's population. Since Harney is the largest county in America, you can imagine how thinly-populated the rest of the area is!

A glimpse at a map will tell you that Burns is one of the most isolated towns of its size in the state. It's also the consummate cowtown, with a dusty old fashioned business district and more tack shops and Western wear shops than food and variety stores. Incorporated in 1891, it was named for Scottish poet Robert Burns, at the urging of its Scottish postmaster George

WHAT IN TARNATION IS A COWBOY?

Nothing has captured the world's fancy quite so much as the American cowboy. Much of eastern Oregon is cattle country, and many folks there feel they're a part of the Old West. You'll find no shortage of ten-gallon hats and jingling spurs in towns like Pendleton and Burns.

However, even though the cowboy is considered an American institution, he has his roots in Mexico. And the famous trail-herding era—which endures in books, movies, TV shows and in romantic hearts—lasted less than 25 years.

It was the promise of fertile farmland and gold that lured the first flood of Americans west, not cattle. When the Oregon Trail pioneers and California's Forty-niners hurried out here in the mid-1800s, they'd never heard of ten-gallon hats, lassos or blue denims.

The first big cattle spreads were developed in the 1870s in the open rangelands of Arizona, New Mexico and west Texas. Those early ranchers marveled at the skill of the *vaqueros* of next-door Mexico, who could catch a running steer with a length of braided rawhide called a *riata*. Their saddles had high backs to help them keep their seats, and snubbing horns for their rawhide ropes. The *vaqueros* wore broad-brimmed *sombreros* for sun shelter and leather leggings—or "chaps"—as protection from scratchy chaparral. These outfits made sense, so the gringos adopted them. American ranchers also hired many of the Mexican cowboys to run their herds.

To reach Eastern markets, livestock had to be herded to railheads, and the romance of the great cattle drives was born. Yes, they *did* sing to calm the spooky critters at night—and they were probably terribly off-key.

Spreading railroads soon eliminated the need for cattle drives, and straight-shooting marshals eliminated most of the bad guys in rowdy Western towns. Settlers fenced in much of the open range. By the 1890s, the era of cattle drives and range wars was over. Although herds are still run in remote regions such as southeastern Oregon, the beef you barbecue today probably came from a feedlot.

What about those blue jeans, which are *de rigueur* for every cowboy from Pendleton to Pomona? Well, dang my britches, they weren't even produced until 1874, well after the "cowboy period" had begun. When Levi Strauss began producing britches in the 1850s, he used gray tent canvas. The denim—which originated in France—came much later. Besides, Levi's pants were for California gold miners, not Western cowpokes.

McGowan. To learn more about the old cowtown's past, stop by its yesterday archive:

☺ **Harney County Historical Museum** ● *18 West D Street (573- 2636). Open mid-May to mid-October, Tuesday-Friday 9 to 5 and Saturday 9 to noon. Adults $1.50, couples $2, kids 50 cents, families $2.50* This interesting small museum captures Harney County's Old West past, with artifacts from Peter

340 — CHAPTER TEN

French's ranch, early cowboying photos and other ranching lore. Exhibits also include some nice handmade quilts, a turn-of-the-century kitchen, a diorama of area birds and a shed full of old wagons.

WHERE TO DINE

The Powerhouse ● △△ $

305 E. Monroe; (503) 573-9060. American; full bar service. Daily 9 a.m. to 10 p.m. MC/VISA. Western style restaurant built into the 1924 city power station, trimmed with barnwood and ranch regalia. Simple American menu varies from steaks to chicken to chops; noted for its prime rib, homemade bread and pies.

Pine Room Café ● △△ $

Monroe at Egan; (503) 573-6631. American; full bar service. MC/VISA. Folksy family-style café featuring fresh cut steaks and homemade bread and desserts; German potato soup is a specialty. Novel preparation of conventional chickens, chops and steaks make this 30-year-old diner a cut above average.

Jerry's Restaurant on the south edge of town at 937 Oregon Avenue (573-7000) is open 24 hours—a good place to fuel up for the long haul eastward. For light fare and good sourdough bread, try **Steens Mountain Café and Bakery** at 54 N. Broadway (573-7226); open Monday-Saturday 8 a.m. to 5 p.m.

WHERE TO SLEEP

Orbit Motel ● △ $ Ø

Highway 20 and 395, Burns, OR 97720; (800) 235-6155 or (503) 573-2034. Couples $30 to $35, singles $25 to $30. Major credit cards. A 31-unit motel with TV movies, room phones and pool; some room refrigerators. **Restaurant** adjacent.

Silver Spur Motel ● △△ $$ Ø

789 N. Broadway, Burns, OR 97720; (503) 573-2077. Couples $33.25 to $34.75, singles $24.10 to $26.75. Major credit cards. A 26-unit motel with TV, room phones and spa. Rental refrigerators available and health club privileges.

A long drive from Burns will express you to the chalky-white alkaline **Alvord Desert** and an impressive lower view of the Steens Mountain eastern escarpment. Head 70 miles southeast of Burns on State Route 78, then follow a rough dirt road 40 to 50 miles into the desert. En route, pause near **New Princeton** to see the unusual **round barn,** built by cattle baron Pete French a century ago. Note the hundreds of initials carved into corral posts by working cowboys. Incidentally, you also can reach the **Diamond Craters** area (mentioned above) by driving south from New Princeton.

Once you hit the Alvord Desert, the view up to Steens Mountain is awesome. It might even be worth the long and dusty drive. You can wash some of that dust away at **Alvord Hot Springs.** It's an informal, free spa a few miles north of the tiny town of **Andrews** on the edge of the desert.

Back in Burns, you'll have to cover 114 miles of high desert and prairie on Highway 20 to reach **Vale,** gateway to the Owyhee Country. The only town you'll encounter on this stretch is **Juntura** (properly pronounced *Wan-TU-ra* by locals). It's a small trading center for a sheep growing area.

(If you've done the Alvord Desert trip, you can go straight north from New Princeton and pick up the highway 23 miles east of Burns.)

Approaching **Vale,** you'll enter rich farmlands irrigated by the damming of the Owyhee River. The sprawling acres of sugar beets, alfalfa and potatoes offer refreshing contrast to the dusty desert behind you. If you come during harvest time, you'll know this also is onion country! The Oregon Trail crosses the Snake River at **Nyssa** (*NI-sah*), southeast east of here, and swings inland through Vale. A roadside monument marks the spot on the Malheur River near Vale where pioneers rested and prepared for the dry crossing north to **Farewell Bend.**

☺ From Vale, turn south on a paved country road toward **Keeney Pass** and follow signs to **Owyhee Dam and Lake Owyhee.** The highway parallels the Oregon Trail and a monument marks Keeney Pass, where some of the wagon ruts are still visible.

Owyhee Dam, completed in 1932, is an imposing affair—a 405-foot concrete spade wedged into a narrow ravine. Hike across its face for impressive views of the steep-walled, sculpted Owyhee Canyon. A paved road continues south for several miles along the twisting canyon shoreline to **Lake Owyhee State Park.** It offers RV sites with water and electrical hookups for $11 and tent sites for $9. Other facilities include showers, a boat launch and hiking trails around the shoreline. To complete your southeastern Oregon tour, retrace your path from the dam, then follow signs east to **Adrian** and turn south onto State Highway 201.

☺ After eight miles, signs will direct you to the **Succor Creek State Recreation Area.** This is one of Oregon's often-overlooked jewels—a beautiful desert canyon cut by a small tributary of the Snake River. The drive is dusty and at times bumpy, but it'll carry you past an imposing parade of spires, terraces, ridges and serpentine dry washes.

Deep within the canyon, you can park your RV, pitch your tent or picnic at a primitive campground. Seventeen miles below the camp, another road—somewhat rougher—will carry you through wild geological shapes of **Leslie Gulch** to an overlook of Owyhee Canyon. The banded, multi-colored sandstone formations are worth the jolting and the bumps. If you're in an ordinary sedan, scout the route carefully, to make sure you can get through.

The 34-mile-drive through Succor Creek Recreation Area merges onto U.S. Highway 95 at Malloy Ranch. A swift 18-mile run south takes you to an oldstyle community that retains much of its distinctive European ancestry.

Jordan Valley

Population: 400   **Elevation: 4,389 feet**

This well-kept town was founded by Basque shepherds in the 1890s. It later became a trading center when California miners headed north to newly-found gold discoveries in Idaho. As you pass through, note the *pelota fronton,* the traditional Basque ball court in the center of town. Pelota is a fast-moving game similar to our handball.

For a sample of traditional cooking, try the **Old Basque Inn Restaurant** at the north end of town; (586-2298). Huge family-style dinners, featuring a mix of spicy Basque entrées (usually lamb) and hearty American fare, will sink your boat. Try a *Picon* punch to work up an appetite and some hearty red wine—traditionally served in water glasses—to wash it all down. Then plan to spend the night. Two modest, inexpensive lodges, **Basque**

Station Motel (586-9244) and **Sahara Motel** (586-2500) can probably put you up.

Southwest of Jordan Valley on Highway 95, **Antelope Reservoir** offers a place to picnic, camp and launch your boat. Four miles beyond, a dirt road to the south leads you about 20 miles to another overlook of the dramatic spires and ridges of **Owyhee Canyon.**

After 15 miles, you arrive in **Rome.** This tiny farm community on the banks of the Owyhee River certainly could have been built in a day—in an afternoon, for that matter. The name is appropriate. Imposing sandstone bas relief columns in the nearby Owyhee Canyon resemble those from a Roman temple. These **Rome Columns** can be reached via a three and a half mile dirt road, off U.S. 95 just northeast of town.

Rome is the rendezvous point for several commercial outfits that run wild and scenic stretches of the Owyhee River Canyon. Since this is desert country where streams shrivel quickly, river trips are made only in the spring. One outfit tackles these rapids in small, nimble dories, providing a particularly wild ride. For information, contact: **Northwest Dories,** 1127 Airway Ave., Lewiston, ID 83501, (800) 877-DORY or (208) 743-4201 or P.O. Box 16, Altaville, CA 95221 (209) 736-0805.

This Rome may not be the crossroads of the world, but it's the division point for your southeastern loop. Highway 95 heads south through Nevada and California, and north into Idaho and eastern Washington. If you have more to discover in the Emerald State, you can branch northwest at **Burns Junction** to get back into the heart of Oregon.

SOUTHEASTERN OREGON EVENTS

Migratory Bird Festival, early April at Malheur National Wildlife Refuge, Burns; (503) 573-2636.

Jordan Valley Rodeo, May; (503) 372-3091.

Thunderegg Days, early June in Nyssa; (503) 372-3091.

Obsidian Days rock and gem exhibition, mid-June in Hines; (503) 573-2636.

Harney County Pioneer Day, mid-June in Burns; (503) 573-6517.

Nyssa Nite Rodeo, late June; (503) 372-3091.

Lake County Junior Rodeo, late June in Lakeview; (503) 947-3427

Hang Gliding Festival, early July in Lakeview; (503) 947-5040.

Oregon Trail Days, early July in Vale; (503) 473-3800.

Malheur County Fair, early August in Ontario; (503) 889-3431.

Lake County Roundup and Fair, early September in Lakeview; (503) 947-2925.

Harney County Fair, mid-September in Burns; (503) 573-6166.

Jordan Valley Basque Festival, September; (503) 372-3091.

Chapter Eleven
AFTERTHOUGHTS

THE VERY BEST OF OREGON

AFTER SPENDING the previous chapters exploring Oregon's diverse lures, let's have a bit of fun and select the very best of the Emerald State. We'll pick our favorite in each category, followed by the other nine in alphabetical order. Thus, we have no losers in *The Oregon Discovery Guide,* only winners and runners up.

THE TEN BEST ATTRACTIONS

1. **Crater Lake National Park**; chapter 2, page 56
2. Columbia River Gorge waterfalls; chapter 8, page 241
3. Fort Clatsop National Memorial; chapter 7, page 233
4. Fort Stevens State Park; chapter 7, page 231
5. Newberry Crater National Volcanic Area; chapter 8, page 284
6. Oregon Coast Aquarium, Newport; chapter 6, page 195
7. Oregon Dunes National Recreation Area; chapter 5, page 176
8. Oregon State Capitol, Salem; chapter 3, page 96
9. Silver Falls State Park; chapter 3, page 104
10. Washington Park attractions (zoo, rose gardens and Japanse Garden), Portland; chapter 4, page 121

THE TEN BEST MUSEUMS

1. **High Desert Museum**, Bend; chapter 8, page 271
2. Alsea Bay Bridge Interpretive Center, Walport; chapter 6, page 194
3. Clackamas County History Museum, Oregon City; chapter 3, page 106
4. Columbia River Maritime Museum, Astoria; chapter 7, page 235
5. Douglas County Museum, Roseburg; chapter 3, page 78
6. Old Aurora Colony Museum, Aurora; chapter 3, page 105

7. Oregon Trail Interpretive Center, Baker City; chapter 9, page 317
8. Oregon Historical Center, Portland; chapter 4, page 119
9. Oregon Museum of Science & Industry, Portland; chapter 4, page 119
10. University Art Museum, Eugene; chapter 3, page 86

THE TEN BEST ACTIVITIES

1. **Oregon Shakespeare Festival**, Ashland; chapter 2, page 33
2. Britt Festivals, Jacksonville; chapter 2, page 45
3. Hells Canyonwhitewater trip, Northwest Dories; chapter 9, page 316
4. High Wallowas Tram, Wallowa Lake; chapter 9, page 308
5. Mount Bachelor Summit Lift; chapter 8, page 283
6. Rogue River jet boat trips from Grants Pass and Gold Beach; chapter 2, page 63 and chapter 5, page 155
7. Rogue whitewater trips with Orange Torpedoes; chapter 2, page 63
8. Saturday Market in Portland; chapter 4, page 118
9. Saturday Street Fair in Eugene; chapter 3, page 88
10. The Dalles Dam "work train" tour, the Dalles; chapter 7, page 259

THE TEN BEST VISTA POINTS

1. **Cape Perpetua lookout**; chapter Six, page 189
2. Dee Wright Observatory, McKenzie Pass; chapter 8, page 287
3. Cape Blanco State Park north of Port Orford; chapter 5, page 163
4. Hat Point, Hells Canyon; chapter 9, page 313
5. Larch Mountain, off the Columbia Gorge drive; chapter 7, page 242
6. Oregon Dunes Overlook, Oregon Dunes National Recreation Area; chapter 5, page 181
7. Paulina Peak at Newberry Crater; chapter 8, page 286
8. Portland Women's Club Forum State Park; chapter 7, page 242
9. Rowena Crest east of Hood River; chapter 7, page 257
10. Steens Mountain, East Rim Viewpoint; chapter 10, page 337

THE TEN MOST INTERESTING TOWNS OR CITIES

In selecting our favorite cities and towns, we looked for places with a balance of cultural, scenic and historic attractions—the kind of place one might select for an extended visit or possibly for retirement. Certainly, these would be nice places to live and work as well, although we didn't consider employment or other economic factors.

1. **Ashland**, chapter 2, page 32
2. Astoria, chapter 7, page 229
3. Bandon, chapter 5, page 164
4. Bend, chapter 8, page 269
5. Eugene, chapter 3, page 84
6. Hood River, chapter 7, page 249
7. Oceanside, chapter 6, page 210
8. Portland, chapter 4, page 111
9. Sunriver, chapter 8, page 276
10. Yachats, chapter 6, page 190

THE TEN BEST RESTAURANTS

1. **Atwater's**, Bancorp Tower in Portland; chapter 4, page 128
2. Ambrosia, downtown Eugene; chapter 3, page 88
3. Cafè de la Mer, Cannon Beach; chapter 6, page 219

4. Chata, in Talent between Ashland and Medford; chapter 2, page 37
5. Columbia River Court, Columbia Gorge Hotel in Hood River; chapter 7, page 251
6. Esplanade, RiverPlace Alexis Hotel, Portland; chapter 4, page 129
7. La Serre Seafood Restaurant, Yachats; chapter 6, page 191
8. The Meadows Restaurant, Sunriver Lodge; chapter 8, page 276
9. Pine Tavern Restaurant, Bend; chapter 8, page 273
10. Cascade Room, Timberline Lodge, Mount Hood; chapter 7, page 254

THE TEN BEST HOTELS AND RESORTS

1. **Salishan Lodge**, Gleneden Beach between Depoe Bay and Lincoln City; chapter 6, page 203
2. The Benson, Portland; chapter 4, page 132
3. Columbia Gorge Hotel, Hood River; chapter 7, page 251
4. The Heathman Hotel, Portland; chapter 4, page 132
5. The Inn at Spanish Head, Lincoln City; chapter 6, page 205
6. Inn of the Seventh Mountain, Bend; chapter 8, page 274
7. Portland Marriott; chapter 4, page 132
8. RiverPlace Alexis Hotel, Portland; chapter 4, page 133
9. Sea Quest Bed & Breakfast, Yachats; chapter 6, page 192
10. Sunriver Lodge, Sunriver; chapter 8, page 276

THE TEN BEST HIDEAWAY RESORTS

When you just have to get away from it all, or you want to slip into someplace comfortable with someone special, you might consider one of these places:

1. **The Inn at Otter Crest**, between Newport and Depoe Bay; chapter 6, page 200
2. Black Butte Ranch, between Sisters and Bend; chapter 8, page 274
3. Holiday Farm, Blue River in the McKenzie River Recreation Area; chapter 3, page 92
4. Kah-Nee-Ta Resort, Warm Springs Indian Reservation north of Redmond; chapter 8, page 268
5. Morrison Lodge, on the Rogue River west of Grants Pass; chapter 2, page 68
6. Mount Ashland Inn, north of Ashland in the Siskiyou Mountains; chapter 2, page 39
7. Steamboat Inn, Umpqua River Recreation Area; chapter 3, page 82
8. Tu Tu' Tun Lodge, on the Rogue River, upstream from Gold Beach; chapter 5, page 157
9. Timberline Lodge, Mount Hood; chapter 7, page 254
10. Union Creek Resort, just west of Crater Lake; chapter 2, page 55

OTHER USEFUL OREGON BOOKS
Travel, hiking and dining

The Best of Oregon by Ken Metzgler, © 1986; Timber Press, Portland, Ore.

Driving the Pacific Coast by Kenn Oberrecht, © 1990; Globe Pequot Press, Chester, Conn.

Exploring the Oregon Coast by William L. Mainwaring, © 1985; West Ridge Press, Salem, Ore.

Exploring Oregon's Central and Southern Cascades by William L. Mainwaring, © 1979; West Ridge Press, Salem, Ore.

Exploring Oregon's Wild Areas by William L. Sullivan; © 1988; Mountaineers Books, Denver, Colo.

A Good Rain by Timothy Egan, © 1990; Alfred A. Knopf, New York.

Insight Guides: Northwest, edited by Hans Hoefer, © 1986; Graphic Arts Center Publishing, Portland, Ore.

Off Beat Oregon by Mimi Bell, © 1983; Chronicle Books, San Francisco, Calif.

Oregon for the Curious by Ralph Friedman, © 1972; Caxton Press, Caldwell, Idaho.

Pacific Coast Adventures by Fraser Bridges, © 1991; Western Traveller Press, Vancouver, B.C.

The Menu: A Restaurant Guide to Oregon, edited by Tom Demarre. © 1991; David Thomas Publishing, Hillsboro, Ore.

Northwest Best Places by David Brewster and Stephanie Irving, © 1991; Sasquatch Books, Seattle, Wash.

Oregon Coast Hikes by Paul Williams, © 1983; Mountaineers Books, Denver, Colo.

Oregon Off the Beaten Path by Myrna Oakley, © 1991; Globe Pequot Press, Chester, Conn.

Portland Best Places, edited by Stephanie Irving, © 1990; Sasquatch Books, Seattle, Wash.

History & reference

Oregon Geographic Names by Lewis MacArthur, © 1982; Oregon Historical Society, Portland, Ore.

The Making of Oregon, © 1979; Oregon Historical Society, Portland, Ore.

The Oregon Desert by E.R. Jackson, © 1964; Caxton Press, Caldwell, Idaho.

Oregon: the End of the Trail, edited by Carol Stream, © 1982; re-issue of the Depression era Federal Writers' Project guide, by Somerset Press.

Silent Siege: Japanese Attacks on North America in World War II by Bert Webber, © 1988; Webb Research Group, Medford, Ore.

Sometimes a Great Notion by Ken Kesey, © 1964; Viking Press, New York.

Steens Mountain in Oregon's High Desert Country, © 1967; Caxton Press, Caldwell, Idaho.

Index

Primary listings are in *boldface italics*